ACHIEVING DEVOPS

A NOVEL ABOUT DELIVERING THE BEST OF AGILE, DEVOPS, AND MICROSERVICES

Dave Harrison

Knox Lively

With contributions by Ron Vincent

Foreword by Abel Wang

Apress®

Achieving DevOps: A Novel About Delivering the Best of Agile, DevOps, and Microservices

Dave Harrison
Madras, OR, USA

Knox Lively
Montclair, NJ, USA

ISBN-13 (pbk): 978-1-4842-4387-9
https://doi.org/10.1007/978-1-4842-4388-6

ISBN-13 (electronic): 978-1-4842-4388-6

Managing Director, Apress Media LLC: Welmoed Spahr
Acquisitions Editor: Jonathan Gennick
Development Editor: Laura Berendson
Coordinating Editor: Jill Balzano

Cover designed by eStudioCalamar

Cover image designed by Freepik (www.freepik.com)

Distributed to the book trade worldwide by Springer Science+Business Media New York, 233 Spring Street, 6th Floor, New York, NY 10013. Phone 1-800-SPRINGER, fax (201) 348-4505, e-mail orders-ny@springer-sbm.com, or visit www.springeronline.com. Apress Media, LLC is a California LLC and the sole member (owner) is Springer Science + Business Media Finance Inc (SSBM Finance Inc). SSBM Finance Inc is a **Delaware** corporation.

For information on translations, please e-mail rights@apress.com, or visit http://www.apress.com/rights-permissions.

Apress titles may be purchased in bulk for academic, corporate, or promotional use. eBook versions and licenses are also available for most titles. For more information, reference our Print and eBook Bulk Sales web page at http://www.apress.com/bulk-sales.

Any source code or other supplementary material referenced by the author in this book is available to readers on GitHub via the book's product page, located at www.apress.com/9781484243879. For more detailed information, please visit http://www.apress.com/source-code.

Printed on acid-free paper

Thanks to the giants of our field, including Gene Kim, Gary Gruver, Jez Humble, Martin Fowler, Nicole Forsgren, John Willis, and Damon Edwards. We're so appreciative of the brilliance, energy, and creativity of your work!

Contents

About the Authors

Dave Harrison is a Senior Consultant at Microsoft Premier specializing in DevOps and Agile. As a development lead, architect and project manager, he has spearheaded cultural revolutions in several large enterprises making the leap to agile development and continuous delivery. Dave is an enthusiastic promoter of release management using tools such as Chef, Puppet, Ansible, and Docker. He believes very firmly that, as with agile development, the exact tool selected is less important than having the people and processes in place and ready.

He's the proud father of two beautiful girls, has been married to his lovely wife Jennifer for 24 years, and is based out of Central Oregon in the United States. He enjoys fly fishing, reading history books, and in his spare time often wonders if he should be doing more around the house instead of goofing off. His blog can be found at https://driftboatdave.com.

Knox Lively is Lead DevOps Engineer at Songtrust, a NYC-based Music Start-Up. As a seasoned DevOps Engineer in the entertainment industry, Knox has built out entire DevOps departments, consulted as an architect with various firms, and tried his hardest to automate himself out of a job. Bringing a rather Zen approach to DevOps, Knox enjoys reducing complexity in various environments, as well as increasing visibility into said systems with rigorous and intelligent monitoring.

When not behind the keyboard, Knox spends his time traveling, fly-fishing, and searching New York for the perfect bowl of Pho.

Foreword

The phrase DevOps has been an industry buzzword for quite a few years now, but what exactly is DevOps? If you were to ask ten people in a room today that question, you'll likely get about 20 different answers. Here's our definition of DevOps at Microsoft:

> *DevOps is the union of people, process and products to enable the continuous delivery of value to our end users.*

> —Donovan Brown, Principal DevOps Manager, Microsoft

The key here is continuously delivering value. That is the ultimate end goal.

We have always said that companies who adopt DevOps best practices and continuously deliver value to their end users out-innovate and outperform their competitors. And this is no longer theory. DevOps has now been in existence long enough that we have solid empirical numbers to back this statement up:

High Performance DevOps Companies Achieve...

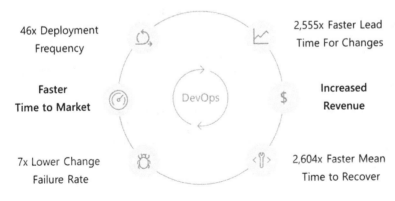

46x Deployment Frequency

2,555x Faster Lead Time For Changes

Faster Time to Market

Increased Revenue

DevOps

7x Lower Change Failure Rate

2,604x Faster Mean Time to Recover

I've been a DevOps practitioner for the past 7 years, helping customers achieve their DevOps goals. Unfortunately, in the enterprise space, most customers are still behind the curve and haven't quite started on their DevOps journey. They know they need "DevOps," but aren't quite sure how to proceed.

The first thing they want to know is, "How can we buy DevOps? What tools do we need to get?" And unfortunately, DevOps is not a magic product. You can't just buy DevOps. Sure, you can buy all the best tools and products, but that's not going to magically fix your organization. You must address all three pillars. That's people, process, and the products you use.

First, you must address the people in your organization. This is the hardest pillar to change because here, you are talking about the culture of your organization. Everybody, from the top, all the way down, must be 100% aligned in continuously delivering value to the end users in whatever way possible.

All too often when I talk to our customers, I ask them why they are doing something the way they are currently doing it. And they respond with, "Because that's how we've always done it." That's not an acceptable answer! If how we used to do things did not let us continuously deliver value to our end users, then we must change how we do things.

As we all know, culture shifts in an organization are extremely difficult to implement. It doesn't have to start from the top down, but it sure is easier when it does start from the top down. Also, plan for some attrition to happen. Not all people in an organization are ready or willing to be part of that cultural shift. And if they aren't, they need to be part of another organization.

Next, the process. Enterprises need to make sure they have a process that will let them iterate fast enough, yet still deliver high enough quality code. Luckily, processes that accomplish this have already been clearly defined. Processes like Agile and Scrum are just some examples.

And finally, the products that help you enable all of this. I'm partial to Azure DevOps (of course), but there are many good DevOps tools out there that can help enterprises be successful.

Once my customers are all onboard with this, the next thing they want to know is, "Where should we start making changes? Should we try to accomplish everything at once?" And my answer is: Let's address one problem at a time.

First, what hurts the most? Depending on what that is, let's fix that one thing.

If the answer is, "We don't even use source control. We just have our code on a shared drive," then let's start by adding in a source control system.

If the answer is, "We can't deliver our work on time and we need 10 months of coding before we can deploy anything," let's adopt a process like Agile and start working in sprints and having deployable goals at the end of each sprint.

If the answer is, "We can't deploy our finished code fast enough," then let's start building out automated build and deploy pipelines.

If the answer is, "We can't QA our finished code fast enough and it's become a bottleneck," then let's start shifting left, moving away from functional testing to automated unit testing.

If the answer is, "We are moving so fast that we don't have time to do our security reviews," then let's shift left, implement security reviews earlier in the process (think each pull request) and start adding security checks into our pipelines.

Find what hurts the most and just fix that. And once that problem has been fixed, find what hurts the most next and then fix that.

The thing to remember is the DevOps journey is exactly that. A journey. It is not a one and done thing. In fact, it is never "done." It is a journey of constant iterative improvements. The only constant is that teams that adopt DevOps best practices out-innovate teams that don't, and quickly render those teams obsolete.

Good luck on your DevOps Journey!

Abel Wang, Principal Cloud Developer Advocate, Microsoft

December 20, 2018

Introduction by Dave Harrison

This book comes from two of my greatest failures, one personal and the other professional.

The first came in fall of 2013, as I was being unceremoniously cut by a sporting apparel company after a disastrous stint as a project manager. It was a miserable trip out to my car, with rivulets of rain streaming off my jacket onto my soggy box of belongings. I felt like I'd been hit on the back of the head with a 2x4. What happened?

Just a year earlier, working at a great company in the same market just down the street, I had managed a team of developers and had enjoyed some great wins in adopting Agile. I had expected this assignment to be the next rung on the ladder and build on this success; after all, I had so much more to work with at this new company. I had a bigger team, which meant more firepower. And the team looked like the perfect group to build on; they were bright, experienced developers with very deep-level expertise in modern web development. My new manager understood Agile and backed my vision 100%. I felt confident, fully expecting a glorious victory; instead, ignominiously, I was having to start over.

The fact remained that though I had been successful with Agile at one company, the same recipe and approach had not gained any traction at another. I remember gripping the wheel in frustration as I drove home that evening, thinking; Dave, you missed your off-ramp.

The off-ramp I had missed wasn't made of concrete. Looking back, I had missed opportunities to really drive a better vision for the team that would have been less risky, incorporated quality as a first-class citizen and built incrementally on success. I had engaged with the testing community and even – halfheartedly – tried to inject some quality initiatives within our team. But the two teams still remained very separate; QA was always lagging by a significant margin behind development, our manual testing took days to complete and leaked like a colander. We had missed several very embarrassing issues that required all-out efforts to mitigate, costing me points in rep that I now realized I couldn't afford to lose. Our poor reliability and lengthening technical debt hurt team morale and was nakedly exposed to the end user community.

Worse, we were dropping stones into a pool with our releases. Operations was also siloed from development. We had no idea what features were working as expected and were often the last to know when key services went down. Our releases were joined at the hip with an older web site that was in even worse shape. We had the capability to roll out multiple times a day, but as we were chained to this old manually tested system, we were forced into a torpid multi-month release timetable. Our weekend releases became crucibles of forced overtime with bad catered food, terrible cat picture slideshows, and short tempers as we had to choose between forcing a humiliating rollback or trying to patch things together in place.

As personally painful as the experience had been for me, one experience stood out that started some wheels turning. I inherited on the team an IT/infrastructure liaison whose main assignment was to write Chef recipes so infrastructure could be rolled out alongside code releases. This was the first experience I had had with Chef and automated infrastructure – and it was a real eye-opener. I remember watching templated environments get rolled out with a single command and being absolutely floored by the repeatability and reliability of that one pocket of our release lifecycle.

This same infrastructure person pulled me aside once and told me – "Dave, sometimes you have to go slow to go fast." In the mad chaos of day-to-day project management, I brushed that aside. Now, thinking back, I realized that I had missed something.

Years went by; I found a great job that was incredibly challenging technically, writing a shop floor application as part of a small three-man team supporting a manufacturing process of large-screen touch sensitive monitors. The days of big battalions and 20-person teams were behind me; here I worked as part of a very tight, close-knit group. Everyone contributed to design and implementation, and we proudly watched our little code baby grow in strength and capability.

But even on this tiny team, the same problems with coordinating releases remained. Most of our releases failed, as the big batches of code that we checked in every few days or so failed to integrate. As a result, several critical demonstrations to our customers abended, and we were forced to scramble to patch together a working fallback. In the end the project succeeded, but only with a lot of unnecessary friction and waste.

Then, I moved into Microsoft as a senior consultant and began working with customers throughout the western United States on their development challenges. However, I never forgot my earlier experiences and kept thinking about better ways of making software releases safer and more predictable.

Increasingly, I could see that the problems I had faced trying to scale Agile in the real world was not an anomaly.

Then, in December of 2017, just as I was beginning to think about what this book would look like, my second great life failure happened. My new doctor required an in-person checkup, so I made a routine visit, had some blood drawn, and left. Two days later I got a call – I needed to come in, as soon as possible. My blood sugar level was through the roof, as was my bad cholesterol levels and blood pressure. In short, I had Type 2 diabetes and would need to change my diet, exercise, and be on medication, for the rest of my life.

I was hit with waves of guilt. Type 2 diabetes is a lifestyle disease; the hectic and stress-filled pace I had set in my life – and the food and drink I used as fuel in coping with it – had finally caught up with me.

This was a different and very personal crisis, but I felt the same reaction – what happened? I thought I was healthy; I had tons of energy, a great gig without too much stress, and a wonderful family life. But as my colleague Aaron Bjork has pointed out – "Just because you're not sick, doesn't mean you're healthy." I had ignored several critical warning signs with my health and now was saddled with a life limiting condition to manage – the physiological equivalent to a disabling car crash.

Looking back, I'm grateful for my failures most of all. I've learned so much from them. My professional failure as a project manager got me thinking about better ways of writing software and coordinating releases, which led directly to discovering DevOps and a brilliant and selfless community of professionals with a powerful mission. Failing at managing my health made me reset the pace of my life and the way I was using and abusing food and drink. I'm calmer now, more empathetic, less focused on "getting stuff done" – more concerned with safety and a sustainable pace.

Giving away the ending of our novel here – but our hero Ben ends the story with a talk about humility, patience, and trust. I've had a great opportunity to share time with some great leaders in our community; they were across the spectrum in terms of their personality types, their favorite choices with technology, and the resources at their command. But those three qualities kept appearing in our conversations, a common thread.

There is no single roadmap to success in DevOps. But, if you get only one thing from this book, remember this – if you make it about learning, and demonstrate humility, patience and trust in your personal behavior, you won't be far off from success.

Introduction by Knox Lively

We live in a time of instant, or at least near-instant gratification with information at out fingertips within 200 milliseconds or less. After reading a book such as this one, or any book for that matter, the reader often assumes that the tightly woven narrative that is portrayed has always been such. It couldn't be further from the truth. A book, as with a career, or anything worthwhile doing is the culmination of many months, and even years of concentrated effort, often by multiple parties. This book was such. Dave and I worked countless hours while managing relationships, families and our day jobs to follow a goal that we thought worthwhile of sacrificing the better part of a year to.

My career, just as with this book, was the product of daily effort multiplied by time. It didn't appear overnight, there were no fireworks, nor did I even realize I had a career until years down the road.

As I suspect how many of the readers careers began did, mine began in the trenches of IT. Helpdesk Tier 1 to be exact. It was my first salaried position right out of college, and I couldn't have been happier. "I made it!" I thought to myself. I couldn't believe they were going to pay me $35,000 no matter how many hours I worked! Let's just say it didn't take long until I began to strive for more.

From helpdesk I began to teach myself programming and worked my way into more of a Junior Sysadmin-type role at the same company. After learning a couple of programming languages and seeing the power it had to transform my career, I was hooked. From there, I continued to work my way up to my first traditional Systems Administrator position. In my career path, and my limited understanding of the field, Senior Systems Administrator was the culmination and ceiling for my career path. After a couple of more years I'd landed at just that, a Senior Systems Administrator role. "This is it, I made it." Once again, I thought. But the truth was it didn't really feel any different from my first position working on the Helpdesk. Instead solving one-off problems with people and their desktops, I'd simply migrated to solving one-off problems with servers. My workflow was still entirely push-based. Work came to me, and typically at the worst time possible. I was a technical firefighter for all tense and purposes.

Enter my "there's got to be a better way" moment. Sick and tired of legacy systems, legacy thinking, and legacy people I pulled up my stakes and set my sight on new career horizons. I spent months of looking for and researching my next career move.

Luckily, not too long into my research I stumbled my way into a DevOps role in Los Angeles. I'd barely heard of the term DevOps, what did it mean? Was it the beta-max of development methodologies, or was there some staying power to this new concept? I wasn't sure, but I sure as hell wasn't about to complain. The money was good enough that I figured I could make myself excited about it for the foreseeable future.

My second stroke of luck was being able to work under a brilliant DevOps engineer. The company was small, so it was just us two. I had landed basically what seemed a paid mentorship. A mentorship is something not easy to find anywhere these days, much less getting paid for it. I learned the ins and outs of configuration management tools, proactive monitoring suites, as well as deploying infrastructure as code. This was everything my career had been missing up to this point, a way for me to proactively design my way around future potential problems. Problems that all legacy systems were plagued by. Problems like, snow-flake systems, or rather systems that needed special hands on maintenance due to drifts in configuration practices across the environment. Other problems like only finding out systems were down only because customers called, or simply trying to keep up with all of the systems we owned seemed to be a thing of the past.

It seemed too good to be true; there had to be a catch. And there was a catch. It required a shift in mindset, specifically the mindset of an engineer or an architect to properly implement and build such systems. The cowboy coder and the typical grump legacy systems administrator mindset was 100% incompatible with this new methodology. I fell into those camps. I hacked my way through every cookbook, recipe, task, you name it. I did so with, not surprisingly, limited success.

I wish I could say I read a couple of books and BAM! I saw the DevOps light, and everything was happily ever after. That couldn't have been further from the truth. It took me the better part of my DevOps career to shift my perspective. Only through diligently reading, educating myself, and working with greater engineers on a daily basis was I able to reshape the way I thought about IT, DevOps, and Software engineering as a whole.

My education and understanding of DevOps is now quite simple. Ask me a few years ago if you came to me looking for a definition of DevOps and what it is I do I would have told you to "google it." Not because I'm a jerk, well maybe, but rather because the concept was so elusive to me. It means something different to each person you ask. So, I'll give you my definition of DevOps.

Firstly, and foremost, DevOps is a mindset. It's not some new-fangled tool made by some trendy software company of which everyone sports their t-shirt. It's a way in which you approach a problem. The tools are, well just that, tools. Pick whichever ones suit you and your organization best. The mindset, however, is the real asset. DevOps, when applied correctly, will help you and your organization architecturally plan around problems before they happen. DevOps, its accompanying methodologies, and tools should help you architect infrastructure that is iterable, scalable, and version-able. No different than software development methodologies such as Agile. Agile for infrastructure if you will.

Secondly, DevOps should empower you and your organization to take on any project no matter how large through the process of breaking large tasks into smaller tasks, delegation, automation, and lastly by using the multiplier of time. Any successful company, no matter the sector, will tell you that this above all is how you build empires.

Thirdly, and perhaps the most important concept DevOps has to offer, is the idea of closing or integrating feedback loops within a tech department, or even across an organization. For far too long departments have been siloed, forced into throwing work over the fence to another, each operating in independence. Even within the tech department processes and technologies are siloed in a way that didn't offer an easy way to see the whole picture. DevOps offers a way of integrating all the various systems and closing the feedback loop for rapid learning, iterating, and re-integration of knew knowledge to systems and processes. DevOps is an organic approach to systems design that has been missing in the tech landscape until now.

My hopes and wishes for the reader are that they understand that DevOps is not only a set of tools and practices, but rather a mindset. A mindset that informs each and every decision for their work and the direction of the organization as a whole. However, in reality, we are dealing with concepts larger than DevOps itself. On a more global scale, whether it be creating a family, growing a garden, or writing a book, each can be achieved by using the same fundamental principles. The principle that through small, incremental, yet measurable changes applied daily can create long and lasting change.

My other greatest wish for the reader is that this book, although loaded with information, quells their fears of mobilizes them to take action on what seems an Everest of tech debt. We all have stared down this mountain and wondered "How can I ever hope to achieve half of what is being asked of me?" Not enough resources, not enough time, lack of knowledge, etc. The excuses are endless. However, they are not unique to any one individual or organization. There is no DevOps "Never-Never Land" where everything works as it should, no practice ages, nor has any consequences upon its failure. Not even the "big guys" you hear about from your favorite Tech blogger operate in a sandbox. They each got to where they were by adopting a certain set of tools and practices, as well as a mindset that worked for them and their organization. They took these resources and simply started. Each and every day chipping away at the mountain. It's the only way anyone could ever hope to achieve what is being asked of them and their department.

What You'll Learn from This Book

In the preface to Lean Enterprise[1], the authors noted that the biggest pain point they saw came from people working at organizations that only could speak for part of the whole:

> Everyone finds it difficult to implement these ideas successfully. In most cases it was impossible to realize anything more than incremental improvements because only part of the organization changed — and that part still needed to work with the rest of the organization, which expected them to behave in the traditional way.

This same pain point exists today, and it's killing us. We find motivated, bright people at every level of the organization and from all walks of life — IT, QA, development, InfoSec. These early adopters catch fire and love the concepts of DevOps from the first day; but as they only can change part of the organization, the underlying issues of end to end delivery remains unchanged. After returning from a great conference, or reading inspiring books like *The Goal*, *Continuous Delivery*, or *The Phoenix Project*, a common reaction seems to be — oddly — depression.

It's what we like to call a "now what?" moment. Unlike the heroes in these stories, we aren't blessed with a magical, all-wise advisor who can lead us in the right direction; we may also not have a small army of bright, capable direct reports that can follow our lead as we try to turn things around.

It's almost cruel. We're being shown a shiny, beautiful car — but we're not allowed to take it for a spin. In conferences and in meetings with customers, we constantly hear from people that love the principles underlying DevOps, but then are slapped in the face with the ugly reality — my place just doesn't work like that. I don't have the kind of authority we'd need to pivot like this.

---

[1]Jez Humble, Joanne Molesky, Barry O'Reilly; Lean Enterprise: How High Performance Organizations Innovate at Scale, O'Reilly Media, 2015

So, what to do?

In Portland, a few years ago, Dave was asked by a good friend to speak at a conference about this shiny new object called DevOps. The auditorium was full, and the audience was engaged and interested in the topic; the time flew by as we went back and forth about different ways of building out an effective, pragmatic roadmap. But one programmer toward the back put up a stumper, asking, "This is all terrific, but on my team I'm just one guy in a group of ten. And we're all heads-down programmers. What can we do to play around with this?"

Dismissively, Dave said, "Well, that's just it. If you don't have executive buy in and a mandate to completely rework the company top to bottom – forget it! If you can't change the company – and at your level you might not be able to – then change your company. Find your way to an outfit that lives and breathes this, and don't settle for less."

On the way home, Dave felt uneasy, like he'd failed a test. The answer seemed to pat, too glib – and it bothered him for weeks. Was that really the end of the story? Did the people in that audience – fellow application developers for the most part – go home discouraged, thinking, "Well, that was super interesting, but ultimately irrelevant. It's not like I personally can benefit from this – it's all strategery stuff for the bigwigs."

Was the answer really wrong? Most of the successful transformations we've seen have been led by visionary leaders who set the pace and could drive change, top to bottom. And there's no question that having a large amount of authority, resources, and a time-capped existential crisis helps tilt things in our favor when it comes to creating change in large enterprises.

So, for the rest of us – let's say we don't have those cards to play. Are we stuck? Is DevOps only possible from the top down? And does it only work for the handful of unicorns out there with the web in their DNA – flexible, nimble companies with rivers of money and oodles of innovative, creative people?

This book is our answer to those questions. Now we're convinced – because we've seen it – that it is totally within our grasp to create change. Each of us has the ability to contribute toward a shift in thinking so that a true large-scale DevOps effort can be successful. And the payoff is immense. We're not talking about productivity or efficiency here; we're talking about leaving work with less fear and exhaustion, with more time for the ones we love, and a deep glow from a job well done. Who doesn't want that?

Let's say you're part of a great team of very capable people – but the way you are working, the environment, is a limiting factor. Changing it seems like too big a task; overwhelming, like climbing a mountain. Where do I start? Am I going to get fired when something goes wrong with this? What about the other areas of the company I need but have zero control over?

We're going to answer these questions by telling a story of a team that's exactly where we suspect your team might be – one that's not at a complete failure state, that actually has some wins under its belt with Agile, but has some significant obstacles in its path. We'll walk along with this team as they begin their journey and, over the course of a year, emerge victorious in their struggle – despite some serious potholes and setbacks as the team finds their way onward and upward. The story ends – if you can forgive the spoiler – with the entire organization beginning to make some visible traction in the right direction. As Winston Churchill put it, "not the beginning of the end but rather the end of the beginning."

We're assuming you know what DevOps is and have read some of the concepts written about by the Mount Rushmore of thought leaders in that arena – which to us includes Gene Kim, Jez Humble, Martin Fowler, and Gary Gruver. We're assuming you have some background in Agile and have even made some strides in applying those principles in your team; now, you are at a plateau stage and are thinking about ramp up your organization's maturity level when it comes to end-to-end delivery.

One caution we feel we have to make right at the beginning. A common ask is for a specific roadmap, a one-size-fits-all recipe that can be followed, along with the "best-in-class" software that will guarantee a bulls-eye in "doing DevOps." That's not in this book; only a circus huckster – or a software vendor! – would try to sell a magic silver bullet. In the world of code, this is called "cargo cult programming" or "implementation thinking." Mindlessly trying to cut and paste what Google does, or Amazon, is the one guaranteed way to fail miserably in your journey; culture can't be grafted.

So, we'll tell a story in this book, but please don't misunderstand us and think that this is YOUR story. The destination the team is reaching for in this book is likely the same one you're thinking of, but how you and your organization will get there will need to be very different from what the team does in this book. Despite what some consultants and software vendors try to pitch in their marketing, you cannot buy DevOps. A single battle-tested, foolproof recipe for success simply does not exist.

But that's not saying that you won't come away without learning something new. The main problem we hope to overcome is what we've called "Baskin Robbins' syndrome," where we're paralyzed by an abundance of possibilities. There's so much to do. And we're so far behind. Where do I start? Stay too long in that state, and there's a very strong and understandable tendency to lapse into apathy, or play it safe and conservative – putting together a large, strategic-level Big Plan stretching across multiple years.

In fact, both reactions are mistakes. Let's say you feel like you're on the outside looking in. Well, no worries, you're not as far behind as you think. It may be true that most companies are attempting some form of DevOps on a trial basis, but how many are really doing it at scale and across the entire company? The number is likely lower than we think – perhaps much less than 10%. Even the "unicorns" we point to with envy had to start somewhere; most as recently as a decade ago were stuck with the same crumbling, error-prone infrastructure and leaky, nightmare-inducing releases that we might be struggling with.

And on the Big Plan, stretching across many years, well – a word of caution. Many executives in desperation or envy have chosen that type of a 90-degree pivot. Some have even kept their jobs! But uniformly – and this is even for the companies where it's worked – we're told that these huge campaigns are high risk, wasteful and very traumatic. Given a do-over, without exception, we're told that they would have gone about things differently – more of a gradual leveling up, a slowly progressing experiment.

So, instead of trying to come up with the perfect plan, this book will show a team that applies Agile and Lean thinking in solving their own delivery issues. They will make some serious mistakes that will cost them – but they will be moving forward, and learning as they go. Imperfectly, they'll begin with what hurts the most – make small investments that help that pain point – then refactor and keep moving up the mountain, one step at a time.

There's a third mistake we'd love for you to avoid – and that's apathy. We commonly think that we have less power than we actually do. But there's a ripple effect from implementing the right behaviors that has immense power over time. Damon Edwards is fond of saying "you can't change culture, but you can change behavior, and over time behavior becomes culture." We live in an increasingly API-centric world – one where we consume services that have bindings, a known engagement protocol and predictable responses in its communications. Our teams – even if we only are responsible for a few people, or part of a small team – can be thought of as being an API-based service. We can change our behavior, and the way those bindings work – our requirements to consume our services – so that quality is built in early, and our services are easier to maintain and support. Fascinatingly, once our behaviors change, we often find our partners adjusting in their behavior as well, creating a snowball effect. Whoa. We have more power than we think!

This book is not a fairy tale. It's based on real stories, from real people working everywhere from small consulting teams to software vendors and large-scale enterprises to pubsec agencies. Each of them has been able to change their organization, often without a strong mandate from top-level executives, starting first with refactoring the way they work as a team. None of their stories are complete, and there's been some bruises along the way that they shared with us as a valuable lesson for others. We're hoping, once you finish reading this, that you'll feel both excited about the potential for DevOps with your company, empowered to make small, incremental changes to your team's behavior and practices – and most of all, confident that your next steps with DevOps are well thought out and will be successful.

Now, let's talk a little about bias. You'll notice some of the authors of this book come from Microsoft. Most of us are fairly new, arriving after the Steve Ballmer era when the company began adopting Open Source aggressively. But there's a residue of mistrust stemming back to the early 2000s that leaves most of the leading DevOps books and speakers to leave Microsoft out or mention them as an afterthought.

This attitude was well deserved back in the mid 2000s when Microsoft's attitude toward Open Source and even release management could best be described as adversarial or primitive; it simply doesn't hold true anymore. Most organizations out there now view their CI/CD solutions and tools as modular and expect Microsoft to compete on merit, not as an all-or-nothing "stack." Every year, tools become more inclusive and can be integrated with minimal effort, at least on a CLI level if not natively as tasks in a release path. Viewing Microsoft as a DevOps backwater is not only dated, but this bias ignores the reality of mixed platforms in most organizations today.

Linux and Open Source tools have shown astonishing reliability and an ability to innovate and disrupt that has been very good for the IT community. They're clearly here to stay, and the disruptive and powerful ideas embedded in that community have bled into every successful enterprise we admire today; Google, Amazon, Netflix, and yes – Microsoft. To survive, Microsoft was forced to look in the mirror and recognize that what used to work no longer held true. It needed to embrace Linux, Apple and Android mobile development, and the OS community and the decentralized way development is handled on these platforms.

We wish that more of the DevOps materials we see out there would adjust their point of view to reflect current reality and not that of the mid 2000s: DevOps is a concept that is not limited to a single company, software tool, programming language, or platform.

We've done our very best to counter any tendency toward bias based on our corporate allegiance and keep true to the open source and community-driven roots of DevOps. You're not going to see us advocating any particular software tool for builds, source control, monitoring, or config management. In fact, most of the solutions we recommend in this book will cost you nothing; they aren't software tools but improvements in process, helping you maximize your investments in tools you already own.

If this book saves you some work, prevents an embarrassing production failure, or improves your working life in some way, we feel like we have reached our goal – regardless of what flag your ship is flying!

Microsoft, Facebook, Amazon, Google, Netflix – all have succeeded in different ways of driving more business value with DevOps. As part of the research for this book, we reached out to all of these companies. The astonishing thing was the openness and direct, frank way thought leaders from these organizations spoke. Consistently, there was a great deal of pride in how their companies met the needs of customers and could innovate at scale.

The flavor of all these conversations was friendly and very open. Without exception, all seemed to have the same basic desire we have; a strong desire to share information and honest lessons learned, motivated by a spirit of community and helping others avoid the bumps and bruises they suffered in figuring out what worked best. We're deeply grateful to be surrounded by such bright and giving people with such unselfish motives in the DevOps and Agile community.

There simply wasn't enough room to print every book and article found in our research; for a more comprehensive list, please check out the "Achieving DevOps: The Back Story" post on Dave's blog, driftboatdave.com: https://driftboatdave.com/2019/02/16/achieving-devops-the-back-story/

Go forth and conquer! We are in your corner, all the way.

Words from the Field

At the end of this book, you'll find a collection of case studies and interviews. One of the most surprising things we found during the course of writing this book was that most of the prescriptive "list" books out there are making a fundamental mistake. There are many possible roads to success, as the experts we met demonstrated. Getting insight into their experiences and perspectives drove home the point that there is no such thing as a "best practice"– only a better practice than yesterdays.

Here's some highlights:

Anne Steiner, DevJam

"I'm always looking for that right kind of leadership protection, a willingness to experiment, and a group that wants to learn and try something different. That's your beachhead!"

Aaron Bjork, Microsoft

"The saying we live by goes – 'You can't cheat shipping.' If you deliver working software to your users at the end of every iteration, you'll learn what it takes to do that and which pieces you'll need to automate."

Tyler Hardison, Redhawk

"A lot of managers don't realize what a fundamental difference it makes – how we react when there's an outage or a failure. Sometimes you'd swear that the poor coder is a puppy and it's everyone's job to rub his nose in it when there's a screwup."

Nigel Kersten, Puppet

"It's all too easy to get bogged down when it comes to automation. DevOps isn't art, it's just hard work. Focus that hard work on the things that really matter. Guard your time and that of the people around you."

John Weers, Micron

"The tool is not the problem, ever. It's always culture and energy."

Seth Vargo, Google

"Often times CTO/CIO's catch fire and announce that they're going to reorganize with cross functional teams. Don't do that! Think about your DevOps or SRE transition in the same way that you'd release software."

Jon Cwiak, Humana

"DevOps is an emergent characteristic. It's not something you buy, not something you do. It's something that emerges from a team when you are doing all the right things behind the scenes, and these practices all work together and support each other."

Sam Guckenheimer, Microsoft

"There was no magical fairy dust for us. It required progressive change, some very conscious hard engineering changes, and walking the walk."

Ryan Comingdeer, Five Talent

"We've tried tiger teams, where we pull in one rep from every department – for us that wasn't a winner. Instead we try to focus on one very specific goal as an experiment."

JD Trask, Raygun

"We're still way behind the times when it comes to having true empathy with our end users. It's surprising how entrenched that mindset of monitoring being an afterthought or a bolt-on can be."

Michael Stahnke, Puppet

"Defining how people should interact and how they optimize their work and collaborate, to me that's the real potential offered with DevOps. It's not tech. Tech is cool, glossy, beautiful, but what's way more important is showing leaks in the process."

Rob England, The IT Skeptic

"I refuse to get entangled in arguments about the pros and cons of various tools. This is really a closed problem: there is always a solution, you just need to find it."

Munil Shah, Microsoft

"People don't want to do testing, it's not glamorous. For us, there was no alternative but to roll up our sleeves and do it. It's been the key factor in everything we've accomplished, the velocity we've been able to reach."

Michael Goetz, Chef

"One of the biggest failure points I see is that people often don't make their work visible enough. If you don't know what people are working on across the team, that creates a natural siloization which reduces ability to collaborate."

Brian Blackman, Microsoft

"The number one point that I want to bring out is waste. Executives get this instinctively. Here's the waste, and if you eliminate this, look as the payoff — that gets you the buy in you needed."

Thank You!

Thanks to the following people who bought time out of their busy lives to review our book and make it better:

- Alexandre Campos Silva
- Claudio Prospero
- Stuart Eggerton
- Greg Duncan
- Matthias Kautzner
- Ron Vincent
- Al Mata
- Donovan Brown
- David Kalmin
- Monu Bambroo
- Rob Smith
- Ethan Smith-Gillespie

We also were blessed with an extraordinary group of interviewees and contributors. This included the following:

Anne Steiner from CPrime, Tyler Hardison from Redhawk Network Security, Michael Stahnke and Nigel Kersten from Puppet, John Weers from Micron, Jon Cwiak from Humana, Sam Guckenheimer, Brian Blackman, Aaron Bjork, and Brian Blackman from Microsoft, JD Trask from Raygun, The IT Skeptic (Rob England) from faraway New Zealand, Michael Kwan from InTimeTec, and Ryan Comingdeer from Five Talent Software, Betsy Beyer, Stephen Thorne and Seth Vargo from Google, and Sam Eaton from Yelp.

A few personal thanks as well:

- Thanks to the lovely Jennifer for being my confidante, my good friend, and such a spiritual and wise person. Thanks for making me laugh and always surprising me, 24 years and counting!

- To Ingrid, who looks at life the way it could be. And to Kai, who I promised to take care of and protect, so many years ago. You are both special beyond words and I am so proud of you.

- Thanks to Ed for the great laughter and floating in the pool with the kids, and for teaching us that "No Peeing From The Porch" is really more of a suggestion.

- A grateful thanks to the good people at Wild Winds Station for their life-affirming bacon breakfast sandwiches, and for putting up with that weirdo in the corner muttering to himself and pounding away on his laptop.

- To Rob, who's taught me so much about fishing and life. One day, I will be as patient and wise a teacher as you are! And I'll never forget your favorite scripture…

- To Curtis and Heather, for the punches in the shoulder and the great cribbage games. That awkward scene at Hamburger Habit I will savor forever.

- To Joel, Amanda, Liam, and Savannah, for the great friendship and above all the fond memories of karaoke championships and some epic clumsy moments on the Nehalem.

- To the early morning chicas – Jorden, Chiara, Keturah, and Nancy – for the encouraging words and making me laugh.

- To Adam Dietrich and the heroic teachers at Metolius Elementary, who first got me thinking about the importance of character traits and keeping those values visible – which led directly to Chapter 7.

- To my mom and dad, for teaching me what it means to be a good parent and life partner.

- To Hany and Nancy, my very best friend (just not in tennis) and his lovely bride. Eventually, that boat is going to get in the water.

- To Don, enemy to Audis everywhere, hunter of elk, a true friend in need, and the best fisherman I've ever met. "We were having to put our eggs on behind the bushes!"

And to Dean and Lisa, for the great advice, wonderful food and warm hospitality!

- To Matt and Zara, for letting me kidnap the big lug and drag him off to the Kenai. And for taunting Joel when he fell into the river like an upside-down turtle.

- To Jake "Muffet Kilmanjaro," for the long insightful talks and a very rewarding friendship. We'll always have Brooklyn!

The Abyss Stares Back

This story isn't true, but it could be.

The conversations in this book we've had in some form many times. The feeling persists at the end of day, rubbing our weary eyes – we were busy today, crazy busy, and it feels like we got a lot done. So, why do we feel like we're treading water? There's all these wonderful things we'd like to accomplish, personally and in our careers – but it feels like they always take the back seat to survival, keeping the wolf away from the door.

At least, that's the position Ben is in. He's come from the development ranks, but his last line of code was written a decade ago. Now, his life consists of meetings and e-mails. And more and more, he feels caught up in a gathering catastrophe. The team is starting to fracture with the stress of long hours and unreasonable expectations; irreplaceable people are defecting to other companies. He's stuck with an IT and Operations team that seems both incompetent and hostile, deliberately sabotaging his team's releases and botching support, while shifting all the blame elsewhere. And management is starting to tune him out and freeze his requests. It seems like, one way or another, he'll need to find another job, or perhaps another career.

In short, it's a mess. He's stuck and isn't sure how to find the way out, or even where to begin.

© Dave Harrison and Knox Lively 2019
D. Harrison and K. Lively, *Achieving DevOps*,
https://doi.org/10.1007/978-1-4842-4388-6_1

Picking Up the Pieces

George sat back heavily in his chair, which groaned in protest. "That was…. Gawd-awful. Honestly, Ben, I don't think I can take another meeting like that."

I grimaced. "Well, you have to admit, it could have gone worse. Our team looks really good by comparison with what our IT *partners* have been delivering." I drew out the word *partners* just enough to give it the right sarcastic flavor. "Or not delivering. I mean, if we can keep up this trajectory, we could get more developers and finally start making real progress."

I've got to admit though – this latest meeting had not gone well. No team had covered themselves with glory in WonderTek's most recent release, and my business partners have increasingly become frustrated. New features – features that our customer base had been asking for months now – had to be rolled back; they were simply too buggy to be shown. Worse, unexpected integration issues that arose very late in the testing phase had caused noticeable performance degradation issues. Customers were now having to submit orders over the phone, while teams worked around the clock to try to get order processing off the ground. Credit card orders were running the risk of expiring.

My last meeting had been with the company CTO and the CEO and several vice presidents I've never met before. There wasn't a smile in the room, except for some sardonic ones when I was laying out my remediation plan. Clearly, people were losing faith, and it was eroding my position.

It seems at times like we are slogging uphill. Since adopting Agile, my team has moved mountains, and we've met all their delivery goals. It simply is not our fault that the last release had not gone well. That message evidently hasn't sunk in, however; the clear chasm between my team and the IT/Operations group was baldly exposed during the meeting. I will need to do something to reverse the tide.

Thankfully, I had a good friend to watch my back. I've known George over the past 10 years; he's my wartime consigliere, to borrow a phrase from *The Godfather*. At the moment, George's thin frame slumped in the chair, head back and eyes closed; the picture of abject dejection. But I knew this was just a passing thing; George was indomitable. And the man had an uncanny sense for what was going on behind the scenes. I will need every bit of his political savvy and knack for pulling on the right strings.

I pinch my nose and try to clear my head. "George – I don't get it. Three months ago, all our teams signed off on this company-wide Agile movement. We have the most expensive and experienced consultants available to help us out. We're churning out more work than we've ever done, so our adoption of Agile is on track. Yet our last release has even more bugs and the business is unhappier than ever. I keep thinking I'm missing something."

George's head lifts slightly, and I catch a glimmer from his slitted eyes. "It's true the developers are working together well and we're producing code at a faster rate. But our testing is in a shambles right now, and operations is dumping bugs on us faster than we can keep up. We are drowning in technical debt, Ben." He sighed. "It's true that we may be winning as a unit, but what good does that do us if we are losing as a team?"

He straightens a little, and now his eyes were open a little. "If success means delivering new features as fast as possible to QA, we are successful. But what if that's not the finish line?" A long pause. I reach over and pat his hand. "George, we're a shared services org. That means our responsibility is to deliver code period. After that, it's just not our responsibility, and eventually people are going to realize that and put the blame where it belongs."

My old friend is shaking his head. "I'm agreeing with you that Agile is working for us, but from what I'm seeing it's actually making things worse down the line. We're burning through our chips, Ben. The people in that room aren't listening, because they view us as failing – our releases aren't making it into production – or once they get there we are drowning in post release cleanup like this." The chair creaked again, and George stands up. "I'm going to go home, make myself an Old Fashioned, and try to forget about this meeting." We say our goodbyes and part ways.

That's the difference between George and me, I think as I head out to my car. Instead of feeling afraid or drained, I was oddly energized by the back-and-forth tug of war in the boardroom. I'd always loved courtroom dramas and enjoyed fighting for my team on the executive level. Still, George had a point; the partnership with Operations had become more strained of late. I resolved to put some feelers out.

A Bad Start to the Day

There was just a little blue softening the black of the early morning sky when I pull into the rain-slicked parking lot at Wondertek. I've learned long ago that 90% of my work gets done before 9 a.m., and it's easily the best part of my day – a chance to reflect a little without distraction.

Usually, that is. I was just stirring around the bubbling coffee grounds in the French press when Douglas pops his head over the cubicle wall. "Ben, can you come into my office for a bit?"

A pang of fear clenches my gut as I follow Douglas back. Douglas is not quite looking me in the eyes, and he is definitely not smiling. We chat uncomfortably for a few minutes about how things were going post release. Then, he begins. "I suppose you probably know why we are having this little chat."

"Um, not quite." I swallow a bit. "I realize things did not go well with the last release, but we are showing progress – "

"Showing progress? Ben, I hired you to make me look good. You told me, don't worry about the team, I've got it under control. From what I hear, this last release was just more of the same." He looked out the window and slowly let out a puff of air. "For the past three years we have been telling people that things will be different, that we're working as partners to get our code out the door faster and better."

My stomach is clenching up, and my throat is dry. This is starting to sound like a pack-your-things discussion, and I'm not prepared. It's a bad economy, my savings account is in tatters, and it would take easily half a year or more to find another job. "I don't understand this. We ARE releasing faster, and I have the numbers to prove it. Agile is working for us, Douglas. The team is pulling together as one, we met all of our goals for this quarter early. My God, we just finished rolling out that footwear survey app two weeks ahead of time – and it's a killer app, Douglas, it uses stuff we've never tried before. Really cutting edge, JavaScript-based, the UI is clean and so responsive."

"Ben." My managers' tone is flat, emphatic, and final. "The footwear people were the first ones I heard from yesterday. They aren't happy, at all. And our relationship with Operations seems to be getting worse as well, they're calling you The Cowboys."

"Cowboys!", I snort. "Do you realize that they've been sitting on our releases for 6 weeks now prepping environments and there's no sign of traction…"

Douglas held out a hand; he's looking at me now, and he's angry. "Do me a favor and just listen to me. We are paid by the business. They want these features out the door. This footwear app that your team wrote, is it in production?" Another silence. "I already know it isn't. Footwear tells me that they've been waiting on it for two months; they're going to miss their window for this quarter to get this to customers for their marketing push."

"Douglas, come on! The app is done, tested and ready to deploy; we are waiting on production environments to get built out. That's not on me! Operations didn't handle their procurement right, and they keep shoving us to the bottom of their priority queue. There is no escalation path or even a way to check status with them without walking down and hoping I can catch someone in their cubicle who's halfway competent." I roll my eyes. "Dear God, I've seen better organization on 16th century whaling ships!"

"Ben, just stop it. Your predecessor talked like that too – it was always the other guys. Well, he didn't last. The business does not care one good goddamn if the issue was Operations or you. In their eyes, YOU are failing – as a group – to get them what they've been asking for."

This is sounding exactly like what George was saying last night. I have to force myself not to lean forward or clench my fists under this barrage. Douglas continues, "All right. I'd be doing you a disservice if I didn't say that you are trying your hardest. I wasn't sure if Agile was going to work for us when you first started on, but now I'm convinced, and I think the business is happier with some things you're trying. But I'd also be doing you a disservice if I pretended that things are going terrific. They're not. We are sitting on a powder keg right now, and the perception is that your team is the place where good ideas go to die. You need to turn this around."

He leans back and pinches the bridge of his nose. "Whatever is going on here, you need to make it right with your partners in Operations and IT. Right or wrong, you won't be able to move an inch without their cooperation, and they're pissed right now. And go to your customers and shore things up there as well. Get me a remediation plan, Ben – I want it in writing, and it needs to be soon."

Back at my desk, I find myself shaking a little; that was a close call. Even the aroma of the coffee can't dispel the sense of gloom from this morning's ambush. I need to come up with some workable ideas, fast. When George comes in, I tell him about the morning's developments. He's back to his old unflappable self; his face never registers even a flicker or a trace of surprise. Instead, he's philosophical. He muses, "I don't think Douglas wants to get rid of us. Actually, I think he's trying to protect us. But like I said yesterday, we're burning out our support."

I'm still a little flummoxed. "I can show that we've made progress. We sold the business on Agile a year ago, and it's worked. The team loves the retrospectives and the planning sessions; we're pulling together well and we're being transparent to our customers. But there's problems down the line. We're releasing to QA every two weeks, right on schedule – but those releases just sit there because Operations can't build out environments fast enough. Our test cycle is completely manual; we've thrown people at it and added an offshore team in Bangalore to push work through faster but it's still a 4-day turnaround. Will somebody please explain to me why blame keeps falling on our shoulders when it's obvious that our turnaround time is not the problem?"

George smiles. "Last night I did a little research and found out something strange. Do you know what our turnaround time was before we started doing Agile?" I shrug, and he continues: "It took about 2 months to get a Hello World type web app out the door and in production, remember? Well, guess how long that takes now, nine months later? … Ben, we haven't shifted the needle at all. It still takes 2 months."

"That's impossible! It would only take our team a few days to crank that website out and get it in test."

"Yes, well, that's the problem, isn't it? The finish line for our team is getting it out the door to QA. But, in the eyes of the business, at that point we're just starting – the real finish line is working as designed in production. And our pain point with production deployments and building environments haven't changed at all. We're still stuck in quicksand."

I smile grimly. "Urggh. A nice little epitaph for my career here at WonderTek. George, I'm in my mid-forties, and I don't want to have to hit the job market as damaged goods like this. It feels very much like we've got a sword over our heads." I drum my fingers on the desk. "That's really true? Our turnaround time hasn't budged?" George nods. "So, that's a number we can start with, and it might explain why the team seems to be moving faster but our success isn't registering. Let's put together some kind of remediation plan to convince people we've got a handle on things. I'll need to spend some time talking to my partners and see if we can salvage things with them."

Operations Piles On

For whatever reason, my latest craze is root beer floats. Lately, and this was something I'm not very proud of, I've been starting the day with one. The mixture of the creamy smooth vanilla ice cream and the fizzy root beer hits my taste buds just right. This morning, I spooned some into my Yeti cup; I found the insulated stainless steel makes the ice cream form a little crunchy crust that was better than any morning coffee. I need to hit the ground running this morning; hopefully, the sugar high will carry me through.

I begin with the most unpleasant task, meeting with Operations. At WonderTek, this group seems to always be complaining about lack of resources. In my eyes, they had a nasty habit of sitting on work to build a case for more people. It was an old game that unfortunately seemed to be working; the department had tripled in size over the past 2 years. Emily, who ran the team, was tough and no-nonsense; she held her team accountable to a high standard but was also fiercely protective and was an implacable adversary when things go wrong. Despite our differences, I respect her, and I've worked hard to build up a good personal rapport with her. If fences needed mending, I was starting at the right place.

But perhaps not this morning. As soon as I walk into her office, she swivels her chair around and gives me a look of pure, white fury. "Is this about last weekend? Ben, I am not – repeat – NOT happy with your team."

"I just got back from my boss, Emily. He tells me you've been complaining about us. He seems to be under the impression it was our guys that dropped the ball. Emily, I thought we were partners. I really don't appreciate being stabbed in the back like this." My jaw sets. "I thought we were past this."

Emily laughs bitterly. "On a personal level, we're fine. I think some of the things your team has done over the past year have been really positive. But this last weekend…" She shakes her head. "I spent most of Sunday, when I was hoping to go wine tasting with my husband, having to talk Kevin off a ledge. He wanted to quit, Ben."

"Kevin? Good God, what are you talking about? My team told me they've been waiting on him to create a VM for the past four weeks. That's a right-mouse click, Emily. And he was a complete dead weight when it came time for our deployment. We gave you guys documentation, we walked you through what needed to happen, and when we needed Operations to partner up with us, they left us holding the bag. We got those environments late, Emily, and we had to spend most of the weekend getting them functional."

Emily's smile widens into a smirk. "Those jokers on your team are selling you a line. Did they tell you when they came by with those setup instructions?" She jabs her index finger on the desk. "Wednesday. Freaking Wednesday, Ben. The rollout was on Friday night! And look at this crap!" She pulls a thick sheaf of papers from a folder on her desk and slaps it down triumphantly in front of me, like a prosecutor with a particularly incriminating piece of evidence. "I'm looking at five pages of itemized directions here. And it's garbage. Look at this one – '5. Set up SQL Server'. What does that mean, exactly? What version, what size, what's the backup/restore strategy – none of that's here, we're left to guess. Ben, you put my guys under the bullseye. This just can't keep happening."

I hadn't been expecting this and find myself stammering a little as I leaf through the handover documentation. "You know, I looked through those directions myself when we were planning the rollout. To me, it looked complete. We even put up a wiki…"

"A wiki! I'd settle for a decent head start. It's time you faced facts. Since you guys made this move to Agile, you've been pushing out releases every two weeks. And each of them requires a touchpoint with my team. You say that we're partners, but you've never asked us if we're ready to handle releases every two weeks versus every 6 months. And we're just not, Ben. We don't have the people – don't you dare laugh, you don't work over here and you don't know what it's like supporting something in production. You talk partnership, but you're not walking the walk, plain and simple. A real partner would never drop something like this on us with no warning."

I stand up. The whole point was to salvage our relationship; if I stay much longer, I'll start throwing some facts of my own in her face. *Remember what your Dad used to say – once you say those words, those angry words, you can't unsay them.* "Emily, I didn't know that you guys felt this way. You know we can't move anything without your help, and it seems like we are missing something as a team. I need to think this over."

"You know me, Ben, I'll always tell it to you straight. We're really sick and tired of being downstream of you guys. I can't lose Kevin, he's my best person and frankly he's done working with your team." She started to put her headphones on. "I've got a meeting, and we need to do a postmortem of this last little misadventure. Let's talk later in the week, OK?"

In Debt up to Our Eyeballs

Things got no better when I walk across the street to talk to the Footwear people. My main partner there, Tabrez, sees me as I come through the lobby doors. He just shakes his head slightly and turns back to his meeting; I will have to try again later.

Back at my office, I get caught up on e-mail. There was a few from my QA lead Rajesh, complaining about being behind on their test cycles as a result of the last push. That was par for the course; it seems like there is never enough resources or time for the QA team. More seriously, my ace BSA, Elaine, left me a short note: *You need to see me, today.* I sigh and say a silent prayer for some energy.

The daily standup gives me just the nice jolt I need. The last sprint ended on Friday – this was Day I of a new effort, and the team is visibly excited to be getting to work on some new features. I listen and make a mental note of some blockers looming up ahead. For the first time in days, I can feel my shoulders unclench. *God help me, I love these guys. We've come so far.*

A year ago, Agile was just an unproven theory. My team was one of the first to adopt it at WonderTek. Now, of course, I pretend that it was all part of my inscrutable Master Plan, but I remember damn well what led to us adopting Agile: sheer desperation. This was my first taste of management, and for months I had felt completely disconnected from what the team was actually doing. This left me vulnerable to credibility-burning surprises. Agile was a gamble that paid off handsomely for me; I know exactly what the team was committing to and how we were doing. It also helped me gate work; in the past, people would swing by to "check on how things were going" and try to get their favorite developers to prioritize their latest emergency project. Best of all, it gave something a manager can't have enough of – insulation. If anything was stopping our progress, or if it looked like we were going to fall short, I knew well ahead of time and could get ahead of things.

What made the biggest impact was the smallest of things: a few hundred dollars sunk into widescreen monitors. Over a few weekends, I'd read some books on Toyota's Lean movement, including the widespread use of "information radiators" to show progress in common areas. The following week, I had set up a few monitors facing the hallway displaying all the key metrics for the team: a nice burndown chart for the sprint, our progress against their assigned tasks, and the improvement in velocity made as a group over the past year. This helped the team by keeping their commitments top of mind, but the real payoff came with other groups. People kept dropping by and asking me questions – "What's a PBI? Why do you guys meet every day – isn't that inefficient? Why do you estimate in points instead of hours?"

It was an odd and very human thing. If I had paraded around scrum and Agile concepts, it would have fallen flat as an attempt to make other teams look bad in comparison. Just displaying the work we were doing without pushing caused this kind of snowball effect, where it gathered momentum on its own. Other teams started working in sprints, quietly and without fanfare. They all did it a little differently, but now there wasn't an engineering team at WonderTek that wasn't producing work in short bursts instead of year-long milestones.

I remember very well though being terrified about exposure. WonderTek can be a very political place. At times, my job seems like a game of Donkey Kong with flaming barrels coming at me from all sides. Everything is based on a flawless reputation for competence; a certain level of paranoia can be a healthy survival trait here. Given this operating climate, sending out those first few retrospectives – including our mistakes and where we didn't complete work – gave me pause. Mistakes would be seized upon and magnified by other team leads; I worried about losing face with our business partners.

Astonishingly, no hammers or flaming barrels descended from above. In fact, it seemed like being up-front with where the team was falling short weirdly seemed to increase my credibility. And the team really enjoyed it; several had told me that complete, honest, hold-nothing-back retrospectives were the best side effect of implementing Agile. During sprint planning sessions, it's common to see points being made off a retrospective done months earlier; it had saved us several times from going down the rabbit hole and repeating mistakes.

There were rough points, of course. Agile wasn't free; it required a time investment. Meeting together every 2 weeks for a retrospective session, including a group demo and show-and-tell, took up almost 4 hours; combined with the sprint planning meeting, which took another half day, they were losing too much time keeping the wheels turning. But the business seemed to respond well to the bargain that I put to them during that first trial period with Agile – *if you give us isolation, we will give you transparency and accountability*. I don't see business partners dropping by "just checking up on things" for example, once we gave them a public dashboard to check on their deliverables and explained that work would be gated and planned sprint by sprint.

I still don't like all the time lost with the retrospective and planning sessions. It's unavoidable, and in the end I've decided it's a tax well worth paying. Just being able to plan and commit to a small set of tasks had a transformative effect on what had been a very chaotic and unhappy group. Suddenly, we were in the driver's seat, instead of being a victim of events beyond our control.

This didn't mean that life was bliss. There's a tapping on my office door – Alex, my lead developer, pokes his head in. "Hey, can we talk a second?"

Trouble ahead; Alex didn't do this often. "I think I've got a few minutes before the next beat-down. What's up?"

"Listen, we just finished this big push. We said a few sprints ago that we would buy out some cycles to start paying down our technical debt. Our bug list is through the roof, but that's not the worst of it – our code quality continues to degrade. To get the last few features out, we had to take some shortcuts. I don't even want to show you some of the hardcoding and crappy spaghetti code in the last release, or the new libraries we threw in there completely untested. My suspicion is that's the real cause of some of the performance issues we've been seeing in production. Most of my guys are heads down knocking down bugs, and we likely will be doing that for a few more sprints. We can throw our commitments for this sprint totally out the window – our main priority is keeping our heads above water."

"Well, that's obviously not good." I sigh; this conversation had a déjà vu quality to it that grated. Every sprint I come in thinking we finally have a clean slate to really start knocking down new work and ramping up velocity. And it seems like on day 2 of every sprint, half my firepower bleeds away handling support and post-release fixes. As unpleasant as this news was, it really wasn't unexpected. "Obviously I've got some more damage control to do then with our stakeholders because we're not going to be able to deliver what we promised."

Alex grimaces. "I know you're focused on new work, and I get it – but at some point, we are going to have to say no. We threw architecture almost completely out the window months ago trying to make our dates, and look where that's got us. Our codebase is just a big ball of mud – half the time when there's a problem, it takes us days just to figure out where the problem could be because our releases are so gigantic. And then when we try to roll out a fix, we get all these wonky regression errors. No one really understands how things work end to end because it's held together with baling wire and sealing wax – yes, me too unfortunately – and God help us if one of my people gets sick. Padma was out two days ago; no one else on the team even knew where her work was, let alone how to fix it."

Now, I'm starting to get a little pissed off. This is nothing more than a process problem, and I've told Alex before to set a higher standard when it came to documentation. "Alex, we've been over this before. You need to have better documentation, even a wiki or a SharePoint site for Pete's sake. Your guys should be totally interchangeable – if we're doing what we should be and leaving a better documentation trail, it shouldn't matter at all if someone's sick. We're still thinking like a bunch of skilled individual craftsmen, not a team."

"Ok. Just something to think about, all right?" Alex gets up and says, "Listen, we committed to Agile, and it's working. But our technical debt is rising, and at some point, the bill is going to come due."

I pat him on the shoulder on the way out and then look at my phone. I'll be late for the release recap meeting. I hate coming in late to any meeting, as it puts me on my back foot. This one especially looks like a bruiser, and now I was at a serious disadvantage.

Release Retrospective

Sure enough, there was a set of unfriendly stares as I come into the meeting room. There were about 20 people in the room, about a dozen more than I like for a productive working session. Of course, that wasn't the point today – this was more like a show trial. Emily has a phalanx of IT peeps on her side of the table, whose main purpose seemed to be nodding in agreement whenever she drops a bombshell.

She launches a frag grenade now. "Thanks for joining us Ben – we were just talking with your team about what happened this last launch. It seems like every time there's a new version of this software from you guys, we end up having to work round the clock getting it to work. And then there's dealing with all the support calls afterwards because it's broken. This last one was particularly bad – we're still adding them up, but there's over a dozen major issues we've identified so far in production, and about a hundred minor UI bugs. Ivan tells me that it's going to take his team days just to triage and prioritize the issues. Don't you guys test your code before you send it out the door?"

I fight the urge to roll my eyes with this expression of sympathy for poor Ivan having to actually lift a finger. Ivan was a particularly vocal and nasty thorn in my side. He was in charge of 24x7 support and triage here. So far, all his ideas seem to focus on shifting responsibilities elsewhere. His latest "process improvement" had consisted of buying an expensive trouble ticket software system, separate from the one the development team used. Besides the ongoing drain caused by trying to reconcile two different ticket queues, any bugs called in by customers now passed along untouched to hit my team directly. Ivan views this as efficient; I view it as a naked attempt to shift responsibility and burden my team with production support.

It frustrates me, because easily two thirds of the bugs we face are non–code related – networking issues, trouble with authentication, or good old-fashioned user error. Now, his team had to sort through the bugs themselves and weed out environmental or dead-end problems – a big reason why we are tied down every sprint with unplanned support work. Most of the organization seemed to think that Ivan was the Operations version of Jack Welch, but I think he's a buzzword-quoting career asshole.

Rajesh, on the far side of the table, had his hackles up with Emily's attack on their quality. "Emily, with all due respect, you don't know what we've put into our testing layer. Just with this last release, we had a team of 18 people in Bangalore running smoke-testing against the UI layer round the clock. We've invested heavily in Selenium and our integration test coverage is rising every sprint. The issues with this last release have nothing to do with lack of testing – the dev teams changed the UI significantly, which meant we had to rewrite our functional test layer. Everything was broken – it was a miracle we were able to get our test coverage up to what we did, since we had to start from scratch a month ago."

Elaine, my ace business analyst, is sitting two seats over from Rajesh. She says, "Not only that, but there were the same old problems with what was in the release itself. Our business stakeholders looked at the features we were releasing and there were several that just didn't make the cut from a quality standpoint, and a few had to be rolled back completely because the developers either misunderstood the requirements or the feature itself just wasn't needed anymore. Honestly, some of these requests have been sitting waiting on us for six months or more – I'm surprised any of them had any value at all by the time we got to them." She gives me a glance and says, "Rolling back those bad features seemed to take up a lot of time that could have been spent knocking down some of the bugs our users have been reporting from the last release."

The lone developer at the table, Alex, had been checking his phone, but now his head popped up. "Yes, about that – that code had been in a feature branch that was at least two months old. Keeping that code stable and up to date is killing us, it's going to take me a few sprints just to integrate this with main and nail down issues with conflicting libraries and get the code merged. It didn't help that last Thursday Elaine came over and told me to get rid of the new order submission screens. That late in the game – it's like if a customer comes in asking for a cup of coffee with cream, and then after I make it just the way they wanted they change their mind and ask me to get rid of the cream. Of course, I can do that, but it's going to take me a lot of work. I wish our business people would understand the impacts they're causing when they change their minds – it's directly leading to these stability problems."

"This is exactly why we need to pay more attention to the basics," Emily said, frowning. "We've been saying for months that our current pace isn't sustainable. Our releases are breaking, they're not just high-risk – it seems like every one is a guaranteed fail. One year ago, we started up CAB meetings and for whatever reason it dwindled away due to lack of support. I think we should start them up again – go over defects, run postmortems on more than an ad hoc basis. These breakages are making everyone look bad, not just my team. It's high time we begin instituting a little discipline in these processes. In my last job at Phoenix Insurance, we had a great process – gated releases based on CAB approval, zero defect meetings where all the developers could go over root causes. There just wasn't this Wild West type bad behavior we're seeing with runaway releases..."

Enough – time to start focusing on some kind of outcome instead of this finger-pointing. I've learned a few tricks from a round of marriage counseling that Julie and I went through, and one of them was active listening. I stand up and walk over to the whiteboard and draw a table with three columns:

What Worked	What Didn't Work	What We'll Do Differently

I say, "OK, it's obvious the wheels came off with this last release. We've committed to Agile as a company, so let's handle this like we would any other retrospective – which starts with listening. What I'm seeing here is a few things that are not working."

I add the following to the middle column:

- Branch integration issues
- Integration code coverage dropping
- Business changing its minds about features to deploy
- Too many bugs making it out the door to production (strain on Operations)
- Late or nonexistent communication with IT on infrastructure needs
- Long list of features that are aging
- Crappy release documentation and rollout instructions
- Technical debt rising

I step back and look at the board. I don't necessarily agree with several of the points or their impact, but I figure throwing in the comments about the strain on IT and Operations might help soothe some tempers. I ask, "That last one is something Alex brought to my attention just a few minutes ago – it seems like the quality of our application code is showing some strain as well. Does that cover things?"

Elaine says, "In my view, we need to start training your team more in understanding and eliciting requirements. We only have two business analysts on the team, Ben – a lot of teams have a 1:1 ratio of developers to BSA's, and they don't see this kind of friction. If you aren't going to get me help with people, I am going to need to have your developers start putting in more work into understanding what needs to be done. It can't be just me."

Emily is still folding her arms – the permafrost on her side of the table shows no sign in thawing. "Put under the 'What We'll Do Differently' column the weekly CAB and zero-defect meetings. Attendance should be mandatory. I'm tired of just seeing people from my team in the room."

"Fair enough." The dry erase marker squeaks as I add it to the list. "Before we go any further, let's talk about what is working. I think we can agree that we've got some serious quality issues here. Was there anything that went well for us?"

Complete silence around the table. Even Alex shrugs; he is back on his phone, checking e-mail. Emily, surprisingly, is the first to speak. "You know, I thought putting Kevin in touch directly with Alex Friday night – when it looked like we'd have to roll the entire thing back – really helped things immensely. Once we actually had some back-and-forth going, we were able to find the mismatch in the server configuration that had caused all those intermittent connection issues. We barely made the cutoff to avoid a rollback, which would have really been a nightmare – but at least we made it."

I nod. Time for an olive branch. "I really appreciated having your team available and working with us in the war room, Emily. Kevin put in some heroic work." I sigh and sit down. "OK, let's put cross team collaboration as a win on the left side, and leave it at that. Emily, on the CAB meetings, let me attend to represent our team, so you'll have someone to work with on the dev side of things."

We're out of time for the meeting, which is good – I'd purposely capped it at 30 minutes. Meetings, like all gases, tended to expand to fill the space allocated to them. Emily closes her laptop and stands up. "I look forward to seeing a remediation plan. One thing I think we all agree on here – this can't just keep on happening. It's expensive and stressful."

I nod my head grimly as the meeting breaks up. The feeling I'd had since early this morning of a cloud hanging over me feels stronger than ever. I'm bone tired and still have a long day stretching ahead working on postrelease cleanup. As I leave the room, I look back at the whiteboard. The empty column on the right mocks me. Without a clear problem definition, it was hard to even think about a long-term solution.

What Isn't Working

At 3 p.m. every Tuesday, I sit down with George for half an hour to go over how things were going with our Agile improvements. Of late, these meetings had lasted barely a few minutes as we ironed out some rough spots; given the events of the past week, I have a feeling this one might stretch a little longer.

George begins by drawing up some of the troubles we'd pinpointed during the release recap meeting, then stops. "How are you doing, Ben? You seem tired today."

I lift my eyebrows. "Yeah, guess I am – for some reason." We both laugh. "I keep coming back to that talk we had a few days ago and I'm frustrated. Maybe we've plateaued, and maybe our partners are dropping the ball, I don't know. But this latest crapfest is really undermining my credibility, and George – that's all I've got! Agile has really helped the team, but I can only control this much" – I hold my hands close together – "not the rest of the company. I don't control project management, or IT, or Operations. Even our security and architecture people are siloed off."

We're both silent a few seconds, then I continue: "I don't think Douglas is going to fire us. But it's clear to me that some of the promises we've been making about higher quality with more frequent releases we just can't keep. My gut tells me shifting to longer releases is a mistake, but if we can't get IT to move at the speed we do, we may have to go back to a quarterly release cycle. Development is very much a balance between safety and speed, and right now our Agile velocity is hurting our safety."

"So, it seems like now is a good time to start talking about that next leap forward."

"Ah, you mean DevOps. The latest shiny object." I shake my head. "We're not Netflix or Amazon, George. I don't have a billion dollars, or hundreds of expensive, highly competent engineers. I've got a few dozen people available to me, that's it – and we've got a couple dozen mission critical apps to support. And you know well what a nightmare those apps are. We inherited a bunch of garbage kludged together by people who are no longer here and didn't believe in writing things down. So most of the time, we're afraid to touch them – they're just too brittle, too badly put together."

"And like I said – I only speak for part of the company. If it's related to development and writing code, or testing, you know my people – we can try it and see if we get results. But anything other than that is above my pay grade." I look at George, and my mouth tightened. "You can't ask a supertanker to perform like a sailboat, George. Our turning radius just isn't that small, and we're having problems just getting this jump to Agile to work for us. The perception, as you saw in that meeting, is that we're making things worse. Upper management sees us as being a cost center – WonderTek has always been and always be a sportswear company, first, last, and always."

George is relentless. "I think that attitude about 'we're just a clothing company' is changing, Ben. I was talking to a salesman the other day. Did you know that our sales people are still driving around with vans of samples to show our retailers their spring displays? But our competition is driving around with tablets – they can actually show the store manager how their displays will look, with a view they can rotate and play with, of their actual store. Guess who is going to be selling more clothing next quarter to that store? Under Armour, North Face, and Marmot are all using technology as a differentiator – not just a cost of doing business. I'm seeing signs that we're moving in that direction too."

That's interesting – I hadn't heard that. "That's definitely something to think about down the road. Let's get back to what is in our control. We have this list of trouble areas; Douglas wants a remediation plan. What's something we can promise in the short to medium term that can give people a better level of confidence in us?"

George is smiling at me. I know him well; he's going to hang onto this DevOps thing like a bulldog. "Well, looking at this list, we're seeing some issues like brittle test code, long wait times to get features out the door, integration hangovers, and quality issues. Oddly enough, these are all exactly the kind of problems DevOps was meant to address. We can start by focusing on the main pain point that's hurting everyone, and – without even using that forbidden word 'DevOps' – begin that supertanker turn you talked about."

He goes back to the board and crosses out the right column, "Things We Will Do Differently," and put in all capitals the word "QUALITY." Then, he put the following bullet points in the table:

What Didn't Work	QUALITY
• Branch integration issues	• Code review
• Code coverage dropping	• Continuous integration
• Business changing its mind	• Continuous delivery
• Too many bugs	
• Bad communication prerelease with IT	
• Long list of aging features	
• Rising technical debt	

"Hang on a second, George. We do code reviews already."

"We do – infrequently and very, very briefly as part of a pre-release show and tell. That's great for public speaking practice, but it's not really helping improve the overall quality of your code, does it? I was listening to a talk by

Randy Shoup, who used to work for Google – he said that, if he could go back, that'd be one practice he'd really refactor – he'd have code reviews be more frequent. Like, daily."

"George, you know our situation – the business is waiting on these features. They won't stand for a lot of time lost with handholding."

"Do you think the business is happy now?"

That, I have to admit, is another good point. George continues, "What I'm asking the team is to think about quality, first and foremost. It's obvious that the business is not happy with the way features are being delivered right now. If we want a different result, we are going to have to think about this differently, more holistically.

"Where we are trying to get as a team is to get fast feedback and smaller release bits. The two work together – this last release represented three months of work, mushed into one feature branch, and it was delivered late. It was a tidal wave of crap – we'll be picking up the wreckage from this for weeks. However, if we move the pain forward, and if we do more frequent releases with smaller amounts of changes in each one, our risk level will actually go down. We want small, frequent waves, not huge, catastrophic ones. Faster *is* safer, Ben. I think our goal should be to get to daily releases, and in six months if at all possible."

My jaw drops a little. George might as well be talking about going to Mars. "Daily?! We're having a hard time running out releases quarterly at the moment. It's going to be hard to sell this, George. If the perception out there is that we're a bunch of developer cowboys, this will look as if we're trying to wriggle out of our commitments."

George stares hard at me, that bulldog gleam in his eye. "Here's what I don't understand. Why are you asking permission from others to do your job? You've said to me several times, 'the business has every right to tell me **what** to do, but not **how** to do it – that's *my* job.' So why are you asking for an OK from them now? Everything I heard in that meeting today had to do with quality – improving that is part of our team's core function as professionals. For the next three months, *everything* we do needs to center around that one focus point, and there's no one in the company that can tell you differently."

I lay my hands flat on the desk. "I haven't lost my nerve, if that's what you're asking. But I know this company and what's possible. What you're asking for – we simply don't have the maturity level or the tools to make this happen. Now, I need to put together some kind of realistic plan. Get me something more realistic and we can talk about DevOps once we get our *own* house in order."

The Brain Trust

Every few weeks, I like to get together with a few close friends early in the morning and shoot the breeze. I call them the "Brain Trust" – usually it's just George, Elaine, Alex, and myself. Sometimes, we talk about work and the problems we're facing; other times, we get caught up on the weekend adventures or how our families are doing.

This early in the morning, the only other people here are the earliest of the kitchen crew, arriving for lunch prep. Every table in the large cafeteria space was empty. The clink of dishes and silverware is oddly comforting; it reminds me of my college days. Most of my fellow students loved hanging out at the library. My favorite study area was the local McMenamins brewpub, where I'd study late into the night. I loved the hum and clatter in the background; it helps the nice, relaxed, informal vibe that gets good ideas flowing.

Today, though, I invited Rajesh along and bought him a coffee. Rajesh is a gentle soul and has one of those calm, sensible voices that is easily drowned out. I've run into people like Rajesh in every place I've ever worked. They tend to be silent heroes, not caring overmuch about credit, but in a time of crisis they always seem to be in the right place with a thoughtful, perfect solution. Perhaps, I need to invite him along more often. I like this group small and trim, but if quality really is our sticking point, I need to have Rajesh here and contributing.

George dumps three creamers into his coffee and stirs it contentedly. He seems to be able to eat whatever he wants. I feel a pang of jealousy – for being as thin as he is, George never seems to struggle overmuch with weight as I do. Ah well. "Business today guys, so sorry – we're playing cleanup from the release last week. George, why don't you show us the latest?"

George recaps the to-do items we've uncovered, in a now-familiar litany: branch integration issues, rising technical debt, and the abysmal communications ahead of the release. "Each of these has cost us time, but when we look at the overall picture, the consistent issue that seems to crop up is quality. We're spending weeks testing our code but the features we're delivering are still making it out the door with some pretty significant defects. Do you think that sounds about right?"

I can always count on Elaine to be our conscience and connect us with how the business thinks. She says, "The biggest issue isn't even on this list. My father used to tell me – it takes a lifetime to build up credibility, and 30 seconds to lose it. We are losing credibility with the business by the day – our reputation couldn't be worse right now. They're calling us 'The Black Hole'. Until we start improving our turnaround time on requests and making some headway on these requirements that are piling up on us, that rep is only going to get worse."

Rajesh groaned. "Elaine, we just finished talking about technical debt. We really need to buckle down and pay off that debt before we can expect to move forward. That means getting everyone on the team to commit to quality first. We need to take 3 or 4 sprints and focus on getting our integration testing caught up. This is do or die for us – unless we get our test coverage up, we're never going to be able to produce work at any kind of decent pace. We're just going to keep on churning out defects and hoping for the best."

I straighten up in my chair; a four-sprint timeout – and it'll be at least six by the time all is said and done – was one idea I hadn't seen coming. Elaine counters, "Rajesh, it's really naïve to think that we can take out 2 months of our time and sit on our hands working on buffing up testing when other requests are dying on the vine. The business simply won't stand for it."

George was munching on a cream cheese danish, and now he brushes some crumbs off his chest. "It seems to me like we need to find a better balance between velocity and safety. Right now, Rajesh is saying that our safety is dropping, and our test coverage numbers show that. However, if we focus on testing, our velocity goes to zero. That can't happen."

I don't know what the answer is, and it's making me panicky. I do know, instinctively, that Elaine is right; we can't take ourselves offline for a quarter. They'll dismantle us. Elaine is telling us that the slow rate of progress we're making is alienating the people I most need on our side. Rajesh is saying that we aren't eating our vegetables and that we're paying for it. We have to go faster to survive; but the person I most trust on the team is insisting that we need to put the brakes on. It's an impossible situation.

George is smiling. He says, "I totally understand why we all feel a little overwhelmed right now. When I look at all the things we need to do to get better at once, it looks gigantic. There's a lot that's outside our control right now – which means stress. But last week we isolated a few things that are totally within our control to implement that we can do *today*. We need to implement better peer reviews, like on a daily basis, and look at improving our delivery rate so we have small, testable batches going out the door."

Rajesh looked pained. "Sorry to say this George, but increasing our release rate right now is the last thing we need. The code that the developers are writing just isn't testable. As for full regression testing with our offshore team, every time we do a release – that's three weeks. We can't speed that up until we rethink our testing approach, and maybe change our framework. Implementing continuous delivery – I mean, that's just not realistic given our situation. We don't have a small army of people to throw at this thing, and it's just a pipe dream to even think about continuous delivery as long as what we produce takes so long to smoke-test."

The lunch crowd is starting to filter in; we've run out of time. I sigh, "OK, so let's go through the things George mentioned. Thumbs up or down, your honest opinion." I read off the items George had written on the board again. First was CI/CD, and to my surprise, that didn't get a single vote except for George. Rajesh's proposal to refactor our test framework in a lengthy reset gets shot down almost immediately. That left two items – daily code reviews and peer approval. Both got almost unanimous assent; these were, the Brain Trust agreed, low risk items that could help improve quality without taking away attention from work that needed to be done.

I can tell Rajesh is still frustrated. I grab him by the shoulder before we leave the cafeteria and say – "Rajesh, I know this seems like a step back…"

"It *is* a step back, Ben. You're signaling by your actions that quality just doesn't matter. The developers will continue to follow your lead and throw stuff over the fence." His mouth tightened a little. "I told you before, you have to go slow to go fast."

"Yes, I remember. Look – no one at that table thinks that testing comes second place. I think what you're hearing is a lot of fear and uncertainty. No one wants to be the one to tell the business that we need to stop work for several months to get things right. I definitely can't sell that to Douglas, and I would hate to hear what our business partners would say." I smile. "I'm really glad you came today, and your thoughts were dead on. Let's put some thought into it. Take two weeks – and come to me with a workable proposal. A proposal on specifically *how* to overhaul our testing so we won't continually have QA lagging behind. Pretend like you have no constraints, no sacred cows, and cost and resources aren't a problem. If it's workable, I promise you, I'll do whatever I can to implement it."

Rajesh has stopped seething. "So, in two weeks – you're going to listen to what I have to say. And you'll show it to the team?"

"I promise, Rajesh. Don't give up on me yet, I won't give up on you."

Bleeding Out

Just as I begin navigating to my comfy office chair, my phone buzzes. It's a text from Laure in HR: *Call me. I have some bad news about your team.*

Ten minutes later, my ears still ringing from the call, I stop by Erik's cubicle and tap him on the shoulder. He looks up guiltily then follows me back to the cafeteria. Erik was one of my prize hires. He had been hired on 2 years ago after an exhaustive national search and had quickly proven his worth; he was a top performer on the team and had cutting edge coding skills. Laure's news that Erik was leaving was a real blow; even worse, Erik had apparently decided to burn down every bridge he could on his way out the door.

"Erik, I hear you've handed in your notice. Why didn't you tell me first?"

"Ah, you know how it is man – it was late, you'd already gone home. I didn't want to hurt your feelings. This offer is just too good to pass up."

"Where are you planning to go?" Erik's eyes dropped, but after a slight pause he shrugged his shoulders and said, "Actually, I'm taking on a dev lead position at Netflix. They're going to let me work remote, and I might get some more time with my son."

Erik's son has autism – I had arranged for him to have 2 days a week working from home with that in mind. I say as calmly as possible, "I understand you leaving – the gold watch days are long behind us. But, the way you're leaving – Laure tells me you gave us zeroes across the board. You said we had weak leadership, that we were stuck in the mud, that we waste most of our time with busy work. You even recommended that we get folded into other groups. Erik, this reflects directly on me. I can't understand why you didn't come to me first."

Erik sighs and fidgets in his chair. "Look, Ben, on a personal level – you and I are fine, I like you. But honestly, can you really claim that we are cutting edge? I mean, look at this last release. I see us churning this garbage out, and when I try to point out ways of improving our apps so that they're not constantly breaking, I just get a bunch of head-nods. But nothing *really* changes. I tried to put it as best as I could with Laure, but bottom line – I'm leaving because Netflix is a 1% company. They get it, and they treat development as a core line of business, a vital part of how they do work. We are retail, Ben. It's all about dropping costs as low as possible, and they treat us like peons. It's always 'do more with less', 'we don't have time for that', 'the business expects us to meet these dates.' And it's been one death march after another lately. So then all this talk about partnership is just talk – I'm not a partner, I'm not valued. Thanks, but no thanks – I'd rather go to a company that takes me seriously, that values my time, where I can really make a difference. Here, it's like I'm trying to do open heart surgery in a stable. It's a losing game."

I reply hotly, "Erik, that's great, and we've had conversations about this before. You know, I can't control any of that. But we've created a little oasis of sanity for the team. Things are working better here, and I can't believe you're saying that you're not valued. We made a lot of concessions to get you the working schedule you wanted, and you're paid higher than anyone on my team, including some people that have been here twenty years. I feel absolutely stabbed in the back."

"Well, that's kind of why I ended up going to Laure, instead of talking to you. I knew you'd take it personally." Erik stands up. "Ben, you made me all kinds of promises to get me to come out here from Tennessee. You told me that we were going to be changing, modernizing, that I could control my destiny and change the organization for the better." He pointed to the WonderTek label on his shirt – "You know I love WonderTek, I've always worn this stuff and I'm loyal to what this company stands for. But the way we write software is thirty years old, we're hopelessly stuck in the past. It's the responsibility of the team lead to *lead*, Ben. In my view, and I'm sorry to say this, you smile and say we'll get to that, just as soon as possible, but nothing ever really happens. You're just part of the problem."

We part in icy silence. It would take me a few days to look Erik in the eye. This one stung a little. I owe Laure quite a bit for letting me know, side-channel, that one of my employees was tarring my rep on his way out the door. The team commonly sheds a person or two a year, and it usually seems to be a few weeks after a hard push like their last release. Still, exit interviews were valued very highly by management; Erik's remarks were bound to come up in my next performance eval with Douglas.

And now I have to find a replacement for Erik. It could take me months to find the right person and bring them up to speed. It looks like our team's productivity was going to have to take yet another serious hit.

Dysfunction Thrives on Secrets (Making Technical Debt Visible)

At the next daily standup, there is a definite chill in the air. Everyone rattles through their daily to-do's in a robotic, flat monotone. Even Padma and George, normally the happy bubbles of the group, seem subdued as they talk about their challenges to tackle for the day.

As the group wraps up and starts to disperse, I hold up a hand. "I'm not feeling a very good vibe today from you guys. What's going on?" Silence, but a few people glanced at Erik. I smile. "So, I think it's time to acknowledge the elephant in the room. Does this have to do with Erik leaving us?"

Erik grimaces and rolls his eyes up at the ceiling; George starts to smirk. "How do you like your eggs, Erik? Oh wait, let me guess – Eggs Benedict." Everyone groans, but at least now things are out in the open.

I got to give him credit; Erik is a stand-up guy. He faces the half-circle of his teammates now without flinching. "It's true, I'm leaving. I love you guys, you know that. This is a big step up for me. I'm hoping you can support me instead of acting like I just stabbed you in the back."

George asked, half-jokingly, "Was it something I said?" But I can feel the air of unspoken hostility starting to dissipate. Smiling broadly, I say cheerfully, "I think it'd be really unfair if we acted like Erik was a traitor or leaving us in the lurch. Sometimes we can grow within the company. And sometimes we end up looking for those challenges elsewhere. But that's Erik's right and privilege to map out his own career. Naturally, we'd prefer to keep you Erik, but I'm excited you're going to get a chance at leading a team of your own. That being said – you are going to leave a huge hole. Everyone here is really going to miss you."

For a few minutes, we chat with Erik about his new gig and what he's excited about. Erik purses his lips a little; he's on the spot and doesn't like it. "What I said is true – I'm not leaving WonderTek so much as I found something cool and new that happens to be elsewhere. It's not that big of a deal, people come and go all the time. And the economy's good enough where I'd be a fool not to think about options."

He sighs. "In terms of what the team here can do for the next person, well, I would" – slight pause here as he gauges me a little – "follow through on some of the things I told Ben a few days back. We keep saying we want to be cutting edge, modernize, get out of firefighting mode, blah blah. But the decisions we make are in the exact opposite direction – we are a clothing company not an IT shop, we don't have time for testing, forget about operationalizing, we need to deliver these features on these dates and get it done. Our words and our actions need to line up."

He looked around the group, pointedly. "I also told Ben that I was tired of trying to do heart surgery in a stable; I wanted to join a company where IT and application development are part of the DNA and our skills are really valued. This new spot gives me a chance to really drive and have an input on architecture at a meaningful level, not just trying to patch up a sinking ship."

I keep a calm smile on my face, but inside I'm seething; WonderTek is not the Titanic. I could squelch this, but that would give everyone the wrong message – and maybe lead to more defections. George is one step ahead of me as usual – he chips in, "Erik, you are telling us that the entire organizational culture here is working against the direction of the team, and that's why we keep getting caught in unplanned maintenance hell. That's great, and I actually agree with you, but this is a problem you're raising without a solution. What's something you think we need to improve on as a team that wouldn't require a magical fairy wand of power?"

Erik replies, "It's the exact same thing I've been bringing up in retrospectives for the past year. We need immutable infrastructure, a set of golden images and templates that we deploy as part of our releases. That's the key to eliminating three quarters of the problems we see that are caused by things other than code. If we had more discipline in how we set up and deploy our infrastructure, we'd get meaningful release management, faster dev/test cycles. That's the straw that stirs the drink – infrastructure as code."

Harry, one of my silverback coders, grunts derisively and says flatly, "Erik, like I told you last retrospective, this isn't Amazon. We are always being asked to do more with less, and moving mountains means we have to turn requests over fast. Like it or not we have multiple lines of business to support and hundreds of applications. The kinds of automation you're advocating require a lot of setup and governance and – most of all – TIME. Time we just don't have. What you're proposing might work for a software company, but I have yet to see it working in the real world where we're saddled with tons of legacy code and customers screaming their heads off over every delay."

Rajesh nods in agreement and says, "Yes, and our current pace just isn't sustainable. We need to move more slowly and shore up our testing, so what we push out the door doesn't fall on its face. That kills our rep with the business that's paying the bills. We have to move slow for our apps to have reliability and stability."

Erik says resignedly, "Look, this is exactly the discussion I didn't want to have. This is not a divorce, it's a career decision. You should be able to hear this without getting all up in my face. And why are you selling yourselves short like this?" He looks around the group for a few seconds then continues: "We are a software company that happens to sell clothing; development and IT are a vital part of our business. Pretending otherwise and treating our work as a cost center or a program where risk has to be managed is hopelessly out of touch. I've worked for startups, I've worked for large enterprises, banking institutions with heavy compliance and security requirements, insurance companies, it doesn't matter. We are all software companies, plain and simple, and it's been that way for a long time. In the end our job is to produce high-quality software as fast as possible. I've just mentioned one proven way to do that, something everyone here should be 100% onboard with, and all I'm getting is static, like I have for the past 12 months.

"And is it really a tradeoff between speed and quality – one or the other?" Erik looks around the circle for a few moments. "I don't buy that you have to go slow to go fast – in our industry, right now, we have competitors that are releasing multiple times a day and their quality and stability keeps going up. Don't you guys think our management knows that? At some point, we are going to have to stop trying to find new and ingenious ways to fail, and start thinking at a higher level. You just can't solve these problems we're facing using the same old way, at the same level of intelligence that created them."

There was a long pause following Erik's announcement. I see some angry faces, but at least half of the team is nodding in agreement. And Erik, much as I hate to say it, is right on some points. If I care about honesty, this is the time to show it. I say calmly, "OK, so this is a daily standup that has kind of spiraled a little bit. I'm sorry Erik – I really didn't mean to put you on the spot." I'm lying a little – there's a part of me that enjoys watching Erik squirm in payback for his poisonous exit interview. "I'm accepting that we need to think about new ways of doing things. I think we'll start with putting on paper the values we have as a team."

I draw this on the top of the whiteboard:

What We Value in Our Tribe

Open, honest communication – you will never get in trouble for saying the truth

---

I turn to the group and say, "That's front and center, and I'm going to have that show up in every performance eval and 1x1 we have. As some of you know, I grew up in a pretty dysfunctional family. One thing I've learned is that addictive behavior – whether it's centered on alcohol, drugs, or some form of abuse – thrives in the darkness. In my family, with my wife and kids, I try to be transparent, to be honest. If we have a problem as a team, I don't want to waste time trying to sweep it under the rug or ignore it and pretend like we're perfect. That's a dead-end game. I don't want to be perfect. I want to be better. Everyone of you, I know, feels exactly the same.

"Erik is telling us that we have a problem. And it just happens to match with some of the things we've discovered in our last release, so I know it's grounded in reality. Let's put up here – right in the open, in our team area, the problems we're discussing and some of the possible solutions, so it's not a secret anymore."

What Isn't Working

Branch integration issues

Code coverage dropping

Business changing its mind

Too many bugs – stuck in firefighting

Bad communication prerelease with IT

Long list of aging features

Rising technical debt

Infrastructure creaky, inconsistent, difficult to manage

Alert and monitoring nonexistent

I get general agreement from the group; this isn't a complete list of all that ails us, but a good starting point at least. Now, I ask for some solutions to throw up there – and the board starts to look more complete. This fits pretty well with what the Brain Trust and I were talking about earlier:

Things We Could Try

Continuous integration & delivery

Smaller releases

Refining requirements gathering

Peer review

Version control

Code coverage and testing

Better teamwork with outside teams especially Ops

Paying down technical debt

Infrastructure as code / a set of "golden images"

We all step back and take this in. It's an imposing list. Harry speaks for everybody when he laughs shortly and says, "This is like staring at Mount Everest. Any one of these are monumental tasks. It'll take us years even to scrape the surface."

George steps in with the right words. "Yeah, I agree. Let's not try to cure everything on this list at once. Let's just think about the last release. Which of these items sticks out as being the low-lying fruit?"

Padma says quietly, "I like that point about peer review. You know, where I used to work, we really took peer reviews seriously. I mean, you couldn't check in code unless at least one other person had looked over what you'd done. It forced me to write neater, more well documented code."

Hearing this, I start to smile and can see several others doing the same – it's hard to imagine Padma ever writing a sloppy line of code, even with a gun to her head. She's the ultimate professional; her approaches and techniques are always top-notch, and the thoroughness of her documentation is the stuff of legend. But George is nodding his head, musing: "I kind of like this, because it's low cost, it's something we can control, and it's a way of holding each other accountable to a common standard. In the past, that's worked really well for us."

Alex groans loudly. "I've also worked on teams that tried peer review, and let me tell ya – that's one idea that sounds great, in theory. But it just ends up being a gauntlet for junior programmers to run while they get beaten senseless. All it ever leads to is people being afraid to change the name of a module or else the Grammar Police come out of the walls and start whipping people for breaking their sacred naming conventions."

"I've worked places in the past where things went that way too," I mutter, frowning. But there has to be something here for Padma to bring it up. "It seems to me like your former outfit figured out how to do code and peer reviews right, Padma. Tell you what – let's sidebar this one. Can we talk about this in a week?"

Padma looks relieved; now, she has a few days to prepare. "OK – now on to version control," I nudge. "Now, that's the first thing we addressed with our switch to Agile. Thankfully, this is one area I don't think we need to talk about at length."

Erik coughs, loudly. "Actually, in Continuous Delivery Jez Humble pointed out that most people think their version control strategy is rock solid, but that's rarely the case. Using version control is foundational and it means that you can deploy and release any version of your software to any environment at will using a fully automated process. You know you're doing things right if your process is repeatable and reliable; that's clearly not the case with us right now. We've got our source code in, and most of our config files, that's true. But does that capture everything needed to run things, including systems configuration? And, does that really match what is running on production?"

Uncomfortable silence follows this question. Erik continues: "Let's say that we lost a production server. How long would it take us to rebuild it, and could it be done 100% with what's in our version control?"

Despite myself, I start to laugh. "OK, point taken. Much as I hate it. What bothers me the most about there's a huge amount of work you're talking about, capturing EVERYTHING needed to deploy, build, test, and release in version control. Up to now we've really just thought about version control as being for code. Let's add this to our to-do list then and come back to this again in a week. Erik, could you take point on that one?" He nods, and I move on. "This item on breaking up large features into small, incremental changes, and having them merged to trunk daily. Is that even practicable for us?"

George says, "Well, I know that's a key part of how the big companies we keep bringing up as examples do their work. Engineers at Microsoft, Netflix, Amazon, all have slightly different build strategies – but they all view long-lived feature branches as poison. So their teams check their work into mainline multiple times a day, and they don't seem to have the integration issues we suffer through."

Harry begins ticking off the now-familiar reasons why this could never work for us. "Once again, even if we had the resources to support a refactor – which we don't – we have interfaces and hooks to our mainframe systems that change at different rates, which means a lot of releases stuck in queue waiting on a dependency to finish development. Our current branching strategy isn't perfect but I don't think there's a lot of ROI in refactoring it just to try to make our brownfield applications look like a shiny web-native greenfield app."

There is some back and forth discussions on this for a few minutes, but no clear consensus on whether this was a main pain point. It looks like the costs of implementing continuous integration might not outweigh the benefits for us. With some relief, I put it on the list as a potential future topic and mentally shelve it. We have enough at this point to get started on, even if the crystal ball still looks a little murky. Here's what the right side of the wallboard looks like after our edits:

To Do

Peer Review (Padma)

Version Control (Erik)

Code coverage and testing (Rajesh)

Maybe Later

Better teamwork with outside teams i.e. Ops

Continuous integration & delivery

Smaller releases

Refining requirements gathering

Paying down technical debt

Infrastructure as code / a set of "golden images"

What We Value in our Tribe

Open, honest communication – you will never get in trouble for saying the truth

---

We're now well over half an hour overtime; it's time to wrap things up. I say, "I've heard from some of you that it seems like we write things on sand, never really learning or improving. And Alex tells me that we've never really listed our technical debt in one place; our shortcuts and deferred work end up getting buried in our retrospectives. So, we're going to leave this up here – and I'll put this on our wiki so we can all keep this single list of our problems and potential solutions up to date and prioritized. But I'm not putting anything on this list that we're not serious about, meaning we don't have someone that can drive it start to finish.

"Here's the takeaway message. We won't get anywhere as a team if we don't base everything we do on honesty. Even if its uncomfortable and it's not what we want to hear. So, the sweeping things under the rug days are over, starting today. I'm adding Erik's immutable infrastructure to our list. And I am making our team values explicit and in writing – you will never, EVER get in trouble for saying the truth. It won't show up on your performance eval, it won't be passed upwards with your name attached. We want feedback, we want honesty. I'm going to leave this up here, and we'll have a copy in every retrospective, so you can hold *me* accountable."

There was still a residual air of grumpiness as the team starts to disperse, but oddly enough I feel more cheerful than I have in days. Somehow, making some of those unspoken, implicit team values explicit seems like something of a turning point.

Legacy's Kiss of Death

It's been a long day; I put on my coat and head for the door. It's going to be mostly back roads for me today in getting home. All the roads out of Portland right now are bright red on Google Maps, like the circulatory system of an unhealthy heart patient.

George intercepts me a few steps from the door, and we chat a little as we head to our cars. I ask him what he thinks about the team values and to-do list on the board. Under the hood of his raincoat – no true Oregonian would use an umbrella, that's for tourists – I get the glimmer of a smile. "Well, it's a start… we've had these values for a while, you know. But I think it helps to make sure they're explicit, spelled out, and up on a wall somewhere."

"Yeah, I think it was past time." I pause and decide to confide in George a little more. "Erik leaving really hurts us, and more than just losing his tech skills. He really threw the team – and me – under the bus; made it sound like we were treading water, complacent, atrophying. That's the kind of ammo that our friends out there in Operations would love to get ahold of." I sigh. "As I'm sure they eventually will." I was speaking loudly, I noticed, and I sounded angry. I'm tired of playing defense, and the last few weeks have worn on me.

George pats me on the shoulder and starts to drift toward his own car; a few steps away, he stops. "As great as it looks to have our team values up on the wall, in the end it's just a bunch of feel-good nonsense if we're stuck in quicksand. We still haven't even started to address the main struggle we're having – our massive amount of technical debt, all the legacy applications out there that we know little or nothing about and break down every other day. Until we get our arms around that, we can't make headway with the demands Footwear and others are putting on us for new work."

I grimace. This was exactly what I was afraid of in terms of perception. If the team interprets our discussion today as window-dressing, nothing will change – we'll sink back into complacency, a sure death sentence. And was it really true that our vast amount of legacy support demands means we have no viable options to move out of firefighting hell?

"I agree with you, George. And I need your help. We need to get ahead of Erik's smears. Perceptions are important – I want people outside the team to see that the way we work doesn't jive with the mud he's throwing around on the way out the door. That sinking ship thing – sorry, I don't agree. We are NOT a lost a cause."

We part ways, and I make my way onto the hopelessly clogged Highway 26, heading home. As expected, the drive home was a hellish nightmare of stop and go traffic. It gives me time though to think about the team's feedback and George's comments. Were we hopelessly stuck in the mud?

Behind the Story

The first step Ben's team takes to getting the mastery over their spiraling technical debt situation is to make it visible. Why is that important?

Making Technical Debt Visible

"How did you guys at Microsoft do it?"

"What's the best practices you recommend for us to implement DevOps?"

"Which tools do you recommend for CI/CD?"

"Can you give us a roadmap or recipe so we can reach our goals?"

Some form of such questions gets raised almost every time we meet with a new customer. Perhaps, this is the reason why you bought this book; if so, you're probably wondering why we are answering with a story.

There Is No Single Roadmap or "Best Practice"

It's completely understandable that people want to ask about "best practices" or get a specific roadmap. Uncertainty means risk; actions mean exposure, mistakes, and vulnerability. To remove some of this risk, it's tempting to take what another company has done and try to implement it like a prescription, a recipe. We're going to explore some of the common elements that we found in successful enterprises that use DevOps to innovate at scale. But to quote Aaron Bjork from the Azure DevOps program team, "it would be foolish for me to say, you should exactly do it our way."

Here's the problem with a roadmap: they end up becoming prescriptions. But a roadmap is based on a starting point, and an ending point. And it's a certainty – your starting point, assets and liabilities, product portfolio, and end goals are going to vary dramatically from ours. Let's say you went on a cross country trip, from Seattle to Orlando. How helpful would a roadmap of an earlier trip from Tempe to LA be for you?

In other words, recipes can and do fail us… But experimentation and learning works, always. We believe you'll learn more from how Ben's team goes about solving their problems than we could ever teach by giving you a generic and ultimately misleading checklist.

Just for example, take the groundbreaking book *The Goal* by Eli Goldratt. This is a book that radically refined how we thought about manufacturing in the 1980s and was the inspiration behind "The Phoenix Project." But we often forget that the author was a scientist and interested – not so much in pat answers or a recipe – but in a new way of teaching that used both Socratic questioning and the scientific method.

Asking questions instead of lecturing with "facts" or "best practices" forces us into an uncomfortable area where our preconceptions are challenged. That discomfort leads directly to an environment where failure is welcomed, where we're encouraged to learn from mistakes instead of trying to sweep them under the rug or point fingers. The scientific method teaches us that everything is a hypothesis or a theory, an assumption; we can come up with thousands of trials, but if even one test disproves our theory, it must be abandoned, and we have to rethink our assumptions with a new theory.

One Team, One Year

In this book, we are writing a story that reflects the world that is, not as we would like it to be. In the real world, we aren't blessed with limitless power, a blank slate, and armies of well-trained consultants and employees. No, we are saddled with legacy debt, constrained by limited resources, and often have very limited management buy-in.

In this book, we'll tell the story of a team that overcomes their limitations by learning to experiment. As we go along, the team will gradually go up the mountain, making mistakes along the way – but always moving onward and upward, iteratively building on success.

The methods underlying the works of Eli Goldratt, Gene Kim, and Edward Deming – the scientific method, and Socratic questioning – should always be top of mind, regardless of what you call your transformation or how you go about it. Applying this scientific method however requires a forward-thinking mindset and a group that isn't just tolerant of failure but embraces it as an opportunity to learn. That doesn't describe the vast majority of the organizations we've worked with. With some highly political companies we've engaged with, we used to joke that getting stuff done was like playing Snakes and Ladders – only with no ladders, only snakes!

We can forget about the scientific method in the WonderTek the way things are now. In that environment, it's not safe to make mistakes. Any errors or lack of knowledge will be exploited by other teams; the name of the game is avoiding blame and shifting responsibility elsewhere.

Sure enough, that's what we're finding here at WonderTek. There's a few antipatterns that the team is saddled with that is causing some definite angst:

- Multimonth milestones and long-lived feature branches, leading to painfully long and messy integration phases

- Traditional command-and-control type organization, leading to risk-averse climate where mistakes are punished politically and siloization

- Lengthy feedback cycles and disengaged stakeholders

- Manual, error-prone, and time-consuming release processes and a lack of attention to quality, especially in testing

- Poorly understood and brittle legacy code that is resistant to change and a constant drain on resources with firefighting

- A creaky, inconsistent infrastructure layer that is hard to scale and impossible to manage

It is just starting to dawn on Ben's team how much this is cumulatively impacting them.

Game Attracts Game

And as we see in the section "Bleeding Out" – one of the most insidious effects that's somewhat hidden from Ben is with hiring and a gradual brain drain. As Mary and Tom Poppendieck have brought out, up until a century ago, capital was a critical resource. Now, the largest constraint globally is the passion and energy of bright creative people. It's becoming harder and harder for Ben to hire and keep the best and brightest, as we see with Erik's defection. His best and sharpest minds are walking out the door, to more competitive, fun, capable companies. The people that remain in this environment are atrophying in their skills; Ben is being asked to perform like a thoroughbred, with less and less capable people to do the work.

One decisionmaker we interviewed told us that tech and IT was now a supply problem – companies are finding technical resources and skilled people to be the real constraint. As he put it, "If we're going to recruit and retain world class talent, we have to show we're serious about learning. I absolutely believe that game attracts game, that people want to work with the best. Most of my focus and those of my people is around attracting and keeping the best – that's our firepower."

The enterprises that focus on learning and eliminating stress and meaningless work are outperforming others, because they're able to attract and keep the best people. These are companies that aren't focused on "cloud first" or "doing DevOps" – they are learning focused and invest in continuous training and practice consistently.

Making Debt Visible

In the section "Dysfunction Thrives on Secrets," one of the first steps the team takes is to make their technical debt visible. Why begin with this, instead of better release management practices?

Perhaps, Ben is trying to create a Plimsoll line.

Back in the 17th and 18th centuries, it was very common to lose freighter ships to overloading. In fact, unscrupulous shipowners would often send overloaded aging ships out to sea to collect on insurance money – which led to an appalling loss of life. In 1876, British Parliament passed a bill that made it mandatory to have marks on both sides of a ship. If the ship was overloaded, the load line marks would disappear underwater – and the harbormaster would prevent the ship from leaving port.[1]

---

[1] *"The Secret Language of Ships,"* Erin Van Rheenen for Hakai Magazine, Jalopnik, 4/20/2018, https://jalopnik.com/the-secret-language-of-ships-1825381945.

If we are putting a ship out to sea, it's important to know how much weight we are carrying so we don't risk being swamped. If we're trying to pay our way out of debt, the first step is to track what we are spending and keep up to date a full list of our debts.

In any project, we are going to incur technical debt – improvements we have to defer, the cost of shortcuts made to make our goals. Most of these revolve around improvements in areas like security, performance, and the like. These may not be key technical functions that the business is asking for, but they end up being rocks that our application is wrecked on – the unspoken, implicit expectations that when missed causes our users to hate what we're producing.

We like the neat way the cost of technical debt is defined by Kief Morris:

> *Technical debt is a metaphor for problems in a system that have been left unfixed. As with most financial debts, your system charges interest for technical debt. You might have to pay interest in the form of ongoing manual workarounds needed to keep things running. You may pay it as extra time taken to make changes that would be simpler with a cleaner architecture. Or charges may take the form of unreliable or hard-to-use services for your users. Software craftsmanship is largely about avoiding technical debt. Make a habit of fixing problems and flaws as you discover them, which is preferably as you make them, rather than falling into the bad habit of thinking it's good enough for now.*
>
> *This is a controversial view. Some people dislike technical debt as a metaphor for poorly implemented systems, because it implies a deliberate, responsible decision, like borrowing money to start a business. But it's worth considering that there are different types of debt. Implementing something badly is like taking a payday loan to pay for a vacation: it runs a serious risk of bankrupting you.*[2]

In any project we're involved in, we make sure as one of the first steps that there's a full list of our technical debt exposed and visible to the stakeholders; paying down this debt should be what we choose to invest our time in after the very limited delivery goals for each sprint. Microsoft made paying down this debt one of their top priorities on the Azure DevOps product teams. This was accomplished by means of tracking their BTE ratio – Bugs-to-Engineers – and making sure that this number rarely exceeded a reasonable count. We discuss how the BTE ratio helped give Microsoft clarity in the interviews with Sam Guckenheimer and Aaron Bjork in the Appendix, and in Chapter 6 under metrics and monitoring. Suffice to say – for us, this was a vivid example of a Plimsoll line and the positive behaviors and results gained by keeping technical debt visible.

---

[2]*"Infrastructure as Code: Managing Servers in the Cloud," Kief Morris, O'Reilly Media; 6/27/2016, ISBN-10: 1491924357, ISBN-13: 978-1491924358.*

Another method used very successfully to expose technical debt by large enterprises such as Ticketmaster, CapitalOne, and Exxon is the much-maligned maturity matrix. We can't agree with many of the books out there that flatly call a maturity or capability matrix an antipattern; there's several powerful examples of companies using cloud-enabling capabilities to create self-organizing teams that assess themselves, including recommendations for improvement that fit their specific use case.

The main point is in the section title: Dysfunction does thrive on secrets. Happy families value honest, open discussions – even when this causes some pain in the short term. It's the dysfunctional families that tend to hide problems or minimize them. Left in the dark, these secrets often multiply into a crushing burden.

Exposing the weight that Ben's team is carrying as a list – a Plimsoll line – is a powerful first step to beginning to formulate a better way of lightening the teams' load.

We'll talk more in Chapter 7 about how to recruit that all-important executive support we'll need to start paying down this debt. Suffice to say that it's critical to speak in the language of business, to link our list of debts to quantifiable results: dollars saved, waste eliminated, or opportunities for gain. Michael Stahnke of Puppet told us that it's critical for engineers to learn how to put technical debt in practical terms that executive decision-makers can understand:

> …Think about the way you are presenting this information to the people that matter in your company. You want to steer towards a measurable outcome that matters to people. For example, don't try to sell MTTR by itself. If I say I need to have more worker roles added to this process, or more servers in the background – that's great for techies but not for the people writing the checks. But if I say it costs me this much every time this problem happens, then I get strong feedback. What would it cost to fix this? Then we can talk about our options and have a discussion. But if something's important, I do try to convert it to dollars – that's the universal language of business.
>
> That's something I wish more developers understood. We need to think about the long-term maintenance costs of the things we build more. Over time, the cost of development gets rounded to zero in comparison with the cost of operating and maintaining the system.
>
> Operations teams have a better understanding of business value and maintenance costs than developers do. If we really understood the language of business – we could get the backing we need to produce better quality software and keep our technical debt in check.[3]

---

[3]*Interview of Michael Stahnke by Dave Harrison, see Appendix.*

Where Do I Start?

Autumn had been a train wreck of a season, no question about it.

Ben has suffered a high-level defection, losing a very capable professional that would be tough to replace. The team is drowning in support costs for a creaky set of undocumented legacy systems. And that vital connection with his business customers and his IT/Operations partners is fraying at the edges. The chasm between the developers producing code and the people supporting that code seems to be growing bigger by the day, with constant sniping and nasty politics undermining any hope of cooperation.

As bad as things are looking, they still have some advantages. Ben's team is still able to crank out work thanks to their now instinctive work pattern of daily scrums and honest retrospectives. And most of the tension and drama is being kept external to the team; everyone is drawing together tightly in a circle, guarding each other's back. Ben is proud of his team's cohesion under attack; they were an oasis of sanity and demonstrated a strong commitment to getting better.

It's a new season though. Winter is a time of new beginnings, for gathering strength. Change is in the air for the team…

A Fishing Trip (Ratcheting Change)

January brings some of my best days of the year. When the rains come and drenches the streets of Hillsboro, and the gray clouds lower and shadow the faces of morning commuters, I know steelhead are starting to make their way

© Dave Harrison and Knox Lively 2019
D. Harrison and K. Lively, *Achieving DevOps*,
https://doi.org/10.1007/978-1-4842-4388-6_2

upstream along the Pacific coast. I start to compulsively watch the river levels online and the fishing reports for a telltale spike of flow that could bring with it a strong pulse of fish.

Soon enough, there's a spike on one of my favorite north Oregon Coast rivers near the town of Tillamook, but I'm too slammed to make a getaway. Sure enough, I get the dreaded gloating phone call that afternoon from my friend Dean. "I pulled in yesterday about one in the afternoon, the parking lot was empty, and the water was the color of my morning chocolate milkshake. But, I decided what the hey, and stopped by a few hours later. Let me tell ya – I think I had three fish hooked in the first 15 casts! Big, bright fish – they looked like bars of aluminum." Dean chuckles. "And it's just going to get better, that nice emerald green water... It's going to be so good tomorrow, we'll have to put bait on behind the bushes, or they'll come out of the water and BITE us!"

That was all I needed to hear. The next day, I was on my way west, leaving at 3 in the morning to meet Dean at one of our favorite bankside spots. The clock on my truck was just ticking over to 6 a.m. when I pull up to the parking spot. There was still a light rainfall that dampened my shirt as I hopped out of the truck and began pulling on my waders. I make sure my Simms waterproof backpack and two fishing rods are in the boat and all rigged up and ready to go, and we slide the boat into the inky black water.

The espresso I'd picked up from a roadside stand is warming my tummy pleasantly, and I can feel my heart pounding with anticipation as we slide down into the first run we'll be working. We are just in time. The light was just starting to come into the valley – it was still thirty minutes until the sky would lighten to a ghostly blue-black and I could start casting. This was a bad year for returns but my timing could not have been better – right after a heavy storm, the rain had scoured the river bottom clean of leaves and debris, and I was confident there were dozens of fish moving upstream to complete their life's cycle and spawn. With luck, I will be able to limit out early and bring home some fish for the barbecue.

If only wishes were fishes. After 2 hours, I had succeeded only in losing gear to the greedy river bed. The cold is starting to seep into my bones, and I could feel my casting gradually becoming robotic. I was going "on tilt" – mechanically thrashing water dozens of times, reeling in impatiently, hopelessly going through the motions. Unfortunately, my fishing partner is doing far better today than I am, with two already caught. One was a smaller nickel-bright hen, but the colored-up buck was a real trophy – easily 16 pounds, and more than 3 feet in length. Dean is grinning ear to ear as he tells the story of the line just barely hesitating after his cast; he'd slightly lifted the rod and felt that slight telltale pressure, then set the hook.

The standard, cliched line on the river was "the tug is the drug," yet it was true – that feeling was better than any amphetamine. The fight of a great fish is electrifying and – perhaps because it comes so rarely – can be remembered and retold for years. Dean had to chase the fish downstream after it had neatly wrapped the line around a large rock below the tailout of the pool where it had been hooked. After having to wade out to his waist in the icy water to free up the line from its snag, he reeled in – and miraculously, the fish was still hooked. It was an epic battle and the fish had nearly taken all his line as it thrashed the surface and fought him up and down the creek, but after 10 minutes, Dean was able to tire the giant out and smoothly sweep it into his net.

That evening in the grimy, smelly trailer that we had stashed at a friend's place near the seaside town of Rockaway, Dean's teeth gleamed as he talked about how the fish had thrashed about wildly, leaping into the air and twisting its body several times. The strength and beauty of these fish was always breathtaking.

I feel a familiar wave of admiration tinged with a little envy at my friend's focus. I remember his hand moving almost imperceptibly as the rod slowly sweeps downstream in an arc, the tip twitching like the antenna of a predatory insect. The slightest move or hesitation of the line, and that hand comes up sharply as he brings the line tight and sets the hook. More often than not, the rod bends into nearly a half circle as it bucks under the heavy weight of a very surprised and angry steelhead.

The worst humiliation had come late in the day. Dean had stepped in behind me just as I was leaving a run – one of our favorite spots, a little greasy table-sized patch of slower moving water between two fast current seams. I thought he was wasting his time; I'd thrashed it for an hour with not a nibble. Not even 3 minutes later, I heard a whoop – and sure enough, upstream there was a spray of water and a huge splash as a monster steelhead – the biggest of the day – thrashed and jumped into the air, Dean in hot pursuit. My pocket had been picked.

Fishing had been challenging today and I noticed that most of the fisherman had gone home empty-handed, like me. Small comfort that was, as I watch Dean neatly fillet his fish and slide the carrot-red strips of flesh into Ziploc bags for the freezer back home. As a good friend and longtime fishing buddy, Dean limited himself to just a couple comments about me "needing to use a hook next time" and some helpful hints about me "not pulling your own weight." I feel, as always, a little outclassed; Dean had been a fishing guide for 20 years, still fished almost half the year, and had an almost supernatural ability to snuffle out and hook fish in the worst of conditions.

I grump out some compliments sprinkled with a few comments about a certain blind squirrel finding some random nuts to balance things out as the we close out the evening with a few cocktails. Swallowing a little pride, I finally ask Dean what I'd gotten wrong today.

"Well...." says Dean, staring into his second cocktail, swirling the golden whiskey around in his coffee cup to hear the ice tinkle. He's in a classic Old Man of the River mood. "You know, you're a good fisherman and you've come a long way... Usually, you'd have caught something on a day like today."

"Yeah, I'm a good fisherman, just not great." It eats at me, but I have to admit it – Dean was simply on another level.

Dean chuckles again. "That takes practice. Probably more time than you have at your age and with your career." He takes a long sip from his cup, beaming in satisfaction. "I'll tell you one thing I noticed – you weren't in it today like you usually are. You just seemed to be on remote control. The fish can tell, man. I'd say on most of your drifts, you weren't even close to being in the zone – I looked over a few times and your yarn was right on the surface. There's not a steelhead alive that will bite that."

"What about at that river curve, when you came behind me and pulled out that nice fish? I'd beaten the crap out of that water!"

"Yep... I noticed you were there a while. What do you think I did that you didn't do?"

I shrug again. Dean takes another long sip and leans back in his camp chair, adopting a professorial tone. "You needed to adjust your approach, man. You didn't have enough lead on your line – you were fishing too light to get on the river bottom, so you never even gave the fish a chance to bite. And, one thing you'll notice, I'm always changing things up. I'll try eggs for five minutes – then if that doesn't work, I'll cut over to a yarnball, or a bead under a float. Two weeks ago on the Trask for instance, I hammered this one spot for like ten minutes, and then – I clipped off the bead under my float and put on a nightmare jig. First float through, bang! A big hatchery buck fish grabbed my line and took off for the Pacific. I didn't think I'd ever land that one."

I know what he's talking about. A lot of times, success or failure in fishing just came down to persistence and time on the water. I am a good fisherman, and I catch more than my fair share each year – but to be great, I'd have to learn to stay sharp, be ready to try new things, and not zone out and become complacent. Dean was always laser focused and was constantly changing things up.

"Just remember, I'm just like you," says Dean, putting a comforting hand on my shoulder and looking sympathetically into my eyes. He breaks into a grin: "Only successful."

The next day after the daily standup, Kevin asks me how fishing had was; it's a dreary story of failure that I hastily cut short once I see eyes glazing over. Kevin though has done some fishing in the past with his son, and can relate. "Been there, man. That's why they call it fishing, not catching..." We both laugh.

The next day as we are wrapping up our daily scrum, I get groans as I start to say, "You know, DevOps is kind of like…" Alex fakes slipping into a coma and collapses over his keyboard. "For God's sake, ANOTHER DevOps metaphor? Let me guess, it's like ballet, right? Or a tractor?"

I have to laugh. There's something about DevOps that seems to pick up metaphors like lint. But I forge ahead anyway: "As I was saying… the takeout was really nasty yesterday, because it was low tide. So we had to winch the boat up at the takeout as the bank was at a really steep angle. I will tell you honestly, we never would have made it without the ratcheting winch we had on the trailer."

Some really lucky people have an electric winch on the front of their trucks; we had a manual winch that required a little elbow grease to get the boat up the slippery hillside to the trailer. But without that beautifully simple mechanical design, we never would have made it up the slope. There was a clicking sound as we turned the handle of the winch; with each click, a spring-loaded metal finger or pawl slid into a groove between the teeth of the round gear being turned. We could stop and take a break whenever we wanted; as long as the pawl was engaged, the gear couldn't roll backward.

Looked at linearly, the gear travel could have looked something like this:

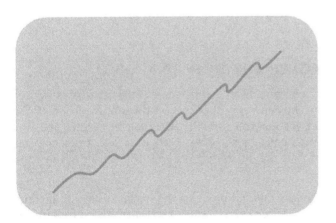

I sketch this on the whiteboard and turn to the team. "All the pending work and improvements we're thinking about kind of become like that hillside in my mind sometimes – indomitable, vast, endless challenges. If I stare at it as a single block, it's an impossible, overwhelming task, and I start to feel stressed and overwhelmed. But I keep going back to that ratchet design. It's mechanically beautiful, because it does one thing and does it well – allowing the application of force in one direction and one direction only. We knew that boat was going to make it up the hill. It might be one inch at a time, but that ratchet design prevented the boat from sliding back into the river."

George sees where I'm going. "So, in your view, it's OK if we slow down or even pause our rate of change. It's all right to change in tiny increments – in fact, that might be safer. As long as we don't roll back to where we started."

"Yeah, that's right. The military has a saying – "slow is smooth, and smooth is fast." It's obvious there's change ahead for us, whether we want to prevent it or not. But the surest way to not meet that challenge is to try to change everything at once. We need to take this nice and slow, one tooth of the gear at a time. But if we find something to be of value in the team, we can't allow ourselves to drop it because there's a new crisis du jour. We keep our standards consistent and reasonable, and gradually inch our way forward."

I get some bemused looks, and at least half the team has stopped listening; it's time to move along. But I remember that winch in the months ahead, and I'm very careful about how I position DevOps. In fact, usually I don't even mention the word; we stick to generic executive-friendly terms like delivery of business value, flow, and elimination of waste as our buzzwords. Going around preaching DevOps as a revolutionary concept is threatening and risky. Instead, we try to take a more experimental approach, one tiny evolutionary step at a time.

The Worst Form of Laziness (Kanban)

A few weeks go by, and we're halfway through the team retrospective; our Kanban board was open, and Alex was checking on the status of one of the features that Padma was working on for HR. As usual for Padma, she was almost frighteningly competent – tests were complete, unit tests created, delivered to production, and the users had looked it over and given it an enthusiastic thumbs-up.

The Admin screens, surprisingly, ended up being the hangup. Harry looked up as Alex was moving the task through to "Done" and said, "Oh, so that means unit tests are written, right? I don't remember a code review either."

Padma grumbled at him, "Harry, you know very well there wasn't time this sprint for that. We got this request right before the sprint began; the idea is just to throw a detail screen out there for admins to update user login information. Nice and simple. It's internal facing only – not anything the customers are going to see. We can add unit testing – even if it's of value, which I doubt – to a future sprint."

Harry's chair creaked as he leaned back and crossed his arms over his bulging midriff. "Padma, it's like being pregnant. Either you're done or you're not done. It's binary. If you don't have any unit tests, you're hurting the team scoreboard, and setting a bad precedent. Sorry, we can't take this off the board yet, and it can't be cleared for release. Let's try again in two weeks."

Padma's jaw gaped. "Are you serious? The customer – HR, I'll remind you, they produce your paycheck Harry – wants this functionality done. I still haven't heard a good reason why we're being nitpicky on an internal-facing detail screen. This is a MVP effort Harry – minimum viable, right? So the emphasis is on getting something out the door quickly, not trying to nail down every detail."

Alex jumped in. "Padma, I hate to say this, but I think Harry's got a point here. It's true that we love prototyping and MVP's, but the word 'viable' there means it meets our standards. We got into this hole through expediency, remember? We always deferred testing and quality always took a back seat to making our dates. We can't just assume that we'll get to this later. To me, I don't think this task is done yet."

Padma's chin was jutting forward. "Look, sit on this if you want. But to me it's a little unfair that you're coming in last second and holding up a release based on a 'tested in production' type requirement. You didn't ask that of Ryan a few weeks back with his app, and he was working with something that was a lot more sensitive. I don't get why I'm being held to a higher standard here – it seems petty."

Alex looked around the room – "Padma, I get where you're coming from. I wouldn't like it if I was given a higher bar to clear than others on the team. It seems to me though that the problem isn't a personal one – you're one of our best coders we've got and your work is always top-notch. I think the core issue is that our process is inconsistent, and our rules are unspoken. I mean, we've never really had a team definition of done. Is this a good time to talk about this as a group?"

Heads nodded in agreement around the table; they'd batted around the idea of a formal definition of done for some time. I was glad this was coming up as a topic. After some discussion, they decided on something simple – "Done" for the team meant that unit tests were written, their functional tests updated, the changes were peer reviewed, and it was tested in a production-like environment.

Harry objected. "We're missing the point, guys. We could get faster releases and much better testing if we adopted feature flags, like I've been saying. That decouples the release of code to when features are actually turned on for our end users. And it means we can roll back with a toggle."

Alex and George looked at each other; George slowly said, "I love the concept of feature toggles and I really want to explore it, Harry, you know that. Everything you said makes sense. But, that's separate from this discussion. It'll take time to prepare the ground and get signoff from our end users on this new way of releasing; I know for a fact HR isn't going to love the idea of using our end users as guinea pigs if we're testing in production. For right now, it's just a bridge too far. Can we nail down a single definition of what 'done' means first before we mix in new release strategies?"

Harry grouched and moaned, but eventually the group conceded George's point and moved on. I'd been sitting in the back of the room observing the conversational badminton match and decided to launch a volley of my own. "People, before we move on, can I ask a question – Padma, how did that task get on the board for this sprint?"

Padma replied, "Well, it seemed like I had plenty of capacity – a few free days at the end of the sprint. When my contact came to me before the sprint with the ask to bump this up in priority, I thought it was a good decision to scoot it forward."

I said, "That's awesome! Really good responsiveness and it shows a commitment to a quick turnaround. But looking at the backlog and what we committed to this sprint, didn't you feel a little pressured?"

"Comes with the territory," Padma laughed. "I had to put in a few late nights because our authentication model changed, and the COTS gridview component we used ended up having some performance issues that we couldn't fix. So yeah, it took longer than I wanted, but the customer is happy – which is all that matters."

"OK, so now I want to widen this – Padma this isn't about you specifically. But we're now saying things are either ready for a production release and tested – or they're not ready, and it gets kicked forward. So I'm taking two things away from this discussion, and I'll put it in the notes.

"First off, and Elaine this will especially interest you, I think we need to split up what we deliver even finer. We can't have more of these bowling ball requirements, where they're large sized and impenetrable. We need to commit to much less if we're truly saying 'done means DONE'.

"Second, I think we need to put a cap on what we're delivering. What would happen if we capped our WIP in the Kanban board, so only 3 tasks could be worked on at a time?"

The group started to laugh. Alex said, "Ben, look around – there's only 7 people here in the room. Just some basic math here, but if you cap our WIP at 3 active tasks, you're handicapping us. We've got about 30 tasks to do every sprint; there's no way we can get it all done and we'll have people sitting around doing nothing all day. I don't think you want that."

I said slowly, "Correct me if I'm wrong here, but I don't think the business loves us for overcommitting and underdelivering. I was talking to Lisa in HR – she loves you Padma, by the way – but overall she gave us a very low grade when I asked her if we follow through on our commitments. I hear that from Footwear and a few other of our customers as well.

"This isn't a criticism of anyone here. In fact I'm commending you – you're taking on a ton of work and it shows with our velocity. But 60-hour workweeks and heroic efforts to push something out the door aren't sustainable. So I'm going to ask again – what would it look like if we capped our active tasks at 3?"

George looked shocked, and his brow was furrowed. "Looking at this last sprint, that means we only would have delivered about half our value. Like Alex said, you'd be crippling our velocity."

Now, it was my turn to laugh. "I'm not doing anything. I'm asking a question, it's up to the team to decide. Using the last sprint as an example, did we take on too much?" Looking around, he smiled – most people, Padma and Harry excepted, were nodding their heads vigorously. "I haven't asked, but I'll bet one of the first things we threw out was that 20% time we've asked you to use for improving our capacity and maturity. That's our seed corn – we're falling back into bad habits. So – if we capped our WIP at 3 – let's say we produce half the work we did last sprint. But most of those tasks that we've moved to 'Done' really aren't done are they for this sprint – there's a lot of carryover work that is spilling into the next few weeks. So I'm thinking, we may do less, but what we do deliver will be bulletproof."

Alex started to smile. "You know, that may not be such a crazy idea after all. I mean, we could try it. Padma, you started talking to us months ago about XP programming and pair programming. We keep saying we're going to do cross training but when it comes right down to it – we never seem to have the time. And that means, if there's a problem with the HR app, we have to go to Padma. She's the owner of the code, and no one else can fix it. That's a huge limiting factor for us."

Instituting the cap limit – once the team was in consensus that they'd try it as an experiment – took a few sprints to settle out. Despite Harry's dour predictions of locust plagues and fired developers due to chronic laziness, the team found that the really important things were getting out the door more reliably. In several projects, their stakeholders noticed they were doing much better in delivering on their commitments. In other projects, having people in a waiting state caused some visible pain, exposing some problems with tasks being handed off either incomplete or needing to be redone; these were discussed in the retrospectives and improvements folded into the delivery cycle. And during standups, they had people available – for the first time – that could hop on open bugs or blocking tasks in tandem, leading to much better thought out solutions.

It was one of those little things that ended up – as I looked back months later – making a huge difference. Capping their WIP, it turned out, forced the team to focus on only the most important things. Their pace after a few weeks seemed much less hectic, more sustainable. As George said just a few sprints after this, "We're off the hamster wheel!"

Setting Up Base Camp (Version Control)

As always, demo day and the end of sprint seemed to be creeping up on us before we were ready. The team was about halfway through their bug list from the last release. As we go through our work items, I see gaps around the table; some of my people have been calling in sick lately. It looks like yet another failed sprint. I'm already dreading writing the retrospective showing the bleeding from our technical debt and how it was impacting progress against our backlog of work.

This afternoon though looked to be trending up a little. The to-dos on the whiteboard continue to mock me; we decided that getting our version control in shape would be our first target. I hosted a brownbag for the team on the subject, with Erik presenting his findings and recommendations. Surprisingly, we get nearly a full audience – perhaps, the free pizza helped.

I splurged for this event with lots of hot pizza pies and Caesar salad from Pizzicato, one of our faves. I love the Roma pie, with the fennel-saturated homemade sausage, red onions, and roasted peppers. Load it up with parmesan and hot peppers, and it's heaven. We're a happy group of locusts now, and everyone is settling comfortably into their chairs as Erik gets his laptop out and starts up his presentation.

"So, you guys asked me to do some work on version control. To me, this is the base camp of software development – if we can't get version control right, we're dead in the water.

"One of the main goals of continuous delivery is the ability for us to deploy and release any version of our software, to any environment, using a fully automated process. People often look at that and think, 'oh, automation!' – and start to think about Chef or buying some release management tool. But application code is just half of the puzzle; the other piece we often forget about, infrastructure. That's basic housekeeping – we need to have everything in version control. That's everything we need to build, deploy, test, and release.

"As you all know, we're not there yet. We've already identified as a major cause in many of our recent tickets that manual fixes were happening in our environments, which don't match each other. And for code – some of our apps have been patched in production. We had two outages in the past three months just because changes we made to fix something in config didn't get rolled back to our other environments or show up in version control. So, the same issue cropped up again in the next build, and it cost us several days to find and reapply the change.

"My recommendation is that we take care of some basic hygiene and make sure we finally have version control that's complete. An authoritative source of record for everything we need. That includes our infrastructure and everything supporting the application. And this needs to be living and enforced – we use this as a base for any release candidates. And any hotfixes use the same repository as a source, and the same build process – no more shortcuts."

Harry, predictably lounging in a dark corner in the back of the room, has his arms folded. "Hey, I'm not arguing any of this, especially for our web-based projects. But like I keep saying, 90% of our stuff doesn't fit in that bucket. We've got a lot of legacy applications – some are in COBOL for God's sake. Our mainframe deployments don't fit in that space either. I just don't see any need for us to launch on a major rewrite effort when we've got bigger fish to fry. I mean, I was here till 11 last night trying to clear the decks – we just don't have the time for this."

Jeff, one of Harry's closest friends on the team, chips in. "Hate to say it, but Harry's right. We're all scrambling and worn out. And it's not like we don't have and use version control here. Maybe it's not perfect, but it shouldn't be the priority for us right now."

My head snaps up – I'm out of my pizza-induced stupor now. "Guys, let's hold on here before we start playing Whack-A-Mole. Erik, I'm struggling to get where you're going here. Jeff is saying we do have version control; you're saying we don't. You guys can't both be right."

Erik rubs his jaw and laughs shortly, then says, "Most of the outfits I've worked at say the same thing – 'oh sure, we use version control'. That means their app code is stuffed into a repository somewhere – but it's incomplete. It's not used as the source of record when there's a hotfix, and what's in production has been manually tweaked to where it diverges from what's supposed to be our canonical build source. In other words, it's an artifact – and an untrustworthy one.

"For example, George, let's take the Footwear app. Next Monday let's say you have a new programmer coming in and she's sitting in my chair, with a brand-new workstation. Can she check out the project's source code, make a single change, and deploy it to any environment he wants? Let's say that our QA environments suddenly evaporate. Can he rebuild it using only what's in version control? Including the OS, patches, the network configuration, OS binaries, and the app config?"

There was an uncomfortable silence; Footwear was a relatively new app, but only the application code was in version control. Builds were manually created and handed off to Operations as a package or executable. And hotfixes were usually manually applied, as there was a lot of variation applied as patches or configuration tweaks in production that didn't show up in source control or in other environments.

It's a sore spot, and George temperature raises a bit. "You know we don't have control over that Erik. We've got what's in our ducks in a row from a coding standpoint, and that's our only responsibility."

Erik says, "I'm not trying to snipe at you George, actually the Footwear app is further along than any of our other apps that we support in terms of completeness. But for us to reach base camp, we have to rethink the way we're using version control and get more of our artifacts in there. At a minimum we need to think about systems configuration and app configuration as equally valuable as source code. We need to be able to answer these questions – I robbed this from Continuous Delivery – with a 'yes':

Version Control – the finish line

- *Can I exactly reproduce any of my environments, including version of OS, patches, network config, software stack, apps deployed into it and their config?*
- *Can I easily make an incremental change too any of these individual items and be able to deploy that change to any environment?*
- *Can I easily see all changes to an environment and trace a particular change back to what exactly the change was, who made it, and when?*
- *Can I satisfy all compliance requirements?*
- *Can everyone on the team get the info they need and make the changes they need to make?*

Henry scoffs. "Again, not all of our applications will support version control. And what you're really talking about here is automated builds. You're saying this will only work if we hook up version control to every build. You're saying everyone needs to have full access to every environment, which is crazy, and we should have these godlike powers to roll back on a whim. Our security governance will never go for that, and we'd be stepping right on Operations toes. They'll murder us. Operations doesn't see the need for automated builds, Erik, like I've told you many times. They just want their WIX package or MSI installer and a script. We hand off the baton like a good boy at the 100-meter mark and" – he slaps his hands – "done, easy-peasy. We might not like it but it is the way things work here."

I can see some red appearing at the base of Erik's neck – a sure trouble sign. The last thing we need is the team tearing itself apart over what should be a very pat discussion over fundamentals. "OK everyone, Erik's made a lot of effort here," I interrupt just before Erik launches into a defense. "I think we owe it to him to at least listen respectfully. And is anyone seriously arguing that we need to improve with how we use version control?"

Even Harry keeps his head down with that question. I continue, "What I'm walking away with from this discussion is, we need to devote some serious effort to getting our quality under control, and that starts with version control. Right now, it can't be trusted, and it isn't complete."

I can see Harry starting to object and decide to cut him off. "Harry, you're making some good points – it's true that we have a huge number of applications to support. It's also true that we control only part of the build and release process. But it does seem like we're impacted directly by a lot of bugs that are caused by environmental changes and patches we're not aware of and that aren't tracked anywhere. That's a bigger governance problem that I think our friends in Security and Operations would want to get ahead of. And our releases keep running red, which means – though we're using version control to create builds – that there's gaps in our testing, and problems with how our environments are being created and our configurations maintained. Right now, no one seems to trust our build process or the environments it's pointing to. I think it's worth some time to address this."

Harry isn't done though. "Again, too much work, too few people. And it's a bad fit for the type of work we do."

George interrupts Harry before he gets a full head of steam. "Yeah, point taken. It's a massive list of applications, and a vast amount of work. So let's focus first on getting our code trustworthy, and then move on to environments and configurations. We already have a list of the applications we support, right? So, let's use that as a starting point and do what my general contractors call 'snapping a line.'"

Blank stares across the room. George patiently explains: "From that long laundry list of applications, I'm guessing most are static or less important. So let's flag the applications that are actually generating a high number of tickets, the ones that have infrastructure that abends frequently, those that are most visible to the business. If we've got a hundred applications to support – well, that leaves 25 or so that we support frequently on a day to day basis. So to get our codebase in shape, we snap a line. We take what's in production, match it up with what's in source control, and overwrite VC if there's a mismatch."

There's some static, and Harry continues sniping a little and prophesying doom from his corner, but – just as I predicted to George ahead of the meeting – there's no serious resistance. Without a reliable source for our builds, we truly are stuck. Erik's right – this is our base camp, and we need to make sure it's in order before we tackle anything else.

As we wrap up, I tell the team that we're going to keep this as a focus going forward. "This isn't something we can dump on one person. I want us to spend 20% of every sprint getting source control up to speed. Harry has made a valid point – this is going to require some kind of agreement with Operations – that's on my to-do list. We're assuming that they don't care about how we deliver work to them. I'm guessing they very much do."

Selling the Plan

On the way back to my office, on impulse I take a sharp right turn and walk by Douglas' office. Douglas keeps odd hours, and his calendar is usually booked wall to wall. Today, though, his office is empty – and he gives me a half smile and motions for me to come in.

We chat a little. Douglas' passion was racing Miata racecars; he shows me some clips on YouTube from last weekend's race. I can see the appeal; it was exciting watching from the helmet camera recording where the little car almost lost traction on sharp turns. It was a little too NASCAR for my taste though and definitely a hobby well above what I can afford.

Finally, Douglas gives me that half smile again and says, "So – have you given any thought to our discussion? You promised me a remediation plan."

"Yeah, so let's talk about that. I've had meetings with the team and I think we have some good ideas." I sum up for Douglas some of the thoughts we've been batting around as a team, especially around source control. Then, I pause. "Listen, last time we talked, we got off to a bad start. You had just had Footwear and Operations climbing on your back about our team and just after a big push – the team and I feel like we've moved mountains and we're not getting credit. That being said – it's obvious there's a kink in our hose somewhere. Value is just not getting out the door. I'm not sure exactly where it lies – maybe it's the way we are gathering requirements and structuring our projects, maybe it has to do with our testing layer dragging us down. Maybe we are shooting ourselves in the foot somehow with the way we're coding.

"But the main point you made with me was that we need to strengthen that bridge with Operations. After having sat through a very uncomfortable recap meeting with Emily and Ivan, it's obvious we have some work to do there. Somehow, our push to go Agile is making things much harder on them. I'm not sure what the answer is there either, but at least we're starting to get a good grasp on where that pain point is."

"I was worried you'd be coming in here with a grand plan selling this magic word, DevOps." Douglas says this with a sideways grin, like a racing champion holding up the trophy. "You know, I just can't see that flying around here."

"No, at least at this point, I have to agree. That being said, I'm giving the team some room to brush up and come to the table with some ideas to straighten out our deployment and quality issues." Now's not the time to dig in on terminology, and I'm not an evangelist.

"Douglas, it's funny – we're a clothing manufacturer. It's not a field I know anything about. But I mean – look at us." I grab my shirt collar. "I mean, I'm wearing WonderTek. You are too. We make good stuff – it lasts, it looks great. There's a lesson there – somehow, our factories and suppliers figured out how to deliver consistency and quality at speed. From what little I know about Lean Manufacturing, this has been going on for fifty years. If the code we were producing had this same quality, we'd be made in the shade."

"At last, we're starting to see things the same way!" Douglas says with a gleam in his eye. "Ben, as you know, I started my career in the Army and I've never forgotten the lessons I learned there – in fact, I run my teams today based on the principles I was taught in my twenties. I look for discipline and loyalty – disagree with me all you want, but outside these doors I expect you to toe the line. That's the biggest reason why you're sitting in this chair now and not your predecessor – I've never caught you talking behind my back.

"That being said, I'm the only one that I know of with that kind of background here. Most of my peers and my manager come from the world of manufacturing, marketing, or have MBA's. They understand Lean intuitively, it's in their DNA. I've been in several meetings recently where our CEO has been talking about realigning along Lean principles, the way he got his Asian factories humming back in the mid 90's. He expects us to perform the same way. If you're talking Lean, then maybe we might have some common ground here. Anything else – frankly, it'll just be seen as another delay tactic, an excuse so you can miss on your deliveries.

"What gives me pause though is that you say you don't know exactly where the problem lies. If you don't know now, after this length of time working for us, when will you know?"

I feel the hairs on the back of my neck stand up; looks like sword is still very much above my head. I hold Douglas' gaze calmly though and reply, "I want to make this metrics based. We'll take the last Footwear release as a case study. Once I go through each step in the process, I'll know exactly where the problem is. And having it based on numbers means there's no emotion, it's objective. Not a finger-pointing exercise. So… one week from now?"

"OK. One week." Douglas turns back to his desk but calls out to me as I walk out the door. "I look forward to seeing what you come up with. And make sure you invite Ops too. Good talk!"

I leave feeling like a condemned man who's just gotten a call from the Governor. That was as good as it was going to get – now to get some kind of agreement set with Emily.

Nice But Not Nicey-Nice (Effective Peer Reviews)

I was one of the last ones into the team meeting room; Padma was at the board shuffling some of her notes. There was the usual few minutes of fiddling around with the projector, and finally the screen showed the following:

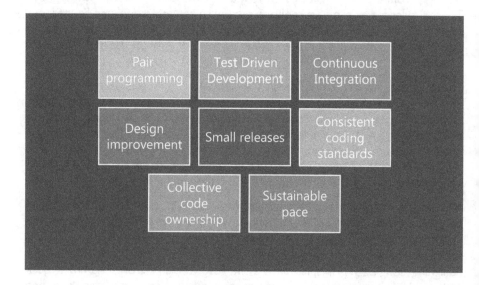

"My eyes!" George yelps. We laugh; the vibrant purple background is burning into my retinas. Padma rolls her eyes and snips, "I forgot I was talking to a bunch of middle-aged white dudes, sorry guys. Next time I'll stick to browns and grays. Anyway – may I continue? – here's the principles stressed with XP programming. You'll notice there's nothing here that is inconsistent with who we are as a team or where we want to go.

"Just for example, take the 'design improvement' item – that means you only build what is needed today, and refactor as needed. That eliminates a lot of wasted time gold plating work on features that are misunderstood or not needed. It also means the customer sets reasonable limits on what they expect and that they're available to us at all times when we have questions." This gets some loud snorts, but Padma soldiers on. "We rely on frequent releases to production and demo to our customer, then we work together on the fine tuning and adjustments we know we're going to make.

"All of these things fit together. Just for example, if we used pair programming, we naturally start growing a culture that favors collective code ownership. The team is working together in teams, one person taking lead, the other person watching and learning, and suggesting improvements. So that second person now understands the system context, they've contributed to the code and helped improve quality; the next time, there's a problem we don't have just one person, and only one person that can help fix it. Once the pair is done with the work, you have a natural code review already done, and it can be released quickly as a single, small change out to where it can be reviewed by the customer. And we rotate the teams so everyone gains knowledge of the work we do as a group, not just our little piece of the puzzle."

George says, "Padma, this is great and I know XP programming is great. It is a big change from the way we have done things as a team though – I thought we were just going to be talking about peer reviews."

"Yeah, and I've done pair programming in the past," Harry chips in. "Suddenly our productivity drops by 50% because we're both chained to a single keyboard. And honestly, I don't know if there's enough breath mints in the world for me to share my terrible coffee breath, day in day out, with anyone." A ripple of laughter.

I'm rubbing my chin; maybe, there's something here that's useful. "I think Padma's on to something here. We just finished a major release beat down, and all of you put in hero type hours. But that's just not sustainable – we'll lose everyone here if we make that a habit. Is anyone seriously arguing that we want to continue with release after release breaking or putting us through hell trying to get it to work in production?"

George says slowly, "We just committed a big chunk of our time to getting our source control in gear, Ben. Do we want to change the way we code and release – at the same time? That seems like a lot to take on."

From the faces around the room, I can tell George isn't alone in his thinking. Padma says, "I wasn't seriously proposing we implement everything on this list, all at once. I was suggesting that we put some of these on the list as things to explore, down the road, as an experiment. XP programming could be a game changer for us when it comes to development. It means we're releasing in lockstep with the customers, small bits at a time. It means no more craftsman-type problems we have with our code – where each of us owns a chunk of code, and if we're hit by a bus or get sick things have to wait. It means that our code is being reviewed early, like before check-in, so we're catching bugs before they ever hit QA. Isn't that where we are trying to go?"

A few smiles now. I can't believe we haven't put collective code ownership on our written list of team values yet. Padma's right – I could think of at least three high-visibility outages recently because people were unavailable and "their" code broke.

George is shaking his head still. "Still too much change at once. Let's say you've got one bullet in your gun, Padma. You know this team. What's the target you'd shoot at?"

Padma answers immediately, "Peer reviews. That's the most bang for the buck. I've worked on teams that have it as part of their standard process, and it's amazing the difference it makes."

"I've also worked on teams that used peer reviews," Alex interrupts. "It just ends up being a code syntax beatdown session – a gauntlet less experienced developers have to run as the senior programmers beat the crap out of them in public. We don't want that kind of negative culture happening here."

"I agree, if we start going down that road it'll make it harder for us to change things out of fear," Padma answers, smiling sweetly. "A lot of companies enforce some kind of static code analysis on check-in, and that should be something to look into. But for now – we need to make sure it's a part of our culture that someone, anyone, looks at our code before we check it in. That's not a beatdown – that's basic due diligence. If we really want to get ahead of our quality issues, it's a have to have."

George is starting to warm up to this. He says, "I don't think this is going to add to our workload if we do it right. It's just a change in the way we go about things. People can choose to work in pairs – that's best practice, because it ensures we have multiple people that can help with the app going forward. Or we can choose to have someone look at our code and provide a signoff in our IDE before we check our code in. But either way, having someone do a peer review is fundamental, it's hard to argue with that."

Of course, we do our best to prove him wrong. There's some grumbling and grim prophecies of doom muttered over the next 15 minutes, but in the end we decided to give this a try as a team – and check in after 2 weeks to see if it hamstrings us. I promise the team that if everyone decides pair programming is not effective, we'll try something else.

On the way back to my office, I stop by the whiteboard in the team area and get it up to date:

What Isn't Working	To Do
Rising technical debt	Peer Review (Padma)
Untrustworthy VC repository	Version Control (Erik)
Branch integration issues	Code coverage and testing (Rajesh)
Code coverage dropping	**Maybe Later**
Business changing its mind	Better teamwork with outside teams i.e. Ops
Too many bugs – stuck in firefighting	Continuous integration & delivery
Bad communication pre-release with IT	Smaller releases
Long list of aging features	Refining requirements gathering
Dependencies holding up releases	Paying down technical debt
Infrastructure creaky, inconsistent, difficult to manage	Infrastructure as code / a set of "golden images"
Alerts and monitoring nonexistent	**What We Value in our Tribe**
	Open, honest communication – you will never get in trouble for saying the truth
	Collective code ownership
	Every line of code checked by a peer before checkin. (Peer review and/or pair programming)

Easy There, Pardner

It was heading toward end of day; I reach for my iPhone and send Emily a quick message: *You available?* Ten minutes later, I'm in the cafeteria. The place was deserted, and all the staff had already gone home for the day. It was a perfect neutral ground for our talk.

We spend a few minutes talking about our teams and how things were going, and our plans for the weekend. Emily has been with WonderTek for a few years longer than me, which meant that at times there was just a hint of condescension; *just teaching the new kid the lay of the land.* Still, at least I get a hint of a smile every now and then, and a more-or-less honest dialogue. Anything is better than the postmortem battle royale both of us are still recovering from. Perhaps, just perhaps, there is something salvageable here.

Finally, Emily leans back and gives me a hard stare. "So, you wanted to talk. I think I've already told you how our group feels and I'm interested in what you want to do to fix things."

Ah, the blame game again; it's a game she never seems to tire of. I bite my lip but reply calmly, "Well, it's obvious that our releases are not well coordinated; you mentioned us handing you documentation two days before launch, and that was the first time your team had gotten notice that a release was coming up. In your shoes, I'd be irate because that means a long weekend running the release and cleaning up messes afterward. You asked for better attendance at your CAB meetings – and I don't think I've missed one since. You also said your resources are stretched thin and with our team's shift to Agile we are putting too much of a strain on your people, including one of your best – Kevin. Did I get that right?"

A slow smile creeps across Emily's face. "Yep, that about covers it. I don't think your team has any concept of how hard it is to roll out and support software in production. It's our job to work with you, but can you honestly say that you're doing all you can to make it easy on us?"

I find myself laughing a little. "You know, I think I understand a little of how you feel. For us, we're downstream of someone too – our business partners and the project management layer – and it really sucks to be responsible for something you had no say in and couldn't control. That's the definition of stress." I glance at Emily again and decide to take a gamble. "Did I ever tell you about my near-divorce, about five years ago?"

Emily looks at me and raises an eyebrow. "You're kidding me – you always talk so much about your family! I thought you and Julie were some of the lucky ones."

"Yeah, it's something I'm not proud of. Julie and I had been married a long time by that point, and of course we had our ups and downs. But we'd been trying to have a child – and when it happened, I found myself on the outside looking in. I started hunting and fishing more; being at home just seemed so BORING, like house arrest. There's only so much burping and diaper changing you can do before you have to get some air. That, and the sleep deprivation, well, we really started fraying at the edges. For a few months we barely talked, just walked around in icy silence – or she would scream at me that I was still trying to act like a single man, and I would storm off, hit the bars. It really got ugly. After a while neither of us really wanted to be together anymore or enjoyed each other's company.

"Like I said, this isn't a part of my life that I am proud of. Both of us at this point were only seeing each other's flaws and the relationship just didn't look fixable. But, as one last try, we ended up going into therapy. I'll never forget on our third session together, the therapist talked about what a dysfunctional relationship is – that it's where both parties feel victimized, held hostage by the other. Neither side is getting what they need, and neither is really taking a good look at what they are bringing to the table. So, long story short, we had this long talk in the car on the way back and really opened up about how hurt and angry we were, and how disappointed we felt. It felt like kneeling on broken glass, but for the first time in months I looked at Julie and said sincerely that my behavior was selfish, that I wasn't being a good partner and that I didn't want to keep on repeating my actions that were so disrespectful, that it wasn't fair to her. And over a few months we set some common goals that we could work towards together."

This is getting a little uncomfortable; I'm revealing a bit more than I'd wanted. "Anyway, no, Julie and I aren't a perfect couple. We really had to work at our marriage to stay together, and it all started back in that talk in the car – saying that we weren't being fair to each other and that we wanted to do things differently."

I sigh. "In a sense, your team and mine are married. And right now it's definitely a dysfunctional marriage, where we both feel trapped and dissatisfied. You're saying your team isn't being partnered with, that we are dropping things out of nowhere on you – I believe that. You've also said we need to coordinate better. I think, with our rush to deliver working software at the end of every sprint out to QA, we have been missing the downstream impacts. So, what does that look like from your perspective?"

Emily is smiling at me and nodding, but there's steel behind her smile. She says, "Well, yes, you're right – this is a dysfunctional marriage." We both laugh, and she grips her cup of tea a little tighter. "I'm just tired of hearing complaints about what it's like running builds for your group, and I don't get this kind of static from the Java team or the SQL folks. There's some basic hygiene that your team needs to think about so we don't get a mess dropped on us every two weeks. And I can't afford to lose someone like Kevin. You know the Portland market – it could take me a year to find someone at his level and then get him or her trained up to that level of competence. I am hearing you say the right things though Ben – for the first time." She looks at me over the rim of her teacup and takes a deliberately long sip. "Now let's see if you can follow through with the actions."

It's hard for me not to roll my eyes a little at Emily's speech. Emily has been trashing my name every chance she can get for months; now the same old tune, my team is always at fault. I have to swallow this though and keep in mind what I want out of our little café summit. "All right, so we have common goals – we want our teams to work together smoothly with less friction. What I'm hearing from this is that your teams and mine are stuck under the same rock. We are both drowning in firefighting, in unplanned work. Every week we lose most of our firepower with handling support and triage, and our broken releases are gobbling up the rest.

"So, Douglas wants me to talk about a plan to move towards a more stable release pattern. I think both of us want to learn some lessons from our last Footwear app release and move onward and upward. So, what do you think about coming up with a plan and presenting it to management together?"

Emily mulls this over and comes up with a winner — we'll pair the two people closest to the last release debacle, Kevin and Alex, and put them in a room for a few days to brainstorm. I have to push back on including Ivan — who would have hijacked any discussion into ticket-routing as a cure-all — but we leave with what looks like the beginnings of an agreement.

Sticking to the 20% Rule (Capacity Planning)

Before I knew it, we were wrapping up another sprint and clearing the decks for the next one.

I find my attention wandering during the sprint planning session. The room has a good energy level though; we can already show some progress, just a few weeks in. Perhaps, most surprisingly — Harry, of all people, teamed up with Padma and came up with the number of tickets created by each app on our list for the previous 90 days, broken into major and minor buckets.

This freaking report, believe it or not, was an actual game changer for us. It looks like George's hunch was right — out of the dozens of apps and services we have to maintain, really only a handful are true problem children — with a high business value and a large number of relatively painful bugs. Wrapping better release management and version control practices around our codebase is now looking a lot more possible. We can focus on just a few of the most temperamental, highly visible apps, and leave the rest for now.

The last of our demos is finishing up; now's the time. "As you know, this is Erik's last meeting with us," I announce. "Erik, I know we're all going to miss your energy and drive. As you are heading out the door, I thought you could tell us up front — how are we doing with our push for better version control discipline?"

"Well, it's still really early on." Erik shoots me an irritated look; once again, I've got him under the spotlight. "It's unreasonable to expect a turnaround in such a short period of time. But yeah, I'm seeing some positive trends. We've got some environmental and config code moving to version control and that's really good to see, and I'm satisfied that what we've got in version control right now matches production for our major headaches. But we still have a mountain of work ahead of us."

The rest of the group is silent. I wait a few beats then say, "I take it the rest of you agree. To me, it's really good news that out of the 80 some apps that we have to support, less than 10 need to be prioritized. That cuts down our to-do list by quite a bit. What about our push for better quality on check-in with more consistent peer reviews?"

There's a little dead space, and then finally Alex pipes up. "Well, I think we're still very early on, but there's some positive signs around the concepts of collective ownership and our peer review system is making some progress. But pair programming, my God..." Loud sounds of agreement were heard around the table.

Padma is fuming. "Alex, pair programming is a key part of XP programming and we'll never have true quality without it."

"With all respect, Padma, I disagree. It means we cut our capacity in half. And there's times when I really need to think about something, focus and concentrate. I can't do that with someone sitting three feet from me. Peer review, yes that's working – pair programming is a loser. We need to drop it."

"Well, I promised you it would be an experiment, one that we could drop if it's not working out," I say brightly. "So the question is, is it too early for us to judge if this is successful or not?"

"I don't think it's too early," Alex replied. "We should know by now if something is actually helping us or not. We've had that time, and it's just not working for us."

Before Padma can break in again, I shrug and reply, "This is a group decision, not something I'm going to mandate. If we see pair programming as something that can help this team improve our quality, we should do it. If we see it as hurting or neutral in its effects, we need to drop it. Let's see a show of hands – how many of you want to continue with pair programming?" I get a few hands up, but most of the devs keep their arms at their sides. "OK, I'll put this in the retrospective – we tried it, it didn't help us, we're going to shelve it. I'm worried though that our customers might see this as us falling back on some commitments we've made around quality. Is every line of code we're committing going through a peer review?"

"Yes, we're doing that," Harry says confidently. "For example, I usually call Rob or Ryan over before I do my daily check-ins for a quick look-see. It's helped a little. Mostly though, it's slowed me down. Sometimes there's no one around and then I have to go ahead and check my changes in solo."

"Harry, either we're doing the right thing or we're not!", Alex snaps in exasperation. "I'd like to see us checking in our code much more frequently, like multiple times a day. Once a day or once a week – and I've seen your check-ins, once a week is more like it – just isn't often enough for us."

"If you want multiple releases a day, Alex, then get us a better test framework." Harry's lip is curling up in disdain. "Right now I'm a little more concerned with not ending my career every time we go to deploy. I have zero confidence that our test layer is going to catch actual bugs and I don't want to spend my life tracking down regression issues."

I can see both Padma and Rajesh starting to bristle now. I spread my hands on the table. "Let's not waste time circling around like this. I'm worried about us falling back into our old habits. We agreed that we would have every change reviewed by a peer. From what I'm hearing, the process right now is informal and ad hoc. It looks like the best fix might be gating our code in some way. Of those apps that we flagged as being troublemakers – how much work would it be for us to enforce some sort of peer review on check-in?"

Padma frowns. "For the apps that we maintain in Visual Studio AND have in source control, it's a checkbox. We could enforce this with approval on a Git pull request for example. But some of our worst apps are more than twenty years old, and it shows – we're talking Coldfusion, COBOL FORTRAN, etc. We build and deploy these manually as executables. Those legacy apps can't be gated, at least not easily."

"I'm the team dev lead and it's my job to make sure that our standards are consistent." Alex looks around the room. "It bothers me that we're not checking in often enough, and that when we do we go to a good ol' buddy to rubber-stamp hundreds of lines of code he or she has never seen before. Any objections to us setting up a policy where any check-in must be reviewed before commit as a gated approval step?"

We get agreement on this; we also put in the retrospective and on the team whiteboard that our check-ins are too large and infrequent. Something keeps weighing on me though – finally I snap my fingers. "That's it – I almost forgot. When we planned out our work this sprint and the last one, we made sure to leave 20% of the capacity – that's two days for each of you – to start to pay down our technical debt. I got a lot of static from our business partners on this, as we're already behind in our commitments. I told them that we would only be able to make real progress on quality if we stopped booking you up 100%. What I want to know is, how is that working for us?"

To my surprise, one of the quieter devs on the team – Rob – offers his thoughts. "Not so great. Yeah, I had two days blocked on my calendar, but we had a boatload of bugs drop the day before. I was going to use that time to shape up the codebase in VC, but I had to drop that to work on the bugs we found with the last release."

As a few others in the room chime in with similar complaints, Alex rolls his eyes. "If it was really that bad, I would have expected to see more of you here Thursday and Friday instead of working from home. I'm just going to say it – that 20% time isn't for us to go home and buff up our World of Warcraft characters. We need everyone to show a commitment to improving our quality for things to get better. Otherwise, we're going to get what we deserve – long painful releases and a never-ending list of bugs."

"We're running out of time here and we need to get back to our sprint planning," George says firmly. "I don't think anyone here interprets those two days as 'Netflix time'. Let's do this – next sprint, for our retrospective, each person can spend five minutes talking about what was done on their 20% time. If it's block-and-tackle stuff like version control and struggling with moving config/environmental code, so be it. If it's something shiny and new you played around with and think could help us, even better. But let's not lose sight of the goal – for us to get out of our rut, we need to be learning continually. That means bringing something new to the table every two weeks, something that can help the person next to you."

Nothing to argue with here. George smiles broadly and says, "One quick story and then we'll get back to it. Back in my early twenties I used to be a section hiker on the Pacific Crest Trail. And I'll never forget when I first tried to put on that 50 lb pack and felt those straps cutting into my shoulder blades. I thought, *there's no way I can carry a mile, let alone a hundred.* And the first few days of every hike was pure torture. But I learned two things – first off, to be successful I just had to keep putting one foot in front of the other and not look up at the mountain in front of me. I kept saying every few minutes, *one step at a time, one step at a time.*

"The second thing I learned was that my biggest blocker was really mental, not physical. Once I stopped comparing myself to other hikers and showed some patience, I got less frustrated. My goal shifted from putting in twenty miles a day to trying to do that day's hike the right way at the right pace for that day. Those little habits started to kick in over time, I got injured less and spent more of my time enjoying the process instead of hating my pack, hating that bland oatmeal, hating the work. I think that's where we are right now as a team – we're learning the little habits it'll take to be successful and a lot less stressed out."

A Focus on Flow, Not Quality (Reliability First)

Today's the big presentation to Douglas; I walk into the conference room a few minutes early. It isn't enough though – Emily is already there, moving briskly ahead with setting up the presentation display. *At least we got them to agree to present off the same deck,* I think and grin a little. Douglas, true to his military background, shows up precisely on time – and motions impatiently for us to kick things off.

Emily begins by recounting some of the issues with the Footwear release, now many weeks back – highlighting the late notice of the upcoming release, the incomplete setup instructions, and the strain the weekend patch work and troubleshooting had put on her team. I have to give her credit here though – she is sticking to facts, and even ends on a somewhat conciliatory note: "Ben and I were joking recently that the relationship between our team is like a dysfunctional marriage – neither side is really getting what they want. I do know that Ops simply isn't ready to handle this kind of a nightmare every two months, let alone every two weeks. We need a renewed focus on quality, which means slowing things down and better planning. We simply can't focus on velocity without thinking about the disruptions it is causing the teams that have to support and operate this code that we're shoveling out the door." She sits down, glowing in triumph.

I stand up and square my shoulders. For the first time in weeks, I felt like I understood where Emily is coming from – and that there might be a way out of this cross-team mudslinging. "First off, I agree 100% with the problems Emily's outlined with this release. Now that we're starting to see problems the same way, we can start to work jointly toward a resolution.

"Let's show each part of our that release – but without any groups or team names called out. Our objective here isn't to pin blame on anyone, but simply to show the flow of work across WonderTek for this one product. Here's what that looked like."

Footwear Release Pain Points

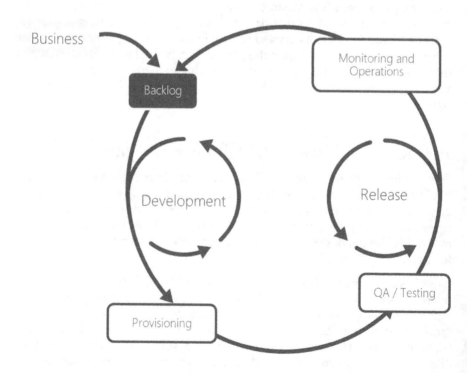

He continued: "Top left is our starting point – where work enters the system and is dropped into our backlog. I'd love to talk about the pipeline of work going into development for a few minutes. We're seeing issues here right off the bat – there's constant churn and jostling over what the right priority should be as everyone champions their favorite pet feature. It's not uncommon for us to bounce from one red-hot, must-be-done emergency project to another from sprint to sprint – enough to give anyone a bad case of whiplash. Having our priorities and focus shift like this is leading directly to a lack of traction as we constantly shift projects back and forth.

"We also have a long list of features waiting on development. Elaine tells me that we have 13 major features under development and about 120 minor features in our backlog, just for one application. That represents in total about 1,300 hours worth of development. Worse, those asks are aging on us – the average time these wait to be assigned to a sprint is stretching out to about 90 days, and that's climbing steadily. You can imagine how that's going over with Footwear." Douglas is nodding vigorously; he's been getting an earful lately. "At least half of the features that we've worked on in the past three months end up being unused or dropped as no longer being of value. A significant amount of our development work ends up on the cutting room floor – by the time we deliver, it's not needed or we've spent a lot of time gold-plating a feature that ends up being a dead end."

That's two weak points already – a long list of aging features that are stacking up on us, and shifting priorities by the business. But I'm not done yet. "Next comes the problems we've seen in writing code. For our last release, we spent a lot of time consolidating our code so it was buildable – we call that integration. That took up a shocking amount of time, about 12 weeks total. And once we were able to get a releasable build ready, our headaches were just beginning. As we're releasing more often, there's less room for us to work on nonfunctional requirements. Some very fundamental aspects like security and performance are dropping by the wayside. If all work stopped now, we'd still have two months of work addressing this technical debt.

"I mentioned earlier how frustrated the business has become as they've seen their requests languish. The reason for that is simple – we're having to pull away from new development work to knock down bugs. We have currently in production about 12 major bugs, and over 100 minor ones – all of which are sapping our firepower when it comes to taking on new development. We started tracking this a few weeks ago and found that about 60% of our team's capacity is spent identifying and fixing bugs. Of these bugs, it turns out that about half were red herrings – either false alarms, environmental or noncode issues, or user errors. Another 20% could have been addressed by the first responder in a few minutes using the runbooks we've provided them. But each issue reported requires us to stop work and triage, since they're passed along to us untouched. More than anything else, getting tied down in firefighting is the single biggest contributor to the perception by the business that work is not getting done. It is – just not the type of work that adds value."

"It sounds to me like your QA team isn't doing their job right," Douglas interrupts. "Why are we sinking the money and time we are into testing, if it's not catching these problems early on?"

"That's a great question." I wince a little. "I wish I had a pat answer for this. Rajesh and his team have moved mountains to get our code coverage up, but still QA seems to always lag behind development by a few weeks. That gap is hurting us – most of the bugs I just mentioned should have been caught on check-in. Instead, they make it out the door into production. By the time they're found and backed out, which is its own nightmare, it's cost us ten times what it should have."

Emily is wrinkling her brow at this. I continue, "Emily, that's not an exaggeration. Rolling selectively back what we think might have caused a problem and then validating our work is a huge overhead cost. I know the QA team is working very hard, and we can't fault their intentions or competence. But there's no doubt about it – our quality is hurting us right now, and it appears like we need to rethink the way we're approaching testing so it's more of a parallel effort with development.

"Making thing worse are our environmental anomalies. Currently when we prepare a build, it's prepped as a WIX package and then sent to the IT/Ops team for implementation. They then take the baton and run with it – spinning up environments based on our instructions and specs and installing the package and libraries it'll require to run. There's a lot of wasted time as people run back and forth trying to get the package to run on a new server as it does on a dev workstation after weeks of tweaking.

"Our environments themselves have become priceless artifacts – we're terrified to make any changes to them. A significant number of the bugs and performance problems we see are actually caused by environmental anomalies. This means whenever we have to troubleshoot something, we first need to figure out if it's caused by non-code issues like a patch to the OS or a networking condition. That can sometimes take days to determine – it's a big reason why our firefighting is so drawn out and costly.

"So there you have it – a nasty little vicious cycle we have going on right now."

Douglas is getting impatient. "OK, I get it, life is tough. Get to the point though – you're presenting this as a set of problems. My ask is for my people to present me with options and solutions, not just problems. What's our way out of this mess?"

Emily slowly stands up and smiles. "Well, Ben and I have been talking about our deployment process. I have to give him some props here, at least he's starting to acknowledge some of the quality issues coming out of the code base. We'd like to tackle this as a joint problem." She shows her next slide:

Issue	Metrics	Options
Aging requests by business	1300 hours development in wait status	Better filter/prioritization and unified view
	90 days avg wait until tasked and in sprint	Improve deployment and dev practices downstream
Low quality – bugs in production	12 major, 100 minor bugs	Peer review
	Unit test code coverage – 25%	Automated builds
	60% of developer time spent on bugfixes	Configuration management
		Source control
		First responder triage training
Integration Issues	12 weeks to integrate code branches	Continuous integration
		Source control
Risky releases	Change failure rate 70%	Release management
	Lead time 3 weeks	Improved diagnostics and monitoring
	MTTR – 8.5 days	Automated builds
	Release frequency – 2 weeks	Source control

"I've put Kevin in tandem with Alex on Ben's team, and they think we can better automate our releases," Emily continues. "There's no reason why the builds for this application can't be better automated so that we have a Christmas-tree like display with green and red builds on a dashboard. And on environment provisioning – we need to stop thinking about code as just being for software. Environments and servers can be scripted, and Kevin's confident that with the current design of the Footwear app, it should be a matter of weeks to get to where we can spin up a VM environment from a script that is capable of running the app. That gives us apples-to-apples conformity from QA down to PROD."

Douglas is looking at the third column and frowning. "Emily, I appreciate you being here and working with Ben jointly on a solution. That more than anything else gives me some hope. But let's be honest here – this is a lot of ideas to take on. I think, maybe too much for where you are right now."

I say slowly, "Yeah, I totally agree. We aren't proposing taking on every aspect of these at the same time – that's just not reasonable. What we'd like to do is focus on one thing – and see if we can't make some measurable improvement, over three months. That one thing is our release process.

"Lack of maturity over how we handle changes and code releases is our limiting factor, and it's tied in to everything else. If we had fewer bugs making it into production, we could focus more on the backlog requests and get the business the features they're asking for. Our Operations and IT team would be a lot happier as they won't be dragged into all-week war rooms trying to fix the latest broken build. Our releases would be safer, so we won't feel like we're making a career ending decision every time we go ahead with a production push."

Douglas is nodding. Things are going well so far; this is running smoother than I anticipated. He asks, "So, let's get down to it. What are you going to do to fix things?"

Emily shows the next slide:

Mission: Improve Release Process

Proposed Fix	Current State	Target State (in one month)
Source control for code and infrastructure	Change failure rate 70%	Change failure rate 35%
	Release frequency – 2 weeks	Release frequency – 1 week
Automated builds	300 hours total release prep time (240 hours integration, 60 hours release)	150 hours total prep time per release
Continuous Integration		
Improved coordination with Dev and Ops with RM Tiger Team	60 bugs caused by noncode issues	30 bugs caused by noncode issues
	MTTR – 8.5 days	MTTR - 4 days

Douglas is frowning again. "Ben, you're already struggling getting your stuff out the door every two weeks. Why are you wanting to push your code out more frequently? And if you want to reduce firefighting – how come I'm not seeing anything here for your QA team?"

I reply, "On that second point about why we're not targeting quality directly – two reasons. First, focus. You said it yourself – we can't take on too much at once, we have limited capacity. Second, we're drowning in bugs, true – but that's a masking symptom, not the cause. The actual cause of all these bugs is lack of process, of automation.

"Our teams are telling us that if we have a pushbutton deployment that's repeatable, to every environment, our rollbacks will be much easier; our firefighting will drop off as we begin using scripts more for templating our environments. We're betting heavily on creating automated builds, running off of source control that's the single source of truth for environments, configuration and code. That will have cascading benefits everywhere, including quality. And if we can turn half of those red dots on our manual releases to green – say get it to a 35% failure rate – I think a lot of the friction between Emily and myself suddenly goes away. We'll know we're making headway if each release carries less of a tax on us – if we're only spending 150 hours prepping and rolling out a release, versus the 300 hours its currently costing our teams."

He's still frowning a little, but I'm getting a little bit of a nod. "OK, good plan. I like this because it's specific and verifiable, we'll know if we're on track or not. I still think this is a lot to take on in one month, but let's see how things go. Emily, are you onboard with this?"

Emily says, "I'm not happy about saying we're going to release more often. Like I keep saying, we're strained to the limit already. But, let's wait and see. The big win from where I stand is the Release Management Tiger Team. This is a few people from my team and Ben's, meeting together weekly to talk about current and future state with our release processes and build automation. Right there, we'll see better communication and less dropped balls between our two teams."

Douglas stands up. "Well, this has been a good discussion. I'm late for my next meeting – but the fact that at least I could get you two in a room to talk about this together was a good thing. Let's move forward along these lines – and see how things go."

Behind the Story

A few concepts in this chapter bear some exploration. For example, why are we discussing boat winches in a book about DevOps and software development? And why was the team's decision to focus on improving velocity so short-sighted?

Lastly, a key part of DevOps is learning how to control queue size and limit work. Let's explore what this process – which in software we implement with a process called Kanban – means in more detail.

Ratcheting Change

Fast is fine, but accuracy is everything. In a gun fight... You need to take your time in a hurry.

— Doc Holliday

Simplicity changes behavior.

— BJ Fogg[1]

The power of sustaining your progress is that you end up blowing away anyone that chased success as fast as possible.

— Rob Hardy[2]

As part of writing this book, we devoured nearly a hundred books on the subject of DevOps. But two in particular had the biggest impact on our thinking: the book *Team of Teams* by General McChrystal and *The Power of Habit* by Charles Duhigg. Neither mention DevOps anywhere in their text. But we suggest that both are essential to understanding why most organizations find the road to better change management and velocity so difficult.

We took an opportunity in the section "A Fishing Trip" to talk about the lessons these books and others reveal about human behavior and the difficulty of overcoming inertia and tradition. Setting a safe pace remains one of the most important factors so often overlooked in the "how-to" recipe books on DevOps.

Slow Is Smooth, Smooth Is Fast

There's a lot of meaning in that classic military saying "slow is smooth, smooth is fast." Moving fast or rushing our pace in any strategic-scale transformation is reckless, potentially fatal. When we move carefully, deliberately, at a measured pace, two wonderful things happen. First off, we avoid many rep-sapping mistakes and limit the blast radius of any missteps — meaning we'll still be around to implement our next incremental change or improvement. Second, our progress actually becomes faster than big-lurch death marches.

---

[1] "Tiny Habits," BJ Fogg, Stanford University, 2018, www.tinyhabits.com/.
[2] "A Counterintuitive Strategy for Building a Daily Exercise Habit," Rob Hardy, Medium.com, 7/21/2017, https://betterhumans.coach.me/a-counterintuitive-strategy-for-building-a-lifelong-exercise-habit-13471da4e49d.

The ingrained nature of habits and organizational culture is why Jon Cwiak of Humana told us the following:

> Some of our teams though have been doing work in a particular way for 15 years; it's extraordinarily hard to change these indoctrinated patterns. What we are finding is, we succeed if we show we are adding value. Even with these long-standing teams, once they see how a stable release pipeline can eliminate so much repetitive work from their lives, we begin to make some progress.[3]

Seth Vargo of Google echoed this:

> ...we have to admit the challenge large, established enterprises face, is huge. The word 'entrenched' doesn't even cover it. We're talking about 150 years of corporate culture, everything based on incentives around competition. Do you want that raise? Do you want more vacation time, a better office? Then you have to step on your peers to get ahead. That culture doesn't just go away overnight. You can't just step in and say, 'everybody get along now, we're all about learning and not using people as stepping stones anymore.' There's a lot of history of unhealthy competition and fear that has to be unlearned first.

> No company starts out with yearly deployments; all these struggling companies, when they first started, were likely incredibly agile – even before that movement existed! Services and software got rolled out the door frequently, but then there's that one customer or account that is such a large value that you'll do anything to keep them. Now we have to start slowing down releases because we care more about availability than we do augmenting these services. It builds up tension between the people that build services and those that keep it running. This ultimately leads to slowing or halting releases and adding unnecessary processes in the release process.[4]

We'll illustrate this with the personal story of a friend of ours, whom we'll call James. James was like most of us in the programming and IT field: almost completely sedentary in his lifestyle, badly overweight, and badly overworked. He told us that he found himself out of breath just crossing the hundred feet from his office to his car. Then, as often happens, the debts his way of life were accruing came due; he had a visit to the emergency room, followed by months of physical therapy. On his first visit post-event to his physical therapist, the man looked at James and told him he had two decisions: "in ten years, do you want to be healthy, alive and well for your family? Or do you want to die?"

---

[3]*Interview of Jon Cwiak by Dave Harrison, see Appendix.*
[4]*Interview of Seth Vargo by Dave Harrison, see Appendix.*

It was one of those dramatic forks in life's road that forces a choice. The interesting thing is that James did not start out with a crash course, a complete reversal of his potato chips-and-the-sofa lifestyle to tofu and 3 hours of hitting the gym a day. Like many of us, James hated working out, but he did like riding a bike from time to time. So, he started a new habit, at the same time each day. He would hop on his bike and ride around his neighborhood, about 3 miles. This went on for a few months. Over time, he started riding with a group over longer distance; an older man was kind enough to hang back with him so he wasn't left in the dust. Gradually, click by click, he was able to ratchet up his activity level till he was hitting almost 5000 miles a year – doing something that he enjoyed, every turn of the wheel.

Two years after this event, James doesn't put on the mileage that he used to on his bike. But he still gets out several times a week, when he's not doing other active things. He's lost 30 pounds, and his health – due to his new lifelong habits – is back in the green.

Start with Tiny Habits

This is why our fathers often told us, "slow and steady wins the race." If James had chosen the path most of us take when it comes to our new year's resolutions, it's safe to say that today he'd be back where he started, if not worse off. Most of us start our personal transformations on a grand scale, with high hopes of dramatic improvements in our health or mindset. Months later, our treadmill or exercise bike languishes unused in the garage, being used as a coat rack. What makes the difference here in having a new habit stick?

The studies and work conducted by Dr BJ Fogg of Stanford are very revealing on this topic. He noted that many of us start out thinking almost entirely about outcomes – "I'm going to lose 20 lbs by March!" There's that familiar initial rush of enthusiasm – we make seismic changes to our lifestyle from top to bottom, a complete renovation for comprehensive fitness. Then, about 3 to 4 weeks later, we find it almost impossible to make that trip to the gym or to down yet another salad. Burnout and lethargy set in; we fall off the wagon. Within a few months, we are back to our unhealthy state; nothing has changed.

The seeds of failure were right there in the beginning when we started out thinking about life-changing outcomes vs. one habit at a time. Those who actually succeed in this very difficult quest tend to think less about outcomes and more in terms of habits. And they tend to build these habits like our friend James did, with a ridiculously easy starting point and very gradual, gentle increases over time.

For example, Dr Fogg found himself wanting to increase his physical fitness as he entered his 50s. But starting with 100 pushups a day – though that might have worked for a week or so – was simply too big a mountain to climb;

10–12 pushups a day was also too hard. He started with an anchor, a physical cue. In this case, it was every time he went to the bathroom. After peeing, he did two pushups. Then, he washed his hands – and felt a little burst of satisfaction.

That's how the habit started – with a simple act, tiny in size, with the same physical cue or trigger – an anchor, as Dr Fogg calls it. Now, after months of gradually stepping it up, Dr Fogg does between 40 and 80 pushups a day – often outperforming his students. Dr Fogg calls these "Tiny Habits," and it's a proven way of encouraging lasting personal change at a sustainable, safe pace.

James Clear found the same thing to be true in his work. For example, he wanted to increase the weight he was able to lift in squats to 300 pounds. He did this by starting with lifting an easy amount of weight a few times a week, about 200 pounds. That was way too light for his capacity and added hardly nothing to his weekly routine. Every few weeks or so, he kicked up the weight by no more than 5 pounds – what he called a "small upper bound." Within a year, he was up to that 300 pound goal. As he put it:

> I never followed a magical program. I simply did the work and added 5 pounds every two weeks or so. Sure, the lower limit was important. I had to keep adding weight in order to get stronger. But the upper limit was just as critical. I had to grow slowly and methodically if I wanted to prevent inflammation and injury.

> There were plenty of days when I could have added 10 pounds. Maybe even 15 pounds. But if I aggressively pursued growth I would have quickly hit a plateau (or worse, caused an injury). Instead, I chose stay within a safety margin of growth and avoided going too fast. I wanted every set to feel easy.

> The power of setting an upper limit is that it becomes easier for you to sustain your progress. And the power of sustaining your progress is that you end up blowing away everyone who chased success as quickly as possible.[5]

You'll notice a theme beginning to emerge here with these success stories:

1. Commitment: There's a personal commitment and accountability – often communicated to others – to make a change.

2. Habit Not Outcome Oriented: This change is communicated in the form of a habit ("I want to squat 300 lbs") vs. an outcome ("I want to lose thirty pounds").

---

[5]*"Do Things You Can Sustain," James Clear,* https://jamesclear.com/upper-bound.

3. Simple, Clear, and Unambiguous: The habit is easily understood and something that can (and should) be done every day.

4. Small and Achievable: Instead of being epic level achievements, successful changes begin with tiny nudges – perhaps only minutes a day – that are gradually ramped up over time.

Activation Energy, Bright Lines, and the Single Pushup

It's natural to think big and try to set ambitious goals. But thinking only in terms of life-changing outcomes and setting these big lifetime-changing goals can set us up for failure. James Clear compared the costs of starting a new habit to activation energy, the minimum amount of energy required for a chemical reaction to occur – like when we strike a match. The energy in striking the match creates friction and heat, just enough energy needed to trigger a reaction and light the match on fire. As he says,

> The problem is that big goals often require big activation energies. In the beginning, you might be able to find the energy to get started each day because you're motivated and excited about your new goal, but pretty soon (often within a few weeks) that motivation starts to fade and suddenly you're lacking the energy you need to activate your habit each day.

> …Smaller habits require smaller activation energies and that makes them more sustainable. The bigger the activation energy is for your habit, the more difficult it will be to remain consistent over the long-run. When you require a lot of energy to get started there are bound to be days when starting never happens.[6]

That's why, if you want to get stronger, it's better to start with one pushup a day instead of 80. One pushup a day will be like striking a match, nice and easy – a very low activation energy. It's going to take a lot more activation energy to start with 80 pushups a day – and the odds tell us that within a week, maybe two, we'll find the price too high to pay and keep motivated. We'll miss a day, then two… and our old negative habits will reassert themselves.

Beyond just being bite-sized, the habit we're trying to instill uses what is called in the world of contract law "bright lines" – a clear, unambiguous standard, or guidelines. Rules and commandments are easy to get around or subvert; deciding ahead of time that we are committed to a very specific change in our behavior – and making preparations so our environment encourages this change – is something else entirely.

---

[6]"Do Things You Can Sustain," James Clear, https://jamesclear.com/upper-bound.

Alcoholics Anonymous, for example, has found that it's almost impossible to tell people to stop doing bad things or habits and hope for success. Instead, they try to replace bad habits with good ones. As Charles Duhigg brought out in "The Power of Habit," they incrementally try to replace bad habits with good ones. For most alcoholics, as an example, the bar is more of a social draw than anything else. Having a clear personal commitment, regular group discussions in a warm community, and an assigned mentor that a recovering alcoholic can call during moments of temptation replaces that bad habit of hitting the bar with a positive habit build on our natural social needs.[7]

DevOps really at its heart is really about changing habits at scale. Refinements like breaking down siloed walls, eliminating the "blink" or handoffs between groups, and improving the flow of communication and work are all changes in human behaviors and habits. This kind of dramatic change in human behavior is extremely challenging and comes with a high recession rate. Otherwise, there wouldn't be a thriving $30B a year fitness and health industry in America alone!

We tilt the odds in our favor when we take into consideration human psychology and the nature of building positive habits. Thinking that releasing 10,000 times a day like Amazon, Microsoft, or Facebook will fix things is really just outcome-based thinking. And, fundamentally, that kind of an imitation-based goal has nothing to do with delivering value or solving a specific business problem. The same is true of CIO-driven initiatives to become "cloud-native," without thinking of the capabilities and advantages that would make such a movement desirable or even possible.

There's a hidden pitfall here in subconsciously trying to follow a pattern set by another company's winning recipe. Michael Stahnke of Puppet told us that habits like continuous learning (which we discuss in Chapter 7) are far better than a cookie-cutter approach born out of envy:

> *Usually when things go off the rails with DevOps it's because incentives are misaligned with what you're trying to do. To me it comes down to internal motivation – do you want to be demonstrably better today than yesterday? Everything is culture side for me.*
>
> *You can't pattern yourself after Etsy or Google. Guess what – they're terrible at certain things, the same as you are. They just don't talk about it onstage. The big unspoken secret of our movement is, no one, absolutely NO ONE is the best at DevOps. Everyone is still learning and trying to do their thing.[8]*

---

[7]*The Power of Habit: Why We Do What We Do in Life and Business*, Jan 2014, Charles Duhigg, Random House, ISBN-10: 081298160X, ISBN-13: 978-0812981605
[8]*Interview of Michael Stahnke by Dave Harrison, see Appendix.*

Some very big epic-level concepts being batted around in this book: configuration management; comprehensive automation and a robust test and release cycle; microservices and domain-driven design; small, cross-functional teams with production support responsibilities; feature flags and continuous delivery; and hypothesis-driven development. These are all big goals involving months or years of work – like doing 100 pushups a day, or trying to lose 40 pounds.

This book is about "one team, one year," and it's technically possible to make progress in all of these things in a year. But we aren't seriously suggesting you SHOULD do all these things in a year. It's better to think less of these big-scale capabilities and epic improvements and more about some small, tiny habits you can instill tomorrow that won't roll back, that can be something to build on. Something like a single pushup.

What does "one pushup" look like in the DevOps world? Perhaps, this could be having your developers begin meeting once a week with Operations for lunch, or dedicating some cycles to sharing production support. Perhaps, it's instilling a better peer review process or experimenting with pair programming to produce better quality code. Maybe, you'll spend a day or two and build out a map showing the delivery of value across one of your workstreams, from idea to product. Or – our personal favorite – you'll take the advice of John-Daniel Trask and invest some time into setting up better instrumentation and monitoring. Any small, bite-sized habit that can give your team that quick positive burst of energy that comes from doing the right things the right way.

Changing habits is what led Ticketmaster to create an objective list of practices they wished to encourage in their maturity matrix model, which built toward their epic-level goal of self-disciplining teams.

Changing habits is what underlies Microsoft's push toward forcing a release every 2–3 weeks across all their delivery teams for Azure DevOps. Aaron Bjork told us, "you can't cheat shipping," and said that this forced pace promoted "righteous behaviors," good habits that avoided piling up technical debt and deferred work. That's a bright line that actually helped resolve a true business problem, and it wasn't allowed to be rolled back.

A consistent theme in our interviews was that the best roadmaps built positive habits that accrued gradually. Think less about grand imitative outcomes and more about changing habits with bright lines and a lowered activation energy.

Ben's on the right course when he is thinking about change in terms of the principles behind the click-and-pawl ratchet. Habit changes work along similar lines: small, incremental gains that are gradually ramped up over time. It's the only way to ensure that the changes in behavior we are trying to instill actually stick.

Kanban

The two pillars of the Toyota production system are just-in-time and automation with a human touch, or autonomation. The tool used to operate the system is kanban.

— Taiichi Ohno, Toyota

Controlling queue size is an extremely powerful management tool, as it is one of the few leading indicators of lead time – with most work items, we don't know how long it will take until it's actually completed. … it also makes it easier to see problems that prevent the completion of work. ….Bad multitasking often occurs when people are assigned to multiple projects, resulting in many prioritization problems.

— Dominica DeGrandis[9]

Kanban is another one of those unglamorous topics; there's not a lot of techy glitter about it, once the novelty of moving sticky notes about the screen fades. But the odds are that – just like with version control – you think you're doing Kanban, but you're not doing it right. And it's one of those secrets hidden right in the open that separates the high performers from the imitators.

In the section "Behind the Story – The Worst Form of Laziness," Ben's team first begins to experiment with Kanban and limiting work.

The Software Hierarchy of Needs

Let Dave explain with a little story from his past: "A few years back, I was leading a team that was swamped in debt. Very little new work, was going on as our mission mostly was supporting creaky old orphaned applications. The perpetrators that created this swamp of undocumented, untestable, kludgy garbage had long ago fled the scene, of course. Every day was a terrifying nightmare of uncertainty; important things were breaking, and we had no clue of how to fix them. To say we were stuck in neutral would be too kind; we were stuck in the mud, with no way of getting out.

What got us out of that negative cycle of fear and uncertainty? One morning I read a post written by Scott Hanselman on Maslow's hierarchy of needs. If you're not familiar with it – here's the original hierarchy:

---

[9]*"The DevOps Handbook: How to Create World-Class Agility, Reliability, and Security in Technology Organizations,"* by Gene Kim, Patrick Dubois, John Willis, Jez Humble. IT Revolution Press, 10/6/2016, ISBN-10: 1942788002, ISBN-13: 978-1942788003.

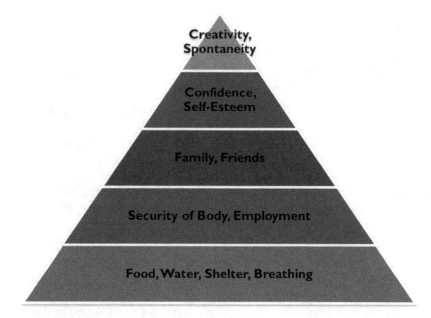

The essential point is that all of those great and lovely things we enjoy about culture is built on something. If our basic needs aren't being taken care of, if we're not safe and have a healthy network of supportive friends and family, the top of the pyramid is weak. Scott applied this to programming in a way that immediately caught our attention:

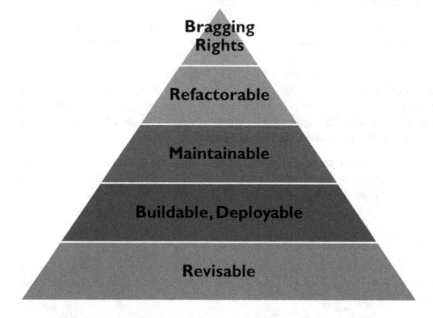

Scott's point was that it makes little difference what shiny new tech we're using – if the base of the pyramid isn't stable, we're stuck. If we can't deploy and roll back on a whim, if we are terrified of changing anything because of runaway environments and brittle, tightly coupled architectures – we're cavemen, living day to day, just trying to survive. You can't boast about all the cool stuff your apps do if you haven't taken care of the foundation. And you can't blame other groups either – this stuff is fundamental and is your responsibility to provide with every single line of code.

That morning, before our daily standup, I went over the article with my team and we mapped out what that meant to us. Over the following 30 minutes – and for the first time – we talked honestly about our applications big picture. Where were we falling short in having our code be revisable, buildable, maintainable, and refactorable? For us, it was clear – we had lots of room for improvement in having more productive design and peer reviews, and we desperately needed better tooling around our build process with CI and gated check-ins.

Here's the whiteboard drawing that resulted, in all its kludgy glory:

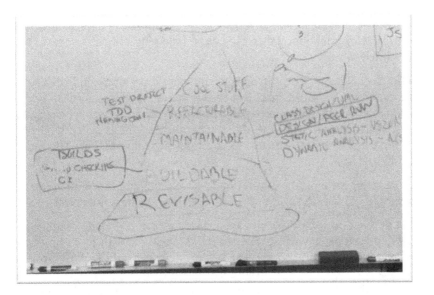

We called this misshapen wizard hat – sorry Scott! – our "Harry Potter Hat of Greatness." I can't tell you what a powerful impact that article had on my entire team, and myself personally. For the first time, as a group, we stopped pissing and moaning about all the things those other bad people were doing and started focusing on what we needed to change. Now, that we had named the problem, it couldn't hide anymore – we started making steady progress toward mastering our environments, making them more safe.

I remember going home that evening for the first time in months with a huge smile on my face; I was taking control of my destiny and finally earning my title as a team lead.

From this, I learned two lessons:

1. We were too busy to be effective at anything. If things were going to get better, we'd need to focus less on the urgent and more on the important things that were getting back-burnered.

2. For me to earn my pay as a lead, I'd need to set the example. That meant drilling in on one thing and one thing only.

Both of these lessons I should have learned months earlier; this is all Kanban 101. I was going through the motions of Kanban but not understanding the real intent."

Kanban Is About WIP

Interestingly, if you had talked to anyone at Dave's team at the time, they would have told you very confidently that they were following Kanban process. Yet, the team clearly wasn't.

To be effective, Kanban isn't just about showing your work and making it visible to everyone – though that's a nice side benefit. Kanban is really a tool to limit your WIP, your work in progress. You and the team decide how many things you can focus on at a time. As a general rule – if it's more than one task per person on the team, or five to seven for a group, you have too much work in play at once.

Why such a stringent limit? Isn't it better to have multiple tasks in progress at once, in parallel, so we don't have dead time waiting on dependencies?

First, the bar must be set low for a reason. Teams – and engineers especially – habitually underestimate what it takes to drive a task through to completion. (Remember the old general contractor's rule, that the last 20% of the project inevitably takes up 80% of the project time?) And we buy into this myth of multitasking – that we can juggle seven to eight things at once and do justice to them all. Inevitably, telling ourselves this lie means we pay a high price in terms of stress and waste due to context switching. Worse, we end up surrounded by projects and work that is half-done, disappointing the very people we were trying to please by overcommitting.

Noncoders frequently underestimate the costs of context switching and interruptions on flow. The book *Peopleware* was one of the first that took the time to describe flow and how it relates to programmers. Flow is an ubercreative, Nirvana-like state where we are solving problems and creating cool new functionality almost effortlessly. But as Peopleware brought out, it's not easy to get into that state; for most of us, it takes at least 15 minutes. Any break causes another 15 minute (minimum!) reset to get our mental train going again; a handful of interruptions can easily cost you a day's work. (This is why we are not big fans of modern "collaborative" software that forces popup toast messages or IM windows on our screens; they kill productivity and creativity.)

One of the best parts of Agile was that it finally gave us a break from constant interruptions by our stakeholders – "is it done yet? Hey, can you do this little task here this afternoon?" Agile gave us a safe little bubble of isolation that coders and engineers need to work on a set list of defined tasks – a bubble (hopefully) free of interruptions, which we pay for with accountability and transparency through our regular planning sessions and retrospectives.

In the majority of the time where teams struggle in their adoption of Agile, the common factor seems to be not gating or limiting the amount of work in flight. Kanban drives that next step up in isolation and helps eliminate the waste caused by context switching. After a settling-in phase, we bet that you'll notice is how much more seems to get done, with a lot less wear and tear on your people.

So if you're really doing Kanban, take a second look at that board and the tasks that are in flight. You should only have a few, and the entire team should be focused on them and pitching in together to drive them to "done" status.

Capacity Planning and In-Parallel Work

This brings us to our second point – parallel vs. in-series work. Immediately you'll hear cries of complaint when you institute these limits as a hard cap. It looks inefficient to have people waiting on work or complete artifacts – "people aren't busy! They're waiting on this other dependency to start work!" However, this is a very good thing – you're exposing a weak point (what the military calls a "limfac") in the process flow and forcing improvements at that constraint point in the value stream.

Remember that efficiency is not our goal – we are not trying to fully utilize our staff, to 100% of capacity. A fully utilized freeway is completely useless – it's jam-packed with cars, but nothing is moving. We want flow. That means limiting the number of cars on the road.

As Dominica DeGrandis pointed out:

> *Controlling queue size is an extremely powerful management tool, as it is one of the few leading indicators of lead time – with most work items, we don't know how long it will tke until it's actually completed. ...It also makes it easier to see problems that prevent the completion of work. It's tempting to start new work during that idle time as we are waiting – but a better action would be to find out what is causing the delay and help fix that problem. Bad multitasking often occurs when people are assigned to multiple projects, resulting in many prioritization problems.*[10]

Surprisingly, the cries of complaint you're going to hear loudest aren't going to come from outside your team. The loudest and most passionate arguments against capping work will come from the Atlases within your team – those long-suffering heroes who singlehandedly support everything. In the book *The Phoenix Project*, this much-hated person was called Brent; nothing could happen if Brent was sick or gone. He was a human limfac!

These people are often highly competent and very wide based in their tech judo as well as company lore. And the more difficult the assignment, the tighter the deadline, the less known the problem, and the more obscure the fix, the better! Secretly, these people – and you have at least a few in your company – LOVE the long nights, the weekend runs for pizza, kibitzing in the war room during a broken deployment.

It seems like these people are everywhere, with their hands on everything. Rarely is there time to document anything for the "next guy" – it's on to the next crisis du jour! They are taking point, fighting their way out of ambushes, getting things done – usually nine things at once, and that's on a Saturday. Saving the day comes with a significant payoff in terms of self-esteem and satisfaction – enough, perhaps, to justify in their minds the high price they often pay in terms of neglected relationships and their own health. Left to themselves, these self-sacrificing, highly competent heroes will lead the team into disaster; their work simply can't be recreated by anyone else.

Before we jump in with cries to "fire Brent!", let's take a good long look in the mirror first and admit that there's a secret adrenaline junky – a hidden Brent – in all of us. We check e-mail compulsively, monitor our work accounts during vacation, pride ourselves on our fast response time for any request, and a spotlessly clean inbox. We have to-do lists a hundred items long. We read websites on how to maximize our productivity and pride ourselves on how booked solid our calendars are – wall to wall meetings, everybody! And

---

[10]*"The DevOps Handbook: How to Create World-Class Agility, Reliability, and Security in Technology Organizations,"* by Gene Kim, Patrick Dubois, John Willis, Jez Humble. IT Revolution Press, 10/6/2016, ISBN-10: 1942788002, ISBN-13: 978-1942788003.

we start each morning and end the day with hours of streams of information and news that leaves us stressed and agitated. We move faster and faster; living the "full catastrophe life" to its fullest. We're crazy busy, which makes us irreplaceable. Is it possible though that in reality we are being… lazy?

Being Busy Is the Worst Form of Laziness

Timothy Ferris in the book *The Four Hour Workweek* made a very strong point: that we "busy" people are actually very lazy. Being busy is actually the worst form of laziness. Being busy is often caused by a failure to set priorities (despite the excuses we offer); our actions are indiscriminate, and we aren't putting any effort into separating out the important things. We are too lazy to check ourselves and ask – Am I being productive or just active? Am I inventing things to avoid the important?[11]

Truly effective people know innately the 80/20 rule – and they limit tasks to the 20% of things that will pay off long term, the truly important things. Keeping in mind Parkinson's Law – that tasks (cough, meetings!) expand to fill the time we allot for them – they hardcap their commitments ruthlessly. And they never even attempt multitasking. The book recommends that we have, at most, two goals or tasks to do each day – and they should be driven through to completion. If that isn't happening, we need to commit to less.

We'll get more into monitoring and dashboarding later. But it's worth saying that Kanban by itself is only a piece of the puzzle:

What is most interesting is that WIP limits on their own do not strongly predict delivery performance. It's only when they're combined with the use of visual displays and have a feedback loop from production monitoring tools back to delivery teams or the business that we see a strong effect. When teams use these tools together, we see a much stronger positive effect on software delivery performance… [So beyond limiting WIP, effective teams] make obstacles to higher flow visible, and if teams remove these obstacles through process improvement, leading to improved throughput. WIP limits are no good if they don't lead to improvements that increase flow.[12]

This doesn't have to be hugely complicated. For Dave's team, they kept that crude little Dr Seuss hat up on the whiteboard for 30 days and kept it front and center in our discussions and sprint retrospectives. Straightening out our flow pinch points was a longer journey. But, at least we were having the discussion, and the team was focused on a single mission.

---

[11]"*The 4-Hour Workweek: Escape 9-5, Live Anywhere, and Join the New Rich*" by Timothy Ferriss, December 2019, ISBN-10: 9780307465351, ISBN-13: 978-0307465351.
[12]"*Accelerate: The Science of Lean Software and DevOps: Building and Scaling High Performing Technology Organizations,*" Nicole Forsgren PhD, Jez Humble, Gene Kim. IT Revolution Press, 3/27/2018. ISBN-10: 1942788339, ISBN-13: 978-1942788331.

Do One Thing

As long as we're talking about focus, you'll forgive us for a short rant. One of the disturbing trends we've seen recently in tooling is how many Kanban boards out there are missing the point. The cards themselves are displaying way too much text and attributes that should be kept in drilldown, which makes the screen cluttered and difficult to grasp at a glance. And what started as a simple three-lane board – "To Do," "In Process," "Done" – now is sprouting all kinds of extra alleys. We commonly see "In Integration," or "Staging," "Dev Design," "Implementing," or "Data Modeling" lanes. Not surprisingly, these same teams struggle with showing their actual progress in a single board, or with straightening out their limfac points. They've fallen in love with the allure of a complicated display and lost sight of the end question – which is binary. Is the work done or not?

Many farmers focus on "one thing." If they get that one thing done a day – whatever is highest in priority – they can go to bed at night and sleep with a good conscience, knowing that they're making steady progress in chipping away at the work and constant maintenance that comes with the job.

For our team, we decided that "one thing" was peer and design reviews as a regular part of our working routine. For 30 days, we just focused on that as a team. Every meeting, every day, I found some reason to bring this up as a theme. Steadily, slowly but surely, "one thing" at a time, we started knocking down some of that overwhelming technical debt until we could get to the point where as a team we could finally brag about our progress. We were out of the mud!

Reliability First

Simplicity is prerequisite for reliability.

— Edsger W. Dijkstra

It is not the strongest of the species that survive, nor the most intelligent, but the one most responsive to change.

— Charles Darwin

In the section "A Focus on Flow, Not Quality," Ben opts to drive on flow and increasing velocity. This is a prime example of the numbers we choose to focus on having unintended consequences, and the biggest "road not taken" missed opportunity in the book. What would Ben's journey would have looked like if they had chosen a different KPI that focused more on reliability and service availability?

Thankfully, we have a stellar example of a very successful movement that chose to do just that: the Site Reliability Engineering (SRE) movement, founded by a little startup called Google. What can the SRE paradigm teach us about the value of building quality and reliability into our development processes and team values?

DevOps and the SRE Movement

Google faced a serious problem in 2003; as a consequence of their exponential growth, their large-scale services and data centers were beginning to show signs of wear, and their operational teams were overburdened. How could they continue to grow and add new features without sacrificing quality and reliability?

Enter Ben Treynor and his group of software engineers, driven by a single mission: to make the company's services run more reliably and at scale. Starting with a single team of seven, this group has now expanded to well over 1500 at Google. As a model, Site Reliability Engineering (SRE) is no longer unique to just Google; SRE teams have sprung up at companies like Apple, Microsoft, Facebook, Amazon, Target, IBM, and Dropbox.

Although Google's success with the SRE model has led many to label SRE as being "DevOps 2.0" or "the future of DevOps," interestingly, the people we interviewed at Google did not agree. At its core SRE is a very specific, proscribed implementation of DevOps principles. SRE happens to embody the philosophies of DevOps but has a much more prescriptive way of measuring and achieving reliability through engineering and operations work.

For example, the following table – courtesy of Seth Vargo, whose interview is in the Appendix – illustrates five DevOps principles and their corresponding SRE practices:[13]

DevOps	SRE
Reduce organization silos	Share ownership with developers by using the same tools and techniques across the stack
Accept failure as normal	Have a formula for balancing accidents and failures against new releases
Implement gradual change	Encourage moving quickly by reducing costs of failure
Leverage tooling and automation	Encourages "automating this year's job away" and minimizing manual systems work to focus on efforts that bring long-term value to the system
Measure everything	Believes that operations is a software problem and defines prescriptive ways for measuring availability, uptime, outages, toil, etc.

---

[13]"SRE vs. DevOps: competing standards or close friends?", Seth Vargo. Google Cloud Platform Blog, 5/8/2018. https://cloudplatform.googleblog.com/2018/05/SRE-vs-DevOps-competing-standards-or-close-friends.html.

SRE teams are "*responsible for the availability, latency, performance, efficiency, change management, monitoring, emergency response, and capacity planning of their services. We have codified rules of engagement and principles for how SRE teams interact with their environment – not only the production environment, but also the product development teams, the testing teams, the users, and so on. Those rules and work practices help us to maintain our focus on engineering work, as opposed to operations work.*"[14]

DevOps and SRE are not two competing methods for software development and operations, but rather close friends designed to break down organizational barriers to deliver better software faster.[15]

We don't envision SRE being "the way things are done" 10 years from now, as it's just one possible way of implementing DevOps. We do see it becoming more of a standardized role within many companies; its growth is only going to increase. It's a fantastic idea to have dedicated teams with a single obsession around reliability. Too many development teams out there ignore the maxim that over time, the cost of writing code compared to the cost of supporting it shrinks to zero. SRE forces a very rigorous and constant awareness of the cost of operability and the impacts of risks and cutting corners on quality with our releases.

If you are a heavily services-oriented company and want to put some teeth behind your customer-facing SLA's, SRE is a proven and very robust model. It makes implicit, unspoken expectations around availability and velocity more explicit, forcing a consensus around a common set of goals – defusing much frustration and conflict. And the stress SRE puts on the real value of automation in reducing waste and meaningless repetitive work – toil – is dead on. And we love the very pragmatic and prescriptive way the SRE movement uses numbers to better balance out the power struggle between change agents and sysops.

Transferable Lessons from SRE

Here's the key components behind Site Reliability Engineering that we feel translates very well to other enterprises:

- Have a single team(s) focused entirely on reliability
- Use error budgets and gate launches on them

---

[14]"Site Reliability Engineering: How Google Runs Production Systems," Niall Richard Murphy, Betsy Beyer, Chris Jones, Jennifer Petoff, O'Reilly Media; 4/16/2016, ISBN-10: 149192912X, ISBN-13: 978-1491929124.
[15]"SRE vs. DevOps: competing standards or close friends?", Seth Vargo. Google Cloud Platform Blog, 5/8/2018. https://cloudplatform.googleblog.com/2018/05/SRE-vs-DevOps-competing-standards-or-close-friends.html.

- Have development teams share the pain of production support

- Cap operational workloads

Let's break this down piece by piece and see what we can learn.

A dedicated team focused on reliability

Most companies would agree that reliability is the single most important quality they are looking for in their software, much more important than adding new features. Yet open discussions setting expectations around this important metric rarely seem to happen; it's also the first thing thrown out the door in the rush to get new features delivered. Worse, by the time an app becomes unreliable, it's very challenging to recover; it can take months or years to isolate and roll back the changes that have introduced instability.[16]

Because reliability is so critical, SREs are focused on finding ways to improve the design and operation of systems to make them more scalable, more reliable, and more efficient. However, we expend effort in this direction only up to a point: when systems are "reliable enough," we instead invest our efforts in adding features or building new products.[17]

The SRE movement began and is centered around having an explicit SLA for every service; reliability is set and enforced as a budget based on availability. SRE teams don't perform risk assessments or try to avoid outages. It forces a brokered conversation around reliability based on that single, explicit SLA.

Use error budgets to gate launches

There's no denying that change introduces risk; every change introduced by developers is a potential source of an embarrassing, expensive outage – directly impacting the workload and often bonus levels of the IT/Operations people providing frontline support. So a kind of war begins; Operations institutes risk-mitigation methods like zero defect meetings, CAB reviews, launch reviews, and change review boards, all of which slow down or gate change. Development teams counter with end-run tactics around these obstacles – "dark launches" and feature flag/canary releases, "experiments," "minor routine" changes – all intended to slip changes over, under, or around these barriers to release.

---

[16]"Keys to SRE," Ben Treynor. SRECon 2014, 5/30/2014. www.usenix.org/conference/srecon14/technical-sessions/presentation/keys-sre.
[17]"Site Reliability Engineering: How Google Runs Production Systems," Niall Richard Murphy, Betsy Beyer, Chris Jones, Jennifer Petoff, O'Reilly Media; 4/16/2016, ISBN-10: 149192912X, ISBN-13: 978-1491929124.

Google noted early on the built-in conflict created by the way companies incentivize their development teams to introduce change – which threatens directly the people incentivized to maximize stability, the Ops teams. It also recognizes that this is actually a three-way tug-of-war, with the business weighing in and either pushing for an unsustainable pace of development or requiring absurdly high reliability levels

> *You might expect Google to try to build 100% reliable services – ones that never fail. It turns out that past a certain point, however, increasing reliability is worse for a service (and its users) rather than better! Extreme reliability comes at a cost: maximizing stability limits how fast new features can be developed and how quickly products can be delivered to users, and dramatically increases their cost, which in turn reduces the numbers of features a team can afford to offer. Further, users typically don't notice the difference between high reliability and extreme reliability in a service, because the user experience is dominated by less reliable components like the cellular network or the device they are working with. Put simply, a user on a 99% reliable smartphone cannot tell the difference between 99.99% and 99.999% service reliability!*

> *…The use of an error budget resolves the structural conflict of incentives between development and SRE. SRE's goal is no longer 'zero outages'; rather, SREs and product developers aim to spend the error budget getting maximum feature velocity. This change makes all the difference. An outage is no longer a 'bad' thing – it is an expected part of the process of innovation, and an occurrence that both development and SRE teams manage rather than fear.[18]*

The SRE approach makes the often unstated, implicit battles around expectations of reliability and pace explicit, bringing the conflict out in the open where an objective, specific goal can be agreed upon in consensus vs. waged in protracted wars of political attrition. It also encourages thoughtful risktaking; availability targets can be exceeded by ideally not by much, as it would waste opportunities to clean up technical debt, reduce operational costs, or add new features. Just the fact that these conversations around risk vs. reward are happening is a huge step forward in collaboration.

---

[18]"Site Reliability Engineering: How Google Runs Production Systems," Niall Richard Murphy, Betsy Beyer, Chris Jones, Jennifer Petoff, O'Reilly Media; 4/16/2016, ISBN-10: 149192912X, ISBN-13: 978-1491929124.

Why the obsession with numbers and metrics? As Seth Vargo explains:

> It can be challenging to have a productive conversation about software development without a consistent and agreed-upon way to describe a system's uptime and availability. Operations teams are constantly putting out fires, some of which end up being bugs in developer's code. But without a clear measurement of uptime and a clear prioritization on availability, product teams may not agree that reliability is a problem. This very challenge affected Google in the early 2000s, and it was one of the motivating factors for developing the SRE discipline. SRE ensures that everyone agrees on how to measure availability, and what to do when availability falls out of specification.[19]

Like with most successful efforts we've seen, this strategy is self-sustaining and grassroots in implementation. Product development teams manage their own risk and share responsibility for uptime; so they begin pushing for slower velocity or more testing, as they don't want to risk stalling a launch, and encourage a culture of quality by having developers challenge each other so they can get high-priority changes out the door. And if the expectations around availability are too high and throttling the pace of innovation, the error budget can be increased by stakeholders. Outages are recognized as a cost of doing business; postmortem discussions with stakeholders become much less toxic and more focused on increasing MTTR.

It also doesn't attempt to change human nature or assume either bad or good intentions. It gives the same incentive to both devs and operations people; how can we maximize reliability so we can release more?

We love the idea of an error budget and wish it was used more often. It's fascinating that Microsoft and Google faced the same problem with runaway code / spiraling technical debt and resolved it with caps using two entirely different metrics – Microsoft capped the number of bugs as a ratio to the number of engineers; Google focused on meeting a SLA as a percent of availability. Both ended up being valid; both show the benefits of making numbers the issue, not teams or people.

Have development teams share the pain of production support

At Google, this works by having a common staffing pool for SRE and the development team. Excess work (i.e. a creaky, unreliable service) overflows to the development teams once it passes the operational workload limit – more on this later. And at least 5% of production support is handled directly by the

---

[19]"SRE vs. DevOps: Competing Standards or Close Friends?", Seth Vargo. Google Cloud Platform Blog, 5/8/2018. https://cloudplatform.googleblog.com/2018/05/SRE-vs-DevOps-competing-standards-or-close-friends.html.

devs. Ben Treynor has brought out that there is no shortcut for this – without handling at least some production support workload, it's a natural tendency for developers to lack empathy and think support is easy. Some pain has to be experienced by the development teams for SRE to work.

This is the one issue where you will likely get the most resistance; developers will come up with all sorts of creative and dramatic reasons why production support is a no-go for them. The underlying fear here is that their lives will shift from coding to support, 100%. Thankfully, this is rarely or never the case; Ben noted that after 6 months of engaging with SRE teams and handling support, the dev teams he's worked with can't imagine doing their development work any other way.[20]

One of our favorite sayings comes from the unofficial SRE motto at Google: "Hope is not a strategy." We'll get into this later in the book, but SRE teams take disaster planning and wargames very seriously. SRE teams constantly look for possible sources of outages, trying to get ahead of incidents before they lead to outages. Annually, they perform Disaster Recovery and Training (DIRT) drills to stress test production systems and try to inflict outages, looking for weak spots in their critsit handling and their ecology. And many of these events are treated as open labs where critsit triage and recovery approaches are discussed openly, ensuring that first responders are better informed and supported.

Cap operational workloads

The official workload cap at Google is no more than two events per oncall shift, and no more than 50% of an engineer's day; in practice, it ends up being averaged out at about 30% across the team. Google hires coders for their SRE team and uses this cap to lure best-and-brightest people; they want their SRE teams to have plenty of time to work on code so the operational load doesn't grow out of control.

> *Without constant engineering, operations load increases and teams will need more people just to keep pace with the workload. Eventually, a traditional ops-focused group scales linearly with service size: if the products supported by the service succeed, the operational load will grow with traffic. That means hiring more people to do the same tasks over and over again. To avoid this fate, the team tasked with managing a service needs to code or it will drown.*

---

[20]"Keys to SRE," Ben Treynor. SRECon 2014, 5/30/2014. www.usenix.org/conference/srecon14/technical-sessions/presentation/keys-sre.

…So how do we enforce that threshold? In the first place, we have to measure how SRE time is spent. With that measurement in hand, we ensure that the teams consistently spending less than 50% of their time on development work change their practices. Often this means shifting some of the operations burden back to the development team, or adding staff to the team without assigning that team additional operational responsibilities. Consciously maintaining this balance between ops and development work allows us to ensure that SREs have the bandwidth to engage in creative, autonomous engineering, while still retaining the wisdom gleaned from the operations side of running a service.[21]

---

[21]"Site Reliability Engineering: How Google Runs Production Systems," Niall Richard Murphy, Betsy Beyer, Chris Jones, Jennifer Petoff, O'Reilly Media; 4/16/2016, ISBN-10: 149192912X, ISBN-13: 978-1491929124.

Shifting Left

And now, it's spring – everything is awakening!

Let's skip forward 3 months in time and check back in on Ben and the team. They've made some positive strides forward, as they are beginning to wrap their arms around the following:

- Using version control as the authoritative source for everything: code, config, and infrastructure

- Improved code quality through practices like gated check-ins based on automated unit tests or static code analysis, approval by peer on pull request

- Continuous integration and delivery

- Automated builds and release management

- Leaving capacity open to pay down technical debt

The most encouraging progress so far has come from the people and process side of things. For example, they're improving their coordination with the teams handling IT and Operations – a must-have if they are to attain their goal of smoother, less disruptive releases.

The team has chosen to focus not so much on external factors beyond their control, but on what they are bringing to the table – especially improving their quality of code very early on using practices like peer review and pair programming. Even better, they've brought several underlying problems out in the open and made them explicit. It's now a team value that no single programmer can "own" code or an app, creating a dangerous situation where a single missing or overloaded resource can cause a severe outage and limit learning by the rest of the team.

D. Harrison and K. Lively, Achieving DevOps,
https://doi.org/10.1007/978-1-4842-4388-6_3

Also, Ben has made a firm commitment and promise to the team that problems should be shared openly and honestly, instead of the time-honored tradition at WonderTek of blame-shifting and minimizing or trying to hide problems. He's even made sure that the team has the capacity to work on their RM maturity by ensuring that 20% of their time is set aside to work on nonfunctional requirements.

Still, as you'd expect in Oregon, there are some big clouds on the horizon. The team has chosen to focus on increasing their number of releases – their flow – without tackling the thorny issue of quality. We already know that their QA team is overburdened and lagging behind the development team. What consequences will this decision to prioritize based on release frequency have?

Also, there are some significant challenges still to face with that still-strained partnership with Operations. Emily is focused primarily on operational metrics such as reducing the number of outages and increasing their SLA; stability remains their byword, while Ben and the developers are still laser focused on velocity and speed – delivering new features. Both teams are still using different dashboards and ticketing queues, and bugs are still flowing through first responders with little to no attempts to triage. And their primary stakeholders remain unengaged and disenchanted with how things have gone with the project.

The team has made some strides, but their core issues around delivery remain. Can they turn these negative factors around?

Spring Comes to WonderTek

I grab a quick yogurt at the cafeteria before sitting down with the Brain Trust. The last 3 months have definitely gone by in a flash; I'm eager to get some thoughts from the group on how things were going.

Rajesh isn't here yet, but Elaine, Alex, Kevin, and George were already at the table and talking animatedly. We had an outage yesterday that had led to some dropped orders as credit card processing had timed out. This was very high visibility, and I've been fielding angry calls from Tabrez and some of his people all day.

I pop the lid on my strawberry yogurt and savor the first spoonful. "Well guys, it's been a crazy few months. I know our outage yesterday is probably all we can think about, but this is a chance for us to step aside from the issues of the day and think a little more big picture. Three months ago, we made some big promises to our management layer – that things would get better if we placed these bets on building up our maturity level with release management. I think it's safe to say that we've seen some progress, but not what we would like. Is that about right?"

There is a short silence and finally Elaine starts to laugh. "Well, we've been talking about how important it is to be open and honest in our communication, not nicey-nice. I guess that about sums it up. Ben, from the business' perspective, we've been making a lot of noise but things really haven't gotten any better. If we were to get a grade from them today, I think it'd be a D+, at best."

George rolls his eyes. "Ben, you've seen our latest scorecard. I think it's hard to argue that we haven't made progress if we're talking objectively. Simply put, they're not grading us, and they don't know or can't see what we've done ground-level to deliver faster and more efficiently for them. Maybe this is just a hangover from the past, and their perception is lagging behind reality."

I smile, but I'm really not worried. Perhaps I did overpromise a bit to Douglas – and I've paid for that several times. But I like the way we've stripped things down to their essentials. We're tracking our key numbers and show them on every release retrospective; it's had a noticeable change in our behavior.

Right on cue, Alex pulls up the latest sprint retrospective on his phone, and our progress over the past quarter was right at the top:

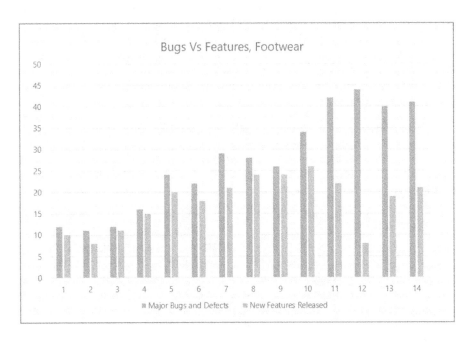

It was a nice and much simpler way of showing our progress in a way that matters to our customers. If the core complaint was slow turnaround on releases, or that bugs were being ignored in favor of shiny new features, the chart showed that they were making some headway. Still, our bug count was way too high, and it seemed like our velocity was stuck in neutral after some initial gains.

Just in time, Rajesh plops down at the table. I show him the chart, and we talk a little about those stubborn blue bars.

Rajesh looks pained. "It's actually even worse than this appears, Ben. If we were to show all the bugs, minor issues that we can live with, the number would be off the charts, like in the thousands. We're now 5 weeks behind in our integration testing; we've thrown more people at it in Bangalore and even added a nearsite support center in Guadalajara. But right now it does seem to be a losing battle. To be honest, I'm really getting tired of working 16-hour days."

I wince at this; Rajesh isn't exaggerating. He has two young children, both under the age of five. His family is paying too high a price for the lack of quality around our codebase. I know it's bad in QA, but as usual Rajesh is stoically taking on a heroic amount of work without complaint. I think, *If I'm not careful, I'll lose him. The team can't afford to lose someone as dedicated and smart as Rajesh.*

I say, "Let's circle back to that later. For now, I'm taking this as the numbers show – we're releasing features more often but problems with our health, our bug count, is rising out of control. Let's talk about our releases. We said we would implement continuous integration and delivery and invest in release management and automated builds. I pushed hard to get our releases to weekly as a target over the quarter, and we've met that." I know damn well that our releases aren't really "continuous" yet – but they are faster, and that's something.

One of my brighter decisions over the past quarter was to pull Kevin into our meetings. Having him as a liaison to Emily and the Operations team has been valuable; he's caught several potentially very damaging oversights. I ask Kevin what he thinks so far of our partnership and our release management maturity.

Kevin is a thoughtful, deliberate kind of guy, and he mulls my questions over carefully before he responds. "From the release perspective, I think things are… improving," he replies. "We've started moving more configuration into source control and at least now we've got visibility into how our releases are going. I think Emily really likes being able to roll back a release on demand, that's saved our bacon more than once. But the heat level over in Ops hasn't dropped much. It's still taking us way too much time to handle problems when we release, and there's a lot of releases we handle for you guys that are still very manual."

George chips in, "Yeah, we can see that with the scorecards. Just look at the last one – I know you've seen this Ben, it's up on our team monitor in the daily standup room. Anyway, we're still not where we want to be – our changes still fail too often, and it takes too much time for us to prep a release. I don't know how to get us better numbers here, but maybe it's a good time for us to talk about slowing down our releases or giving us a few months to stabilize."

I glance at the team monitor, which was just barely visible from where I sit at our café table:

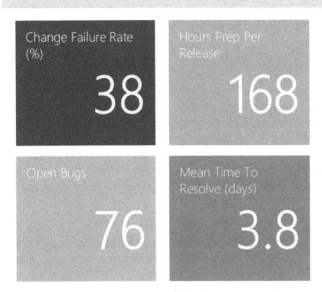

I muse, "Are we paying attention to the right things?"

"Yeah, I think so," George answers. "I mean, we really wanted to drop the waste we were seeing with firefighting right? That's why we've got the bug count as an indicator there, and the amount of time we're taking to triage and resolve issues. If we're doing well on that front, those numbers should drop, and we already know quality and stability is important to our business. And we are focusing on making our releases smaller and easier to troubleshoot, meaning we're investing pretty heavily in release management and reducing the time we spend integrating and prepping a buildable release. Theoretically, that should have good impacts across the board, with less failures and easier rollbacks."

Elaine says, "I still find it so hard to believe that it's taking us 168 hours total to handle a release. Is that actually true? I mean, how much of this is Ops side and how much is preparing the build?"

Kevin says grimly, "That's an actual number. I'd say it's probably mostly cost on our side of things, which is why I say your rep is still in the trashcan over in my neck of the woods."

I can see Alex's hackles rising a little and step in hastily; the last thing we need is another dev/IT squabble in what's supposed to be a friendly space. "So, let's remember our values here – open and honest, no finger pointing, and we have to think global not local. If Kevin is saying that our quality is still iffy and it's costing us with failed releases and time lost to firefighting and bug triage, well, I'm taking that as being the way things are. Thoughts on some possible solutions?"

"If we had those two months to get caught up," Rajesh interjects, "we could improve that perception of quality and get the bug count down to a manageable level."

"OK, I'll put a code freeze down as an option. Anything else?"

George pipes up, "Our environmental anomalies are killing us. I would love to see non-code or environmental issues versus code related bugs for example on this dashboard. I think about 90% of the time when we have a problem reported it comes down to the fact that our servers and environments have a significant amount of drift in their config, they're all unique – DEV doesn't match QA, Staging, or Production. And our builds are only going all the way to QA and Staging, not to Prod. We need to make our deployment process and environments much more consistent."

"George, we've been over and over this," Kevin groaned. "We don't have the money to build out every environment just like production, and I don't think your developers would appreciate having their environments taking 16 hours to prep and populate with test data. Let's not forget – our security people will not allow you guys to do self-service deployments all the way to production. We have auditors and SOX compliance to think about."

"I totally hear you and understand that – but the fact remains, we need templated environments and automated builds end to end – that includes Production – if we're going to need to get to where we need to be. I refuse to just throw up my hands and give up on this because of some auditor says we can't perform the way I know other companies in our space do."

Part of me wants to come off the pylon and join George in pointing the finger squarely at Operations; he's not wrong in his points. But his timing might be; I can't risk losing Kevin to a blowup. I put my hands on the table and say calmly, "That's enough. I think we'd be missing the point if we walked away from this table thinking that we're failing. We're not failing, we are learning, and at the very least our releases are making it out the door with less friction, and we've got some visibility and control. Let's see what we can do to improve our quality now – I think that should be our theme for the next quarter."

Unusual for our little group, there's an undercurrent of hostility and dissatisfaction hanging over us as we start to break up. Did I make a mistake by not pushing harder for more control over our environments?

Killing Our Integration Woes (Continuous Integration)

It's been a few days; I'm enjoying the new green on the budding trees as I make my way from the parking area to my desk. I'm humming "Paint It Black" by the Stones as off-tune as loudly as I can; nothing can kill my good mood this beautiful spring day. But, on cue, I get waylaid by Alex, who is deep into a cubicle rant with Harry and Padma. "Ben, can you stop by here and help us out with this?"

I glance regretfully at the wisps of steam leaving my coffee cup. Sighing, I sit it down at my desk and walk like a condemned man back to Alex.

"We've been talking about that 168 number you keep bringing up – the hours we spend prepping a build for release," Alex says. His blood was up this morning; few things in life give Alex more heartburn than the integration period proscribed by the ubiquitous PMO team. "Emily and the RM team are even talking about an extended code freeze period of two weeks to stabilize and mitigate risk."

I sigh. "Yes, that's correct. So far we're just discussing it; Emily is fronting this as a way of getting more reliable releases."

Harry's lips tighten in disdain. "Ben, that number of hours shown on the dashboard is mostly wait time. We have a mandated three-day period where we're not allowed to touch a line of code. Sometimes we're actually doing meaningful work like merging and making sure our versioning and library references are valid, but mostly we are just waiting on the go signal. Until we tighten this up, we can't move faster."

"Well, it's hard for us to argue the point right now that we need more stability. I mean, is there an alternative?"

Alex says, exasperated, "Of course there is. It's called Continuous Integration. We've had it on our to-do list for months. But this direction you are talking about taking – with a long stabilization period – it's the exact opposite of where we want to go. I think you and Emily think this will lead to more stability; I'm here to tell you today that the exact opposite is true. The bigger our releases and the less frequent they are, the riskier they are. I thought we'd agreed on this. Got to be honest, I'm a little shocked that you're caving in with a single push from Ops."

"OK, hold on here. I haven't had my coffee yet, unlike some people, and I might get a little snippy here. First off, I'm not siding with Emily against you. I'm in favor of whatever gets our releases out faster and with higher quality, period. And I don't think Emily and Ops is against Continuous Integration per se. We just need to present a different way of working. Right now, our release process seems a little haphazard; if I had to guess, I'd say they're trying to inject a little more consistency into the way we release our apps."

Padma is calmer than Harry and Alex, as I'd expect, but there's a firm set to the corners of her smile that let me know that she's deadly serious. "Two months ago it would have been totally valid for them to call us out like this. But we've done a lot of foundational work Ben – we've finally got some form of comprehensive version control including config, and our release pipeline is looking much better. It's time to let us off the leash, not tighten it up just as we're starting to get some traction."

"So, come at me. What are we going to propose then?"

Alex says shortly, "We're not going to propose anything, Ben. You keep going back for approval to this outside group. I don't think you get it – we don't need to ask for approval on how we produce our software. If we choose to produce releasable bits multiple times a day, and we can show that it leads to better reliability and more velocity, that's all you or anybody else needs to know. No other engineering team at WonderTek is under this kind of scrutiny, and frankly I'm kind of tired of it."

I feel the first stabbings of a morning migraine right between my eyes. Perhaps my fist comes down on the table a little harder than I had intended, but it does cause them to jump a little. "Jesus Christ! All this emotion and drama at 8 a.m. in the goddamn morning?" I slump into a chair. "OK, I can see we're running a little hot this morning. Let's say you're 100% correct, and we have carte blanche, and godlike powers to wave our magic wand and the CI fairy will appear and make everything better for us. What model are you proposing?"

Padma says, "If we go with GitHub Flow as our release model, it dovetails nicely with our push to get better shared knowledge and peer review. We can tag peers on the team when we create a pull request, those reviewers add their feedback early on when feedback is useful, and over time we'll get a set of living documentation and a more useful, efficient peer review."

Harry nods. "For once, I totally agree. Most of our integration problems come from not checking in our code often enough. And we've got feature branches now on some of our projects that are practically pets, they've been around so long. This means hours of frustration merging, cherry-picking, and trying to resolve inconsistencies and breaking library references when we're trying to integrate code branches. If we used any form of CI, and GitHub Flow is pretty popular these days, we could cut that integration time by 75%, easy."

I smile. Maybe there's a way back to my coffee in time after all. "That's a pretty big bet there Harry! So, you're arguing that long code freezes are actually riskier, and that if we as a team adopt continuous integration we can bring that 168 hour number wasted currently with each release down to – let's say 40 hours. That's total time, start to finish, from developer check-in to a functioning green release out the door to Dev. I'll take that bet. So, let's start with Footwear. If you can cut it down to 40 hours, and prove to me that our quality doesn't drop, that's all I need to stave off a mandated code freeze from up above."

The conspirators are glancing at each other nervously; no one expected me to cave in this quickly. Alex says, "It would be a huge mistake to think that we just need to implement this as a tool and wait for our integration pain to drop, Ben. CI is a practice more than it is a tool. This means the team needs to start thinking about the other pieces around CI that support it. Our deployment pipeline needs to be more robust, which begins with a fast, reliable, and comprehensive testing protocol and gated releases. And we're going to need to get serious about changing some of our behavior – that means you and I following up when we see long-lived feature branches. I'm a little concerned about using GitHub Flow as it could allow us to fall back into sloppy practices where our feature branches hang around for weeks."

Kevin pops his head over the cubicle wall; he had been working with Rob, but evidently the temptation to listen in had been too great. "The real test for you guys is going to be when something breaks. In the past, you've shoved production bugs unless they were livesite outages to the back of the queue. You can't do that anymore if you're going to be serious about continuous integration. If you see a red build in the pipeline – either from a broken build, a failed test or a problem in the release pipeline itself – the team is going to have to commit to dropping everything to either fixing it or reverting back to a known good state, within minutes."

I fidget nervously; I had forgotten that Alex had been spending most of his time in their area recently. It would be a disaster if my team's badmouthing of Emily somehow got back to her. "OK, so let's talk about this at our next team meeting this coming Friday. If everyone signs on and can commit to this, including Alex's comment about hopping on failed tests and builds as a group commitment, I say let's go ahead. We can check back in on this in one month and see if it makes an appreciable dent in our integration headaches. The exact model you select is – well, I don't care. Just make sure that you keep it simple and right down the middle. I want little changes; if we're running around everywhere making grandiose promises and wreaking havoc it'll cost me too much with our " – I glance at Kevin – "valued service partners."

Back at the safety and comfort of my own desk, I sit down wearily and take that long-awaited first sip of coffee. As expected, it was barely warm.

Quality Is a Function, Not a Title

I sit down at the conference room table. For this meeting, I need it to be as small as possible – in this case just Alex and Rajesh. This was a painful subject but I'd deferred it long enough, and one way or another we need to find a better way forward on QA.

Once my leads file in, I begin by saying, "A few months ago we made the decision to focus on flow over quality so we could relieve some pressure from the business. At the time that looked like a solid decision, now I'm not so sure. Our change failure rate keeps rising – last I checked nearly half our releases are running red – and both our bug count and our MTTR keeps rising. I'd like your thoughts on why, and what you think we should do about it."

Rajesh looks pained. "It's exactly as I showed you last week, Ben. The developers are racing ahead, and my QA teams can't keep up. I'm 6 weeks behind right now just with Footwear. We need that code freeze to get us in a stable condition and allow my people the time they need to get our acceptance test coverage up to 80% or better." He passes around a printout from their last retrospective:

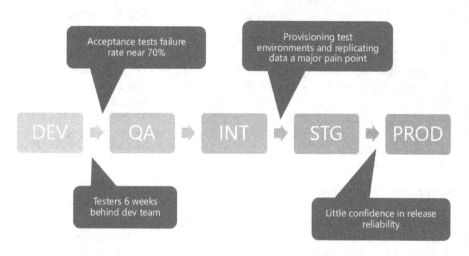

This is a nifty little graphic, and the points are valid, but it continues the QA-As-Victims theme that I'm starting to find a little tiresome. Time to shift this a little. "I should have said something earlier, but here goes – quality is a function, not a title," I say heatedly. "If our code coverage is dropping, it's a 'We' issue, not a 'Rajesh' issue. We're not pointing fingers at QA here as the culprit, Rajesh; this is not a 'pin the tail on the donkey' type discussion. With that in mind, does everyone agree here with the problems Rajesh is describing? That our problems with unreliable releases are caused by a lack of automated test coverage and is made worse by the amount of time it takes to spin up new test environments and replicate data?"

Alex says, "I'd definitely agree that we're behind on our testing and it doesn't seem to be for lack of effort. Kevin might not agree on this, but I'd even say the comment on provisioning environments and getting reliable data is dead-on. We've had a ton of issues come up that we didn't catch in QA because the data was inconsistent or a problem only happened under load. On everything else though – I know for a fact my guys have been complaining for a while about getting very late feedback from the QA teams though, and when we do get bugs they're anomalies because of something funky going on with the environments or a data mismatch. The false alarms are driving us crazy."

"OK, totally valid." Rajesh nods his head vigorously. "But you have to admit, we talk a good game about quality but rarely follow through. Just for example, our acceptance tests are failing 70% of the time. We're trying to refactor and fix our older tests, while adding new tests to every new feature your guys are spinning out. But we're getting snowed under and there's no end in sight. And you devs aren't helping us – we're adding bugs to the queue but they're just sitting there. It's like you've moved on."

"Rajesh with all due respect – you're not a coder, so you don't understand." Alex's tone has just a hint of condescension. "We don't have a choice. We can't sit and wait for 6 weeks every time we have a new feature to implement. And asking my team to run back a few weeks or months and fix something you just found – that's ancient history by that time. Having us break concentration by pulling the ripcord every time there's a hiccup with an acceptance test would force us to a standstill, always waiting on your offshore teams to get up to speed. You keep asking for a code freeze, and we keep telling you – the business won't accept it."

It seems like there's no end to the dysfunctional marriages around here. Time to bring our attention back to the process instead of people. "Rajesh, you're saying that our releases are breaking because our test coverage is shoddy. It also seems like we're causing a lot of false alarms because of bad data or environmental mismatches, and that it's taking us too long to spin up a production-like environment to test against. And it's obvious that too many bugs are getting out trhe door that we're not catching – right?" Both Rajesh and Alex are nodding in agreement. "OK, so now we have a real problem. We have a fault in our release process because our testing is inadequate, which causes a lot of risk and fear. We're basically driving without a seatbelt. Do I have that right?"

Alex isn't done yet. He says, "Yes, but our whole approach to testing needs to be rethought from the ground up. We do most of our testing offshore, either in Guadalajara or in Bangladesh. There's a significant language problem especially with the India based team, and the timezone difference. We're getting very late feedback and it's causing lots of interruptions and static. Also, the tests are brittle and expensive in terms of time. We're doing most of our acceptance testing either manually with smoketesting or by using recorded tests against the UI. Every time we do a refactor the entire test suite abends and the entire QA team has to scramble to rerecord tests."

Rajesh stands up a little straighter in his chair. "Yes, that's something I've been thinking about – there are some patterns we can follow so that our code is more inherently testable. And we can implement some more object-oriented approaches in our test suite so that we're a little more abstracted away from the UI layer, and using mocks and fakes more in handling dependency points. As far as the offshore teams go – we're talking about dozens of people here, Alex. They don't grow on trees, and we can't easily get them onsite. That's the reason we outsourced this to begin with."

In the flurry of issues, there's no way I can make out what the solution is just yet. But it's obvious to me that the problem isn't that the QA team is based out of Mexico or India. Rajesh is right when he points out that the QA team is lagging behind – and that the problem is growing. Our release panel right now is loaded up with red "failed" builds that we're pushing out anyway, because of known "false positives" and flaky tests that everyone ignores. Our charts tell the story – our release pattern is stalled out because we just keep pushing more bugs out the door to production with every release. We need a more reliable, stronger test layer that's keeping up with code, step for step.

A week ago, I stopped by Footwear and talked to them about our bug infestation in our development life cycle. The weirdest thing happened – they started to laugh!

It turns out they were having quality problems with their factories in the mid-1990s, and it was all because of two factors – delays and handoffs. Because audits and inspections happened at the end of the production line at a separate station, root causes often weren't tracked down – they just yanked defective shoes as they were caught. This worked for a time but ended up being both expensive and imperfect; they started to lag against top-level competitors like Nike. Their quality levels didn't budge until they actually made ongoing process improvements a regular part of day to day work for everyone on the team. If there was a problem with a shoe, the whole line was stopped until a fix was made to whatever material, component, or machine tool was allowing the defect. Getting faster feedback fixed the delay component, and building quality into the process as part of everyone's daily work fixed the handoff piece.

We may not be cranking out sneakers, but there's a lesson there for us; I'm still trying to put my finger on it. But I'm not going to steamroll either of my leads until they at least have a chance to work together on a viable solution.

I give each of them my best sunny smile. "Thankfully, I've hired really smart people that can solve these problems for me. I've learned a few facts here – that our feedback loops are too long, that QA is falling behind dev, that our acceptance test layer is creaky, costly and unreliable. So, treat me like a customer and put on your engineering hats. I'm coming to you with this as a problem – how would you solve this, given our constraints? Think it over for a few days and come back to me with how you want to get quality back on track."

Testing My Patience (Shift Left on Testing)

The day before the retrospective, I hold a special joint meeting with the entire engineering team and include a few people from Emily's team, Ivan and Kevin. Due to the size of the combined group, we are using the special amphitheater room. I hate the room layout; it's impersonal, and the central stage is set so Emily and I are sitting on stools under the glare of harsh lighting with everyone above us, looking down. Sadly, it's the best option that we've got. It's not like the ground isn't prepared; I've spent the last few days hashing over with my leads – and with Emily separately – going over the options we thought were available to us. Now, it was time to put this to the team and gauge their reaction.

Rajesh, Kevin, and Alex each stand up and give their perspectives on our quality issues to date. The problem set glares at us from an imposing height, impassable and immovable. It's depressing and monstrous – the long, delayed feedback loops; our manual smoke testing not catching production issues but slowing up the release cycle; that flaky tests are causing most releases to run red. The communication lag and gaps with offshoring are up there but last. In my view, the exact location of the testing team isn't nearly as important as the fact that QA, the caboose on a very long train of work, is uncoupled and falling further behind every day.

Alex is just finishing his turn. "OK folks, those are the problems we've identified. Any comments or thoughts before we go on? You'll notice, we're not talking solutions yet, just listing the main pain points we're feeling as a team around quality."

One of the junior devs raises a hand, smirking. "It seems to me like this is an opportunity for addition by subtraction. If QA isn't doing its job and it's holding up our releases, we need to unhook them from our process."

My teeth grind; when are we going to tire of pointing fingers? I'm about to stand up, when – gratifyingly – Alex smiles and calmly answers, "Folks, there's two things to keep in mind here. First off, bad organizations tend to blame people. Good organizations blame bad processes. We want to be a good organization. The QA team has been doing heroic work, but the process we're using is letting them down. It would be a huge mistake to blame the QA team; I think it doesn't help that a lot of the work they do around quality is hidden from us, as it's being done off-hours and remote."

I'm full of gratitude at Alex's response; it's exactly the tone we needed. Rajesh stands up and thanks Alex then moves on to the next slide showing the solutions we were discussing to our quality problems:

Problems	Options
Late feedback on issues	Shift left with unit testing / TDD
Acceptance tests are brittle, unreliable, expensive	The whole team is responsible for tests and releases running green as top priority
Releases running red – broken builds or flaky tests ignored	Monitored and visible – how?
Offshoring and team size	Testing Center of Excellence

Rajesh continues: "We mentioned earlier that our acceptance testing is always lagging behind. I've proposed many times a stabilization period – a code freeze – but it seems like that's not a viable option for us at the moment. One option that is completely in our wheelhouse has to do with unit testing. Some large organizations have been stuck in the same swamp we are, and they've dug their way out by making unit tests a part of the definition of done for any new code. We know that right now our biggest pain point is that no one has any confidence that green releases are safe to promote, and that we have a lot of flaky tests that run green MOST of the time, or run red because of false positives."

He then goes on to explain our proposed solution. Keeping in mind the lessons we were learning from our manufacturing friends when it came to waste around delays and handoffs, we were proposing stopping handling QA as a late-game, separate stage by a separate, dedicated team. Instead, we were going to have quality built into the process early on by requiring unit tests to be associated with every code check-in, at a bare minimum. And to address the issue with handoffs – that gap between Dev and QA that caused out of synch work and miscommunications – we were going to merge the two groups together.

How this would work exactly, we were still in the process of defining. Alex, Rajesh, and I were still in the process of figuring out how to best redistribute people in both teams so that every workstream or vital component could be covered by that ideal team size of 8 to 12 people. I don't allow any debate or discussion on this one topic, making it clear that the old way of doing business was dead and gone. "I think you're going to like working in smaller groups with a clearer mission. But regardless, we no longer have a QA team, or a Dev team anymore. We all have the same title – engineers. This may seem to some of you like we're just shuffling cards around, but I can assure you that how we define our roles is fundamental in how we view each other and our work. The root problem that keeps coming up here is that we are building quality in too late in the process, and we're making it somebody else's job. That isn't working for us, and it ends – today."

I explain that we're forming a Center of Excellence (CoE) around quality. Rajesh will be the nominal lead, but his role is more shepherding; we want this to be a community-driven effort, centered around the mission we're setting around driving down our firefighting drain. We get some substantial objections and agree – a reshuffle won't magically solve our brittle and expensive test layer, or fix the 6-week lag in our acceptance testing suite. But Rajesh says emphatically, "We're not throwing anyone into the deep end, and we understand this isn't something that we've asked before. Over the next few weeks, we're going to have demos on how to go about test driven development and what good unit testing looks like, and we'll keep up this as a refresher training course every so often. We'll also make it a prereq for any check-in, and a part of our peer review."

Harry speaks up, from his favored position in the back of the room. "This is exactly the wrong direction to be going. We're already struggling to meet the customer's expectations; this will slow us down to a halt. I mean, unit testing? First off, it's useless – all it does is tell us if something works in isolation, but it'll never catch the integration and UI issues we're seeing in production. Second, TDD is a total joke. No one uses it in the real world; it's the kind of thing that sounds better taught in a college class but doesn't work in practice. And how on earth are we supposed to implement that when we're talking about a ColdFusion app written in the 90's? Or some of the sites I'm responsible for that have thousands of modules, spaghetti business logic splattered all over the place, a complete mess. As far as I'm concerned, it's pie-in-the-sky to think that we can just pivot and sprinkle some unit testing fairy dust on these, and suddenly every release will magically just work."

Padma replies, "I don't think they're asking us to implement TDD across the board. That's just for new projects, right? All they're saying is that any new functionality we add comes with a unit test. So, for your website app, if you're implementing a fix you need to have a unit test done – either before you write the code, which I like, or after to prove that it works. You can call that Defect-Driven Testing if you want. But it's hard to argue that the way we've been writing code is sustainable."

Harry's arms are still folded, and his chin is sinking in disdain into his misshapen fuzzy sweater. When he gets this way, he always reminds me of a grouchy, under-caffeinated Wilford Brimley. "Padma, you've already slowed us to a walk with the peer reviews. It's really disruptive. This sets us back to a crawl. And how does this help us with the mismatches we see in our environments, or the amount of time it takes us to spin up a test environment and populate it with data? Kevin, you've been pretty quiet – what are you guys planning on doing to fix that?"

"Look, I'm mostly an observer here," Kevin says, shrugging his shoulders. "I know right now we need to make our environment buildouts and releases more prescriptive and less manual, but we don't have our arms around that yet. Self service provisioning and templated environments, those things are coming. I do know it would be great to know on our release dashboards that if a release is green that it's safe to release."

There's a lot of chatter and noise in the room, which was a good sign. Alex says a little more about Mike Cohn's test pyramid and why enforcing automated unit testing with every check-in was a necessary first step to catch issues early on, before they hit the more expensive and longer running acceptance test process. "We're not saying we're going to stop our smoke-testing or our acceptance testing, because Harry's right – there are some issues that only a human can catch, or problems with the UI layer or integration that unit testing won't touch. Besides, those tests represent a lot of time we've invested, too much to just throw away. And we're never going to be able to automate everything. But everyone in this room should be onboard with this – for us to survive we are going to need to shift left and make strengthening our test layer a part of our daily work."

Harry points a fat finger at me, quivering in full on Angry Quaker Oats Guy mode. "Ben, did you get permission from the stakeholders on this? What about Douglas? Do you think they're going to be happy when I tell them that they're only going to get half the features I promised them because we're waiting on peer reviews and unit tests?"

I lift my chin a little. Harry must think I'm an idiot to not have talked this over with my boss first. "Actually, I have discussed this with Douglas, and yes he's onboard with this. He's happy with some of the gains we've made with our velocity but he's also aware it's come with a high price – the defects that we're pushing out the door, more and more every month.

"But Harry, if you're asking if I asked for permission – of course I didn't! We don't ask for *permission* on how we go about our jobs, Harry. Anything we need to do to drive value faster and with more quality we don't NEED to ask for permission for. The same thing goes with our stakeholders. We're professionals. A professional doesn't ask how to go about his or her job. Our stakeholders and managers have every right to define *what* we do, but we decide *how* that work should be delivered."

Rob is looking thoughtful. He says, "I don't mind adding unit tests to my daily work, in some ways that'll make things easier with getting signoff from my stakeholders. But for this to work right, we're going to need to rethink the way we write our applications. If we can't trust our Selenium code or its too brittle, fine – but we still need some way of verifying if a page is responding the way it should. That means writing it so it's loosely coupled, where both the UI and our test layer hits the same API based communication layer. Not all of our apps are web-based and many of them just can't be refactored so they're testable on that level."

Rajesh nods. "Great point, Rob. If we had just one app to maintain, or if it was greenfield, yes we could make sure it was inherently testable. We don't have that luxury. Thoughts?"

"Of course I agree that we need more testable architecture," Ryan muses. "It's not a bad idea to make that a part of our design review process. But most of our apps aren't API-driven and can't be rewritten in that way, there's just no ROI for that."

We bat the problem around for a few minutes, then decide to shelve it for now. We have consensus that testability should be a design review checkpoint – and that a better, more specific definition of what that implementation might look like could be the first subject for the new Quality CoE to tackle. I trust Rajesh's pragmatism; he'll be able to keep the new group on point and get something workable up that can be used as a point of reference and refined over time.

Then, we move on to the second bullet point on the whiteboard. Rajesh explains that one of their main blockers currently to a consistently green build process are those pesky flaky or long-running tests. "Gary Gruver and his team at HP had to refactor and wipe out thousands of acceptance tests that weren't consistent or weren't reliably detecting problems. In some cases, they started over completely – they looked at errors and livesite failures they experienced over the past six months, and came up with the tests they'd need to write to capture just those problems, and junked everything else. We may need to do this to move forward. The point is, until people can trust our test layer as an effective beg detection and regression safety net, we're not at the finish line."

Ryan interjects, "Why are we saying that a green build is the team's top priority? What if it's not a big deal and won't really hurt the release?"

"Good question!", Rajesh responds. "The fact is, sometimes there's going to be problems we'll find late in the game with an acceptance test that we can and should gloss over – maybe it's a minor hiccup or the UI not looking quite right, but delaying the release will cause greater harm than good. That's pragmatic. But our position is that unit testing is a fundamental. If a unit test fails, ANY unit test, the build fails, right then and there. That means if your changes cause your test to pass but some unit tests elsewhere fails, the build fails and the entire team needs to take responsibility to fix it so the tests run green. Keeping the builds running green is now our top priority – that deployment pipeline is our jugular, and it's more important than the apps that we are supporting."

Rob asks, "What about our offshore teams? Are we taking this all in-house? Seems like if we do, we really will be grinding to a halt." Every eye turned to me. I find myself stammering, "Ah…on that one, I'm going to be up front here, I don't know. I hear from some of you that the delayed feedback is an issue. Others seem to work just fine with remote testers. I do know it'd be better if we were all collocated, but we can't find enough good people here in Hillsboro to keep up with the demand. I don't think the exact location of where work is happening is a major problem… can I just say that I don't know?

"I realize that this will have a big impact on our velocity, especially at first. I'm betting that if we try this 'Shift Left' approach, things will start to get better. Our bug count will drop, our releases will run green and STAY green. I am hoping it also means more time on the weekends and evenings with our families, and a lot less stress. So, what I'm asking for is a little trust. We're making a guess here, an assumption. Let's try this for a few months and see how things go."

I get challenged on whether our plans are to grow the team in Hillsboro. I simply repeat that we are going to be treating quality as an investment, and no longer optional. "I do know that good companies don't try to operationalize and do more with less. The real market leaders I know of do more with more – they don't just talk quality but they hire and keep the best people they can find and think strategically about quality. What that will look like over time – well, it's just too early to say. Now, I've got a question for the group – here's the KPI's that we think represent quality. Is this accurate, or do we need to tweak some things?"

Tech Lead Scorecard

Change Failure Rate (%)	Hours Prep Per Release
49	110

Open Bugs	Mean Time To Resolve (days)
148	6.4

Most agree that MTTR and change failure rate are a good general detector; Rob and Ryan feel that "Open Bugs" is a red herring. "I mean, I could have a dozen major bugs open, or 100 minor oopsies and CSS or formatting issues. Which is a better, more stable app?" Ryan asked.

The group ended up with some decision points – including making sure unit tests were monitored so build times wouldn't balloon out and cause frustration. Alex is of the opinion that anything longer than 6 minutes is unacceptable; "If I make a tweak to some HTML, run a commit and go get a cup of coffee and come back – I'm going to be pissed if it still hasn't finished."

Our session ends up running overtime, which isn't surprising. It's worth it – we are having a good, vibrant discussion with lots of opposing views, exactly what I've been looking for. And the Quality CoE is especially encouraging as a step forward. If the team perceives this effort as being top-down or a Douglas-driven mandate, they'll give it lip service and carry on as before. If they see it as a joint experiment that everyone can contribute to, one that can be adjusted as needed in our mission to improve our quality of life and work, we'll be successful.

Are We Done Yet? (Definition of Done, Family Dinner Code Reviews)

Now that we've put a line in the sand about regular peer reviews, I've made up my mind to attend as many as I can. One of our first ones ends up being a real doozy.

I'm about 5 minutes late, and the three developers – sorry, *engineers* – in the room are already finishing up their discussion of the ground rules.

"OK, so every time there's a check-in we have a peer look over what we've done – that's part of every pull request we do," Alex says. "This is a little more involved though – here we're adding a whole new application and so for that we do a more formal inspection where we walk through the code and the application in detail. Ryan and Harry have done most of the work so they're steering, and I'll be the moderator. Guys, take it away."

Ryan begins by pulling up the requirements documentation and coughs nervously. "Uhmmm… kinda wish I had more coffee in my bloodstream right now. Anyway, we're adding a whole new application here, one that shows the worker conditions in our factories in Indonesia and China based on independent audits. This is how our leadership wants us to track and improve conditions at our footwear factories. Even though these are usually subcontractor owned and operated, they're producing our shoes and the worker conditions there reflect on WonderTek directly. I've been told repeatedly that the data here is highly sensitive – if it was to leak, the press could make us out to look like monsters and it'd be a PR nightmare. So, we need to think about security early and often."

Ryan walks us through the business logic, the data model and how the programmers had implemented the UI layer and authentication/authorization. Everyone in the room has already taken a look at the code and the requirements, so the walkthrough is quick. Things are going swimmingly for the first 10 minutes, and I'm starting to drift off a little when Harry suddenly says sharply, "What's going on with your class design here, Ryan?"

Ryan looks like a faun spotlighted in the headlights of an oncoming Mack truck. "Um, well, we tried to follow SOLID principles here and to me it looks like this is good OO compliant design…"

Harry snorts derisively, and he stabs a finger angrily at the code on the screen. "Dude, this is 101-level programming stuff here that you're mangling. I mean, your naming conventions are all over the board. You should be camelcasing your class names, your variables should begin with a lower case letter, your constants should be upper case, your interfaces are named all wrong – I mean use some adverbs like I've told you before. Your segmentation is OK but there's zero documentation in the code – this is a nightmare for anyone coming after you and it doesn't fit the rest of the codebase. There's no way I'm going to OK this crap."

Ryan visibly wilts under this barrage, as Harry continues: "You've been here now two years, and I'm still seeing the same hacky crap with style that you had when you first came here. I'm really disappointed that this keeps on coming up with you, Ryan."

Alex says, "Hold up there, Harry – before we start tearing each other apart here, what are you getting at? I'm looking at the same code you are, and I don't see anything substantial to pick apart."

"Alex, this just keeps coming up and I'm tired of it always getting swept under the rug," Harry grimaces. "Naming conventions and style are important, and it's a signaler for quality and forethought in design. Any programmer that ignores them creates work for everybody else. And Ryan here should know – if we allow this to go out the door, the next time there's a call for a change or a sitedown issue, it'll take us two or three times longer than it should have because the code is illegible and inconsistent."

Ryan says, "I guess I could have spent a little more time tidying up. But we've never made a specific naming convention part of our definition of done as a team. In fact, we don't even HAVE a definition of done. Seems to me like if I'm going to get put on the spot for missing a standard, that standard needs to be in writing and enforced across the board."

Harry says, "For once we agree. Yeah, we definitely need a formalized definition of done. I don't want to have to keep playing whack-a-mole with this sloppy crap every week. Ben, we need to stop putting this off – can we get a decision on this today?"

All eyes swivel to me. I start to laugh and throw up my hands in surrender. "Hey guys, I thought we've been over this already. We decided on what needs to be done around quality, and all of you know the numbers I'm looking at every day as a manager. That's unit test coverage, our bug count and our release success rate – those three things tell me if we're making progress or not. But I'm not mandating anything – how you reach these goals is entirely up to you. If you think a formal definition of done is important, go for it. If you want these peer reviews to be more formal and less GitHub-by, fine. My advice to you is to make sure that whatever you decide on is simple, easy to enforce, and consistent with our team mission and values."

Alex is frowning as he opens the conference door and calls the team in. "Harry has brought up the need for a definition of done. Apparently this is too important to wait, and it is a team decision. Do you think we need a better, more defined list of what 'done' means for our code?"

Harry injects, "Specifically I'm asking for a lot more discipline around style and naming conventions. It may seem like a small thing but it's making our code an unreadable hodgepodge."

"I actually think our reviews are going well," Padma says. She looks a little amused. "On check-in, we just have someone pop by and look over what we've done before we commit code. It's informal and lightweight – efficient."

Harry retorts, "Padma, it's toothless. Everybody just brings over their best buddy who does a looks-good-to-me signoff. Our commenting and documentation is nonexistent, and our code – well, you see what's going on here with Ryan's hunk of crap." He's smirking, triumphant, lounging in his chair. King Nerd.

But George is looking at the code, and he's frowning. "Geez, Harry, take a chill pill. I'm not seeing anything here that's as bad as what you say."

There's some more discussion about having the need for an explicit, defined definition of done. Padma is adamant – "I don't agree that our review process is toothless but I do think it could be more effective. I don't want a stone tablet of the 10 commandments of coding showing up on my desk. That inhibits everything we're trying to do as a team."

Alex comments, "This is good enough for me. Harry – you've made a point that our commenting and our styles differ from person to person – I'm not convinced yet that it's painful enough to warrant a fix. I will say this much – I agree with you that we need to add some better checks and balances.

"We're going to come up with a checklist for our reviews. One of the main things is testing. I'm embarrassed to say this, but I didn't ask to see unit testing and whether we were capturing all the scenarios that were likely to come up. We keep saying that every change we produce needs to have unit tests against it – so it needs to be part of our checks. And any demo needs to run on a production-like environment, otherwise it doesn't count. We'll check back on this in a few weeks, and see if we need to add static code analysis requirements on every check-in."

Harry is groaning. "So, we're just staying the course huh? If you don't put it in writing, Alex, all we can expect is just more mediocrity."

Alex's chin juts out, and he says firmly: "Correct me if I'm wrong Harry, but we took the time out of everyone's day to discuss your concerns around style and conventions. The team decided that it wasn't an issue serious enough to warrant a formal change, but we ARE going to be paying more attention to the test layer, linter and static analysis checks, and our documentation and commenting styles going forward. I'm NOT going to dictate anything unless it's truly an issue and not one person's pet peeve.

"One last thing – Ryan, I really appreciate you bringing your code to the group like this. Thank you for being willing to show us your work, and I think the business is going to be very happy with what you've delivered in such a short period of time. I love the new security framework you're experimenting with, and maybe for our demo on Friday you can go into that in more detail. I think I could use that in my own work."

As the team files out, I tap Harry on the shoulder and ask him and Alex to remain. As much as I sometimes enjoy watching him squirm a little, Harry is a good member of the team, and he's visibly frustrated. "Ben, like I said, this is just more nicey-nice. Discipline is important and you guys are sandbagging."

Alex sighs. "Actually Harry, I agreed with a lot of what you said. But the way you said it made it impossible for me to side with you. You were personally attacking Ryan, which means the next time we do a review session with him he'll either turtle up or wait much longer until his code is absolutely perfect. I'd rather have good code sooner than perfect code never."

I say slowly, "If you feel like we need to tighten something up, Harry, I trust your judgment. Next time we have a demo – why don't you give us an overview of how we can get more consistent in our code? If the group decides – we'll just add it to our new checklist."

Harry doesn't agree, and we go back and forth for a few minutes. Finally, Alex closes by saying, "I think this is a good learning experience for all of us, Harry. The tone that we want comes from the 'family dinner' you see at most good-quality restaurants. Chefs know that to get better you have to be willing to experiment and learn- so once a week they get together and serve a meal from a new recipe. And I thought it was so cool – people were tasting this food and asking if a little more vanilla might be a good thing, or if it was overcooked or flawed in some way. That's the tone we're looking for – where someone is serving something they created out of love and offering it up to the group, so it can be made a little better."

Behind the Story

Three new aspects are introduced in this chapter: continuous integration, shifting left on testing, and more effective code reviews. Let's explore each in more detail.

Continuous Integration

Programmers don't burn out on hard work, they burn out on change-with-the-wind directives and not shipping.

— Mark Berry

The team is getting to the point where releases are rolling out the door with better repeatedly, at least from a tools perspective. But they are still investing way too much time into getting their code to a point where it's releasable. In this case, no one is seriously arguing about whether Continuous Integration is necessary; the way it should be implemented however is very much in debate.

Enough time has passed by since the landmark publication of *Continuous Delivery* where we can make some authoritative statements:

Code Freezes Are Evil

Code freezes and long stabilization phases are evil; continuous integration is the cure.

We've worked on projects with multiweek and sometimes multimonth integration/stabilization periods where code development is frozen or long amounts of time are spent merging long-lived feature branches. Without exception, the significant amount of pain this caused (in terms of lost hours and opportunity cost) was both underestimated and completely avoidable with better hygiene; the freeze period was masking serious underlying cultural issues preventing faster releases that needed to be exposed and resolved by practicing continuous integration.

We're not saying that frequent check-ins to trunk by itself is enough. But in combination with a strong, comprehensive test harness and complete version control, it's a proven winner. The "magic triangle" of a good test layer, trunk-based development, and version control has been established as leading directly to lower levels of deployment pain, higher throughput/stability, and lower change failure rates.[1]

Notice how these really come down to practices, which is just another word for hard work. For your developers to agree to having every change kick off a build, they'll need to have a solid test layer — which means more of their time devoted to strengthening up their "test pyramid." For their releases to be more reliable, the deployment pipeline needs to be rock solid, and more thought needs to go into keeping the configurations of the environments consistent.

---

[1] "Annual State of DevOps Report," unattributed author(s). Puppet Labs, 2015. https://puppetlabs.com/2015-devops-report.

And, worst of all, any failed build for any reason needs to jump to the front of the line. This is the equivalent of the iconic "green Andon cord" that Toyota put in their factories, where workers could stop the line for any reason until a defect was resolved. This caused pain – deliberately – which forced attention on every level to permanently resolve the problem at its source so the line could continue moving.

There's no question that having consistently "green" running builds will require more work and attention by your team. We suggest the pain will decrease with practice, and it will lead to fundamentally better quality. Pain leads to change and a better daily focus on improvement. Practice and culture trumps tools, any day of the week.

Set up some team rules to make it consistent: no commenting out failing tests; fixing a broken build is everyone's responsibility, and if a build can't be fixed within a reasonable timeframe – say 15 minutes – revert. (Another reason to practice frequent check-ins!)

Remember – by "continuous integration," we mean frequent check-ins to mainline. By "version control," we mean comprehensive usage in every environment and every deploy – everything needed to run an app, including system/environment config, can be pulled from VC as an authoritative source of record. And by a good test layer – this means something that runs on every check-in and validates every build, against a production-like set of environments, giving us a good level of confidence and high visibility on failures. (More on this, later!)

You're Probably Doing CI Wrong

It's impossible to overstate both the importance of Continuous Integration (CI) – it's been called "the most important technical practice in the Agile canon" – and how badly it has been implemented in many enterprises. CI has been defined as the practice of working in small batches and using automated tests to detect and reverse changes that could have introduced a regression error. Some have gone a little further and, besides requiring that everyone check into mainline (i.e., no feature branches), add the need for a meaningful Definition of Done.

Regardless of how you define it, the fascinating thing is that most organizations that say they are practicing continuous integration actually aren't. As brought out in "Continuous Delivery," Continuous Integration means the following:

1. Is all development checked into trunk – not just merged from their branches?

2. Does every change to trunk kick off a build process including automated tests?

3. When the build and test systems show a fail, does the team fix the build within a few minutes either by fixing the breakage or reversion?[2]

Many of the teams and organizations that say they are practicing either CI or the next step up – Continuous Delivery – often cannot answer positively to those three critical questions. Testing is rarely in place or provide adequate coverage and builds are consistently running red as the team's priorities and focus lie elsewhere.

The word "continuous" means every check-in triggers a build – no shortcuts. Scheduled builds running once a night (or once daily) can't be considered "continuous." What happens when there's an issue with a broken build involving perhaps a hundred different commits over a day? More sifting, diagnosis, and hassles with rollbacks.[3, 4]

Usually, the need for a scheduled build arises because the test layer has bloated out to the point where it can't be run on check-in. We'll get into this later – and please see our interview with Munil Shah in the Appendix – but several companies we spoke to, including Microsoft, chose to invest a vast amount of management time on a continual basis to watching build times, creating a set of tests that could run in parallel or cover just a component, and weeding out or refactoring long-running tests. Once a build cycle starts exceeding 10 minutes, your developers will start to find creative ways to avoid frequent check-ins and the hit their productivity is taking. Show you value their time by keeping your tests lean and mean.

Munil Shah told us that having the mainline always be in a shippable state is critical for Microsoft:

> Another common mistake are these deep, really complex branching structures. We used to do that, and it was like death by a thousand cuts – the integration debt from all these low-lying branches that we'd have to pay against constantly.

> Now, it's a different story – every engineer merges against master. That's indispensable – to merge to master, you have to be absolutely sure you won't break it – so that forces a large amount of automated unit tests to prevent problems on check-in. And for that to work, you need to make sure these tests can run fast, every time you do a pull request. So, only the fast and reliable tests survive, everything else you weed out.

[2]"Continuous Delivery: Reliable Software Releases through Build, Test, and Deployment Automation" by Jez Humble, David Farley. Addison-Wesley Professional, 8/6/2010. ISBN-10: 9780321601919, ISBN-13: 978-0321601919.
[3]"Building Microservices: Designing Fine-Grained Systems," Sam Newman. O'Reilly Media; 2/20/2015. ISBN-10: 1491950358, ISBN-13: 978-1491950357.
[4]"7 Signs You're Mastering Continuous Integration," Brian Dawson. DevOps.com, 7/18/2018. https://devops.com/7-signs-youre-mastering-continuous-integration/.

All that good behavior comes from having the master, the mainline always being in a shippable state – that concept is crucial for us. We do use and ship from release branches – we have to have those for hotfixes and to simulate a particular version on demand. But the concept of a feature branch is verboten to us, every engineer knows they can trust and build from master and know it has the same level of quality as any release branch.

Think about it this way. Let's say you're an engineer, and you just wrote some code and check it in. But there's this long integration cycle and test cycle that then kicks off. Two weeks later, someone comes to you with a list of bugs. That's very interruption-driven and disruptive to your workflow; by that time, you may not even remember why you made those changes, or even where they were. But if you get feedback almost immediately – say within 90 minutes that your checkin is integrated to mainline, and it looks good – that gives you confidence that you can change things, safely. And there's a lot less waste due to context switching.[5]

Keep It Simple, Sweetie

One of the most common attractions for many engineering teams is a very complex, branching source control tree. We caution against this in most cases. For example, the book *Accelerate* notes the following:

*Developing off trunk/master rather than on long-lived feature branches was correlated with higher delivery performance. ....It's worth re-emphasizing that these results are independent of team size, organization size, or industry. ....**Many software development teams are used to developing features on branches for days or even weeks. Integrating all these branches requires significant time and rework.** Following our principle of working in small batches and building quality in, high- performing teams keep branches short-lived (less than one day's work) and integrate them into trunk/master frequently. Each change triggers a build process that includes running unit tests. If any part of this process fails, developers fix it immediately.[6] (note, emphasis ours)*

---

[5]Interview of Munil Shah by Dave Harrison, see Appendix.
[6]"Accelerate: The Science of Lean Software and DevOps: Building and Scaling High Performing Technology Organizations," Nicole Forsgren PhD, Jez Humble, Gene Kim. IT Revolution Press, 3/27/2018. ISBN-10: 1942788339, ISBN-13: 978-1942788331.

The Puppet/DORA 2017 Annual State of DevOps report echoed this:

> While our experience shows that developers in high-performing teams work in small batches and develop off of trunk or master, rather than long-lived feature branches, many practitioners in the industry routinely work in branches or forks. Last year's results confirmed that the following development practices contribute to higher software delivery performance:
>
> - Merging code into trunk on a daily basis.
>
> - Having branches or forks with very short lifetimes (less than a day).
>
> - Having fewer than three active branches.
>
> We also found that teams without code lock periods had higher software delivery performance. (The ability to work without code lock periods is supported by the practices described above.) … There's clear guidance to offer from these findings: **Teams should avoid keeping branches alive more than a day. If it's taking you more than a day to merge and integrate branches, that's a warning sign, and you should take a look at your practices and your architecture.**[7] (emphasis ours)

You might question the thresholds mentioned here – less than a day for any branch lifetime might seem absurdly short. But the general guideline of any integration/merge stage taking longer than a day being cause for concern is valid. Long feedback loops are the bane of our development life cycle; long-lived feature branches inevitably lead to "big bang" merge efforts that are risky and time-consuming to debug and cause developers to hold back on refactoring or cleaning up code due to fear of inducing breakages elsewhere on checked-out code.

Even better than that one day warning threshold for integration is tracking your resource drain. We suggest that if you have a "build master" running integrations full-time or a team of specialists just watching the deployment pipeline, more thought needs to be put into your deployment processes. For DevOps to work well, everyone involved in producing work needs to understand how deployments work, have those deployments visible, and potentially be able to push off a build themselves. A team of "deployment specialists" is really just another silo, creating a gap between work being produced and the act of it going out to production.

---

[7]"Annual State of DevOps Report," unattributed author(s). Puppet Labs, 2017. https://puppetlabs.com/2017-devops-report.

Sophisticated, complex build processes with branching per environment – one common antipattern – sounds great in theory, but in practice opens the door to environment mismatches in our version control repository. Despite the most exhaustive tests, there's no guarantee that the test results are valid – because changes can be induced on any branch independently, so QA/STG may not necessarily reflect production. Inevitably, as hotfixes are rolled out to production branches, these changes and environment tweaks fall between the cracks – lurking, unnoticed, waiting to cause variance and regression errors down the road.

Don't take our word for it though. If you have a branching structure that your team finds appealing, count the cost and perform a basic check, as suggested by Kief Morris:

> *Measure the cycle time and analyze the value stream for a single change… Consider how much of the cycle time is spent in activities due to merging and post-merging testing activities. Moving to [a trunk-based approach] should completely eliminate the need for these activities. If your team uses short-lived branches, and spends little or no time merging and testing after merges, then there is not much to be gained by switching. But most teams that use branches routinely spend days or weeks massaging the codebase after merges before they're able to put them into production.*[8]

I don't think we can stress enough the need to keep things as simple as possible from the get-go. The innate tendency is often to overcomplicate. As Edward Thomson of Microsoft pointed out:

> *The more I talk to developers, the more I've observed something that tends to happen to teams that don't do trunk-based development. No matter how organized they think they are, in fact, they tend to structure their branches in the same way. It's a bit of a corollary to Conway's Law: Organizations tend to produce branching structures that copy the organization chart.*[9]

For our team, it's going to be critical that they – one way or another – kill off that lengthy code freeze and stabilization period, as that's the single biggest contributor they have currently to their wait time and its throttling their release momentum. Now that they're going to pay some serious attention to this, they'll have more bandwidth to use for more rewarding work.

---

[8]"Infrastructure as Code: Managing Servers in the Cloud," Kief Morris. O'Reilly Media, 6/27/2016. ISBN-10: 1491924357, ISBN-13: 978-1491924358.
[9]"Release Flow: How We Do Branching on the VSTS Team," Edward Thomson. MSDN Blogs, 4/19/2018. https://blogs.msdn.microsoft.com/devops/2018/04/19/release-flow-how-we-do-branching-on-the-vsts-team/.

GitHub Flow Can Be Awesome

On Harry's arguments about GitHub Flow, there's definitely some solid reasoning behind his arguments that led to him winning his case. We're not going to be dogmatic on how you should go about practicing CI, other than it must fit the three criteria discussed earlier – merge to trunk daily at a minimum, branches with short <1 day lifetimes, and less than three active branches. If it fits this criteria, experience shows you'll have a much smoother release cycle and little of the pain so common in our industry around getting code to a releasable state.

Far from being just for open source or informal projects, GitHub Flow can actually help improve some of the basic hygiene points we're trying to stress – collaboration and frequent peer reviews, short feedback loops, and a viable, living documentation trail.

William Buchwalter noted the following:

> *GitHub Flow is all about short feedback loops (everything in DevOps mostly is, actually). This means work branches ('work' could mean a new feature or a bug fix – there is no distinction) starts from the production code (master) and are short lived – the shorter the better. Merging back becomes a breeze and we are truly continuously integrating.*

> *Collaboration is the other cornerstone of the GitHub Flow. Everyone agrees that code reviews are a good thing, but few will actually do it seriously. In many cases this is simply because it takes too much time: most developers will wait until they think they are done to open a pull request (or Merge Request if you use GitLab). How can we review 3 weeks of changes in a reasonable amount of time? We cannot, so we just skim over the surface and approve.*

> *A better approach is to open a pull request as early as possible and code in the open, discuss implementation details and architecture choices as you go, tag people that can help you while you're coding. This has the side effect of creating a living documentation for you: wondering why someone made a particular decision? Check the discussion in the related pull request.*[10]

That's not saying that this particular pattern is perfect or bulletproof. The Azure DevOps team for example is very complimentary to GitHub Flow in general. However, given their specific use case, they found it not practicable for large teams due to contention during a production deployment:

---

[10]"A Git Workflow for Continuous Delivery," William Buchwalter. Microsoft TechNet, 6/26/2016. `https://blogs.technet.microsoft.com/devops/2016/06/21/a-git-workflow-for-continuous-delivery/`

Overall, I really like this system [GitHub Flow]; it's lightweight and with good tooling and automation, you can be very productive. This system works pretty well for GitHub, but unfortunately, it doesn't scale to the Azure DevOps team's needs. That's because there's a subtlety to GitHub Flow that often goes overlooked. You actually deploy your changes to production before merging the pull request... This system is extremely clever: when you're ready to check-in, you get immediate feedback on how a pull request will behave in production, and that feedback happens before you complete the pull request. So if there's a problem with your code changes, you can simply abandon the deployment, and your bad code never got merged into master. This lets you take a step back and look at the monitoring data to understand why your changes were problematic, then iterate on the pull request and try again.

The problem with this development strategy is that it scales extremely poorly to larger teams, because there's contention when you're trying to deploy to production... When you have a few developers, you're going to need a deployment queue to ensure that only one pull request can be deployed at once. This is great, but as you start to grow and hire more developers, there are more people in the queue. As your codebase grows, builds start to take longer. And as you get more popular, your infrastructure grows and with it, the time it takes to deploy.

Azure DevOps has hundreds of developers working on it. On average, we build, review and merge over 200 pull requests a day into our master branch. If we wanted to deploy each of those before we merged them it, it would decimate our velocity.[11]

Where do we stand on GitHub Flow? Time has shown that GitHub Flow will work very well with teams that will be onboard with frequent check-ins; the GitHub Flow model is very lightweight and well thought out and can make your collaboration/documentation more intuitive and seamless. It can also run out of control and cause integration pains if discipline is not followed with creating pull requests early and tagging your peers for input, and not allowing feature branches to age. So, it all depends upon your team's makeup, mission, and level of maturity. "Your results may vary."

There are other patterns that can be used in combination with trunk-based development, and some will be considered later. Feature flags, branch by abstraction, and splitting your work by domain boundaries and components –

---

[11]"Release Flow: How We Do Branching on the VSTS Team," Edward Thomson. MSDN Blogs, 4/19/2018. https://blogs.msdn.microsoft.com/devops/2018/04/19/release-flow-how-we-do-branching-on-the-vsts-team/

microservices, essentially – can all play a role in limiting your "blast radius" and lessening the fear factor your development teams may be going through every time they check in their changes.

We can't improve on how it's put in *Continuous Delivery*:

> *Our proposal is not a tech solution but a practice – always commit to trunk, and do it at least once a day. If this seems incompatible with making far-reaching changes, perhaps you haven't tried hard enough. In our experience, although it sometimes takes longer to implement a feature as a series of small incremental steps that keeps the code in working state, the benefits are immense. Having code that is always working is fundamental – we can't emphasize enough how important this practice is in enabling continuous delivery of valuable, working software.*[12]

Shift Left on Testing

> *Regardless of your plans, production is the ultimate testing environment.*
>
> — J.T. Wall

Quality comes first – except in software development, it seems. You'll notice in "Testing My Patience" the continuing theme that the team is paying lip service to quality; they've deferred paying attention to testing in favor of other priorities with a quicker payoff and less drudgery. The negative impacts this has had on their release cycle and regression issues has reached a point where Ben can no longer ignore it; he chooses to make quality part of the job description of every member of the team.

The Most Important Part of Continuous Delivery

Many organizations focus only on the profit line and minimizing costs when it comes to their IT and development operations, treating technology investments as a cost center. In particular cries of outrage are often heard when the team objects to tight, mandated deadlines as it won't allow enough time for a functional test layer to be written. This shortsighted focus on velocity at all costs often ends up hamstringing their growth and potential. John Seddon once pointed out that "the paradox is that when managers focus on productivity, long-term improvements are rarely made. On the other hand, when managers focus on quality, productivity improves continuously."

---

[12]"Continuous Delivery: Reliable Software Releases through Build, Test, and Deployment Automation," Jez Humble, David Farley. Addison-Wesley Professional, 8/6/2010. ISBN-10: 9780321601919, ISBN-13: 978-0321601919.

Putting quality first – which in the software world means testing – is hardly a new concept. The revered father of Lean, Edward Deming, famously made building quality into a manufacturing line an emphasis. The third of his 14 key principles for management emphasized ceasing "dependence on mass inspection to achieve quality. Improve the process and build quality into the product in the first place." In the Japanese automotive plants built according to Lean principles, less work was needed to inspect and catch defects in the cars at the end of the assembly lines – because work was continually going on behind to scenes to catch and remediate issues early on, when they were cheaper to fix permanently.

The 2017 Annual State of DevOps report noted that four factors positively impacted continuous delivery:

- Comprehensive version control
- Continuous integration and trunk-based development
- Integrating security into software delivery
- Test and deployment automation

Of these, which would you put first in importance? The shocking statement for us came immediately following that list: "Of these, test automation is the biggest contributor."[13]

This begs the question: if testing – and specifically automated tests – are such a boon to quality, why are we so terrible at it as a community? It's shocking how many large and business-critical applications have manual acceptance testing as the only layer. Any automated tests that exist are usually ineffective in their coverage and out of date. Without an effective and automated testing layer, any adjustments made to the release pipeline may actually make things worse.

The situation has hardly improved since Continuous Delivery noted this gap, back in 2010:

> *Manual testing in the software industry is the norm and represents often the only type of testing done by a team. This is both expensive and rarely good enough on its own to ensure high quality.*[14]

---

[13]"Annual State of DevOps Report," unattributed author(s). Puppet Labs, 2017. https://puppetlabs.com/2017-devops-report.
[14]"Continuous Delivery: Reliable Software Releases through Build, Test, and Deployment Automation," Jez Humble, David Farley. Addison-Wesley Professional, 8/6/2010. ISBN-10: 9780321601919, ISBN-13: 978-0321601919

It's hard for a team to claim it is being "Agile" and producing value when they've gone from releasing code every 3 months with no automated testing to releasing every 2 weeks with no automated testing. Speeding up the release cycle in this way usually just improves the rate of delivery of bugs to production!

We've experienced this firsthand even with very small teams. For example, once Dave worked on a team consisting of exactly two developers, working 5 feet apart. However, each had different versions of Visual Studio, and the project's library versions were completely out of synch. Testing consisted of creating an executable, unpacking it manually on a QA webserver, followed by poking around with a few canned scenarios. The day before a critical demo to key business stakeholders of the new manufacturing shopfloor system, guess what happened? You guessed it – somehow the exhaustive "smoketesting" missed a critical bug around authentication. Without users being able to get into the system, the demo went down in flames, and the team suffered a huge hit to our reputation that the project never fully recovered from. Only two developers, and somehow they had managed to stomp on each other's toes!

Gary Gruver in "Start and Scaling DevOps in the Enterprise" wrote about one organization's seemingly robust test layer being a paper tiger:

> ...I worked with one organization that was very proud of the fact that they had written over one thousand automated tests that they were running at the end of each release cycle. I pointed out that this was good, but to see the most value, they should start using them in the DP [delivery pipeline] every day, gating builds where the developers were required to keep the builds green. They should also make sure they started with the best, most stable tests because if the red builds were frequently due to test issues instead of code issues, then the developers would get upset and disengage from the process.

> They spent several weeks trying to find reliable tests out of the huge amount available. In the end, they found out that they had to throw out all the existing tests because they were not stable, maintainable, or triagable. Don't make this same mistake! Start using your test automation as soon as possible. Have the first few tests gating code on your DP, and once you know you have a stable test framework, start adding more tests over time.[15]

---

[15]"Start and Scaling Devops in the Enterprise," Gary Gruver. BookBaby, 12/1/2016. ISBN-10: 1483583589, ISBN-13: 978-1483583587

Common Blockers to Effective Testing

Repeatedly, we hear the same set of objections raised to investing in a testing framework:

- "We don't have the licenses to run tests against our code – there's only enough for the QA team."

- "Our application architecture (or data layer size) doesn't allow our acceptance tests to be run on a dev environment."

- "We really don't have the time for this – we need to focus on delivering. The business won't stand for this."

- "Our legacy application is a nightmare; it's completely untestable."

- "We only control part of the application. We have to coordinate any testing and releasing with them, and it's killing us."

- And most surprisingly – resistance from the developers: "This is going to slow us down, break up our flow, and prevent us from thinking big picture. It's a total waste of time and effort."

It's common that cost is cited as a factor for not providing a near-production like replicated environment for testing. This usually ends up as a case study in false economy; horror stories abound of systems with tight SLA's around performance failing because of problems exhibited at loads that couldn't be applied in the lower-spec, QA type environments.

As *Continuous Delivery* puts it:

> *A common complaint [is that automated tests] are too expensive to create and maintain. The cost of this is much lower in our experience than performing frequent manual acceptance and regression testing or releasing poor quality software. They catch serious problems that unit or component tests can never catch. Manual testing usually happens at a late date where teams under extreme pressure to get software out the door. There's no time to fix these bugs – they're added to a list. Where defects are found that require complex fixes, odds of integration/ regression problems rise.*

> *… The cost of maintaining complex acceptance tests is a tax, an investment which is repaid many times over in reduced maintenance costs, protection that allows you to make wide ranging changes to the app, and significantly higher quality – "bringing the pain forward".*

> *Without excellent automated test coverage, one of three things happens: a lot of time is spent trying to find and fix bugs at the end of the process, you spend time and money on manual and regression testing, or you release poor quality software.*[16]

Struggling with Legacy Code

The legacy code argument is perhaps one of the stickiest, one of the reasons why we often call our pet monster apps "Big Balls of Mud." There's no question that legacy code is often not well structured, meaning we're always terrified of breaking things unexpectedly with the smallest of modifications. There's little value in adding comprehensive testing in most these cases, even if it was possible. This is something Michael Feathers called the Legacy Code Dilemma: *When we change code, we should have tests in place. To put tests in place, we often have to change code.*[17]

This doesn't mean that we should just throw up our hands, think *poor me*, and suffer in silence as our days are spent harnessed to an uncontrollable and temperamental ball of mud. This problem is not much different in shape than trying to test against other notoriously "untestable" elements such as frontend GUI forms, dialog boxes and widgets, device drivers, transactional components, IO interactions, asynchronous threads and processes, transaction controllers, etc.

Legacy code, as Michael Feathers has aptly defined it, are simply systems that do not have automated tests. That's a changeable condition, and if we are forced to introduce changes, we need to validate that the app is functioning as expected. In many cases, it is possible to add tests for any new features we introduce by using a shell that we gradually enhance over time – more on this later when we talk about scaffolding. But very rarely do we come across a system that cannot be testable in some way, perhaps by using mocks or the Humble Object pattern.

Think about what a high price we pay with those mission-critical apps we call "legacy," throw up our hands on as "untestable," and end up supporting with no automated testing layer. For these apps, there is no useful bug detection. Bugs cannot be found and fixed quickly, leading to expensive and embarrassing regression errors in production. And without confidence in our bug detection, we have no courage to make large-scale changes or refactors, or even add new features in many cases. Without refactoring, the codebase rots in quality and development grinds to a halt as the team treads water, fearful to touch either the app or the environments it runs on.

---

[16]"Continuous Delivery: Reliable Software Releases through Build, Test, and Deployment Automation," Jez Humble, David Farley. Addison-Wesley Professional, 8/6/2010. ISBN-10: 9780321601919, ISBN-13: 978-0321601919.
[17]"Working Effectively with Legacy Code," Michael Feathers. Prentice Hall, 10/2/2004. ISBN-13: 978-0131177055, ISBN-10: 9780131177055.

Automated testing immediately tilts the balance in our favor. Suddenly, we know both when a problem is being introduced – very early on – and we often can identify where the bug was introduced, or at least the release version when it first cropped up as an issue. Knowing when and where in the codebase a regression issue is happening cuts down our firefighting time significantly, by 50% or more.

To be blunt – the mindset of "our code isn't testable" is often more a mental blocker than it is fact-based logic. Often, this complaint is just a smokescreen for developers not wishing to change the way of writing code the way they always have – throwing it over the wall, and moving on to the cool next thing.

Testing is the first and often only weapon that can win the battles against legacy code:

Why don't we clean up code that we know is messy? We're afraid we'll break it. But if we have the tests, we can be reasonably sure that the code is not broken, or that we'll detect the breakage immediately. If we have the tests we become fearless about making changes. If we see messy code, or an unclean structure, we can clean it without fear. Because of the tests, the code becomes malleable again. Because of the tests, software becomes soft again.[18]

What Does an Effective Test Layer Mean?

A functional testing system could be divided into the following categories:

- Unit tests – do small pieces of the app behave as expected in isolation?

- Integration testing – do the different parts of the application or service interact as expected?

- Functional acceptance tests – does this deliver the expected business value expected?

- Nonfunctional tests checking capacity, availability, security.

- Exploratory testing – how does the app look from a user perspective?

Perhaps, for your applications, as with ours, it's rare to have every component of this in place and providing good coverage. But that critical first layer – the unit test – is the most important, and the one we stress highly in our architecture. There's no way around it if you want safety with speed – your

---

[18]"The Three Laws of TDD," Robert Martin. ButUncleBob.com, unknown date. http://butunclebob.com/ArticleS.UncleBob.TheThreeRulesOfTdd.

automated tests need to be run regularly, on every commit. That usually means a very high reliance on unit testing. The goal here is feedback, as fast as possible, to the people making the changes.

Why Unit Testing Is Important

Very few of the applications that the WonderTek teams support are completely without a test layer. But as Ben and Alex keep bringing up, these tests rely heavily either on UI tests or manual smoketesting – which are costing the team heavily both in maintenance and build times, brittle and often unreliable. Without knowing it the testing pattern was looking more and more like the dreaded ice cream cone first conceived by Mike Cohn:[19]

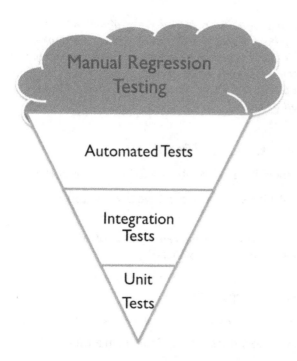

Both in the real physical world and in software design, the ice cream cone is a very unstable structure and melts down over time. We propose the same pattern used with great success by many leading enterprises: "shifting left" to have most of your tests running on every build as unit tests, directly against your code before any commit.

---

[19]"Testing Pyramids & Ice-Cream Cones," Alister Scott. Watirmelon, unknown date. https://watirmelon.blog/testing-pyramids/.

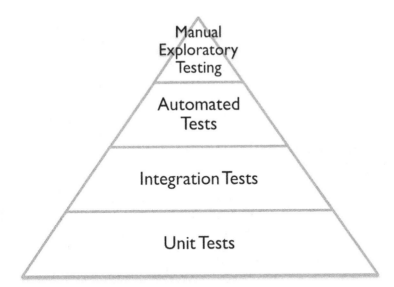

As we mentioned earlier, unit test coverage is a tried and true metric and usually a good measure of how effective your vital first line of defense is.

There are some key principles we can derive for our ideal, reliable test layer:

1. Build commits need to run as fast as possible. (This means your commits should not test against the UI layer at all.)

2. Unit tests should not hit the database, filesystem, external systems, or integration (use mocks or test doubles instead)

3. Ideally, your unit test coverage should be high – like 75% or better – and any failure at this level breaks the release.

4. Dependency injection or inversion of control is a useful design pattern to create testable units of code by removing dependencies.

Unit Testing to the Rescue

Where any automated testing exists, in many shops, the focus is on the UI layer, perhaps using Selenium (which we love, btw). Integration testing and unit testing are often neglected – a dangerous imbalance. We've even heard architects proclaim grandly at conferences, "Unit tests are worthless!" To these grandstanding "experts," we counter with the Azure DevOps story at Microsoft, where (as of mid-2018) 41,000+ unit tests are run every check-in in under 6 minutes. That can't be done purely with integration tests or testing against the UI layer.

Microsoft made a shift to unit testing a key part of their reengineering effort with the Azure DevOps team starting in 2007. As Munil Shah told us afterward:

> *There was a lot of skepticism when we first published this idea, that we'd be relying more on unit testing going forward. We got a lot of 'we tried this before, it didn't work' and 'unit testing won't work in this case' type responses. We tried to avoid a lot of religious debate about this and made it pragmatic. And we didn't try blowing away our 27,000 integration and functional tests overnight – that was a huge investment that we couldn't remove overnight.*

> *But we did put a stake in the ground, insisting that any new code going out the door had to be accompanied with unit tests. And we invested in showing teams how to write unit tests effectively, that are extendable and actually work. We spend time showing how we run testing, deployment, architecture, and security – but we don't get prescriptive. We don't straitjacket our people into one specific way of writing a unit test.*

> *We used to do a crazy amount of performance testing and integration testing in lab environments, simulating real world usage with synthetic loads, and it was killing us. What's more we weren't finding a lot of actual bugs with it! We spent so much time trying to maintain those expensive integration environments and chasing bugs that weren't real. For us, we've found no substitute for actual, real world production environments – testing in production is a big part of moving at speed.*

> *We run bug bashes too – that's where teams take a few days and try to find as many bugs as they can. We give awards out – gold medal for finding the most bugs, or the most bugs in other teams' work. Gamifying things like this helps us avoid that kind of blinders-on way we view our product when we're just testing our own feature, or treating bugs as a hateful flaw that must be hidden from others. No, it's a byproduct of our work! It's kind of like cleaning up a messy room – you just have to roll up your sleeves and tidy up, that's a bug bash.*[20]

As Munil discussed, the fact that Microsoft's old test layer was both expensive to maintain and ineffective was a powerful motivator to shift the emphasis away from performance testing and comprehensive integration and UI testing. This is why Brian Harry of Microsoft has been quoted as saying, "We unashamedly test in production" – for more on this, see the section on "Continuous Delivery and feature flags" in Chapter 6.

---

[20]Interview with Munil Shah by Dave Harrison, see Appendix.

UI-Driven Acceptance Tests Still Matter

This doesn't mean throwing all acceptance tests out the window, replacing them whole cloth with unit and component tests along with pair programming and exploratory testing. We go into this more in the interview with Munil Shah from the Azure DevOps team, but it's wise not to swing the pendulum too far in the opposite direction. Unit testing does not cover user scenarios, and it won't help you catch architectural mistakes, environmental or config issues, CSS or display problems, or threading issues.

Michael Stahnke from Puppet told us that unit tests make a great litmus test but are far from perfect by themselves:

> Let's take unit tests. It's fantastic you've got 90% code coverage, that's great – but does it do what you want? Are you invoking the code at the right spot? By far, the hardest part of continuous delivery is testing and everyone, I mean EVERYONE just glosses over it. It's damn hard, unglamorous work, and there is no generic way of testing everything. But testing is where it starts and ends – let's say you're deploying ten times a day, are you that confident in your tests, or in your ability to rework?
>
> I'm going to risk the pitchforks and torches here and just say, I honestly care a lot less about unit tests than most. They're great as specifications and to demonstrate something works as its designed – but we've had times where Puppet's had 16K unit tests running and the build still fails in prod, so it didn't catch what we needed. We use it as a litmus test, and it gives our devs fast feedback. But I stress with our engineers to spend time at the system and integration level – are we actually solving the problem for the customer?[21]

One company that our friend Donovan Brown engaged with made the common mistake of confusing DevOps with automation. They created thousands of unit and integration tests, and a shiny deployment pipeline where code would flow with no human intervention from commit to production. As soon as they released a minor tweak to some style rules to production, they started to lose money off their production site. It took a person to check out their eCommerce website manually to find that a change to a CSS style sheet had an interesting side effect where the final order button color and text was the same color – resulting in a blank button! This naturally passed all their test layer with flying color, but it caused them to hemorrhage orders until exploratory testing late in the game could isolate the problem.

---

[21]Interview of Michael Stahnke by Dave Harrison, see Appendix.

The lesson here was, automate everything you CAN – but not <u>everything</u>. This echoes the thoughts in Continuous Delivery: "It is important to note that acceptance tests are expensive to create and maintain. They are also regression tests. Don't follow a naive process of taking your acceptance criteria and automating every one."[22]

Another story Donovan likes to tell is of a team where the developers were not allowed to write a line of code until they wrote a UI test – this would fail initially, then the code was refined until it passed. This was handed off to a stakeholder along with a manual test case, written in plain English. These automation and UI tests were admittedly brittle, but it forced the dev team – which was working in 1-week sprints – to do the right thing early. And, as you might expect, a valuable side benefit was the creative ways the stakeholders – coming in green, with no knowledge of the underlying code or design – found cool and exciting ways of breaking the app. This was outstanding feedback that could then be folded back quickly as actionable bugs – along with matching test cases to prevent the UI fails from reoccurring.

Martin Fowler, while stressing that UI tests should be run relatively less often, states that we very much still need that expensive layer of acceptance testing as a second line of defense:

> I always argue that high-level tests are there as a second line of test defense. If you get a failure in a high level test, not just do you have a bug in your functional code, you also have a missing or incorrect unit test. Thus I advise that before fixing a bug exposed by a high level test, you should replicate the bug with a unit test. Then the unit test ensures the bug stays dead.[23]

Applications written with testability in mind will have an API that both the frontend GUI and the test layer can interact with; in these cases, running tests against the business layer gives a good level of confidence. Besides segmenting out API vs. UI-based testing, to speed things up, some companies have had great success with parallelizing their testing with multiple test clients running Selenium tests against the UI layer, or isolating and refactoring their slowest tests.

[22]"Continuous Delivery: Reliable Software Releases through Build, Test, and Deployment Automation," Jez Humble, David Farley. Addison-Wesley Professional, 8/6/2010. ISBN-10: 9780321601919, ISBN-13: 978-0321601919.
[23]"TestPyramid," Martin Fowler. MartinFowler.com, 5/1/2012. https://martinfowler.com/bliki/TestPyramid.html.

This is the unglamorous, dirty secret about DevOps; it relies on testing, which is less about brilliance and more about daily practice and maintenance. Keeping your test layer lean, mean, and effective will require constant oversight and refactoring. This isn't glamorous work, it's one of those boring fundamentals – like blocking and tackling in football – that happens to separate well-performing organizations and code from the mediocre ones. As *Continuous Delivery* points out, however, it has positive holistic benefits for your codebase:

> *Comparing codebases that have been developed using automated acceptance tests from the beginning with those where acceptance testing has been an afterthought, we almost always see better encapsulation, clearer intent, cleaner separation of concerns, and more reuse of code... this really is a virtuous circle, testing at the right time leads to better code.*[24]

No Skeletons in Our Closet

We mentioned earlier the objection – which Harry echoes – of cries of anguish by stakeholders over any delay in delivering features because of testing investments. In most projects we've been associated with, allocating time for testing and quality is typically the first "extra" that the business seeks to eliminate in the drive to lower costs and improve delivery dates. How as professionals can we meet this concern head-on?

We suggest not allowing the cost of tradeoffs on quality to be hidden. In one very cost-driven and high-visibility project Dave once managed, the code had been written at a furious pace to please the resident 800-pound gorilla stakeholder. Naturally, the QA team was left to fend for itself and play catchup. It didn't take much digging to determine that test coverage was plunging – and that the true cost and risk implications of this was not known by the business partners and decision makers we were trying to please.

To solve this issue, we made it visible. In every retrospective, we put on the top left a simple set of boxes – one showing our integration and UI acceptance test coverage, and the percent coverage of our unit test layer – and the percent change from the last release.

This sudden burst of sunlight caused a startling transformation. Miraculously, our often absentee stakeholders began popping by on an almost daily basis, asking why the numbers on our test layer looked as bad as they did. Over the next few months, we took some of the steps discussed in "Testing My Patience" to better integrate QA and more than double our test coverage to >80%.

---

[24] "Continuous Delivery: Reliable Software Releases through Build, Test, and Deployment Automation," Jez Humble, David Farley. Addison-Wesley Professional, 8/6/2010. ISBN-10: 9780321601919, ISBN-13: 978-0321601919.

Dave learned a valuable lesson: business people understand intuitively numbers and risk. Once the consequences of short-term decision-making around quality and the costs of operationalizing software become clear, much of the resistance to investing in a robust test framework drops away.

A good indicator of trouble that could be broadcast is an imbalance in staffing. Our good friend Mike Kwan likes looking at the team makeup to identify an underinvestment in QA. It's common to see no or very few QA specialists, perhaps a 1:4 ratio of QA engineers to devs. Bringing that ratio into balance – where the ratio is 1:1 or even five QA engineers to every four developers – often shows dramatic turnarounds when it comes to being able to scale with quality and deliver in a timely manner.

Another approach is just plain not to ask. As Donovan Brown put it:

> The next time you are asked for an estimate, make sure you add time to write unit tests. Do not explain your estimation. Stop feeling the need to justify doing the right thing. Stop asking for permission. If you do not stop the bleeding, you will forever be waiting for the time to write unit tests.[25]

Watch Those Build Times

To avoid howls of complaint, you'll want to monitor your check-in test exec times frequently. Remember that you are asking the team to commit more regularly, perhaps several times a day. The tipping point seems to be about what it takes to grab a cup of coffee from the café – about 5 to 10 minutes – anything longer than this and it will be harder to justify the price paid with every build as worth the cost. In fact, Robert C Martin – aka "Uncle Bob" – has said that "the time between running tests is on the order of seconds, or minutes. Even 10 minutes is too long."[26]

Munil Shah told us that build times is one of the main KPIs that managers and architects at Microsoft obsess over:

> ...First comes monitoring and visibility. We have dashboards to show our CI runs and we keep them visible. If there's a broken build it shows up big and red and gets a lot of attention. But a bigger worry for us is bloat; let's say you've added tests to where your pull requests now take 15 minutes, and then 30 minutes. If an engineer has to wait half an hour for a pull request, or to merge to master, I guarantee you they will find a way to get around that.

---

[25]"No more excuses," Donovan Brown. Donovanbrown.com, 12/12/2016. http://donovanbrown.com/post/no-more-excuses. Our personal battle cry when it comes to "asking for permission" to write unit tests.
[26]"The Three Laws of TDD," Robert Martin. ButUncleBob.com, unknown date. http://butunclebob.com/ArticleS.UncleBob.TheThreeRulesOfTdd.

So, we very carefully monitor the time it takes to create a pull request; the time it takes to self-host; the time it takes to merge back to main. We constantly talk about ways to trim that time down in our engineering staff meetings – dropping or refactoring tests, or new tech that can speed things up. It does require a constant investment of time and money to keep things running fast – so an engineer can create a pull request in 5-10 minutes, for example – the time it takes to get a cup of coffee.[27]

The insidious, creeping nature of bloated test layer leads some companies to fail builds if performance tests deviate by more than 2% from the previous run. Pruning and optimizing testing practices requires some thought. Etsy for example splits their trunk tests into subsets, so a test battery that would require 30 minutes in its entirety is segmented into three portions that each can run below 11 minutes. Although the exact test module being run varies by check-in, the main purpose is met; code is being tested regularly, and there's a good level of assurance that the builds will not break.

So, do everything possible to keep this stage as fast as possible without losing the main point – getting fast feedback on costly, high profile errors. There's no question that the team is going to chafe especially initially – their development firepower is now reduced, quite significantly. Ben is hoping that this constraint will encourage better development processes. And he's going to need to watch that build commit time like a hawk to make sure long running tests aren't burdening down the pace of his developers.

Why Killing Flaky Tests Is Important

When tests are reliable and "green means go," teams gain confidence that their software is releasable; they're also sure that their time isn't being wasted chasing down ghosts. Flaky, unreliable tests that produce false positives and negatives should be your first priority to prune. Some quarantine these into a separate suite; others remove them ruthlessly until a more reliable test can be substituted.

Rajesh mentions the example of one of our personal heroes, Gary Gruver. Gary oversaw a massive refactoring of HP's very complex testing architecture, a situation that initially looked almost unsolvable. He made a cornerstone of that effort weeding out ineffective and flaky tests, and in some cases completely starting from scratch.[28]

---

[27]Interview with Munil Shah by Dave Harrison, see Appendix.
[28]"Leading the Transformation: Applying Agile and DevOps Principles at Scale," Gary Gruver, Tommy Mouser. IT Revolution Press, 8/1/2015. ISBN-10: 1942788010, ISBN-13: 978-1942788010. An in depth exploration of how HP was able to pull itself out of the mud of long test cycles – even with a labyrinth of possible hardware combinations.

The HP story is one of many we could mention where eliminating flaky tests was the turning point. The Azure DevOps team, in its "Shift Left" movement, didn't have the luxury of blowing up their entire massive, time-sucking test layer and starting over; it represented too great an investment of time. Instead, in parallel with improving their unit testing and testing framework, they used build and test execution data to refactor their integration and functional test layer, dropping or rewriting the worst offenders in terms of build time or reliability. If a test ran green 499 out of 500 times, but that 500th run would show red – for whatever reason – the developer would be asked to create a new test that would not fail under load.

The discipline called out by Alex and Rajesh for the team to collectively take ownership of the build process and drop what it's doing and fix a failed build test is a vital principle. As Martin Fowler eloquently put it, the consequences of ignoring a flaky red test in the release pipeline are endemic:

> *Non-deterministic tests have two problems, firstly they are useless, secondly they are a virulent infection that can completely ruin your entire test suite. As a result they need to be dealt with as soon as you can, before your entire deployment pipeline is compromised. ... The trouble with non-deterministic tests is that when they go red, you have no idea whether its due to a bug, or just part of the non-deterministic behavior. Usually with these tests a non-deterministic failure is relatively common, so you end up shrugging your shoulders when these tests go red. Once you start ignoring a regression test failure, then that test is useless and you might as well throw it away.*

> *Indeed you really ought to throw a non-deterministic test away, since if you don't it has an infectious quality. If you have a suite of 100 tests with 10 non-deterministic tests in them, than that suite will often fail. Initially people will look at the failure report and notice that the failures are in non-deterministic tests, but soon they'll lose the discipline to do that. Once that discipline is lost, then a failure in the healthy deterministic tests will get ignored too. At that point you've lost the whole game and might as well get rid of all the tests.*[29]

Test-Driven Development

Test-Driven Development (TDD) is one of those nifty little practices that initially feels awkward but soon becomes a natural integral part of our daily work. This practice has a long and successful story, coming in part from XP where unit tests are written before any actual application code work begins.

---

[29]"Eradicating Non-Determinism in Tests," Martin Fowler, 4/14/2011. https://martinfowler.com/articles/nonDeterminism.html.

Under XP's doctrine, a programmer is not finished until she cannot come up with any further conditions under which the code can fail. The goal is to force us to think about failure conditions of any line of code very early on. Like the body's immune system, following this practice provides a seemingly small incremental gain that accumulates over time as the system grows in competence; the next time a defect of this type comes up, our code's "antibodies" have a good chance of picking up on this early on and the defect can be quickly identified and removed.

The steps in TDD follow a logical path:

1. A new unit test is written that covers the asked-for functionality.

2. The test is run and verified that it does fail as expected.

3. Just enough code is written to verify that the new test will pass.

4. The test is run again – does the new test pass? Are any other tests failing?

5. Refactoring – remove any code smells from the production and test code and run tests again.

We personally love Uncle Bob's Three Rules of TDD as a touchstone:

- You are not allowed to write any production code unless it is to make a failing unit test pass.

- You are not allowed to write any more of a unit test than is sufficient to fail, and compilation failures are failures.

- You are not allowed to write any more production code than is sufficient to pass the one failing unit test.

Uncle Bob – otherwise known as Robert C Martin, one of the original signers of the Agile Manifesto – made it clear that the order of these rules was a deliberate choice:

I have often compared TDD to double-entry bookkeeping. The act of stating every bit of logic twice, once in a test, and once in the production code, is very similar to the accounting practice of entering every transaction twice, once on the asset side, and once on the liability side. The running of the tests is very similar to the creation of the balance sheet. If the balance of assets and liabilities isn't zero, somebody made a mistake somewhere. So stating that there are places that TDD doesn't work may seem like stating that there are places where double entry bookkeeping doesn't work. [30]

---

[30] "When TDD doesn't work," Robert Martin. The Clean Code Blog, 4/30/2014. https://8thlight.com/blog/uncle-bob/2014/04/30/When-tdd-does-not-work.html.

TDD has some notable benefits. First, it's a known pattern and easy to add as part of your team's Definition of Done. With TDD, tests are not being run once every week or so, but many times a day, potentially thousands of times. With each programmer checking his changes often, we get a fast feedback loop – and it's easier to back out changes instead of trying to track down root cause and try a different approach. TDD tends to encourage thinking about testable design – decoupled, with a clear separation of concerns. Our test code also can become a kind of living document defining how the system was designed and supposed to work – right down to the creation of objects, API invocation, etc.

Brian Blackman loves TDD as a practice and told us that it goes with DevOps like peanut butter and jelly:

> You have to figure out where you're going to get the most value from testing and focus on that. With TDD, you're working on test layer while the development is happening because both those roles are embedded with the team – DevOps and TDD go together like peanut butter and jelly. The cycle is so short now that testing the UI layer and lots of brittle acceptance tests makes almost no sense.

> That shift has been a huge challenge for most organizations I visit. We still see siloes where testing is kept separate and code is thrown over the wall – even if the developer and the tester are one cubicle apart. I think there's one team I worked with in Portland that had integrated testing teams with the developers – their code coverage metric was 100%, and they always kept it at that level. But that's just one company out of the hundreds of companies that I've worked with! Every other customer I've worked with, they box off the testers and keep them separate. And it just doesn't work... Let the deep testers do what they do well – higher level integration level testing, and testing in production.[31]

Tyler Hardison of Redhawk loves TDD especially for greenfield projects:

> I absolutely follow TDD if I can start the project from the ground up. Using it is terrific practice, and it's definitely less overhead than pair programming – you're going to be more disciplined about how you're structuring your functions, and it's actually a protection for the developer – now we can deliver results to spec, we can prove the solution is working exactly as designed. But if you're going into a project late game, it's very difficult to ramp up to that level.

---

[31] Interview of Brian Blackman by Dave Harrison, see Appendix.

I'm facing that now with one of my projects. Once we hit a point of stability and the feature sets are locked, we'll likely peel them off into microservices, each with a battery of unit tests. We'll put in the results we want, have it run red, then add the code to make it green. But you don't always need that kind of overhead, and sometimes you truly can't control the environment. You won't need TDD if you're writing a report off a SQL database for example. But if you're working on a true backbone system, definitely go down the TDD road.[32]

We acknowledge that there's some pains that come with TDD. There is usually a steep learning curve where it feels awkward, slow, and granular. Over time, in most cases, the patience pays off – developers begin to think about testable architecture. Structures begin to be shaped with high cohesion and low coupling; well-defined interfaces start becoming the de facto means of communication with independent layers, and more testing is done against APIs instead of the UI layer.

We're not going to say that you're missing the boat if you're not doing TDD. Some have found TDD to not fit their particular use case; the most substantial argument we have heard is that it doesn't catch one of the most frequent sources of errors, config mismatches, and data mismatches. There will never be a single universal engineering method that will work in every and all cases; the point is that your team buys into the principles behind quality and continual improvement. As long as every member of your team is factoring testing and quality into their daily work habits, it's a win regardless of how your testing looks or is called in theory. [33]

What About Pair Programming?

We'd be remiss as well if we didn't mention another practice we've inherited from XP, pair programming. Several companies we spoke to found that code reviews were causing work to pile up as their more experienced developers were in short supply; they found pair programming to be an invaluable substitute. In one study, paired programmers were found to slow up work slightly – 15% slower than two individual programmers – but increased the amount of error free code by 70–85%. The study found that pairs consider more design alternatives and end up with more maintainable, simpler designs than solo coders, design defects were caught earlier, and it acted as a great knowledge spreader. After some initial bumps, 96% of those surveyed said that they enjoyed their work more.[34]

---

[32]Interview of Tyler Hardison by Dave Harrison, see Appendix.
[33]"Giving Up on Test-First Development," Luca Molteni. iansommerville, 3/17/2016. http://iansommerville.com/systems-software-and-technology/giving-up-on-test-first-development/.
[34]"The Costs and Benefits of Pair Programming," Alistair Cockburn, Laurie Williams, 1/1/2001. https://collaboration.csc.ncsu.edu/laurie/Papers/XPSardinia.PDF.

But we also want you to keep in mind that principle of autonomy and self-governing teams; be careful about the tendency to regulate "best practices" across delivery teams. For example, Aaron Bjork told us that the shift to unit testing has paid off handsomely for Microsoft, but that management deliberately chose not to mandate practices like TDD and pair programming:

> We've gone through a big movement in the past few years where we took our entire test bed, which was largely automated UI focused, and flipped it on its head. Now we are running much fewer automated UI tests and a ton of what we call L1 and L2 tests, which are essentially unit tests at the lowest levels checking components and end to end capabilities. This allows us to run through our test cycle much faster, like every commit. I think you still have to do some level of acceptance testing; just determine what level works for your software base and helps drive quality.
>
> …Pair programming is accepted widely as a best practice; it's also a culture that shapes how we write code. The interesting thing here is we don't mandate pair programming. We do teach it; some of our teams have embraced pair programming and it works great for them, always writing in tandem. Other teams have tried it, and it just hasn't fit. We do enforce consistency on some things across our 40 different teams; others we let the team decide. Pair programming and XP practices are one thing we leave up to the devs; we treat them as adults and don't shove one way of thinking down their throats.[35]

Defect-Driven Testing

One very pragmatic approach – and the one Ben's team ends up going with – is to tip your cap to TDD in principle but apply it only to new feature work or where defects arise in existing code.

Jared Richardson has found success in many cases by not insisting on a complete refactor with TDD of an existing codebase, but by something he calls "Defect-Driven Testing" – focusing a team's testing efforts on any new bugs that appear. When a bug is reported, the team adds a test that catches the defect. This way, instead of drowning in a neverending to-do list of tests to write for a large codebase, the team is focusing on the areas that are causing trouble. We like this approach as it honors the basic principles of TDD – start

---

[35]Interview of Aaron Bjork by Dave Harrison, see Appendix.

first with a failed test covering the asked-for functionality or broken code – and builds in quality as an incremental program, without having to launch an all-hands-on-deck type war on untested code.[36]

Jon Cwiak from Humana stated to us that testing remains the most obvious culprit in slow release cycles. He has found the self-documentation aspect of a well-designed unit test framework to be a valuable selling point. He also found defect-driven testing to be a viable approach:

> *The big blocker for most organizations seems to be testing. Developers want to move at speed, but the way we test – usually manually – and our lack of investment in automated unit tests creates these long test cycles which in turn spawns these long-lived release branches. The obvious antidote are feature toggles to decouple deployment from delivery.*

> *…A big part of the journey for us is designing architectures so that they are inherently testable, mockable. I'm more interested in test driven design than I am test driven development personally, because it forces me to think in terms of – how am I going to test this? What are my dependencies, how can I fake or mock them so that the software is verifiable?*

> *The carrot I use in talking about this shift and convincing them to invest in unit testing is, not only is this your safety net, it's a living, breathing definition of what the software does. So for example, when you get a new person on the team, instead of weeks of manual onboarding, you use the working test harness to introduce them to how the software behaves and give them a comfort level in making modifications safely.*

> *The books don't stress enough how difficult this is. There's just not the ROI to support creating a fully functional set of tests with a brownfield software package in most cases. So you start with asking, where does this hurt most? – using telemetry or tools like SonarQube. And then you invest in slowing down, then stopping the bleeding.*[37]

---

[36]"Defect Driven Testing: Your Ticket Out the Door at Five O'Clock," Jared Richardson. Dzone.com, 8/4/2010. https://dzone.com/articles/defect-driven-testing-your. Note his thoughts on combating bugs, which tend to come in clusters, with what he calls 'testing jazz' – thinking in riffs with dozens of tests checking an issue like invalid spaces in input.

[37]Interview of Jon Cwiak by Dave Harrison, see Appendix.

What About Outsourcing?

Ben's experience of constantly hearing objections about offshoring or nearshoring QA is quite common nowadays. He's correct in his guess that the real issue is that quality is being envisioned as that other person's job, vs. the exact location of the team.

The book *Accelerate* draws on almost a decade of annual surveys to state that outsourced third party testing programs and separate QA teams are both equally ineffective. The optimal solution is always to have the people writing the code also write the testing harness accompanying the code – it forces more testable software architecture and, even more importantly, makes developers care more about the quality of their work:

> *It's interesting to note that having automated tests primarily created and maintained either by QA or an outsourced party is not correlated with IT performance. The theory behind this is that when developers are involved in creating and maintaining acceptance tests, there are two important effects. First, the code becomes more testable when developers write tests. This is one of the main reasons why test-driven development (TDD) is an important practice – it forces developers to create more testable designs. Second, when developers are responsible for the automated tests, they care more about them and will invest more effort into maintaining and fixing them.*[38]

Continuous Delivery repeats this:

> *A common practice in many orgs is to have a separate team dedicate to the production and maintenance of the test suite. Devs then feel they don't own the acceptance tests, so they don't pay attention to failure at this late stage, so it stays broken for long periods of time. Acceptance tests written without dev involvement tend to be tightly coupled to the UI and thus brittle and badly factored.*[39]

Munil Shah of Microsoft told us it was shocking how many companies treat QA as a second-class concern:

---

[38]"Accelerate: The Science of Lean Software and DevOps: Building and Scaling High Performing Technology Organizations," Nicole Forsgren PhD, Jez Humble, Gene Kim. IT Revolution Press, 3/27/2018. ISBN-10: 1942788339, ISBN-13: 978-1942788331.
[39]"Continuous Delivery: Reliable Software Releases through Build, Test, and Deployment Automation," Jez Humble, David Farley. Addison-Wesley Professional, 8/6/2010. ISBN-10: 9780321601919, ISBN-13: 978-0321601919.

It boggles my mind when companies tell me, "Oh we have a team in India that does the testing, and we get a report back on bugs." To me that's a fundamental part of the engineering system that you are choosing to ignore, to outsource – you just can't do that. Think about all the real problems that get swept under the rug, the opportunity cost from all the feedback you're never seeing![40]

So, offshoring or nearshoring is not a bad practice in itself; nearshore programming teams have saved our bacon several times where dates were fixed and resources limited. However, when we start to see functional splits where code is being written in one area and tested in another – that's where quality, inevitably, becomes someone else's job. And that, time and again, is where testing starts inevitably to lag behind.

Is a QA Team an Antipattern?

Ben's diagnosis of the issues with his late-stage QA processes being linked to the friction and waste associated with delays and handoffs is rock-solid. As we've discussed earlier, good testing isn't a separate phase of software development. It also requires some heavy thinking about software design and architecture. It's impossible to create an effective test suite unless QA/testers and developers are collaborating and working together on a daily basis. It's also important to curate and weed your testing garden to get rid of flaky or broken tests. And coming up on the horizon for our team – testing just gets better when combined with infrastructure as code and provisioning environments (including test) on demand, corralling the issues of runaway configurations and unrepeatable snowflake environments.

So, in Ben's specific situation, breaking up QA – as was also done at Microsoft – made great sense. That's not saying that a QA team is an antipattern or a bad thing in and of itself, as Tyler Hardison told us in our interview:

I don't agree that it's necessarily an antipattern to have a separate QA team. For example, we used to have BSA's acting as QA internal in every team. Well, a BSA's goals primarily are to get product out the door as soon as possible – that's not a great position to focus on quality.

So for the first time we created a QA team that would service both the internal and eCommerce web development teams. This QA team had an entirely different direct report, so you'd think we'd be at odds right away – that's a silo right? Only, we made it very clear that QA would need to be involved in the development work from the first day. So as they're meeting

---

[40]Interview of Munil Shah by Dave Harrison, see Appendix.

with the business stakeholders and mapping out their requirements, you'd have the devs madly scribbling out the functional expectations – and the QA person was taking notes about what the final product should look like; and they'd be there at standups and at followup meetings, writing their tests and refining them in parallel with the code being stood up, and participating in peer reviews. We didn't have siloing, and our quality really took off.[41]

We'd be horrified if someone read these words and came away with the message that *"QA is ineffective!"* or *"Let's fire our QA people and replace them with coders who test!"* QA people are valuable resources and subject matter experts that the entire team needs to learn from. The move to distribute QA so that testers are working alongside developers is an important step to remove their testing bottleneck; it'd be irresponsible for Ben to do anything else. But the work these testers will do is now going to change; their main focus will be helping to create a viable set of automated unit tests alongside coders and refining their test layer.

Definition of Done, Family Dinner Code Reviews

When we can no longer change a situation, we are challenged to change ourselves.

—Viktor Frankl

Learn from the mistakes of others. You can't live long enough to make them all yourself.

— Eleanor Roosevelt

Rules are for the obedience of fools and the guidance of wise men.

— Douglas Bader

Does it seem odd we're bringing up the unsexy topic of peer reviews so much?

While release management software is getting all glammed up and hitting the town at midnight, peer reviews are settling into a frumpy sweater and downing some warm milk for a good night's sleep. And yet, without getting this practice squared away, Ben's team will quickly slip back into a rut. There's a huge potential advantage in learning and sharing information across the team that is being squandered.

---

[41] Interview of Tyler Hardison by Dave Harrison, see Appendix.

As Jeff Atwood once wrote:

> *...I believe that peer code reviews are the single biggest thing you can do to improve your code. If you're not doing code reviews right now with another developer, you're missing a lot of bugs in your code and cheating yourself out of some key professional development opportunities. As far as I'm concerned, my code isn't done until I've gone over it with a fellow developer.*[42]

And Nathen Harvey of Chef went so far as to say that effective code reviews are the foundation of continuous delivery:

> *If you want to get to continuous delivery, you start with effective code reviews. Of course you should have a release pipeline. But that's meaningless until you can assess what the code is doing, and if it's not too clever. Clever code is terrific until it breaks, and then you need that genius engineer that wrote it 6 months ago to fix it, because they're the only one that can understand it!*

> *Once you're doing regular code reviews, you can come up with practices, opportunities for improvement or automation. Can we bring in static analysis tools? Should we use spaces or tabs with our conventions? Pick one, and then build it into the pipeline as part of a release gate. I do think you need to enforce it – it really helps if you have some clear rules in place, a guardrail.*[43]

Peer Reviews Are the Point of the Spear

Once when Dave was working for a large insurance provider, he was given the task of coming up with coding standards. He sunk weeks into producing a hefty, thick binder covering any and all aspects of coding in excruciating, eye-numbing detail, from naming conventions to secure code guidelines. Predictably, it went directly to his manager's bookshelf as an official "standard" that never saw actual use – except as a trump card in case an argument was being lost with a fellow manager over process. Those several weeks of effort went almost completely to waste.

Almost. That dusty binder was a complete timesink, true, but the peer review step we rolled out afterward paid off in ways that shocked everyone. Having changes checked over forced everyone to produce better quality

---

[42]"Code Reviews: Just Do It," Jeff Atwood. Coding Horror blog, 1/21/2006. https://blog.codinghorror.com/code-reviews-just-do-it. A true classic!
[43]Interview of Nathen Harvey by Dave Harrison, see Appendix.

work. Applications that were formerly shrouded in mystery became more transparent, both in their purpose and how to maintain them safely. And the team started to play more like a team – with idea sharing and little course corrections becoming a part of the way we did our work daily. Like compound interest, the payoffs seen with peer reviews seem minor but aggregate powerfully over time.

We won't discuss the difference between an informal walkthrough, an inspection (three to eight people with a moderator), and a full-on peer review here. For every positive example of where enterprises have over time adopted a strategy using all three of these, there's others where the review process is overbaked and actually impedes velocity without improving quality – usually due to underlying political or personality issues. The team's approach to tuning their existing informal approach so it's got a little more teeth is incremental and has a much better chance of achieving its goals than a full-scale jump to Orwellian bureaucracy.

Keep It Positive

Key though is to prevent the "gauntlet" antipattern that Harry is attracted to in "Are We Done Yet?":

> *Keep your ego out of reviews! This isn't an arena for oneupmanship. If you go in with the intent to show your brilliance, tear down another coder, or otherwise beat them over the head with your experience, do everyone a favor and don't bother reviewing the code at all. A code review with ego attached is far worse than no review at all.*[44]

Harry's points on style conventions and commenting actually have some validity. The way he was conveying them though did not fit the learning-oriented culture that the team is striving for. Perhaps, down the road, the team will experiment more with having specific style guidelines, and linter checks form a part of their pre–check-in process so the review process becomes more consistent, productive, and relatively painless. Having each person come into the review prepared with a checklist (to catch errors of omission, what's been left out) and checking code for quality (for example, ensuring that demos are run in production like conditions with well designed automated tests) seems like an excellent step forward.

---

[44]"Humanizing Peer Reviews," Karl Wiegers. Addison-Wesley, 11/2/2001. ISBN-13: 978-0201734850.

Some companies we spoke to found tools like CheckStyle and SwiftClean to be particularly valuable in enforcing some consistency with distributed teams and producing high-quality code. Failing builds for warnings and code style breaches comes with a cost; these enterprises found the rewards in terms of less time spent refactoring and cleaning up code smells to more than outweigh the tax paid on check-in.

Tyler Hardison of Redhawk gave us some great pointers:

> *Team dynamics can be fragile and you have to work to keep the dynamic positive. For example, we knew regular code reviews were important and wanted to make them positive and upbuilding, a learning experience versus a beatdown by the silverback devs. At the time we had about 4 or 5 projects running at a time. Each week we would either nominate a volunteer or have a specific developer scheduled if it involved some cool new feature or library. The way we set up our weekly code reviews was with the clear understanding along kindergarten rules – everyone has to be polite. You're picking apart someone's sandcastle, something they've spent time on and are proud of. So don't go kicking it down; play nice.*

> *It's a balance – you want it to be useful and have some teeth to prevent bad code smells from replicating, but you also don't want to show disrespect or be overly critical. Sometimes there's legitimate reasons why the person writing that code approached it from a completely different perspective, and his or her solution is perfectly valid. So we would encourage questions that would gather detail about the context, questions like:*

> - *"Have you considered ..." (not, "Why did you...")*
> - *"What was your thought process when you started this?"*
> - *"Why did you choose that particular library over others?"*

> *...We encouraged empathy; everyone in that room had released horribly visible and embarrassing bugs at some point in their career. The point was to learn for next time, not to crucify the poor guy.*

> *... A lot of managers don't realize what a fundamental difference it makes – how we react when there's an outage or a failure. Sometimes you'd swear that the poor coder is a puppy and it's everyone's job to rub his nose in it when there's a screwup. It leads to people being afraid to do anything, it leads to strained or blocked communication and collaboration, and inevitably to a lot of turnover. That banking team I mentioned happens to work in a very challenging environment, where there's all*

kinds of security constraints and regulatory standards – but they have very low turnover. That trust is part of the team fabric, and it all starts with showing mutual respect during the tough times.[45]

Peer Review Do's and Don'ts

We believe the following practices and patterns are good guidelines to follow to keep your peer reviews helpful, kind, and learning-focused:

Family Dinner Code Reviews – Guiding Principles

Have them, and have them more often.

Make sure that they have teeth.

Timebox and scope what is under review.

Have a focus or theme.

Don't make assumptions – ask.

Don't nitpick – play nice with others.

This is about learning and getting better.

Let's discuss these in more detail:

- **Make sure you have them.** The worst peer review is a gauntlet dominated by style thugs more interested in supremacy games vs. learning and teaching. The second worst is none at all. Resist the pressure to cut the peer review process due to time constraints – remember, "quality can't shift."

- **Do peer reviews more often.** This means at least once weekly, but hopefully more often. This is the backbone of your pipeline and release process so make it a priority. Ideally, it will be a part of your daily routine. Try doing this for half an hour each day for a sprint as a trial and see if you don't get better results.

- **They need to have teeth.** Remember it's just as much of a mistake to make your peer reviews freeform and informal as it is to build a nightmarishly bureaucratic and document-driven process. A simple review checklist updated by the entire team helps ensure consistency and fairness, and especially helps catch missing pieces

---

[45]Interview with Tyler Hardison by Dave Harrison, see Appendix.

and omissions. Good code reviews take time and are worth the effort. If you haven't found anything specific to improve on, odds are you didn't spend enough time and missed something.

- **Timebox and scope what's being reviewed.** We do better with smaller amounts of functionality to review and in limited timeboxes. It's good to limit what you review to no more than 400 LOC (200 is best), 60 minutes at a time (10–30 minutes is better).

- **If you don't understand, don't make assumptions – ask.** Devs need to consider better commenting to make it easier on "the next guy." If you're having trouble understanding some new functionality or change as a reviewer, don't move on. Make sure you ask the questions needed to understand what goal the code is trying to address and how it goes about that task. Some reviewers ask questions – "how will this code work in the real world? Does it handle bad input/user error? Does it play well with the rest of the app?"

- **Don't nitpick or forget priorities.** First comes functionality, then maintainability, last comes optimization. Don't obsess over your favorite style if it can and should be caught by your automated CI tooling with lint scanning. Code reviews should be about larger things than the type of nitpicking Harry is obsessing about in this section; consistent styles can and should be enforced as part of a ruleset as part of every check-in.

- **Kindergarten rules – play nice.** If people are leaving these meetings feeling bullied or humiliated by senior or alpha-type chest-thumpers, your review process is getting subverted by politics and personalities. Management and the team needs to catch this behavior early on and nip it in the bud. Stress at each meeting that this is a chance for everyone to learn and share information. We like Paul Saffo's quip that at Google they favor "strong opinions that are weakly held."

- **Have a focus.** This isn't a design review – that's a separate step that happens much earlier. You could have separate reviews focusing on performance, another on security, or globalization, or supportability – folding in the right people who've made that area their niche.

- **Remember this is all about learning and getting better.** So managers should never use code defect density in performance evaluations or to provide negative feedback later on. Instead, show by conduct and words that defects are positive, and the point of the process is to find and fix as many of these as possible. Who "caused" them is not the focus.

We agree with Kief Morris in calling this renewed focus on producing clean code a return of craftmanship – and that a tradeoff between velocity and quality is a false choice:

> In the past few years, there has been a renewed focus on "clean code" and software craftsmanship, which is as relevant to infrastructure coders as to software developers. Many people see a trade-off between pragmatism (i.e., getting things done) and engineering quality (i.e., building things right). This is a false dichotomy. Poor-quality software, and poor-quality infrastructure, is difficult to maintain and improve. Choosing to throw something up quickly, knowing it probably has problems, leads to an unstable system, where problems are difficult to find and fix. Adding or improving functionality on a spaghetti-code system is also hard, typically taking surprisingly long to make what should be a simple change, and creating more errors and instability.
>
> Craftsmanship is about making sure that what you build works right, and ensuring that loose ends are not left hanging. It means building systems that another professional can quickly and easily understand. When you make a change to a cleanly built system, you are confident that you understand what parts of the system the change will affect.
>
> Clean code and software craftsmanship are not an excuse for over-engineering. The point is not to make things orderly to satisfy a compulsive need for structure. It isn't necessary to build a system that can handle every conceivable future scenario or requirement. Much the opposite. The key to a well-engineered system is simplicity. Build only what you need, then it becomes easier to make sure what you have built is correct. Reorganize code when doing so clearly adds value – for instance, when it makes the work you're currently doing easier and safer. Fix 'broken windows' when you find them.[46]

---

[46] "Infrastructure as Code: Managing Servers in the Cloud," Kief Morris. O'Reilly Media, 6/27/2016. ISBN-10: 1491924357, ISBN-13: 978-1491924358.

The Value of a Written Definition of Done

It's normal for the team's Definition of Done – a simple declaration of what complete code means – to change over time. Microsoft's Azure DevOps team began with their DoD stating that code should be "potentially shippable"; over time this evolved to "shipped." After introducing better telemetry and hypothesis-driven development, the delivery teams changed their Definition of Done to "Live in production, collecting telemetry that examines the hypothesis which motivated the deployment." This sets a customer-focused finish line: work is not "done" until it is live in production and telemetry is being gathered to demonstrate whether desired goals are being reached.

One of our favorite authors, Gary Gruver, pointed out that an explicit Definition of Done and canary releases can be your best protection against having poor-quality "hot" projects sabotage your release velocity:

> [Hot] projects tend to come in with the worst quality, which means every other project on the release has to wait until the really bad project is ready before the release branch can go to production. This type of behavior tends to lead to longer release branches and less frequent releases.
>
> To address this, the organization needs to start changing their definition of done. The code can and should be brought in but not exposed to the customer until it meets the new definition of done. If the organization is going to move to releasing more frequently, the new definition of done needs to change to include the following: all the stories are signed off, the automated testing is in place and passing, and there are no known open defects.[47]

Remember that military axiom, "the standard you walk past is the standard you accept." Keeping consistent, easily enforceable standards as embodied in an agreed upon Definition of Done and enforced on check-in will go a long way toward correcting quality issues early on before they become expensive problems in production.

---

[47]"Start and Scaling Devops in the Enterprise," Gary Gruver. BookBaby, 12/1/2016. ISBN-10: 1483583589, ISBN-13: 978-1483583587.

Besieging the Mountain

Another 3 months goes by, and spring gives way to the full heat of summer. After a difficult adjustment period, some of the efforts that the team has put into a "shift left" movement – including breaking up their siloed QA team – starts to bear fruit. Both their defect rate and release velocity numbers show significant improvement after a slight sag early on. Even better, that vital connection to Ben's customers and stakeholders seems to be thawing somewhat. Putting quality first instead of speed, it turns out, enabled the team to deliver both.

Some of the changes that they've made that had great impact include

- A start in mapping out the flow of value with their more sensitive work streams, identifying limiting factors, and pain points

- More productive code reviews, catching defects earlier in the delivery cycle

- Shifting left – beginning to move toward test-driven development and a more robust automated test layer

- A community-driven Center of Excellence (CoE) around quality, exploring more testable app designs and improving reusable test frameworks

- Scorecards tracking technical debt and quality, visible to all

© Dave Harrison and Knox Lively 2019
D. Harrison and K. Lively, Achieving DevOps,
https://doi.org/10.1007/978-1-4842-4388-6_4

This doesn't mean smooth sailing however. Ben's team still hasn't done enough when it comes to engaging with stakeholders. They're still spending too much time on gold-plating features that are delivering negative value, and their infrastructure provisioning process is still manual, time-intensive, and error-prone. There is still a lot of debt to pay down. And they aren't really paying any kind of attention to improving the limiting factors constricting their flow around provisioning environments.

Will Ben and his team be able to keep ratcheting forward on their quality-driven initiatives, or will old habits and the politically charged atmosphere of WonderTek start to drag on their progress?

No Shame, No Blame (Blameless Postmortems)

"I was up most of the night on the Slack channel war room, so if I'm a little groggy you'll have to forgive me." Emily smiles grimly. She doesn't look tired, I think. She looks angry. "So once again, we find ourselves in this room trying to figure out how to dig our way out of the mess the development team has made."

We are making some progress but critsits still happen, and it's become obvious that we'll need to change some of our behaviors and reactions on a fundamental level. Thankfully, I've been preparing the ground for this for some weeks now. Elaine nods and gives me a slow smile, and says to Emily brightly, "Well, we know many of us were up for much of the night, and we appreciate you attending this meeting now while it's still fresh. I'm the facilitator of this meeting, which means I'm responsible to enforce our ground rules. But anyone and everyone in this room can call out when we start straying." She displays the following slide:

Blameless Postmortems – our rules of the road
"Your organization must continually affirm that individuals are never the 'root cause' of outages."
– Dave Zwieback

- We know that everyone here in the room today had good motives and were making the best decisions they could with the information they had on hand.
- Our mission is to identify root causes, not find culprits.
- We want to learn from this so our processes are safer and more reliable.
- Counterfactual language is not allowed in this room.

Meeting Format	
9:00-9:30	Event Timeline
9:30-9:45	Open Discussion
9:45-9:55	Remediation Items

Emily snorts contemptuously. "Sounds like this is a pretty weak attempt to get out of accountability, Ben. I've never run a retrospective like this – if we don't hold people responsible, our failure rates are going to get worse, not better." She leans back, folding her arms and glaring at me. "I'm not leaving this room until we know who caused this failure and what they're going to do to fix it."

Alex says, "I think we all know that in complex systems there's rarely one root cause. I'm agreeing with the ground rules here – we need to explore what happened, and get the facts straight. But I'm not worried about our people, whether they're wearing an Operations hat or a Developer hat, being accountable. I know everyone here made decisions last night the same way they do every day, based on what they thought was right for the company. It's our processes that may need some tweaking, so those decisions are better informed. Usually that means putting up some guardrails."

Emily is smirking contemptuously at what she clearly thinks is a bunch of hippie nonsense. Her back is to the door, so she doesn't see Douglas coming in as she says, "On my team and on the systems we support, we've found that things don't just break on their own. Someone rolled out a patch, or someone changed an application, and due diligence wasn't done. If you don't want these things to repeat over and over again, we have to bring them out in the open."

Elaine says evenly, "I completely agree. We're not going to sugarcoat what happened or try to sweep things under the table. Our objective here is to collect a full account of what happened – in fact, we're going to spend the next hour coming up with a complete timeline of the facts. We won't move on until the events and contributing factors are listed and we agree on them. But we're not going to name, blame or shame anyone for what happened yesterday.

For us to collect all the detail we need, everyone here needs to understand and agree that failure is a normal part of maintaining complex systems. Our objective is not to punish but to learn what we can do to prevent this from reoccurring or limit the blast radius next time.

"Now, first and most important question – is everyone that we need here in this room?"

Emily stabs her finger at me. "Hang on. My people were up most of the night because of the devs pulling their usual cowboy shenanigans. These problems aren't going away and they need to be addressed, with names. If we're not going to drill down to who did what and when, why for God's sake are we even here?"

Like I said before, I respect Emily, and she does a fantastic job of protecting and supporting her team. But her instinct to point fingers when something goes awry is hurting us, and I decided weeks ago to put some countermeasures in place to head off any Ops-instigated witch hunts.

For the past quarter, we've put our focus as a team on testing early and often, with the goal of improving our release reliability and frequency. Alex, George, and I have been talking for weeks at changing the way we react to mistakes and outages. I remember in particular in a past company a manager I used to work for named Cliff, who believed whole-heartedly in the "bad apple theory" – that a little public shaming was key to prevent people from making errors in judgment. If a build broke, Cliff would bring by a dancing chipmunk doll and leave it at the desk of whoever broke the latest release. Anyone who wanted to could walk by that cubicle and hit a button, and the chipmunk would start jiggling around, singing "I'm All Right." He'd also hold weekly "Zero Defect" meetings where upper level management would call in the offending developer and put them through a gauntlet of would-have, should-have interrogation.

This drive for "better visibility and accountability" had an immediate impact, but not like Cliff expected. His team's releases dried up almost immediately, going slower and slower as people tried to keep their heads down and avoid the dreaded dancing chipmunk. But this caused more work to pile up and the release changes to get bigger, increasing the risk of breakages and lengthening resolution time. And root causes were rarely addressed; by making the person the problem, they missed opportunities to improve their process.

I learned a lot from how Cliff's worldview impacted his team. One thing was – it's never people that are the problem – there's always something missing or flawed with the process. The team is starting to reduce its technical debt, but I can't let what I call process debt accumulate unseen. Process debt is as big a problem as technical debt in every company I've ever worked for, and it always seems to come down to how we view errors, and whether learning is safe. Right now, our lack of automation or controls in several spots in our release process makes learning a very risky proposition.

I pick my battles but decided a month ago that this was one that was worth fighting. I lean forward and address Emily directly. "There's two ways of looking at faults like these. We can say, these people are bad, our systems would be fine if we didn't have these careless, incompetent people messing around with them and creating work for everyone else. By calling them out and shaming them, we'll prevent this from happening again and make them be more careful. That's a very comforting, satisfying way of looking at things, and it's how we've run our postmortems in the past. Like Elaine says, though, it won't help us in prevention down the road because we haven't identified the root cause."

Emily smiles like a cat with a fresh bowl of milk. "It sounds to me like you don't like process period, Ben. I've never seen you at our CAB meetings, or at the Zero Defect meetings I've held."

I actually have attended a few but stopped after a few rounds when it became clear what the tone would be. I have to tread lightly here though; both of these meetings are held in high esteem by some of our management team. Calling them out as unproductive snipe hunts will not win me any friends in the executive suites. "The company is asking us to do work, Emily. Mistakes are a byproduct of work. I'm OK with people making stupid mistakes – because I do too, every day. But a zero-defect meeting is coming at things from the wrong angle. I'm not a zero-defect person, and you're not either.

"What I'm not OK with is people making the same stupid mistakes as last time. That means we will be sharing this openly with everyone. That kind of transparency requires us to be honest and focus on the context of good people making decisions based on limited information and complex and imperfect processes. Now, these rules shouldn't surprise anyone. They're right there in the meeting agenda. If anyone disagrees with them, they need to either adjust their thinking or leave the room. Can we move forward now?"

While I've been talking, Emily has been scanning the room and spots Douglas, who has a carefully neutral expression on his face but is paying very close attention to this showdown. She smiles sweetly at me, all sugar and sparkles. "Of course! Just as long as we make clear exactly what happened and publish it, I think that would satisfy everyone."

Elaine continues to explain the meeting structure. For the next 30 minutes, we're going to reconstruct a timeline of what happened. Here, our goal is not to rush to any fixes – we're just listing what happened, what our expectations were and assumptions that were made, and what effects we observed. Until the timeline and events are agreed upon, the meeting will not move forward to potential remediation items.

The engineer who made the changes in this broken release, Ryan, groans softly. With slumped shoulders, he begins displaying the release notes and logs. Most of the great programmers don't exactly have the presentation skills of

Steve Jobs; that, combined with the harsh glare of being under a microscope, is definitely working against Ryan. His forehead is sweaty, and he's having trouble looking anyone in the eye, the picture of guilt and shame.

The facts as they are don't reflect particularly well on anyone. Ryan had been working on a change that involved trimming some user accounts and adding a new column to the users table. The PowerShell script implementing this had been tested and was checked into source control as part of a scheduled build at 5:30 p.m., about the end of the working day. At 7:45 that evening, they started getting reports from users that logins were not working, neither were payments or searches. The support team had tried reaching the on-call developer, Alex, but he was at the gym and had his phone on airplane mode.

Rolling back the release failed to resolve the issue, as the database model changes weren't rolled back to the previous version and it left the UI in an inconsistent state. It took several more hours for the developers on call and the support team to track down the account issue, get Ryan on the phone, and get the website back to a stable state.

I'd been on the war room channel along with several others, but felt helpless to influence the outcome. It looked for a while like the website might be out for an entire day, a very visible disaster and one their competitors were sure to capitalize on. Douglas had been surprisingly calm when I updated him on what had happened, and I took the opportunity to explain to him how we were going to handle the postmortem process.

Ivan from the Ops team was filling out some events for the rollback timeline. My head snaps up as he finishes by saying, "It seems pretty obvious from the logs that Ryan should have noticed this flaw earlier in the release process, and we wasted hours trying to get ahold of him. The fact that he went dark like he did really slowed us up."

Elaine, who has been writing down some notes, stops and says, "OK, so we all remember the ground rules right? Here, let's display them again." She shows the first screen and the item about counterfactual thinking being verboten. "My job as a facilitator is to make sure we don't say anything like 'could have' or 'should have'. That's hindsight bias – it assumes that there's a neat, linear, predictable path where everything goes perfectly if X didn't happen."

Emily laughs shortly. "Elaine, with all due respect, all WOULD have gone perfectly if Ryan hadn't kicked off a release that he hadn't tested thoroughly and then gone to polish his guns at the gym."

I say sternly, "It seems to me like we keep getting back into this rut of trying to blame and punish, and that's not productive. Maybe we need to change our habits so we are checking in and pushing releases earlier in the day, but I don't remember us ever making that a written rule in the past. Ryan didn't do anything that I and a few others haven't done in the past."

George is nodding his head in agreement. "Decisions aren't made in a vacuum. We're trying to understand the context better and what we knew at the time, and dig a little behind the obvious. It's what Etsy calls 'second stories' when they're doing their postmortems."

"If that rollback script had been checked over by anyone with an eye for detail, it would have clearly obvious that it was removing some admin level accounts," Ivan counters. "And not checking for the database rollback script was a particularly egregious oversight. I wish you guys would fold us in earlier when it comes to these deployments. It leaves us holding the bag when things break."

Alex and Elaine's face both go scarlet in unison, but before they can respond, Douglas slams his hand on the table. "Stop. Everybody just STOP."

The entire room goes silent, and Douglas stands up. His jaw is set, and he's glaring at Ivan and Emily. "In the military, we commonly did after-action reports. The one thing we NEVER did was to assume infallibility or perfect knowledge by the operatives. And we're looking for actionable, specific goals to target so problems don't reoccur."

He looks directly at Emily again, and there's not a trace of a smile. "Ben has been talking to me about this for the past few weeks, and I'm in agreement with him that this is the way our postmortems need to go. I'm comfortable that he's not trying to deflect responsibility or point fingers. If anyone here – anyone – is putting their political position ahead of the company's wellbeing, or trying to position this as a developer vs. operations problem, they're not thinking in terms of the team. And they don't belong here. Does everyone understand?"

Douglas' stance isn't a surprise to me; he cares very much about team cohesion and preaches unity and consensus. Ivan has gone silent under the assault; Emily is white-lipped with anger. I've never seen her at a loss for words like this, but I have to give her credit; she's unsinkable and unrelenting in her stance, even when her direct manager is in opposition.

Elaine begins the open discussion part of the meeting, and people began bringing out some options for fixes. Ryan offers that they should have considered doing additive changes only to the backend update script, where entities and columns can be added but never deleted – that way a database side rollback would be unnecessary. On changing the test layer, the group agrees that the unit tests had passed – the issue was higher level, something had broken major pieces of their functionality and had not been caught with their integration testing.

I decide it is time to offer an olive branch. "Ivan, Kevin, and Emily – I know you were all on the hot spot when this was going on. Did we detect something was wrong fast enough?" It turns out that alerts had gone out soon after the site went dead – but they were buried in thousands of other low- and midlevel alerts that day. The Operations dashboard showed all server-related metrics, like CPU and disk utilization. But there was no display of the uptime of the main site, response time for users displayed across all regions, or cart transactions per hour – any of which would have caught the issue several hours earlier.

As Elaine is writing down the need for a consistent dashboard showing the actual user experience – and an alerting system that isn't yipping like a hyperactive chihuahua – Emily interjects again. "Am I allowed to point out that this is not my team's responsibility? We build and provision the servers according to specs, keep our operating systems up-patched and maintain security of the network and infrastructure. That's it. We build the house, and we keep it standing, but we're not responsible for anything going on inside."

I've rarely seen Douglas this angry. "Emily, we seem to keep coming back to this. Ivan said a little earlier that Ops didn't feel included in this change. I'm confused – did Ben not invite you or anyone on your team to their daily sprint? Their retrospectives? What about their release planning session?" Emily's lips compress again into a thin white line, as Ivan mumbles something about being too tied down with an OS upgrade project. Douglas continues, "It seems to me that if our main site is down, then WE – the entire team – has a problem. And it seems to me that there's likely room for improvement across the entire team. Now if out of this mess we end up with a less noisy, more effective alerting system, that alone is worth it. I'd be delighted to see everyone looking at the same screen too. If all Operations is looking at are server uptime metrics, we're missing the point. Not one of our customers cares about our CPU utilization. Elaine, make sure that gets in the notes you send out." He looks at his phone, and says, "I have to go; thanks for inviting me. I am very interested in what you decide to implement so that this doesn't happen again. Remember, keep it small, keep it actionable, and make sure it gets done."

After he leaves, there's a silence that stretches on for a few uncomfortable moments. Emily and Ivan are on a slow simmer, Kevin is avoiding eye contact, and Alex and Elaine look unsettled and upset. Only George seems to have that unflappable calm that he wears like a coat.

We finally move on to discussing remediation steps around our on-call process. Kevin muses, "It seems to me like any release process where we have to hunt down a single developer to figure out what happened and how to reverse it has some weak points." This gets a general agreement, but we don't seem to have any specific ideas on how to address that; we put this as an open issue in our report and move on.

The subject of feature flags and canary releases came up – would the release have been safer if it could have been toggled or released out to specific customers in rings? Ryan says, "I really love the thought of being able to run out a release in one sprint – and then turning it on when we're good and ready. I'm not sure how that will work with a database model change like we're discussing though." This also gets added to our growing list of things to explore.

Another area of concern – the initial responders, it turned out, had not known how to do even basic troubleshooting or triage, and their contact list was months out of date. Alex takes as a to-do to meet with them next week and show how they could do some basic smoketesting and diagnose a few common issues.

As the meeting begins to wrap up, I add one more item to the to-do list. I say, "Ivan brought up that these changes came out of nowhere for the Operations team; I'm accepting that. I could have been involved in the weekly release planning meetings. I'll start attending, beginning next week."

Emily replies, "I thought you didn't like 'pin the tail on the donkey' games, Ben." Her smile is all honey and arsenic. Even as I grit my teeth, I find myself admiring her toughness; she's an indomitable political machine. If I don't mend some fences, I'm risking a very bloody trench war with my delivery partner that very well could end with my departure. I say quietly, "I'll cut you a deal. It might be too much to ask someone from your team to attend every single daily scrum we have. But it seems to me like we both need to work harder at coordination. So how does sound: if you attend our retrospectives and demo sessions, I'll attend the weekly release planning session. That way our retrospectives will have the whole story, including Operation's point of view. And I can keep your team better informed of what's going out the door."

I keep my promise and rarely miss a release planning session from that day on. Elaine's writeup is posted on our wiki, and we make sure that our bite-sized remediation steps are dropped onto our backlog.

I'd love to say that this ends the cold war, but old habits die hard. Emily's default position is – and probably always will be – to point fingers; it makes her a challenging and unreliable partner. But Douglas seems to be satisfied with our remediation steps, especially with the new dashboarding that began to appear in both the developer and support work areas. Showing numbers that mattered – like site response times and availability – and having the same displays in both areas began to have a subtle and very positive impact on how problems are handled at WonderTek.

When Is a "Requirement" Not a Requirement? (Hypothesis-Driven Development)

Padma has been working on a certification site for Human Resources for several months now; the design has gone through several changes, and it looks like at least another few sprints will be required to reach "feature complete" stage. At her request, I sit in on the next design review meeting along with Alex and their stakeholders. Invited to the meeting are a few people I have met only a few times in the past – the project business analyst, Torrey, and their HR stakeholder, Lisa.

The first thing I notice is that Lisa's chair is empty. Later, I find out from Padma that this was not unusual; Lisa had stopped attending after the initial design and planning sessions.

Padma finishes a quick demo of the previous sprint's work. We have come a long way from the wireframe stage, and to me the site looks 90% complete. Padma is most excited about the nifty look and feel of the UI and its responsiveness and mobile-friendly CSS theme. Much of the features and settings on the site could be customized by the user, including sliders that concealed or exposed the data behind each of their subsidiaries, contractor facilities, and warehouses.

Torrey, however, is not as thrilled, and he makes it clear that the demo was falling well short of HR's expectations. Torrey's rep is that of someone that's determined, highly competent, and a stickler for detail. He has a strong background as a DBA and even provided SQL snippets for Padma to follow in creating detail and summary views. This was his pet project, and he's vocal in his disapproval; he wants the entire detail page for the main user view redone and several admin screens to be refactored. I grimace; this was setting us back to square 1, and Padma was badly needed elsewhere.

Finally, I speak up. "Hey, Torrey, I love the work you've put into this and the passion here. Can I ask though – what's the actual customer problem we're trying to solve here?"

Torrey smiles condescendingly and runs a hand through his thinning blonde hair. "Always great to have management come in several months after the fact and start questioning things. As you might have heard, WonderTek makes things like shoes and athletic apparel. We have factories and subsidiaries overseas that are producing our goods. Auditors need to come in and mark off safety and occupational health risk factors, and track progress on action items we've identified. If we don't see improvements, we need to be able to make that visible so we can sever ties. We need this app to be highly secure and segmented by user and role, but really ethics is the main driver. And it needs to be performant, hopefully with offline availability – a lot of our records are going to be entered in very remote regions with limited 3G wireless access connectivity. We discussed all of this back in the design stages months ago, Ben – you were there."

Fair enough, I tell him. "So then I have to ask – is this solving a problem for a customer? How is it going to make us money, or save us money?"

Torrey looks at me with the expression you'd use with a fairly dim 6-year old. "Ben, that's a really naive question, and like I said – it's months too late in the game. Like I said, this is about ethics. We just can't spend enough on something like this. A leak or a perceived deaf ear on this could set us back potentially years in the market and leave us open to all kinds of liability. You remember what happened to Nike in the late 90's when they were accused of running sweatshops in China and Vietnam, it really damaged their brand. We have VP's and division leads asking for this information; giving them a secure view of our compliance status is considered top level in priority."

I say, "With that kind of visibility, I'm a little surprised we didn't investigate further the possibility of buying this as a COTS product instead of trying to build something custom to fit our own internal preferences." Torrey rolls his eyes contemptuously again; this is an old argument I was digging up. He had gone back and forth multiple times on funding and resources during the planning stages months ago, with Torrey eventually carrying the day by insisting that it could be done with two people in three months. With Lisa and HR, a powerful proponent, taking his side, the project was pushed through. Five months later, we are still looking for an endgame.

Torrey says flatly, "Ben, this is dead ground. We've gone over this, and you lost. So live with it. These are the requirements, and they come from Lisa. Now, Padma, when are you going to get these new screens done? And these reports – I have to have them for our upcoming delivery view in three weeks."

I don't like to play trump cards like this, but this project is tying up several of my best people, and we need to put a bow on it. "Hang on one second Torrey – I'm totally appreciative of where you're coming from and I know you have the best interests of the company at heart. That being said – I only have so many people, and this effort is already several months behind schedule. It's my responsibility to make sure we're aligning ourselves with the delivery of actual value to our customers. This is an internal application, and internal apps are often most vulnerable to time drains like gold-plating and endless scope creep. So, do we really need to have all these features delivered to know if this is going to take off or not? What's really our minimum viable product here, and how are we going to measure if it's going to be a success?"

Torrey's jaw drops. "Gold-plating – are you serious… dammit, this isn't a game. Lisa expects these screens, soon. Are you really going to make me go back to her and tell her that our development team is dragging their feet on something the business needs?"

I reply calmly, "Correct me if I'm wrong, but I don't believe those screens were part of the original ask, at all. It's not in anyone's best interests to have our commitments spiral upward endlessly. We need to have a clear finish line everyone agrees on."

"I thought you guys were Agile," Torrey snorts. "I kept on hearing about how you didn't want me to give you a full-size requirements doc, like I typically do, just a PowerPoint wireframe. The customer's needs have shifted, and it's your job now to roll with the punches and deliver according to the new ask. Anything else – well, we'd need to take that up with Lisa." He sat back in his chair, grinning triumphantly.

I decide to call his bluff. "Yes, I think that'd be a great idea. Let's get Lisa in here, I want her to look over what we've delivered to date and what you're asking for here and see if it's weighted correctly."

At least I've stopped the eye-rolling; Torrey is suddenly almost angry at being defied. "This is exactly why I wanted to take this to a third party. You guys are just too slow and inflexible to get this done on the timeline HR needs."

"I agree with that first statement," I said. "When this project came up for review, I argued against it. I said that this doesn't give us any kind of a competitive advantage; to me, it was a textbook use case for a third-party app. That option is still open to us, by the way. If we truly are back to square one after this design session, six months in, I think we definitely need to present this to Lisa and our HR partners and have them make the call."

"I never said we were back to square one," Torrey says. He frowns and mutters disgustedly, "We just need to finish up these reports and these two admin screens and we'll be good to go."

"Ah, now we're starting to get somewhere," says Alex, leaning forward. "On these two screens – getting back to that minimum viable product question Ben asked – do you really need to have them for the application to work?"

Torrey hems and haws, but finally it comes out – yes, we have enough functionality to deliver something useful to our factory auditors for their reports. As Alex and I had guessed, the current "requirements" were both admin-facing features that Torrey had tacked on, likely without Lisa even knowing about them. I shiver. This is looking more and more like one of those dreaded headless zombie projects, with an absentee stakeholder and a shifting mission. The delays for the past few months as new requirements kept stacking up suddenly made sense – Torrey has hijacked the design UI based on his own personal point of view. Perhaps, his hunches were right; but with no way of verifying or validating them, his tacked-on features and stories remained guesses.

All that being out in the open, I have no more intent of scrapping months of work than Torrey does. I do need to cap things though and get this out the door, so we can get usable feedback. "Let's assume that you're right Torrey, and we really are almost there. We need a finish line to this race. That means a true, defined minimum viable product. Let's say we only have two sprints more of work available. What features could we squeeze into that time?"

Torrey takes two deep breaths, 10 seconds to pull himself together. He's not accustomed to being defied like this. "We need to have those two reports at a minimum. Without it, there's no aggregate way to display results. We won't be able to filter out the worst performing factories and mark their progress. That's the key answer HR needs to have answered, and without it the app is DOA."

Padma says, "Torrey has already given us the SQL for the reports, and we can use a third-party extension to provide both a web and a printable report view for our admins. I'm pretty sure we can knock both out in a few days, maybe a week."

Most of my engineers tend to underestimate work by a factor of 2-5x; Padma may be the lone exception. She's amazingly accurate, even with large unknown areas in the technical specs; I'm confident she can deliver what's needed in a week. I ask Torrey and Padma to demo the app to Lisa as it currently works and let us know if she agrees – that with those two reports we have a complete MVP that's customer-ready.

I continue, "Now, something else I want to talk about, this whole idea of 'requirements' being a fixed, immovable object. I don't buy into that. We don't know if this will meet our true business needs, and it seems like we don't have our assumptions and the problem we are trying to solve written down anywhere. Torrey, is that correct?"

Torrey throws up his hands in frustration. "Ben, with all due respect, I don't think the seagull treatment is helping here and I don't appreciate you coming in here, 11th hour, and treating my project like a statue." He starts speaking slowly and stressing every syllable – "No, of COURSE we didn't do any of those basic, fundamental things at inception, because I'm a horrible mean person who likes to force nerds to break a sweat and I'm terrible at my job. If you had bothered to look at the documentation link in each meeting agenda, you'll see that the mission statement was set the first week."

Padma breaks in, "That's true, Ben – we've got a clear problem statement and we've tried to adhere to it from day 1." She pulls up the following on her screen from the project wiki:

"We believe that delivering this application for our Human Resources administrators will achieve a better safety and humane working conditions at WonderTek. We will know we are successful when we see a 95% compliance record with our factories and subcontractor manufacturing plants, with a zero red flag count three years after rollout."

Padma explains that red flags were the truly sensitive, worst case safety or inhumane working conditions. Currently, HR suspects that at least five and as many as eight of our suppliers and subcontractors fall under this category; giving them clear notice and enforcing it as a program will allow WonderTek to phase out these underperformers and replace them with more progressive factory plants.

Torrey says smugly, "That is business value, Ben. Not having our name in the papers as an exploiter of our workers is business value. If we want to be mentioned in the same sentence as Columbia Sportswear or Patagonia with the upscale, socially progressive market that we are targeting – that means caring about ethics, right down to the materials we source and the way we run our factories."

"Let's stop trying to score points against each other, Torrey," I reply. "I've acknowledged that you have good motives and I'd appreciate you giving me the same benefit of the doubt. This project is getting a reputation of being a money-losing time suck, and Douglas wants me to scrub our involvement in it. I can go back to him with a counterargument – two more sprints worth of work and we'll have a product that can stand on its own. That's a better outcome than pulling the plug on months of hard work from you and the team. But I have to cap it at two sprints – that's four weeks, Torrey. It's all we've got, we need to make it count."

Padma says, "It'll take us at most a week, possibly a week and a half to do these last changes. So why are we asking for a month?"

Alex answers, "Because we're not sure if this project is going to be viable yet, Padma. Maybe what we roll out won't be usable by our auditors over a thin pipe. Maybe the report data won't be usable by HR – in fact I'd bet dollars to donuts that they're going to want to refine the audit reports significantly after seeing what people are turning in from the field. And maybe they'll find a third-party product that's more flexible and doesn't require two developers to build and maintain."

I say, "In short, we're making a bet. We're thinking that this is going to give HR the data they need to ensure compliance, and it's usable by our auditors. But we might be wrong. So we get this MVP out to our end users globally as soon as we possibly can. And then we need to see how our bet is doing. That means a way of collecting measurable usage data and incorporating what we learn into our workflow. So last question from me – what have we done as far as monitoring?"

The answer with some hedging was – very little. Now, even Torrey is showing some signs of interest; as a technical BSA, he loves data and ways of proving value to his partners. Padma muses that – given those two or three weeks – they could look into providing monitoring that would give HR a viewable dashboard of the site's response times by region, and for admins a better view of security and threat monitoring. I'm relieved to see that she has no intention of rolling her own monitoring framework; there's several SAAS-based monitoring solutions available that can provide what we need for what amounts to a few thousand dollars a year.

At this point, Torrey objects to what he sees as an unnecessary cost in setting up monitoring as a service. I tell him, "Torrey, you keep saying that this is a high priority project and very visible to the powers that be. So let's give them some credit. By the time all is said and done here, we'll have sunk almost a half year of development time into this from two developers, and it'll cost us another year or two easy in providing post-rollout support and tweaks. That's conservatively speaking about a million dollars just in direct labor costs. Are you telling me that HR – who knows exactly what a good developer in the Portland job market costs nowadays – won't be willing to sink $1,000 a month into providing some basic monitoring?"

Torrey and I argue about this a little more; I flatly refuse to deploy anything to production without a healthy monitoring system in place. Torrey threatens to bring in Lisa again. I offer to bring in Douglas as a mediator on scrubbing the project – which settles things nicely. Torrey acts as if he's being stonewalled but finally accepts my conditions with good grace.

He's a cagey negotiator, and we both know that Douglas' two-sprint mandate is a paper tiger; this project will likely spin along for some time. But I'm happy with our beta program approach, and I'm looking forward to a few months from now when we can finally put this zombie project back in the grave.

Finding the Real Bottleneck (Value Stream Map)

It's been a few weeks since monitors started popping up like mushrooms in the IT and development areas. Douglas gave us some pretty firm guidelines – he wanted our release failure rate, frequency, and our defect count showing. Our recovery time, MTTR, still isn't up there despite a few tries on my part; we also haven't been able to figure out how to show the hours spent prepping each release or separating out noncode from code related defects.

As I feared, it doesn't take long for some to figure out how to game the system. Alex has found a few cases where engineers are gating bugs so their overall defect rate looks better than it is. And some teams are focusing too much on keeping their releases green, which is slowing them down.

So, it's not a perfect view of what is actually happening out there. But it's better than what we had before, which was a murky view at best of one piece of the system. George gives me a huge grin one morning as we look over our release rates. "It's like I keep telling you Ben – if you give an engineer a number, he'll kill himself trying to make it better." And I have to say – ramping up our release rates may not mean much by itself, but in combination with our other KPI's it seems to be promoting some of the behavior we are looking for.

We try to use these numbers, not as a club, but as a start to a conversation with our teams, and not overreact to "red" values. If we start clamping down on negatives, we're sure to get fake numbers and evasion – we want honest discussions and a better understanding of what's blocking us. Often, there's contributing factors we can help resolve as management that would remain hidden if we brought out the pitchforks and torches.

It's a mixed bag as yet. I can't claim any magical transformations as yet with this drive for transparency, but it does seem to be driving home the main message Douglas wants us to send: team first, no more localized incentives and KPIs.

I still have fences to mend with Footwear, my primary customer. I start making the trek across the street to their offices a part of my daily ritual; usually I can catch a few minutes with Tabrez first thing in the morning. It takes a few weeks of relentless pestering and a few lunches, but finally Tabrez and I are able to come to an agreement; yes, releases are happening more often and with fewer defects, but new features are still rolling out at an almost glacial pace. Tabrez and I agree that it's past time that we take a second look at the overall flow of work and see if our constraints have changed.

This time, we decide to make the assessment and audit more of a metrics-based approach and done in a less home-grown way. For this exercise to work, we are going to need a truly neutral third party that can cut across team and department barriers with a clear, unbiased mandate. So I ask Emily to come up with a list of three consulting agencies that she had worked with in the past and trusted; after a round of interviews, Tabrez and Douglas select a well-known San Francisco based consulting firm that has an excellent track record.

I had some initial reservations, but I end up very impressed with the consultant they select for the audit. Karen comes from the manufacturing world and understands Lean theory very well; she's sharp as a tack and has an impressive track record. No doubt the assessment will be both comprehensive and somewhat painful. Still, Tabrez is enthusiastic about the effort. Emily, somewhat mollified as I've been following through in participating in her release planning activities, is onboard as well.

By the time Karen is able to come onsite, I've almost forgotten about the audit and have to scramble a little to clear up room on my calendar. Surprisingly though, Karen doesn't spend a lot of time interviewing the division heads or the team leads to get their thoughts. Instead, she mainly sits in the team areas as they conduct their daily scrums, or sets up shop on Emily's side of the building. I catch a glimpse of her once talking animatedly to Elaine, and we pass each other in the corridor once when I'm leaving the Footwear offices. Otherwise, she's a complete cipher to me. I have no idea what she's going to put in her report; I'm worried about damage control in case she digs up something unpleasant about our team.

When I mention to George that I'm a little worried that Karen might not be getting the right strategic view of things, George chuckles and says, "Ben, I've been watching Karen, and I think you've got nothing to worry about. She doesn't miss a trick. Let's just watch this play out and see what she comes up with."

At the end of the second week, Karen calls a leadership meeting with Tabrez, Douglas, Emily, and myself to go over her assessment. She begins by covering some of the changes that had been made over the past few months to their release management processes. "From what I can gather, a few months ago you determined that your releases were the likely pain point, but that seemed more of a guess than anything else. No one ever seems to have looked at the entire release process start to finish and put some numbers behind why features were creeping out the door. We did come up with some numbers that showed a lot of pain around integration and stabilization, and a very fragile release process." She displays the following:

	Original State	Target State	Current State
Change Failure Rate	70%	35%	20%
Release Frequency	2 weeks	1 week	9 days
Release Prep Time	300 hrs (240 integration, 60 release)	150 hours total prep time per release	25 hrs (5 integration, 20 release)
Bugs Caused by Noncode Issues	60 bugs	30 bugs	70 bugs
MTTR	8.5 days	4 days	6.5 days

She continues, "Obviously wasting almost 300 hours getting a release ready and then having most of them fail – or have to spend more time trying to fix bugs post-release – isn't sustainable. So the changes we've made to date – investing in version control as an authoritative source for all your releases, using automated builds and continuous integration, and a better partnership between Dev and Operations seems to be paying off. But we're obviously not there yet – even with releases happening more often, new features still are not making it out to production fast enough for us to innovate and keep ahead of WonderTek's competitors."

Emily interrupts, "Nancy, with all due respect, you never took the time to meet with me and you couldn't possibly be aware of all the history going on here in just two weeks. We have a track record of bringing in changes late that are unreliable and that force long war room releases that stretch on for days, into the evening and over weekends. No Operations team can survive this. I'm a little disappointed that you didn't take more time to show a holistic view of what's going on."

Nancy replies smoothly, "My mission here – and we discussed this well ahead of time – was to cut through all the clutter of that history that you mentioned, Emily. We're trying to make this as facts-based as possible, from the point of view of your end customer, Footwear. As I said, no one has ever mapped out the entire release cycle – that's from inception to entering the dev backlog, to it going out the door in a release to production and then post-release support. In the companies I've worked with, the problem is never a 'bad' team that is deliberately obstructing work; it's usually a flaw in the process, where we aren't seeing things in global context. Making this flow of work visible usually is the first step to making real progress.

"In the past few weeks, I've spent time with your business analysts, Footwear management, your architects, some developers and UAT people, and the Operations people handling release and infrastructure builds. Here's the process from start to finish with the most recent release:"

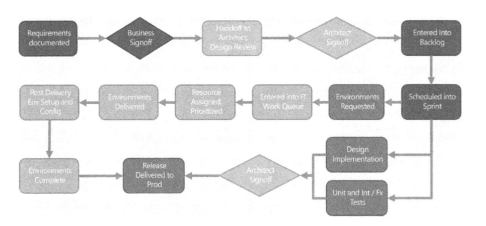

"Above, I put BA-centered activities in purple, architectural gates in green, development centered tasks in blue, and IT/infrastructure tasks in orange. You could argue that this isn't a true end to end scenario, as I'm not covering the 'fuzzy' parts like initial conceptualization and post-release monitoring and operations. However, I think – big picture – this does capture every step needed to bring one release out the door. Did I get this about right?"

After a few seconds pause with no objections, she continues: "So, the Business Analyst documents requirements; these are signed off by the customer, at which point an architect looks over the requirements and drafts a design. That design might include libraries, a recommended web framework or programming language, or a specific design pattern that the architect favors. After this design is signed off by the architects, the BA enters it into the backlog and its prioritized. For this particular release, the changes requested were important enough that it was entered into the next sprint right away.

"From here the developers ask for new environments from the IT/Ops team if needed. In this particular case, we did need a full set of environments created for DEV/QA/STG/PROD to host the new services requested. While the new environments are being built out, the programmers begin work on creating the code implementation. I talked with Rajesh and some other QA people about the change made to create unit tests and integration/functional tests in parallel with code development; it seems like creating test code along with application code as part of every release is making a real difference in improving overall quality. But I'll get back to that later.

"A few interesting things here though – for this most recent release, creating those environments caused an almost four week delay in the project. During this time the code was actually done for several weeks – that's why the dashboard shows a 9 day release cycle, which looks terrific. That's deceiving, because the actual release date was much, much longer than that. Because environments were not ready, the release had to be delayed. Putting some numbers behind these steps exposed the problem even more clearly. Here I made the steps a neutral gray, put wait times in blue and process or work times in pink on the top right."

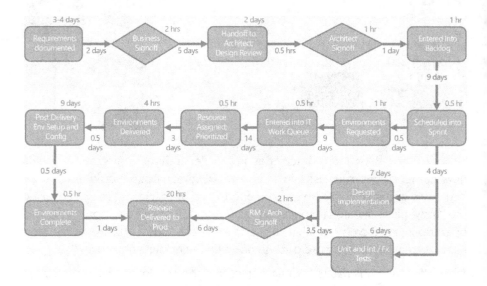

She continues, "If we compress this down even further, we get a much better picture of the entire release cycle:"

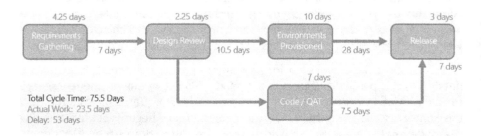

I could see jaws drop around the room; Tabrez looked like he'd been hit with a 2x4. He sputters, "This is our cycle time? I mean, I'm not surprised that it is taking almost a full quarter to get work done for even the most minor request, that's not anything new. But are we really spending more than two months with work just sitting there waiting on a handoff?"

Douglas looks almost sick. "I set a really high standard of delivery for my teams, and this is a complete surprise for me. And I hate surprises. Which team is responsible for this awful performance?"

Karen replied, "Well, this will all be in my audit report. I can tell you, it's not one particular team or person that is causing a problem. The process itself has gaps that we will need to close for the system to work efficiently. Here's a few notes I took showing some of the positive and negative attributes of each step of the release cycle. You can see here, no single team is 'the problem'. If you were thinking that releases and CI/CD was going to magically make things better – perhaps that was true six months ago, but it's no longer true now."

	Work (days)	Delay (days)	% of Total Time	Notes
Requirements Gathering	4.25	7	13%	Good use of wireframes/storyboards by BSA
				Usage data missing in prioritizing work
Design Review	2.25	10.5	15%	Ad hoc "emergency" requests filling up capacity
				Team's firepower eaten up by firefighting
Environments Provisioned	10	28	44%	Long delays in getting in queue, post delivery config tweaks
				Environments manually provisioned, source control not used for config
				Mismatches in environments wreaking havoc with triage times
				Separate work queue with IT, Ops and Dev teams
Code / QAT	7	7.5	17%	Test layer stabilizing
Release	3	7	12%	Better CI/CD processes helping reduce integration/stabilization time
				Little to no preparation or documentation for support teams and first responders
				No monitoring on availability or user experiences
	23.5	53		78 days total

I feel a little bonked on the head as well. We've been working so hard for the last few months to get our house in order; how could we have made so little progress? I ask, "Are you saying that all our improvements have not budged the needle at all? That we're stuck in a swamp? Because that doesn't reflect what I hear from the team."

Karen smiles consolingly and replies, "I think it'd be easy to look at this and feel discouraged. There are some positives and a lot of progress that we should celebrate. For example, it does seem like not having long stabilization periods and a better focus on delivering test code along with application code is helping. And there's some real positives outside of the dev sphere – for example, the BSA's are doing a great job of having their specifications be in wireframes or PowerPoint storyboards before vetting it with the stakeholders. That's a real timesaver as it's easier to rewrite or throw away a wireframe than it is code. IT is starting to use more version control when it comes to configurations and in templating out environments, although we're only seeing this for just a few applications to date. It's anecdotal, but I do hear from the IT and Operations team that there is a better handoff and coordination happening with the programming teams."

Nancy continues, "There's some problems we're not showing. For example, I mentioned that there's little to no prep work happening with the first responders. That's having a direct downstream impact on your developers, Ben, in the form of false alarms and firefighting easily triaged bugs that are passing along untouched to hit the engineers directly. It also means customers are having to wait a frustratingly long time when their problems could be easily diagnosed and resolved within minutes by the first or second support level.

"There's a few stage gates here that I think could be rethought – for example that 23 day period from requirements first being gathered to the design being written up. In the case I looked at, the design went through a lot of revisions during implementation, so most of that time spent coming up with an optimal design ended up in the trash can. With such a long approval cycle, we think it would be a good idea for you to explore concepts like a true minimum viable product. Because of that delay, work is finding its way in ungated through side doors. Each day I kept seeing people "just dropping by" to their favorite developer's desk and asking for little tweaks or asks as a favor; it's a rough estimate but I imagine at least a quarter of your team's time is dribbling away here unseen, Ben. There's a lot of disruption caused by these ad hoc requests and it shows the process as it currently stands isn't lightweight enough if so much is coming in by a side door.

"But the overall picture shows these gaping holes that need to be closed by the management team. Let's show them here."

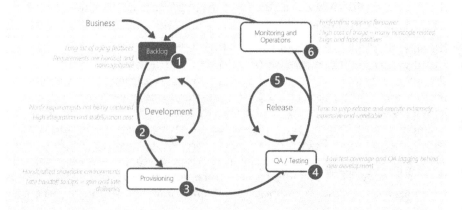

Footwear Release Pain Points

"Working backwards, you have a long list of aging features because the team is getting gobbled up by firefighting and fixing bugs from the last release. Because there is no effective usage monitoring for any of your applications, you have no idea what should be prioritized and what should be abandoned, so you are flailing when it comes to what little feature work is being done. Because your environments are inconsistent from PROD to DEV, there's a lot of rework when it comes to setup and then separating out noncode related issues and bugs caused by patches or failing infrastructure. And you need a better prepared front line response so the team can spend more time on productive, innovative work.

"Like I said at the beginning, there's not one particular culprit; the problem is systemic. If we are thinking of the release process end to end as a train, the problem is that there is no coupling between the groups handling the design, spinning up the environments, writing the code, and operationalizing and supporting the work. Each thinks they are doing the best they can, which they likely are – locally. But globally, because the train cars are uncoupled, work is not able to be delivered safely and on time."

The next slide causes another ripple of discussion throughout the room. As I said, I've been working hard on building a better relationship with Emily and the Ops team. But it doesn't take a genius to see that provisioning environments seemed to gobble up half our time on the project.

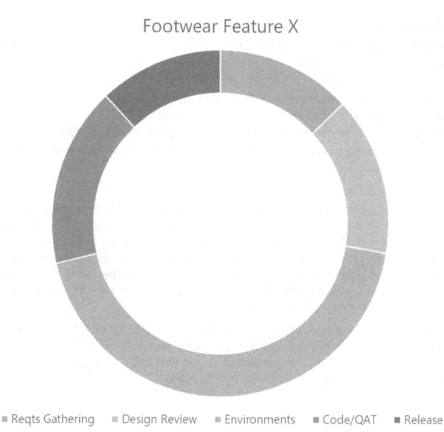

Footwear Feature X

■ Reqts Gathering ■ Design Review ■ Environments ■ Code/QAT ■ Release

Karen has seen our dashboards, but she asks anyway how we measure what value means. I make my pitch for MTTR again, as resilience is something I definitely want showing. Douglas says, "I think that our change success rate is the key number. If we're reliable in what we release, then we have happier customers and I get more sleep."

Emily chips in, "We like CPU and memory counters to get ahead of problems, but it all comes down to reliability and availability. Three 9's to me is a good baseline to start with – and it's likely all we need to look at. If the environments aren't available, then the applications won't run."

Karen says, "I see all kinds of metrics being thrown around, and it all comes from what you choose to value – is it speed to market? Security? Stability? There's no wrong answer – but the fact that you are all coming in with a different answer of what value means should tell us that we're not on the same page yet, that each team is thinking locally. We shouldn't see the problem as 'fixing' IT or Operations,. The problem is the gap – that interstitial space between the boxes that I put in blue. In 'Team of Teams' Stanley McChrystal called this the 'blink', and he made closing these gaps the centerpiece of the fight against Al Qaeda. As long as your teams are seeing their mission as being '99.9% uptime', or 'coding done in two sprints', you won't be able to win the battle."

My head is hurting, and I pinch the bridge of my nose to try to think clearly. "If we get a thousand to-do's thrown at us, I guarantee you that nothing will be done. I refuse to accept that this is an unfixable situation, and I don't want us to get stuck in the mud here. Karen, we came into this meeting with a clear mandate from Footwear – they want more frequent releases, more reliably. So, Tabrez, am I correct when I say that if we could deliver an end to end release – that's from concept to delivery – in two weeks, that this is the target we should be shooting for?"

Before Tabrez can answer, Emily starts to laugh. "Ben, more frequent releases by itself is where you guys were six months ago. That didn't win you anything but a skyrocketing bug count, remember?"

I shrug off the migraine that's hammering between my eyes, and say firmly: "From what I can see here, Emily, it looks like none of that time was wasted. In fact, it's given us the foundation we needed to come up with a solution that can deliver real value, at tempo. As long as we're pitching this as being the fault of one team and one team only – and pretending that our systems are perfectly safe as long as 'bad people' stop touching it – we'll never make real progress. The enemy here isn't anyone in this room – it's the delays and waste whenever we pass work from one team to another."

Douglas breaks in. "Obviously we're still seeing some different point of views here that need to be reconciled. But that's not the point of this meeting and I don't want us picking out solutions when the problem itself isn't defined clearly. Karen, thanks for coming and for this presentation. You've posed some good questions here that we will need to answer, and I'm looking forward to that audit report. Let's talk again once it's ready."

Behind the Story

Three big hurdles were jumped in this chapter; holding blame-free postmortems, developing software features using hypothesis-driven development, and mapping out the flow of value comprehensively. What value are these three concepts going to offer Ben's team in their journey?

Blameless Postmortems

> *Underneath every simple, obvious story about 'human error,' there is a deeper, more complex story about the organization.*
>
> —Sidney Dekker[1]

> *By removing blame, you remove fear; by removing fear, you enable honesty; and honesty enables prevention.*
>
> —Bethany Macri[2]

Jeff Bezos famously once said that "failure and invention are inseparable twins." Yet for every company like Amazon that handles mistakes and failure as an opportunity to learn, we see a hundred others that follow instinctively JFK's saying after the Bay of Pigs fiasco: "Victory has a hundred fathers and defeat is an orphan."

A few years ago, Dave was heading in to work and decided to stop by and grab a coffee at one of his favorite joints. He glanced at the paper by the checkout stand, and there it was – his company, right on the very front page, top and center. A recent mailer had accidentally printed the customer's date of birth and social security number, right on the mailing envelope; it had been sent out to tens of thousands of people. This was a very public and visible gaffe that would require months of damage control; whoever made this mistake could look forward to weeks under a very public magnifying glass, at the very least. A cold wave of fear ran down his spine – *oh crap, was that me?*

Turns out the inadvertent leak wasn't his fault, but it very well could have been. Those of you who have been in the room when a deployment fails and a rollback is not working know that sense of fear well.

How We Respond to Mistakes Defines Us

How organizations and leaders deal with bad news, outages, and uncomfortable facts – let's call them outliers – is actually a defining quality. The 1998 Ron Westrum study has been cited many times, especially in the excellent book *Accelerate* and the DORA annual reports; it remains the best way we've seen yet of grouping organizations based on how failure and messengers are treated:

---

[1]"Behind Human Error," Sidney Dekker, David Woods. CRC Press, 9/30/2010. ISBN-13: 978-0754678342, ISBN-10: 0754678342. Etsy and other companies has mentioned this book and its discussion of First Stories vs Second Stories many times.
[2]"The DevOps Handbook: How to Create World-Class Agility, Reliability, and Security in Technology Organizations," Gene Kim, Patrick Dubois, John Willis, Jez Humble. IT Revolution Press, 10/6/2016, ISBN-10: 1942788002, ISBN-13: 978-1942788003.

Power Oriented (Pathological)	Rule Oriented (Bureaucratic)	Performance Oriented (Generative)
Low cooperation	Modest cooperation	High cooperation
Messengers shot	Messengers neglected	Messengers trained
Responsibilities shirked	Narrow responsibilities	Risks are shared
Bridging discouraged	Bridging tolerated	Bridging encouraged
Failure ➤ scapegoating	Failure ➤ justice	Failure ➤ inquiry
Novelty crushed	Novelty ➤ problems	Novelty implemented

source: [3, 4]

We find this study best combined with the infamous "Five Dysfunctions of a Team" by Patrick Lencioni:[5]

1. Absence of trust (unwilling to be vulnerable within the group)

2. Fear of conflict (seeking artificial harmony over constructive passionate debate)

3. Lack of commitment (feigning buy-in for group decisions, ambiguity)

4. Avoidance of accountability (ducking responsibility to call out peers on counterproductive behavior)

5. Inattention to results (focusing on personal success, status, and ego before the team)

---

[3]"A typology of organisational cultures," Ron Westrum. BMJ Quality & Safety, 2004;13:ii22-ii27, https://qualitysafety.bmj.com/content/13/suppl_2/ii22.
[4]"Annual State of DevOps Report," unattributed author(s). Puppet Labs, 2016. https://puppetlabs.com/2016-devops-report.
[5]"The Five Dysfunctions of a Team: A Leadership Fable," Patrick Lencioni. Jossey-Bass, 4/11/2002. ISBN-13: 978-0787960759, ISBN-10: 0787960756.

Notice anything interesting? Let's match up the sick organization on the far left – the power-based Pathological one – with that list of five dysfunctions:

Westrum – Pathological Orgs	Lencioni – Five Dysfunctions
Low cooperation	Absence of trust
Messengers shot	Fear of conflict
Responsibilities shirked	Lack of commitment and buy-in
Bridging discouraged	Avoidance of accountability
Failure leads to scapegoating	Inattention to results
Novelty crushed	

The two very neatly overlap, as you can see. Pathological and bureaucratic organizations – the type where we've unfortunately spent the majority of our careers! – lean toward power/personality politics or a set of departmental fiefdoms governed by "rules." This directly impacts how well information and work flow inside the organization and how trust, openness, and collaboration are actually valued.

Ultimately, this has a major impact on how well the company ship is run. If employees are aligned on a single mission, less effort is wasted on departmental infighting and blame-fixing exercises. Leaders in trust-based, generative cultures have better information available to them so they can follow up on good bets – and abandon bad ones without fear of taking a political hit.

In practice, we find that the Westrum study makes a great rear-view mirror but is a crappy windshield. It's very helpful in diagnosing why poor performing companies tend to veer toward shame, name, and blame games when there's failure – but depressing as hell when it comes to thinking about the future. In many cases, the cultural traits of an organization and how it responds to failure can be very ingrained and – in Ben's case – well above his pay grade. What's a mortal team lead or divisional manager to do?

Taking a lesson from SOA principles, it is possible – we've seen it many times – where even on a team level it is possible to create an oasis where the right behavior is encouraged; this in turn can have ripple effects elsewhere. Obviously, WonderTek is not generative by the way that high severity outages are being handled; mistakes are either minimized, blame is shifted, or a big red hammer comes out to punish the guilty. But Ben is starting in the right place by changing his behavior and that of his team when things go wrong, and expecting his partners to toe the same line.

This isn't something that can wait; how Ben's team and he react to this high-visibility outage could undermine months of work as they try to grow toward a more transparent, honest, and productive flow of work.

Postmortems with Teeth

You'll notice that Ben's team ends up with several action items that are immediately added to the developer work queue. John Allspaw was famous for not allowing people to leave postmortems at Etsy until remediation tasks were identified and dropped into their Jira work backlog. All of these items were typically actionable in 30 days, and it was rare for them to take longer than 6 months. These remediation steps followed the SMART rule established by George Doran – Specific, Measurable, Assignable, Realistic, Time-Related.[6]

Keep the meeting to open to all – especially your stakeholders, the people that introduced the defect, the team that identified it, and those that came up with the resolution. A facilitator should be present, and possibly a notetaker. The facilitator's role is to keep the discussion productive and fair. That means calling out cognitive biases, like the following:

- Hindsight bias (assuming events are predictable despite incomplete info)

- Confirmation bias (find and favor facts that support your pet theory)

- Outcome bias (evaluate decisions based on bias and not info available at the time)

- Recency bias (recent events are given more emphasis than those further in the past)

- Fundamental attribution error (other people's faults are intrinsic, due to personality or bad intentions, vs. situational)

The group will have a trend to slip into this type of bias instinctively, which is why Etsy forbids using terms like "could have" or "should have" during postmortems.[7] The facilitator should state this during a brief introduction, and anyone should feel comfortable to call out bias to get the postmortem back on track.

---

[6]"There's a S.M.A.R.T. Way to Write Management's Goals and Objectives," Doran, G. T. Management Review, Vol. 70, Issue 11, 1/1/1981. https://community.mis.temple.edu/mis0855002fall2015/files/2015/10/S.M.A.R.T-Way-Management-Review.pdf.
[7]"Morgue: Helping Better Understand Events by Building a Post Mortem Tool," Bethany Macri. DevOpsDays.org, Vimeo, 10/18/2013. https://vimeo.com/77206751. How and why the Morgue postmortem tool was created at Etsy. This tool is publicly available on GitHub; see https://github.com/etsy/morgue.

The meeting could be set up similar to the following:

- Part 1, 30–40 minutes: What happened. Build a timeline of events, using logs, chatroom records, and release notes. Describe what happened – what was known at that time, and why the decisions made sense at the time. The goal here isn't to come up with remediation steps – that comes later – but simply to get better understanding of the context. Consensus on these facts must be agreed to before the group can continue.

- Part 2, 10–15 minutes: Open discussion. This is an exploration of what could make the organization better prepared for the next event. Many times the issue comes down to decisions being made with partial information or the "fog of war" – gaps in runbooks or documentation need to be improved, handoffs or support triage improved, better notifications and visibility to customers, stakeholders, or troubleshooting personnel. Any and all ideas here are welcome – anything that can especially improve the application's robustness, lessening the time to detect problems and implement a fix. In this step – if the root cause is found to not include some tweak to sharing knowledge, adding better alerts and monitoring, or improving support triage – we suggest you haven't dug deep enough into the "second story."

- Part 3, 5–10 minutes: Remediation items. These are usually actionable in 30 days, and typically not more than 6 months. Remember the SMART rule we mentioned earlier – Specific, Measurable, Assignable, Realistic, Time-Related. If the group leaves without having at least 1–2 new work items dropped into their work backlog – including hopefully some way of measuring if the changes are producing the desired outcomes – the meeting has not reached its objective.

One last comment – the results of this need to be broadcast, searchable, and transparent to everyone – including the business/stakeholder partners, and the teams both developing and supporting product work. Some groups have been very successful using some form of the Morgue OS tool; others use Wikis or the application knowledgebase. Any good postmortem will end up with at least one actionable and practical follow-up point; that's the entire point of the exercise. Toothless, inconclusive retrospectives and postmortems are as useless as having a buddy rubberstamp a peer review.

A Focus on Guardrails Not Punishment

We've been in many postmortems and "zero defect meetings" that seemed to begin and end at the human factor; a gauntlet of blame and punishment, an inquisition to root out the guilty sinners who so thoughtlessly put the company at risk. It's a vicious cycle – blame leads to fear, which leads to dishonesty, minimization ("what outage?"), and stonewalling. You'll know this by the way mistakes are handled; engineers become defensive, reluctant to divulge facts that could lead to a quicker diagnosis or better process next time. Over time, pathological type responses to failures lead inevitably to a strangled development process. Who wants to lose their job over even minor changes if the threat of punishment and public embarrassment is so drastic?

> In "the traditional way of handling the aftermath of such an outage – we would now come together and yell at the person who was maintaining the system that broke. Or the one who wrote the code. Or the one working on fixing it. Surely if they had just done a better job, we wouldn't have had that outage. This usually ends in a very unproductive meeting where afterwards everybody feels worse. And on top of that you didn't even find out what really happened."[8]

It's immensely satisfying and very easy to buy into the "bad apple" theory and try to make an example of someone who made a mistake. In pathological organizations, this is the currency of the realm; team leads and directors score points against other fiefdoms by successfully pinning blame and responsibility for mistakes elsewhere. Good organizations dig deeper than that; they begin every postmortem with the mindset of building guardrails. Acknowledging that these are complex systems and we have an imperfect understanding of our current state and dependencies, how do we make our changes safer, and provide more information for the next time?

Google's postmortem culture follows these principles closely. The approach is simple: when something goes wrong, the team does an in-depth analysis with an emphasis on process over people. They write down everything they learned and share the document as widely as possible to make sure it never happens again.

---

[8]"Practical Postmortems at Etsy," Daniel Schauenberg. InfoQ, 8/22/2015. https://www.infoq.com/articles/postmortems-etsy.

These postmortems are blameless because we assume everyone makes mistakes from time to time. Post mortems aren't criminal investigations, they're an affirmative process designed to make us all a little smarter:

A blamelessly written postmortem assumes that everyone involved in an incident had good intentions and did the right thing with the information they had. If a culture of finger pointing and shaming individuals or teams for doing the "wrong" thing prevails, people will not bring issues to light for fear of punishment.

…When postmortems shift from allocating blame to investigating the systematic reasons why an individual or team had incomplete or incorrect information, effective prevention plans can be put in place. You can't "fix" people, but you can fix systems and processes to better support people making the right choices when designing and maintaining complex systems. When an outage does occur, a postmortem is not written as a formality to be forgotten. Instead the postmortem is seen by engineers as an opportunity not only to fix a weakness, but to make Google more resilient as a whole.[9]

Google's Seth Vargo told us:

People won't take risks if there's a fear of drastic failure. If we want people to experiment to get better performance, we have to convince them that if they mess something up, they won't get fired. If every outage is treated as opportunity to blame someone, we'll never learn anything.

There are some very well publicized incidents where an engineer caused a major outage by running a command against production. If you go into the postmortem looking to blame the engineer, that's the wrong approach. This was fundamentally a problem with the architecture, with safety, not a human problem. Why did this user have read/write access to every row and table in the production system? Why does the staging database live on the same subnet as the production database? These questions become action items or specific steps that can improve the overall reliability and health of the system. But if your developers are afraid that if they break something they'll get fired – they're not going to be on the top of their game, they're going to suck at their jobs, because you have a fear-based culture.[10]

[9]"Site Reliability Engineering: How Google Runs Production Systems," Niall Richard Murphy, Betsy Beyer, Chris Jones, Jennifer Petoff, O'Reilly Media; 4/16/2016, ISBN-10: 149192912X, ISBN-13: 978-1491929124. Appendix D has an excellent sample postmortem.
[10]Interview of Seth Vargo by Dave Harrison, see Appendix.

Ryan Comingdeer of Five Talent echoed this thinking when he shared with us the missed opportunities that come with blame:

> *It's never the fault of Dave, that guy who wrote the horrible code – why did we miss that as a best practice in our code review? Did we miss something in how we look at maintainability, security, performance? Are lead developers setting expectation properly, how can we improve in our training?*
>
> *Blame is the enemy of learning and communication. The challenge for us is setting the expectation that failure is an expected outcome, a good thing that we can learn from. Let's count the number of failures we're going to have, and see how good our retrospectives can get. We're going to fail, that's OK – how we learn from these failures?*[11]

What About Accountability?

Doesn't a blame-free postmortem really just mean that no one is accountable or held responsible? Etsy in particular has found that not to be the case; management (in particular John Allspaw) took great care to set up what they called a "just culture" that balanced safety and accountability. John noted the negative effects of blame culture, where details are hidden out of fear of punishment/CYA type actions, and its acidic effect on trust. "Less-skilled companies name, blame, and shame," he noted.

It's important to remember that the concept of blameless postmortem didn't originate in software but was borrowed from the aviation and healthcare industries – two fields where accountability and learning from mistakes can have life-impacting consequences. Etsy found that in blameless cultures, it was far easier for people to take responsibility for their mistakes and learn for them.[12]

> *A funny thing happens when engineers make mistakes and feel safe when giving details about it: they are not only willing to be held accountable, they are also enthusiastic in helping the rest of the company avoid the same error in the future. They are, after all, the most expert in their own error. They ought to be heavily involved in coming up with remediation items.*

---

[11]Interview of Ryan Comingdeer by Dave Harrison, see Appendix.
[12]"Etsy's Winning Secret: Don't Play The Blame Game!", Owen Thomas. Business Insider, 5/15/2012. http://www.businessinsider.com/etsy-chad-dickerson-blameless-post-mortem-2012-5.

So technically, engineers are not at all "off the hook" with a blameless postmortem process. They are very much on the hook for helping Etsy become safer and more resilient, in the end. And lo and behold: most engineers I know find this idea of making things better for others a worthwhile exercise.[13]

Far from preventing accountability, blameless postmortems may be the best way of maximizing a team's effectiveness. In a recent 5-year study, Google found that a great team depends less about who was on the team, and more on intangible characteristics – how the team works together. Top on their list of five characteristics was psychological safety – an environment that is judgment free and where thoughts can be shared without fear, and where mistakes are learned from instead of punished.[14]

It's no coincidence that many of the high performers we try to emulate – companies such as Netflix, Google, Etsy, Facebook – all had moments in their past where they were colossal dumpster fires from a maturity standpoint. What set them apart from their competitors is their ability to learn fast – both to acknowledge and learn from mistakes, a strong ability to improve. Dig far enough and you'll find under each of these very different companies is a single common thread – a blame-free culture; an eagerness to acknowledge and learn from failure in a scientific way.

Your grandfather might have told you once that how we handle adversity shows character. How we handle mistakes as a culture is also often the ceiling of our organization. It could be the most common limiting factor that we see, regardless of size or company type. Without a healthy, generative approach to handling mistakes, any DevOps movement you initiate will end up being just words on the wall.

Hypothesis-Driven Development

The cheapest, fastest, and most reliable components of a computer system are those that aren't there.

—Gordon Bell

---

[13]"Blameless PostMortems and a Just Culture," John Allspaw. Code as Craft / Etsy, 5/22/2012. https://codeascraft.com/2012/05/22/blameless-postmortems/.
[14]"What Google Learned From Its Quest to Build the Perfect Team," Charles Duhigg, 2/25/2016, NY Times Magazine, https://www.nytimes.com/2016/02/28/magazine/what-google-learned-from-its-quest-to-build-the-perfect-team.html.

A complex system that works is invariably found to have evolved from a simple system that worked. The inverse proposition also appears to be true: A complex system designed from scratch never works and cannot be made to work.

—John Gall

The code you write makes you a programmer. The code you delete makes you a good one. The code you don't have to write makes you a great one.

—Mario Fusco

Let's say you're absolutely killing it at a big-money Texas Hold 'Em Tournament – made it to the second day with a nice pile of chips, about $51,000. And things just keep getting better – you look at your pocket cards and two aces are staring back at you. This is the proverbial "bullet" or "rocket" hand – the strongest starting position in the game, a 221:1 lucky break. If you win the pot at this point, you'd nearly double your stack. Should you go all in?

That's exactly the position Benoit Lam was in on the second day of the 2017 Poker Stars Monte Carlo championship. Most players with pocket aces would go all-in in his position; it's easy to fall in love with the beauty of a strong opening hand like this and get locked in, "married to the hand." Yet as other cards came down and it became obvious that his hand was weakening, Lam chose to fold his hand in as a bad bet.[15]

Knowing when to fold 'em, as Kenny Rogers put it, is the mark of a professional in the poker world. One commentator later said:

> *Any investment is about betting when you have an edge and folding when you hold no advantage, or in poker terms, you have poor cards... Without getting clouded by the beauty of the Aces..., clearly focus on hand ranges and likely ranges just as you always do with any other starting hands and make your decision based on those facts rather than anything else. ... Sometimes it's not only fine to fold Aces, but essential if you are to become a winning poker player.*[16]

---

[15]"Would You Fold Pocket Aces Postflop In This Spot?", Martin Harris. PokerNews, 5/8/2017. https://www.pokernews.com/strategy/would-you-fold-pocket-aces-postflop-in-this-spot-27861.htm. The source for the pocket aces fold story comes from this article.
[16]"When is it OK to Fold Aces?", Malcolm Clark. PokerTube.com, 6/22/2016. https://www.pokertube.com/article/when-is-it-ok-to-fold-aces.

In the poker world, the bets you choose not to make is what sets you apart. The same thing is true in football – if distance thrown or arm strength were what counted, we'd have gunslingers like Jeff George and Brett Favre at the very top of the NFL pyramid. Instead, we consider accurate, rock-steady throwers like Tom Brady and Joe Montana the best of all time – judged by their touchdown-to-interception ratio, especially in crunch situations. In other words, just like with poker hands, it's the throws you DON'T make that set you apart as a quarterback.

We wish that kind of dispassionate, logical decision-making – being willing to walk away from a bad bet, or throw the ball away instead of taking a sack or throwing a pick – was more common in the software world. Instead, companies often end up falling in love with a bad hand. In the section "When Is a "Requirement" Not a Requirement?", Ben is trying to instill some more discipline around intake so the limited capacity of his team isn't thrown away on bad bets. In the process, he's taking head on a major source of waste in most software development teams – eliminating unwanted features.

Software Features Are Bets

We're all well familiar with the 80:20 rule; it's a maxim in software that 20% of the highest priority features will satisfy 80% of customer needs. That same 80:20 rule also comes into play with the bets we choose to make with features; one study showed that only 20% of a software's features are frequently used; by far, the majority (64%) of the features developed were rarely or never used.[17]

The features your team is working on are really bets. Forty years of software development demonstrates conclusively that most of these bets are in fact losers – offering negative or neutral value. Each feature or line of code we write in these dead-end missions ends up costing us time we could have invested elsewhere – we will now be building and maintaining vast rooms completely empty of customers, while actual viable and productive ideas languish, buried deep in the dusty caverns of our backlog.

Perhaps, the issue lies with that inflexible word "requirement." Lean Enterprise made the following statement:

---

[17]"Standish Group 2015 Chaos Report - Q&A with Jennifer Lynch," Stéphane Wojewoda, Shane Hastie. InfoQ, 10/4/2015. https://www.infoq.com/articles/standish-chaos-2015. From 2011-2015, the number of "successful" vs challenged/failed projects held rock steady at about 29%. Interestingly, the smaller the project was, the greater its chance of success; small projects had a 62% success rate versus only a 2-6% chance for grand/large sized projects

We should stop using the word 'requirements' in product development, at least in the context of nontrivial features. What we have, rather, is hypotheses. We believe that a particular business model, or product, or feature, will prove valuable to customers. But we must test our assumptions. We can take a scientific approach to testing these assumptions by running experiments.[18]

The Tools for Agile blog once noted that when you hear comments like "wouldn't it be cool if...," or "if only we had this one feature," that alarms should be going off:

Quick – what's the biggest waste in software development? Defects? Rework? Documentation? Work in progress? Communication? Coordination?

Those are all big wastes for sure. But the biggest waste is building features that nobody wants. We can put up with rework and defects if we at least get something useful at the end of the day. The problem with unwanted features is that you not only incur all the other wastes, but you end up developing nothing useful. Worse, you could have the best delivery process in the planet, and it still won't save you from incurring this waste.[19]

Both poker pros and manufacturing mavens would find our obstinate reliance on hard-set "requirements" and long delays in getting customer feedback incomprehensible. Unlike cars or virtually anything else, code is cheap and easy to play with; tailor-made for experimenting and prototypes. Early on, typically within a few weeks, we should be able to come up with something usable that can demonstrate an idea. Once we show this to a customer, there's nothing stopping us from getting their input and quickly folding it into the next version of the design. It's hard to imagine – with this kind of a safe, incremental, experimental approach – that our current rate of project success would stay as miserable as it currently is.

Yet, too often, there is no feedback loop set up to tell us early on if a product or feature will have the results we expect. And often, "agile" development teams are not allowed to change requirements or specifications en route without approval or authorization from some external group – usually, a

---

[18]"Lean Enterprise: How High Performance Organizations Innovate at Scale," Jez Humble, Joanne Molesky, Barry O'Reilly. O'Reilly Media, 1/3/2015. ISBN-10: 1449368425, ISBN-13: 978-1449368425.
[19]"The biggest waste in software development," Siddharta X. Tools For Agile blog, 3/26/2010. http://toolsforagile.com/blog/archives/260/the-biggest-waste-in-software-development.

project management team or executive board. Being handcuffed like this to a bad hand often results in a development team that is hopelessly out of touch with the customer base, working on features that will be rarely or never used.

Hypothesis-Driven Development

Thankfully there's an alternative approach to this kind of joyless toil, and it isn't a long jump from where Ben's team already is. A team that is strong at decomposing work into small batches and making the flow of work visible to all is likely not far off from what we call "hypothesis-driven development."

The 2017 Puppet/DORA "Annual State of DevOps" report noted a strong link between viewing software development as a series of experiments and DevOps tools and practices:

> *Improving your software delivery pipeline will improve your ability to work in small batches and incorporate customer feedback along the way. If we combine these models across years, it becomes a reciprocal model, or colloquially, a virtuous cycle.*

> *In software organizations, the ability to work and deliver in small batches is especially important, because it allows you to gather user feedback quickly using techniques such as A/B testing. It's worth noting that the ability to take an experimental approach to product development is highly correlated with the technical practices that contribute to continuous delivery.[20]*

This experimental approach to software – something called hypothesis driven development – is really just a matter of treating each "requirement" for what it really is – a guess – and setting in controls early on so you can tell if your guess is dead on or needs to be reworked. In short, hypothesis-driven development really comes down to knowing when to fold a bad bet.

Implementation is oh so easy. You simply gate any new story, feature, product backlog by asking a standard set of questions. PMI has long advocated the A3 system, which sounds intimidating but is really just a single piece of paper covering the project goals and experiment conditions at a high level. Others favor the Lean UX template, which is the one Ben's team chose:

We believe that [building this feature] [for these people] will achieve [this outcome]. We will know we are successful when we see [this signal from the market.]

---

[20]"Annual State of DevOps Report," unattributed author(s). Puppet Labs, 2017. https://puppetlabs.com/2017-devops-report.

That's short and sweet, and fine for the use case earlier. Microsoft chose to riff on this with the following feature template for the Azure DevOps teams:

- *Hypothesis: We believe {customer segment} wants {product/ feature} because {value prop}*

- *Experiment: To prove or disprove the above, the team will conduct the following experiment(s): ...'*

- *Learn: The above experiment(s) proved or disproved the hypothesis by impacting the following metric(s): ...*

Again, quite nifty; it states explicitly that this is an experiment and provides a clear go/no go indicator to show whether the experiment is worth continuing.

We discuss this in Chapter 3, but Microsoft has found HDD so valuable that it has folded it into its official Definition of Done for code check-ins. Validation is so inexpensive compared to the cost of creating and supporting a new feature that we believe it should be a required part of any backlog item before any actual coding work is done.

Do We Still Need Project Managers?

It's a common misperception among both Agile and DevOps devotees that project management – including PMO and the business analyst layer – is suddenly a thing of the past. We couldn't disagree more. In fact, it's been our experience that strong delivery-focused organizations rely more heavily on the strategic planning, resourcing, coordination, and customer engagement skills that both the beleaguered project manager and BSA bring to the table. Without strategic or epic-level guidance and budgeting, larger enterprises would suffer chaotic, incoherent product development and waste from cross-team friction and overlap. And a great BSA is the everyday hero and conscience of the team; they engage constantly with the customer to better identify and prioritize work, act as a team advocate to keep expectations of management in line with reality, help shape acceptance testing that is focused and value driven, and act as a guardrail to keep the product's featureset useful and valuable to the end user.

Good project managers keep that engagement with your business partners and stakeholders humming. Mike Kwan once explained that as a PM, one of his most valuable lessons "wasn't how to schedule better; it was how important it is to be in constant communication with sponsors, to document, to communicate. It's incredibly important to define your success criteria right at the beginning."[21]

---

[21]Mike Kwan, Intimetec, interview with Dave Harrison.

And BSAs are a great check and balance on self-inflicted wounds by the devs. We should note here that – despite our using the big bad BSA as the black hat in this section – one of the most frequent culprits in dragging out project timelines are not PMs but – gasp! – the engineers. In the military, brilliant inspirations about the magical benefits of a new tool are said to be inspired by the Good Idea Fairy – a malignant creature definitely not friendly to humans or project timelines. In the DevOps world, we often see the Good Idea Fairy whispering in the ears of engineering teams with the promotion of some fantastic, world-changing language, holistic platform or toolset. A good BSA or PM will make sure that the team stays focused on driving true business value with each sprint, instead of working on a technically driven wish list of cool, cutting-edge glitter.

Breaking Down Bowling Balls

The natural enemy of the development team is the infamous Bowling Ball Story that we often receive unfiltered from customers or stakeholders – a big, heavy, impenetrable, seemingly indivisible requirement. Left alone or unquestioned by that hero BSA or by the team in its sprint planning, these "requirements" will act as a cover for all kinds of unintended scope creep. Basic Agile hygiene tells us to work with our stakeholders to follow the INVEST principle – Independent, Negotiable, Valuable, Estimable, Small, and Testable.

Again, the hero BSA can come to our rescue, by starting with acceptance criteria – what does the finish line look like from their perspective? – and working backward to small, bite-size stories that can be delivered in stages. This will also streamline the automated acceptance testing suite – as Continuous Delivery pointed out, "blindly automating badly written acceptance criteria is one of the major causes of unmaintainable acceptance test suites…. It should be possible to write an automated acceptance test proving that the value described is delivered to the user."[22]

Limiting scope is something that is often preached but incredibly difficult to implement in practice – both developers and stakeholders are eager to deliver as much as possible. The road to hell is lined with good intentions and runaway scope creep. We're reminded of one episode of the TV show "30 Rock," where the executive Jack Donaghy and his design team set out with the desire to build the perfect toaster for GE and end up with design plans for the Pontiac Aztek!

Internal-only projects in particular seem to be particularly susceptible to runaway feature creep. We've worked on several projects with internal customers who insisted on unrealistic uptime SLAs and gold-plated

---

[22]"Continuous Delivery: Reliable Software Releases through Build, Test, and Deployment Automation," Jez Humble, David Farley. Addison-Wesley Professional, 8/6/2010. ISBN-10: 9780321601919, ISBN-13: 978-0321601919.

requirements that were expensive to implement – and impossible to test and support. One project in particular involved working with a very headstrong – and politically powerful – business analyst, who constantly tacked on pet features and extra requirements – and contemptuously waved developers aside with a sweeping motion when we'd come with questions, saying "Just go do it." Another project we were on overran its timeline by 6 months because the BSA on the project kept changing requirements. With no direct customer feedback to inject reality, and no written list of goals, objectives, or success standards to guide us, the project was finally scrubbed as a failure. One manager we talked to recounted a story of laboring for months on a requirement from Marketing around reverse translating CAD models to a previous version – with very little supporting evidence that this was a viable scenario, or even something asked for by customers.

Here, thank goodness, that close and constant link to the customer – something we inherited from the original Agile Manifesto – comes to our rescue. Forcing the ritual of asking the Hypothesis/Experiment/Learn questions at the onsite forces us to think about where exactly the finish line is, what our assumptions are, and how to get feedback in measurable terms from our end user community, early and often.

If a requirement or story can't be delivered in weeks or months, call it out in the planning/prioritization meeting for what it is – a bowling ball. Take the time to refactor and split that big, indivisible object into chunks. Our focus needs to be on solving a real and urgent customer problem as quickly as possible. If we can't quantify what that means, it needs to be refined or dropped.

The Value of a True MVP

Ryan Comingdeer of Five Talent told us that a true MVP can be both a compelling DevOps proof of concept, and a little embarrassing:

> The first sprint is typically just a proof of concept of the CI/CD tools and how they can work on that top #1 feature we've identified. The development team works on it for perhaps 2 days, then sysops takes over and uses our tooling to get this feature into the sandbox environment and then production. This isn't even a beta product, it's a true MVP – something for friends and family. But it's an opportunity to show the business and get that feedback that we're looking for – is the UI ok? How does the flow look? And once the people driving business goals sit down and start playing with the product on that first demo, two weeks later, they're hooked. And we explain – if you give us your suggestions, we can get them to staging and then onto production with a single click. It sells itself – we don't need long speeches.

The typical reaction we get is − "great, you've delivered 5% of what I really want. Come back when it's 100% done." And the product is a little underwhelming. But that's because we're not always sticking to the true definition of a minimum viable product (MVP). I always say, "If an MVP is not something you're ashamed of, it's not a MVP!" Companies like Google and Amazon are past masters at this − they throw something crude out there and see if it sticks. It's like they're not one company but 1,000 little startups. You've got to understand when to stop, and get that feedback.

I've seen customers go way down in the weeds and waste a ton of money on something that ends up just not being viable. One customer I worked with spent almost $250K and a year polishing and refactoring this mobile app endlessly, when we could have delivered something for about $80K − a year earlier! Think of how the market shifted in that time, all the insights we missed out on. Agile is all about small, iterative changes − but most companies are still failing at this. They'll make small changes, and then gate them so they sit there for months.[23]

Don't Shift on Quality

As long as we're on the subject, let's talk about how we handle setting expectations on deliveries with that vital PM/BSA layer. Date-driven discussions seem to be a common failure point in software development. Donovan Brown once said that leading with a date is a huge mistake − to the point where he would sit down with product owners and demand that dates were not mentioned in planning meetings:

The first problem is most conversations begin with a date. That is the first mistake. When you lead with a date then ask if can we make it, developers start to subtract back from that date in their heads and start making compromises. The first time-saver is to cut out testing, which will lead to customer satisfaction issues and technical debt. Technical debt, like credit card debt, accrues interest that you must pay eventually. The hit to your reputation with your customers will take even longer to repair.

…What I needed was the teams honest, unbiased opinion of the effort of each task. Once that was established, the onus was on the product owner to set the priority of the items such that they got what they needed by the date only known to them. Dates became forbidden. The simple fact was if you need 9 days' worth of work in 5 days, you were not getting it.

---

[23]Interview of Ryan Comingdeer by Dave Harrison, see Appendix.

...We have all seen quality suffer to make a date. If anything should be nonnegotiable, it should be quality. ...I know dates exist, but many are not as important as we are first led to believe. They are used to motivate but do more damage than good. How many times have you been told the date cannot be moved, but when you fail to deliver, the date moves?[24]

That's not to say that dates aren't to be discussed, ever. Every organization we've worked with has a different view of what is important in the famous "Iron Triangle" of project management – Dates, Resources/Cost, and Functionality. Some enterprises demand a full set of features but are willing to add more resources and can shift on the dates. Other companies require a full production release by X date but can be negotiable on which features roll out the door. Quality however should be a fixed, nonnegotiable point. The date can get scooted, or we can reduce the feature set; but how work is delivered shouldn't change. After all, how many civil engineers or architects do you know that change the approval protocols or specifications for a building or bridge because "we don't have time for testing"?

Good vs. Bad Documentation

We're asking people to write down more with HDD, which seems odd and a little anti-Agile. Wasn't one of the best bits of the Agile Manifesto about favoring "working software over comprehensive documentation"? Are we creeping back to the bad old days creating reams of requirements and feature documentation?

Hardly! But there's no denying it – documentation at the right time and place can be a real life-saver. For example, one project we worked on involved creating a data warehouse and a REST-based API displaying products, sales information, and images for a company site. The project had a reputation as being an albatross after several failed tries – nothing like it had been done before, the performance requirements were tight, visibility to a reactive management layer was red-hot, and it involved integrating five very different data stores.

Instead of rolling up our sleeves and beginning "real work" on Day 1, we took the time to write down in a single one-page document everything we knew about the project at an executive level – and had it signed off by our executive sponsors. This was a very simple statement of the problem or goal and how we meant to go about solving it with our experiment. We listed the problem statement and performance requirements and desired outcomes, any

---

[24]"Stop Getting Stuff Done After You Said You Couldn't," Donovan Brown. donovanbrown.com, 3/17/2017. http://donovanbrown.com/post/Stop-Getting-Stuff-Done-After-You-Said-You-Couldnt.

assumptions we were making, and how we were going to go about trying to reach this goal. We also showed specifically how we would know if this was a viable solution, including some risks that could end up causing us to scrub the effort.

It's not an understatement to say that this single page saved the project. Having a defined finish line and conditions of acceptance in writing meant we could work on the problem without worrying about the finish line moving on us. When an architect dropped by midproject with an added "enhancement" that would have bloated out our data store, we used that document as a shield, an agreed upon contract. The project was delivered as a successful prototype in the third week – almost 3 months ahead of schedule, and the only effort in several years to come in ahead of time and under budget.

The Deming cycle that so revolutionized the Japanese car industry in the 1970s – and in turn came to software development in the form of Lean – is embodied in the Plan-Do-Check-Act cycle. As some have said, we're very good at the Plan and Do portion – coming up with a hypothesis, and designing an experiment to test it – but not so good at the Check-Act portion, where we go over the results and change our model and approach. Having in writing our understanding of the problem or goal, and our conditions of success, is GOOD documentation that keeps us in a learning and experimenting mode, following up on success and abandoning failure quickly.

The Cutting Edge of the Saw

Hypothesis-Driven Development tends to lead to and complement the use of something we'll be discussing later in more detail – feature flags. Once teams start adopting feature flags as part of their release cycle, they also gain the ability to tweak and test usage and adoption of new features. As any new feature wrapped in a flag can be easily killed, it leads to a more experimental-focused delivery with shorter validation windows – a nice, natural transition to hypothesis-driven development. Netflix, in particular, is an outstanding example of a company that uses feature flags and frequent updates based on usage validation from their customers.

The ability to be able to ideate – whip up a prototype, push it to a small subset of users, and get feedback – can be the cutting edge of your DevOps saw. Your product teams will be happier and more energized with that short turnaround time and narrow focus, as they'll see the benefits from their work and a comfort level that they are not investing their time in dead ends. Your PMO team and stakeholders will know which features deserve refinement and promotion, and which to drop. And your customers will be delighted as the things they want appear instead of gathering dust in a backlog.

Value Stream Mapping

An army may be likened to water, for just as flowing water avoids the heights and hastens to the lowlands, so an army avoids strength and strikes weakness.

—Sun Tzu

One of the biggest failure points I see is that people often don't make their work visible enough. If you don't know what people are working on across the team, that creates a natural siloization which reduces ability to collaborate. Not being completely transparent across the org is one of the biggest pitfalls that I've seen.

—Michael Goetz, Chef

We're still very much in trouble, as you can see from the section "Finding the Real Bottleneck." The team is still completely blind about what features are useful and valuable to their end users, so their development and support is likely going to the wrong places. Mismatches in their environments – and the fact that each environment is a hand-created work of art – are wreaking havoc in terms of setup and maintenance costs, not to mention creating constant overhead when tickets come in as a significant number are caused by noncode-related issues; this also is likely causing a significant amount of distrust in their release testing as their test environments do not reflect production loading or configuration. Leaving aside the troubling anomalies and manual toil this creates, the developers are almost completely tied down with firefighting because their first and second line of defense – the Operations response team – isn't trained or prepared to handle any kind of support.

The main issue though as Karen is bringing out in her assessment is what the book *Team of Teams* calls the "blinks" – the spaces between teams. It's clear no single team is the "problem" – each is trying to do the best they can, and each is tasked up well past 100%. But Ben's development team still sees their mission as writing code; Emily's IT team as standing up environments with high availability; the BSAs and PMs as scoping and delivering requirements from the business; and the Operations team as creating and then reassigning tickets as fast as possible. Each group is describing value as part of the elephant; none can describe their mission in terms of the global whole. The fact that IT, Operations, and Developers all have completely separate work queues and dashboarding is a dead giveaway – there is work still to be done in embracing value delivery from one perspective, the customers.

Finding the Pinch Point

The value stream analysis does point out that one of the main pain points in terms of flow does come down to the way WonderTek is provisioning environments. Defining the pinch point is a key part of Lean and is defined as the "Theory of Constraints." It can be compared to an actual bottleneck or dam on a stream – if we try to improve the flow of water upstream of the dam, it simply piles up more water as a load on the constraint downstream. If we try optimizations after the dam, they'll be ineffective as the overall flow won't change. The theory of constraints teaches that any changes outside of that single pain point are ephemeral and that local optimizations ("we're releasing to QA twice as fast now!") can actually destroy global optimization.

Value stream exercises are helpful in pointing out waste in the form of rework – that's why many recommend showing numbers like %C/A (% complete and accurate), which tells us how much waste is being caused by incomplete or wrong information. But the key value that we look for is delays. Nonvalue-added activities and waiting times, the days that a task awaited work by the next team – those are the holes you want to expose and eliminate:

> If developers are practicing continuous integration, ending each day with a build ready to test, and if the test organization is unable to test at that rate, then it needs to be addressed. If Dev-test is running two-week sprints but the Ops team takes three weeks to provision a new test server, it needs to be addressed. If Dev-test teams are able to operate continuously, delivering code with a high velocity through two-week sprints, but the business analysts are providing new user stories in large blocks once a quarter, which is slower than the delivery velocity, it needs to be addressed. If the security team is only able to run their security tests on new apps, only once per release cycle, and take 5 to 10 days to run their tests, it needs to be addressed. If integration builds are taking hours to complete because they build every component and module, even those that did not change, it needs to be addressed. If the lines of business expect projects to operate on project plans with fixed, gate-based schedules but in reality their requirements are not well understood, the project plans need to be addressed.[25]

Our value stream here is fairly big picture and imperfect. It's perfectly OK to have a very big-picture first draft that you refine over time. Mike Kwan told us that he instinctively doesn't like value stream mapping as an exercise, because it tends to get bogged down in the weeds. The whole aspect of

[25]"The DevOps Adoption Playbook: A Guide to Adopting DevOps in a Multi-Speed IT Enterprise," Sanjeev Sharma. Wiley, 2/28/2017. ISBN-10: 9781119308744, ISBN-13: 978-1119308744

quantification and finding out which aspect is causing the most pain in a process can be like playing whack-a-mole. He does favor what he calls **progressive elaboration** – where the entire process is mapped out very top level, say depicting the flow of information/artifacts or a dependency mapping, and it's progressively refined as more information is known or the team tries different solutions to see if they're a good fit.

> *I love that phrase of progressive elaboration, and I use it all the time. So start by rolling it backwards. Start with getting it in the hands of your users – without even talking about what it is they're doing. How frequently are you going to deliver it? How are you going to ensure that what you're delivering is what the users expect? What's your acceptance test on product features? How are you going to define quality?*
>
> *Progressive elaboration allows us to learn from doing. Execution yields insights that just weren't possible from extensive upfront planning – which is often informed by assumption or old experiences. It allows us to start, learn, and avoid being paralyzed by trying to completely plan upfront based on information that is likely to change or become stale.*
>
> *These methods didn't exist when we ported project management methods from hardware to software. The hardware development ramps included long lead time and expensive tooling and manufacturing costs. But software isn't like that. We can write code early, and then throw it away if we learn something. And we can change it right up to the last moment.*[26]

We're guessing that very few if any of your team has a clearly mapped and visible view of the flow of work end to end, from idea to product. Coming up with this picture isn't a matter of a few minutes, but it also shouldn't take more than a few days with the right people in the room and a little digging. We favor permanent markers and giant sticky notes to keep the moving parts as simple as possible so the group doesn't bog down in minutiae.

The map doesn't need to be revisited daily, or even weekly. But it's an excellent idea to revisit it from time to time and see how things are improving. For shared services organizations, some have found it helpful to hold a regular collaboration workshop, where the leaders review the stream and commit to optimization steps as a group.[27]

---

[26]Mike Kwan, Intimetec, interview with Dave Harrison.

[27]"Making Matrixed Organizations Successful with DevOps: Tactics for Transformation in a Less Than Optimal Organization," Gene Kim. IT Revolution DevOps Enterprise Forum 2017. https://itrevolution.com/book/making-matrixed-organizations-successful-devops/ A good discussion on how and why to form a cross-functional team, starting with the leadership level.

Jon Cwiak of Humana uses two now-familiar metrics to identify constraints in their value stream mapping exercises:

> There's lots of metrics to choose from, but two metrics stand out – and they're not new or shocking. Lead time and cycle time. Those two are the standard we always fall back on, and the only way we can tell if we're really making progress. They won't tell us where we have constraints, but it does tell us which parts of the org are having problems. We're going after those with every fiber of our effort. There's other line of sight metrics, but those two are dominant in determining how things are going.
>
> We do value stream analysis and map out our cycle time, our wait time, and handoffs. It's an incredibly useful tool in terms of being a bucket of cold water right to the face – it exposes the ridiculous amount of effort being wasted in doing things manually. That exercise has been critical in helping prove why we need to change the way we do things. Its specific, quantitative – people see the numbers and get immediately why waiting two weeks for someone to push a button is unacceptable. Until they see the numbers, it always seems to be emotional.[28]

The pain point (what the military calls a "limfac," a limiting factor) may surprise you. Perhaps, the main pain point is at the very beginning – what we call the "fuzzy front end," the length of time ideas and features spend in limbo until they're assigned to a developer's work queue as a backlog item. One leader we spoke to started out considering lead time as being relatively unimportant; once he realized how much his business partners were frustrated by apparent delay and slow progress on mission critical ideas, displaying progress in terms of lead time became his touchstone. It could also be the testing cycle, or a manual stage gate preproduction. Other times, as we see in this book, the time spent provisioning and readying environments is the limfac. The point is – until you measure it, and keep it displayed, it won't get better.

Local optimization has a long tradition and showing performance improvements across just a portion of the flow – the one you happen to be responsible for – can be tempting. John Willis shared a story about the hazards of doing a partial value stream map:

> I had lunch a few weeks ago with a CIO of a Manhattan-based Fortune 500 company in which I tried to help him understand his DevOps questions. I asked him if they had ever tried to use the Lean Value Stream Mapping process to understand their overall cycle times. He proceeded to give me a tongue lashing about how he has been studying Lean Sigma for

---

[28]Interview of Jon Cwiak by Dave Harrison, see Appendix.

over 1000 years and they had tried every trick in the book. I mention a few other DevOps hacks but we seem to be going nowhere fast. However, near the end of the conversation he says something about his operations team that gives me a clue to ask one more last question. I asked him, 'When you did the Value Stream Mapping, did you do it across engineering and operations?' After about 15 seconds of dead silence he sheepishly answered, 'Shit, we never thought about that.'[29]

Value stream mapping are typically a very revealing exercise; for most people in the room, this may be the first time they've seen the amount of hard work and heroics required to get a release out the door. The amount of thrash and stress caused by long lead times and handoff delays is exposed in stark detail, with nowhere to hide. It could just be the ticket to get executive awareness of the price being paid with clunky manual processes and siloed entrenched teams of specialists – a great catalyst for change based on objective data.

---

[29]"DevOps Culture (Part 1)," John Willis. IT Revolution, 5/1/2012. https://itrevolution.com/devops-culture-part-1/ This is an extremely influential and powerful article; we turned back to it many times.

Drilling In

It's halfway through spring, and the delivery teams at WonderTek are just starting to realize how much of their work is falling between the cracks.

That's not saying there haven't been some encouraging signs of progress. By setting up and enforcing blame-free postmortems, they've made significant headway in encouraging a culture that is more focused on learning from mistakes instead of punishment, blame, and evasion. They're cutting down the time they spend on dead ends and red herrings by treating their development stories and features as guesses – experiments – bets that they can either double down on or abandon if they don't hit predetermined marks.

By far, the best changes are in the fundamental way that Operations and Development are learning to work together. Ben and Emily are starting to show a commitment in the things valued by their other partner – well coordinated and thought out release plans by Ops and delivery retrospectives and planning by Dev. Having displays everywhere that focus on business-centric KPIs like response time, availability, and defects is having a subtle but penetrating effect; developers and operations are starting to see problems from a common, global point of view.

As positive as these developments are, there's still so much work left undone. Engineers are still drowning in tickets turfed to them by Operations, who are using a completely separate ticket queue. Security is still an afterthought. Most seriously, a seemingly positive and long-overdue development – a true value stream map – threatens to break up that fragile truce that he and Emily have established.

It's clear that testing and quality, which used to be the limiting factor in their delivery life cycle, has become much less of a problem. Taking its place as a constraint is infrastructure – the time it takes to spin up environments and

© Dave Harrison and Knox Lively 2019
D. Harrison and K. Lively, *Achieving DevOps*,
https://doi.org/10.1007/978-1-4842-4388-6_5

configure them properly. WonderTek is still very much a political swamp in many ways, and old habits die hard. Will that tenuous working relationship between dev and IT fall back into the old game of finger pointing and blame?

Leaner and Meaner (Small Cross-Functional Teams)

Karen's audit and the aftermath hit us like a bomb. It was like somebody had poked a stick into an anthill.

Emily and I had talked with Karen shortly after her presentation, and we started to form a plan. Over the next few weeks, I was very busy talking to security and our architects, often folding Karen in over the phone. I also stepped up my discussions with Tabrez. I felt confident that once the audit report appeared, we'd be ready.

A few weeks later, the audit report came in. Thankfully, it wasn't a tree-killing dictionary of "best practices" – just a few dozen pages summarizing Karen's assessment of WonderTek's delivery cycle and some simple steps she recommended to resolve our current delivery bottleneck. Most of this was around infrastructure.

In the old days, not so many months ago, getting ammunition like this to use against my rival would have been cause for rejoicing. But Emily and I have been having lunch or coffee together a few times a week, and she and Kevin have been incredibly busy trying to wrap his arms around how to best create immutable infrastructure on demand. Somehow, I can't find it in myself to start putting in the dagger on a problem that both of us share.

Not that there aren't temptations. During my weekly 1x1 with Douglas, he brought up the audit again, and you couldn't have asked for a better opportunity to throw IT under the bus. He begins by complaining, "You know, I told you a year ago that WonderTek just isn't ready for this DevOps thing. I think we've gone a bridge too far here, Ben. It's time to scale this back, we shouldn't have to deal with this much stress and friction."

I have to walk cautiously here. Douglas has a point that there's a strong undercurrent of suspicion that "this DevOps thing" is a fad, and we've gotten a lot of resistance. I've been very careful to narrow my focus to specific workstreams, not even using that loaded (and imperfect!) word "DevOps" in any meetings. Instead, I put things in terms like "delivering value," "driving efficiency," or "eliminating waste." We've found that if we keep a laser focus on delivering business value and streamlining our release pipeline, and back it up with monitor displays of our current and desired future state, we win. But if it comes across as a dev-centered movement around better tooling or process refactoring, it falls flat.

I tell Douglas that we aren't trying to do DevOps – just straightening out the kinks in the hose that are preventing us from delivering value. This particular morning, that isn't working for me. He stares at the ceiling, eyelids half closed, jaw jutting out. "Don't piss on me and tell me it's raining, Ben. I'm telling you, every organization has a turning radius. WonderTek isn't a sportscar, it's a supertanker. You're risking the ship by trying too much change, too fast."

I get the message, and I'm concerned about where this is coming from; we've been very careful with our bets and have tried to keep a low profile. He's evasive about where he's getting this information, and ultimately it doesn't matter; I have to bring our attention back to the future we're trying to create and leave the office scuttlebutt alone. I reply, "You've read the audit – the numbers speak for themselves. We don't have an Ops problem, or a Dev problem, or a PM/BSA problem – regardless of how people try to frame things. The issue is the blinks – the spaces in between these different delivery groups. If you want faster and better delivery of value, we need to seal those gaps."

I just get a groan in response; his eyes are still on the ceiling. Time to try a different tack. "Douglas, you're a military guy. What do you think about Grant's campaign at Vicksburg during the Civil War?"

This gets his attention, and he arrows a sour look in my direction. It's an irresistible gambit; Douglas loves military history and especially the Civil War. He slowly says, "Vicksburg? Ah, that was kind of genius. You know, people think General Lee was the dominant military genius of the war, but I always say that if those two men had switched places, Grant would have acted exactly as Lee had. Both could take great risks when they needed to."

Bait taken! "If I remember right, Grant didn't succeed the first time, did he?"

"Ha! No, far from it. He failed so many times. He had to cross the Mississippi river against a prepared enemy that outnumbered him. First he tried approaching from two sides; that failed, twice – then he tried digging canals to bypass the city's forts, which failed... shoot, had to be a half dozen different things he tried. All losers, and it cost him months." He's starting to warm up and then catches himself. "Why?"

"What ended up being the winning formula for Grant?"

"Ah... well, he did the bold and unexpected thing. He risked crossing the river, completely away from his supply lines and any hope of retreat, and fought a series of battles away from the city that forced the enemy commander to make guesses. His opponent guessed wrong, and the North ended up defeating them in detail. It was the biggest turning point of the war, in my opinion."

I'm not Douglas' match when it comes to history, but I have read enough to try to make my point. "So, let me put this to you – Lee said Grant would 'hang on like a bulldog and never let go.' Grant's greatest quality was persistence, even when things looked grim. Grant tried, what, six different approaches at Vicksburg and they all failed miserably – everyone but the last. Any other general would have quit months earlier. Can we take a page from his book and show some persistence and courage here? To try to do something different?"

The sour look is gone; Douglas looks intrigued. "You mean, Karen's SWAT team recommendation?"

"That's exactly what I'm talking about." I open my tablet to that page of the report:

SWAT Team

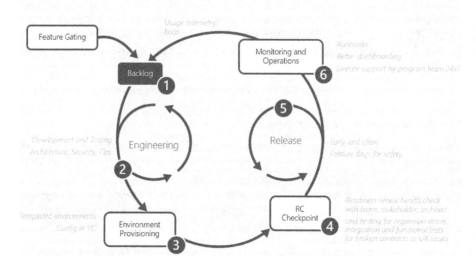

"Karen is proposing that we try something new," I continue. "She's asking us if we're ready to cross the river. The report proposes that for our future releases with Footwear, we try using a very small team – like under 10 people – that can deliver a single feature end to end in two weeks. With this, we close the 'blinks' – we should have none of the delays or lost information and rework that we've suffered in every release in the past."

I build up some steam as I continue talking about some of the benefits; it's something Emily and I are starting to get excited about. We already have a lot of the building blocks in place with better version control and continuous integration.

Better yet, I might have some very powerful allies in the wings. I know that our architects – who always complain about being brought in late or not at all – are very enthusiastic about this as a concept. We're still working out how this might look, but it could be in the form of part time involvement –

maybe a day each sprint, more if needed – by an architect embedded with the product team directly. Security is also onboard; they're thinking about a similar engagement model, where they give us some best practices training on folding security in as part of our development life cycle. Music to my ears, they're even floating ideas around about making this as painless as possible to implement by creating a community-curated security framework.

As I expected, this resonates with Douglas as we're talking better-integrated teams – and reducing the hassles and static he gets from both of these very vocal groups. Still, the core problem remains. "Ben, what worries Emily and I the most is how this report is sandbagging on her IT team; it's divisive and doesn't take into account how hard her people are working. And Karen's recommending that we make the jump to the cloud, which is off the table. It's a massive security risk, not to mention throwing away the millions of dollars we've invested in our own datacenters. Yet this is one of the key recommendations in the audit – saying moving to the cloud is the only way we'll be able to deliver truly scalable and resilient infrastructure in the timeline that Footwear is wanting. That's just not based on reality, at all."

I'm going to need to sidestep a little; any mention of the cloud provokes a strong allergic reaction from anyone at IT and Operations. But I also know how long it takes us to spin up a single VM and get it configured correctly, and the beating our availability takes due to untested patches and configuration changes that are impossible to roll back. I'm convinced that Karen is right; we are going to have to step away from our supply lines and try something new. My guess is, if we empower our teams to handle end-to-end support and deployments and not mandate one specific platform, exactly where our services are hosted will cease to become such a contentious question.

"Karen recommended that we have at least one and preferably two Operations specialists on each team," I reply. "That's like a quarter of the team, Douglas – so it's not like Emily's people aren't being involved enough. Just the fact that we're going to be in the same room and talking to each other is a huge win. When it comes to the cloud – I agree with you, whether the apps run there or on our own datacenters is not the question to be asking. I think we should have as a goal that faster end to end delivery cycle that Tabrez is asking for. Anything that gets in the way of that turnaround needs to be eliminated, without remorse.

"Right now our scoreboard is saying we're taking 9 days for each release, but that's just out the door to QA. That's not the actual finish line – when our bits make it out the door to production. And you know what that number actually is – we're talking in months, not days. 23 days of work – and 53 days of delays due to handoffs. I think we can cut that delivery time in half, or better, if we adopt some of Karen's proposals."

There's a pause for a few seconds as Douglas scans me. "Have you talked to Tabrez about this?"

"Yes. He's totally onboard. He has a space available – a large conference room, really comfortable, big enough to fit 20, right next to his designers there in Footwear. He loves the thought of having the team close by and accessible."

"I'll bet he does." Douglas groans again, "You realize you're opening up your team to all kinds of problems, don't you? They're going to be interrupted ninety times a day now with Tabrez and his people stopping by with their little requests."

"Maybe." That's something else I haven't thought about; I like our little cocoon of silence. Was that mystery voice right – am I introducing more chaos in our work patterns than we can handle? I decide to brazen it out. "Our thinking is, the closer we can get to the customer, the quicker we can understand what they really want. I'm confident they'll play by the rules, and personally I'm excited about seeing them more at our retrospectives as stakeholders. I'm getting pretty tired of presenting our work to an empty room, Douglas."

"Mmmmm." Douglas is looking back at his monitor display. "You know, I don't agree with everything Karen said, and I agree with Emily that she should have talked more to senior management ahead of launching this little bombshell. But, I like the thoughts in here about first responder training. I know for a fact that our customers are complaining about their tickets waiting around for days or weeks for a developer to get to them; we'd be much better off if we could knock down the easy stuff in a few minutes. You know, I've said to Ivan a hundred times, having his team act as some kind of glorified turnstile that churns out bugs isn't helping us at all. Lack of good triage has always been a pain point."

I propose a weekly review where the team can present progress transparently. "Let's be up front and tell people that this is an experiment, an open lab. We're going to be trying some new things and making some mistakes, and we want to share our wins and losses openly with everyone. For example, how do we use feature flags? We think it'll really help us be able to safely toggle new functionality on and off so our releases will be less disruptive – but that's just a guess right now. And what about monitoring – do we go with a vendor or roll our own? How do we set up dashboarding so everyone is looking at work the same way? How do we fold usage data back in to our backlog prioritization before each sprint? What about – well, you get the idea. We're going to try a different approach, because we're wanting a different result."

It takes another hour of back-and-forth negotiations, but I walk out with what I needed. We're going to give the SWAT team a 3-month try. Our judge will be Footwear; if after 3 months the needle doesn't budge or if there is excessive thrash, Douglas will pull the plug.

McEnvironments (Configuration Management and Infrastructure As Code)

Like I said, Kevin and Emily had been talking about immutable infrastructure. But talk it seems was still a long way from action, and for the next few weeks we suffered through incident after incident caused by environmental instability.

First, we had a charming outage caused by a distributed denial-of-service attack against our DNS nameservers; it took some scrambling to figure out what was going on, and a few days more to figure out a fix with our caching and a failover strategy for what had become a sneaky single point of failure for our network. Then, we had one of our production services not restart after the host servers were up-patched; our monitoring missed that completely. In an embarrassing repeat of the Footwear services abend a few months earlier, it took some customers calling in to realize that the service was unresponsive and force a restart. And we kept having to spend valuable time determining if an issue was code related or environmental related. As none of our environments really matched each other as yet, piecing together what had happened and when took much longer than it should. If I was to take George and Alex at their word – easily 75% of our ticket resolution time was spent isolating problems and turfing server or environmental-related problems back to Operations.

This made for a somewhat chilling impact on my lunches with Emily; no doubt, she was getting an earful from her people as well. After our postmortem on the DDoS attack, Emily agreed quickly to a powwow on our next step with infrastructure as code.

I got in a little late, just in time for Kevin to hit his concluding remarks. "Alex, Ivan and I have been looking over our production-down issues from the last three months. It's very common for networking elements like routers, DNS, and directory services to break our services and apps in prod, as well as causing ripple effects with our network availability and performance. Our recommendation is that we beef up our network monitoring software to catch these issues while they're still in a yellow state, and make sure that every time a connection times out or is closed our apps need to be logging warnings. And our test environment topology needs to be beefed up so that we've got more assurance that what works in QA will perform similarly in production."

Alex nodded. It was a good sign that he and Kevin were sitting next to each other and both relatively calm. "One other aspect that Kevin and Emily are in favor of is making sure every part of our networking infrastructure is in version control. That means that we need to make sure that our switches, routers, everything can be externally configured, and that we are able to roll out changes to these elements using code. That's true of a lot of our infrastructure but not everything; it's going to be a gradual process."

If this is like our move to version control, I'm confident that what seems to be an overwhelming task will end up being triage. We'll take one batch of networking elements at a time, starting with the most troublesome, and gradually isolate out and shoot the parts that can't be configured and updated externally. Just the fact that we're talking about automation and infrastructure as code is a positive step. Still, this isn't a postmortem about one isolated incident; I'm hoping that we can begin a larger discussion around enabling self-service environments. After saying that, I offer up some tech candy: "Do we have the tools we need to recover faster from failure?"

Ivan snorts. "You're talking about configuration management, right Ben? Well, we've had Puppet here for about three years. We spend a fortune on it with licensing every year, and frankly it fails more often than it works. If we can't get it to work reliably outside of ad hoc script commands, we're going to scrap it in favor of something cheaper." His tone is flat and emphatic.

A few more ideas get batted around of different software solutions. As people talk animatedly about their own pet favorites – containers, Packer, Terraform, Ansible – I stay silent and absent-mindedly swirl my coffee cup around. I keep thinking back to that value stream map that's taunting me from the conference room; 53 days of delay caused by handoffs and delays in provisioning infrastructure. The problem isn't that Emily's team is lazy or incompetent; I know from my visits over there that they're constantly under the gun and putting in long hours. The problem is that gap, the blink between the developers needing new environments and the way software is built out at WonderTek. We need to figure out a better way of closing the gap, something that can please both sides. I'm not convinced that new software would actually help, but my guess is that it's our use of that software – our process – that needs to get tightened up.

I look up from my coffee cup just in time to catch Emily giving me a significant look. We've been talking about better ways of configuring our servers over the past few weeks. She reaches out and pats Ivan on the hand; it's not a condescending gesture, but it does get his attention and stops him mid-rant. "I'm not sold on the idea of Puppet being a loser yet, Ivan. Right now, we're running Puppet on an ad hoc basis, for a few workstreams in our portfolio. And we use it to maintain an asset library and catch licensing compliance issues. That's a good start, but I think we need to trust the tool more, and use it like it's designed to be used."

Ivan is incredulous. "Emily, we've never been able to get it to work. It seems to break down after a few weeks on any of our servers, and it's a nightmare trying to find out what the proper template is for our environments. Sorry, but configuration management given our working constraints – and the constellation of servers and environments we have to manage – is a dead end."

Alex's eyebrows go up at this conversational hand grenade, but before he can get a word out Kevin speaks up: "Agreed, it's going to be challenging finding the proper source of truth with our environments. But we all know that configuration drift is a problem that's not going away, and it seems to be getting worse. Puppet – really any configuration management tool, but that's the one we've got – is purpose built to fix this problem."

Alex chimes in, "We had to force ourselves to use version control as the single point of truth for all our application builds. Yeah, it wasn't easy, but we started with the most fragile, important workstreams – and one at a time, we put up some guardrails. We didn't allow any manual config changes and used our CI/CD release pipeline for any and all changes, including hotfixes. No change, no matter how small or how urgent, was allowed to be rolled out manually. Could we use the same approach in managing our infrastructure?"

Ivan puffs out his cheeks in disbelief and says slowly, "Once again, we can't get it to work. It breaks. What works on one app server, doesn't run green on another – the Puppet run fails, and we even had a few servers go down. And we're too busy to invest more time in this. Now, maybe if we had the people I've been asking for…"

Emily is drumming her fingers on the table. "Ivan, we gave you more people, three months ago. Is anyone here seriously arguing that setting up and keeping our machines configured using automated scripts a bad idea?" Ivan starts to speak, then snaps his jaw shut as Emily gives him a hard look. "On this subject, Ben and I have been in agreement for some time. If we tighten things up so we run our environments through the same release process we do code – with a pipeline, one we can roll back or inspect – I'm betting we'll knock out most of the trouble tickets your team is loaded down with, Ivan."

Kevin says, "What would happen if we let Puppet run unattended across our entire domain?" There's now a few people shaking their heads no; there was just too much variance for this kind of a switch-flip to work. He squinches up his face a little, in thought. "OK, then we run this in segments. Let's take a single set of servers handling one workstream – make sure that our configuration definitions are set and work properly, and then we let Puppet run unattended on them. If that works, after two weeks, we start rolling this out to other batches."

Ivan is fighting a rearguard action now; he allows that, if Kevin is willing to try this experiment first with the apps he's managing, including Footwear, then perhaps it wouldn't be a complete disaster. I suppress an irritated twitch to my mouth; Ivan's fear of automation is almost pathological. I keep telling myself that servers and environments are complex and unsafe, with lots of moving breakable parts; his caution is a learned behavior from years of dodging hammers.

If this gets us to where our environments are more consistent, it's a big win. Perhaps, I should be satisfied with that, but there's still that vision of true end-to-end responsibility, where the SWAT teams handle both production support and maintain their own set of environments. There's so much left to be done for us to get to where we are self-service. It's clearly the elephant in the room; of those 53 days of delay, most is wait time on provisioned environments. I could make my delivery promises with room to spare if we had more direct control and responsibility.

The thought of being able to create a new set of environments with a pushbutton script, without waiting weeks on the infrastructure CAB process and coming up with business case justification arguments, is just too appealing to pass up. Best of all, it'd give Emily's infrastructure team a higher purpose and more rewarding work, overseeing and strengthening the framework instead of doing low-level work like spinning up VM's manually.

However, Emily and I are not there yet, and I have no desire to continue pressing the point if it'll cost us our gains. Last week, she told me point-blank that she didn't think our developers can or should handle infrastructure support directly; she still clearly views provisioning as being the exclusive domain of her team.

I have to give her credit though — in a conciliatory move, Emily has been working with our cloud provider to allow us to select from one of three possible templates on demand. As a first effort, it's a start, but these approved images are so plain-vanilla and locked down that Alex told me that they were functionally useless as true application servers. In a rare burst of humor, he called them "McEnvironments" — fast, mass-produced, and junky.

So, half a loaf it is. I'll keep the pain points we have around provisioning environments visible. I'm convinced that over time those self-service options will become less rigid, and that core question — who has responsibility over creating and maintaining environments? — will be resolved in a way that will help free up the infrastructure team from tedious grunt work and help the coders take more ownership over the systems their applications and services run on.

An Insecurity Complex (Security As Part of the Life Cycle)

Brian, a balding middle-aged man who always reminds me a little of Elmer Fudd, sighs deeply. "Like I told you, this software can't be released. Your version of Bouncy Castle has a weak hash-based messaging authentication code that's susceptible to cracking." He sees my blank look and tries again, his voice having just a tinge of a whine — "Your application uses a cryptographic API called Bouncy Castle; the version you chose is not on our list of approved versions, for good reason – we've known for several months now that it can be brute forced in just a few seconds by a hacker using a hash collision attack. It's beyond me why you guys chose it."

Try as I might, whenever I talk with Brian, I can't help but think of Looney Tunes and "Wabbit Season"; it makes it nearly impossible to take what he says seriously. I swivel to Alex and ask: "I have no idea really what's going on here, but Brian seems to think that we have a problem with our authentication library. How widespread is this?"

Alex is slouching in his chair, slumped in frustration. "For this application, updating this out of date library to a more current version is just a few keystrokes. Then we have to kick off a whole new round of testing – not that big of a deal, thanks to our shiny new release pipeline. But it's not just this application – we have dozens to support, and we'll have to check each one. Most of them don't have any kind of a release pipeline other than walking over with a thumbdrive to Ops, and there's no test layer to protect us. Honestly, it could take us weeks, more likely months. This is going to kill our velocity, Ben."

The teeth-grating whine again, this time a little louder: "That's hardly MY fault! We've asked you guys for months to do a little better checking on your deployments using the known Top 10 threats published by OWASP. That's a basic level of competence, Alex. If you would have thought ahead even a little, this update would have been easy!"

I cut him off. "Brian, I'm convinced you have our best interests – and the safety of our users and our data – at heart. You don't have to worry about us shooting the messenger; we're better off knowing about this than living in ignorance."

George interrupts, "I'm not so worried about this particular attack vector. I know this will get fixed, now that we're aware. I'm worried about the next one. It seems like these vulnerabilities keep popping up more and more often. It's causing us a lot of headaches, usually right before a release. And it seems like our dependencies are usually the vulnerable spot – stuff like this Bouncy Castle API. Brian, do you have any ideas on how we can get a little ahead of this?"

Brian says slowly and patiently, "Just the things you already know about. Your team needs to make security a first-priority concern. Right now it's last, and that's why this release is going to miss its dates."

Brian may know security, but he doesn't understand the repercussions of missing dates and how that's viewed here. I counter, "Brian, I don't miss dates. We can scale back on the features we deliver, but two things don't change on my teams – quality and the delivery date. The business cares very much about getting what they need out on time. To me, something like this security bug is a quality issue. So, we'll fix it – and we'll make our date."

George breaks in again. "Brian, help us out a little here. This isn't something written in COBOL back in the 70's. We've got a lot of cutting edge stuff packed into this site and it's rolling out fully automated. We can make changes on the fly, safely – nothing is fixed in stone. So how can we get a better picture of these security gaps early on?"

Brian waves a pudgy hand and says dismissively, "Well, not knowing your code or anything about the design, I really can't say. Just stick to what the checklist pointed out in my latest security scan."

"Brian, that security scan is three weeks old," Alex says, grating his teeth. "That's a lifetime ago when we're talking about software – how do I know that when you run your audit again, that we won't have other holes pop up?"

Brian looks like he has Bugs Bunny staring right down the barrel of his 12-gauge shotgun. "You don't. But I don't think you want to get your name on the front page of the paper, do you? Or hear from management after I submit my report?" He gives us a self-satisfied, smug, almost sleepy grin. Classic Elmer.

Once we pledge fealty and promise to address this new vulnerability as our "top priority," the meeting peters out and Brian shuffles off to his next victim. Alex throws his notepad at the whiteboard. "Dammit! We were almost there! Now, I have to waste days satisfying this bureaucratic nightmare of a checklist! And I guarantee you, that's not the end of the story. He'll find something else."

I say, "You know, I'm not so sure. I've been talking to Erik about this – he's a lot more helpful than Brian is, and it helps he's an actual decisionmaker with InfoSec. They're onboard with the idea of having someone from their team bundled up with our new SWAT teams, a half day a week."

I get a suspicious sideways glance from Alex. "It's not Brian, is it?"

"I don't know. For God's sake, let's not make Elmer – I mean Brian, sorry – the problem here. He's not telling us anything we didn't need to know. We just didn't hear it soon enough. Now, how are we going to get ahead of this next time?"

George looks thoughtful. "You know, we've been getting pretty slack lately with some of our basic hygiene. There's no reason why we can't gate our check-ins so that it looks for those top 10 vulnerabilities. That would give us early feedback – and it won't allow checking in code we know is insecure. And it's a lot more objective than Brian coming in at the 11th hour with a red octagon sign based on his vulnerability du jour."

"Will this lengthen our build times?" Alex wonders, his brow furrowed. Alex watches check-in times like a hawk and is merciless about forcing developers to rewrite slow-running tests. He was the originator of the now-infamous "Nine Minutes Or Doom" rule at WonderTek – throwing a royal hissy fit and hunting down culprits if it took longer to check in code than it took to grab a cup of coffee from the cafeteria.

Both George and I chuckle, remembering the last particularly epic tantrum with great fondness. "No, it takes almost no time at all to run some basic security checks," George says. "If we're smart, we'll need to augment this with some penetration testing. We can't keep on trying to harden our apps when they're 90% baked like this."

I ask, "Isn't this overkill? I mean, is there any information here that someone would actually WANT to steal?"

"On this app, no." Alex smirks wearily. "This is what I mean – those security guys have a hammer, every single frigging thing is a nail. There's absolutely no proprietary information here at all. No sensitive records, no socials, no credit card info, nada. We're clean."

"OK, so there's no PI data. But we still have information in there we need to keep private," George muses. "Otherwise it'd be an open system and you wouldn't need to authenticate at all. At the very least, we need to make sure the user information we use for logins is protected and that the site itself doesn't get hacked and users get directed elsewhere."

I'm convinced this is a gap that we need to fill – and that it'll bring a powerful advocate to my side. "I'm convinced this is a gap we need to fill. Security reviews need to be a part of every feature design – Erik will totally be behind that. But we can't do it ourselves, and static scans aren't enough. We need a better framework that's preauthorized – make it easy on our guys to do the right thing."

Alex says, "These guys see themselves as gatekeepers, Ben. They're not going to want to sink time into being at our design sessions and looking over our deployment code."

If we were talking about Brian, Alex's assumptions would be dead on. Thankfully, Erik's made of different stuff; since our talk he's been five steps ahead of me, championing the creation of a curated framework that was community-owned and blessed by our security gods. But I just smile and say, "Give them some credit. I think they're ready for a more cooperative model. I'll meet with Erik later today and see what his thoughts are. I'll tell him we want to do the right thing – and that we need his help. He'll love that – especially if I make him think it's his idea!"

Like magic, a few weeks later Brian starts appearing at our biweekly design sessions. The hated checklist stops making such frequent appearances as we begin folding in security scans into our check-in gating.

We're still a ways away from a comprehensive security framework – but I trust Erik and I know it'll come, soon. And now we're getting regular feedback on security as part of our development life cycle.

Effective First Response (Automated Jobs and Dev Production Support)

Ivan takes a long slurp on his coffee and lets the silence build a little. As usual, his hackles are up. "Folks, I'm a little surprised to see this meeting fall on my calendar this week. We weren't given any time to prepare and I don't like the agenda, to be honest. Seems kind of dev-driven to me. Is this another pin-the-tail-on-the-Ops guy session? If so, I'm walking."

Try as I might, our relationship with Ivan and his support team hasn't thawed like it has with Emily; my charm offensive (such as it was) was stopped in its tracks. I'm not giving up yet on the campaign, but it does look like we've got at least one very vocal detractor who's dug in.

I lean forward and say, "I appreciate your concern, Ivan – I've been in a few meetings like that here myself. This isn't a blame session; we're trying to figure out ways we can work together better in handling support."

"Yeah, that seems like the same thing." Ivan takes another long sip, drawing it out to show his contempt. "My people are already working very hard, round the clock, to try to support your crap. Forgive me for being blunt here, Ben, but it seems to me like you're angling to shuffle more support work on my guys. That's not going to fly with me, and I think Emily will back me up on that one."

Tabrez, our Footwear stakeholder, now steps in. "I'm sure we'd all love another round of Ops and Devs playing tag, but that's not the point. I called this meeting for one purpose. We're seeing a lot of tickets lately with our new app; our customers are getting angry that these tickets just seem to sit there in queue, awaiting developer attention. And we've had a few high-profile outages that seemed to drag on and on. What can we do collectively to turn this situation around with our support system?"

The charts Tabrez displays tell the story, and it's a grim one. "As you can see, we seem to be treading water. Our response time on our high severity tickets are getting worse, and those third tier tickets – things like customers getting authentication errors or timeout issues – they're totally circling the drain. It's taking us on average more than 10 hours to knock down these local issues, by which time the customer has often moved on to other, more reliable apps.

"I don't even want to read to you the comments we're getting in the app store for both Google and Apple – they could remove paint. Our ratings are in the toilet. We're hemorrhaging customers. This just can't go on."

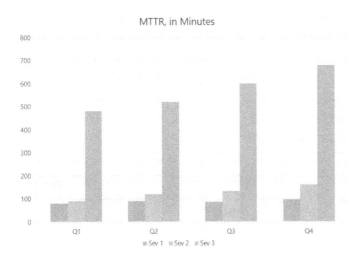

MTTR, in Minutes

Ivan snorts derisively. "See, that's exactly what I'm talking about. For this app, we received zero training. Ben's team just dropped it on us, out of nowhere. And you'll notice, the changes I instituted about three months ago are working. We're processing more tickets than ever, and it's automated – meaning less time per ticket by the Ops team. That's nearly doubling our efficiency. We're a multibillion dollar company with a global scope, and I have a lot more apps to support than just Footwear. I don't think anyone here has any idea of how difficult it is to be in the firing line like we are, 7 days a week."

I'm wearing my best poker face but have to fight not to roll my eyes. Ivan's claims of weary serfdom and powerless victimhood are starting to wear a little thin. We did training, exhaustively, and Alex tells me that we've provided a list of "Top 10" issues that we expected Ivan's team to help knock down.

"As you can see, our ticket numbers are escalating," Tabrez says, continuing with the next slide. "If we view success narrowly as being 'efficiency in intake of tickets,' then maybe this is a win. But from the customer's point of view, this is a disaster. We do need to provide true global support, 24x7, and if the ticket has to wait for the next available dev – that's just too long for most of our customers."

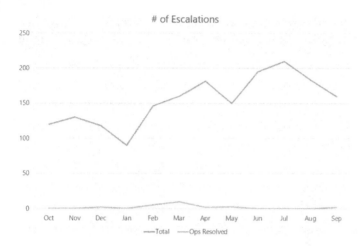

Ivan smirks derisively, looking thoroughly unimpressed. "Again, sounds like a problem for the coders to figure out. Reliability is all about architecture; maybe a better thought out design would give you the numbers you need."

I say flatly, "We aren't breaking out separately here the number of noncode related problems; we can do that if you want. I don't think it'd be productive personally. But a large number of these escalations were caused by patches to the infrastructure. And Ivan, a win for us here has to be global. The tickets are spending too long in queue, and our first touches aren't helping knock down easily triaged bugs – look at that flag green line there on the bottom. We need a better definition of success here, one that's more customer-driven."

"Well then, put your money where your mouth is, Ben. Start sharing the load. If you want better first-touch resolution rates, put your people in the call center."

Tabrez and I start to laugh. After gathering myself, I say sunnily, "Great minds think alike! That's exactly what we're talking about, Ivan – sharing the load. What if we made support and reliability more of a commitment for everyone, not just your Operations team?"

Finally, the cat-with-a-mouse smirk was gone. "Still seems like an end-run to me. What are we talking about here exactly?"

We start to outline the plan that's been taking shape over the past few weeks. As I said, we've gone over the support tickets for the past quarter and found that most fell into one of three categories:

1. Noncode-related issues (OS patches, networking or config issues, or scheduled downtimes)

2. Code changes or deployment-related issues

3. Interrupts

I say, "That last one is important. These are the bulk of the service requests we're seeing for the app. These are the Sev 3 tickets Tabrez mentioned earlier – user login issues, timeouts, caching problems. Most of these problems are small, and they're repeatable – they could be fixed with a simple service restart or a job that updates login credentials for example. In fact, if we had those documented 'Top 10' issues available as automated jobs for your support team to remediate, almost 75% of these incoming tickets would have been resolved within 15 minutes. That's very low-hanging fruit, Ivan. It's a win for you, as we can close tickets faster. We'll have happier customers – and my team spends less time playing Sherlock Holmes with long-dead tickets."

Tabrez is smiling in agreement. "Ivan, up to now we've been defining success in narrow, localized terms, like lines of code delivered for devs; or availability and server metrics for Ops. We need to change our incentives and our point of view. Success for our customers means reliability, pure and simple. How fast can a user authenticate and get to the second screen of the app? That's something they actually care about. And if there's a problem – how long does it take for a ticket to get fixed? Not just put in a queue, but actually addressed and done? If we can fix this – we'll get the app back on track and our user base will start growing instead of cratering."

Ivan is smirking again; the well of sarcasm runs deep with him. "Yeah, like I said – an end-run. I love how you put noncode related problems up top. What about all those problems with deployments? What are you going to be doing to stop these bugs early on, Ben?"

I exhale in frustration; I've given it my best. "Ivan, cut it out. We're trying to partner with you here so we can better meet our customer's needs. So let's drop the 'tude. Here's what we're thinking – and this is a rough sketch at the moment, so everyone in the room here can come in with their thoughts:"

A New Response Model

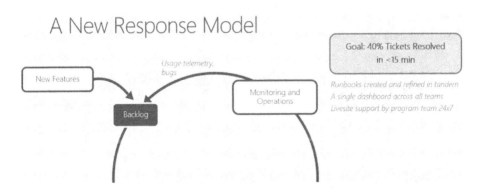

I continue: "You say we – meaning the devs – haven't been stepping it up when it comes to production support; I'll meet you halfway and agree with you. Right now everything you're seeing in red doesn't exist at the moment. We aren't getting any usage information, bugs are flowing through untouched, and we have completely different metrics and dashboarding than your support teams. Even our ticket queues are separate.

"So let's start over with a fresh approach. Let's say I put some skin in the game. I dedicate two people on each team to handle livesite support. They work with your team, in the same room, and for 4 hours a day they take incoming calls. I think, with a little time spent in the foxholes, they'd have a much better appreciation of what it takes to create and support highly available software."

I've screwed up. Emily, George and I have been going over this, but I forgot to include Alex – and now his mouth drops in shock. "Ben, you can't ask us to do this. We'll be stuck in the mud. Our people are very expensive, highly trained specialists. You're yanking them into a call center? They'll quit, Ben. And I shouldn't have to tell you, it'll take us months to find a replacement. A call center person takes a single phone call, and we can get them the next day – 16 bucks an hour."

I tell him as best I can – we can't continue begging for more coders and complaining about the tickets we're drowning in and refusing to make any tradeoffs. "Ivan is right when he says we're not doing enough. I want to try this – as an experiment."

Alex says desperately, "Ben, once again, we'll lose these people. No one wants to work in a call center. No one. For us to do our jobs effectively, we need to not be interrupt driven. Come on, you know how context switching works – it's slow death for any programmer. I can't imagine anyone on our team being willing to swallow this."

I reply firmly, "We can talk about this later if you want – nothing's been decided. But if we want something to change, we're going to have to stop thinking of support as being some other person's job. And you can't tell me this isn't costing us anyway. Last sprint, we lost half the team to firefighting on the third day of the sprint. What would you rather have – a 25% reduction in firepower, or 50%?"

Gears are starting to turn, so I press my advantage. I explain that we'll rotate support on the team so no one is stuck with a pager full time. And the people embedded with the support teams will be spending at least half their time doing what they've always done and are best at – coding. This means automating those manual tasks – creating runbooks and jobs that can be executed single-click. I make some headway with Alex, but you can tell he's still convinced we'll see a mass exodus of talent once we saddle them with any amount of livesite support.

Ivan, for once, is also thinking. "So you're to help with support. What's this going to cost me in trade?"

"What's it going to cost you? Information. We need information, Ivan, because we're working blind right now. We need to know what's working and what isn't for our customers, and your team is closer to that source than anyone.

We need your teams to commit to using those runbooks as they're created – and then help us make them better. We're not trying to automate everything here – just the most common, manual tasks that crop up repeatedly. The kind of stuff that's better done by a machine than a human being."

Ivan isn't smirking anymore, but he's still deeply suspicious. "Really. Hmm. So if we go ahead with this – attempt – this means you'll meet, every week, for an hour with us? We'll go over all the bugs opened in the past week and work together on these automated jobs? Come on, Ben, some new crisis will pop up and you'll flit off elsewhere. I doubt you have the attention span for this kind of effort. Really, don't you think it's smarter not to start?"

I tell him to put me to the test – for 3 months. We'll experiment with creating these runbooks and a single queue displaying open support tickets that's the same as the work queue for the devs. I even offer to pay out of my budget for new monitors in their war room. "And yes, the entire support team – that includes you and I – will meet every Monday for one hour and go over the tickets, just like you said. I'll bet you a steak dinner Ivan – in 3 months, we'll hit our target. That means 40% of our tickets resolved in less than 15 minutes."

The only thing that kept Ivan in the room long enough to broker a deal was the fact that Tabrez was there. Even then, it takes a few more haggling sessions with Ivan – and finally a Come-To-Jesus moment with Emily – to kick this off as an experiment. I'd love to say it took off like a rocket, but Alex's concerns about developer grumbling were well founded. Our first few rounds of support were a little ragged, and there was still too much cross-team sniping.

But in the end, no one walked out the door. There would come a time when it was hard to believe that we'd ever worked any differently; it made a fundamental difference in getting us a better connection to the customer and knocking down our firefighting costs. And best of all, I got to enjoy an enormous T-bone steak, medium rare, courtesy of Emily and Ivan.

Behind the Story

During this chapter, Ben introduces the concept of working in smaller-sized teams that have true end-to-end-responsibility, in an effort to reduce the waste they are seeing because of handoffs between siloed groups. The role of security as part of their "Shift Left" movement makes an appearance, as does improving their initial support and remediation capabilities through the use of runbooks and automated jobs. Let's go into a little more detail on each of these topics.

Small Cross-Functional Teams

My own version of the networked system is small, multidisciplinary teams focused on solving a particular business challenge. As the requirements of the company shifts, the initial teams might be joined by more small teams, each tackling a different problem. ...Simple physics tells us that change requires energy, and I think there is far more momentum created when people are minded to want to go in a particular direction rather than being told to. It's heart, and not just head, supported by a big opportunity that people can believe in. – Neil Perkin[1]

You know, I'm all for progress. It's change I object to. – Mark Twain

The team's first foray into a value stream map was way back in Chapter 2, in the section "A Focus on Flow, Not on Quality." Now, months later, they're doing a second pass. This actually isn't unusual; in fact, it's healthy to do a reassessment from time to time. It never ceases to amaze us what an immediate impact a simple sticky-note flowchart can have, especially on numbers- and results-oriented executives. Most of us have never seen what it actually takes in effort to move an idea from concept through to delivery. Value stream maps expose friction and gaps in our processes and can become a powerful catalyst for global-scope improvements.

We're indebted to the books *Making Work Visible* and *The DevOps Handbook* for their much more detailed discussions on creating actionable and useful value stream maps. *Making Work Visible* in particular outlines an alternative approach that seeks to engage that vital upper stratosphere we'll need to create lasting change. Instead of an outside agent proscribing a course as in our story, which can backfire badly, the committed leadership members are "locked into a room" and build the flow map themselves over several days. Having an enterprise diagnose itself using nonbiased elapsed time metrics – vs. a report coming from a disengaged outside party – creates a much better environment of buy-in and cooperation. Often, the coordinators will have to put on the brakes, forcing participants to finish mapping out the problem before driving to potential solutions – an excellent problem to have![2]

---

[1]"Structuring for Change: The Dual Operating System," Neil Perkin. Medium.com, 4/11/2017. https://medium.com/building-the-agile-business/structuring-for-change-the-dual-operating-system-78fa3a3d3da3.

[2]"Making Work Visible: Exposing Time Theft to Optimize Work & Flow," Dominica Degrandis, 11/14/2017, IT Revolution Press; ISBN-10: 1942788150, ISBN-13: 978-1942788157.

Finding the Blinks

Ben's proposal to Douglas in the section "Leaner and Meaner" gets the winning nod for a few reasons. First, this is a timeboxed trial period of 3 months only. After 3 months, if there's not improvement, rolling the attempt back won't come with a huge cost in terms of rep. Secondly, he did his prework. Soliciting and getting the buy-in from the architects and security auditors made for some nice trump cards in his discussion, and it will set the groundwork for a much better holistic solution down the road.

But the biggest single reason why the SWAT team proposal won out was that it had the strong backing of the business, Footwear. They're clearly not happy with the cost, lack of transparency, and the effectiveness of the siloized process as it currently stands. Each group has been trying to do their work in a vacuum with a local mandate and criteria for success; with Tabrez's backing, Ben can try as an experiment delivering value with very small cross-functional teams – and get feedback from Tabrez on a regular basis so they can make adjustments on the fly.

Ben is betting that if they break down feature requests to very small pieces of functionality – there's only so much work that can be done with a 6–12 person team after all – and focus all their efforts on a successful release to production in 2 weeks, Tabrez and his Footwear customer base will start to see some improvements, and they'll start to pick up speed in a meaningful, sustainable way.

We commonly see executives drilling into deep-level detail about the individual artifacts and steps themselves, even on the first few passes. However, the primary value of the value stream map is to expose, not what's working, but what isn't working – waste. This can be in the form of manual information flow, but more than likely – as we've mentioned before – this waste is happening as work is handed off to a separate team's work queue – what was called "blinks" in the book *Team of Teams*.

WonderTek is no exception. Most of their waste has come in the form of delays due to handoffs. Ben is proposing a change where delivery is happening across a single cross-functional team. It comes with a cost; the delivery teams will have to accept directions from the stakeholder much more frequently, and the stakeholders will need to invest time into providing accurate and timely feedback, so the work stays on course.

This is comparable to a restaurant breaking down the walls between the kitchen and the seating area and having all the meal preparation happen in the open. This can be undesirable; it exposes a lot more mess and noise and can be limiting. However, many top-end restaurants have found an open and transparent kitchen to be a deciding factor in having a clean, safe, and productive working area; the lack of physical walls leads to a stronger connection between the people preparing the food and those enjoying it.

Expectations are being set up front that this is a learning opportunity and that mistakes will be made. There's simply too much unknown at the starting line; they don't know yet how to set up robust monitoring, or feed usage back to set priorities in their work. Runbooks and better job automation are still a blank page. Using feature flags is still an unknown space, as is templated environments for the most part.

Still, this is a huge turning point. A smaller team will be much tighter knit and lose less due to communication overhead than a larger bloated team. They're getting early feedback from security and architects – meaning fewer heart attack-inducing surprises late in the game as the application is halted just before release for refactoring. Karen is proposing a readiness review as part of an ongoing effort – where the team, stakeholders, and architects jointly review self-graded scorecards and flag a few priorities to address over the next few sprints – meaning quality and addressing technical debt won't be victimized by a single-minded focus on flow.

The SWAT Team Model

No doubt, there's a lot of detail in Karen's report about how this proposed SWAT team would work. What are the main principles behind this dramatically new culture built around delivery?

- **A separate offsite location.** In this case, Tabrez is hooking the team up with a common work area very close to their end user base. Despite Douglas' objections, we think a closer tie to Footwear will in the end be a net positive – there'll be less delays in communication and the developers will feel and be seen as part of the business flow, vs. an isolated, remote group.

- **Work is visible, and there's a single definition of value.** WonderTek has already made some advances in this area; Karen's proposal takes this even further. We can't overstate the importance of displaying the flow of work and finding ways to continually make those displays powerful and omnipresent. Toyota made information radiators and omnipresent displays a key part of their Lean transformation. In the fight against Al Qaeda, General McChrystal broke down calcified organizational silos with a constant barrage of information and huge war room displays in one common location.[3] This new

---

[3]"Team of Teams: New Rules of Engagement for a Complex World," Stanley McChrystal. Portfolio, 5/12/2015. ISBN-10: 1591847486, ISBN-13: 978-1591847489.

SWAT team will have large displays showing their key business-facing metrics everywhere as well. Operations might have special modules or subdisplays showing numbers like availability or CPU metrics, or page response time. Developers might have their own minidashboards showing bug counts and delivery velocity. But the real coin of the realm, the common language and focus, will be the numbers that matter to the business – in WonderTek's case, cycle time, global availability, response time, and # of unique logins by month.

- **A common work queue.** Bugs, feature stories, and tasks, and environment and configuration requests are all the same thing – work. Having a single queue showing work for an entire project across every delivery team will be key for them to expose cross-team blockers quickly and maintain that open, honest, transparent behavior in working with their customers. And as we discussed earlier in Chapter 4, there's going to be a strong need to gate the work the team is acting on. BSAs and PMs will still very much be needed to help shape requirements into actionable work and ask the hard questions:

  What business problem are we trying to solve?

  How will we know we're on the right track?

  What monitoring do we have in place to gather this information, and what numbers do we need to track to confirm our assumptions and validate the design?[4]

  Hopefully, this gating will turn away a significant amount of work before a line of code is ever written. Studies have found that lead time – not the number of releases a day – is one of the greatest predictors of both customer satisfaction and employee happiness. A large backlog of work waiting in queue, which we used to think was a comforting sign of job security, is as damaging to a software delivery team as a huge inventory sitting on shelves are to a manufacturer.

---

[4]"DevOps Cafe Episode 61 - Jody Mulkey," John Willis, Damon Edwards. DevOps Café, 7/27/2015. http://devopscafe.org/show/2015/7/27/devops-cafe-episode-61-jody-mulkey.html.

- **A learning friendly environment.** Besides a blame-free postmortem ethos that favors learning from errors, the team is committing to regular weekly demos that are open to all in the company. Some argue that having a single "DevOps team" is an antipattern; we do not agree. Past experience shows that having several pilot teams experimenting with DevOps is a much less disruptive and necessary part of the "pioneers/settlers" early on growth phase. One definite antipattern we'd want to avoid is exclusiveness; if this new team is showered with all kinds of attention and shiny new gadgets while the rest of the organization languishes as "legacy," resentment will build. Treating this work as an open experiment can help spread enthusiasm and defuse potential friction.

- **Destructible, resilient environments.** What form this will take is still unknown. Will the team use Chaos Monkey or Simian Army type approach to force high availability on their production systems? Will they explore Docker or Kubernetes? Will their architecture use worker roles to help with scalability? Will they end up using Chef, Puppet, or Ansible to help configure and script their environments and enforce consistency? All of this is still in the gray areas of the map still; but early on, with global availability being a very visible indicator, the entire team will be thinking of ways of taming their ecosystem problems.

- **Self-organizing, self-disciplining teams.** They didn't propose blowing up the organization – an idea completely above their grasp. Instead, each SWAT team is both small and virtual, with each team member having the same direct report they did previously. Ben for example might have two to three engineers on each delivery team that still reports to him, and he handles resourcing and administration. Architecture might have one architect spread out among five or six of these virtual teams, spending perhaps one day every 2 weeks embedded with them. And Emily's IT team may have two or more people writing environment and configuration recipes alongside the developers; perhaps, over time as the need for new environments drops, their involvement could shrink to a single halftime IT admin on the team.

Are Shared Services Models a Dead End?

The point earlier about a virtual self-organizing team is important. The proposal doesn't depend on breaking up the organization into horizontal small delivery groups – a reshuffle that isn't always possible with many organizations. We've seen several examples of "virtual" cross-functional teams that have different direct reports – but still function as a single unit, with the same incentives and goals. This is imperfect, but workable, and far from a serious limitation.

As Mike Rother put it in *Toyota Kata*, even Toyota is structured around a "shared services" model:

> *As tempting as it seems, one cannot reorganize your way to continuous improvement and adaptiveness. What is decisive is not the form of the organization, but how people act and react. The roots of Toyota's success lie not in its organizational structures, but in developing capability and habits in people. It surprises many people, in fact, to find that Toyota is largely organized in a traditional, functional-department style.[5]*

We do feel that having the physical org match the way software is being delivered is a powerful asset and works in line with Conway's Law – as powerfully demonstrated by Amazon. Reshuffling the delivery teams, removing the middle layer to make the org more horizontal, and creating a new standard common title were identified by the Azure DevOps management team as key contributors to instituting real change and improving velocity. But we won't be dogmatic on the subject; there's too many winning examples of teams that made their delivery teams work without a complete reshuffle.

Aaron Bjork told us that same-sizing was an important catalyst in getting the Microsoft Azure DevOps product teams at Microsoft to deliver at scale:

> *Every Azure DevOps program team has a consistent size and shape – about 8-12 people, working across the stack all the way to production support. This helps not just with delivering value faster in incremental sizes but gives us a common taxonomy so we can work across teams at scale. Whenever we break that rule – teams that are smaller than that, or bloat out to 20 people for example – we start to see antipatterns crop up; resource horse-trading and things like that. I love the 'two pizza rule' at Amazon; there's no reason not to use that approach, ever.[6]*

---

[5]"Toyota Kata: Managing People for Improvement, Adaptiveness and Superior Results." Mike Rother. McGraw-Hill Education, 8/4/2009. ISBN-10: 0071635238, ISBN-13: 978-0071635233.
[6]Interview of Aaron Bjork by Dave Harrison, see Appendix.

You could argue that the decisions Ben made in this section should have happened much earlier. And perhaps, Ben missed an opportunity by not folding in the business earlier and taking a more holistic view of things. But, no one gets it perfect right out of the gate – and the pieces they put in place around source control, release management, and CI/CD were all necessary leaps in maturity they had to make to get to where global problems with delivery could be addressed. It's hard to dispute with the careful, conservative approach of taking it one step at a time and choosing to focus first on what Ben's team was bringing to the table.

You'll notice, at no point did the proposal mention the word "microservices" or even "DevOps." The SWAT team proposal is really a Trojan horse, introducing not just those concepts but also enabling a better way of handling legacy heartburn with the strangler fig or scaffolding pattern. Reasonably sized teams using services-oriented interfaces and responsible for smaller capsules of functionality are not far off from our ideal of Continuous Delivery and microservices, with little or no delays due to handoffs, unstable environments, or outside dependencies.

Configuration Management and Infrastructure as Code

Your greatest danger is letting the urgent things crowd out the important.

– Charles E. Hummel

Provisioning new servers is manual, repetitive, resource-intensive, and error-prone process – exactly the kind of problem that can be solved with automation.

– Continuous Delivery

Consistency is more important than perfection. As an admin, I'd rather have a bad thing done 100 times the same terrible way, than the right thing done once – and who the hell knows what the other 99 configs look like?

– Michael Stahnke

This book is written primarily from the perspective of a group of developers moving toward the DevOps model. We've discussed at length topics like peer review, Kanban, continuous integration, MVP, and hypothesis-driven development – all are coding-centric attempts to try to catch defects earlier and deploy software in smaller, safer batches.

Putting the onus on the development team was a deliberate choice. There's a common misperception among the development community that DevOps means "NoOps," and they can finally throw off the shackles of IT and manage their own environments independently. It's important for development teams to realize that for DevOps to work, producing quality code becomes much more important. It's a massive shift in thinking for most development teams to have to worry about customer satisfaction, feature acceptance, and how their apps are actually performing in the real world; ultimately, that's what true end-to-end responsibility means. Far from "NoOps" or "ShadowOps," coders will need to find ways to engage more frequently with their compadres that are handling infrastructure and operations support.

We're only able to spend a few pages skimming the basics of configuration management software and infrastructure as code, a vast and fast-moving landscape. But it was important that we give it some consideration, as arguably this is the best bang-for-the-buck value that the DevOps movement offers. As our software has gotten better and containerization and cloud platforms have matured, there are fewer and fewer obstacles to having servers and environments maintained with code just as we would software.

In the book, the single biggest crimp in the delivery pipeline that Ben's team was experiencing revolved around environments; getting servers procured, provisioned, and properly configured took weeks of effort. We've experienced that pain point ourselves and keep hearing horror stories of "lazy, obstructive, incompetent" IT teams delivering faulty environments late on a recurring basis. In every case, it doesn't take much digging to find that IT and Ops teams are far from lazy; in fact, they're usually overburdened and insanely busy, performing heroics that is rarely noticed or appreciated by the people depending on their infrastructure. Because of lack of capacity, they often lack the space they need to come up with creative solutions to the problems caused by proliferating systems. This bandwidth situation is a constraint that the arrival of cloud platforms has actually made worse:

...Even with the latest and best new tools and platforms, IT operations teams still find that they can't keep up with their daily workload. They don't have the time to fix longstanding problems with their systems, much less revamp them to make the best use of new tools. In fact, cloud and automation often makes things worse. The ease of provisioning new infrastructure leads to an ever-growing portfolio of systems, and it takes an ever-increasing amount of time just to keep everything from collapsing. Adopting cloud and automation tools immediately lowers barriers for making changes to infrastructure. But managing changes in a way that improves consistency and reliability doesn't come out of the box with the

software. It takes people to think through how they will use the tools and put in place the systems, processes, and habits to use them effectively.[7]

And that's the problem – we rarely give these people the bandwidth to think about anything beyond the short term. Most IT teams are suffering from the tyranny of the urgent, where important things that bring long-term benefits are constantly being deferred or shuffled to the back of the deck. As with the problems we've experienced with software delivery teams, the issue is rarely the people – it's the processes and tools we give them to work with. Poor performing IT and Operations teams rarely have the capacity to think beyond the demands of the day.

As with software delivery teams, delivering infrastructure more reliably and repeatably comes down to better automation and better process. Having infrastructure teams track their work and make it visible in Kanban promotes transparency and helps drive tasks through to completion – and limits work in progress so people are not overwhelmed with attempting to multitask multiple critical tasks at once. Managers and orgs that truly care about their people will take care to track the amount of time they're spending on urgent, nonvalue added tasks – what Google's SRE movement appropriately labels toil – and make sure it's capped so that at least 20%, and preferably 50%, of their time is spent on more rewarding work that looks to the future. Better process and tools in the form of infrastructure as code – especially the use of configuration management and scripted environments, containers, and orchestration – promote portability and lessen the problems caused by unique, invaluable, and brittle environments.

Either You Own Your Environments or Your Environments Own You

At his first day at one former assignment, Dave was shown his desk workspace. Oddly, there was an antique desktop computer humming away below his desk, but it didn't appear to have any monitor display hooked up. When he asked what the desktop was doing under his desk, he was told, "Don't turn that off! The last time we powered that desktop down, it shut down parts of our order processing system. We're not sure what it does, and the guy that set it up left a long time ago. Just leave it alone."

That server was a scary black box, kept in the corner; it had a name, and everyone was terrified of what would happen if it ever went offline. That's an extreme example of the famous "Pets Versus Cattle" analogy that Randy Bias came up with back in 2011. As he put it:

---

[7] "Site Reliability Engineering: How Google Runs Production Systems," Niall Richard Murphy, Betsy Beyer, Chris Jones, Jennifer Petoff, O'Reilly Media; 4/16/2016, ISBN-10: 149192912X, ISBN-13: 978-1491929124.

In the old way of doing things, we treat our servers like pets, for example Bob the mail server. If Bob goes down, it's all hands on deck. The CEO can't get his email and it's the end of the world. In the new way, servers are numbered, like cattle in a herd. For example, www001 to www100. When one server goes down, it's taken out back, shot, and replaced on the line.[8]

Mainframes, servers, networking components, or database systems that are unique, indispensable, and can never be down are "pets" – they are manually built, lovingly named, and keeping these static and increasingly creaky environments well fed and happy becomes an increasingly important part of our worklife. Gene Kim called these precious, impossible to replace artifacts "works of art" in the classic *Visible Ops Handbook*; Martin Fowler called them "snowflake environments," with each server boasting a unique and special configuration.

The rise of modern cloud-based environments and the challenges of maintaining datacenters at scale has led to the realization that servers and environments are best treated as cattle – replaceable, mass-produced, modular, predictable, and disaster tolerant. The core tenet here is that it should always be easier and cheaper to create a new environment than to patch or repair an old one. Those of us who grew up on farms knew why our parents told us not to name new baby lambs, goats, or cows; these animals were here to serve a purpose, and they wouldn't be here forever – so don't get attached!

The Netflix operations team, for example, knows that a certain percentage of their AWS instances will perform much worse than average. Instead of trying to isolate and track down the exact cause, which might be a unique or temporary condition, they treat these instances as "cattle." They have their provisioning scripts test each new instance's performance, and if they don't meet a predetermined standard, the script destroys the instance and creates a new one.

The situation has gotten much better in the past 10 years with the rise of configuration management. Still, in too many organizations we find manually configured environments and a significant amount of drift that comes with making one-off scripting changes and ad hoc adjustments in flight. As one IT manager we talked with put it, "Pets?! WE are the pets! Our servers own us!"

---

[8]"The History of Pets vs Cattle and How to Use the Analogy Properly," Randy Bias. CloudScaling.com, 9/29/2016. http://cloudscaling.com/blog/cloud-computing/the-history-of-pets-vs-cattle/.

What Is Infrastructure As Code?

Infrastructure as Code (IAC) is a movement that aims to bring the same benefits to infrastructure that the software development world has experienced with automation. Modern configuration management tools can treat infrastructure as if it was software and data; servers and systems can be maintained and governed through code kept on a version control system, tested and validated, and deployed alongside code as part of a delivery pipeline. Instead of manual or ad-hoc custom scripts, it emphasizes consistent, repeatable routines for provisioning systems and governing their configuration. Applying the tools we found so useful in the "first wave" of Agile development: version control, continuous integration, code review, and automated testing to the Operations space allow us to make infrastructure changes much more safe, reliable, and easy.

IAC is best described by the end results: your application and all the environmental infrastructure it depends on – OS, patches, the app stack and its config, data, and all config – can be deployed without human intervention. When IAC is set up properly, operators should never need to log onto a machine to complete setup. Instead, code is written to describe the desired state, which is run on a regular cadence and ensures the systems are brought back to convergence. And once running, no changes should ever be made separate from the build pipeline. (Some organizations have actually disabled SSH to prevent ad hoc changes!) John Willis once infamously described this as the "Mojito Test" – can I deploy my application to a completely new environment while holding a Mojito?

It's a movement that is gathering momentum. Jon Cwiak told us that it took aggressive effort over a long period of time to tame their "config drift monster" at Humana, but the results were well worth it:

> It took some bold steps to get our infrastructure under control. Each application had its own unique and beautiful configuration, and no two environments were alike – dev, QA, test, production, they were all different. Trying to figure out where these artifacts were and what the proper source of truth was required a lot of weekends playing "Where's Waldo"! Introducing practices like configuration transforms gave us confidence we could deploy repeatedly and get the same behavior and it really helped us enforce some consistency. The movement toward a standardized infrastructure – no snowflakes, everything the same, infrastructure as code – has been a key enabler for fighting the config drift monster.[9]

---

[9]Interview of Jon Cwiak by Dave Harrison, see Appendix.

Russ Collier agrees and says that configuration management is the root cause of most of our problems with software delivery:

> *We keep beating the configuration problem drum, but we truly believe it is the root cause of many organizations' software problems. Instead of treating configuration like a software development afterthought, treat it like the first-class citizen that it is. By solving the configuration problem, you ensure a consistent process which will inevitably lead you towards software that is easy to operate.*[10]

As Continuous Delivery put it, preventing configuration drift means making sure all changes are handled with a script-based, auditable process:

> *While in general we are not a fan of locking things down and establishing approval processes, when it comes to your production infrastructure it is essential. And since you should treat your testing environments the same way you treat production – this impacts both. Otherwise it is just too tempting, when things go wrong, to log onto an environment and poke around to resolve problems. ...The best way to enforce auditability is to have all changes made by automated scripts which can be referenced later (we favor automation over documentation for this reason). Written documentation is never a guarantee that the documented change was performed correctly.*[11]

This was what Gene Kim was referring to when he spoke about "stabilizing the patient." Keeping all the changes and patches the Operations team is rolling out as part of a script in VC and deployed as part of a pipeline means there's a reliable record of what is being done and when, which dramatically simplifies reproducing problems. Having all your configuration information in version control is a giant step forward in preventing inadvertent changes and allowing easier rollbacks. It's the only way to ensure our end goal of easier to operate software; this depends on a consistent process and stable, well-functioning systems.

It also keeps your Ops teams from going crazy, spending all their time firefighting issues caused by unplanned and destructive changes. Changes to systems change from becoming high-stress, traumatic events to routine. Users can provision and manage the resources they need without involving IT staff; in turn, IT staff are freed up to work on more valuable and creative tasks, enabling change and more robust infrastructure frameworks.

---

[10] "It Takes Dev and Ops to Make DevOps," Russ Collier. DevOpsOnWindows.com, 7/26/2013. www.devopsonwindows.com/it-takes-dev-and-ops-to-make-devops/.
[11] "Continuous Delivery: Reliable Software Releases through Build, Test, and Deployment Automation," Jez Humble, David Farley. Addison-Wesley Professional, 8/6/2010. ISBN-10: 9780321601919, ISBN-13: 978-0321601919.

As Yevgeniy Brikman put it:

> *There is another very important, and often overlooked, reason for why you should use IAC: happiness. Deploying code and managing infrastructure manually is repetitive and tedious. Developers and sysadmins resent this type of work, as it involves no creativity, no challenge, and no recognition. You could deploy code perfectly for months, and no one will take notice – until that one day when you mess it up. That creates a stressful and unpleasant environment. IAC offers a better alternative that allows computers to do what they do best (automation) and developers to do what they do best (coding).* [12]

One often overlooked benefit is the way it changes the Development and Operations dynamic to a virtuous cycle. Before, when there was problems, it was hard to tell if the problem was caused by server variability or an environmental change, which wastes valuable time and causes finger pointing. And in "throwing it over the fence," developers often miss or provide incomplete setup information to the release engineers in charge of getting new features to work in production. Moving to coding environments and IAC forces these two separate groups to work together on a common set of scripts that are tracked and released from version control. There's a tighter alignment and communication cycle with this model, so changes will work at every stage of the delivery plan.

Infrastructure as code leads to a more robust infrastructure, where systems can withstand failure, external threats, and abnormal loading. Contrary to what we used to believe, gating changes for long periods or preventing them ("don't touch that server!") does not make our servers and network more robust; instead, it weakens them and makes them more vulnerable, increasing the risk of disruption when long-delayed changes are rolled out in a massive push. Just as software becomes more resilient and robust as teams make smaller changes more often, servers and environments that are constantly being improved upon and replaced are more ready to handle disaster. Combined with another principle we learned from software development – the art of the blameless postmortem – IT teams that use IAC tools properly focus on improving and hardening systems after incidents, instead of patching and praying.

It's a huge change in mindset for most IT/Ops teams to move beyond ad hoc scripts and manual commands into the world of IAC tooling and automation. For Ryan Comingdeer at Five Talent, he's found the benefits in terms of speed to be well worth the cost:

---

[12]"Terraform: Up and Running: Writing Infrastructure as Code," Yevgeniy Brikman. O'Reilly Media, 3/27/2017. ISBN-10: 1491977086, ISBN-13: 978-1491977088.

For us, automating everything is the #1 principle. It reduces security concerns, drops the human error factor; increases our ability to experiment faster with infrastructure our codebase. Being able to spin up environments and roll out POC's is so much easier with automation. It all comes down to speed. The more automation you have in place, the faster you can get things done. It does take effort to set up initially; the payoff is more than worth it. Getting your stuff out the door as fast as possible with small, iterative changes is the only really safe way; that's only possible with automation.

You would think everyone would be onboard with the idea of automation over manually logging on and poking around on VM's when there's trouble, but – believe it or not – that's not always the case. And sometimes our strongest resistance to this comes from the director/CTO level![13]

IAC and Configuration Management Tools

There's some subtle (and not-so-subtle) differences in the commercially available products around IAC in the market today. Server provisioning tools (such as Terraform, CloudFormation, or OpenStack Heat) that can create servers and networking environments – databases, caches, load balancers, subnet and firewall configs, routing rules, etc. Server templating tools like Docker, Packer, and Vagrant all work by uploading an image or machine snapshot, which can then be installed as a template using another IAC tool. Configuration management tools – among which are included Chef, Ansible, Puppet, and SaltStack – install and manage software on existing servers. They can scan your network continuously, discover and track details about what software and configurations are in place, and create a complete server inventory, flagging out of date software and inaccurate user accounts.

Ansible, Chef, Puppet, and SaltStack all use externalized configuration files. Some (like Ansible) use a push model, where a central server pushes updates to servers. But most still use a pull model, where an agent on each server runs periodically and pulls the latest definition from a central repository and applies it to the server configuration.

Enterprises often mix and match these tools. Some use Terraform to provision servers and Chef to keep them configured properly. Others use Docker or Packer to create a library of images, which are then used as a source when new servers are rolled out with a tool like Ansible.

Using any of these tools gains reliability, reproducibility, consistency, and better governance over your entire system; new instances can be spun up on demand and changes can be pushed out en masse.

---

[13]Interview of Ryan Comingdeer by Dave Harrison, see Appendix.

Which of these is best? We'd be doing you a disservice by anointing one of these IAC tools as the "best in class," as these packages are maturing so quickly. There's a bit of an arms race going on at the moment as each vendor tries to assert dominance and leapfrog the competition. And it only takes a little poking around to find out that the "best choice" is a highly subjective thing.

We interviewed several brilliant people from leading configuration management software companies in writing this book and expected them to have been very vocal and opinionated on why their particular software was the unequivocal best choice. No doubt they felt that way – but to our surprise, we kept hearing variations on the same theme: it's not the software choice that matters as much as the process. Having people buy into the need for configuration management and IAC, and be willing to change the way they're used to working, is far more important than picking a particular "best in class" vendor.

It feels like cheating to say "any of these will work for you" – though that might very well be true. We'll just say about IAC and change management software what we say about CI/CD software: if your people feel they had a voice and were able to choose the best tool for the job, they'll work hard to make it a success. If one single tool is mandated and forced externally upon IT teams from on high, it'll end up being used incorrectly or not at all.

We can judge the effectiveness of an IAC team – not by the awesome capabilities of the configuration management system they're using – but by results. For example, we know that a software development team is truly successful with CI/CD when they can handle change better; safety and velocity both go on the uptick. Lead time drops and as new requirements are broken down into bite-size pieces and rolled out frequently, minimizing the impact of change. Recovery time improves as monitoring, automation, and postmortem processes tighten up and harden applications, making them more portable and reproducible. Instead of MTBF, they focus less on avoiding failures and more on improving their recovery time, MTTR.

The same is true with how infrastructure and IT are managed in an organization. Highly effective IT/Ops teams are able to rebuild any element of infrastructure at a whim and with a single command – perhaps while holding a Mojito. The infrastructure team is never needed to handle common requests like building out a standard set of environments, and there's no waste in the form of service tickets to external groups; environments can be tailored and provisioned within minutes by the teams themselves, self-service. Most work is done during the day; there is rarely or never a need for a maintenance window. Systems are up to date, consistently up-patched, and kept consistent with automated tools running constantly in the background. Failures are treated as an opportunity to learn and improve recovery time for the next incident.

If It Ain't Within Minutes, It Ain't Self-Service

Infrastructure as code in practice means that environments are provisioned with a self-service, on-demand model. Many IT organizations today boast of having self-service and on-demand infrastructure capabilities, but still fall well short of the "Mojito Test" standard. As the wonderful book *Infrastructure as Code* by Kief Morris put it:

> *In the 'iron age' of IT, systems were directly bound to physical hardware. Provisioning and maintaining infrastructure was manual work, forcing humans to spend their time pointing, clicking, and typing to keep the gears turning. Because changes involved so much work, change management processes emphasized careful up-front consideration, design, and review work. This made sense because getting it wrong was expensive.*[14]

There's still more than a few Iron Age processes still lying about in many IT shops, even the ones that boast of cloud capabilities. These artifacts show up in various ways: teams are allowed one of a very narrow set of choices (such as a web server, app server, or a database server), but have no ability to customize or optimize these vanilla choices. Or a new environment request requires a detailed request form and specifications and an implementation plan, followed by a review period and weeks of delay. Even if the delay from creating a ticket to getting back login information is only a few days, this is far from an autonomous, self-service model. The end result is the same: environments can't be spun up on demand, quickly and with a single command, and they can't be customized to fit the needs of the solution.

Here, our old friend from Chapter 4 – the value stream map – again proves its worth. Make sure the time it takes to provision environments is mapped out and kept visible. This will tell you where to invest your energy: if making a change takes 45 hours to make it to production, and tasks that can be automated only take up an hour of this, there is little value in sinking time and money into speeding up automation. And remember that we are looking for wait time and wastes due to handoff; it's not uncommon that 95% or more of cycle time for a task or change is spent waiting on other requirements. So, a "cloud-ready" infrastructure team may boast a 5- to 10-minute turnaround time to stand up a new environment, but the actual turnaround time to from when an environment is needed to when it's fully available could be much later. It's not unusual to see that 10-minute turnaround time, once we factor in the time it really takes to get that environment ready – filling in a business case and a request ticket, setting up networking and adding user accounts, and performing post-provisioning testing – is actually better measured in weeks.

---

[14]"Infrastructure as Code: Managing Servers in the Cloud," Kief Morris. O'Reilly Media, 6/27/2016. ISBN-10: 1491924357, ISBN-13: 978-1491924358.

Slow and clunky provisioning processes are usually the culprit behind weeks-long turnaround times, as Gary Gruver recounts:

> One large organization ... started their DevOps initiative by trying to understand how long it would take to get up Hello World! in an environment using their standard processes. They did this to understand where the biggest constraints were in their organization. They quit this experiment after 250 days even though they still did not have Hello World! up and running because they felt they had identified the biggest constraints. Next, they ran the same experiment in Amazon Web Services and showed it could be done in two hours. This experiment provided a good understanding of the issues in their organization and also provided a view of what was possible.[15]

Infrastructure as code requires that teams have the ability to use scripts to automatically provision resources and custom fit it to their needs, instead of having centralized teams act as gatekeepers. Provisioning a machine should not require any human involvement; there should never be a need to create a ticket or a change request, and provisioning requests should be handled within minutes at most. As Carla Geisser from Google put it: "If a human operator needs to touch your system during normal operations, you have a bug."

If your IT department claims to have self-service capability but still requires days or weeks for approval and provisioning, it's quite likely that either an overly rigid cloud provider agreement, a threadbare resource pool, or antique Iron Age manual processes are holding them back. These need to be reexamined for infrastructure provisioning to be truly on-demand and able to keep up with the pace of application development.

Golden Image Libraries and Immutable Servers

One concept in many DevOps books from a decade ago that has not weathered particularly well in practice is that of the concept of the library of golden images. We know it's much easier to operate and govern complex systems if we keep the variance to a bare minimum. With a very limited set of available images to select from, as the theory goes, it should be much easier to troubleshoot and keep configurations from drifting. This also fits the traditional way IT teams have worked; architects come up with a single "optimal" server environment to support web services or a database server, and this design spec is handed off as an approved, fixed template; any variance is verboten.

---

[15]"Start and Scaling Devops in the Enterprise," Gary Gruver. BookBaby, 12/1/2016. ISBN-10: 1483583589, ISBN-13: 978-1483583587.

The library of golden images sounds like an excellent idea in theory; in practice, we've found most enterprises pay lip service to the concept but found it difficult to implement. Part of this has to do with the nature of self-service and on-demand provisioning as we discussed in the previous section. Teams need to be able to take responsibility for their own environments, and – unless lack of governance is demonstrably hurting the org – tweak them as they go, so they are optimized for the applications they support.

It's a common misperception that every time a code deploy happens, every target server environment should be destroyed and rebuilt. In this strategy, servers are immutable; nothing is changed, any new build requires a complete teardown and recreation of environments from that "golden" set of images. There's no question that this practice will increase predictability and offers a cleaner slate. Although there's nothing wrong with immutable server theory and some enterprises have found success with it in practice, others have found it to be unacceptably slow as part of a code delivery cycle. A typical team doing CI/CD might be deploying dozens of builds a day; building a new server template for each build might be impractical.

As Michael Goetz of Chef told us, often the best practice is a multistep process; first, snap a "chalk line" and create a set of images, then enforce consistency with configuration management software – and have your servers rebuilt from these images using any schedule you desire:

> There's always a strong pull to this concept of a set of golden images. Of course this is a solid concept but in actual practice, many companies struggle with it. Much like the container wave – they're immutable, you build them, it does its thing, and then you kill it. But this assumes a level of maturity and rigor that most orgs can't handle. Even in the cloud, most simply aren't ready for the rapid creation and destruction of resources like this, and you get old defunct instances spiraling out of control, a maintenance and governance nightmare.

> A common misunderstanding is that you need to rebuild your environments every time you do a build from that "golden image" template. Well, if it takes you 45 minutes to install software on a system, no amount of automation will make that go faster if you're installing from scratch every time. We say, build it with a tool – a dry run build – and use that to snap a chalk line: these are our build times on this date. Now you have your first step, the image creation process. But you won't do that every time, that's just a process you will run on a regular schedule – perhaps daily, or weekly, or monthly. To cover the gaps in between destroying and recreating these images, you go to step 2 – configuration management.

Run software that detects variances and enforces it, bringing your systems in line. If you don't follow something like this process, almost immediately you'll have drifts. How our software works at Chef is – you form a policy set, configure your system to match that, detect changes and correct them. Four phases essentially. Chef's perfectly capable of detecting and correcting variances immediately. It's very common for companies to want a pause button though – they want to know, but they also want to decide when that correction happens.[16]

The root problem with the concept of the golden library was that in application it ended up being driven more by architectural desires for purity and ease of operability than it was about fluidity in servicing business needs. Difference in the form of varying server configurations isn't bad by itself; the problem is when the server is a black box – no one understands how or why it's different from a standard image and can't rebuild or replace it easily. If there's no confidence that an environment can be quickly rebuilt or replaced, creating a process that can reproduce that environment reproducibly should be a top priority for the application team. As Michael Stahnke from Puppet told us:

I'm not a big believer in the mythical golden set of builds. First off, stability by itself is a really crappy goal. A better question is – what's your current state? Where do you want to be? What are the characteristics you're after? I'm betting you don't really want to have a golden image of Windows that stays static for months. You want a Windows image that's up to date and conforms to all your standards. You want up to date user accounts and security patches. In almost zero cases, a set of golden images is really not the destination you should be shooting for.[17]

This isn't to say that there's no value in enforcing some form of consistency; perhaps, for enterprises drowning in troubleshooting and operational complexity, the pendulum needs to swing more in the direction of an approved set of templates – hopefully, with a lot of room for variation. Just make sure to allow enough room for your teams to innovate and experiment with the servers you are charging them to support. Nathen Harvey from Chef told us the following:

Do you need to really clamp down and enforce a set of "golden images"? Well that's a tradeoff. If you allow a hundred different versions of Tomcat, or the .NET Framework, you're increasing your operational complexity. If you choose to constrain these and enforce some consistency, you're going to help reduce complexity, but you're also reducing your developer's capacity to innovate.[18]

---

[16]Interview of Michael Goetz by Dave Harrison, see Appendix.
[17]Interview of Michael Stahnke by Dave Harrison, see Appendix.
[18]Interview of Nathen Harvey by Dave Harrison, see Appendix.

Trust the Tool

Much like with CI/CD software, the odds are that the software itself already exists in some form in your company; it's just not set up properly. This often comes down to lack of trust. It's common for organizations to start with a "graduated" approach with configuration management; they have manifests checked into source control, but these are only used when a specific change needs to be made, and only to a targeted set of machines. This is like buying a Porsche and only using the radio; IAC tooling can and should go far beyond being a simple scripting tool used on an ad hoc basis. Kief Morris called this the "Audit and Fix Antipattern" in his book on IAC; his position was that too many Operations teams – even those with advanced configuration management software – use an auditing process, where inconsistencies are flagged in an audit report. This adds a constant stream of reactive, tedious, manual work – toil – for the team in catching and resolving these inconsistencies. Kief likened his server proliferation situation at one company to that faced by Mickey Mouse in Fantasia:

> We found ourselves a bit like Mickey Mouse in "The Sorcerer's Apprentice" from Fantasia. We spawned virtual servers, then more, then even more. They overwhelmed us. When something broke, we tracked down the VM and fixed whatever was wrong with it, but we couldn't keep track of what changes we'd made where. ...The problem was that, although Puppet (and Chef and the others) should have been set up and left running unattended across all of our servers, we couldn't trust it. Our servers were just too different. We would write manifests to configure and manage a particular application server. But when we ran it against another, theoretically similar app server, we found that different versions of Java, application software, and OS components would cause the Puppet run to fail, or worse, break the application server.
>
> ....I used automation selectively – for example, to help build new servers, or to make a specific configuration change. I tweaked the configuration each time I ran it, to suit the particular task I was doing. I was afraid to turn my back on my automation tools, because I lacked confidence in what they would do. I lacked confidence in my automation because my servers were not consistent. My servers were not consistent because I wasn't running automation frequently and consistently.[19]

Kief described this downward spin as the "automation fear spiral"; it leads to using automation selectively, in certain cases, such as spinning up a new server, but ultimately doesn't address the problem of configuration drift. Teams stuck

---

[19]"Infrastructure as Code: Managing Servers in the Cloud," Kief Morris. O'Reilly Media, 6/27/2016. ISBN-10: 1491924357, ISBN-13: 978-1491924358.

in this vicious downward cycle should attempt a graduated experiment to get out of the shallow end of the pool; pick a set of servers, ensure the configuration definitions you have work properly, and schedule your tooling to run unattended on them. If this experiment is successful – as we predict it will be – then begin with the next set of servers, until all your environments are being continuously updated.

Nathen Harvey recommended using postmortem reports to build confidence in your software-enabled ability to manage and govern automated infrastructure:

> One of the common problems I see is fearing the system. For example, with Chef, or Puppet, or any other config management tool out there – we can automatically remove any variances with your systems, easily. At one place I used to work, we had infrastructure as code, with an agent running and keeping things up to date. But we got scared of the risk, so we turned it off. And any time we'd make a change, we'd have to add new code, spin up an agent to test against to confirm it was good – and then apply it to production. But by that time there could have been all kinds of changes in production that weren't in that test. So we made a change – we decided to run config management all the time in production, trust our monitoring, and trust our reaction time and our ability to recover.
>
> To get to that point where you really trust the tool – and trust yourself – probably the best place to start is looking at your last outage and the postmortem process you followed. Can you now detect that issue faster, recover faster? Zero in on those questions, and if there's a gap in tooling – THEN you buy software that will fill that particular need.[20]

Trusting automation begins with a level of confidence that every server can be rebuilt from scratch as needed using the tools and resource database you have available. From there with some steady work, it should be possible to get to the point where all your servers are having configuration tooling running continuously. If automation breaks with some edge case server, either the process needs to be modified to handle the new design or the server needs to be paved over and replaced with something that can be reproduced with the automated IAC system.

One of the most consistent feedback points we received from configuration management vendors was to trust the tool and move away from ad hoc usage. If environments are being created with an automated process – as they certainly should be – then it's a simple matter to track down with your scans environments that are out of spec, those that weren't built or configured with automation. These can and should be either brought into the automated

---

[20]Interview of Nathen Harvey by Dave Harrison, see Appendix.

fold or replaced with conformant systems; it's the only way to prevent the Sorcerer's Apprentice nightmare facing many Ops teams.

Docker and the Rise of Containerization

We're enamored by containers – which today is nearly synonymous with Docker – and the potential that this brings in the form of reproducible infrastructure and portable applications, especially in combination with microservices. The rise of containers and orchestration software happened after most of the configuration management software we know and love today was developed. Arguably, using an image created from a Dockerfile or a Packer template eliminates a host of problems that was traditionally handled by configuration management tools.

Tyler Hardison was very enthusiastic about Docker for internal development at Redhawk:

> Docker I just can't say enough about. Rolling back is so easy – when there's a problem, we pull the cord and revert back to an older version of the container. That takes all the pressure off of trying to run out a hotfix with a production down system.[21]

Since container template files are code, they can be managed in a version control system; this means the stage is set for gaining most of the positive benefits with infrastructure as code, including testing and automation. Container images can be run on any host server that supports the container runtime, creating a consistent environment – reducing or eliminating the problem of apples-to-oranges systems anomalies. The risk of environmental inconsistency is greatly minimized with the advent of containers.

With containers, moving applications from a developer's laptop out to test and production, or from a physical machine out to the public cloud, a much easier barrier to hurdle. And it has demonstrably helped reduce the problem of cloud vendor lock-in; app-specific configurations are kept separate from the underlying host environments, making it – at least in theory – easier to jump ship when you want to move your datacenters to a different cloud vendor.

It's been said that containers are the "next wave" of virtualization. It can take a VM minutes to spin up; startup of a container can take just a few seconds. This has some obvious advantages when it comes to scalability and handling high loads; while VMs allowed us to scale capacity in minutes, containers can do the same in seconds. And with the smaller footprint, server hardware resources can be much better utilized. It opens up new possibilities in the

---

[21]Interview of Tyler Hardison by Dave Harrison, see Appendix.

form of finer-grained control and optimization; it's easy to tweak settings in the containers internally without impacting other services and jobs.

Perhaps, best of all, having that clean separation of concerns between infrastructure and applications drastically simplifies our infrastructure governance problemset. A clean host system can have the bare minimum needed to support the OS, perhaps some monitoring and logging libraries and a few other admin agents, and the container runtime software itself; all the applications and services and its dependencies, including language runtimes, OS packages, and libraries, are encapsulated in the container. This eliminates or simplifies a whole set of problems with conflicting dependencies and "DLL hell" and reduces the maintenance needs and vulnerability points in the host. A simplified, hardened OS/host layer with fewer moving parts will require fewer changes, moving us much closer to the immutable infrastructure model where servers can be easily destroyed and replaced. It also frees us from having to optimize each server or VM to fit the needs of a single application or service.

That's not saying that there aren't some downsides with containers and orchestration. Although there's some benefits in reducing the host surface area exposed to threats, there's still much weaker isolation with containers vs. a traditional VM because containers share a common OS kernel; a virus that can infect one container puts other containers sharing that kernel at risk. (It's likely for this reason that containers are still relatively little used in production systems at the time this was written.) Untrusted code should be partitioned onto different environments than those running platform services.

Contrary to popular belief, containers do not magically solve the "it works on my machine" problem, as Tyler Hardison told us:

> [Containers and orchestration] allows developers to be lazy and think they can just plop their laptop on production. So they do all these things that are really horrible and think containerization will make their work portable and secure. My prediction is, we're going to see some major security issues over the next few years. It won't be the fault of Docker or Kubernetes, but it'll be an exploit based on a vulnerability with the images themselves.[22]

Containers also move some of the complexity of managing systems upward instead of eliminating it entirely. With hundreds of containers in play, each running a single service, the operating landscape becomes much more complex. Provisioning large numbers of containers running these services and scaling them up and down dynamically, as well as managing the interaction

---

[22]Interview of Tyler Hardison by Dave Harrison, see Appendix.

between them, can be a daunting task. (Not to say that there aren't solutions for this problem, especially with the rapidly maturing orchestration tools such as Kubernetes; just that this needs to be allowed for in your planning.)

It'd be a mistake to "lift and shift" a monolithic app onto a container and think it will yield magical results. Data persistence and storage will still need to be planned for, and if the application is running just fine on a VM, there's little reason to port it to a container. Certainly, it's possible to lump together all your processes together into a single container – as Tyler brought out earlier – but that may not pay off as much as you'd expect. Containers are really best used as a way of packaging a single service, app, or job; the end state you want is multiple containers each running a single process, which can then be individually managed and scaled.

Don't let us rain on your Docker parade though. Containers would be a natural choice as a new way to cut that mammoth legacy app down to size. We'll get into this more in Chapter 7 as we discuss microservices – but Docker/Packer would be a natural fit for the "strangler fig" pattern many have used to gradually pare down troublesome monoliths.

Containers and microservices go together like peanut butter and jelly. Containers can scale stateless tasks or small units of functionality very well. The fact that containers come with a very well documented set of APIs makes operability a much easier task; administrators can be comfortable that the containers they are running have a set of common characteristics and interfaces.

Uber, eBay, Yelp, ADP, and Goldman Sachs – all have found great success in using containers and orchestration to provide a standardized infrastructure for packaging, shipping, and running applications. It's proven itself as a powerful way of eliminating many of the obstacles to true self-service environment provisioning. We see its adoption continuing to skyrocket and grow as more enterprises become comfortable with running them in production environments.

Security as Part of the Life Cycle

> *I think computer viruses should count as life. I think it says something about human nature that the only form of life we have created so far is purely destructive. We've created life in our own image.*
>
> – Stephen Hawking

The sad thing about most of the data leaks and vulnerabilities you've read about is how many could have been prevented very easily and with minimal work. For example, in 2014, 97% of successful attacks were traced to ten vulnerabilities, all known. Of those ten, eight had fixes in place for over 10 years.[23]

Too Important to Come Last

This isn't a book on security. In fact, security makes us fidget a little in our chairs. We're used to churning out code, by the bucket; "security" was always something we were asked to do, usually in the form of an audit just before a release. It didn't help that as a specialty field (as we thought) the threat landscape seemed to always be evolving in new and terrifying ways that put our users and data in peril.

Our distrust and antipathy to security was understandable; like cooking or sex, security is one of those things that gets better with practice. We simply had not done it enough so that it wasn't painfully awkward.

It became increasingly obvious that security deserved a place in this book. We can't be confident in our code if we don't run checks early and often to make sure there's no gaping security holes, or that users can see data or perform actions that they aren't authorized for. And our systems and network need to be protected and monitored.

Security is one of those things that we often add as a bolt-on – part of an infrequent, last-second audit – as seen in the section "An Insecurity Complex." The people conducting these audits are often in separate, insulated groups and are welcomed with as much warmth and enthusiasm as an IRS auditor. This afterthought type mindset of security being this "other person's job" really belongs to another era. Nowadays, there is just no excuse for not doing some level of security checking – even just a routine vulnerability scan – as part of the normal development life cycle.

Shifting Left with Security

For software to be secure, code needs to be reviewed early and often for vulnerabilities and gaps. For this to happen, it needs to be a part of every check-in. This means a similar "Shift Left" movement to what WonderTek has done earlier with QA and testing – no longer can security be a disconnected, late-game process.

---

[23]"DevOps Cafe Episode 63 - Josh Corman," DevOps Café, 9/2/2015, http://devopscafe.org/show/2015/9/2/devops-cafe-episode-63-josh-corman.html.

Tyler Hardison at Redhawk made it clear that there is no reasonable excuse to not build security into the development life cycle:

> *Security should be a byword and it's never been easier to integrate. There are good frameworks that can help us identify security risks that didn't exist 5 years ago, and there's just no excuse for not using one. OWASP with its top 10 proactive security controls is the best – it's even ranked in order, from most important to least. But when you talk to DevOps gurus about security, they just roll their eyes – security is something pushed on them, and it cramps their style.*
>
> *But really it's no different from code development, and done right it actually adds a little excitement to the routine. Do it at the very beginning and start with a risk assessment of the data. What are you trying to protect? If you're trying to map stars or you're storing GIS data, that's no big deal. But if it's healthcare related or you've got credit card information you're handling, your security protocols had better be at the top of its game. And with most teams you don't have to do it all. If you love data, focus on that – or if you're more of a UI specialist, that's what your security efforts should target.[24]*

The Security Development Life Cycle

Some key dos and don'ts for your own SDL adoption:

- **Flow is the word.** Security reviews need to happen especially on new feature work, but they can't slow down your velocity. So, instead of an approval gate or a bolt-on, security needs to be part of the life cycle early on. Root causes need to be identified and folded into a revised release process.

- **It's not just one thing.** Over time your security controls should be getting better and more comprehensive beyond just static code analysis for known threats. This includes threat modeling, defensive design and secure coding training, and risk-based security testing.

- **Integrate Infosec people.** Infosec in this "shift left" movement are no longer "gatekeepers" handing down edicts from on high; similar to QA and architecture, their feedback comes in early and often as an integrated part

---

[24]Interview of Tyler Hardison by Dave Harrison, see Appendix.

of the team, as peers. This means conversations early and often between your developers and your InfoSec teams, who should have a representative at key points reviewing the security protocols used in the design implementation.

- **Dashboarding and quick feedback are vital.** Developers should have quick visibility into the vulnerabilities in their code on check-in, not late in the cycle.

- **Another argument for microservices.** Smaller codebases (cough, microservices!) tend to be much easier to keep compliant and monitor than monolithic applications.

- **Threat intelligence needs to be shared openly.** This is still very much debated in the community, as there are obvious reasons why enterprises hesitate to air their dirty laundry from a political and a threat containment standpoint. But hiding security flaws rarely pays off in the long-term; instead, it prolongs the exposure window and widens the damage.

Make It Easy to Do the Right Thing

The companies that we've seen be successful with this make it easy for people to do the right thing – providing a well-documented, usable framework so that security checks can be run on check-in and lots of ongoing training and interaction with InfoSec experts during design and product demo sessions.

Zane Lackey at Etsy found that more attention needed to be paid to the libraries and tools they were asking their development team to use. "We can't just say that security is everyone's responsibility and then not give them visibility or tools for security. The way in which you actually deliver on that as a security team is by bringing visibility to everyone... In the old secure development life cycle model, we built a lot of security controls that were very heavyweight and top-down. And they require a lot of investment to tune and work correctly; and in the end, we would get a report once a month or longer."[25]

That lack of visibility and instant feedback was crippling their security improvements at the source; creating easier to adopt frameworks that gave instant, visible feedback – including feeding security bugs directly into the developer's work queue – became a fulcrum point at Etsy.

---

[25]"DevSecOps: How to Use DevOps to Make You More Secure," Zane Lackey. IT Revolution, 8/26/2018. https://itrevolution.com/devsecops-zane-lackey/.

Josh Corman, one of the cofounders of the Rugged Software movement, essentially gives developers and architects a Robert Frost-type "two roads" to choose from – one where the design team can choose a library of their choice or pick one of their approved libraries. He explains the cost-benefit analysis of each – including the importance of reducing attack surfaces in mapping vulnerabilities. Not choosing from one of their selected templates is possible – but it takes longer for approvals, and the implications of higher cost are explained in the form of a higher elective attack surface and for developers, unplanned, unscheduled work trying to resurrect what was done years ago in patching. He noted:

> *Any strategy that depends on a change in human behavior is going to fail. So stop talking about what you care about, talk about what they want to care about.*[26]

It's Not Just Your Code That's Vulnerable

Our applications are made up of more than just our code. We rely on frameworks and libraries that were written by others; even the environments we deploy to, and those deployment processes themselves, use packages and services written by others. These need to be scanned to make sure they are up to date with the latest bug fixes and security patches.

Engineering choices can create a security nightmare for Infosec teams that are invited late to the party. For example, at the 2016 RSA conference, one security engineer told a story about a bank that used a particular Java library. Across all of its products, the developers used 60 different versions of this library. Of those, 57 had published security vulnerabilities.

J. Paul Reed noted that both release and security engineers actually have much in common – and that putting the two together could help reduce your threat attack surface:

> *Ask the two engineering groups [release and security] to research your software supply chain. One of the core tenets of rugged DevOps is that you should know where your software components come from and reduce those components to a minimum number in your software supply chain: the group of well-known, high-quality vendors with which you work. A good first step here is to have your release and security engineers look at your flagship products and determine which libraries they use.*

---

[26]"DevOps Cafe Episode 63 - Josh Corman," DevOps Café, 9/2/2015, http://devopscafe. org/show/2015/9/2/devops-cafe-episode-63-josh-corman.html.

> This type of excavation is where release engineers excel and security engineers know how to make sifting through the results more actionable. That might mean addressing an incompatible licensing issue or updating to a newer version of a library that has had a critical security vulnerability fixed. Finding out what code is lurking in there is likely to be a revelation, and the exercise is highly valuable to boot.[27]

Threat Vector Analysis

Talking about security in terms of costs and liabilities instead of audit checklists makes conversations easier, as it's less subjective and more concrete. Once cost implications are explained, it's easier to weed out and constrain insecure libraries and dependencies. For Paul, this transformed the way security used to work – the drag, the prohibition, the "you guys are sure a drag to go drinking with," to the good parts – the stuff that enables more secure code and less unplanned work.

Like goalies in soccer, security people and the costs of maintaining secure code are often ignored or left in the background, until something happens – in which case, the InfoSec team ends up taking the heat. In response, some auditors have taken a very conservative and prohibitive stance – *lock down everything! No exceptions!* – without an understanding of what the true risks are, which leads to constricted performance, flow, and even available features. It helps to think of security as being not a binary flag but more of a spectrum:

> Security is a matter of assessing threat and risk and deciding on compromises. Think of security as a continuum: on one end you have "wet paper bag," and on the other you have "Fort Knox." You wouldn't implement Fort Knox– level security for storing $100, nor would you leave it in the open on the center console of your car while shopping at the mall. In these cases, you're assessing the threat (theft of your $100) and the level of risk (leaving it unattended while shopping at the mall). It doesn't make sense to spend $1,000 to protect against losing $100. In other cases, the level of security is too intrusive and cumbersome on how you work.

> Can you imagine if you had the same level of security at home as found at the White House? Wearing a badge around the house at all times, checking in and out with security staff, pat-downs, metal detectors, bulletproof glass... seems a bit much for the home, right? A good lock on the doors and windows would work much better for the annoyance factor.[28]

---

[27]"Want rugged DevOps? Team up your release and security engineers," J Paul Reed. TechBeacon, unknown date. https://techbeacon.com/want-rugged-devops-team-your-release-security-engineers.

[28]"Practical Monitoring: Effective Strategies for the Real World," Mike Julian. O'Reilly Media, 11/23/2017. ISBN-10: 1491957352, ISBN-13: 978-1491957356.

In the design sessions, the InfoSec representative needs to discuss with the team the risks associated with each new feature. Is there something about this particular change that could require deeper inspection? Is there sensitive data like credit card or social security numbers? How do we know data or the identities used for authentication aren't altered or fake? What protections do we have on the servers and network – such as a host intrusion detection system, or a network intrusion detection system running via a network tap? Do we ever actually check the logs and monitor what these systems are finding?

In the application release cycle itself, having that InfoSec representative present and checking over the release pipeline will help ensure that penetration testing is happening as an ongoing part of the product development – no software is ready for release unless it is hardened and user information and data kept private.

Netflix has taken a very careful position to empower their development teams without encouraging codependence. Diane Marsh, the Director of Engineering Tools at Netflix, has said that the engineering team's charter is to "support our engineer teams' innovation and velocity. We don't build, bake, or deploy anything for these teams, nor do we manage their configurations. Instead, we build tools to enable self-service. It's okay for people to be dependent on our tools, but it's important that they don't become dependent on us." Ernest Mueller from Bazaarvoice echoed this by saying that they are careful to segregate architectural and foundational work; platform teams can accept requirements but not work from other teams.[29]

Think Rugged

We won't hide our disdain for the clunky phrase "DevSecOps," though it seems popular these days. (Where does this end exactly? DevArcDevTestSecOps?) Maybe, we're being a little fussy here, but it seems like this misses the point. DevOps is just a metaphor for an inclusive culture. Language and terminology are important, and DevSecOps as a phrase seems to represent more of a divergence than we're comfortable with.

Instead, we've adopted the Rugged Manifesto as our own personal working mantra in designing applications, and we encourage you to take a look at this as well. The Rugged Manifesto acknowledges that our software is going to be used in unexpected ways, that it will be submerged in a hostile environment

---

[29]"The DevOps Handbook: How to Create World-Class Agility, Reliability, and Security in Technology Organizations," Gene Kim, Patrick Dubois, John Willis, Jez Humble. IT Revolution Press, 10/6/2016, ISBN-10: 1942788002, ISBN-13: 978-1942788003.

and subjected to unending malicious attacks. This is, like it or not, our reality – the Rugged Manifesto challenges us to face that reality and pledge to do something about it.[30]

To us, this embraces the true spirit of folding security into part of the development life cycle, as a personal responsibility – without having to coin ugly new movement titles.

Automated Jobs and Dev Production Support

Simply put, things always had to be in a production-ready state: if you wrote it, you darn well had to be there to get it running!

— Mike Miller

It seems like hours until help arrives, but it was probably only a few minutes. As you are pulled from the wreckage of your car and placed on a stretcher, someone is at your side telling you that everything is going to be all right. You're carried to the ambulance and as it speeds off in the direction of the hospital, you weakly ask if you can be given some painkillers, or at least stem the bleeding from your broken arm. "I'm so sorry," the EMT person says, sadly shaking her head. "I'm not allowed access to painkillers, and we don't have tourniquets or bandages in this vehicle. It'll have to wait till we get to the hospital."

As ridiculous and potentially tragic as this scenario is, it plays out every day in our service support and Ops centers. And it causes a huge drain on your development firepower, as we see in the section "Effective First Response." If you find yourself tired of support demands bleeding away your work on new features, you're likely stuck in the same situation as that faced by Ticketmaster not too long ago.

It's a story that most of us can relate to. The Operations team at Ticketmaster was suffering a slow death by a thousand cuts – drowning in tickets and manual interventions, trying to support applications that each required a unique set of processes and tools. Deployments were a nightmare of handoffs and delays, with each environment from dev to production requiring a different team to deploy. There was no single place to look at the status of current or previous builds; no way of knowing what had been done or by whom, and what had happened pre- and postdeployment. The nightmare that resulted of support calls spilling directly onto the development teams created long delays that were expensive, painfully visible, and enraged their customer base.

---

[30]"The Rugged Manifesto," unattributed author(s). RuggedSoftware.org, 1/1/2010. www.ruggedsoftware.org.

You'd think the cure for this situation would have been a shiny new CI/CD tool and a years-long effort to force compliance. But the eventual solution they identified was both humbler and lower cost: providing better support for their first responders in Operations.

The Case for Runbooks

Runbooks – automation scripts that can be executed with a single push of a button – were introduced for most of the routine operations tasks, including service restarts, rebooting VMs, and performing cleanup jobs. Delivery teams started working with Operations to provide them a set of jobs that were continually refined and expanded. Operations provided reports back to the delivery teams so customer needs could be anticipated and bugs added to the queue.

As a result of these efforts, first responders gained a broad knowledge of the entire ecosystem and could knock down up to 80% of incoming tickets without the need for escalation. Helping first responders in Operations handle triage and remediation created dramatic results: a 40% drop in escalations and a reduction in time to recover (MTTR) by 50–150%. Overall support costs dropped in half.

We've worked in several enterprises where the team is drowning in firefighting. Often, leaders and the teams involved recognized that better training was called for; lip service was paid to creating automated jobs and enabling effective triage by the support/Ops team. This often ended up consisting of a few halfhearted training sessions and then a handoff of "Top 10" issues documentation – no meaningful ongoing collaboration with Ops or change in behavior followed. Predictably, the needle didn't budge, and problems continued flowing through untouched.

Nigel Kersten of Puppet told us that self-service jobs and runbooks are a force multiplier:

> Take that list and work on what's causing pain for your on-call people, what's causing your deployments to break. The more you can automate this, the better. And make it as self-service as possible – instead of having the devs fire off an email to you, where you create a ticket, then provision test environments – all those manual chokepoints – wouldn't it be better to have the devs have the ability to call an API or click on a website button and get a test environment spun up automatically that's set up just like production? That's a force multiplier in terms of improving your quality right at the get-go.[31]

---

[31]Interview of Nigel Kersten by Dave Harrison, see Appendix.

And Gary Gruver pointed out that automation works to reduce waste in three distinct ways:

> *First, it addresses the obvious waste of doing something manually when it could be automated. Automation also enables the tasks to be run more frequently, which helps with batch sizes and thus the triage process. Second, it dramatically reduces the time associated with these manual tasks so that the feedback cycles are much shorter, which helps to reduce the waste for new and unique work. Third, because the automated tasks are executed the same way every time, it reduces the amount of triage required to find manual mistakes or inconsistencies across environments.*[32]

How Important Is Shared Production Support?

Is production support and end-to-end responsibility by the team for their production running services and applications a must-have? We would answer: maybe, production support isn't a requirement, but it's damn close.

Some will argue that development resources are too scarce and offshoring support is so scalable and inexpensive that it makes no sense to hand any support work off to coders. And some smaller shops we interviewed chose to limit drastically the involvement by their development teams, to perhaps 5% of incoming calls.

But we never encountered a single successful, robust DevOps movement that didn't have some involvement by the devs in helping share the load of production support. Not even one.

We feel that's not a coincidence. Several people we spoke to mentioned the shocking lack of empathy that happens with the traditional "heads-down" programmer; introducing some type of regular support schedule caused immediate positive changes in the team's view of quality and service availability. Having the team hold itself accountable, it seems, is worth more than any number of speeches or quality-driven initiatives instituted from higher levels.

For us personally, although "pager week" was never something we looked forward to, it undeniably helped us to connect better to the world of our customers. Much as we hate to admit it – some share in production support forced us to care more about defects and work harder on permanent fixes instead of one-off patches. Sam Newman agrees:

> *This increased level of ownership leads to increased autonomy and speed of delivery. Having one team responsible for deploying and maintaining the application means it has an incentive to create services that are*

[32]"Start and Scaling Devops in the Enterprise," Gary Gruver, BookBaby, 12/1/2016. ISBN-10: 1483583589, ISBN-13: 978-1483583587.

easy to deploy; that is, concerns about 'throwing something over the wall' dissipate when there is no one to throw it to! … It pushes the decisions to the people best able to make them, giving the team both increased power and autonomy, but also making it accountable for its work.[33]

Google has also found production support to be a valuable crucible for their development teams. Contrary to common belief, most teams at Google handle most support independently, without an SRE involved; and before any SRE can be assigned to a team, they require that the team self-manage their service in production for at least 6 months. There are several review stages that the teams are also required to perform before handing support duties off or launching a new service. All of this drive home the message that operability and effective defect tracking and resolution are not somebody else's job.

The payoff of thinking through remediation paths and recording best practices in a playbook was found to be massive for Google; roughly a 3x improvement in recovery time (MTTR). As the book *Site Reliability Engineering: How Google Runs Production Systems* stated:

The hero jack-of-all-trades on-call engineer does work, but the practiced on-call engineer armed with a playbook works much better. While no playbook, no matter how comprehensive it may be, is a substitute for smart engineers able to think on the fly, clear and thorough troubleshooting steps and tips are valuable when responding to a high-stakes or time-sensitive page. Thus, Google SRE relies on on-call playbooks, in addition to exercises such as the "Wheel of Misfortune," to prepare engineers to react to on-call events.[34]

It's easy to see the impact that a well-thought-out playbook can have on your support team. When a first responder gets an alert in the early morning, she'll have immediately available a link to the playbook. At a glance, she will be able to understand what the service is, what its functionality includes, any dependency points, infrastructure supporting it, contact information and responsibility chains, and metrics and logs that can help with remediation. She also may have been in several rehearsal sessions earlier that went over restart scenarios to help with her diagnosis.

Ideally, she'll have available one of the excellent support-oriented software available such as PagerDuty, VictorOps, and OpsGenie. Your support teams should have one of these tools available to help with reconstructing incident

---

[33]"Building Microservices: Designing Fine-Grained Systems," Sam Newman. O'Reilly Media; 2/20/2015. ISBN-10: 1491950358, ISBN-13: 978-1491950357.
[34]"Site Reliability Engineering: How Google Runs Production Systems," Niall Richard Murphy, Betsy Beyer, Chris Jones, Jennifer Petoff, O'Reilly Media; 4/16/2016, ISBN-10: 149192912X, ISBN-13: 978-1491929124.

timelines and handling escalation paths. A clear timeline and an abundance of information available to first responders are critical to reducing MTTD and MTTR; the value of the recordings and automation capabilities with these software packages cannot be overstated.

A Real Partnership with Ops

The success story at Ticketmaster wasn't an accident; it began with a plan backed by senior management and a significant commitment in time and energy to improve the response process. Specific metrics were watched very carefully over time at the highest levels. The partnership with Operations and support was more than a gesture; it was a viable two-way flow of information and coordination of work.

The DevOps Handbook recounts the story of one sysadmin and the nightmares they experienced being at the end of the development chain:

> In our group, most system admins lasted only six months. Things were always breaking in production, the hours were insane, and app deployments were painful beyond belief... during each moment, we all felt like the developers personally hated us.[35]

That kind of havoc is the recipe for a poisoned, toxic relationship between your support and delivery teams. We'll talk more about this in Chapter 7, but any DevOps movement that doesn't tackle the problem of trust head-on is in trouble. As Sanjeev Sharma pointed out in *The DevOps Adoption Playbook*:

> Why don't Ops teams in large organizations give direct self-service access to the production environments to developers, to deploy continuously, as many startups do? The reason is simple: they don't trust Dev teams to deliver stable, secure, and reliable applications. ...This lack of trust in large organizations seems to extend beyond just Dev and Ops. Dev does not trust business analysts. Enterprise architecture does not trust Ops. QA does not trust the developers. The audit and compliance team trusts no one. No one trusts management, and so on. This lack of trust results in teams not being able to effectively communicate and collaborate across functional silos.[36]

[35]"The DevOps Handbook: How to Create World-Class Agility, Reliability, and Security in Technology Organizations," Gene Kim, Patrick Dubois, John Willis, Jez Humble. IT Revolution Press, 10/6/2016, ISBN-10: 1942788002, ISBN-13: 978-1942788003
[36]"The DevOps Adoption Playbook: A Guide to Adopting DevOps in a Multi-Speed IT Enterprise," Sanjeev Sharma. Wiley, 2/28/2017. ISBN-10: 9781119308744, ISBN-13: 978-1119308744.

The best way we've found to break down these calcified walls and build empathy is by sharing the load. Having developers take a portion of frontline support invariably helps build trust between traditionally partitioned functional teams and improves the flow of feedback from customers to the feature delivery team.

Aaron Bjork at Microsoft feels very strongly that having teams own their features as a product is vital, not a like-to-have. As he told us,

> *Our teams own their features in production. If you start having siloed support or operations teams running things in production, almost immediately you start to see disruption in continuity and other bad behaviors. It doesn't motivate people to ship quality and deliver end-to-end capabilities to users; instead it becomes a 'not it' game.*
>
> *In handling support, our teams each sprint are broken up into an 'F' and an 'L' team. The F team is focused on new features; the L team is focused on disruptions and life cycle. We rotate these people, so every sprint a different pair of engineers are handling bugfixes and interruptions, and the other 10 new feature work. This helps people schedule their lives when they're on call.*
>
> *Our teams own features in production – we hire engineers who write code, test code, deploy code, and support code. In the end that's DevOps. Now our folks have a relationship with the people handling support – they have to. If you start with that setup – the rest falls into place. If you have separate groups, each responsible for a piece of the puzzle – that's a recipe for not succeeding, in my view.*[37]

Having a rotating support model like the "F" and "L" support model used by Microsoft might be useful. Or, you might find it better to gate work across the board, so developers have a few hours or a single ticket to support each week. However you choose to go about it, make sure your development teams share some responsibility for how their products are working in the real world. Besides helping us listen to the voice of the customer in our development priorities, this can have a very nice side benefit of helping bring more of a tools and automation orientation to your support team.

If your team is drowning in support costs and irate customer calls, take the same approach used so effectively by companies like Ticketmaster, Microsoft, and Google. Keep visible your metrics around reliability and SLA coverage, exposing the cost caused by pass-through tickets and long remediation times. Provide simple, push-button automation that is self-service or as close to the problem as possible; constantly engage with Ops to keep these runbooks up to date. And empower the people first on the scene to knock down as many problems as they can.

---

[37]Interview of Aaron Bjork by Dave Harrison, see Appendix.

Numbers Lead the Way

With spring giving way to the full heat of summer, Ben is feeling his oats. He's made several big bets – such as promising Tabrez that he can deliver releases to production in half the time they were formerly, in only 38 days! What gives him confidence that he can deliver on this promise?

Perhaps, knowing how bad things were when they started, he's now more comfortable with their capacity to absorb change. Barely under a year ago, they were stuck in the mud. Technical debt was piling up unseen, and his business partners were outraged at their slow time to deliver on promised features. QA was lagging hopelessly behind, catching few serious errors but introducing weeks of delays and high support costs. Releases commonly ran red and required multiple manual handoffs. Rarely were requests prioritized or evaluated from an objective point of view; the concept of Minimum Viable Products and the ability to turn off an unsuccessful feature was completely unknown.

Now though, Ben is feeling like he finally has a place to stand. It began with more of a focus on the work the team itself was producing, instilling quality early on. This meant a team definition of done, enforced with common, well-structured peer reviews run along the friendly but effective lines of a "family dinner." Blame-free postmortems in partnership with Operations led to more emphasis on setting up runbooks and automation to find and fix root problems. Also, helping cut down on their firefighting time was setting aside capacity to work on big-picture delivery pipeline improvements and requiring a healthy level of live site support by the devs.

© Dave Harrison and Knox Lively 2019
D. Harrison and K. Lively, *Achieving DevOps*,
https://doi.org/10.1007/978-1-4842-4388-6_6

Breaking their teams down into smaller "SWAT" teams tasked with supporting a single value stream end to end promises to cut down on some of the significant delay wastes they're suffering and possibly paves the way for microservices and a cleaner services-based architectural model.

Perhaps, best of all, what was a murky "fog of war" is now looking a little clearer. They are starting to have better displays of the global delivery flow and limiting factors, thanks to some careful analysis following several rounds of value stream mapping exercises. There's more work to be done here however until they are truly seeing things from the eyes of the business. And monitoring is still far from being an essential part of any new service or app, which means their available data stores still have significant blind spots.

Can they move closer to a true Continuous Delivery model? Will the shift in focus from velocity and delivery rates to recovery time pay off in the availability-centric metrics that Ben's partners care about? And what happens when the wheels really fall off the bus, and there's a significant, long-term outage?

By the Numbers (Metrics and Monitoring)

"Well, there's your answer, right there. See that? You got the email; I can see the alert right there. Maybe check your spam filter or your inbox rules."

I lean forward, frustration tightening the muscles along my shoulders. "Yeah, we got that alert, along with several thousand others that look just like it. I'm so tired of all this CYA bullcrap, Kevin."

I'm pissed off, and with good reason. I just got out of a severe ass-chewing session with Tabrez, who's asking me why we were the last ones to know that the Footwear app was down. People were locked out all weekend; it was a mess, and we look like idiots. This is just after promising Tabrez and my boss that end-to-end support and smaller, cross-functional teams would fix these kinds of drops. And once again, I'm getting this pass-the-buck attitude by Operations, refusing to take any responsibility for the messes they create.

Enough, I tell myself, is enough. "You keep telling me that things are going to get better. This isn't better, Kevin." I jab my finger into Kevin's chest, twice. My voice is taking on a hard edge. "It's a total lack of accountability, and it's completely unacceptable to me. Understand?"

Kevin looks at me wide-eyed like an owl, but remains silent; the entire room is frozen. Almost immediately, I feel a wash of regret, but it's too late to turn back now. I'm about to drive home a few more points when I feel a hand gripping my wrist, hard. "Ben, can I talk to you outside for a few minutes? ... Excuse us folks."

Out in the hallway, Alex looks around, then impales me with an icy stare. "What... are... you doing here, Ben?"

I make a few noises about how I'm accountable for how the app performs and that my feet that are getting put to the fire. My heart isn't really in it though. I'm in an untenable position; it really isn't like me to lose control as I just did. I finish by stammering weakly, "It's past time for me to stop taking the heat for guys like Kevin..."

"Guys like Kevin are part of the team, Ben. And I'm the team lead for this group. Now you set out the rules for this SWAT team, beginning with honesty and transparency. And you are the one that keeps saying that we're adults, that you trust us to have the right motives and a strong internal work ethic. And we started out this meeting with the slide on having a blameless postmortem – that was something YOU pushed for. Now, how do you think this is going to go over if you come down on Kevin like a bag of hammers when we have a problem?"

I mull this over, my jaw working a little. "All right. Fair enough, I'll back off. Alex, you are the team lead, and I trust you implicitly. But this could not have happened at a worse time. Tabrez and I want to see some accountability here; people need to step up to the plate and take ownership of the problem."

Alex still has a stern look, but he puts a hand on my shoulder. "Ben, you're my direct and you know I follow your lead. You've never had to worry about me going behind your back. But now that you've set the template for the team – I want you to take a step back here and watch how the team chooses to resolve this problem. And I bet you coffee tomorrow that the problem is not named Kevin. OK?"

"Deal." We reenter the conference room; Alex continues. "All right, now where were we... oh yeah, let's talk about monitoring and alerts. Do we have the response team people here in the room?"

For this week, it was Ryan that was on point for live site support. He confirms what I'd been saying earlier; "Yeah, there was that alert, in an email on Saturday night. It went out to every dev on the team, and Ops got it as well. The problem was, it wasn't acted on – it was buried in a snowdrift of other email alerts. It had about nine exclamation points in the subject line and was flagged Important, but that was also true of about three hundred other emails over that time period. There just isn't a way I can see, going back in time, where any support engineer could have known something was seriously wrong."

Kevin sighs in frustration. "So, Microsoft in their infinite wisdom chose to roll out a security patch that forced a restart on Saturday about 3 pm. When that happened, for whatever reason IIS didn't restart, which meant the Footwear authentication service abended. From our perspective in Ops, this was just a short downtime, and all the server metrics looked great across the board.

CPU, memory, disk health – all looked green. Why IIS didn't restart, as it should have, is still a mystery I'm trying to resolve. So far I can't simulate that when I run manual restarts on staging."

Padma says, "This looks like a masking problem to me. Yes, it's terrible that the service was down, and we need to look into why it didn't restart. But fixing this one problem doesn't guarantee something else just a little different won't reoccur. So the problem we should be drilling in on and focusing our efforts is our monitoring. Right now, it's too noisy to be effective. People are oversaturated with old-school email alerts and are tuning it out."

Vigorous head nods can be seen around the room; Alex says with a smile, "Yeah, I can see that's the consensus feeling here. This isn't the first time we've pointed out a need to reset with our alerts and monitoring. Kevin, you're our resident SME on that subject, what's your thoughts?"

Kevin, after hemming and hawing a little, finally allows that – at ten years old and counting – their homegrown monitoring system is starting to show some signs of age. "When we first wrote this, none of the SaaS stuff we see out there was in existence, and I think we all looked at email or pages as being the best way to raise alarms. I think it'd be very dangerous to turn it off though."

"No, no one is saying that – we need to know what's going on." George, who's been silent most of this time, is now drumming his fingers on the table, deep in thought. "It's becoming clearer that this is a bigger problem than just this one isolated incident. Tuesday we're meeting with our frontline peeps to go over the issues for the week. I think that'd be a great time to talk about a reset on our alerts. If they're truly as noisy and ineffective as the group seems to think – maybe we look into tuning these alerts so they only happen with the truly high priority conditions. I'd be willing to bet our support people would love it too if we could log more diagnostic information and embed as much of that as possible in that very first triggered email."

"Does everybody realize what we're asking for here?" Harry looked around the room, in full Grumpy Oatmeal Guy mode. His bushy white mustache quivers in indignation. "Are we seriously thinking about shotgunning logging statements throughout our apps and services? That's crazy talk. Monitoring agents will kill our latency numbers; people will be more upset about our performance, not less. And it gives us yet another set of systems to worry about when it comes to keeping our configurations consistent and up to date."

Alex says, "I'm not worried about some supposed massive overhead from monitoring agents; this is not the nineties, our systems are much more powerful and the agents are much more lightweight."

Harry's on the top of his game. "This is a lot of work we're talking about, and I don't think anyone is thinking enough about costs, you just want to plunge ahead and think this will work out of the box. I mean, Etsy says to measure anything and everything – which is great if you're a storage vendor! That data that we're talking about collecting and monitoring, we don't have anything set up yet to handle it. It'll take us weeks, months to get logging set up across all our systems, especially our legacy stuff. This is difficult and EXPENSIVE, guys. The business won't stand for it."

George counters, "Fair enough. Maybe we need to think a little more about what we can cover without having to run out and buy anything. How does this sound – on Tuesday, we go over with the response team the last ten issues that have cropped up, and which could have been detected with better monitoring or logging. Then we go back and add that to our existing engine, and keep repeating that question every week. In a few months, we should have MOST of the common scenarios covered, without having to kick off a massive rewrite like you seem to be worried about."

This doesn't fly so well; most people in the room are wanting a new framework that's more extensible and powerful. As you'd expect with a gaggle of engineers, we go right to tooling and software options. Ryan likes Pingdom; Padma favors the ELK stack, and others are weighing in for Raygun. For a few minutes, we bat this around, but in the end George's suggestion – which happens to be lowest cost – carries the day. We agree that if the support teams find serious gaps that our homespun logging and aggregation system can't handle, we'll begin investigating some of the newer SAAS-based monitoring options as a replacement.

Ryan says, "I'd like to see our scoreboard change a little. We need to have metrics that actually matter showing on those damn screens in the team meeting room. I'm just going to say it – we don't need to have server metrics staring us in the face every time I look at the application health. Let's take this outage as an example – what we should be measuring is our page response time and success/fail rates on user logins. This is a global app and if we know a page is suddenly taking 10 seconds to load, where yesterday it was taking half a second, we know there's a problem."

I've cooled off a while ago, and Ryan's thought makes me grin; it's something Tabrez and I have spent a lot of time on lately. I send him a text: *Hey, get over here, this is interesting.*

Harry is really starting to get some traction with a particularly epic rant on a favorite topic, On The Cluelessness Of Managers. "Well, that's the problem with WonderTek, isn't it? A lack of focus? I mean, they tell us they want us to drive things through to completion, and the next day we get handed down nine different numbers as some kind of half-assed quota to meet. It's ridiculous!", he harrumphs. "Better not to give us anything at all. I swear to God, this company has a severe case of ADD. Every new manager we get seems to have the attention span of a meth-addicted hamster..."

Harry's air of wounded outrage finally breaks me, and I start to laugh, just as Tabrez slips into the room and takes a seat. "Ha!! Well, call me guilty on that, I guess. Harry, you've got a point, but with all due respect I get a few hundred more emails a day than you do, which might explain some of that distraction. Anyway, we're not trying to create world peace here, we just want to talk specifics about our monitoring and alerts. Does everyone agree with Ryan? Do we need to change our displays so they're showing our user's actual experience across every region?"

The group kicks around some more ideas. Padma is advocating for us to make reliability and availability our lingua franca. "After all," she says sharply, "if an application isn't available, anything else doesn't matter. The question we should always be asking is, how are we going to improve our availability? Right now our standards are impossibly high. We have a SLA but it's totally unrealistic; a single five-minute outage would put us over the edge. We need to rethink how we measure and enforce reliability – even if that means capping our releases, the same way Google does, if we're out of our budget on availability. Right now it's just a paper tiger."

Tabrez finally speaks up. "I agree with you, Padma, and maybe showing our current SLA is a good thing. And I agree that our current SLA standards need to be rethought; I'd settle for 99% availability at this point."

"Padma has a point when she says that our expectations are too high," George replies. "We keep getting mixed signals from you, Tabrez – you say you want velocity, and we have a pile of features you've put on our plate. Which is great – but then you are also asking for 99% availability. The only way we can meet that is to freeze all changes – to the environments, network, or the app itself. You don't want us grinding to a halt, but you don't want any downtime. We can't do both."

Surprisingly, Tabrez yields on this point, allowing that perhaps we need to rethink our availability SLA's during beta periods. But he presses for a more valuable dashboard in business terms: "If we want this dashboard to answer the key question of the application's health, then I think displaying a chart showing successful vs failed logins every day over the previous 30 days is a great place to start. And I'd love to see a global map, where if the average page response takes longer than 5 seconds, it turns the region yellow or red."

Alex brings up the concern from earlier that the team is being given too cluttered a dashboard to monitor and that the metrics we're tracking are constantly being swapped out.

Tabrez laughs. "Well, yeah, I'd have to agree. So let's simplify. I'd say, yes show the current SLA as a reference point, say top right. But I'd also like to see our bug trends as we've done in the past. Maybe transaction rate as well. For our customers... what matters also is our communication when things go haywire. That means we need to get them talking to a human being in 15 minutes or less – and hopefully their problem resolved in that time. I keep bringing this up but – that's why we're tracking our long-running tickets, those longer than 15 minutes. If we've guessed right with this new, more direct support model, I'm hopeful we can cut these in half over the next few months."

Alex says, "Well, I see we're almost out of time, but this has got me thinking. I'll say this – while I want to see some of the user-centric numbers that Tabrez is talking about on some displays, I do think we're not breaking rules by having some developer-centric screens. Our SLA itself, that's important but we need to keep in mind that's the effect, not the cause. Some block-and-tackle work in knocking down our most frequent errors and bugs is where we'll actually see results. I'll be a fly on the wall with tomorrow's talk with the critsit response team. But we should be careful not to focus on mean time between failures – that'll just make us conservative, as Tabrez has said, and I know we're going to have more outages."

It looks like I'm going to have to buy Alex coffee tomorrow, but I'm OK with that. I chip in, "For my part, I'm hearing that it's frustrating to constantly have the goalposts get moved. This outage – as embarrassing as it was – just shows us how vital it is to minimize the impact of any outage. That question we need to keep asking hits the nail on the head: 'How long does it take us to detect and restore service?' So – despite Harry here calling me a methhead rodent" – some laughter ripples through the room – "I'm not changing direction. We're staying focused on the one number we agreed weeks ago as a delivery team, and that's MTTR."

Ryan can't leave well enough alone and says, "So are we going to stick with Kevin's bubblegum-and-popsicle-stick monitoring system, or are we going to get Raygun set up as I've been pushing for the past two years?"

Before I can speak, I feel that grip on my wrist again; Alex replies crisply, "Let's not skip ahead to a solution until we've defined the problem better. There's all kinds of great vendors out there, and it looks like everyone here has their favorite. If there's truly a gap that's causing a blind spot, we'll identify it and buy a better tool, I promise."

George stands up. "One last thought – was the problem here that the tool we currently have is hopelessly inadequate? Or is it that we've spent the last decade thinking that setting up monitoring and alerts is someone else's job?"

He looks around the room. "I don't know what the solution is going to look like here, but I do know the problem we experienced over the weekend was just a symptom. For that symptom not to be repeated, we need to make sure that monitoring is seen as everyone's job. So if Tabrez says availability and long-running tickets are a problem for the customer, that means our dashboards need to show this. If it's not visible, we can't improve it. And we'll make this a part of our weekly review – seeing how useful our alert thresholds are, whether we can improve in the data we're storing, and how easy we're making it for the coders to implement this as a reusable framework. Does that sound like a good action plan?"

As the meeting breaks up, a beaming Tabrez gives me two jarring pats on the shoulder on the way out of the room. "Hey, this is the first time I've seen any kind of customer focus from you guys. And it seems like you're asking the right questions. Keep it up!"

I find myself whistling all the way back to my office. Alex had been right; in the end, the team had stayed on course and was finding solutions to their own problems. Things were starting to really click!

Letting Our Freak Flag Fly (Feature Flags, Continuous Delivery)

This morning, I thought I'd shake it up a little bit and invite Alex in on my daily trek over to Footwear. They had an upcoming launch of a new shoe line set for mid-September, and Alex had some interesting new ideas on how we could better coordinate on the release. After Alex had explained his thinking, I could hear the devious MBA side of me starting to cackle with glee. This was the juiciest opportunity to build a better relationship that I've seen in months.

"So, you're saying you want us in the driver's seat for this upcoming release? And you want to kick it off next week?" Tabrez gives us a heavy *are you serious?* look and sighs. "Look, we've come a long way, and I trust you guys. But I kind of feel like you're asking me to stand on a red X right now. And from what you showed me last week, what we have just isn't ready for prime time."

I laugh; in Tabrez's place, I would have reacted exactly the same way. "Hey, I totally get where you are coming from. Relax, we're not asking you to do anything groundbreaking or risky. In fact, I think you'll find that Alex's suggestion here is going to make our lives a lot easier."

Tabrez's eyebrows are still arched, but he allows us to continue. Alex pulls up a new release dashboard he's been working on for the past week. "So, we've been talking about our release patterns, and it's clear we still have a lot of work to do. For example, right now we're checking in our work many times a day – but we're still releasing once every three weeks or so. That's just not a quick enough feedback cycle for us to catch problems early enough."

Tabrez interrupted, "I thought that was why we invested as much time as we have into bumping up our unit test coverage. You told me that was the big pain point and it'd help us get earlier detection on bugs."

"Yes, you're right, and you know from our retrospectives and our scorecards – our revised testing harness is catching more bugs early on, at check-in. But this is just like with your factory manufacturing floor – once we knock down one constraining point, there will be another constraint we'll have to focus on. Right now, it looks like that's centered around the way we are rolling out our releases. Right now, they're too big to fail, and that's costing us."

Tabrez nods his head slowly. "Yeah, I think I understand that. I'm thinking back now to two months ago, when Tina on my team asked you to roll back that user forum feature that was flatlining. It took about two weeks to pull out that code as I remember. But you still haven't answered my question; how does this new project dashboard make my life easier?"

I decided to break in. "That's a great example. In fact, it was that same messy rollback that got us thinking about feature flags and a more gradual way of rolling out changes behind the scenes. Going back in time, what if we could have made that feature exposed only to your Footwear people for their acceptance testing? Or maybe exposed it just to a set of beta users that you trust?"

Tabrez smiled. "Of course, that would have been terrific. But for this particular launch – this is very sensitive information, Ben, and we can't risk our competitors getting ahold of it. It's much safer for us to lock down this functionality until we can turn it on as part of a coordinating marketing launch. With this new line of shoes – I can't go into details on what makes it special, but if it takes off like I think it will, it could mean hundreds of millions of dollars. We're talking about three years of global effort here at stake – it's an amazing innovation."

I try a different tack. "Totally understood, and you're right. Up to now, you've handed work off to us and we come back weeks or months later – and there's this messy back and forth on coordinating the release. There's an opportunity here to kill two birds with one stone – with feature flags or toggling, my team can introduce changes sooner for your Footwear people to review – which will make our release cycle tighter and give us the feedback we need. And we think once your Footwear team experiments with this dashboard, you'll get addicted – it'll be so much easier for you to gate and control who sees what with these high-profile launches. With this much at stake – wouldn't you feel better if Footwear was at the wheel?"

Alex presses the advantage a little. "As you can see from this dashboard, it's really easy for us to show every flag we're using with the app in one list. We can turn them on or off with a single click; but we're only allowing you and a few people you delegate to have that kind of control. We can set up tags so our sysops people can filter out their environmental config changes as a toggle, and have a flag so we can put the site in maintenance mode during our database refreshes. You can see here – we've already got snippets set up in the code so the new shoe line launch pages can be viewed by Footwear, and only Footwear, with a single click." He catches Tabrez's look and hastily adds, "These are blank pages so far with nothing sensitive or proprietary until you give the OK, Tabrez. But our thinking is, it'll be much safer for you to be at the helm of this launch than us. You know which users should be granted access, and what level of access they should have."

Tabrez had pulled Alex's laptop away and was messing around with the dashboard as he was talking. He looks up and gives me that half-smile that I've learned was a good sign; *maybe this will work.* "It looks like we've even got an audit trail here, so we can track who's changing things. Hmmm... you know for a few months now I've been wondering how we can do a pre-launch and demo for a few of our top retailers, three weeks ahead of the general release. This could be what I've been looking for."

His eyes keep going back to the slick dashboard and the list of toggled release features. "Hmmm. I'm willing to give this a try, but if you're asking us to share the responsibility around the release – and that's exactly what you're trying to do, Ben – you need to step up to the plate. Give us training and a clear set of documentation. I'll have my team play around with this for a week, and they'll give me a yes/no call on going forward with this. If it looks like it's just more of a headache or a distraction from our actual design and planning work, I'll drop this thing like the world's hottest potato."

I smile. "OK, so we've got a plan then." I'm quietly confident that we won't be scaling this back in a week. Tabrez is going to find this very impactful in terms of better coordination on upcoming releases and having complete control over when and who sees his new features. Once we get him and his team in charge of selectively turning on new features to beta groups, he won't want to turn us back.

Alex looks a little depressed on the way back across the street, though. I pat him on the shoulder. "Look, that was the best reaction we could have hoped for. Tabrez has been around the block a few times, and he's not going to be dancing with happiness about any proposed solution from us that looks like more work for his people. He didn't say no, Alex. In fact, I think he's going to say yes – just because it gets him the beta program he wants."

Alex replied, "You know as well as I do, this is something we need if we're going to get out of this 'push and pray' cycle. We shouldn't let Tabrez be the decider on something that matters this much to the team. I can't believe I have to go back to them and announce that we're waiting on a yes decision on a bunch of shoe designers."

I stop in the pathway. "Alex, two things. First off, Tabrez very much is our boss. He has every right to tell us what to do, because the shoes his team produces and markets pay our salaries. If we say we want to partner better with them, we need to act like it and get their input instead of just pushing things on them.

"Second, I think you misunderstood the whole point of that conversation. We already know these massive tsunami releases aren't working for us. Tabrez is making the call on how much control he wants his team to have over the release pace, but I never said we would be rolling back any of the things we've been talking about as a team – feature flags, canary releases or blue/green deployments. It's clear to me we need all of those things, and it's a core competency that we own, the way we handle our business. I'm not asking for permission on how we do our work, OK?"

Alex looks relieved, and we head into the café to grab some sandwiches. We talk a little more shop about the upcoming feature launch, then get caught up a little with our home life. As we chat, I can't stop smiling. I feel very confident that Tabrez and his team would find the fine-tuned control and segmentation capabilities around feature flags and controlling releases addicting.

This would solve so many problems for us in coordinating releases, getting better feedback, and help in breaking down more barriers. Being able to decouple our deployments from feature releases was going to be a huge step forward.

Backlash (Disaster Recovery and Gamedays)

As I've come to expect, 3 days after the outage I get a single agenda-less meeting invite from Emily. Normally, I might have ignored it, but in this case, she's invited both Douglas and Tabrez; all managers, not a single technical person in the room. *It's time for another discussion around better discipline with our releases*, was all she'd say when I asked her the purpose of the meeting.

So, I was going in blind and unprepared, a nice little sacrificial lamb – and given some recent problems we've had, it didn't take a Rhodes scholar to guess her real aim.

Worst of all, it looks like I'm walking into an ambush on ground she's prepared well in advance. Emily had evidently met with Douglas privately earlier. They were already in the conference room, chatting and smiling, as Tabrez and I walk in. Emily gives me her very best Cheshire cat grin; I could almost see feathers poking out of the corner of her mouth. I smile back evenly with as much false warmth as I can manage.

Emily and I have come a long way, but we don't see eye to eye on everything; she can be a dangerous opponent. I remind myself, *don't show weakness, let her make the first move.*

Emily wastes no time chatting about the weather and just launches right in, confident of success. "As I was just explaining to Douglas – we really need to rein in some of the bad traits we've been seeing with this Footwear application.

It's a disaster and the support costs to my team have been skyrocketing. You can't believe how angry your customers have been on the phone – honestly, it just seems so sloppy."

She taps a set of papers on the table and smiles again. "With Sysops, we're in a better position and more experienced to provide availability support. I really regret your not involving us earlier, it could have brought the site up hours earlier. And the SWAT teams you instituted don't seem to be working out very well in practice. When I went to your engineering team, they seemed completely at a loss as to what to do. There wasn't a runbook or a plan – people were running around like chickens. It took me several hours to regain control."

I resist the urge to snort. Alex had come to me later in a rage. "You should have seen it, Ben – she was like Christ coming to cleanse the temple. You would have thought she was riding in a chariot pulled by four white horses. And she immediately starts running from engineer to engineer, bellowing out about needing a status, and what the ETA was." Alex said that by the time he was able to gently ease her out of the room to allow the team time to work the problem, Alice had cost them about an hour.

That was a card I could play, but for now it stayed in my hand. "That's a little different than how I heard it, but don't let me stop you. Let's say our response wasn't perfect – which I certainly agree with. And I know you have the best interests of WonderTek at heart." I gave her my best guileless smile, trying to get a glimpse of her endgame. "What's your proposed solution?"

Emily turned to Douglas with an upraised eyebrow in mock surprise. "Really? I would have thought this would have been more familiar to you by now but – if you want me to repeat myself, here goes. As I was telling Douglas, we've seen great results so far with that Change Authorization Board. In fact, we have 70% of the company's assets now being released under this process. It's past time that Footwear gets folded into this company-wide mandate." She goes on for a few more minutes, and I found myself dozing off a bit as she was describing the new authorization forms we'd need to complete, and the approval chain before any production release – "minor or major, we can't have any deviances!" – and of course her personal favorite, the Zero Defect Meetings.

In the end, she was right – this was a familiar argument, and by now I found it tediously repetitive. I'd been able to fend this off in the past with a sincere effort to collaborate, though admittedly I'd missed a few of the release planning sessions.

What made this uncertain was the Douglas factor; I have no idea which way he'll swing. *He values teamwork,* I tell myself, nodding brightly as she wraps up her speech with a glorious vision of how effortless and problem-free our lives will become under this new program. *Speak and think in terms of the team and the best interests of the whole.*

Douglas is watching me carefully but so far has not given me any signs; the man had the perfect poker face. I've seen pictures of Half Dome that looked more expressive. "So, Ben, I'm curious about your position on this. We've talked several times about folding in a more rigorous change control process. In light of… recent events… do you think it's time that we put that back on the table?"

I remember the tap dance act that Richard Gere did in the movie Chicago and decide to use one of Emily's favorite tactics: the endless monologue. "Absolutely, it should be. I think all options should be on the table – if we can prove they add value and are solving the problem. Emily, if I understand your position right here, it seems like you are advocating for a better change control process, correct? Meaning a weekly change approval process and zero defect meetings, perhaps a change window for a gated release in the evening hours. Did I get that about right?"

Emily's smile takes on a hint of exasperation; she's wondering about my next move, too. "Yessss, Ben, exactly the same process that the rest of us have been following for the past three months. You know this. I shouldn't have to go into all the benefits this offers again in terms of compliance, security, better governance. I'm frankly a little shocked it's taken your team this long to come to the table."

Last week, I caught a glimpse of the poor saps dragging themselves out of Emily's vaunted Zero Defect Meeting and suppressed a shudder. Ukrainian serfs dragging around wheelbarrows of potatoes looked happier and more fulfilled. Time to get back to the tap dance. "Ok, so we did have an outage a few days ago – one that took us the better part of six hours to resolve. And it's even worse than you've described."

I ask if they've taken a look at the postmortem; as I suspected, neither Douglas nor Emily had taken the time. I call in Alex, Rajesh, and Rob, who had been handling live site support that week. They took the team through the findings, including the timeline of what had happened and the root causes that the group had identified so far.

As I'd admitted, it didn't look pretty. We had checked in a change to our shopping cart processing routines, one that was fairly minor in scope in handling payment processing. Unfortunately, we'd missed some dependencies where this same module was used elsewhere by the WonderTek apparel team. The modification immediately froze all transactions across WonderTek's eCommerce sites; in-process orders began timing out, and carts were stuck in an in-process state. Worse, our end-to-end testing had not anticipated this specific scenario, and our peer review had missed the hidden dependency.

Once the problem had been detected – which according to the timeline had taken nearly 90 minutes – the team had immediately flipped back the feature flag covering the change. But our old enemy the data model once again proved to be a sticking point; the changes to the backend entities could not be rolled back, and shopping carts were still in a halted state. It took a full recovery of the database from the most recent backup to bring the backend to a stable, operable state that was consistent with the UI and service layer. Several hours' worth of transactions had been lost or compromised, which translated to nearly $200K in lost revenue.

Tabrez chips in once Ryan and Alex were finished with their recap. "Even worse for us was the gap in communication. It took us far too long to realize something was wrong, and to track down and isolate the issue and roll it back. In the meantime, we didn't have a good communications chain with our customers, who were left nearly completely in the dark for almost half a day. I've been fielding angry calls for the past several days on this, and it's been all over the news. We've been able to soothe some hurt feelings, but there's no question that our rep has taken yet another hit from this."

Time for another round of tap dancing. "OK, so now we've got a much clearer idea of the problem. I'm still a little unclear though – you say the rollbacks weren't clean because of the data layer component. Does that mean that we should consider feature flags and continual delivery ineffective for us?"

Alex smiles. "Well, we're still trying to determine why this didn't come up with our beta customers. But I would say there's not just one single root cause here. We've identified six action items, which you'll see in the report." He passed around a written copy of the postmortem and explained some of the areas that were exposed as weak points. "We know our time to detect was laughably slow here – 90 minutes. Ideally, we'd have eyes on the order processing rate; that's our lifeblood, but it's not a part of our current dashboard, and it needs to be. We would have seen this almost immediately if we'd had that showing, and it will also help keep our team better focused on the business impacts of the features we're working on. Also, we feel that entity changes in the future should always be additive, never destructive – in other words, we can add columns but never change or remove them in a table. That should help with making rollbacks less painful. We've added all of these as items to our upcoming sprint as tasks."

I flip Emily an olive branch. "Another concern I have is that broken communication chain. Let's start with internally. For example, Emily came in and started cracking the whip to see what our current state is. But ideally, we wouldn't have needed that. We had some team members in the room, and others were calling in to a conference call that we'd set up. But as a manager I can't tell what the status is from a conference call, and we can't use an audio call to come up with a timeline and order of events easily. Do you have any thoughts about how we can knock down that issue?"

"Yes, since we're distributed at times, it'd be a good idea for us to have a virtual chat room, open and available for any high severity problem," Rob answers. "That's in the report and we're looking into some different lightweight chat solutions now."

I feel badly for Rob; as the primary live site engineer that week, he'd taken the brunt of the impact. He looks hollow eyed and haggard, completely spent. "I also like some of the concepts behind a self-healing, unbreakable pipeline. There's no reason why we can't have our software notice a dramatic shift in a KPI like order processing and trigger either an alarm or automatically roll back to a previous version. Investigating that as a potential solution is tops on my list for next sprint." His laugh has just a slight bitter edge. "I can tell you honestly, I hope it's a long time before we have another release like this one. Once we refactor our testing, I doubt this exact same issue is going to crop up again – so we need to make sure anything we come up as a fix is looking ahead, not backwards."

Tabrez says, "That covers our internal communications lag, but it doesn't address our customer relations issue. I'm working on some ideas now where we can provide better notification during an outage." Tabrez told me that one of his new business KPIs was MTTN – Mean Time to Notify. I laughed, but it turned out he was serious. What hurt us wasn't so much the downtime, but the long lag between our services being back up and customers finding out we were back open for business.

Emily says in a flat tone, "Gentlemen, we're really getting away from the point here. This change would never have made it out the door with the company's CAB review process in place. We're just buying time until the next high-visibility outage."

I'm tempted to call out her counterfactual reasoning; instead, I spread my hands out in surrender. "Emily, if I thought a weekly CAB meeting would help solve this problem, I'd jump on it with both feet. But it sounds to me like all a weekly off-hours change window would do is hold up our releases so they're larger in size – meaning there's a greater chance that things would break. We want to be releasing more often, not less. So far, our customer has been happy with our release pace and the greater safety controls we've put in place by gradually toggling new features in release rings."

I turn to Tabrez for backup, who responds with a strong affirmative nod – our partnership is still going strong. "The problem here wasn't that we didn't have governance or a strong, well thought out release process. I mean, we were able to identify a fix and come back to a stable state using artifacts only in our version control and our standard release process; that proves it's viable. What we've identified is some gaps in our testing and in the way we make changes to our data layer, along with some changes we need to make to monitoring and log aggregation. But we can't say that these controls weren't in place, or that they're insecure, not auditable, or unrepeatable."

"I would be angry if they were either minimizing this problem or trying to point blame elsewhere. But we've asked them to take on a greater share of production support and solve their own problems; to me, this is a good example of that. We're not perfect, but we aren't making the same mistakes twice." I look now at Douglas, our judge and jury. "If we're thinking in terms of the team… If we're putting their best interests and those of the business first, then we should probably take their recommendations into account. There's several items here in their action list that I will make sure gets followed through on – in particular, I'd like to see us put our availability more to the test. We need to have a monthly DR exercise, where we're whacking environments or deliberately redlining a release and seeing if our rollbacks are working as they should. The team calls this a Gameday, and I'd like Emily's help in coming up with a few realistic scenarios for next month."

Finally, the hint of a smile on that granite face. "Hmmmm… well, Tabrez, what do you think? We had this outage, and it impacted your team most of all – do you have confidence we're on target with our solutions?"

Tabrez says, "I'd say there's still work to be done when it comes to communication. We needed better visibility during the event of what's going on, and a better coordinated response post-event. That's for Ben and I to take on and resolve. But yes, I'm actually pleased with the items I see here in this plan."

All the work I've put into my relationship with Tabrez is paying off now; Emily is facing a phalanx. She rocks back in her chair in disbelief as she sees her chances slip away. "Douglas, I thought we were on the same page here. Are you going to allow things to drift like this – "

Douglas turns to her, and now she's getting the full weight of his stare. "Emily, we are not drifting. I wanted a solution that the team could back, and it seems like Ben has a workable one ready. That's very different from what you were describing to me earlier." He stands up and says to me – "Ben, give me a report in a month and tell me how these action items are progressing. And Tabrez, you know I'd value your feedback as well."

Emily grabs me by the arm, just as I'm leaving the room, still trying to salvage a victory. "Ben, I don't understand why you're digging in like this. You know that until we have better controls over releases, you'll never have a stable app, and it's embarrassing the company."

Once again, I find myself admiring her unsinkable determination – time to show a little iron of my own. "Emily, I don't agree with you that we lack controls, but we do lack manual controls. You and I are on a good road now, and we're cooperating better when it comes to standing up infrastructure and coordinating releases. So let's not fight now. If you could prove to me that this rigid approval process will prevent issues, I'd buy in – tomorrow. But I trust my eyes, and the numbers show that our stability and resilience are rising."

She's still angry, and for a few days we grump at each other in the hallways and avoid eye contact. But give her credit; Emily is a good manager, and she's all about protecting her team. Better DR doesn't take much salesmanship, and soon enough it becomes her baby. She and Kevin start putting together some fascinating Gameday disaster recovery scenarios, which are first attempted – with great hesitation – on some staging environments.

Months later, when we finally get the nerve to go live ammo and start knocking out some production environments during the day, her team handles coordination and recovery from the aftermath brilliantly. We bring beer and pizza by for her entire team and give them a standing ovation. We've crossed a major milestone, and she's glowing with pride.

I'm glad I sunk the time I did into trying to understand Emily's position; I'm also glad that we kicked back on a new manual gate. It's almost certain that this would have slowed down our release rate. Worse, it was kicking us off in the opposite direction from where we wanted the team to go; it was fear motivated, not trust motivated. And I had that bet with Tabrez to think about.

I have to hand it to the guy – when we blow our 38-day release cycle goal a few months after this and get our releases out on a weekly cadence, Tabrez takes us all out to celebrate – on his dime. Indian food, at one of Padma's favorite places – the heat of the spices was almost enough to make me call in sick the next day. I know we've still got a ways to go in improving our release turnaround time, but for now – I'm satisfied.

Behind the Story

Dashboarding and monitoring should have been far more prominent in the team's journey; in this chapter, they finally begin to pay more attention to the numbers that matter most to their business partners, which reflect global value. Why is this important? And how do feature flags help enable a more continuous flow of value without increasing risk?

We have yet to see any major DevOps transformation that didn't hit some major roadblocks, usually cultural. In this chapter, Emily's drive to instill better governance through a manual approval process is in direct conflict with the team's mandate to control and optimize their flow rate. What's the best way to handle the massive cultural shifts required for any comprehensive DevOps movement?

Metrics and Monitoring

Engineering is done with numbers. Analysis without numbers is only an opinion.

—Akin's 1st Law of Spacecraft Design

One accurate measurement is worth a thousand expert opinions.

—Grace Hopper

The lateral line is how a fish can survive in a very harsh, always-changing environment; without it, a fish is "blind" and cannot survive. In a trout or a salmon's sphere, sudden pressure change is the KPI that alerts them to potential danger or food. As James Babb wrote in *Fly Fishin' Fool*:

> *The lateral line, a kind of fish-length marshaling yard conveying vibrations from a receptive network of neuromasts to central data analysis quartered in the head, constantly monitors water for changes in pressure, telling fish not only where they are but also what's around them and what it's doing. A fish blinded by sadistic scientists with too much time on their hands can still find its prey through the lateral line. But leave the eyes alone and block off the lateral line, and the fish starves.[1]*

For fish, weightlifters, and DevOps devotees, the statement holds true; if you can't measure it, you can't improve it.

Most people would not argue with this statement; yet coming up with the right numbers to track or even having a common measurement of what success looks like is a real struggle for many organizations. In the section "By The Numbers," Ben's team is just starting to come to grips with this problem. It's in the nick of time; with hindsight, the team will come to realize that waiting so long to address transparency was their single biggest mistake.

What are some keys to keeping the lateral line feeding the information you need to survive and thrive in a hostile and complex operating environment?

Pervasive Information Radiators

Let's take the topic of pervasive information radiators as an example. We've already mentioned that Toyota made pervasive information displays a cornerstone of their Lean manufacturing process. Quality and the current build process state were constantly updated and available at a glance from any point on the factory floor.

---

[1]"Fly-Fishin' Fool: The Adventures, Misadventures, and Outright Idiocies of a Compulsive Angler," James Babb. Lyons Press; 4/1/2005. ISBN-10: 1592285937, ISBN-13: 978-1592285938.

When it comes to using displays to create a common awareness of flow, software appears to be lagging badly behind manufacturing. In most enterprises we've engaged with, monitors are either missing or only displaying part of the problem. Every team gathering area and war room should have at least one and preferably many displays.

Gathering metrics is too important to be optional or last in priority. We would never get in a car that didn't have a speedometer and gas gauge front and center. Constant real-time monitoring and dashboarding is a critical part of safe operations for any vehicle. The same is true with the services and products we deploy; none are "fire and forget" missiles. If it's running in production – it must be monitored.

It's not an overstatement to say instrumentation is one of the most valuable, impactful components of any application we build. Without it, we won't know what aspects of the app are in use – meaning our backlog will be prioritized based on best guesses. And that "thin blue line" of initial support will have no information on hand to triage and knock down common problems; second and third-tier responders will waste hours trying to reconstruct performance or operating issues because of blind spots in activity logs and a low signal-to-noise ratio.

And yet it's often the first thing that's thrown out when budgets are tight. Here's where an effective project manager or team lead earns her pay; stand your ground and don't allow short-sighted project time crunches or cost constraints to sabotage a crucial part of your architecture.

A clean dashboard showing valuable numbers is a first-class citizen of the project – the veins of your app's circulatory system. Your code reviews and design reviews should drill in on how monitoring will be set up and what alert thresholds are appropriate.

Aaron Bjork told us that the Azure DevOps product teams at Microsoft use one simple, easy to understand number as a barometer – the Bugs-To-Engineer ratio. This helps them keep the pain point they wanted to expose – mounting technical debt – front and center on their radar:

> *We do track one metric that is very telling – the number of defects a team has. We call this the bug cap. You just take the number of engineers and multiply it by 4 – so if your team has 10 engineers, your bug cap is 40. We operate under a simple rule – if your bug count is above this bug cap, then in the next sprint you need to slow down and pay down that debt. This helps us fight the tendency to let technical debt pile up and be a boat anchor you're dragging everywhere and having to fight against. With continuous delivery, you just can't let that debt creep up on you like that. We have no dedicated time to work on debt – but we do monitor the bug cap and let each team manage it as they see best.*

I check this number all the time, and if we see that number go above the limit we have a discussion and find out if there's a valid reason for that debt pileup and what the plan is to remedy. Here we don't allow any team to accrue a significant debt but we pay it off like you would a credit card – instead of making the minimum payment though we're paying off the majority of the balance, every pay period. It's often not realistic to say "Zero bugs" – some defects may just not be that urgent or shouldn't come ahead of a hot new feature work in priority. This allows us to keep technical debt to reasonable number and still focus on delivering new capabilities.

We have an engineering scorecard that's visible to everyone but we're very careful about what we put on that. Our measurements are very carefully chosen and we don't give teams 20 things to work on – that's overwhelming. With every metric that you start to measure, you're going to get a behavior – and maybe some bad ones you weren't expecting. We see a lot of companies trying to track and improve everything, which seems to be overburdening teams – no one wants to see a scorecard with 20 red buttons on it![2]

This isn't saying that the scoreboard and dashboard displays for the Azure DevOps team are simplistic. There's thumbnail charts showing pipeline velocity (time to build, deploy, test, and failed/flaky automation), live site health (time to communicate, mitigate, incident prevention items, SLA per customer), and those powerful business-facing metrics – engagement, satisfaction, and feature usage. It tells an engaging and comprehensive story, and even better – it's actually used, serving as a touchstone as their small-sized delivery teams align around that centrally set mission and purpose.

But to us the better story is what you don't see – what the Azure DevOps management team chooses NOT to watch. They don't track story point velocity. Team burndowns are nowhere to be found on any scoreboards, or the number of bugs found. They don't show team capacity, or the lines of code (uggh!) delivered, or even original vs. current estimates. If a KPI like the preceding doesn't matter to the end user, and it doesn't drive the right kind of behavior, it should be dropped – pronto!

---

[2]Interview of Aaron Bjork by Dave Harrison, see Appendix.

It's Not As Hard As You Think

One common fear we hear often is that it's somehow difficult and time-consuming to get monitoring set up. Actually, setting up monitoring is almost frighteningly easy. (Setting up the right kind of monitoring is where the pain comes in. We'll get into that later!)

As with all things, starting simple is the key: what about timing how long database queries take? Or how long some external vendor API takes to respond? Or how many logins happen throughout the day?

Like we said earlier – the single biggest mistake Ben makes in this book is waiting so long to get to monitoring. It honestly should have been first and would have saved the team some time-wasting cul-de-sacs. The most formidable enemy in any transformation on the scale that DevOps demands is inertia. And the most powerful weapon you have to wield against falling back into old habits is the careful and consistent use of numbers to tell a story.

Once you start instrumenting your app, it becomes addictive. App metrics are so useful for a variety of things, you'll wonder why you didn't get started sooner. Your business partners, who usually were completely in the dark before, will welcome more detail around issues and changes shown in your information radiators. And it's a key part of completing the feedback cycle between your development and Ops teams.

There's a variety of great tools out there; it's almost impossible to pick a bad one. Do what our friend JD Trask of Raygun recommends – take a Friday afternoon, and just get it done.

Monitoring Is for Everyone

Similar to security, if left as a late-breaking audit step monitoring can gain a rep as just another painful gate to hurdle.

Monitoring is a skill, not a job title. It's far too important to be relegated to one "monitoring expert" to handle; everyone on your team should know and be familiar with setting up instrumentation.

The successful companies we interviewed all made monitoring a first-class concern – and they made it a breeze to wire in. Engineers will always find the shortest distance between two points. Most of the winning strategies we've seen made it easier to do the right thing, providing a clear, constantly improving library with usage guidelines and an ongoing training program. Many were flexible and collaborative, allowing extendability or completely different approaches – as long as it provided a similar level of coverage.

Creating a pipeline of flowing customer feedback to your product teams is electrifying, like plugging a fan into the wall. Without it, we're left to guess, and our energies will be dissipated into nonproductive areas and dead ends. Yet, for most enterprise products, there is no reliable feedback loop in the life cycle, as Brian Blackman told us:

> We talked about flow – another key piece is getting feedback. Most companies simply don't think to implement things to see that they're getting consistent, frequent feedback from customers. In your customer facing apps, do they have a way of providing feedback – a smiley face, or a direct way to call on a new feature? I don't see orgs doing enough around the feedback loop; if they do have a feedback loop its manual, with long delays and full of waste and misinterpretation.[3]

Ryan Comingdeer makes sure that some level of logging and monitoring is built into every project at Five Talent:

> Monitoring is too important to leave to end of project, that's our finish line. So we identify what the KPI's are to begin with. Right now it revolves around three areas – performance (latency of requests), security (breach attempts), and application logs (errors returned, availability and uptime).

> ...Sometimes of course we have customers that want to go cheap on monitoring. So, quite often, we'll just go to app level errors; but that's our bare minimum. We always log, sometimes we don't monitor. We had this crop up this morning with a customer – after a year or more, we went live, but all we had was that minimal logging. Guess what, that didn't help us much when the server went down!

> Going bare-bones on monitoring is something customers typically regret, because of surprises like that. Real user monitoring, like you can get with any cloud provider, is another thing that's incredibly valuable checking for things like latency across every region.[4]

What Numbers Matter?

The WonderTek team could have chosen any one of a number of KPI's. If the issue was testing and a lack of quality around release gates, automated test coverage could have been shown. If defects and bugs continued to skyrocket, defect counts, the amount of unplanned work, or build failures could be highlighted. If development velocity was waning, velocity in function

---

[3]Interview of Brian Blackman by Dave Harrison, see Appendix.
[4]Interview of Ryan Comingdeer by Dave Harrison, see Appendix.

points could have been shown, sprint by sprint. If infrastructure is creaky and environment changes are hurting service availability, the number of unique environments in production or server/sysadmin ratios could be shown. Or – Alex's white whale – if developers are sullen and mutinous over excessive build times disrupting their work flow, daily average build times could have been monitored carefully. If the problem was failed or incomplete transactions, failed orders could be displayed. Google for its service layer focuses on what it calls the four "golden signals" – latency, traffic, errors, and saturation.[5]

The best metrics we've seen aren't generic but are very specific answers to a very unique problem the company has identified. For example, a little more drilling into the issue of configuration drift by Emily's team could have shown a large number of unique, snowflake servers that were brittle and irreplaceable, "pets." Showing the number of unique configurations in production as a trend over time could help spur visibility. Tracking the number of times a VM had to be logged onto directly in remediation vs. remote diagnosis could point the team toward the need for better configuration management and more complete log aggregation. Showing the number of sysadmins per server can expose lack of automation around standing up and servicing IAAS environments. For Ben's team, showing the amount of unplanned work each sprint will indicate if the improvements they've planned around live site support are helping reduce the burden of firefighting on feature development.[6]

The team started out with a complex dashboard and a slew of numbers to watch; over time, they've winnowed this down to one key aspect that seems to matter most to the business – MTTR, or recovery time. That doesn't mean that they're not watching other numbers, too. The displays for an Operations person may not show the exact same set of metrics that a developer's screen would. But, MTTR is emerging for WonderTek as the single number that should matter most to everyone in their delivery chain.

It seems like an excellent place to focus on; Google, for example, has made reliability and availability the centerpiece of their famous SRE program. Interestingly, considering how different Microsoft and Google are in their DNA, both companies chose to start with reliability as a touchstone. Sam Guckenheimer from Microsoft has said that for the Azure DevOps team,

---

[5]"Site Reliability Engineering: How Google Runs Production Systems," Betsy Beyer, Chris Jones, Jennifer Petoff, Niall Richard Murphy. O'Reilly Media, 4/1/2016. ISBN-10: 9781491929124, ISBN- 13: 978-1491929124.
[6]"The Visible Ops Handbook: Implementing ITIL in 4 Practical and Auditable Steps," Kevin Behr, Gene Kim, George Spafford. Information Technology Process Institute, 6/15/2005. ISBN-10: 0975568612, ISBN-13: 978-0975568613. We wish this short but powerful book was better known. Like Continuous Delivery, it's aged well – and most of its precepts still hold true. It resonates particularly well with IT managers and Operations staff.

a tight focus on reliability as a single, specific metric was the touchstone for their transformation:

> I think telemetry is the first thing. If you don't get the telemetry right, everything, all bets are off. I'm sorry. If you cannot measure it and you can't see what's actually happening in your system... we rely on that first and foremost. You've got to make sure that you're hitting that reliability number for your customer... From there, I think it depends on the product.[7]

Resilience was the right choice for the team given their current state and operating conditions, but that may not be the case months down the road. You'll find the KPIs that matter most to your enterprise might shift over time, and it's easy to be glib and understate how challenging and difficult it is to articulate and then capture that powerful business-facing metric.

We commonly see lead times ignored in value stream maps and KPI charts, for example, because it's difficult to measure and has such a high degree of variation. But two of our biggest heroes, Mary and Tom Poppendieck, have pointed out the lessons from manufacturing in identifying lead time as a key metric, going so far as to say that it identifies more about the delivery process health than any other metric. Asking, "How long would it take your org to deploy a change that involves a single line of code?" pinpoints issues with tooling and process that are hurting delivery times; asking "Can this be done on a repeatable, reliable basis?" brings to light gaps in areas like automated testing that are impacting quality.[8]

John Weers in guiding the DevOps transformation at Micron found it necessary to tune their KPIs over time as they experimented with what worked best for their enterprise. At Micron, lead time and production impact emerged as the best customer-facing indicators:

> We focus on two things – lead time (or cycle time in the industry) and production impact. We want to know the impact in terms of lost opportunity – when the fab slows down or stops because of a change or problem. That resonates very well with management, it's something everyone can understand.

---

[7]"Moving 65,000 Microsofties to DevOps on the Public Cloud," Sam Guckenheimer. Microsoft Docs, 8/3/2017. https://docs.microsoft.com/en-us/azure/devops/devops-at-microsoft/moving-65000-microsofties-devops-public-cloud.
[8]"DevOps Cafe Episode 62 - Mary and Tom Poppendieck," John Willis, Damon Edwards. DevOps Café, 8/16/2015. http://devopscafe.org/show/2015/8/16/devops-cafe-episode-62-mary-and-tom-poppendieck.html.

But I tell people to be careful about metrics. It's easy to fall in love with a metric and push it to the point of absurdity! I've don't this several times. We've dabbled in tracking defects, bug counts, code coverage, volume of unit testing, number of regression tests – and all of them have a dark side or poor behavior that is encouraged. Just for example, let's say we are tracking and displaying volume of regression tests. Suddenly, rather than creating a single test that makes sense, you start to see tests getting chopped up into dozens of tests with one step in them so the team can hit a volume metric. With bug counts – developers can classify them as misunderstood requirement rather than admitting something was an actual bug. When we went after code coverage, one developer wrote a unit test that would bring the entire module of code under test and ran that as one gigantic block to hit their numbers.

We've decided to keep it simple – we're only going to track these 2 things – cycle time and production impact – and the teams can talk individually in their retrospectives about how good or bad their quality really is. The team level is also where we can make the most impact on quality.

I've learned a lot about metrics over the years from Bob Lewis' IS Survivor columns. Chief among those lessons is to be very, very careful about the conversation you have with every metric. You should determine what success looks like, and then generate a metric that gives you a view of how your team is working. All subsequent conversations should be around 'if we're being successful' and not 'are we achieving the metric.' The worst thing that can happen is that I got what I measured.[9]

Keep It Customer Facing

It bears repeating: it'll be harder than you think to come up with the right numbers. More than likely, your initial few tries will be off target and your KPI choices will need to be tweaked significantly.

The Azure DevOps management team, for example, struggled to come up with numbers and metrics that accurately reflect customer satisfaction; see the interview with Sam Guckenheimer in the Appendix for more on this. They would tell you that the payoffs are well worth it. Most companies are still aligned around localized incentives and rewards that pit groups against each other or are otherwise disconnected from the actual success of the work in the eyes of customers. Changing incentives and management attention to global KPIs revolving around customer satisfaction, retention, and adoption elevates creates a startling change; no longer are we fighting against the current.

---

[9]Interview of John Weers by Dave Harrison, see Appendix.

Seth Vargo of Google drove the importance of customer satisfaction home in his discussion with us:

> ...It frustrates me that people focus on number of deployments a day as a success metric. 'If you're deploying 10 million times a day, you're doing DevOps!' No. That doesn't matter to your customers at all. They want value.
>
> So, does your site work? Are you delivering the features they want? Don't get caught up in the wrong metrics. Things like test code coverage, build deploy numbers, even build failures – they don't mean anything compared to customer satisfaction. Find out how to measure that – everything else is just signals, useful information but not the real definition of success.[10]

John-Daniel Trask of Raygun found that conference booths can be a great way of encouraging pride of craft and forcing empathy with end users:

> It's quite shocking how little empathy there is by most software engineers for their actual end users. You would think the stereotypical heads-down programmer would be a dinosaur, last of a dying breed, but it's still a very entrenched mindset.
>
> I sometimes joke that for most software engineers, you can measure their entire world as being the distance from the back of their head to the front of their monitor! There's a lack of awareness and even care about things like software breaking for your users, or a slow loading site. No, what we care about is – how beautiful is this code that I've written, look how cool this algorithm is that I wrote.
>
> We sometimes forget that it all comes down to human beings. If you don't think about that first and foremost, you're really starting off on the wrong leg.
>
> One of the things I like about Amazon is the mechanisms they have to put their people closer to the customer experience. We try to drive that at Raygun too. We often have to drag developers to events where we have a booth. Once they're there, the most amazing thing happens – we have a handful of customers come by and they start sharing about how amazing they think the product is. You start to see them puff out their chests a little – life is good! And the customers start sharing a few things they'd like to see – and you see the engineers start nodding their heads and thinking a little. We find those engineers come back with a completely different way

---

[10]Interview of Seth Vargo by Dave Harrison, see Appendix.

of solving problems, where they're thinking holistically about the product, about the long-term impact of the changes they're making. Unfortunately, the default behavior is still to avoid that kind of engagement, it's still out of our comfort zone.[11]

A Single View of Success

What's it worth to have that single view of success? For Alaska Air, keeping their eyes on takeoff time and shaving a few minutes per flight save them enough to buy a few more Boeing 737's for their fleet every year. For Amazon, keeping order rates front and center in displays at every level keeps their distribution centers humming and spurs creative new ideas.

The only thing worse than misusing metrics as a stick instead of a carrot, it seems, is not gathering any at all and hoping for the best. One person we interviewed told us that any data gathered has to focus on the question, "Is what I'm doing getting us closer to a desirable customer outcome?" Process improvements, project objectives all should take a back seat to that customer focus. Yet, in some organizations, he saw an almost allergic response to metrics – "we know this is the right thing to do, we're not going to measure anything – just tell stories and hope things will get better." Incredulously, he asked: "In that case, how do you know things are actually improving?"

It can't be overstated the power that a single highly visible number can have. In one previous company, we knew that our automated testing was lagging months behind new feature development, but there we were in the middle of a death march to make our promised delivery dates. There simply was no appetite for sparing any work toward improving quality as the team was falling behind.

The solution was simple: visibility. We put the automated test coverage on the top right of every retrospective in a big 2-inch square box, in bright purple. Suddenly, executives and sponsors were dropping by worriedly several times a day, concerned about the lack of test coverage and asking what could be done. Now our project could get the resources and attention needed to raise our test levels up to an acceptable state.

Metrics are a two-edged sword, however. Several that we talked to mentioned the dangerous allure of trying to track too much, or tracking the wrong thing. Try to expose everything as an improvement target, and the effort will stall out due to lack of focus.

---

[11]Interview of John-Daniel Trask by Dave Harrison, see Appendix.

Lack of a single mission defined by clear numbers is a common stumbling point:

> *The area that causes the most inertia is a lack of right measurements for practitioners and teams. People will not change their behaviors, unless the way they are being measured matches the new, desired behaviors. Furthermore, to deliver true collaboration and a sense of a single team working toward a singular set of goals across silos, these measurements of success should be the same among all practitioners. Dev, test, and Ops need to have common or at least similar metrics that their success is measured on. Everyone – and I mean everyone – has to be made responsible for deploying to production.*[12]

What's the solution to what Puppet has called the "land and expand" issue – where people are overwhelmed by a maelstrom of issues and choices and don't know where to start? We're betting that out of the seemingly endless cloud of problems facing you, there's one workstream in particular that is a recurring pain point. And with that app or service, there's likely one thing that in particular sticks out as being a pervasive, time-sucking mess. Perhaps, it's latency in your app; perhaps, it's dropped orders, security, availability, or hassles with deployments. Whatever that one single pain point is, and assuming it's low-hanging fruit, build your monitoring around that.

Michael Stahnke of Puppet advised against using generic KPIs or canned monitoring scenarios, but instead thinking in terms of what a correctly running and well performing system means and working backward from there:

> *I love monitoring and I hate how often it gets put last or gets swept under the table. If you think about it, it's just testing but it's done in production. So just like with testing – don't think plain vanilla metrics – but think about what you need to do to make sure the application is running correctly from the user's perspective. Then implement some way of watching that in your monitoring.*[13]

Alcoa and the Keystone Habit

Enterprises that struggle with dashboarding tend to clutter up their displays with nonessential or generic data. That kind of complexity dilutes the impact of information radiators and doesn't force behavioral changes; any message is lost in the noise. In contrast, Microsoft in their dashboarding has a variety of

---

[12]"The DevOps Adoption Playbook: A Guide to Adopting DevOps in a Multi-Speed IT Enterprise," Sanjeev Sharma. Wiley, 2/28/2017. ISBN-10: 9781119308744, ISBN-13: 978-1119308744.

[13]Interview of Michael Stahnke by Dave Harrison, see Appendix.

KPIs exposed, but typically one in particular dominates the screen. Most of the successful companies we've seen choose to focus on one particular KPI at a time as a primary theme.

As an example, let's take a close look at the how the aluminum manufacturer Alcoa was transformed in the late 1980s. The company was in trouble, and a new CEO, Paul O'Neill, was brought in to right the ship. He found a deep chasm between management and the union workers. To bridge the gap, he made safety the problem – the single mission for the entire company. He stood before investors and announced:

"Every year, numerous Alcoa workers are injured so badly that they miss a day of work. Our safety record is better than the general American workforce, especially considering that our employees work with metals that are 1500 degrees and machines that can rip a man's arm off. But it's not good enough. I intend to make Alcoa the safest company in America. I intend to go for zero injuries."

The Wall Street audience was expecting the usual comforting talk about revenue growth, profit, and inventory levels, and was completely stunned. When asked about inventory levels, O'Neill responded, "I'm not certain you heard me. If you want to understand how Alcoa is doing, you need to look at our workplace safety figures."

This message caused a minor stampede with the shareholders at the meeting. As weeks and months went by and O'Neill's attention didn't shift off of safety, it looked like O'Neill was completely disconnected from the realities of running an enterprise as complex and threatened as Alcoa.

Yet, the continued emphasis on safety made an impact. Over O'Neill's tenure, Alcoa dropped from 1.86 lost work days to injury per 100 workers to 0.2. By 2012, the rate had fallen to 0.125. Surprisingly, that impact extended beyond worker health. One year after O'Neill's speech, the company's profits hit a record high.

Focusing on that one critical metric, or what Charles Duhigg in *The Power of Habit* referred to as a "keystone habit," created a change that rippled through the whole culture. With Alcoa, O'Neill's focus on worker safety led to an examination of an inefficient manufacturing process – one that made for suboptimal aluminum and danger for workers.

By changing the safety habits, O'Neill improved several processes in the organization. When he retired, 13 years later, Alcoa's annual net income was five times higher than when he started. He said later:

> *I knew I had to transform Alcoa. But you can't order people to change. So I decided I was going to start by focusing on one thing. If I could start disrupting the habits around one thing, it would spread throughout the entire company.*[14]

O'Neill's single-minded focus on worker safety initially looked like a terrible decision. But his success at Alcoa shows the transformative power of clarity around one carefully chosen number.

What's Happening with Your Error Logs?

We cover this in greater detail in our interview with John-Daniel Trask of Raygun in the Appendix. But we're betting that there's a treasure trove of valuable customer data that is being ignored and gathering dust in your release cycle: the error and application event log. As John-Daniel explained to us:

> *…I think we're still way behind the times when it comes to having true empathy with our end users. It's surprising how entrenched that mindset of monitoring being an afterthought or a bolt-on can be. Sometimes we'll meet with customers and they'll say that they just aren't using any kind of monitoring, that it's not useful for them. And we show them that they're having almost 200,000 errors a day – impacting 25,000 users each day with a bad experience.*

> *It's always a much, much larger number than they were expecting – by a factor of 10 sometimes. Yet somehow, they've decided that this isn't something they should care about. A lot of these companies have great ideas that their customers love – but because the app crashes nonstop, or is flaky, it strangles them. You almost get the thinking that a lot of people would really rather not know how many problems there really are with what they're building.*

> *…This isn't rocket science, and it isn't hard. Reducing technical debt and improving speed is just a matter of listening to what your own application is telling you. By nibbling away on the stuff that impacts your customers the most, you end up with a hyper reliable system and a fantastic experience, the kind that can change the entire game. One company we worked with started*

---

[14]"The Power of Habit: Why We Do What We Do in Life and Business," Charles Duhigg. Random House, 1/1/2014. ISBN-10: 081298160X, ISBN-13: 978-0812981605

to just take the top bug or two off their list every sprint and it was dramatic – in 8 weeks, they reduced the number of impacted customers by 96%!

…Real user monitoring, APM, error and crash reporting – this stuff isn't rocket science. But think about how powerful a motivator those kinds of gains are for behavioral change in your company. Data like that is the golden ticket you need to get support from the very top levels of your company.[15]

It's easy to get overwhelmed when we're talking about wading through error logs with six-figure error counts. But we love the pragmatic approach John-Daniel explained in great detail in his interview with us, of grouping and prioritizing these problems in terms of customer impact – not the number of occurrences! – and dropping the top two or three onto the work queue for the next sprint. Talk about a game changer in terms of actionable customer feedback!

Beware of Misusing Metrics

Numbers make a great flashlight, but a terrible club. A common pitfall with KPIs involves their misuse as a "motivational" tool. The book *Accelerate* pointed out two key aspects of a KPI and how nonforward thinking orgs often misuse these:

A successful measure of performance should have two key characteristics. First, it should focus on a global outcome to ensure teams aren't pitted against each other. The classic example is rewarding developers for throughput and operations for stability: this is a key contributor to the "wall of confusion" in which development throws poor quality code over the wall to operations, and operations puts in place painful change management processes as a way to inhibit change. Second, our measure should focus on outcomes not output: it shouldn't reward people for putting in large amounts of busywork that doesn't actually help achieve organizational goals.[16]

Metrics are often misused by pathological or bureaucratic cultures as a form of control; it's clumsy and in the end counterproductive. In fulfillment of Deming's warning that "wherever there is fear, you get the wrong figures," valuable

---

[15]Interview of John-Daniel Trask by Dave Harrison, see Appendix.
[16]"Accelerate: The Science of Lean Software and DevOps: Building and Scaling High Performing Technology Organizations," Nicole Forsgren PhD, Jez Humble, Gene Kim. IT Revolution Press, 3/27/2018. ISBN-10: 1942788339, ISBN-13: 978-1942788331.

information begins being spun or filtered. Once people start being punished for missing target metrics, data is inevitably manipulated so targets are met and blame is shifted. Typically, the numbers selected by these orgs reflect the goals and values of a single functional silo and are rarely updated or changed.

Generative, forward-thinking organizations don't measure results by KPIs — we heard from several high-level executives that they use these numbers as a starting point for conversations to better understand the current state and make improvements vs. blind punishment. (One went so far as to say to us, "We love it when teams report red — that means they're being aggressive, and honest!") They're never used as a hammer — only as a frame for a conversation about current state and blockers.

So, be careful about what you choose to show on your dashboards; it may have long-lasting unintended consequences. When Dave was first experimenting with Agile as a team lead, he started carping on burndown charts. Surprise — suddenly the team's burndown charts became beautiful, flawless, 45-degree angle lies!

The Hawthorne Effect (also known as the Observer Effect) tells us that what we choose to measure has an enormous influence. Organizations that choose to focus on lines of code delivered as a measure of velocity will suddenly see those numbers jump as developers churn out lots of short lines of sloppy code to "make their numbers." If the focus is ticket elapsed time to resolution, testers will log easily fixed bugs and close them out in droves, requiring multiple tickets to be opened for the same problem.

These are both examples of "vanity metrics" — numbers that are easy to measure and gather — but solve essentially local problems and encourage fudging. If a number we're tracking changes and there is nothing we can do in response, it's a vanity metric. Before setting up any KPI, it's important to check and ask: "What will we do differently based on changes to this metric?"[17]

For example, let's take the popular metric of server response times. This is a very easy number to collect, but does it really show the actual user experience — say of a customer trying to log on from a remote location in Indonesia, on a 7-year-old phone, connecting via a 3G network? Operations teams in particular lean strongly toward OS metrics like CPU, memory, network, disk, etc. Yet, these metrics by themselves don't answer the key question — "is the app working? What's our customer experience like?" Of course, these numbers have value, especially in diagnostics, and we want to store them — but they shouldn't be key drivers out of context for any decisions, and we need to be careful about the alarms triggered from these events as they may just add noise.

---

[17]"Customer focus and making production visible with Raygun," Damian Brady. Channel9, 2/8/2018. https://channel9.msdn.com/Shows/DevOps-Lab/Customer-focus-and-making-production-visible-with-Raygun?WT.mc_id=dlvr_twitter_ch9.

Douglas Hubbard pointed out that it's key to start from the desired end result and work backward:

> *If you can define the outcome you really want, give examples of it, and identify how those consequences are observable, then you can design measurements that will measure the outcomes that matter. The problem is that, if anything, managers were simply measuring what seemed simplest to measure.*[18]

It's easy to see why complicated or ultimately meaningless displays are often the default behavior. SAAS software vendors make selecting from specific canned, generic scenarios very easy. (Which, by the way, we're fine with – as a starting point!) The alternative of drilling into what success means exactly and what numbers should define risk – let alone how to gather this in an actionable way – involves an incredible amount of work over long periods of time. Yet, despite this hassle and expense, uniformly the experts we spoke to considered useful monitoring to be not just worth it but vital – the single underlying foundation of every improvement made.

Don't Forget About the Pipeline Itself

Before we leave this topic, we should discuss the one part of your software you might be tempted to overlook – the build process itself. It's tempting to think of this as being ultimately not as high a priority to watch as our application facing KPIs. However, if your current release process can't tell you when deployments started, when they ended, who deployed it and which build was triggered – and if it can't send out alarms or fail builds where SLAs are at risk and regressions are likely – this is a threat to the jugular vein of the enterprise, and addressing this should be first and foremost. Keeping the build pipeline green and humming should be every delivery team's top priority, far more important than delivering new features.

Adrian Cockroft has mentioned that one of his favorite metrics is how many meetings and work tickets are required to perform a release. Publishing this widely exposes pain and helps to reduce the effort required to deliver work.[19]

---

[18]"How to Measure Anything: Finding the Value of Intangibles in Business," Douglas Hubbard. Wiley Publishing, 3/17/2014. ISBN-10: 9781118539279, ISBN-13: 978-1118539279.
[19]"DevOps Cafe Episode 50 - Adrian Cockcroft," John Willis, Damon Edwards. DevOps Café, 7/22/2014. http://devopscafe.org/show/2014/7/22/devops-cafe-episode-50-adrian-cockcroft.html. We love this interview in part for Adrian calling out teams that are stuck in analysis paralysis – and the absurdity of not giving teams self-service environment provisioning."First I ask… are you serious?"

Buy or Build?

Should you buy a solution or build your own? There's successful examples we could to point to from both camps; Etsy loves the flexibility its custom solutions (including StatsD) provide; Google enthusiastically promotes Borgmon or Prometheus. Other companies such as Target, AirBnb, Pinterest, and Yelp rave about the power and ease of implementation that comes with SAAS-based solutions like New Relic.

We'll bow out of this argument, but not without making this observation; as with all other strategic decisions around COTS products, beware the hidden opportunity costs. It's frighteningly common to underestimate the amount of work it takes to build a truly robust and flexible enterprise-ready monitoring system. Let's say you make the decision to build out a custom solution from scratch, which ends up requiring almost six people at $200K apiece to develop and support. Was that $1.2M annual operating cost worth it, vs. paying $150K a year for a SaaS package? And how valuable would those six people have been elsewhere on the delivery teams – creating something that could actually give your company a competitive advantage? It does seem to us that, as SaaS solutions become more powerful, robust, and adaptable, most companies should put more thought into this analysis before attempting to build their own custom monitoring solution.

Brian Blackman of Microsoft seems to agree with us:

> Another short-circuit to the learning process some companies fall into is with analytics. I'm still seeing a lot of people rolling their own analytics. That's ridiculous – they really need to be using a vendor! I don't care who you use, dammit, just use pick one. Trust with one vendor is a key aspect of Deming's teachings. You really can't put enough stress on how important it is to get feedback, more often, more accurately to the people that need it. In Lean Manufacturing this isn't as big of a deal – you can't change a car platform every month – but in software you can and should be adjusting and changing almost by the day.[20]

Like a broken record, we'll just repeat that it's not about the tool, ever. As the book *The Practice of Network Security Monitoring* brought out:

> Too many security organizations put tools before operations. They think "we need to buy a log management system" or "I will assign one analyst to antivirus duty, one to data leakage protection duty." And so on. A tool-driven team will not be effective as a mission-driven team. When the mission is

---

[20]Interview of Brian Blackman by Dave Harrison, see Appendix.

defined by running software, analysts become captive to the features and limitations of their tools. Analysts who think in terms of what they need in order to accomplish their mission will seek tools to meet those needs, and keep looking if their requirements aren't met. Sometimes they even decide to build their own tools.[21]

That being said, there is no silver bullet or single magic solution. You'll have to balance between the extremes, of one tool that pleases no one and a chaotic silverware drawer of overlapping tools. As Mike Julian put it in the classic *Practical Monitoring*:

Anything worth solving takes a bit of effort, and monitoring a complex system is certainly no exception. Relatedly, there is no such thing as the single-pane-of-glass tool that will suddenly provide you with perfect visibility into your network, servers, and applications, all with little to no tuning or investment of staff. Many monitoring software vendors sell this idea, but it's a myth. Monitoring isn't just a single, cut-and-dry problem – it's actually a huge problem set... If you are running a large infrastructure (like I suspect many of you are), then paying attention only to your servers won't get you very far: you'll need to monitor the network infrastructure and the applications too. Hoping to find a single tool that will do all of that for you is simply delusional.

My advice is to choose tools wisely and consciously, but don't be afraid of adding new tools simply because it's yet another tool. It's a good thing that your network engineers are using tools specialized for their purpose. It's a good thing that your software engineers are using APM tools to dive deep into their code. In essence, it's desirable that your teams are using tools that solve their problems, instead of being forced into tools that are a poor fit for their needs in the name of "consolidating tools." If everyone is forced to use the same tools, it's unlikely that you're going to have a great outcome, simply due to a poor fit. On the other hand, where you should be rightfully worried is when you have many tools that have an inability to work together. If your systems team can't correlate latency on the network with poor application responsiveness, you should reevaluate your solutions.[22]

---

[21]"The Practice of Network Security Monitoring: Understanding Incident Detection and Response," Richard Bejtlich. No Starch Press, 7/15/2013. ISBN-10: 1593275099, ISBN-13: 978-1593275099.
[22]"Practical Monitoring: Effective Strategies for the Real World," Mike Julian. O'Reilly Media, 11/23/2017. ISBN-10: 1491957352, ISBN-13: 978-1491957356. I think this may actually be a little better than *The Art of Monitoring* – though that's also a book we loved and found value in – just because there's less of a narrow focus on the ELK stack.

Be Thoughtful About Alerting

Practical Monitoring also pointed out that many misunderstand the purpose of monitoring, perhaps because of older tools like Nagios, and think its primary purpose is to generate alerts when things go haywire. But monitoring's purpose goes well beyond that of being an annoying squawkbox. Instead, monitoring is for asking questions. Alerts are just one possible outcome. Perhaps, immediate action is needed; maybe, a PagerDuty or SMS alert needs to be sent. Or the logs generated could be sent to an internal chatroom or custom website app. Or the information should just be stored, quietly, for when it's needed later.

But alerts in particular need to be thought about constantly and kept trimmed back so it doesn't overwhelm and desensitize:

> *Noisy alerts suck. Noisy alerts cause people to stop trusting the monitoring system, which leads people to ignoring it entirely. How many times have you looked at an alert and thought, "I've seen that alert before. It'll clear itself up in a few minutes, so I don't need to do anything"? The middle ground between high-signal monitoring and low-signal monitoring is treacherous. This is the area where you're getting lots of alerts, some actionable and some not, but it's not to the point that you don't trust the monitoring. Over time, this leads to alert fatigue.*
>
> *Alert fatigue occurs when you are so exposed to alerts that you become desensitized to them. Alerts should (and do!) cause a small adrenaline rush. You think to yourself, "Oh crap! A problem!" Having such a response 10 times a week, for months on end, results in long-term alert fatigue and staff burnout. The human response time slows down, alerts may start getting ignored, sleep is impacted – sound familiar yet? The solution to alert fatigue is simple on its face: fewer alerts. In practice, this isn't so easy. There are a number of ways to reduce the amount of alerts you're getting: Go back to the first tip: do all your alerts require someone to act? Look at a month's worth of history for your alerts. What are they? What were the actions? What was the impact of each one? Are there alerts that can simply be deleted? What about modifying the thresholds? Could you redesign the underlying check to be more accurate? What automation can you build to make the alert obsolete entirely?*[23]

The scene in the section "By the Numbers" comes from a real experience we endured, and it's a classic example of the siloed thinking that DevOps is meant to target. One Monday morning, not so very long ago, we came in to find our customers screaming that our service had been unresponsive for most of the

[23]"Practical Monitoring: Effective Strategies for the Real World," Mike Julian. O'Reilly Media, 11/23/2017. ISBN-10: 1491957352, ISBN-13: 978-1491957356.

weekend. After some diagnosis, we determined that a weekend patch of the server OS had shut down IIS, and the service hadn't restarted. "Well, yeah," said our IT partner who had run the patch and then walked away. "Didn't you get the alert?" And there, of course, sitting patiently in our inbox was that alert – buried with several hundred other alerts that looked exactly the same that had been generated that day.

This was patently a dangerous and unreliable monitoring system; normal operations were generating a flurry of ass-covering alerts, which in turn both overwhelmed and desensitized support teams and masked actual customer problems.

We're with Mike – noisy alerts suck. The alerting system we just described was a Chihuahuua – yippy and highstrung. When it comes to alerts, we want big dogs – German Shepherds, Dobermans. When a big dog barks, you know there's a real problem, and it raises an actionable alert. Kill noisy or ineffective alerts with a weekly review by the on-call team; go through the weekly alerts generated with a mission to either turn off as many alerts as possible, or improve the quality of the signals being generated.

Feature Flags, Continuous Delivery

A phased approach to continuous delivery is not only preferable, it's infinitely more manageable.

—Maurice Kherlakian

The most powerful tool we have as developers is automation.

—Scott Hanselman

Automating chaos just gives faster chaos.

—Mark Fewster

On the surface the section "Letting Our Freak Flag Fly" is discussing feature flags, but really it's about the team making it that last mile – where value is being deployed continuously.

We didn't want to cover feature flags at all when we first started this book; it became increasingly obvious that it couldn't be avoided. There's just too many companies out there that have found feature flags to be invaluable when it comes to making their releases safer and faster – a catalyst for true continuous delivery.

We covered this somewhat in Chapter 3 in discussing Continuous Integration. But as Nigel Kersten of Puppet told us, CI/CD should in most cases be our target state from a technical standpoint:

> *The end goal though is always the same. Your target, your goal is to get as close as you can to Continuous Integration / Continuous Delivery. Aiming for continuous delivery is the most productive single thing an enterprise can do, pure and simple. There's tools around this – obviously working for Puppet I have my personal bias as to what's best. But pick one, after some thought – and play with it. Start growing out your testing skills, so you can trust your release gates.[24]*

Continuous Means More Often Than You Think

Can we just say this – it's very common for thought leaders and architects to hit the lecture circuit boasting about their company's high-performing CI/CD pipelines and best-of-breed DevOps culture – while there's some very ugly things happening behind the curtains to get things to actually work.

We talked to many developers who claim vigorously – *yes, of course we do continuous delivery!* But it turns out that while they may be checking in code perhaps many times a day, that's not when releases actually happen to production. Usually, these are gated in some way for reviews or approvals, or there's some kind of lengthy handoff process – and is bundled into a larger release including hundreds of other changes as a scheduled build over a weekend, or at night. This simply is not continuous delivery.

Releases may be happening more often, and it's noticeably easier with more automation, but we have a long way to go to meet the true test of CD – the dreaded Mojito Test from Jez Humble:

> *We're in this position where people feel they ought to be doing continuous delivery, but are people actually doing it? In my experience no. I think that it's very patchy. I have a friend Mike Roberts who I used to work with when I was at ThoughtWorks, and he says "Continuous is much more often than you think." And I think that applies very much to this.*
>
> *I have a test for continuous delivery, which is, 'Could I, at any point in time, press a button, and take what's in version control and ship it, with a Mojito in my hand?' That's my continuous delivery Mojito test. A lot of people don't pass that. A lot of people are still doing releases evenings and weekends. And while they might have automated it, and while they*

---

[24]Interview of Nigel Kersten by Dave Harrison, see Appendix.

might be doing it more often than they used to, this idea that at any time in the day I can press a button and push to prod whatever's in trunk right now, I don't think there are actually that many places that could put their hands on their heart and say they're doing that.[25]

That frustration is echoed in Jez's earlier book: "We can honestly say we haven't found a build or deployment process that couldn't be automated with sufficient work and ingenuity...It's hard to argue with the value of automated releases – but it's amazing how few production systems we've encountered are fully automated."[26]

What Stops Us

If a fully automated and continuous release cycle is so desirable and wonderful, why aren't we seeing it more often? Why isn't this every DevOps implementation moving toward CD as a technical goal?

No surprise, the culprit is usually fear. There's such a high element of risk associated with changing any truly complex system as we have with software. Software releases can become a dragon with a long and destructive tail; we've all been in big-push war room releases and have scar tissue to show from the bloody aftermath. Worst of all is the icy stabbing shivers down our spine when something inevitably doesn't work as we expected: *Can we roll this back? What happens if we've hosed the entire app and we can't salvage our data? Is this going to kill our entire update and push this thing out another year? What am I going to tell my boss, what are our customers going to say?*

This fear is both understandable and sometimes a little dated. Software and the way we can deliver it is more malleable than it used to be. Fifteen years ago, when software was developed and deployed in multiyear releases as shrink-wrapped CDs, we had some real obstacles to being able to deploy software safely and at velocity. With long testing and integration cycles, every release was "push and pray," a massive effort to get to launch – and weeks or months of death marches to provide postrelease support and hotfixes. The penalty for failure was high – rolling back features involved an update or patch, which of course carried its own risks and embarrassment. Releases were either on or off – if bugs were serious enough, the team would have to kill the new feature for the entire userbase until the next gigantic launch milestone.

---

[25]"An Interview with Jez Humble on Continuous Delivery, Engineering Culture, and Making Decisions," Kimbre Lancaster. split.io, 8/16/2018. www.split.io/blog/jez-humble-interview-decisions-2018/.

[26]"Continuous Delivery: Reliable Software Releases through Build, Test, and Deployment Automation," Jez Humble, David Farley. Addison-Wesley Professional, 8/6/2010. ISBN-10: 9780321601919, ISBN-13: 978-0321601919.

Dave remembers very vividly being asked to pull out part of a new application as it was deemed not yet ready for prime time. Of course, three months in, that was a little like saying *hey, great coffee, but I really didn't want half-and-half in that. Can you take that out?* And the answer of course is – yes, but it'll take some work. Weeks of work, as it turned out.

Controlling the Blast Radius

Thankfully, since then both our tooling and the way that software is being delivered has closed the gap. We're getting better at hiding new functionality until it's ready; we use components or microservices to decouple parts of the application that change faster; and simpler but more powerful branching strategies allow us to roll out new features much more smoothly from mainline. We can control the blast radius of any new release by using deployment rings, allowing us to see how our software is actually holding up under production load by gradually releasing it outward, starting with internal or beta customers – a canary release. And failover can become a configuration toggle; we can use load balancing and deployment slots to shift some users to a newer (green) version while keeping the older (blue) version live; monitoring allows us to quickly turn off traffic to the green environment until serious problems are debugged and resolved.

Blue/Green releases, canaries and deployment rings, components, self-healing "unbreakable" release patterns – they're all terrific, amazing, and you should be experimenting with them. But it's feature flags or toggles that we're really in love with. And we're not alone. Just to pick one example, Google relies very heavily on feature flags to mitigate outage risks – and they've found it vital when it comes to performing experiments. And Flickr has found it vital in using a no-branch repository:

> *Flickr is somewhat unique in that it uses a code repository with no branches; everything is checked into head, and head is pushed to production several times a day. This works well for bug fixes that we want to go out immediately, but presents a problem when we're working on a new feature that takes several months to complete. ...Feature flags and flippers mean we don't have to do merges, and that all code (no matter how far it is from being released) is integrated as soon as it is committed. Deploys become smaller and more frequent; this leads to bugs that are easier to fix, since we can catch them earlier and the amount of changed code is minimized.*
>
> *...This style of development isn't all rainbows and sunshine. We have to restrict it to the development team because occasionally things go horribly wrong; it's easy to imagine code that's in development going awry and corrupting all your data. Also, after launching a feature, we have to go*

back in the code base and remove the old version (maintaining separate versions of all features on Flickr would be a nightmare). But overall, we find it helps us develop new features faster and with fewer bugs.[27]

Flickr's implementation of feature flags worked such wonders that John Allspaw once commented that it "increases everyone's confidence to the point of apathy, as far as fear of load-related issues are concerned. I have no idea how many code deploys were made to production on any given day in the past 5 years… because for the most part I don't care, because those changes made in production have such a low chance of causing issues."[28]

Feature flagging is not a new concept; developers have been wrapping sections of code with targeted if/else statements for decades to control releases. It was stunningly easy to implement; the problem was administration and governance as part of a life cycle. Managing these flags, handling access permissions, and controlling their lifetime were a logistical challenge. That's all changed in the past decade; a variety of great open source and SaaS software exists that allows us easy visibility and administration of flags.

Decoupling releases from feature deployments can change everything. Now, we have a pragmatic, controlled way to get to continuous deployment and delivery without causing people to think that they're on a runaway train. Rollbacks and hotfixes are less stressful, involving a ramp down or feature toggle "kill switch." Every phase of planning, writing, testing, launching, and collecting user feedback is more controllable, giving us confidence that we are in charge of the entire release cycle, and how and what our customers are able to see.

Feature flags tie in very well with all the nifty little release gimmicks we discussed earlier – deployment rings, A/B or blue/green releases, automated rollbacks, and self-healing release pipelines. We can roll out our changes to a small group of people and slowly raise the exposure level to 100% as we grow more confident that things aren't breaking. We can form a beta or preview user group for our experiments, quickly and easily; allow early access for power users; or set up a premium plan. In short, the collection of launch techniques revolving around feature flags allows us to learn and experiment.

Feature flags allow us to do more work against mainline or trunk, eliminating the problems caused by long-lived feature branches. By using blue/green releases, we can see how a new feature is being received – and if it's hitting our KPI targets

---

[27]"Flipping Out," Ross Harmes. 12/2/2009, Flickr. http://code.flickr.net/2009/12/02/flipping-out/. A very influential post (if short!) that describes Flickr's release patterns and use of feature flags.
[28]"The DevOps Handbook: How to Create World-Class Agility, Reliability, and Security in Technology Organizations," Gene Kim, Patrick Dubois, John Willis, Jez Humble. IT Revolution Press, 10/6/2016, ISBN-10: 1942788002, ISBN-13: 978-1942788003.

better than the older system. Testing in production is now a possibility, reducing our reliance on building expensive staging environments that imperfectly and expensively attempt to simulate production conditions. And it's been used successfully with that most powerful form of version control – helping IT teams make structural changes or updates to infrastructure and assisting with validation and rollbacks of configuration and environment changes.[29]

Jon Cwiak of Humana told us the following:

> *Using feature toggles changes the way we view change management. We've always viewed delivery as the release of something. Now we can say, the deployment and the release are two different activities. Just because I deploy something doesn't mean it has to be turned on. We used to view releases as a change, which means we needed to manage them as a risk. Feature toggles flips the switch on this where we say, deployments can happen early and often and releases can happen at a different cadence that we can control, safely. What a game-changer that is![30]*

Controlling the Life Cycle

We're enthusiastic about feature flags and everything they can enable in terms of positive behaviors and capabilities around releases. But, we admit they're not a panacea. If left untended or implemented without thinking about controlling their life cycle, feature flags can clutter up your codebase and become a tangled, unmanageable mess of technical debt. It doesn't eliminate the need to think about domain-driven design, components, or microservices.

When used as a kill switch, they can be vulnerable to cascading or dependency failures; it doesn't eliminate the need for planning and practicing DR; regular and realistic gameday practices may be a more effective practice in terms of reducing fear and improving MTTR. They won't provide much insulation when it comes to overcoming sloppy code or ineffective testing. They make a terrible crutch in trying to compensate for a lack of automation. Just as an example, the famous Knight Capital debacle in August 2012, which bankrupted the company after an out of control release ate up nearly $400M in bad trades, was a high-visibility disaster triggered by an engineering team that used feature flags.[31]

---

[29]"Use Cases," unattributed author(s). LaunchDarkly.com, unknown dates. https://launchdarkly.com/use-cases/?utm_source=launchdarkly_blog&utm_medium=organic.

[30]Interview of Jon Cwiak by Dave Harrison, see Appendix.

[31]"Feature Toggles are one of the worst kinds of Technical Debt," Jim Bird. SwReflections. Blogspot, 8/6/2014. http://swreflections.blogspot.com/2014/08/feature-toggles-are-one-of-worst-kinds.html. It's hard to argue with Jim's list of risks: that feature flags are meant to be short-lived and represent technical debt if left untended; if overused they can become an antipattern. Once again, there are no silver bullets.

So, treat flags or toggles like anything else, a useful tool but one that requires some thought in its application. Remember that their intended purpose is to be short-lived, transient. Many development teams do a kind of three-step dance – rolling out a release at the end of a sprint with any new functionality turned off; then the following sprint turning on the functionality; and the sprint after, removing the tags or markup created.

Much like with monitoring, you may find maintenance and administration of this to be worth investing in with a COTS or SaaS product, vs. trying to spin up a homegrown solution – especially where a slick user-friendly dashboard is needed in partnering with a business stakeholder.

Regardless of your choice of management tools or implementation style, we predict you'll find feature flags to be one very nifty little trick that can move you closer to a safer, more controlled release pattern.

Disaster Recovery and Gamedays

I confess plainly not to control events but to being controlled by them.

—Abraham Lincoln

Simple, clear purpose and principles give rise to complex and intelligent behavior. Complex rules and regulations give rise to simple and stupid behavior.

—Dee Hock

Bad managers believe in the illusion of control – there's lots of meetings, trying to break a complex system down into simple disconnected parts. Good managers on the other hand have a shared consciousness but decentralized control.

—Damon Edwards[32]

---

[32]"DevOps Cafe Episode 65 - John interviews Damon," John Willis, Damon Edwards. DevOps Café, 12/15/2015. http://devopscafe.org/show/2015/12/15/devops-cafe-episode-65-john-interviews-damon.html. A great discussion about the antipatterns around the releases and the dangerous illusion of control that many managers suffer from. In one company, they had less than 1% of CAB submittals rejected – out of 2,000 approved. Those that were rejected often had not filled out the correct submittal form! As Damon brought out, all this activity was three degrees removed from the keyboard – those making the approvals really had very little idea of what was actually going on.

We had a friend get into a very serious car accident not too long ago in New York; thankfully, she emerged from the wreckage with no life-threatening injuries. But long after the physical trauma was over, her body continued to "overclench" as her body's nervous system tightened up and sent false alarm signals in a protective instinct. This led to over a year of painful and intensive physical therapy, as she fought to relax the stressed muscles and nerves in her neck and shoulders.

In the wake of a disaster, the human biological response is often to overcorrect. If you've ever broken a bone, you know the feeling; long after the cast is off and everything is back to 100% health, we treat it gingerly, carefully, like the bone is made of balsa wood. Both organizations and people carry a strong and long-lasting memory of traumatic events, and it's hard to shake it off and get over the mental aftereffects of a catastrophic failure.

Counterfactual Arguments Around Failure

In *Backlash*, Emily is championing what appears to be a powerful argument for better change controls and release management. And yet – for WonderTek to continue on in its upward trajectory, the solutions she is fighting for represents a kind of overclenching. Thankfully, Ben and Tabrez had some strong arguments ready that focus less on instituting artificial gates and reducing failure rates, and more on increasing recovery times.

John Allspaw noted that in the wake of a major disaster, there are two counterfactual narratives that spring up:[33]

1. Blame change control. "Hey, better change management practices could have prevented this!"

2. Blame testing – "If we had better QA, we could have caught this before it hit production!"

It's hard to argue with either of these seemingly logical stances – especially early on in the recovery cycle. But as Gene Kim has noted, "in environments with low-trust, command and control cultures, the outcomes of their change control and testing countermeasures end up hurting more than they help. Builds become bigger, less frequent and more risky."[34]

---

[33]"Blameless PostMortems and a Just Culture," John Allspaw. Code as Craft / Etsy, 5/22/2012. https://codeascraft.com/2012/05/22/blameless-postmortems/. John Allspaw's seminal post on how "blameless postmortems" actually work at Etsy. Note how they openly discuss attribution bias and how they plan to counter it.

[34]"The DevOps Handbook: How to Create World-Class Agility, Reliability, and Security in Technology Organizations," Gene Kim, Patrick Dubois, John Willis, Jez Humble. IT Revolution Press, 10/6/2016, ISBN-10: 1942788002, ISBN-13: 978-1942788003.

Huh? If the goal is more safety and reliability, why are these countermeasures so ineffective?

The Vicious Cycle of MTBF-Centric Thinking

Let's say Emily wins this round, and immediately management begins imposing long and mandatory weekly change control every week to approve releases and go over defects from the previous week. We all know how hard it is to kill a committee, and their mandates and scope always seem to grow over time. Soon enough, we'll begin seeing perhaps dozens of attendees being hauled in front of a kind of inquisitorial Star Chamber. The reviewers are usually managers or director level executives, far removed from the actual process of writing and deploying code; they'll have little ability to prevent errors from happening. But they do have the power to hold up releases pending their seal of approval and punish the guilty in front of their peers. Worse, this is a hard stop; there's a physical limit to how many CAB meetings that can be held, and releases can't be sped up past this gate.

A manual approval process for any change leads to increased batch sizes and deployment lead times – which leads, inevitably, to larger, more risky deployments that are much harder to troubleshoot when things go wrong. As the feedback loop is so stretched out at this point, developers have a much more difficult time detecting when errors are being introduced; they learn to "play it safe" and minimize any changes in this new climate of blame and distrust. Under great pressure, the QA team begins to clamp down and add more manual, time-consuming exploratory, and end-to-end tests as a part of a longer gated release process.

Change windows get tighter, forcing work at a fevered pitch – and often moving releases to a "safer" window late at night, when human systems are at their lowest point biologically, when mistakes can slip by us. (Often, we've noted that one of the biggest signs of dysfunction with a release process is when they are scheduled – nighttime or weekends vs. a middle-of-the-day release speaks volumes about how the organization views safety and velocity.)

In short, it's a reactionary, 180-degree backlash to the kind of trust-based, automation-enabled flow at the heart of the DevOps movement. Delays are introduced at every point of our release process:

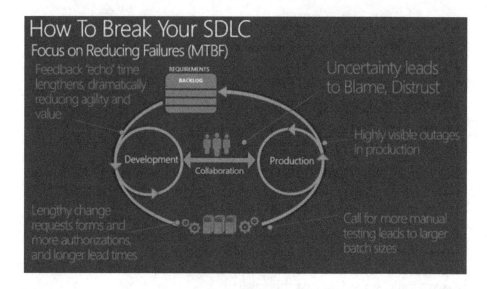

The main issue causing this vicious cycle is that the executive layer is focusing on reducing MTBF, or the mean time between failures, and is trying to bring the number of defects to zero – a practical impossibility. Management's drive for improved "transparency" and "accountability" is setting the team up for failure due to unreasonable expectations – and setting the conditions for higher-risk releases with a larger blast radius.

This is well backed up by evidence; a key finding of several studies is that high-performing orgs relied more on peer review and less on an external, gated approval of changes. The more organizations rely on change approval, the worse their IT performance in both stability (MTTR and change fail rate) and throughput (deployment lead times and frequency).[35]

Recovery and Detection Time Is a Better Choice

That's not the way that we see successful DevOps companies operate. Instead of a drive to reduce their failure counts, these organizations are learning centric and recognize that failure is inevitable – that outages will happen, despite every precaution. Instead, they try to treat each failure as an opportunity – what test was missing that could have caught this, what gap in our processes can address this next time?

---

[35]"Accelerate: The Science of Lean Software and DevOps: Building and Scaling High Performing Technology Organizations," Nicole Forsgren PhD, Jez Humble, Gene Kim. IT Revolution Press, 3/27/2018. ISBN-10: 1942788339, ISBN-13: 978-1942788331.

Especially, they focus on improving their reaction time – improving their time to recovery, MTTR (Mean Time to Recover), which often begins with better detection mechanisms and dropping the time to detect a problem (MTTD). Testing and infrastructure as code – that famous passage about wanting "cattle not pets," that is, blowing away and recreating environments at whim – form the heart of a more adaptive, flexible response strategy.

If we're truly interested in improving our MTTR and MTTD metrics, the annual State of DevOps report from DORA has over many years built up a convincing data-backed case that two factors stand out as being most important in reducing recovery time:

- **Use of version control for *all* production artifacts** – This includes everything you'd need to roll out an application – including every artifact needed for infrastructure and networking config. When an error is identified in production, this means you can quickly either redeploy the last good state or fix the problem and roll forward, reducing our time to recover.

- **Monitoring system and application health** – Logging and monitoring systems make it easy to detect failures and identify the events that contributed to them. Proactive monitoring of system health based on threshold and rate-of-change warnings enables us to preemptively detect and mitigate problems.[36]

A Change to a Virtuous Cycle

There's many areas we could focus on in describing a better, virtuous cycle in improving reliability, as follows:

---

[36]"Annual State of DevOps Report," unattributed author(s). Puppet Labs, 2016. https://puppetlabs.com/2016-devops-report.

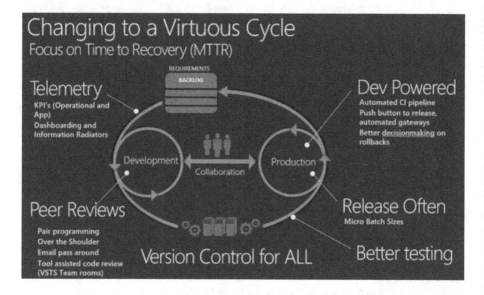

The virtuous cycle earlier is based on instilling quality as early as possible in our development cycle – just as Toyota focused less on late-inspection and audits of cars rolling off the assembly line, and more on identifying and resolving the source of defects very early on in the process. It begins with the realization that smaller is better – that we want our releases coming early and often and sized very small so we'll be able to make cleaner rollbacks if needed. So, there's a careful focus on making sure our alarm systems and telemetry is in place and is detecting problems as they should – and false positives and unnecessary alerts are being weeded out on an ongoing basis.

We have better, more effective peer reviews in place to catch problems early – and we don't allow untested code or flaky tests to make it out the door. Even our infrastructure and systems configuration are kept in version control – no one is logging onto VMs and making manual, unauditable, unrepeatable changes. And perhaps in our release strategy, we are using feature flags or canary releases to carefully gauge the impacts of our changes and roll them back with a single config change if there are problems.

It's important to make clear that we are not proposing to take away the safety that a lengthy manual review cycle appears to offer. Instead, we're replacing these controls with something more data driven. If we can demonstrate a low MTTR and a high success rate with our build pipeline, that's the best argument possible that we possess an auditable, effective control environment that accomplishes the desired goal.

It may seem like allowing pushbutton releases straight to production in this way is a dangerous amount of control to give to the program teams. But remember we still have our postmortem process – which may be blameless but are wickedly effective in tracking down and eliminating root causes. By forcing the devs to carry a portion of the production support burden, and by making their technical debt visible with public scorecards and dashboarding, there's a strong internal motivation to keep services reliable and available. And this is the best way of allowing teams to be self-policing; the people running the deployments know the code, are familiar with its operation and failure points and interdependencies, and will be in the best possible position to handle rollbacks and recovery.

Practicing for Armageddon – Gamedays

Backlash also discusses the vital role of Gamedays, which we wish we could have spent more time on. Netflix was one of our first leaders in this area, with the notion of whacking production artifacts at whim and en masse with products like Chaos Monkey and Simian Army.

At Amazon, they sometimes power off a facility with no notice and then let the systems fail naturally and allow people to follow their processes. This helps expose latent defects and new points of failure that were unexpected – such as people not knowing how to access a conference bridge call.

Google similarly practices gamedays that simulate earthquake, DCs suffering complete loss of power, and even aliens attacking cities. For more on this, there's more about Gamedays in Chapter 5 on production support and in the Appendix with our interviews with Seth Vargo, Betsy Byer, and Stephen Thorne of Google.

One consulting firm we greatly respect, Five Talents, makes gameday DR scenarios a cornerstone of every initial few releases. Their CTO, Ryan Comingdeer, told us the following:

> *Most of my clients aren't brave enough to run something like Simian Army or Chaos Monkey on live production systems! But we do gamedays, and we love them. Here's how that works:*
>
> *I don't let the team know what the problem is going to be, but one week before launch – on our sandbox environments, we do something truly evil to test our readiness. And we check how things went – did alerts get fired correctly by our monitoring tools? Was the event logged properly? How did the escalation process work, and did the right people get the information they needed fast enough to respond? Did they have the access they needed to make the changes? Were we able to use our standard release process to get a fix out to production? Did we have the right amount of*

redundancy on the team? Was the runbook comprehensive enough, and were the responders able to use our knowledgebase to track down similar problems in the past to come up with a remedy?

The whole team loves this, believe it or not. We learn so much when things go bump in the night. Maybe we find a problem with auto healing, or there's an opportunity to change the design so the environments are more loosely coupled. Maybe we need to clear up our logging, or tune our escalation process, or spread some more knowledge about our release pipeline. There's always something, and it usually takes us at least a week to fold in these lessons learned into the product before we do a hard launch. Gamedays are huge for us – so much so, we make sure it's a part of our statement of work with the customer.

For one recent product, we did three Gamedays on sandbox and we felt pretty dialed in. So, one week before go-live, we injected a regional issue on production – which forced the team to duplicate the entire environment into a completely separate region using cold backups. Our SLA was 2 hours; the whole team was able to duplicate the entire production set from Oregon to Virginia datacenters in less than 45 minutes! It was such a great team win, you should have seen the celebration.[37]

The Price of Failure

We put this section in the book as a reminder – as if we needed one – that people are not angels. Any DevOps implementation that pretends that people have inherently "good" motives or ignores the human factor in making large course corrections is likely doomed from the start.

Emily's drive for more control makes perfect logical sense from an Operations point of view; instituting better "process" and a public review and approval gate will lead directly to better stability, in her view. This is classic red-tie MBA/Six Sigma thinking, and it's in the DNA of most executives for the past 70 years: identifying the constraint or problem and instilling better process to reduce defects and variance.

Emily is just doing what she's always done – making some political hay out of a highly visible misstep by a peer, widening her power base. You could call it mean-spirited, selfish, short-sighted, or Darwinian – or simply the way successful managers get ahead in most of the organizations we've known. Angelic it ain't – but it is how things work. This is an old game, and it's an integral part of life in the corporate world – an undertow that needs to be taken into account in any push for change.

---

[37]Interview of Ryan Comingdeer by Dave Harrison, see Appendix.

Executives and managers instinctively understand the political costs of mistakes from a survival perspective. We wish that more DevOps disciples and engineers took this into account in their thinking. Be pragmatic and conservative: take care in choosing what bets are worth making in your transformation, how much risk you can afford to take. Ben's efforts to have the business be his protector and limiting impact by making any changes revolve around numbers and experimentation – vs. a contest of wills between entrenched groups – are good survival strategies. Numbers, as we've already discussed, make excellent insulation.

The arguments Emily is making appear to be both sensible and safety oriented. But the immediate effect would be a flow-killing dam that will actually increase risk and instability. Involving Ben's business partner Footwear in making the big-picture decisions around risk and a viable release strategy pay off, as Tabrez has gained a better comfort level with a faster release cycle and more reliance on automated testing and rollbacks. (Having the stakeholder involved in risk discussions and setting error budgets is a fundamental part of the growing SRE movement.)

By now, we know that CAB meetings are more than likely a bad thing. That doesn't mean you necessarily need to go to war to cast off your shackles. As Gary Gruver brought out in *Starting and Scaling DevOps in the Enterprise*, a manual approval process may not necessarily be your pain point:

> *The key is to make sure you are prioritizing improvements that will do the most to improve the flow. So, start with the bottleneck and fix it, then identify and fix the next bottleneck. This is the key to improving flow. If your test cycle is taking six weeks to run and your management approval takes a day, it does not make any sense to take on the political battle of convincing your organization that DevOps means it needs to let developers push code into production. If, on the other hand, testing takes hours, your trunk is always at production levels of quality, and your management approval takes days, then it makes sense to address the approval barriers that are slowing down the flow of code.*[38]

If you're at an organization where CAB reviews or "zero defect" meetings are institutionalized, make visible the high cost of delayed feedback and the fallout from big-delta "tsunami releases." Challenge the value of any unnecessary artifacts or gates that are building up pressure. Go through the last few hundred approvals and ask – how many were rejected, and why? Are we adding value or introducing delays? Keep complaining, loudly – show in your value stream maps the waste caused by these artificial gates, and don't rest until they're removed.

---

[38]"Start and Scaling Devops in the Enterprise," Gary Gruver. Bookbaby, 12/1/2016. ISBN-10: 1483583589, ISBN-13: 978-1483583587.

To Build a Fire

Autumn arrives, and the team is celebrating a year into their journey. They can claim some real victories. They've really stepped up their game with monitoring and gathering metrics; just in the past few months, they've investigated some cool new SaaS-based monitoring services, which has improved their visibility into their application's actual performance in the field. Better yet, they're actually caring about the right things; showing business-facing metrics like their order processing rate is helping everyone visualize the part they're playing in a very long delivery chain.

The team isn't quite there yet with continuous delivery – in fact, just cutting down their release cycle to once weekly required moving mountains – but there's some wins in that area, too. Using feature flags allows them to decouple releases from turning on functionality and brings the ability to limit the blast radius by gradually revealing features to select groups of customers or internal users. Their goal over time is to move more toward a self-healing pipeline, where serious faults can be detected and rolled back without any need for human intervention.

They've also taken a few hits. There's been more than a few highly visible critsits; the postmortems identified the need to improve in their detection time and in handling communications with their users. And the dysfunctional marriage that's formed the heart of this story – the strained, toxic relationship that's formed between Ops and the development teams – isn't healed yet. Long simmering resentments almost blew up again in a dramatic showdown between Ben and Emily over their release process.

© Dave Harrison and Knox Lively 2019
D. Harrison and K. Lively, *Achieving DevOps*,
https://doi.org/10.1007/978-1-4842-4388-6_7

Their applications are still too big to be well supported with WonderTek's smaller-sized SWAT delivery teams. And Ben's efforts to improve delivery are still very limited in scope and vulnerable without true executive buy-in. How are they going to get the air cover they need to protect their gains?

How Small Is Too Small? (Microservices)

I found myself relaxing in the wake of our blowup, which I nicknamed Hurricane Emily; the team was really bonding together. I've decided to take a step back and watch as the team followed through on the action points from the postmortem. By now, I shouldn't have been surprised, but I still found myself amazed; within a few sprints, every item was either done or well in progress. Things were not falling between the cracks anymore.

I'd like to say that my initial mania about speeding up releases was the ticket, but that was only a piece of it. Our detection times are better now that we're paying more attention to the flow of orders and our other business-facing metrics. And Emily's drive for more realistic Gamedays – including the gutsiest call I've seen yet here, knocking out live production systems to check our failover and remediation process – has paid off in spades.

It's been good for our people, who now feel much more prepared for livesite failures. Our business partners have noticed in how our detection and recovery times have improved progressively, and our rep with them is getting better and better. It's also been very good for Emily's career. I rarely see her anymore; she's been hitting the press circuit lately about her innovative ways of improving IT and Ops and even talking about writing a book.

I found myself almost humming on my way to the team standup; in terms of resiliency, we'd come so far in a little under a year!

Of course, my moment of Zen was destined to be just that. Harry's voice carries well above the cubicle walls; he is worked into a fine lather this morning. "Like I said, microservices are a fad! We're just trying to imitate Amazon here. Well, last time I checked, we aren't Amazon and I don't think we should try to be. We aren't scaled for it and not every design is a good fit for that kind of an approach. And Footwear – we're still in beta, for God's sake. Most of our features are still rolling out and we don't know which ones are going to be successful. How can you possibly pretend that we know the domain boundaries yet?"

Alex looks at me unhappily and gives me the hand signal; *I need more coffee for this.* I plop myself down in a seat and say more brightly than I feel, "So, what'd I walk into this morning?" Harry rolls his eyes and tells me in flat tones, "I don't know when we turned into a bunch of freaking magpies, but the guys here seem to be in love with the latest shiny object. They're already talking about breaking Footwear down into microservices, which I think is a huge mistake."

For once, I found myself going along with Harry's compulsive hand-wringing act at this latest feat of hype-driven development. The architecture for Footwear is less than a year old, which seemed a little early for a complete rewrite. Thankfully, Alex beat me to it. "So, let's get to our standup. Harry, I'm not sure what you ate this morning, but we have time to go over this AFTER our DSU."

For the next few minutes, everybody on the team goes through their status. I take my turn as well – I may have only a few hours a day available compared to the more heads-down people like Rajesh or Ryan, but I've learned that Agile is a participatory sport. I've come to enjoy giving a quick recap of what I've done and what I'm doing over the next 24 hours. Maybe I'm not churning out new code like I used to, but there's usually one or two items I can push through in a day that can help move blocked tasks forward to an active state.

Interestingly, Jeff is there at the standup. Jeff's an architect at WonderTek, and a very long-suffering one. He's been with us for about 4 years now; it seems like every year his face looks more and more like Sophie, my basset hound – forlorn expression, droopy jowls, and all. Despite his hangdog appearance, he's been a stalwart advocate for many of the new experiments we've been trying over the past year.

I'd found out that he had been talking to Douglas in my support for weeks ahead of my proposal with the SWAT team model, and it was his advocacy that had helped sway the argument my direction. Since the restructure, I'd see him about one day out of every two sprints. Unlike a lot of fearless-leader types that seemed to crowd that field, as an architect Jeff had gotten raves from the developers he was working with. The models and frameworks coming out of our design reviews showed a steady progression in adopting cutting-edge tech, along with a pragmatic approach that left enough free room for the developers to innovate – a nice balance. No doubt it was Jeff's presence that had sparked our little friendly discussion.

I turn to Alex and Harry after the group starts to break apart and give them a little smile. "OK, I know this team well enough by now that usually these blowups don't just happen for no reason. Harry, do we really need to talk about microservices now?"

Harry was fond of little outbursts from time to time, and I'd found myself getting used to his little conversational hand grenades. And as I expected, given a couple minutes to cool down I see him ramping down a bit from what Alex and I called his PJC act – short for Peak Julia Child, complete with hand-wringing and a high-pitched squeaking tone.

But his lips are compressed together tightly still, a white line of offended righteousness. "Ben, if we're going to make any headway with the business, we need to think about stability. That means we can't be scrapping our architecture every year and breaking things up unless there's a damn good reason. But every time I turn around, there's some awesome new game-changing framework that people are raving about. This week, it seems to be microservices. Jeff and Ryan here seem to think that it's the way we should be doing everything from this day on; I'm saying that's a disaster waiting to happen. They're not a silver bullet, and we're risking losing everything we've gained over the past year by even attempting it."

Unless I missed the mark, it wasn't just Jeff and Ryan; I could see four or five heads turned in our direction and listening intently. I kept that smile on my face and suppressed a heavy sigh; yet another fun-filled day on the WonderTek rollercoaster was about to begin. "First off, if microservices are a fad, it seems like Amazon and Google owe us an apology, don't they? And can we really just flatly say, 'that won't work here?'"

Jeff gives me his patented mournful look. "I never said we should be using microservices everywhere and anywhere. But it's past time we started using them on your team, Ben. You already have the small-scale, end to end support model in place, so Conway's Law is working in our favor. In fact, with that small of a team size, I think it's inevitable that you're going to want to fragment your service domains so they're truly supportable by the team, instead of the monolith n-tier structure that seems to be our default here. I'm suggesting that you have the Footwear team start spinning off some functionality by business domains and make them API-based in their interactions. That's all, and it's really not that revolutionary."

Thankfully, I didn't have to expose my ignorance on that point; I knew just enough about Conway's Law to be dangerous. It said that the organizations produced software that copied their organizational structure. Essentially, you always end up shipping your org chart as a product.

Alex chips in. "There's really not a logical argument out there I can think of against microservices, Ben. Right now our teams are ideally sized at about 8-12 people, but for how long? As our traffic and featuresets expand, we'll need to add on people. So we'll end up right back where we were, with massive 30-person teams and a siloed Operations team handling support. For us to make this change stick, we have to start thinking small."

Harry throws up his hands. "Guys, you're trying to do heart surgery in a pig pen! Assuming we can just change our architectural model midstream to a distributed approach— a huge risk in itself – have we thought about the bigger picture? Let's say we start out with 6 or 7 small services around domains like Customer or Purchasing. How do we handle latency and asynchronous processing? How do we handle communication across teams? What about keeping some form of consistency in the language and frameworks we're using? We're already maxed out when it comes to the impacts our design and peer reviews have on our schedule."

Jeff said, "I would think anyone here would be down with a model where it's easier for us to scale and experiment. I'm not just talking about the latest and greatest JavaScript framework – I'm talking about people. Last time I checked, we're having a hard time finding qualified people in the Portland market. Well, what would happen if we could hire outside of that very narrow spectrum of coders that we're looking for? We could experiment outside of .NET with a new language that we think might fit the task better – Go, Erlang, Java, what have you. And we could bring people up to speed so much easier if they have 100 lines of code to look through, not 100,000. That flexibility alone should be enough I would think."

Ryan said flatly – "And it means more reliability as well. Feature flags and dark launches become easier – hell, our entire release cycle becomes so much more lightweight when we're talking about less functionality in play. It is something we could play with – see if it works for us, see if our releases don't become much easier with less moving parts to break. I really think this gives us a level of nimbleness and flexibility that we just won't get any other way."

Harry's still upset. He spread his hands out on the table, palms up, in a beseeching manner. "Guys… seriously… don't do this. It's a bridge too far for us. We're just not ready. Let's leave aside all the questions and complexity around load balancing, service discovery, and monitoring that we're just sweeping under the rug. Think about the pain point right now. Provisioning environments is still a major pain point for us. If we are barely keeping our heads above water now, with a few dozen applications to support – what do you think is going to happen if we suddenly start throwing hundreds or even thousands of APIs at them? And what about when things go bump in the night? Our monitoring and alerts are just not there yet, we're still hours and sometimes days behind the game. And I'm not relishing the thought of trying to track down a problem across dozens of services with an asynchronous model; we just won't have a neat go-or-no-go transactional model to lean on anymore. I'm telling you – I'm begging you – please don't do this. We're just not there yet from a maturity perspective."

I didn't agree with Harry's thinking that microservices was only for the privileged few. But I knew enough to see that he was making some valid points. We have gone through so much change and disruption – I didn't want to overtax people with trying to take on too much at once. Harry was right, when he said months ago that we kept moving the goalposts. A team needs some amount of stability to thrive.

Still, if we waited until the conditions were perfect, we'd never begin. It wasn't like microservices were new and untested; we knew already that all the arguments Ryan and Jeff were making had weight. In the end, microservices might be the only truly sustainable model that would reinforce the end-to-end, full lifecycle support and small team size dynamics that were working so well for us. Was this the right move, at the wrong time?

Then, it comes to me, and I find myself blurting out, "Kudzu!"

Jeff and Ryan turn to me. "The vine that ate the South?", Jeff asked. I knew the metaphor would hit home – Jeff often talked very fondly about his native Georgia, where the vine is everywhere.

Kudzu had an interesting history. It was introduced to America on its hundredth birthday in 1876. The Asian plant had beautiful large green leaves and purple blooms, so it caught on quickly with gardeners. It was the Dust Bowl years in the 1930s though where kudzu really took off. The government was seeking an effective way to prevent soil erosion and recommended it as both high-protein cattle fodder and a cover plant to help control the erosion of slopes; they distributed almost 100 million seedlings and funded plantings across America, but especially in the South. It seemed like a miracle plant, a godsend to farmers, and a beautiful addition to the landscape.

It was thought that once the soil was restored, farmers could go back to planting cotton, soybeans, or corn. But it turns out that the southeastern United States was the perfect environment for kudzu to grow – and keep growing. Once established, Kudzu is able to grow incredibly quickly – as fast as 12 inches a day. Its vines take root deeply and spread in all directions, outstripping any attempt at control through burning, pesticides, or physical removal. It's also a structural parasite, growing on top of other plants and buildings to reach light. Those beautiful purple blossoms and green leaves have come to coil and slither their way across the Southern landscape, devastating the environment and costing up to half a billion a year to the US economy. In fact, there are two outbreaks of the invasive plant not too far from where we are in Hillsboro.

I nodded at Jeff and smiled. "Kudzu started out as a great idea, a wonder plant. The problem was, it was allowed to explode out of control. That's the way that microservices CAN be if there's not some form of governance. Have you read Susan Fowler's book on 'Production Ready Microservices'?" Getting a bunch of headshakes, I continue – "Well, I'm going to buy a copy, for everyone on the team to look through. Susan isn't a naysayer – she loves microservices, and got them to work very well at a little startup called Uber. But she was really careful to put some controls in place. Maybe, for this application, microservices are a good fit. But Harry is making some solid arguments here about our own readiness and how much harder it can be to track down issues that we need to address head on. And especially I want us to think about governance. It's true that splitting up apps into smaller pieces like this is a great idea – but it doesn't eliminate complexity, it just moves it upwards. If we take this on as a default or recommended model, we need to have our ducks in a row."

Ryan looks crestfallen; Jeff's mournful expression is getting deeper. Jeff says slowly, "Ben, I'm the architect, and I'm responsible for a high-quality design. You can't just unilaterally put a brake on a direction that we need to go in. That's actually my decision."

Careful stepping now; I didn't want to ruffle Jeff's feathers or disrupt our budding relationship. "All I'm saying is, we need to look before we leap. If everyone on the team reads that book – or maybe Sam Newman's – and then we get together and decide this is where we need to go, of course I'm giving it my full support. Can we give this four weeks? We assign this as something to take home or read through as homework – or on our 20% time. And in four weeks we do a half day discussion on what we've learned, and how we'd apply this."

This idea gets some nods from everyone but Harry, who is still ramping down from PJC mode. "We're just going to drift into this decision, whether or not we're ready, aren't we? It's like asking someone to go from the couch to running a marathon in two weeks. Guys, it can't be done. We're making a gigantic mistake and we'll end up looking terrible."

Alex says calmly – bless him – "Harry, you know I respect your opinions, and you've been right more often than you've been wrong. I'm glad you're acting as our conscience here. But I don't know if we can just say 'not until everything is perfect', when I think about what microservices have done to companies like Netflix, Amazon, Google – companies that were stuck in the mud and needed a way out. I honestly think that we can move towards this model without causing a lot of disruption."

Harry says bleakly, "And what if you guess wrong, Alex? How many people on our team are good at understanding how to partition an application into seams based on domain boundaries? And let's say you make a mistake in this refactoring – which you will, don't kid yourself. How many dev cycles are we going to pour down the drain trying to get our domains right, how much ground are we going to lose with the business as we're moving our little toy soldiers around?"

A few seconds pass after Harry's pronouncement of doom. We've heard by now of some wondrous benefits in helping even gigantic enterprises pivot with the adoption of microservices; we've also seen more than a few train wrecks.

I decide it's time for us to move on to the day's work and not get overwhelmed with what-ifs. "So, this is the classic 'fog of war' situation, where unknown risks and uncertainties are clouding our judgment. Let's table this for now, and take on more knowledge – I'll set up that architectural half-day talk for a month from now. I will say this – there's another parasitic plant called the strangler fig that could help us out with our legacy support. Take Mark for instance."

Everyone shudders. Poor Mark is saddled with maintaining our legacy AS400 mainframe. Mark's been with us for twenty-some years; he's paid more than anyone else on the team, including me. Every year, as I'm allocating bonuses, I make sure Mark gets the max amount allowed. This isn't out of generosity but simple self-interest; it would be a catastrophe for us to lose Mark. Most of the systems he works with are undocumented, and – of course – remain stubbornly untestable and very complex in their processes and effects. Yet hundreds of millions of dollars of our eCommerce revenue flows through the backend servers that Mark administers.

WonderTek is like many enterprises in that behind its shiny frontends lurks a 1970s era backbone, a greenscreen dinosaur that requires constant feeding and care. Mark is the sole caretaker for that dinosaur. It helps that Mark has both an admirable work ethic – I can count on him to knock down tickets quickly and effectively, and our sales teams rave about his proficiency and understanding. He's kind, competent in his field, and expert in diagnosing trouble spots in our pet AS400 labyrinth; I wish I could clone ten more people just like him.

The problem of course was that I couldn't clone Mark, or create more people like him. I couldn't find anyone with his skillset anymore in the open market, even after several involved searches across the west coast. I'd even attempted hiring a few people fresh out of college and pairing them with Mark. None lasted more than a few months; pay didn't seem to be the problem, but the work. No one wanted to have AS400 programming work on their resume. So, Mark toiled on alone, the unnoticed Atlas of the company – and the one person on the team that was truly irreplaceable.

"You guys know this is a problem that isn't going away – Mark is a human single point of failure. If he gets sick or hit by a bus, we are hosed. In THIS case – a massive legacy system that we can't change or replace – the strangler fig is a great pattern that we can apply. Any new work that comes in, we can roll it out as a proxy-called service that runs its commands as a shell against the mainframe. The idea is, over time, we'll have created a set of services. Our untamable mainframe becomes just a black box, with encapsulated inputs and outputs. The services we build out can be monitored, they'll be testable, and we can deploy them using the same RM tooling we use everywhere else.

"That means we can start supporting it with more people than just our one lone AS400 guru, which means I can start sleeping easier. And over time we can start lessening our dependence on the mainframe or even transitioning it."

Alex looked a little happier at this. "OK, so let's go back and think this over, and we'll talk about it in a month." The group started to dispel, and I headed back to my desk.

Nothing was really solved, of course. I didn't know if microservices would be the next thing for us. Maybe, that was still a few steps down the road. But I had the feeling that eventually we'd go that direction. Sooner or later, we'd get mastery over that greenscreen monster in the back room.

Air Support (One Mission)

I settle myself into a cushy conference chair and found myself grinning. Alice was onstage, working her magic. I've got to hand it to her – she knew how to command a room, and right now you could hear a pin drop.

It wasn't our first DevOps Days in-house conference, but this was the best yet. At first, we'd been worried about presenting to an empty room. But we'd made it team-centric; the only rule was *Demos only, no slides*. I felt like we'd turned the corner when one of Alice's IT people, sweaty neckbeard and all, got up on stage and talked for 5 minutes about how he'd figured out how to get an older network switch configuration into version control and deployable.

Gradually, people started bringing their own bright ideas, challenges, and triumphs to the stage; Ryan's walkthrough of Terraform for example was just 15 minutes long but had almost half an hour of questions. I congratulated Ryan right after he got off the stage. The transformation was remarkable; Ryan, usually a very shy wallflower type personality, was almost glowing with energy.

The presentations were raw, sometimes with painful silences and awkward gaps. No one was going to mistake Henry's speaking style for Winston Churchill or Steve Jobs. But ideas were kicking back and forth, and people kept coming back. Now, we have more great presentations than there is time in the agenda; there was talk about starting an annual DevOps Contest celebrating the most original and productive ideas. Douglas was typically a no-show but had given me a healthy budget to begin holding the event offsite in a big auditorium.

Alice was talking about a new initiative they were thinking about, with self-forming teams – a little idea we'd stolen from Microsoft. Not that Alice of course was admitting that. "One of the things we've noticed is that once we hire someone, we peg them. If they're an IT or a first responder, or a coder" – she looked down and smiles at me – "well, they tend to stay that way. It means that people have to move on, switch companies, to grow.

"Three months ago, we took a great big whiteboard and split it up into columns, one for each of our program teams. Then, we had each of our program team leads stand and present for five minutes on what they were doing – what their services did, what new functionality they were looking to take on over the next year. And we let people put their names on three sticky notes, numbered 1-3 for their preference – and put them on the whiteboard under the teams they were interested in.

"We treated it as an experiment, and were bracing ourselves for chaos. And we weren't always able to allow every request. But as it happened, only about 20% of the teams ended up moving, and it all balanced out nicely. The leads are reporting that the infusion of new blood has led to a nice burst of productivity.

There's no reason why we should be stuck doing the same-old, same-old – and we know from employee satisfaction surveys that our people appreciate having the opportunity to take on new things."

There was a nice little burst of applause, and Alice smiled triumphantly. "It's not just for the developers and program teams, either. As some of you know, we've been driving more livesite support to the program teams themselves, but many of our applications are still being supported by a central Operations team. We've had some great wins over the past year as we've done regular analysis of the most frequent errors and built in more automation in the form of runbooks. As a result, some of our Ops people have picked up quite a bit of coding experience, to the point where we've learned to pull from them regularly when we need more good people on the program teams."

She continued on for a few more minutes, but I was only paying half attention. It was almost time for my turn, and I'd promised my team it was going to be a little different than the rah-rah ones I'd delivered earlier.

I gave Alice a big smile and a high five as she stepped off the stage; as difficult as our partnership has sometimes been, we are definitely trending upward. Alice has her faults, but in the end we had more in common than we had differences. And nothing that we've accomplished over the past year would have been possible without her support.

I look up at the audience and found myself gulping a little. The stage lights felt bright and hot; a trickle of sweat ran down my cheek. I wished I'd had more time to practice.

"Well, I would love to stand up here and take a bow, but I don't feel like we've accomplished anything yet. It still feels like we have so much progress left to make – but looking back we've made a lot of changes that have added up over time. We're starting to play around now with Docker and containers, and our release management pipelines get stronger every day. The decisions we're making are smarter, because we have more data available to us.

"That's not what I want to talk about today though. I want to talk about where we screwed up, the mistakes we've made, because I've always felt that you learn more from errors than you do from victories.

"So let me tell you about our mistakes, and I'll start with me. As a manager, my training is to focus almost exclusively on efficiency. I'm always looking for ways we can cut costs or increase our revenue. That led me down the road to Agile – where we were producing work faster. But what we found was that work wasn't making it out the door. It was held up in QA, or waiting on environments to get built out.

"Then this magic little word called DevOps came around, and I thought – aha – here's the trick. So we hitched our cart to that horse, and waited for it to take us where we needed to go, at speed.

"And it worked… kind of. It was easy for us to get our work into source control, and build a great CI/CD pipeline so changes could flow right out the door to production. But what we ended up doing was shooting ourselves right in the foot. Looking back, it was so obvious – we weren't walking around with USB drives anymore doing x-copy deployments, but our testing level was as manual and slow as it always was. So all we were really doing was accelerating the flow of bugs into production."

I begin walking through our slow, halting steps forward in that difficult first year. Shifting left on testing – where writing unit tests became a part of everyone's daily work. Family dinner code reviews, so the group could learn from each other, and comb out issues early on before they hit prod. Dedicating 20% to paying down technical debt. Giving first responders the tools they needed to effectively triage and knock down the most common problems – and iteratively improve their knowledgebase and automated jobs. Their first forays into microservices, building small autonomous teams that could handle deployments and support end to end, and knocking down their reliance on aging legacy systems with strangler fig SOA.

I continue, after pausing, "This is starting to sound more like a victory lap, and that's – again – not what I want to talk about. Going back, I missed something. I wish I would have made it more about safety. We always talk about people, process, and tools with DevOps – but in the end, we spent a lot of time trying to buy our way out of our broken state. And we wasted a lot of time trying to fix a people problem with software. It's about safety – how safe is it for us to make changes to our applications? How safe is it for us to scale or roll out bug fixes?"

"So as time went on our scorecards – how we measure efficiency, productivity – started to get simpler and simpler. We stopped hyperventilating about our release counts, and learned to drill in on what was really important.

"There's really only one number that I feel matters, and that's our recovery time. Showing the number of releases a day is a great metric; it shows that we are accelerating more and delivering value. And availability is also a great indicator, but there are times and places where we want to bend on availability if it helps us push something the business needs out the door sooner. We realized that trying to focus entirely on driving value out the door as fast as possible in a mad rush was a dead end. We also realized that having 100% availability and uptime usually means we're paying too heavy a price in terms of innovation and velocity.

"So we kept coming back to safety. We should only release as often as we safely can, and that's indicated by our MTTR – our mean time to recover. Velocity without safety is a mirage. Everything we've tried in the past year, as I look back on it, has either improved our safety level – or it's stalled out and gone nowhere. As soon as I stopped trying to drive efficiency and velocity as a goal by itself, we found our recovery numbers getting better – and, oddly enough, our velocity and technical debt improved as well."

I talked for a few more minutes about the mythical green andon cord at Toyota, that any employee once they found a problem could pull the cord – and stop the entire production line. That got people's attention, and almost instantly there would be five or six managers looking over the problem and tracing it back to a root cause. "From Toyota, we learned that problems are solved by swarming. It's a myth that any one person, if he's a manager or CXO, can be perfectly competent in every area and always have the right answers."

"So here's where I'll tell you a little secret, and it has to do with who we look for when we hire. What we're looking for is three qualities: humility, patience, and trust. Without humility, we can't admit our mistakes and what we don't know – and we won't be able to avoid repeating our mistakes. Patience for us is not just passively shrugging your shoulders and putting up with something substandard; no, it's a confidence that where we are going is the right direction, our North Star. We knew for example that we needed to improve the quality of our releases, but how we'd get there didn't become clear until almost a year went by. Patience is understanding the limitations of imperfect, human enterprises and working steadily, relentlessly, toward our North Star.

"And trust. Before, we were all pointing guns at each other. Each unit was doing an excellent, efficient job of handling work in its queue – but we were losing overall. Until we looked at the way people were being paid and incentivized, it became very obvious where the problem was – lack of trust. We needed to change the way that work was being handled so that we were all looking at things the same way.

"I said earlier that we often expect our managers to have all the right answers. Well, my job is not to have all the right answers. My job really comes down to two things – to protect, and to hold accountable. Protection and accountability begins with making sure that we follow up on problems and that they get nailed down, not just gloss over things. So we instituted blameless postmortems, and I dedicate time every week to going over the action items and making sure that they're not slipping off our radar. In general, if they're not moved on in at least 6 weeks, that's a warning sign to me, and it kicks off a conversation with the program team.

"Usually, when we have made a mistake, it's because we did not make those standards clear enough, or there was a gap in what our expectations were. Our people are great problem solvers, once I learned to give people more autonomy and freedom to resolve their own problems, with tools of their choice."

"Another big turning point for us was when we didn't pay attention to results. Einstein said that insanity means doing the same thing over and over again and expecting different results. Well, I can tell you this – Einstein was never a fisherman in winter for Oregon steelhead!" A polite laugh, but the joke falls flat – I hurry on quickly. "Um, but we see this so often with some outfits I've worked for, where we forget and keep trying the same old failed methods. There's a book I read once called *The Five Dysfunctions of a Team*, and it brought out inattention to results as the fifth dysfunction, a sign that something's broken. So we decided to invest some effort into mapping out the flow of our work and it was shocking. I almost wanted to throw it away – no one could believe that there was all this waste as work was being handed off from group to group. But we kept that map of work up to date and visible for everyone to see.

"Alice talked a little earlier about people, and how vital it is to keep them. As time has gone on, I find myself in interviews asking less questions about C# or CLR internals, or top 50 programming questions. What we've found is that the best people we've found are problem solvers. To find these people, it's very simple – I take a design problem that our customers have brought to me, bring it in there, and ask them to map out a design. Within a few minutes, it becomes very obvious their technical ability – and more important, the approach they are taking to this request. Are they asking enough questions, demonstrating curiosity? Are they jumping right to a specific application, or are they spending the time it takes to understand what the customer is really asking for?

"We don't want a bunch of touchy-feely hippies on our teams, so of course we vet people for their technical skills. But what we've found is that the best candidates are learners. They're curious. They read, they keep up to date, they are always looking for something new to sharpen their teeth on.

"When we were kids, we asked all kinds of questions. Why is the sky blue? Why this, why that... and eventually, we ask one question too many, and someone laughs and tells us how stupid we are for asking such an obvious question. And so we learn to keep our questions to ourselves, it's too risky. No one wants to be laughed at! So we learn to stop asking questions, or to admit we don't know something – that's a weakness.

"We want it to be safe here to keep asking questions. We need to admit that we're incompetent – that we don't know enough, and need more information to make better decisions. Admitting what we don't know requires humility, and it's not comfortable. But it's the only way we've been able to keep growing and learning.

"So keep remembering those three qualities – humility, patience, and trust. And please – stay curious!"

Behind the Story

The team has already made some moves toward dividing up their workflow support into smaller sized teams; now, they are thinking about taking another next step forward with microservice architecture. What are the pros and cons of this powerful newer way of delivering applications and services? And what are the ways that Ben and his fellow managers can demonstrate more visionary leadership, and recruit the executive level help they'll need to keep moving forward?

Microservices

> *The best path to clear accountability is to empower small teams that own something end-to-end, which in this example is a service. A service does one thing and one thing well, a concept based on Robert (Uncle Bob) Martin's single responsibility principle. Whether you call it a microservice or not doesn't really matter.*

—Neil Gehani[1]

> *It's not what we don't know that hurts. It's what we know that ain't so.*

—Will Rogers

Dave remembers visiting Jamaica as a 16-year-old kid; it's a beautiful country with some of the kindest, most friendly people on earth – and don't get him started on the wonders of Red Stripe beer! But the shantytowns that Bob Marley sang about in the 1960s were very much the same in the 1980s when Dave last visited; they are still there today, little changed.

Everyone seems to agree that shantytowns are a terrible idea, but still they appear, all over the world. You'll find them in Columbia, in South Africa, in Kenya, Brazil, Haiti, and – yes – in America as well. These sprawling semipermanent camps are set up alongside rivers, under freeway overpasses and in palm tree-dotted jungles alongside the ocean.

Bringing this topic up at a conference causes immediate discomfort. Slums represent a clear failure of government policy and planning, and of our care of the mentally ill, the disadvantaged, minorities, and sometimes the just plain unlucky. Shantytowns appear though for a reason – they're expedient,

---

[1]"Want to develop great microservices? Reorganize your team," Neil Gehani. Mesosphere, unknown date. `https://techbeacon.com/want-develop-great-microservices-reorganize-your-team`. He calls a cross functional delivery team of 6–12 people a "build-and-run" team, which we kind of like.

require little or nothing by the way of architecture, capital investment, or policy investment, and require only cheap, readily available materials to setup. To maintain a shantytown requires little other than a little elbow grease to stand everything up and then maintenance – lots and lots of maintenance. It takes a shocking amount of both drudgery and creativity to keep the walls up and the water outside.

Legacy Slums in IT

The primary characteristic of a shantytown is the complete absence of planning or infrastructure. These are structures that have grown out of control, and which barely fit the basic needs of the people that depend on them.

If you're in the IT industry, likely you have spent most of your life living in a kind of shantytown. We often find ourselves inheriting a slum – sorry, let's call it a "legacy" system – that requires constant maintenance and clever improvisation. The tools and processes available to us are incredibly primitive – nothing is repeatable, especially around releases, dashboarding, and monitoring. Scary undocumented alleyways lurk everywhere; you're afraid to touch anything and risk a global collapse. Architecture and planning are nonexistent. Growth happens in fits and bunches, with little use of frameworks or extendable libraries. Workarounds, shortcuts, and tribal knowledge is the coin of the realm; the application owns us, as deadlines strike like monsoons, changes cause erosion and pollution downstream, and we struggle under a mountain of technical debt.

In short, it's livable – but only just.

What Are Microservices?

If you're stuck in this kind of an application slum, as Ben's team is in "How Small is Too Small?", there is a proven way out: microservices. We always go back to James Lewis and Martin Fowler's very nifty definition:

> *Developing a single application as a suite of small services, each running in its own process and communicating with lightweight mechanisms, often an HTTP resource API. These services are built around business capabilities and are independently deployable by fully automated development machinery. There is a bare minimum of centralized management of these services, which may be written in different programming languages and use different data storage technologies.*[2]

---

[2]"Microservices," James Lewis and Martin Fowler. MartinFowler.com, 3/25/2014. https://martinfowler.com/articles/microservices.html.

That's one very good and comprehensive definition; it won't surprise you that there are others. Adrian Cockroft for example has defined a microservices architecture as being *a service-oriented architecture composed of loosely coupled elements that have bounded contexts.* All the big pieces are there – as microservices are loosely coupled, they can be updated independently. (Meaning, no shared databases – a common culprit in creating "semi-independent" weak points.)

Bounded contexts are drawn along the business capabilities that Fowler and Lewis referred to, as first described in the classic *Domain-Driven Design* by Eric Evans.[3] A microservice with a correctly bounded context is self-contained for the purposes of software development.

Commonly, we're asked how big microservices should be. Jon Reaves at RealEstate.com.au characterizes a microservice as something that could be rewritten in 2 weeks. Sam Newman often puts this as "just small enough and no smaller... We seem to have a very good sense of what is too big, and so it could be argued that once a piece of code no longer feels too big, it's probably small enough." Many microservices we've seen are no more than 100 lines of code; these can be deployed and – even better – destroyed at a whim, when they're no longer useful.[4]

Positives and Benefits

The list of benefits for microservices goes on and on. You limit your risks, as a microservice can be designed to degrade or fail without affecting other parts of the application. They can be scaled independently as demand increases – no longer do we have to we have to tune for performance or availability as a single toggle. We can experiment and adopt new technologies without worrying about disrupting a massive amount of vital functionality. Unlike some highly touted and now somewhat faded patterns like ESB, we know of many companies that have realized great benefits in reuse, cutting down on the amount of code they have to maintain.

Since we have less functionality in scope, it's demonstrably much easier to understand and master a microservice. This means we can onboard new team members and cut down on that steep learning curve. In fact, the fabled Shangri-La of project managers everywhere – being able to drop resources

---

[3]"Domain-Driven Design: Tackling Complexity in the Heart of Software," Eric Evans. Addison-Wesley Professional, 8/30/2003. ISBN-10: 0321125215, ISBN-13: 978-0321125217. This is the gold standard and should be required reading for anyone considering microservices – or indeed just plain well-defined systems architecture.
[4]"Building Microservices: Designing Fine-Grained Systems," Sam Newman. O'Reilly Media; 2/20/2015. ISBN-10: 1491950358, ISBN-13: 978-1491950357.

onto a project to make milestone dates – was actually achieved in several cases, only through the use of microservices. Because the individual services were so bite-sized, several companies could airdrop several dozen green programmers into a late-running project, get them up to speed and contributing in a timeframe simply impossible with a big-block application.

Microservices also seem to be the best fit to eliminate one of the most little-known drags on productivity with the way people communicate and work together. Studies have shown that in large primate groups, 40% of their time is spent in grooming just to maintain group stability. In humans, this is classic water-cooler type behavior – gossip, meetings, hallway chats – you know, communication. If a group gets large enough, both in tribes of monkeys and humans, we see less effort going into work – and more on team-building and the social aspects around that work. This led to Jeff Bezos famously quipping, "no, communication is terrible!", and limiting team sizes at Amazon to 5–12 people – his famous two pizza rule, meaning no team should grow beyond the size that can be fed by two pizzas.

That sizing of 5–12 people does seem to fit what we are looking for – a very high-trust, low-conversation type size for a team. Human organizations and services are often like vines, growing endlessly without some kind of limit. Many organizations find microservices to be a nifty way of constraining growth. Once a service grows in popularity so it can no longer be serviced by a small, collocated, cross-functional team – it's time to talk about splitting the service up again along another domain-driven seam so the team size can be kept in check.

Microservices nicely complement the cultural and process effects we're looking for with DevOps. They make our deployments and rollbacks much, much easier; this may be the best way for organizations to reach that desired outcome of continuous delivery without risking too much.

One of our mistaken preconceptions was the idea that microservices were only for big-battleship outfits, the giant companies that have to operate at scale across dozens of teams. After a few conversations with Ryan Comingdeer of Five Talent Software, we had to change our tune. He finds the reusability and cleaner design aspects of microservices a powerful advantage:

> *Microservices are all the rage right now as well, and in many cases they work great. I'd say at a large scale it's almost a requirement. How else are you going to get 1,000 engineers to work together on a single monolith? The only real answer is to have your interaction points become an API.*

> *It also makes sense at smaller scales. With startups for example, you're iterating and moving so quickly – changing the payment process for example without changing the frontend is such a great win for enabling velocity.*

> ...*You can't just say 'microservices are only for Netflix and other big companies.' It's not the size of the team, but the type of the project. You can have a tiny one-developer project and implement it very successfully with microservices.*

> ...*Microservices are definitely a winner and our choice of architecture. Isolation of functionality is something we really value in our designs; we need to make sure that changes to invoicing won't have any effect on inventory management or anything else. It pays off in so many ways when it comes to scalability and reliability.*[5]

There's other advantages as well. Failure with microservices can have less dramatic of consequences with a smaller sized service; less risk favors innovation and experimentation, the kind of entrepreneurial drive-your-own-business spirit we are looking for.

The API-based communications structure of microservices complements the feature flag discussion we had earlier in this book; clusters of loosely coupled services are much easier to version and roll out new functionality without disrupting the existing customer base. Companies are starting to apply the expand and contract pattern in building out new services, where capabilities are expanded in a new version of the API that supports both the old and new methods. Once customers are transitioned, the API can be contracted, and the old methods and functionality can be removed without disrupting your customer base.

It's a practice that seems built for the cloud. Modern cloud platforms are API-friendly and are a natural fit for implementing event-driven programming and autoscale scenarios, as well as circuit breaker patterns to handle failure gracefully. Microservices in practice often use containers and orchestration to provide packaging, deployment, and isolation; for many teams, some form of Docker or Kubernetes becomes a standard part of the deployment lifecycle.

So, we love microservices. It's not just a pattern, but a practice, and in its DNA are a lot of the success factors we point out in this book: self-reinforcing discipline and positive habits, small-sized teams, a learning culture, and the use of automation and tools to reduce toil and manual work. They're awesome, amazing.

We can't say that if you use microservices you are "doing DevOps" – that would be ridiculous. But if you implement it well, they may be as close to a desired end state in terms of architecture that we can get. There's many examples we can point to where they reinforced and became an integral part of a truly sustainable delivery and feedback cycle.

---

[5]Interview of Ryan Comingdeer by Dave Harrison, see Appendix.

Drawbacks

Wait, hold on – that's not saying there's not drawbacks. Most of the positives we mentioned earlier come with some pretty powerful caveats. Resiliency doesn't come cheap, and it'll take a lot of work to get your systems to truly scale. Deployment, testing, and monitoring all become much more critical if you want to unlock the benefits mentioned. Distributed transactions cause their own unique headaches. There's a higher chance of cascading failure, too. As Sam Newman points out, it's much harder to diagnose root cause with a bird's nest of services:

> In the world of the monolithic application, we at least have a very obvious place to start our investigations. Website slow? It's the monolith. Website giving odd errors? It's the monolith. CPU at 100%? Monolith. Smell of burning? Well, you get the idea. Having a single point of failure also makes failure investigation somewhat simpler![6]

We talk more about Gamedays in the section on "Backlash" in Chapter 6. But Google's Seth Vargo was very honest with us about some of the DR measures that Google has found important in supporting a microservices architecture:

> Part of the SRE discipline is preparing for disaster, so we often do internal drills to see if our fail safes actually work. As more organizations adopt microservices and containers, the probability for failure increases. With tools like Kubernetes, auto-healing is easier… but the probability for cascading failure actually increases. We often have linchpins in these complex large systems – a single point of failure – where a single subsystems dies and brings down the entire system as a result.

> This is why testing in production and introducing chaos is so important. If you practice high availability concepts – redundancy, failover, all the theory in the world – but never test, you don't know if it's actually going to work! I often work with organizations that have very clear processes for backing up and restoring data. When I ask them if they ever run DR scenarios, I get a blank stare. 'No, we've never done that'… so, how do you know if it works?! What happens if halfway through your recovery, you realize your backup has corrupted data? Suddenly what you thought was an hour or so of work turns into days of downtime as you manually repair data. That false sense of security can be incredibly damaging to an organization.

---

[6]"Building Microservices: Designing Fine-Grained Systems," Sam Newman. O'Reilly Media; 2/20/2015. ISBN-10: 1491950358, ISBN-13: 978-1491950357.

Escalation paths are also really important. In a large distributed system, the things that breaks first might not be the thing that's actually broken. Having a tiered response model – who do I go to if I get paged, and if I realize it's a problem with another system – what's the handoff process? You can't have an incident sitting there for 45 minutes while you're trying to locate the team on point.[7]

We said earlier that since each service is smaller, it's easier to understand. But that doesn't mean the complexity around these services goes away – it just moves upward, to the interconnections between services. This can be managed of course with better tooling, automation, and process. But that won't change the fact that the architecture becomes much more complex as the services themselves get simpler.

Another potential downside that's commonly underestimated in its effects; deciding wrong on our service boundaries – which we undoubtedly will with a true greenfield app or startup company – can become a painful nightmare to refactor. (It's for this reason that many believe that a new application should start with a monolith-type architecture as best practice; domain seams often only become apparent after some time.)

See the following section on Conway's Law, but there's a reason why Ben's team waited so long to begin experimenting with this. Microservices were designed to be implemented by teams that reflect that structure: small, cross-functional, independent. You should have everyone on the team needed to design, implement, deploy, and support that microservice in production as a distinct, independent product. And the tooling you have around release management, including your deployment pipeline, configuration management and testing, just can't be a pain point. You'll be releasing early and often with this model; lack of maturity around your environmental ecology will become jarringly evident with a microservice topology.

Another hidden pitfall is the concept of "eventual consistency." With a monolith application, we can use transactions to guarantee consistency. But most microservice architectures are transactionless, which require compensating operations and a tolerance for inconsistency. This isn't a deal-breaker for many organizations; obviously, companies like Amazon have learned to value the ability to respond quickly to demand over the costs of inconsistency. But it's hard to get an idea of the current state of any system with this constellation of pieces in motion; the business has to be prepared for this and have repair or reconstruction abilities prepared in advance as a remedy.

---

[7]Interview of Seth Vargo by Dave Harrison, see Appendix.

This is why Martin Fowler pointed out, "I'm always reluctant to play the distribution card, and think too many people go distributed too quickly because they underestimate the problems." And Susan Fowler, who oversaw a very successful microservices implementation at Uber, wrote: "Ultimately you must come to terms with the fact that asserting control and management of a microservices team is more expensive than with other architectural styles."[8]

Michael Stahnke echoed this in his interview with us:

> *I will say though that it is much harder to have many things online and available versus a few things online and available. And people underestimate that complexity with distributed computing, all the time.[9]*

And Ryan Comingdeer gave us a very balanced view of some of the overhead costs he's seen:

> *…It does add quite a bit of overhead, and there's a point of diminishing returns. We still use monolith type approaches when it comes to throwaway proofs of concept, you can just crank it out.*
>
> *And it's a struggle to keep these services discrete and finite. Let's say you have a small application, how do you separate out the domain modules for your community area and say an event directory so they're truly standalone? In the end you tend to create a quasi-ORM, where your objects have a high dependency on each other; the microservices look terrific at the app or the UI layer, but there's a shared data layer. Or you end up with duplicated data, where the interpretation of 'customer' data varies so much from service to service.*
>
> *Logging is also more of a challenge – you have to put more thought into capturing and aggregating errors with your framework.[10]*

---

[8]"Production-Ready Microservices: Building Standardized Systems Across an Engineering Organization," Susan Fowler. O'Reilly, 12/1/2016. ISBN-10: 1491965975, ISBN-13: 978-1491965979. Susan points out that there's always a balance between speed and safety; the key is to start with a clear goal in mind. Her thoughts around alerts and dashboarding are very well thought out. Even better, it hits perhaps the one true weak point of microservices right on the head: the need for governance. She found it most effective to have a direct prelaunch overview with the development team going over the design on a whiteboard; within 10 minutes, it will become apparent if the solution was truly production-ready. If you have only one book to read on microservices – this is it.
[9]Interview of Michael Stahnke by Dave Harrison, see Appendix.
[10]Interview of Ryan Comingdeer by Dave Harrison, see Appendix.

We're not trying to rain on your parade here, honest. But just keep in mind that while wonderful, microservices are not a cure-all.

The Ongoing Domination of Conway's Law

You may never have heard about it, but we guarantee that you've lived it; it's an inescapable principle that seems to govern any organizational structure: The architecture of a system will be determined by the communication and org structures of a company. Or, as Melvin Conway first put it in his amazingly influential paper back in 1968, "Organizations which design systems... are constrained to produce designs that are copies of the communication structures of these organizations."[11]

Since that statement was made famous in the classic *The Mythical Man-Month*, many thought leaders have taken this principle and run with it. There's a reverse Conway's Law as well, which states that the size, membership, and location of teams will impact team choices and ultimately the team output.

As the saying goes, sooner or later, you end up shipping your org chart.

The statement that the way a company looks is mirrored by its product architecture has become a truism borne out by 40 years of observation. In fact, Microsoft's structure as a model looks remarkably like its products. Google, Amazon, the same thing. This was famously skewered in a fabulous comic in 2011 by Manu Cornet of some modern org charts:

[11]"The Mythical Man-Month: Essays on Software Engineering, Anniversary Edition," Frederick P. Brooks Jr. Addison-Wesley Professional, 8/12/1995. ISBN-10: 9780201835953, ISBN-13: 978-0201835953.

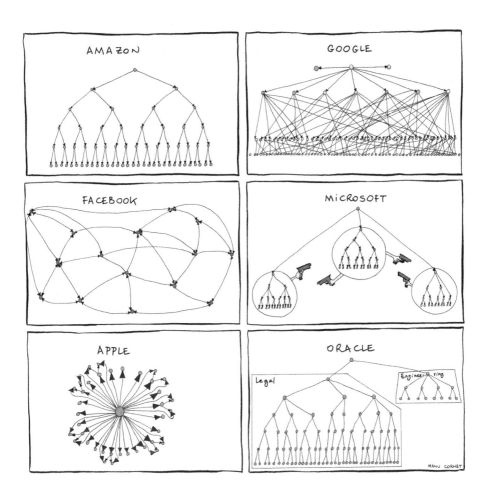

above courtesy Manu Cornet[12]

I should say that this picture represents things as they were, at least at Microsoft. Not too long after this cartoon was published, the company realized that their org structure – the "battling business units" hierarchy lampooned by Dilbert – was not a spark for innovation and healthy competition, but instead a serious constraint on innovation. So, most of the organization – especially the product engineering teams – have been completely reworked to look more like the web-native software and microservices they're producing: self-supporting, modular, very small, tightly knit, flat, and – yes – collocated.

---

[12]"The Google Doodler," Manu Cornet. Ma.nu, 2011. http://ma.nu/about/aboutme/ 2013.07.15_theartofdoing_googler_doodler.pdf.

But the fact is – to make better software, to deploy faster – Microsoft did have to change, from the ground up. It would have been incredibly foolish to split up Azure DevOps as a microservice-based application without changing the way the underlying program teams were structured; the different reporting structures and values (and eventually tools and work queues) would have inevitably caused a fallback.

Here we're bleeding a little into our earlier conversation in Chapter 5 about forming small, cross-functional teams. But Conway's Law tells us that any organization that uses microservices successfully will look very different from a typical top-down, command-and-control, functional or shared services type organization. We should see a large number of very small independent teams and a very flat hierarchy.

As we discussed earlier in the section on Value Stream Mapping, if your organization currently has a set of vertical teams supporting an application, think about the negotiation and handoff costs inherent with that model. Each team has their own priorities, so a change has to be coordinated between the team that handles the API layer, the team that controls the business logic, and lastly the dreaded DBAs that lock down the data layer.

A true cross functional team supporting a microservice doesn't suffer from that kind of a logistical drag. A single team owns the API, business logic, and data layer end to end; they aren't dependent on any other team and can release at will, on their own schedule. The API itself forms the contract between these different vertical teams; each can move at their own pace and use the API to leverage services from other teams.

As one writer put it:

> Microservices are 'Conway's Law as a feature.' They can help you scale your engineering organization, not your product. Smaller, more nimble teams are created to support the individual microservices – thus reducing communications overhead and increasing team efficiency. When properly designed, microservices only communicate with a small number of adjacent microservices – per Brooks, this reduces the drag of human communication patterns.[13]

This switch to high-trust, low-conversation type groups – SWAT teams, as Ben puts it – comes with some great benefits, but as always there's a catch: isolation. We'll need to put more effort and thought into communicating across teams to prevent siloing and sprawl and catch potential disruptions early on. Teams working with microservices don't live on an island, and there's always some

---

[13]"The Only Good Reason to Adopt Microservices," Vijay Gill. LightStep.com, 7/19/2018. https://lightstep.com/blog/the-only-good-reason-to-adopt-microservices/.

level of interaction and interdependence despite our best efforts. Without thinking about how to break down walls and keep communication up cross-group, you could end up with a worse silo problem than when you started.

Perhaps, you have the power and the existential crisis needed to rework the org chart to fit the microservices model, as Jeff Bezos of Amazon did back in 2002. If not, keep Conway's Law in mind when it comes to your application design and the promises you make around microservices. There's been many successful examples of architects harnessing the org chart to their advantage, splitting up a design to fit the current structure of a company. The final solution may not have been a true "microservice" – but it was supportable, and mirrored the way the company was wired to think and act.

Ignore this law at your peril – it's outlasted Moore's Law and many others in the computer science field, because it seems to describe an immutable fact of human nature, with the way we communicate and think and how those patterns leak into the designs we create. Creating a software model that is outrunning the capabilities or shape of the organization is tilting at windmills – over time that neatly structured set of services will drift slowly but surely back into a set of monoliths.

Amazon and Microservices

There's a 2011 post by Steve Yegge, a software engineer that worked for years at both Google and Amazon, that has since grown to near legendary status. It's one of those rare grab-your-popcorn lawn chair type moments, where someone really loses it and brings out all the dirty laundry in an epic blowup. If you're stuck with a bad case of "microservices envy" it might make a comforting read – proof that even our most beloved DevOps unicorns have saddlesores.[14]

After some stone-throwing at Google's ability to create platforms as compared to Facebook, Amazon or Microsoft, Steve turned his attention to Amazon and its charismatic, brilliant founder. After complaining about Amazon's chaotic architecture, he bashes Jeff Bezos' controlling/micromanagement nature – at one point calling him "Steve Jobs without fashion sense." Then, almost in the next sentence, he talks about how that same supposedly negative quality worked in Amazon's favor. Specifically, a directive from Bezos around 2002 kick-started a seismic change with Amazon's services and the way the entire company was structured.

---

[14]"Stevey's Google Platforms Rant," Steve Yegge. Gist.github.com, 1/11/2011. https://gist.github.com/chitchcock/1281611. A now legendary rant about platforms by a software architect that worked early on at both Google and Amazon. Steve did NOT get fired for his little "reply all" oopsie, shockingly – which tells you a lot about the positive traits of Google's culture right there.

As Steve put it, the mandate went something like the following:

1. *All teams will henceforth expose their data and functionality through service interfaces.*

2. *Teams must communicate with each other through these interfaces.*

3. *There will be no other form of interprocess communication allowed: no direct linking, no direct reads of another team's data store, no shared-memory model, no back-doors whatsoever. The only communication allowed is via service interface calls over the network.*

4. *It doesn't matter what technology they use. HTTP, Corba, Pubsub, custom protocols – doesn't matter. Bezos doesn't care.*

5. *All service interfaces, without exception, must be designed from the ground up to be externalizable. That is to say, the team must plan and design to be able to expose the interface to developers in the outside world. No exceptions.*

6. *Anyone who doesn't do this will be fired.*

This undoubtedly wasn't the exact wording of the directive, and some points have been tweaked since then – for example, I seriously doubt that Amazon hasn't tightened up on the tech and frameworks used by their teams under the covers. But nearly two decades later, it wears well – this is exactly what we want to see out of microservices.

It also echoes what we know from interviews with Werner Vogels, Amazon's VP and CTO, who made "you build it, you run it" a mantra at Amazon. Steve Yegge and Werner in several interviews pointed out one of Amazon's ongoing characteristics: platform development requires bringing developers into contact with the day to day operation of their software, and with the customer. Every team is effectively involved in product development – Amazon from almost the very beginning has considered this customer feedback as essential for improving quality of service.

Viewing accessibility as a key characteristic and an obsession over building platforms has been Amazon's strength and competitive advantage for two decades and counting. Realizing that small teams work faster and that they should own the entire lifecycle of their services led directly the realization that they needed to provide better tooling so teams could be self-sufficient. This led in turn to the creation of Amazon Web Services (AWS) – which as of April 2018 generated $1.4 billion in revenue for the company in just one quarter, almost 11% of its total revenue. That's a jaw-dropping amount of money, and it all came from thinking in terms of platforms and self-sufficient teams.

Amazon may be the most prominent example out there but they're hardly the only ones. Netflix for example has structured itself in small, independent teams – so the software that they produced would also be independent and optimized for innovation. The essence is the same – both Amazon and Netflix knew and took into account Conway's Law; both retooled their organization so it matched the system architecture they wanted with microservices.

The Strangler Fig Pattern

Let's talk about one of the best ways to apply microservices that's had phenomenal success: a design pattern called the Strangler Fig.

That memorable name was coined by – of course – the ubiquitous Martin Fowler, who on a trip to the Australian coast noticed these parasitic plants in abundance:

> One of the natural wonders of this area are the huge strangler vines. They seed in the upper branches of a fig tree and gradually work their way down the tree until they root in the soil. Over many years they grow into fantastic and beautiful shapes, meanwhile strangling and killing the tree that was their host. [15]

It's a very simple pattern in concept: first you add a proxy, that sits between the app and its user. All the proxy does is pass on all traffic, as-is, to the original legacy app. Then, next time you get a new functionality request, you add it as a new service and link it to the proxy. The proxy happily goes on servicing customers as it always has – except for any new user activity against these new pages and services, which it routes to your new shell service endpoints. Gradually, over time, more and more traffic will be routed to your spiffy new set of services, at which point you can switch off your old monolith.

In many cases, you'll find this to be the superior way to put an ailing legacy monolith out to pasture. It's much less risky than a big-shift rewrite or lift-and-shift effort. You don't stop delivering value so there's no buildup of pressure (and resulting conflict) with your business stakeholders. And you are drawing a clear line in the sand and sending a strong message to the delivery team: quality comes first, from this day on. You can gate releases for code coverage, TDD, and behavior-driven development from Day 1, and set up the automated CI/CD pipeline and immutable infrastructure of your dreams.

---

[15] "StranglerApplication," Martin Fowler. MartinFowler.com, 6/29/2004. www.martinfowler.com/bliki/StranglerApplication.html.

And we humbly suggest that it's a great jumpoff point for microservices. Implementing a microservice isn't hard, even the first time; any small team can implement a "Hello World" type API in just a few hours, leaving you days of time to nail down a good automated CI/CD pipeline for your MVP all the way through to production. Now note here, we said "good," not "perfect" – the tools, process, and the product itself are very bare-bones and imperfect for our first effort. But the point is, we're off and running.

Susan Fowler in *Production-Ready Microservices* tells the story of one company that used this pattern successfully after an initial stumble:

> ...the first attempt was explicitly focused on changing the architecture from monolith to service-enabled software system. The results were not positive. However, when they evaluated the main issues with the application – particularly the operational inefficiencies around it – they changed their approach from refactoring the existing architecture to automating the problematic deployment process. Through a small investment, they were able to take their service platform deployment downtime from 5 days to 30 minutes. Their next iteration will focus on reducing QA time through automation and a switch in methodology from white-box to black-box testing. ... Following this they will identify the domains in their monolithic application that require the greatest speed of innovation and unbundle these first. By taking an iterative approach tied to clear goals, they are able to measure success quickly and change course if needed.[16]

In our experience, you might never get to the point where you can turn off that monolith; they're amazingly stubborn, and there just might not be the ROI to completely rebuild what amounts to decades of business logic and untestable application detritus. In the end, that may not matter as much as you might think. You'll keep your coders happy – they can work with a clean slate, in a modern system that's open and safe to change, is testable, and automated. And you'll keep the wolves from your door because the flow of work and value won't suffer a big hit.

This is an approach that has proven its worth over time. Just as an example, Bob Familiar (formerly of BlueMetal) discusses using this type of an approach to shrink dependence on a massive legacy system:

> One of the benefits of microservice architecture is that you can evolve towards this approach one service at a time, identifying a business capability, implementing it as a microservice, and integrating using a

---

[16]"Production-Ready Microservices: Building Standardized Systems Across an Engineering Organization," Susan Fowler. O'Reilly, 12/1/2016. ISBN-10: 1491965975, ISBN-13: 978-1491965979.

loose coupling pattern, with the existing monolith providing a bridge to the new architecture. Over time, more and more capabilities can be migrated, shrinking the scope of the monolith until it is just a husk of its original form. The move to microservices will open the door to new user experiences and new business opportunities.[17]

And Phil Calcado of Soundcloud mentioned that the first step for their successful leap to microservices wasn't a big-bang effort, but simply a line in the sand – saying anything new would not be added to their huge monolith, affectionately called the Mothership:

Big-bang refactoring has bitten us in the past, so the team decided that the best approach to deal with the architecture changes would not be to split the Mothership immediately, but rather to not add anything new to it. All of our new features were built as microservices, and whenever a larger refactoring of a feature in the Mothership was required, we extract the code as part of this effort.[18]

In short, there's a lot to recommend in the microservices approach and the strangler fig pattern. Sam Newman likened a classic monolith to a literal block of marble, and architects as a sculptor:

We could blow the whole thing up, but that rarely ends well. It makes much more sense to just chip away at it incrementally… I would suggest finding ways to make each decision small in scope; that way, if you get it wrong, you only impact a small part of your system. Learn to embrace the concept of evolutionary architecture, where your system bends and flexes and changes over time as you learn new things. Think not of big-bang rewrites, but instead of a series of changes made to your system over time to keep it supple.[19]

Every application, no matter how bloated or fragile, likely began as a very well-structured application that solved a specific business problem very effectively. Due to lack of attention, planning, or foresight, it then grew out of control and now requires almost constant upkeep. This is a situation that was created due to the lack of infrastructure and good architecture; given that root cause,

---

[17]"Microservices, IoT, and Azure: Leveraging DevOps and Microservice Architecture to deliver SaaS Solutions," Bob Familiar. Apress, 10/20/2015. ISBN-10: 9781484212769, ISBN-13: 978-1484212769. The best book we've seen out there on IoT in the Microsoft space, by a long shot. Bob Familiar does a terrific job of explaining IoT and microservices in context.
[18]"Building Products at SoundCloud – Part I: Dealing with the Monolith," Phil Calcado. Soundcloud, 6/11/2014. https://developers.soundcloud.com/blog/building-products-at-soundcloud-part-1-dealing-with-the-monolith.
[19]"Building Microservices: Designing Fine-Grained Systems," Sam Newman. O'Reilly Media; 2/20/2015. ISBN-10: 1491950358, ISBN-13: 978-1491950357.

we can only solve it with a fresh start, where the basic framework of infrastructure and architecture is in place at the very beginning.

So, if you are stuck in a shantytown of your own, don't despair. You may find that microservices and services-oriented architecture may be an excellent solution to your unlivable legacy woes.

One Mission

I don't divide the world into the weak and the strong, or the successes and the failures... I divide the world into the learners and nonlearners.

—Benjamin Barber

To be authentic is to be imperfect.

—Simon Sinek

You can't directly change culture. But you can change behavior, and behavior becomes culture

—Lloyd Taylor, Ngmoco

Be humble, communicate clearly, and respect others. It costs nothing to be kind, but the impact is priceless.

—Addy Osmani

One of the major problems we faced in writing this book was making the team's transformations believable when Ben and his group represented only a tiny cog in the enterprise machine. How can just one part of the system change? Doesn't any DevOps transformation require a strong mandate and top-down commitment from the very highest levels?

This is the frustration mentioned by Jez Humble as a major motivation in writing Lean Enterprise:

A large number of companies have achieved measurable benefits [with DevOps], yet gains are limited. It was impossible to realize anything other than incremental improvements because only part of the organization changed – and that part still needed to work with the rest of the organization, which expected them to behave in the traditional way.[20]

---

[20]"Lean Enterprise: How High Performance Organizations Innovate at Scale," Jez Humble, Joanne Molesky, Barry O'Reilly. O'Reilly Media, 1/3/2015. ISBN-10: 1449368425, ISBN-13: 978-1449368425.

It's tempting to shrug our shoulders and sink back mentally into the cushions of our safe and familiar ways, waiting on a magical uplift dictated by our executive level. We've all been there – coming back excited to work after reading a great book or going to an amazing conference, full of possibilities and great ideas – which gets quickly squashed by the realities and grind of our day-to-day worklife. That hidden drag is front and center in the section "Air Support."

Again, it's comforting. No sacred cows get tipped over, and the unspoken rules and truces that govern our workplace remain inviolate. It's also a complete abdication of our responsibility as free agents. If we have a fixed mindset and can only see things as they are, then our current situation will mirror that – remaining permanent, intractable, wasteful, but – safe.

There's another way though. In the military, a common saying goes, "the standards you choose to walk by are the standards you accept." In other words, we can choose to accept what is as what must always be, and try to ignore that the bulk of our day is full of toil – unproductive, boring, wasteful. Or, we can choose to not walk by – to change our behavior, the standards that we set and enforce in our dealings with others.

It's not realistic for Ben and his team to change WonderTek as a whole overnight. But we do know that it's possible to create change, great change, over time with just a tiny spark.

The Three Stages of Growth

Let's say you're camping, in a beautiful spot by a rushing river. But it's been pouring for the last 3 days, and everything you brought is soaked through. Your sleeping bag, your hiking boots and socks, all your gear is sopping wet, and getting musty smelling. But you're struggling getting a fire started because all the wood is cold and wet. What to do?

You'll need three types of materials to get out of your soggy condition – tinder, kindling, and fuel wood. Tinder is stuff like dry leaves, wood shavings, grass, maybe some bark. Next comes kindling, which has a little more substance. That's stuff like twigs and branches – about pencil width. Make a little bundle of your tinder, and over that stack a little teepee with some kindling – leaving an opening for air to get in to feed the fire – with very small twigs and branches. Light that – and gradually, as the fire's warmth builds and the flames get stronger, begin adding larger branches until you get to the third stage – logs and bigger branches, or fuel wood.

One of the biggest mistakes you can make is to try to go too quickly from tinder to fuel wood. Fires have to grow over time, especially when wet. Pile on the big wood too fast and you'll end up with a smudgy pile of cold, wet wood – a failed fire.

In the past 10 years, we've seen enough examples of DevOps movements to realize that it's much like building a fire – there's usually progressive stages, and you can't skip them.

Settlers of DevOps

In a very influential 2015 article, Simon Wardley compared this three-phase growth model to what we'd see in a boardgame like "Settlers of Catan" with Pioneers, Settlers, and Town Planners. Organizations begin with just one or two very experimental and risk-friendly innovators, using very crude or custom-built tools. This spreads organically over time as different teams "borrow" (OK, steal) ideas from these innovators and make them a little more customer-facing. Tools get better, the processes get ironed out. Last comes what we call the "fuel wood" stage – where the executives, the Town Planners, really operationalize things and create a more standardized, ordered framework.

Rob Cummings delivered a brilliant presentation that elaborated on this theme, arguing that – just like with our fire – each phase is important and builds on the last. In the first phase, pioneers explore the complete unknown – there's a lot of failure, but a lot of growth and innovation as well. In the second phase, we see settlers "borrowing" from that work and making it more of a customer-facing product. Town Planners operationalize – processes and tools become faster, better, more efficient.

The important part though is learning. This is a progressive – not perfect – but steadily growing path upward. Rob argues that winning DevOps organizations often have a theft-based economy – we borrow freely from other groups, try out a little variation of our own. Gradually, over time, we get that enterprise-wide buy-in and executive leadership that we need to really get that fire cooking.

Here's the point though – it all started somewhere, with one team, or even just one person. Every fire begins with a single spark.

We're probably all aware of the infamous "Innovator's Dilemma" stage, describing how over time even the most innovative and nimble companies can become mired in bureaucracy and stagnation. This was studied at depth in the book *The Other Side of Innovation*, which explored why it is so difficult for large organizations to do disruptive things. The authors explored three examples of teams that successfully created disruptive, innovative solutions while working as part of a large enterprise. This included the creation of a small tractor line at John Deere, the first BMW electric car project, the first profitable digital news operation at the Wall Street Journal.

It turns out that these projects all began with a single spark – a small, dedicated team that was held accountable for a specific result. And they weren't chained to that Town Planner model – they didn't have to work under the burden of processes and regulations that governed the rest of the business. In other words, they started small – as pioneers.[21]

It turns out that success comes with a significant overhead cost in the form of rules, standards, and bureaucracy. We might call this the Town Planner stage. But Town Planners are not innovators, and the rules and frameworks they put in place can actually work against change, against disruption. Town Planners lean toward process, rules, and laws, and every law to some extent restricts freedom. Large enterprises need Town Planners to operationalize and be efficient at scale; successful large enterprises look for ways to keep their innovators engaged so new, risky ideas can have room to grow. Microservices and the smaller sized teams we've been discussing in this book can imbue more of that innovative spirit even in larger, successful organizations.

So, you may not have the most amazing, enlightened leadership at your back. You may have to work at proving the value of this over time. But given time and a little patience, it can be done. Especially if the enterprise is wise enough to incubate some select teams that have the freedom to innovate under Pioneer and Settler type conditions.

Finding Your Champion

The question comes up all the time: We're true believers, we love DevOps and know it can really help us. But our managers, the director level people – how do I get their buy-in?

Perhaps, you are still at the tinder/kindling stage, where ideas are still bouncing around and gaining traction. Once it starts spreading beyond those initial few pioneering teams, it's quite common for someone with those broad-level executive powers – or a business person who's frustrated by the slow rate of change – to come in as a champion and assume the leadership role we need. At that point, we don't need to "prove value" to anyone; we've demonstrated it in practice, shown that it works regardless of legacy support or application framework.

And we do need engaged leaders for that third "town planner" stage. We're making seismic changes at this point to the way code is delivered with mission critical software, cutting very close to the jugular of the enterprise. For this kind of surgery, we'll need authority and budget to back us, provide visible support, and air cover when things go awry; to preach, evangelize, and really drive culture change at scale.

---

[21] "The Other Side of Innovation: Solving the Execution Challenge," Vijay Govindarajan, Chris Trimble. Harvard Business Review, 9/2/2010. ISBN-10: 1422166961, ISBN-13: 978-1422166963.

Most of all, we'll need to change the unwritten rules and truces that have governed the organization, and that means changing the way we're incentivized. We've already discussed that the main barrier between the people writing new features and the people supporting applications in production often comes down to incentives – the developers are paid based on velocity, on delivering change – and the operations/IT teams are focused and incentivized entirely on stability, on reliability. Stability and change are at opposite ends of the spectrum – it creates immediate conflict.

A good leader can do more than just preach the values of DevOps – they can make sure that everyone is dancing to the same tune, incentivized the same way, speaking the same message. That's when we've hit the "fuel wood" stage of maturity, and the fire really builds heat.

There's lots of ways you could seek out that "hero" for the third stage and recruit their help. You could pitch the benefits of innovation, the ability to ship features quickly – and the ability to invest more effort into bets that pay off, that our customers need, that we can validate with actual usage data. You could mention safety – less manual work, meaning less waste due to rollbacks and failed deployments, and a quicker recovery time. The improvements that Abel Wang mentions in the Foreword are based on real numbers and empirical data. We are far enough along to where questions about DevOps being a fad or ephemeral to real business operations should have been settled long ago.

For leaders that care more about the health and welfare of their teams, you could use the Tillamook Cheese argument – that happy cows make better cheese. DevOps practices have been proven to greatly increase employee satisfaction. This leads to less turnover, to a more profitable company, healthier teams, and a happier workplace. This in turn leads directly to better business outcomes – and greater longevity and success at the executive level!

Good leaders will quickly catch on that this is a wave they'd like to get behind – faster delivery of value, quicker lead times, less failures, a quick recovery time. What's not to love?

You Have More Power Than You Think

The lack of executive support shouldn't stop us from exerting control over HOW our work gets done. If we're professionals – and we call ourselves "software engineers" or "operations engineers," which seems to imply that – then we have a responsibility to produce quality work to a consistent standard. Executives and leadership have the right and responsibility to tell us WHAT needs to happen, and WHY – but the HOW is completely in our ballpark.

Remember that saying at the top of this chapter from Lloyd Taylor – "You can't directly change culture. But you can change behavior, and behavior becomes culture." The idea that our behavior – and the standards we set – has a powerful ripple effect is a complete game-changer. Jannes Smit of ING Bank for example said: "Before, I never discussed culture... it was a difficult topic and I did not know how to change it in a sustainable way. But I learned that when you change the way you work, you change the routines, then you create a different culture."[22]

Think about teams in an organization as like endpoints in a services-oriented architecture. Each team has a set of capabilities or services available – a contract. The services that we provide and the applications we support come with a very specific way of invocation – maybe that's creating tickets in a queue for support, or a regular stakeholder meeting to review and schedule new work. Let's call that our address and binding, where we define how to communicate with the team and provide status of ongoing work.

The great thing about services though is the ability to change and grow. We can change that contract, the work we do, or even the way we gate and handle our work more or less independently. If we choose not to walk by a wasteful process but instead enforce a change in behavior – and make it consistent – over time, we're told, that can actually impact not just our interactions with outside teams but over time influence the entire culture.

This is why our engineering instinct to buy better tools or perfect processes often misses the point. Michael Stahnke of Puppet stressed in his conversation with us how people work together and collaborate remains the essential sticking point:

> *Today DevOps is still talked about like it's a software delivery style. I don't see it that way – I see it as defining the way people work together. You can do DevOps with a mainframe and COBOL and JCL, I don't need CI/CD for that.*

> *But defining how people should interact and how they optimize their work and collaborate, to me that's the real potential offered with DevOps. It's not tech. Tech is cool, glossy, beautiful, but what's way more important is showing leaks in the process. What handoffs are there? Why are they there, and have you tried getting rid of them? How do you handle security audits and change control boards, and what cost do they have with your workflow? To me that's a much more interesting problem than boasting about using Chef, Puppet, blah blah.*

---

[22]"The DevOps Handbook: How to Create World-Class Agility, Reliability, and Security in Technology Organizations," Gene Kim, Patrick Dubois, John Willis, Jez Humble. IT Revolution Press, 10/6/2016, ISBN-10: 1942788002, ISBN-13: 978-1942788003.

I'll say it again – tech isn't all that important for how DevOps works. It's an enabler and change agent – a powerful engine – but the key part really is optimizing how people work together and collaborate.[23]

Remember, behavior becomes culture. Waste lurks unnoticed in every dark corner, and it's likely that your management layer has no idea of how much time and money is being dribbled away in handling manual, repetitive work. Google calls this "toil," and reducing it has become the cornerstone of the SRE movement. Keep that waste visible, complain loudly and often about the cost of toil. There's no need to be unpleasant or pushy about it – waste is everyone's enemy, and it's something that every executive should innately understand. By making it visible as a quantifiable drag on your team's work, you're helping the bottom line of the enterprise.

Beyond exposing waste in the value stream, change comes much easier if we avoid the friction that comes with politics. That means that we make solving a problem, one specific problem, as the sole focus. It's not about dev over ops, or one team's best way of doing things winning out. Making one specific number the problem, and not a team or group, helps avoid the conflicts that come with ego and turf wars. For example, see the section about the transformation Alcoa made in the late 1980s, all around worker safety and a single number – injury rates.

John Weers told us that this same principle guided their transformation efforts at Micron: "We did one thing to improve quality so we'd have a better business outcome, then another, then another. We learned and talked and then picked something else to go after. That first try though should be about where things aren't going well, and not just DevOps for DevOps sake. Pick something that can deliver a real change for your organization."

The standards you walk by are the standards you accept. Even if you're not a big wheel, you have the responsibility as a professional to expose waste like handoffs, rework, and manual toil. Pick a problem that is ruining your day and a lot of others, and keep hammering on the problem until it's gone.

Humility-Based Mission Command

One of the most shocking things we discovered in the course of writing this book was that our perceptions of the military and how orders are actually handled in practice was completely backward. Anne Steiner told us for example that the lowest private often has more ability to question directions and ask about intent and mission more than the average developer or IT professional does. Brian Blackman at length went into his experiences and

---

[23]Interview of Michael Stahnke by Dave Harrison, see Appendix.

how – instead of being asked to "follow orders" like robots, which gets good people killed – the military asks and expects its people to interpret orders based on the realities of complex situations, within the framework of the mission and a clearly explained purpose.

That kind of leadership still remains truly rare in most organizations we've worked with:

> *Executives like to tell people what to do and to get it done, rather than to paint a picture of where you want to go and let teams work out how they're going to get there. That's still very, very rare. It's not that the tools don't exist. It's just that they're tough to implement.*[24]

It's common in executive-facing books and web sites to see long lists of qualities and character traits that a "transformational leader" must have. This is all well and good, but it doesn't jive with what we see in the real world. Good leaders seem to have a spectrum of qualities – good luck finding a common set of personality traits between visionary leaders like Steve Jobs, Jeff Bezos, Jack Welch, Satya Nadella, and Mark Zuckerberg!

It's enough to observe that leadership comes down to actions and behaviors, not personality traits or qualities that are often inborne. Good leaders, like good parents, really do two things: protect their people and hold them accountable. This means giving clear direction about mission and operating values, and then giving teams the autonomy – freedom and responsibility – to accomplish this mission within the guidelines you've established. Those powerful third-stage leaders we are trying to recruit should be managers, not bosses, and know how to build resiliency through trust.

Ryan Comingdeer of Five Talent told us that humility at the top is often sets the ceiling on what can be accomplished in changing the way an organization works:

> *Usually our chances of winning come down to one thing – a humble leader. If the person at the top can swallow their pride, knows how to delegate, and recognize that it will take the entire team to be engaged and solve the problem – then a DevOps culture change is possible. But if the leader has a lot of pride, usually there's not much progress that can be made.*[25]

---

[24]"An Interview with Jez Humble on Continuous Delivery, Engineering Culture, and Making Decisions," Kimbre Lancaster. split.io, 8/16/2018. www.split.io/blog/jez-humble-interview-decisions-2018/.
[25]Interview of Ryan Comingdeer by Dave Harrison, see Appendix.

Patience and "To Build a Fire"

If buy-in seems slow, and our leaders seem to be taking a wait-and-see approach, remember the qualities of patience and humility that Ben talked about in his presentation.

History is rife with examples where impending disaster was masked by spin and skewed or omitted data, from the Challenger shuttle disaster to the quagmire of the Vietnam war. In a famous 1969 study of a telecommunications company, the researchers found that communication in most organizations worked much like water:

> Downward communications are usually better than anyone realizes and frequently more accurate than those at higher levels want them to be. Conversely, upward communications have to be pumped and piped, with a minimum of filters, in order to be effective. The reason for this difference is a phenomenon of human perception whereby persons in a subordinate position must, for survival or success, develop a keen understanding of the true motives, character, and personality of those in positions of power over them.

> Applying the theory of up-and-down communications to a business organization, we determine that subordinates "read" their bosses better than is usually realized and bosses "read" their subordinates less well than they think. Yet most management methods run counter to this theory; for example, formal job appraisals are always the boss's appraisal of the subordinate. Further, we have all noted that when bosses complain about communications in their organizations, they invariably mean that their subordinates have not heard them clearly and effectively. Most formal company communications programs and media are aimed from the top down. Few formal programs are designed so that subordinates can talk and bosses listen.[26]

Information is like water – it flows very easily downhill, but only can be pumped up with great effort. Most of the managers you and I know are suffering from a kind of information poverty – they are bombarded with hundreds of trivial tasks mandated by their direct reports, all urgent, and rarely have the attention span or availability to understand what the daily life of their team is like. It may require patience and repeated discussions to drive home the value of working toward better resiliency instead of efficiency.

---

[26]"Up and Down the Communications Ladder," Bruce Harriman. Harvard Business Review, 9/1/1974. https://hbr.org/1974/09/up-and-down-the-communications-ladder. The original HBR study from 1969. We'll call out one key point – that the feedback program must not be an endcap, but product visible results.

Here, I'm reminded of the classic story "To Build a Fire" by Jack London. A man falls into a frozen-over river; desperate, afraid of death, he scrambles to build a fire. But he doesn't notice the overhanging tree branch directly over him, which – just as the fire just starts to gather strength and heat up – drops its load of snow on the fire, snuffing it out. Like with most disasters, that fatal mistake was really just the last in a chain of mistakes made due to overconfidence. The man had chosen to travel alone in unknown country, against the advice of a more experienced older man. In the end, he freezes to death, the victim of his own arrogance.

Sometimes, by pushing ahead, we put ourselves into a dangerous situation much like in "To Build a Fire." We've all seen the horror stories; someone tries to make big changes, highly visible ones – and enemies come out of the woodwork to pounce once the inevitable mistake is made. Damon Edwards calls these the "corporate antibodies" of culture – it's a riff on the "snow load" that can sometimes put out even the most promising start. Enterprises, especially well-established ones with decades of history, are like supertankers – they can only accept so much change, and the turning radius must be gradual. Gaining that director-level "air support" and finding a way of sustaining that vulnerable fire and protecting it becomes much harder in an enterprise with a ton of legacy code and a set, established way of doing things.

We're not saying this to be discouraging, and we're not saying it's an effort that won't be successful. Just be aware of overhanging branches, of the culture and change capacity of your organization, and remember humility. This means being reasonable in what we expect of others. One of our programming mentors once said, "be externally accepting, and internally rigorous." That's a recipe for much less frustration – a steady demonstration of the right behavior, which over time is much more convincing than any waving of the flag.

As Rob England told us:

> In organizations, if you're too much of an irritant, there's a kind of organizational immune system – all these white cells come out of the woodwork and shut you down, smother you, even eject you. So one of my first learning lessons was to slow down the pace to what the org can handle.[27]

Trust-Based Leadership

Good leaders protect in part by guarding their peoples' time as they do their own, and watching overhead.

---

[27]Interview with Rob England by Dave Harrison, see Appendix.

Eliminating toil became a kickstarter for a vast change with the Microsoft Windows development team back in the late 2000s. A survey was done of over 4700 engineers in the Windows development team, separating out overhead from actual engineering work. Shockingly, the study found that almost half – 40.5% – of an average developer's day was spent keeping internal tracking systems up to date, not coding! Across 25K developers in the WDG group, this represented an astounding amount of wasted time. This sparked the start of a massive overhaul effort led by a "Jedi Council," where the Windows Development Group completely reworked and eliminated as much of this overhead as possible. The company continues to survey their engineer's happiness level and use that feedback to adjust the pace and direction of its DevOps experimentation.

Sam Guckenheimer told us that the principle of servant leadership was part of the DNA in the transformation on the Azure DevOps team at Microsoft:

> We knew that would be our most important and critical win – making sure the delivery teams were onboard and happy with what was going on. We measured this as one of our first KPI's. We would do regular surveys of engineering satisfaction and go into depth about their jobs, how tooling was supporting their jobs, the process was supporting their jobs – and what we saw was a steady rise in satisfaction.

> Just for example on this, one of the things we measured was alerting frequency – are we getting to the right person the first time? That's something we are always watching – if you're waking people up at 2 in the morning, it had better be the right person. We needed to make sure that we are paying attention to the things that matter to people's lives and their satisfaction with their jobs.

> When you're genuine, you get a genuine response. This all helps build that high-trust culture that Gene Kim and others have emphasized as key.

> The concept of servant leadership has been a big part of our change; good managers care about their team and look for ways to make their jobs easier. That's the Andon cord philosophy – anyone on the floor can pull that cord, stop the line if needed – and the manager comes over, the root cause is identified and rolled into the process so future incidents don't happen. So in our case – we don't close out livesite incidents for example until the fix is identified and in the backlog so it won't happen again.[28]

Microsoft isn't the only company that chose to build trust by demonstrating care for how their employees' time is being respected. Google has made eliminating toil an essential component of their SRE movement, of which we

---

[28]Interview of Sam Guckenheimer by Dave Harrison, see Appendix.

wrote about at length in Chapter 2. Management constantly tracks the amount of time being sunk into repetitive, non–value added tasks and works actively to automate these pain points away and cap the amount of time engineers are allowed to spend on this type of nonrewarding work.[29]

As we brought out earlier with John Deere and other success stories with large conservative companies, sometimes this means being willing to play the maverick card and punch through the way things are. Rules and processes often spring up as a kind of scar tissue post crisis; in an attempt to prevent problems, they act instead as a brake on innovation.

In many companies, looking through the binder that HR gives you on your first day at the job can be a kind of tree ring, showing you a historical record of everything that has ever gone wrong at the company. But these manuals won't tell you what you really need to know in order to survive and thrive at the job; who holds the most power, how to push work through the DBA's without it taking months, how to get some heat on a purchase order for some badly needed dev environments. And left to grow as an endless list of "don't-do-this" rules and processes, they can choke off the oxygen to your growing little fire.

High-trust orgs don't rely on a huge binder of commandments as a substitute for trust. Netflix for example does not have a HR manual; instead, they have a single guideline: "Act in Netflix's best interest." This simple rule is enough and doesn't work against the high-trust culture we want:

> *The idea is that if an employee can't figure out how to interpret the guideline in a given situation, he or she doesn't have enough judgment to work there. If you don't trust the judgment of the people on your team, you have to ask why you're employing them. It's true that you'll have to fire people occasionally for violating the guideline. Overall, the high level of mutual trust among members of a team, and across the company as a whole, becomes a strong binding force.*[30]

---

[29]"The Site Reliability Workbook: Practical Ways to Implement SRE," edited by Betsy Beyer, Niall Richard Murphy, David K. Rensin, Kent Kawahara, Stephen Thorne. O'Reilly Media, 8/4/2018. ISBN-10: 1492029505, ISBN-13: 978-1492029502.
[30]"Adopting Microservices at Netflix: Lessons for Team and Process Design," Tony Mauro. Nginx, 3/10/2015. www.nginx.com/blog/adopting-microservices-at-netflix-lessons-for-team-and-process-design/. A very good article, covering Netflix's use of the OODA loop in optimizing for speed vs. efficiency, and creating a high-freedom, high-responsibility culture with less process.

And Courtney Kissler (formerly of Nordstrom) made this powerful point about how critical it is to have senior leaders show by their actions that they support their teams – particularly when the crap hits the fan:

> Senior leaders need to demonstrate their commitment to creating a learning organization. I will share the behaviors I try to model with my teams. I believe passionately in honoring and extracting reality. If I am a senior leader and my team doesn't feel comfortable sharing risks, then I will never truly know reality. And, if I'm not genuinely curious and only show up when there's a failure, then I am failing as a senior leader. It's important to build trust and to demonstrate that failure leads to inquiry.[31]

It's a recurring theme – leadership shows itself most in times of crisis: after mistakes are made, how do we react? Poor organizations seek to blame a culprit or shoot the messenger; generative, forward-thinking leaders demonstrate by example a tolerance for risk and error as a price well worth paying for innovation and autonomy.

We discussed earlier Microsoft's scorecards that it uses to track their engineering teams. But unlike many organizations that use numbers like bug counts, velocity, or failed build rates as a hammer to "encourage" or "whip into shape," the Azure DevOps leadership uses them as a chance to start a conversation directly with the team. Maybe, there's a reason why bugs have risen; maybe, there's unseen blockers or a faulty process that needs to be cleared up. So, questions are asked – what's next on your backlog? What's your debt situation? What problems are you facing that we can help with?

Trust and Resilience

What makes for a resilient team? In the book *Drive*, Daniel Pink highlighted three key elements:

- Autonomy – People must be empowered by leaders to have the freedom and power to work autonomously to achieve the team's objective.

- Mastery – the space and opportunity we need not just to muddle along but really master our craft, the tools we need to contribute to the mission.

---

[31]"Accelerate: The Science of Lean Software and DevOps: Building and Scaling High Performing Technology Organizations," Nicole Forsgren PhD, Jez Humble, Gene Kim. IT Revolution Press, 3/27/2018. ISBN-10: 1942788339, ISBN-13: 978-1942788331.

- Purpose – a mission or shared sense of purpose for the entire team. This vision needs to be challenging, sometimes even unattainable in practice – but clear enough so that everyone can understand what they need to do.

The common quality you'll notice is trust. Managers trust their people that they have good motives, want to get better at the things that matter, and that giving responsibility and freedom to act will yield good returns. In turn, employees and team members trust that the mission that they are being given matters, has actual tangible value to the company and perhaps to the world at large. A common purpose, a shared awareness, and empowering individuals to act and make decisions – that creates resilience.

It also ties in very well with the Golden Rule, the way we want to be treated. We all want autonomy, the ability to direct our own lives; the glow of learning something new, of mastering a particular discipline in solving a problem, is also a strong drive for most of us. Underlying this all though is the principle of service to a mission. We yearn to do what we do in the service of something larger than ourselves, something that matters, that adds to the universe.

Thinking deeply about what leadership means, how to set consistency in terms of mission, and how to reinforce team autonomy and responsibility with the right tools and evolving frameworks was a formative part of how the Azure DevOps management team at Microsoft set their mission. As Sam Guckenheimer told us:

You need to have obvious skin in the game from leadership, and initiative from individual practitioners. Think back to that great book "Drive" by Dan Pink, which stressed the leadership value between Autonomy, Mastery, and Purpose. You are going to need to spark people and get them enthusiastic, active, and feeling like they control their destiny – autonomy.

It's really part art and science, because that autonomy has to be balanced with purpose, which is driven consistently and forcefully by management. And if you look at most of the current execs at Microsoft, you will see that they practice both high empathy and engage deep technically.

Mission is key for us but it goes beyond just a few words or a slogan. We put up guardrails, very clear rules of the road that specifies "here is what you need to do to check your code into master." We have a very clear definition of done that is common in every team – "code delivered with tests and telemetry and deployed in production worldwide."

This is the exact opposite of "it works on my machine" – and everyone knows it. If you're doing new work, there's a set of common services we provide, including sample code and documentation. So no one has to reinvent the wheel when it comes to telemetry for example – you might improve on it, but you would never have to deliver this from scratch, it's reused from a common set of services.[32]

This concept of purpose, of a common vision and understanding both of the problems we want to solve and the goals we want to drive toward, is a common underpinning of the truly "elite" performers.

The problem is that most organizations are built for efficiency, not trust. In terms of their structure, they inherit from the scientific management theories of Frederick Taylor, who revolutionized manufacturing with breaking down complicated processes into discrete parts and optimizing them for maximum efficiency.

Take a minute to look at the command-and-control, top-down structure at the top of the "DevOps and Leadership" section by Ron Vincent. That orderly, neat, pyramid shape on the left reflects the people and technology of the times – it looks very much like a secretarial pool in the 1950s, with the mechanical perfection of a classic black Royal typewriter. It's an efficient structure and worked very well where processes and variables could be defined and optimized as a hard-set process. But in the age of the services-oriented web, that same structure looks hopelessly archaic, a relic; our working conditions, challenges, and tools are all much more modern, fluid, dynamic.

So, contrary to that beautiful, rigid triangle so beloved in the 1950s, the quality we are striving for is not efficiency – it's resilience, which comes from trust.

Sanjeev Sharma of IBM related a story that shows the powerful impact of trust with something as small as listening during standups:

> *I had been asked by the architect on the account to meet with the Director of Dev and the Director of Ops for a client of his. We met for lunch, with the architect and me on one side of the table and the two directors on the other. I knew right away that all was not well on their home front. They were leaning away from each other. The Dev director complained about how Ops was not agile, and the Ops director said that Dev sent them garbage that would not even run without crashing servers. They even looked at their hands while speaking about the other. I felt I was in couples' counseling.*
>
> *The solution plan I recommended to them was to begin with small steps, by shifting left when Ops was engaged. Their main challenge was a total lack of visibility between the Dev and Ops teams, till it was time to deploy to production. The suggestion I made was to pick one critical project and,*

---

[32]Interview of Sam Guckenheimer by Dave Harrison, see Appendix.

once a week, have the Ops team send one resource to the Dev team's daily standup meeting and have them just listen, without needing to engage, and see if things improved.

I had a follow-up meeting with the same two directors less than three months later at a conference. They were happy to report that the Ops team now had a presence at the daily standup meeting, and Ops not only listened, but actively participated, sharing their progress, plans, and blockers. Ops engagement had shifted left. They had achieved collaboration.[33]

Shared meetings like this are not efficient. Hosting a weekly shared lunch with a separate team would make an industrial efficiency maven like Frederick Winslow Taylor roll in his grave. But, again, efficiency is not our target— building resiliency and trust is. That requires a sincere, ongoing effort to build relationships and see things from the other side's point of view.

Indicators of lack of trust usually show up in a lack of collaboration around process. When an Ops team hands off extensive release checklists and procedures as sacred writ to the development team, that's an antipattern. When developers treat configuration management and deployment as "the release team's job," that's also a problem. Lack of involvement in other teams' planning sessions – as Sanjeev noted earlier – is a telltale sign of siloization.

Trust-based, resilient teams care about making their software easier to deploy, configure, and operate. As Russ Collier pointed out:

Your development teams need to seriously listen to the operations group. They need to treat the operations team's concerns just like they would treat any end-user feature request or bug request. After all, your operations team is simply another type of user of the development team's software.[34]

It's Really About Learning

Humility, patience, and trust – it turns out – are vital prerequisites for making the true, often unspoken objective of DevOps: *is it safe for me to learn?* Amazon and Google, for example, have made some disastrous mistakes in their history; yet both have shown an amazing ability to learn, not repeat mistakes, and keep experimenting and following up on what does work. Their thinking has been

---

[33]"The DevOps Adoption Playbook: A Guide to Adopting DevOps in a Multi-Speed IT Enterprise," Sanjeev Sharma. Wiley, 2/28/2017. ISBN-10: 9781119308744, ISBN-13: 978-1119308744.
[34]"It Takes Dev and Ops to Make DevOps," Russ Collier. DevOpsOnWindows.com, 7/26/2013. www.devopsonwindows.com/it-takes-dev-and-ops-to-make-devops/.

influenced by Lean, which favors the idea of kaizen – continuous improvement. As Taiichi Ohno put it:

> Whether top management, middle management, or the workers who actually do the work, we are all human, so we're like walking misconceptions, believing that the way we do things now is the best way. Or perhaps you do not think it is the best way, but you are working within the common sense that "We can't help it, this is how things are... It is important to have the attitude in our daily work that just underneath one kaizen idea is yet another one..."[35]

Kaizen or continuous improvement is based in turn on kata, a routine that is practiced repeatedly until it becomes a habit. Think of the classic martial arts movie "Ip Man," as Donnie Yen practices with a wooden dummy going through blocks, attacks, defense. The goal is to make continuous improvement a habit, so when – in an uncertain situation – we have an instinctive, unconscious routine to guide behavior. Kaizen, learning, is based on Kata, practice – which means a deliberate repetition to improve skills until they become a habit.

Let's say that again. Learning is a habit. We gain it through practice. Practice in turn involves learning from failure.

Dave once noticed a sign at his kids' elementary school saying: "I see value in failure because I learn something new!" The school goes so far as to have their monthly get-togethers with all the students and their parents begin with a 10-minute talk about a specific quality or value and how they contribute to learning. With that poster, the school is encouraging a growth-based mindset.

In the book *Mindset*, Stanford psychologist Carol Dweck presented several decades of research showing that children commonly think about success in two ways: fixed and growth. A "fixed mindset" assumes that character, intelligence, and creativity are all static values that can't be changed in any meaningful way. Success is the affirmation of that inherent intelligence, an assessment of how those givens measure up against an equally fixed standard. When we praise our children for getting an "A" on their report card – "You're so smart!" – instead of praising them for the effort they put into their work, we are actually encouraging a fixed-based mindset.

A "growth mindset," on the other hand, thrives on challenge and sees failure not as evidence of stupidity but as a springboard for growth and stretching our existing abilities. Growth mindset is fueled by a passion for learning, rather than a hunger for approval. This springs from the core belief that intelligence, creativity, and ultimately success can be cultivated through effort and deliberate practice.

---

[35]"Workplace Management," Taiichi Ohno. McGraw-Hill Education, 12/11/2002. ISBN-10: 9780071808019, ISBN-13: 978-0071808019.

Dweck's research demonstrated that the number one trait underpinning creative achievement is the kind of resilience and fail-forward perseverance attributed to the growth mindset. As the book pointed out:

In one world — the world of fixed traits — success is about proving you're smart or talented. Validating yourself. In the other — the world of changing qualities — it's about stretching yourself to learn something new. Developing yourself.

In one world, failure is about having a setback. Getting a bad grade. Losing a tournament. Getting fired. Getting rejected. It means you're not smart or talented. In the other world, failure is about not growing. Not reaching for the things you value. It means you're not fulfilling your potential.

In one world, effort is a bad thing. It, like failure, means you're not smart or talented. If you were, you wouldn't need effort. In the other world, effort is what makes you smart or talented.

Why waste time proving over and over how great you are, when you could be getting better? Why hide deficiencies instead of overcoming them? Why look for friends or partners who will just shore up your self-esteem instead of ones who will also challenge you to grow? And why seek out the tried and true, instead of experiences that will stretch you? The passion for stretching yourself and sticking to it, even (or especially) when it's not going well, is the hallmark of the growth mindset. This is the mindset that allows people to thrive during some of the most challenging times in their lives.[36]

We wish this type of worldview was more common at the enterprises we engage with. Yet the value of practice and learning from failure is often the first casualty of office culture wars. Here, the culprit is not hard to identify. Invariably, teams that demonstrate this fixed-based mindset are mimicking the values and behaviors that are rewarded by an upper management indoctrinated in the value of a "little healthy competition."

Nigel Kersten of Puppet told us that too many organizations are still stuck in neutral instead of practicing, failing, and learning:

In most larger enterprises aiming for complete automation, end to end, is somewhat of a pipe dream – just because these companies have so many groups and silos and dependencies. But that's not saying that DevOps is impossible, even in shared services type orgs. This isn't nuclear science, it's like learning to play the piano. It doesn't require brilliance, it's not art – it's just hard work. It just takes discipline and practice, daily practice.

---

[36]"Mindset: The New Psychology of Success," Carol Dweck. Random House, 2/28/2006. ISBN-10: 1400062756, ISBN-13: 978-1400062751.

> *I have the strong impression that many companies out there SAY they are doing DevOps, whatever that means – but really it hasn't even gotten off the ground. They're still on Square 1, analyzing and trying to come up with the right recipe or roadmap that will fit every single use case they might encounter, past present and future.*[37]

Michael Goetz of Chef told us that learning-based organizations are consistently more successful:

> *You really can't stress this enough – the companies I've seen that are successful take learning seriously and build a plan around it. They run bootcamps or dojos – where they take groups at a time and say, for the next two weeks we're going to teach you about CI/CD and version control, and we're going to work in this way – from today forward.*
>
> *This must be internally taught – it can't come from the outside, from consultants. We try to do a training or engagement with a dedicated group of people – and get them to a place where they're dedicated to it, living it, in their house. Then leave them with the path to set up their own internal consulting agency or center of excellence.*
>
> *Some people get a little allergic when I say CoE or communities of practice because they've been burned in the past. If you organize it where it's a top-down, very rigid, outward focused – this is your coding style, your pipelines will look like this, if you have any questions come to us and we'll give you the right answer – yeah, that is a problem. Those efforts tend to die out pretty quickly.*
>
> *The ones that live longer are where there's a few people in the core – the visionaries – kind of helping move things along and give structure, but it is set up as a kind of organic movement, a potluck, where everyone is bringing something to the table to discuss.*[38]

DevOps Dojos and Self-Forming Teams

Nathen Harvey echoed the importance of learning in having internal challenge and DevOps Dojo type events – something that is part of the DNA of DevOps since its inception:

> *We strongly recommend running DevOps Dojos – a program where you can run through all the tools and learn by doing for 6 weeks – the same startup program I mentioned earlier. Then the people you've invited to this program go back to their original team and bring this new way of doing things.*

---

[37]Interview of Nigel Kersten by Dave Harrison, see Appendix.
[38]Interview of Michael Goetz by Dave Harrison, see Appendix.

Just as an example – Verizon runs an annual DevOps Challenge contest. They set out some cool, aggressive goals at the beginning of the year – maybe a focus on CI/CD, or security, a big theme – and they give out projects for teams to self-select. As the year goes on, they start winnowing down the finalists – from 64, to 32, to 12. And then they bring in outside panelists... to judge their finalists and choose a winner.[39]

DevOps Dojos aren't the only way to spread information. For example, at Google, the SRE teams have created a program called "Mission Control," where developers can join a SRE team for one to two quarters. Mission Control has been very effective in getting coders to see what the SRE role is like in practice and helping disseminate better practices and process. Sam Eaton told us that they run a similar program at Yelp called Deputy, where a developer works alongside the SRE team and receives the training they need to be the link between the SRE teams and the program groups.[40]

Cross pollination and the opportunity to try new things kept coming up in our interviews as a key factor in success; less happy companies tend to have unhappy employees that are stuck in one role that they may not like, have outgrown, or be well suited for.

One of the most crazy and innovative practices we've seen to encourage cross-pollination is a practice that appears to be unique to Microsoft: the self-forming team. As Brian Harry explained it, back in 2008, Chris Shaffer came up with a seemingly insane idea that grew into what is now called the "yellow sticky exercise." It's quite simple: managers derive a list of features needed and team sizes in their planning process. Then, each engineering/program manager pair for each feature team does a "sales pitch" on what the feature development will look like to the combined team.

After a few days of thought, the whole team is brought back together, and everyone is given three sticky notes where they put their names and a number – 1,2,3 – showing their order of preference. Everyone goes to the whiteboard and puts their sticky notes next to the teams they want to be on, in order of preference.

There's a little more to it than that, but in essence that sums it up. After 3 or 4 days, everyone has the ability to jump ship to something they consider new or more exciting. This doesn't happen every month or even every year; as of 2018, the company has done this three times in about 7 years.

---

[39]Interview of Nathen Harvey by Dave Harrison, see Appendix.
[40]Interview of Betsy Byer / Stephen Thorne by Dave Harrison, see Appendix.

(courtesy Brian Harry)

This sounds like a recipe for chaos; surprisingly, Microsoft has found the "yellow sticky" exercise to be amazingly effective. It ties in well with the principles of autonomy, alignment, and team balance the company was looking for in its transformation. Looking back, Brian says it's led to people feeling more empowered, that they have more choices in their career growth within the company:

> It's amazing how organized it is. We've found, pretty consistently about 20% of the org decides they want to change what they are doing and work on something else and about 80% decide to keep working on what they are working on. That provides a nice ratio of continuity, fresh perspectives, opportunity to try new things, etc.
>
> After each of the exercises I go around and take an informal poll... I ask them all what they think of the experience. I ask them if they are happy with both the process and the outcome. The overwhelming response I get is that people love it. Even people who choose to stay on the same team say they are grateful for having the opportunity to learn about all of the other feature teams and to make a decision about what they want. ...I can't promise it will work as well in every org but I can't think of any reason why it can't.[41]

As we discussed in the section on blame-free postmortems in Chapter 4, the costs of faking perfection accrue with interest – the classic pathological organization never learns from past mistakes, since mistakes mean failure.

---

[41]"Self Forming Teams at Scale," Brian Harry. Microsoft Developer Blog, 7/24/2015. https://blogs.msdn.microsoft.com/bharry/2015/07/24/self-forming-teams-at-scale/.

In contrast, forward-thinking, progressive enterprises show a healthy appetite for mistakes as a chance to learn; a fundamentally different way of viewing failure.

This is the part of DevOps cultural change where executive buy-in is essential. If bad behaviors are leaking in under pressure, we likely need to look at the way we approach learning – and if we're allowing enough room in our expectations and work queue for people to truly master their craft, to practice.

Leaders can help here by demonstrating the flexibility and eagerness to learn that they wish their people to emulate. Several leaders we spoke to said that they positioned their transformations as an experiment – something that we're going to try to improve things in a certain way, and see how it goes. That's much less threatening than a mandated, permanent initiative that's set in stone. Others agreed with the teams to look at a new process after a wait period, say 3 months from now – and that any changes would be revisited after a given time period. If it wasn't seeing the desired results, dropping it sent the message that change is just an experiment, and that we're flexible enough to admit when things aren't working and turn our attention to something else.[42]

As our story wraps up, it's nice to see a real commitment to learning on the part of WonderTek with a DevOps Dojo. As it's grown in popularity, we've seen conferences and knowledge-sharing events like DevOps Days spring up across the globe. Many of the people we've talked to have enthused about the value of building support through internal hackathons, brown bag events, or having teams participate in a larger community event as speakers.

For example, Target used DevOps Dojos as a catalyst to spread information and excitement around their services-driven transformation. Nationwide Insurance does a "Teaching Thursday," dedicating time each week for their associates to teach, learn, mentor – learn. At Google, using grouplets has been a part of their DNA from early on – where one day a week (that 20% time we talked about earlier in capacity planning) is dedicated to a project unrelated to their primary area of responsibility. And at Capital One, SMEs have open office hours where people can drop by and ask questions and share stories.[43]

If the fire you're trying to build in your company is kind of smoldering along and executives have their eyes elsewhere, don't fret. Be internally rigorous; externally accepting – demonstrate the behaviors you wish others to emulate as a consistent kata. Take on a new book or two a week and show that obsession with continual learning and improvement as you gain mastery over new fields and techniques.

---

[42]"DevOps and Change Agents: Common Themes," Eliza Earnshaw. Puppet, 12/3/2014. https://puppet.com/blog/devops-and-change-agents-common-themes.
[43]"The DevOps Handbook: How to Create World-Class Agility, Reliability, and Security in Technology Organizations," Gene Kim, Patrick Dubois, John Willis, Jez Humble. IT Revolution Press, 10/6/2016, ISBN-10: 1942788002, ISBN-13: 978-1942788003.

And remember the power of humility, patience, and trust. It takes time for large organizations to change. Demonstrate the value of your experiments in saving money or improving services, and show flexibility and patience as that fire slowly gains intensity and heat.

DevOps and Leadership

By Ron Vincent

Ron is the author of "Learning ArcGIS Runtime SDK for .NET" from Packt Publishing. He currently works as a Senior Consultant for Microsoft Premier, helping organizations to deliver high quality, faster delivery, world-class stability, reliability, availability, and security. Through custom technical workshops, management consulting, architecture reviews, and custom solutions, he helps customers digitally transform via the cloud, system integration, geospatial, augmented reality, IoT, and custom software development.

DevOps requires a different approach to leadership. In this article I'll explain where our modern concept of management came from, and a better model in the age of rapid innovation.

For decades now, the American corporation has been modeled after the concepts of Frederick Winslow Taylor, who back in 1910 studied how workers did their work at a steel company. "In Taylor's view, the task of factory management was to determine the best way for the worker to do the job, to provide the proper tools and training, and to provide incentives for good performance. He broke each job down into its individual motions, analyzed these to determine which were essential, and timed the workers with a stopwatch. With unnecessary motion eliminated, the worker, following a machinelike routine, became far more productive."[44]

---

[44]"Taylorism," unattributed author(s). Encyclopaedia Britannica, unknown date. www.britannica.com/science/Taylorism.

Taylor's approach became a craze and was adopted in every industry, from General Motors to typists to surgeons. There were other leaders in this movement; one such individual was Henry L. Gantt, a name anyone will recognize that's ever created a project management scheduling chart. It's no wonder that project management and Taylorism go hand in hand, as they were part of the same thought movement.

Some examples of how Taylorism reveals itself in today's companies include

1. Board level or bankers controlling the day-to-day business affairs.
2. Publicity or vanity driven metrics influencing business decisions.
3. Organization shuffles, reorganizations as a substitute for improvements.
4. Yearly employee ranking systems, management by objectives, and quotas to improve efficiency.
5. Measurement systems that ignore variation and process control.
6. Treating management as the customer as opposed to treating the customer as the customer.
7. Putting people in competition with one another and not promoting collaboration.
8. Advocating and even cultivating an atmosphere of fear.
9. Rumors and threats of layoffs along with actual layoffs.
10. Rewarding behavior and advocating punishments to gain compliance.[45]

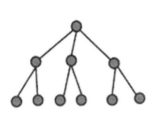

"Top-down"

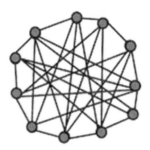

"Bottom-up"

Source above: "The Origin of Society"[46]

Things are different in DevOps. In a world where a single developer can change the world with a few lines of code, we have to think differently about how we manage. Workers are no longer cogs in a machine, automatons to be controlled and directed from on high, as Taylor thought back in 1910.

---

[45]"Neo Taylorism or DevOps Anti Patterns," John Willis. IT Revolution, 10/23/2012. https://itrevolution.com/neo-taylorism-or-devops-anti-patterns.
[46]"The Origin of Society," unattributed author(s). Modern Matriarchal Societies, unknown date. http://mmstudies.com/top-down.

What Makes a Good Leader?

If you take a look at the latest research from Puppet in the 2017 State of DevOps Report, the following leadership qualities have been proven to lead to better IT performance and organization performance:

- **Vision.** Has a clear concept of where the organization is going and where it should be in 5 years.

- **Inspirational communication.** Communicates in a way that inspires and motivates, even in an uncertain or changing environment.

- **Intellectual stimulation.** Challenges followers to think about problems in new ways.

- **Supportive leadership.** Demonstrates care and consideration of followers' personal needs and feelings.

- **Personal recognition.** Praises and acknowledges achievement of goals and improvements in work quality; personally compliments others when they do outstanding work.[47]

These leadership qualities represent a dramatic change from the Command and Control approach of Taylorism. Organizations that apply these have been shown to deliver better results.

The book *Lean Enterprise* echoes this in the following:

> *The most important concern leaders and managers operating within a complex adaptive system face is this: how can we enable people within the organization to make good decisions—to act in the best interests of the organization—given that they can never have sufficient information and context to understand the full consequences of their decisions, and given that events often overtake our plans?*[48]

The Principle of Mission

In *The Principles of Product Development Flow*, Donald Reinertsen presents the Principle of Mission. This principle derives from the military's doctrine of Mission Command, in which the end state and purpose are carefully defined, along with the minimum possible constraints. According to the Principle of

---

[47]"Annual State of DevOps Report," unattributed author(s). Puppet Labs, 2017. https://puppetlabs.com/2017-devops-report.

[48]"Lean Enterprise: How High Performance Organizations Innovate at Scale," Jez Humble, Joanne Molesky, Barry O'Reilly. O'Reilly Media, 1/3/2015. ISBN-10: 1449368425, ISBN-13: 978-1449368425.

Mission, we create alignment not by making a detailed plan of *how* we achieve our objective, but by describing the intent of our mission and communicating *why* we are undertaking it.

> *The key to the Principle of Mission is to create alignment and enable autonomy by setting out clear, high-level target conditions with an agreed time frame—which gets smaller under conditions of greater uncertainty—and then leaving the details of how to achieve the conditions to teams. This approach can even be applied to multiple levels of hierarchy, with each level reducing the scope while providing more context.*[49]

This is great stuff. It allows leadership to determine the "what" and "why" and allows Agile teams to determine the "how."

With that said, I often find that when I visit customers around the world and bring in these concepts and talk about the studies, quote the facts, and attempt to be as persuasive as I can, I still get the sense that many find these new ideas difficult to adjust to for various reasons. Changing an organization's culture is hard work. Often, I find that developers, testers, and midlevel managers all like these ideas, but often top-level management is not involved or just doesn't understand how to go about making these kinds of changes. Taylorism is just how things are done – end of story.

There's another fundamental problem that slows progress: most organizations are practicing Water-Scrum-Fall. The Agile teams are practicing this Mission Command approach in the form of Scrum where teams are self-organizing and self-managing to some degree and actually somewhat adaptive to changing conditions. However, the rest of the organization is practicing the project management-driven approach from Gantt and Taylor. As a result, the organization is running these two paradigms at once. It's no wonder both sides often feel disconnected and frustrated with each other: they have different mental models.

So, how do we merge the mental models both horizontally and vertically across the organization?

We can answer this question with a lesson from the manufacturing world and the Lean movement. Lean theory is fundamental to and inspired DevOps as a movement, and of course Lean didn't start out in software. It started in the automobile industry and has been applied to several industries such as healthcare, government, etc. Furthermore, it turns out that there is an approach to leadership that we can apply to not only software teams but also across the entire organization so that we have a unifying approach to leadership, culture, teams, and individuals no matter their roles and responsibilities.

---

[49]"The Principles of Product Development Flow: Second Generation Lean Product Development," Donald Reinertsen. Celeritas Publishing, 1/1/2009. ISBN-10: 1935401009, ISBN-13: 978-1935401001.

Respect and DevOps

In *The Toyota Way to Lean Leadership*, Jeffrey Liker and Gary Convis explored the way in which Toyota has practiced Lean in great detail. We learn how Toyota applies the principles which has led to Toyota being able to have the wild success they've achieved, using the following principles:[50]

- Spirit of Challenge

- Kaizen Mind

- Genchi Genbutsu, or Go and See To Deeply Understand

- Teamwork

- Respect

I won't explain all of these here, but I will focus a little on respect. Respect in Lean is critical, and in practice it's often ignored.

Let me provide an example. Toyota actually started out as a textile company in the late 1800s. During these early days, the company built mechanical looms. The problem with these looms was that it took a person to stand in front of it to shut it down if it broke. In 1886, Sakichi Toyoda created a new version of the loom that when it broke it would shut down automatically. This meant that you no longer needed all of these people standing around just watching to shut it down to prevent breakage. This increased production and quality, but more importantly it represents the concept of jidoka.

Pretty much everyone knows by now that automation is a key pillar of DevOps, but in Lean it has a slightly different twist. Jidoka means automation + human intelligence. Sakichi Toyoda had such a great respect for people that he didn't want them just standing around watching a machine to make sure it didn't break. He wanted them to use their powerful brains to solve problems. People were not seen as cogs in a machine as Taylor saw them. People were seen as key to innovation.

In other words, Lean is far more humanistic than Taylorism.

There's more too. For Toyota, leadership just doesn't come from the top. It also comes from the bottom of the organization. It's everyone's job to continuously improve (Kaizen) and develop themselves and others around them. It's also the role of leaders at the top to practice Genchi Genbutsu, or "Go and See To Deeply Understand." In other words, leaders at the top must go and see where

---

[50]"The Toyota Way to Lean Leadership: Achieving and Sustaining Excellence through Leadership Development," Jeffrey Liker, Gary Convis. McGraw-Hill Education, 11/7/2011. ISBN-10: 0071780793; ISBN-13: 978-0071780797.

the work is actually being done in order to understand it and help practice Kaizen. In Lean, individuals that are closest to the work garnish the most respect.

Growing Leadership

As *The Toyota Way to Lean Leadership* explains, leaders at Toyota are developed using a specific process dominated by the P-D-C-A cycle. First, leaders should be reflective about themselves and try to improve on their weaknesses. Second, leaders should coach and develop others. Third, leaders and everyone for that matter should practice daily Kaizen. Lastly, leaders at the top should create a vision and seek perfection in eliminating waste in the system. This elimination of waste is central to Lean and is never satisfied, but it sets the organization's True North. For example, True North in software development is to have zero bugs over five consecutive sprints. That's nearly an impossible goal, but in Lean we should still strive for it.

P-D-C-A cycles – Plan-Do-Check-Act – form the essence of each of the preceding steps. This is based on the scientific method of hypothesis-experiment-evaluation, and is applied here to individuals, processes, and teams.

This is quite different from the methods that Taylor came up with. As a true engineer, Taylor was timing how long it took workers to do a job and made changes to improve that cycle time; each worker was given a proscribed set approach to follow, defined and pre-set. That rigid approach was abandoned in Lean in favor of making improvements using the P-D-C-A cycle, which follows an incremental development pattern (as with Agile development) and treats everything as an experiment so that we can improve and learn.

It's important to note that these concepts have been successfully applied to all kinds of industries. No matter what your organization makes or what services it provides, Lean has already been used to make this cultural shift. Also, it turns out that when we understand where we came from (Taylorism), and that there's a better way via Lean, this makes for a deeper understanding than just quoting facts and research.

I invite you to check out *The Toyota Way to Lean Leadership* and learn how to unify your organization around a culture of continuous improvement, so that your enterprise can innovate in the 21st century using the P-D-C-A cycle. This is especially true now given that, as Satya Nadella has noted, "Every industry is now a software industry."

We need new ways to lead, new ways to treat and motivate people, new ways to finance, and new ways to develop and learn so that we can compete in this new era. We need to treat everyone with respect, not as cogs in a machine, but as intelligent and valuable problem-solvers with the power to innovate.

The End of the Beginning

Experience is something you don't get until just after you need it.

—Steven Wright

Management shouldn't inflict sameness.

—Jonathan Smart

If a man is called to be a street sweeper, he should sweep streets even as Michelangelo painted, or Beethoven composed music, or Shakespeare wrote poetry. He should sweep streets so well that all the hosts of heaven and earth will pause to say, here lived a great street sweeper who did his job well.

—Martin Luther King Jr.

If you were to ask anyone on Ben's team how things are actually going, I imagine you'd get mixed responses. Some would be enthusiastic. Others would point to some nasty skeletons in the closet that remain. In other words, work is still work, and it doesn't rain puppies, kittens, and rainbows now that they've discovered this magical word "DevOps."

© Dave Harrison and Knox Lively 2019
D. Harrison and K. Lively, *Achieving DevOps*,
https://doi.org/10.1007/978-1-4842-4388-6_8

Still, most on the team would agree that things are getting better, that they're climbing out of a rut – albeit with a long way to go. Let's take a look back from a year ago and see how the team has grown and the challenges they've faced:

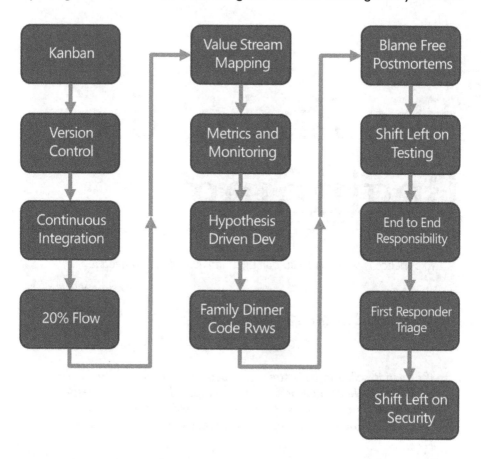

That's a gigantic list when you stare at it, even if their progress isn't perfect on any of these points. Gradually, with fits and starts, an ecosystem is taking shape that's more learning-friendly and robust, resilient, able to cope with disaster and broken releases better.

With **Kanban**, they're limiting WIP, meaning they're causing pain by forcing the team to focus on driving one or two things forward to "done" at a time. This exposes problems with lack of automation, handoffs, bad tooling, signoff hassles, etc. It also means the team is able to work more effectively (less loss due to context switching) and demonstrate what they are working on in dashboards – transparency. Without it, the team is not really a team but a bunch of disconnected siloes, and blockers are not really being exposed as they should be.

With **Version Control**, the team is now storing everything they need to support and extend an application in one place. This is their "base camp" for release management, allowing them safe and easy rollbacks. Without it, they are always having to log onto VMs to figure out what the actual production config is – and no two environments look like another. Having one authoritative source of truth is a huge leap forward for them. (They'll go even further when environment configs are also kept in VC, but that's later.)

With **CI/CD** – that's Continuous Integration / Continuous Delivery – they're eliminating long-lived feature branches and long periods of integration hell and stabilization periods. Smaller batches of work are getting out the door, faster to production. Without this – they'll be wasting half their time or more trying to make the next release semifunctional, and worse – they won't be getting the feedback they need to prioritize their work.

With **20% Flow**, the team now has at least 20% "free" time to work on projects that interest them. This could be improving their infrastructure or RM tooling, or reading a great book on a new design pattern, or participating in a hackathon. This shows the team is serious about paying down technical debt and investing in their people. This is time the team needs to come up with truly ingenious and creative problem-solving ideas – sharpening the saw, as the saying goes. Without buying out this time every sprint, the team is fully allocated – but has no room to breathe or learn, and burning out at an unsustainable pace, like a jammed highway at rush hour.

With **Value Stream Mapping**, they take the time to map out exactly how ideas and requirements flow to them and through to production. This is their first step in actually engaging with a stakeholder and putting the problem in terms they can understand – dollars and waste. Everything up to now has really been foundational – mapping out how business value is driven shows the business partner some startling facts on why even "simple" requests take so much time, and exposes to everyone in the room why a better integrated flow of work is needed. Without this, no matter how efficient the team is, they won't be connected to the actual business problems they're being asked to solve. They'll end up treading water. And they won't have the firepower they need from the business to broker a better partnership with Ops/QA or other siloed teams they're dependent on.

By itself, **Metrics and Monitoring** are very helpful. Having developers know and care more about how their systems are actually performing in production – and staying ahead of trouble with a bad release or a failed infrastructure patch – is a huge leap forward. It also can provide tangible evidence Ben can use to check if the process and people investments they are making are paying off in specific, tangible terms. But paired with **Hypothesis-Driven Development**, and suddenly we're at another level. We can treat each new feature or "requirement" as being what it really is – a guess – and seeing if our guess was right, or if we need to rethink our assumptions. Without good monitoring, we're constantly at the mercy of temperamental and whimsical environments. And without valuable business-driven metrics guiding our decision-making, we're vulnerable to getting hijacked by goldplating or overworked pet projects – or just plain building the wrong thing for the wrong people.

With **Family Dinner Code Reviews**, the team can better share information and work to improve the group's collective body of knowledge. Being able to give insights in a productive, safe environment means far fewer bugs being caught early before making it out the door. Done right – respectfully, following playground rules – code reviews can be the single best way of improving quality of code. Having a consistent Definition of Done that the team maintains will also help maintain fair, clear standards – a self-correcting and improving culture of quality. Without it, the same mistakes will be repeated, and more expensive, time-consuming bugs will leak into production, where they're far more damaging and difficult to fix.

With **Blame-Free Postmortems**, the team acknowledges that the systems they are working on are unsafe and complex, and that problems never have a human source. By making it safe for people to share the details behind mistakes, the company is better able to learn from them. Without this, the underlying causes of problems will be hidden, and changes will slow as people fear the consequences of making a poor decision.

Shift Left on Testing means the entire team assumes responsibility for quality and any new changes (at a minimum) will have fast-running unit tests proving that it works as designed. By using Defect-Driven Testing – or TDD for newer greenfield projects – Ben's team chooses to invest in a growing test suite that runs against every check-in. Without a strong unit test base maintained by the coders, integration and functional tests become increasingly more brittle and expensive to maintain – and lag behinds new functionality, meaning changes are either delayed or safety is compromised.

With a **Shared Responsibility for Production**, Ben's team begins to rotate direct production support of their applications. There's simply no substitute for supporting your own code or having a shared work queue and dashboarding so bugs don't slip behind new, exciting work. This led in turn to the team deciding they needed to better empower their first responder team to assist with triage. **First Responder Triage and Runbooks** means the team will be spending much less time tracking down false positives and fixable issues, and the developers and first responder teams can work together to improve their reliability and response times for their customers. Without this, technical debt will start building up in hidden corners as the developers race ahead – and the Operations team won't have the information they need to knock down common problems quickly.

Looking Backward: As the story ends, there's still clouds on the horizon and a lot of work left undone.

There's so many other things Ben's team could have done – how could we have written a book on DevOps and not written more about configuration management, or infrastructure as code? You would think templated environments would have been first on our list. For Pete's sake, there's not even much mentioned about containers, Docker, or Kubernetes. What the heck?

There's no question, those are all good things – in fact for many organizations, they're essential. But that would come in Year 2, or maybe Year 3, for this particular group. Asking a group that doesn't have its act together to take on microservices or distributed computing is setting it up to fail. All those great, awesome tools and practices depend on a robust ecosystem and learning-oriented culture that in this case just doesn't exist yet. It also means putting tooling as the goal, abstracted from the actual business problem that is constricting value. The "unicorns" we're all so envious of – Microsoft, Google, Netflix – they didn't start out with these tools or practices. They grew into them, gradually, over time, and each of their implementations looks vastly different.

So yes, their lives aren't perfect – but the team is definitely happier with their work as it's gotten more creative and there's much less friction with other groups and fear of breaking an app in prod. Being loosely coupled as a team and enforcing consistent positive behavior with their partners has helped change the culture of the company as WonderTek has moved gradually toward being learning based.

They've also got much better tools/process. Just implementing CI/CD, better config management, and a release process with a weak-but-getting-better automated unit test gating is a huge win for the year. And there's a much better partnership with Operations with a more effective first responder triage/runbook partnership and pervasive monitoring. They're using peer reviews to self-enforce quality and share lessons. Security is in its infancy but now a part of the dev life cycle. They're also turning away more work or abandoning bad bets in the way they gather requirements, use hypothesis-driven development to walk away from failed features / mistaken assumptions early.

Looking Forward: There was a certain amount of navel-gazing as this book neared completion. Where exactly are we going in a few years? What's the future of the DevOps movement as we stretch into a decade plus of actual hands on practice?

Agile was the hot new thing in the 2000s, which ushered in several development practices and tools that are here to stay – including working in short sprints (the scrum cycle) and more comprehensive use of version control. In the 2010s, DevOps became the new fad du jour, and with it the idea of applying version control and code to infrastructure and more rigorous release management and monitoring tools. It seems likely some new movement will take its place. What will that look like exactly?

We'll be honest here in saying that we began this book with the idea of writing a manifesto for the DevOps age. It didn't take us long to realize that this was a naïve and fundamentally flawed concept. The Agile Manifesto remains a remarkably successful charter document and the principles there remain valid to this day. But we agree with Aaron Bjork of Microsoft when he said that the disciples of Agile have turned it into somewhat of a religion:

> It is so shortsighted to say if you follow these practices following this recipe you'll be successful. I don't allow people to start telling me 'we need to do things Agile.' There's just no such thing. Talk to me about what you want to achieve, the business value you want to drive, and that's our starting point.[1]

Coming up with a list of DevOps Ten Commandments on a stone tablet might help us sell some books, but it'd be repeating the mistake we made with Agile: thinking that one size fits all. It's here that our heritage from the efficiency and process-dominated manufacturing world of the 20th century begins to cost us. It's in our DNA to try to mimic a successful pattern used in a company whose culture we envy, or look for a "best practice" – a proven template to follow step by step. This rigid model simply does not fit in the more fluid and creative world of software development and services delivery. As Bob Lewis so famously said, there are no best practices – only a better one than we had yesterday.[2]

One of the companies we think is a success story in process is Micron. The task ahead of them is vastly different and in many ways more complex than the ones the Microsoft engineering teams faced; security, the isolated nature of large chip manufacturing plants, and the rigid and horrendously expensive tooling and hardware being instrumented means a more complex operating environment and a need for wise, conservative bets. They are already showing signs of success in the same way that Ben demonstrated at WonderTek:

---

[1] Interview of Aaron Bjork by Dave Harrison, see Appendix.
[2] "Project Management Non-Best-Practices," Bob Lewis. InfoWorld, 9/26/2006. www.infoworld.com/article/2636977/techology-business/project-management-non-best-practices.html.

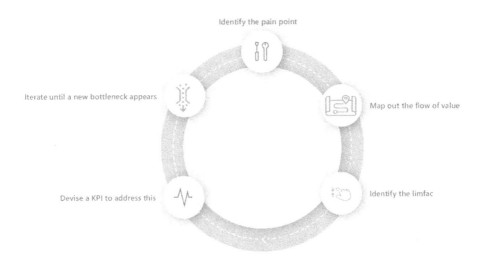

Identify the pain point

Iterate until a new bottleneck appears

Map out the flow of value

Devise a KPI to address this

Identify the limfac

Nothing innovative or flashy here; this is Theory of Constraints 101 type stuff. First, the release cycle is mapped out from idea to product. This leads to an inefficiency being exposed in the pipeline. A metric or KPI is found that exposes that problem. Once everyone understands and agrees with this assessment, it's displayed and tracked on monitors, and different improvements are tried until that KPI is no longer the bottleneck. At that point, we move on to the next weak point in the workstream.

In a company like Micron, this has to be done hundreds of times as the ecology is complex; there are dozens of products and services to support. Remembering our limited capacity for change, Micron is treating this as an evolutionary (vs. revolutionary!) process, one workstream at a time.

We have no crystal ball and won't attempt to play Gypsy foreteller. No one in 2005 could have seen the massive paradigm shift that would be sparked just 3 years later by a few presentations coining this new word "DevOps." It's clear from history that the phrase and movement itself began almost by accident. It also seems likely some new word or movement will be used 10 years from now that will take the spotlight. We believe, just as DevOps built on the principles of Lean, Agile, XP Programming, and other movements that came before, that any new movement will follow the same four-step dance we see taking place at Micron: make the work visible, expose the limiting factor, work to reduce or eliminate it, and iterate.

It doesn't take much foresight to see certain trends continue in their rise. Teams that are guided by the same principles we see in the human body – autonomous, cellular, small-sized, and governed by a central "nervous system" that determines mission and purpose – will become more dominant, as will flatter hierarchies that are more responsive and adaptable to change and less susceptible to the toxic effects of divisional level competition. Microservices and the tools and practices that complement it, including containerization and cloud-based templated environments that are easy to build and replace, will continue to grow in usage. Perhaps most exciting, the tools and monitoring capabilities that allow us to listen to our customers, recover faster from failure, and justify our bets will make quantum leaps in power and flexibility.

In a world that seems increasingly fragmented, selfish, and conflict oriented, the DevOps movement represents a kind of backlash of almost spiritual idealism; how can we get people to work together for the common good? The software may change, but the qualities we've discussed in this book will remain timeless: humility, progressive learning, inclusion, honesty, service-based leadership. Our respect for others shows in the care we take in exposing waste and toil, and the amount of effort we are willing to invest into eliminating waste through automation and better collaboration.

This spirituality is part of the fabric of DevOps, and it's impossible to escape it. There's elements of Zen here as embodied with the shoshin or "beginner's mind" principle, in having an open mind eager to learn new things and a lack of preconceptions. And there's also aspects of the sacredness of work, as Martin Luther King Jr was referring to in his quote beginning this chapter. As wise King Solomon said thousands of years ago:

> So I perceived there is nothing better than for people to enjoy their work, because that is their reward; for who can show them what the future holds?[3]

That inborn, spiritual need to enjoy our work is what sparked this movement – whatever we choose to call it down the road. We believe this very human-based inherent need will become more vital and important in the decades ahead. Enterprises that empower their teams and allow people the freedom to innovate, create, and improve in the way they do work will continue to flourish.

Let's close with some thoughts from the Micron story. Our discussions with their architectural team were very revealing. John Weers, the Senior Manager of DevOps at Micron, told us the following:

> We're starting to realize that software development isn't the same as manufacturing. There are definitely some principles that are shared with manufacturing but it's a different beast. In manufacturing we build identical things. In software, we never build the same thing twice. When

---

[3]New English Translation of Ecclesiastes 3:22. NET Bible Noteless, Kindle edition, 8/26/2005. ASIN: B0010XIA8K.

we try to approach software development through a manufacturing lens, we limit ourselves. The effective ones of us will realize that there is no "best practice", only "better practices" – and they change. What works effectively depends on the software, its criticality, its technical debt, its lifetime, your team, their leader, and their interrelationships. The only people capable of identifying a practice that works well for a team, is the team itself.

At the end of the day it just depends. Because it always depends. Each team is different. People are different. Leaders are different. Technology is different. Companies are different.

That being said, I think these principles are the ones that will guide the winners over the next decade.

Success comes from:

- Small teams that build deep relationships and determine how they work.

- We strive to serve our customers and not just sell or deliver to them.

- We don't take ourselves too seriously, because we all have much to learn.

- We take care of ourselves like we take care of our customers.

- We balance life with work and we strive to live authentically and wholly.

- Whenever possible we have more people contribute to finding a solution than less.

- We don't cheat safety, quality or security for shorter term gains.

- Whenever possible, we choose to learn and experiment and make mistakes, because in the making of mistakes we learn the most.

- We learn that people are more important than work. Our families are more important than work.

Life is about relationships: loving God, loving each other, loving our families.

You only have the one life to live, make sure to spend it on what's important.

Now... Go and be marvelous.

Interviews and Case Studies

When we first started writing this book, we were confident that we had a solid collection of original and brilliant thoughts. It didn't take us long to figure out that some of those ideas were neither original nor brilliant! Thankfully, to the rescue came this great community of fellow practitioners, who gave of their time and experience in interviews and helped us with revisions.

We're in their debt for keeping us honest and on track; it gives this book a depth and perspective that was badly needed. We asked them a variety of questions around DevOps and their views on continuous delivery and what they've seen work best. These experts came from a variety of companies and backgrounds:

- Aaron Bjork, Microsoft
- Anne Steiner, cPrime
- Betsy Byer and Stephen Thorne, Google
- Brian Blackman, Microsoft
- John-Daniel Trask, Raygun
- John Weers, Micron

D. Harrison and K. Lively, *Achieving DevOps*,
https://doi.org/10.1007/978-1-4842-4388-6_9

- Jon Cwiak, Humana
- Michael Goetz, Chef
- Michael Stahnke, Puppet
- Munil Shah, Microsoft
- Nathen Harvey, Chef
- Nigel Kersten, Puppet
- Rob England, The IT Skeptic
- Ryan Comingdeer, Five Talent
- Sam Guckenheimer, Microsoft
- Seth Vargo, Google
- Tyler Hardison, Redhawk Network Security

We did have to trim these down for publication. If you're interested in the complete interview transcripts, please check out Dave's web site, www. driftboatdave.com.

Aaron Bjork, Microsoft

Aaron Bjork is a Principal Group Program Manager at Microsoft working on Azure DevOps Services. He leads all investments in work management, agile project management, reporting, dashboards, and collaboration. Aaron is a 16-year Microsoft veteran who has spent his career building tools to promote and encourage team productivity. Aaron is a recognized Agile thought leader and speaks regularly with companies around the world on how to improve their software engineering practices and culture. When he's not writing code, you'll find Aaron doing projects with his family on their hobby farm or working to lower his handicap on the golf course.

Lessons for Your Roadmap

- *Dance to the same beat. Every team needs to be on the same cadence*

- *You can't cheat shipping. The end of every sprint means a release to production*

- *Each team owns their features as a product – and rotate your livesite support*

- *Feature flags and canary releases are the secret sauce with CI/CD.*

- *Have a "team of teams" meeting to resolve cross team dependencies*

- *Use a "bug cap" to pin down your technical debt and force quality*

- *Use a scorecard – but be selective about what you choose to measure!*

Agile Is Not a Religion

Agile is a culture more than anything else, but – I'm going to be frank – too many people have turned it into a religion, a stone tablet with a bunch of "thou shalts" on it. Some organizations we've worked with bring in multiple rounds of expensive consultants and agile trainers, and they're given an audit: "Oh, you're not doing DSU's, your sprint planning meeting doesn't have the right amount of ceremony, blah blah."

This makes me a laugh. Do I think daily standups are good practice? Yes, I do. But I'm not going to measure a team's efficiency by these things. If the team is struggling producing business value, then we might bring in some of these practices. But it is so shortsighted to say if you follow these practices following this recipe, you'll be successful.

I don't allow people to start telling me "we need to do things Agile." There's just no such thing. Talk to me about what you want to achieve, the business value you want to drive, and that's our starting point.

Just because you have a daily standup doesn't mean you're making the right decisions. Just because you're using containers or adopted microservices doesn't mean you're doing DevOps. Maybe, you're better set up to do Agile or DevOps because of these tools, but nothing really has changed. Agile is very simple and beautiful as a mindset – we are going to deploy as frequently as we can. Too often, we turn it into a set of rules you have to follow.

If you think about it, Agile software books started appearing on the market about 10–15 years ago. That's a different era, when we bought shrink-wrapped packages, vs. delivering software with a single click. The rules have changed since then – but we have a lot of agile zealots out there preaching that same old way it was done 15 years ago. Frankly, often I find they've lost touch with how it's actually done in the real world.

Four Keys to Success

I just want to stress that you can't follow what we did on the Azure DevOps team like a prescription. There's not another product in the world like ours; it would be foolish for me to say, you should exactly do it our way.

That being said, I do see some common elements in teams that successfully make the jump with DevOps:

1. Have a single cadence across all your teams.
2. Ship at the end of each and every sprint.
3. Same-size your teams.
4. Have each team own their features as a product.

In more detail:

- **Have a single cadence across all your teams.** I haven't seen a single place yet where that won't apply. Your teams within that cadence can have significant freedom and autonomy, but we want everyone to be dancing to the same beat.

- **Ship at the end of each and every sprint.** The saying we live by goes – "You can't cheat shipping." If you deliver working software to your users at the end of every iteration, you'll learn what it takes to do that and which pieces you'll need to automate. If you don't ship at the end of each iteration, human nature kicks in and we start to delay, to procrastinate. Shipping at the end of a sprint is comfy and righteous and produces the right behaviors. We started to deploy at the end of every 3 weeks instead of twice a year.

- **Same-size your teams.** Every Azure DevOps program team has a consistent size and shape – about 8–12 people, working across the stack all the way to production support. This helps not just with delivering value faster in incremental sizes, but gives us a common taxonomy so we can work across teams at scale. Whenever we break that rule – teams that are smaller than that, or bloat out to 20 people for example – we start to see antipatterns crop up; resource horse-trading and things like that. I love the "two pizza rule" at Amazon; there's no reason not to use that approach, ever.

- **Have each team own their features as a product.** Our teams own their features in production. If you start having siloed support or operations teams running things in production, almost immediately you start to see disruption in continuity and other bad behaviors. It doesn't motivate people to ship quality and deliver end-to-end capabilities to users; instead it becomes a "not it" game.

How We Handle Production Support

In handling support, our teams each sprint are broken up into an "F" and an "L" team. The F team is focused on new features; the L team is focused on disruptions and life cycle. We rotate these people, so every sprint a different pair of engineers are handling bugfixes and interruptions, and the other ten new feature work. This helps people schedule their lives when they're on call.

Our teams own features in production – we hire engineers who write code, test code, deploy code, and support code. In the end, that's DevOps. Now our folks have a relationship with the people handling support – they have to. If you start with that setup – the rest falls into place. If you have separate groups, each responsible for a piece of the puzzle – that's a recipe for not succeeding, in my view.

Other Changes

We've gone through a big movement in the past few years where we took our entire test bed (see *the Munil Shah interview later in this book*), which was largely automated UI focused, and flipped it on its head. Now, we are running much fewer automated UI tests and a ton of what we call L1 and L2 tests, which are essentially unit tests at the lowest levels checking components and end-to-end capabilities. This allows us to run through our test cycle much faster, like every commit. I think you still have to do some level of acceptance testing; just determine what level works for your software base and helps drive quality.

Another thing was, we moved everyone into the same building and reporting up to the same structure/org. The folks that run our ops are a part of our leadership team just like our engineering and program management team – all under the same umbrella. This started getting everyone bought into shared goals we have. We have monthly business reviews, where we talk about more than just the technical goals, but rather financial, operations, bug health, not just code.

This helps us align on the same goal, bringing people into same umbrella so we are invested in the other side, if you will.

Pair programming is accepted widely as a best practice; it's also a culture that shapes how we write code. The interesting thing here is we don't mandate pair programming. We do teach it; some of our teams have embraced pair programming, and it works great for them, always writing in tandem. Other teams have tried it, and it just hasn't fit. We do enforce consistency on some things across our 40 different teams; others we let the team decide. Pair programming and XP practices are one thing we leave up to the devs; we treat them as adults and don't shove one way of thinking down their throats.

Again, this isn't a prescription, but here's an overview of what our process and organization for the Azure DevOps product looked like, before and after our transformation:

Before	After
4–6 month milestones	3-week sprints
Horizontal teams	Vertical teams
Personal offices	Team rooms
Long planning cycles	Continual planning and learning
PM, Dev, Test roles	PM, Engineering roles
Yearly customer engagement	Continual customer engagement
Feature branches	Everyone in master
20+ person teams	8–12 person teams
Secret roadmap	Publicly shared roadmap
Bug debt	Zero debt
100-page spec documents	Specs in PowerPoint
Private repositories	Open source
Deep organizational hierarchy	Flattened org hierarchy
Success measured by install numbers	User satisfaction defines success
Features shipped once a year	Features shipped every sprint

Fighting Long Integration Cycles

Branching is similar, where we don't have long-lived branches at all. We do have a release branch; our engineers check out their work from mainline though, and they check in their short-lived branches direct to main. In general, I'd say people are checking their changes into their user branch every day;

every other day, they submit a pull request to integrate their user branch back to main. The team handles all merge issues internally; everything is validated that it works before its checked in.

When I think about how we handle releases, a couple things come to mind. First, we want to minimize the time that any code is written is in isolation. We used to have the mindset – at beginning of each sprint, teams would check their code into a feature branch and then integrate back at end of sprint. The problem with this is, the longer you stay away from master, the harder it is to integrate and you pay a massive tax with merge issues. We want to check into master continuously, that's a very important construct for us. Second, we wanted to get into mindset that when a feature is ready, it's easy to put it into production. Instead of the idea that we will put a new feature into production when its 100% ready, move to where the feature is ALWAYS being put into prod. We were trying to get out of engineering mechanics – something we were constantly having to manage, where I felt it should be more a consistent, without thinking kind of mechanical movement. Now, our mechanics are the same whether something is a bug, a critsit incident or a new feature – and we do it without thinking. Getting to that model and think that way required some change – but now, we're always writing code, always deploying code. Feature flags were a big help to us where we felt like we can turn on access to a new feature when we're ready – it's safe, controlled.

Another big help to us is a kind of team of teams meeting, which we have once every sprint. This is not a "get everybody in the room" type of meeting, but its very focused, about four to six people in the room, each representing their team. We don't talk about what we're doing now, but what we're working on three sprints ahead. It always amazes me how many "A-Ha!" moments we have during these meetings. It really helps expose points of dependency that we weren't aware of; "Hmm, we should probably synch up and make sure we have a shared point of view." In my view, this is very agile; it's lightweight, just enough to accomplish the purpose.

Metrics and the Bug Cap

We do track one metric that is very telling – the number of defects a team has. We call this the bug cap. You just take the number of engineers and multiply it by 4 – so if your team has ten engineers, your bug cap is 40. We operate under a simple rule – if your bug count is above this bug cap, then in the next sprint you need to slow down and pay down that debt. This helps us fight the tendency to let technical debt pile up and be a boat anchor you're dragging everywhere and having to fight against. With continuous delivery, you just can't let that debt creep up on you like that. We have no dedicated time to work on debt – but we do monitor the bug cap and let each team manage it as they see best. I check this number all the time, and if we see that number go above the limit, we have a discussion and find out if there's a valid reason for that debt pileup and what the plan is to remedy. Here, we don't allow any team to accrue a significant debt, but we pay it off like you would a credit card – instead of making the minimum payment though we're paying off the majority of the balance, every pay period. It's often not realistic to say "Zero bugs" – some defects may just not be that urgent or shouldn't come ahead of a hot new feature work in priority. This allows us to keep technical debt to reasonable number and still focus on delivering new capabilities.

We have an engineering scorecard that's visible to everyone, but we're very careful about what we put on that. Our measurements are very carefully chosen, and we don't give teams 20 things to work on – that's overwhelming. With every metric that you start to measure, you're going to get a behavior – and maybe some bad ones you weren't expecting. We see a lot of companies trying to track and improve everything, which seems to be overburdening teams – no one wants to see a scorecard with 20 red buttons on it!

Anne Steiner, Cprime

Anne Steiner is the Vice President of Product Agility for Cprime. In her role, Anne sets up cross-team discovery cadences, scales product thinking in large organizations, and teaches and mentors stakeholders in leadership and product roles. Anne and her team have helped companies of all shapes and sizes to transform from traditional, project-thinking to become product-driven organizations that emphasize continuous learning. She also actively promotes building communities of practitioners in the Minneapolis/St. Paul area and frequently speaks at national and regional events. She served in the United States Marine Corps as a logistics/embarkation non-commissioned officer in the early 2000s.

Lessons for Your Roadmap

- *Have one mission. Make sure everyone understands how their work connects to that single mission.*

- *Frame the mission and intent with any new project – and allow the team to find the best solution*

- *Start your pilot with a small team and an engaged leader.*

- *There is no one recipe for success. Adapt, improvise, and overcome!*

The Military's Approach to Orders and Requirements

People think of the military as hierarchical, rigid – but in my experience the military is incredibly flexible and dynamic. It has to be to survive in war, and war is becoming more dynamic. Decision-making keeps getting pushed down to lower and lower levels.

Just for example, look how we start with boot camp. It starts with dehumanization – with the goal of teaching people that we are all the same; nobody's special. We take away your clothes; if you're a guy, we shave off your hair. Then, we teach the lesson – you do everything as a team. The USMC sets up tasks that are impossible to complete in the time allowed alone. For example, the beds are so close together that if you're asked to make a bed – your rack mate has to help you with one side of the lower bunk, and then you help her with your side of her bunk. The lesson is, nobody succeeds alone – in boot camp, you can be perfectly right and still get screamed at. I remember once, I made my bed perfectly; the corners were good, and I still got screamed at because I had known what needed to be done and I didn't help my teammate. The whole process is to drill into your head – this is your family now – you must succeed as a team.

Besides shared values, the concept of how orders are delivered in the military has some application to DevOps. In the military, there's a separation of concerns between the officers who give orders and the enlisted people who carry them out – similar to the division between team members and management. These two groups have very different points of view and misunderstandings or conflicts could hamper an operation or cost lives. To address this – nothing significant happens without a written order describing the commander's intent. It's a standard five-paragraph order that follows the SMEAC format – Situation, Mission, Execution, Administration, and Communication.

Now, the military doesn't expect its people to document every possible scenario or to follow the words in the order blindly – because we need our people to make independent decisions autonomously as the situation ultimately changes mid-operation. So, we don't fill in all the details but provide the high-level intent. The order describes what the commander wants to accomplish, the overall goals, and the time frame – you are following orders as long as you're following the intent and haven't violated some other direction provided. At Cprime, we do the same thing, where we teach product teams something called collaborative framing. That describes what we're doing, why we're doing it, and who we are doing it for. That's pretty similar to the way orders are used in the Marines – the orders provide the high-level strategy and context, and people are allowed to fill in the implementation details later.

I wish this happened more often in the development world. We shouldn't feel like we have to spoon feed everything to dev teams with detailed requirements – what if we just gave them the intent? We could define the operating requirements, the business goals, and allow them to figure out how to solve the problem.

You want to be told why. A lot of times we aren't told "why," just "what" as developers. That's what surprised me about the military – there was never a leader that I worked with that I couldn't ask why, in a respectful manner, and be given context. That helps you understand the mission. It always surprised me how open leadership was to questions about orders.

Now I should say – orders aren't open to question or debate all the time. Sometimes in a crunch we need orders to be followed without question; but that's actually not the norm, contrary to what most people think.

Keys to Success

What separates out the successful orgs? I find three traits winning organizations have in common:

1. Bold leadership that's willing to take risks

2. A culture of agility and learning

3. Starting with a small success story

DevOps culture changes obviously come easier with smaller companies; in larger orgs, you have to find a pocket where it's okay to experiment or where a bold leader can nurture and shelter an effort. Once you get to that point where you can start telling stories – we hit this obstacle, and here we hit some snags, but look at these results – that's where you start to see culture change. You can't just come in the door and say "We're going to take risks and become a learning org!", because you haven't proven yourself yet. I'm always looking for that right kind of leadership protection, a willingness to experiment, and a group that wants to learn and try something different. That's your beachhead!

One of the key factors I see in many successful organizations with their DevOps transformations is to have a legitimate set of shared measures, a shared mission. In the USMC, we have a standard mission – to make Marines, and to win battles. That's the single mission, and if something in the orders doesn't relate to that directly – we throw it out. In the software world, it's not that simple. Every product has a vision, every company has a mission statement. But how many can articulate that simply?

Netflix does a great job with a shared mission for example – their shared goals are to retain subscriptions and to increase subscriptions. Whatever you do needs to be aligned against one of these.

Can you prove that your project aligns against that? Otherwise, you'll see antipatterns like IT teams saying we have 100% uptime. Yeah, that's great, but you've got a crappy product and your customers are unhappy. That's not product thinking, a clear common goal that everyone can rally around.

Flexibility and Innovation

There's a lot of people out there writing books on Agile, and quite a few are well written. But if you slam it on the table, it's not going to work like it says in the book. Then what are you going to do? The teams that are successful are the ones that can implement this or better yet the parts of it that they think will add value, fail, modify it to their situation, and win anyway. That's one of the things I love about the way the Agile Manifesto was written, because it is principle based. We see a lot of organizations struggle because they bring in some "expert" who comes in with a checklist and says, no, you're not doing scrum unless you're doing these things. Well, who cares, as long as you're delivering awesome products?

As a culture, the USMC takes as a point of pride that it is always asked to do more with less – to us, that "Adapt, Improvise and Overcome" mantra is a real point of pride. I think it comes in part from how we were founded. The Marine Corps has the smallest budget of the branches. There's not a lot of money flowing through the organization. So that helps us – we realize, no matter what happens, it's probably not going to work the first time – we'll adapt and change. Traditionally, we think in the software world that change is bad, we have to limit it, a risk. Well, change is inevitable, we should expect it – and win even if we have to come up with a new solution on the fly.

Betsy Beyer, Stephen Thorne, Google

Betsy is a Technical Writer for Google in NYC specializing in Site Reliability Engineering. She co-authored the books Site Reliability Engineering: How Google Runs Production Systems *and* The Site Reliability Workbook: Practical Ways to Implement SRE. *She has previously written documentation for Google's Data Center and Hardware Operations Teams in Mountain View and across its globally distributed data centers.*

Stephen is a Site Reliability Engineer in Google's London office. The book The Site Reliability Workbook: Practical Ways to Implement SRE, *which he co-authored, drew from his work introducing SRE practices to Google customers on the Customer Reliability Engineering Team. He has been an SRE at Google since 2011 and has previously worked on Google Ads and Google App Engine.*

Lessons for Your Roadmap

- *A good SRE knows when to hit the brakes, and when to go for it and speed up the pace of releases.*

- *An explicit, written Error Budget agreed upon with your stakeholders is the foundation of good availability.*

- *Pick out only the most important items for remediation from your postmortems; management must keep these visible so they're followed through on to completion.*

- *The more dev ownership of production you can get, the more you'll be able to sustainably support production.*

- *Cross pollinate knowledge so SRE's don't become just another silo.*

- *Practicing for failure is vital; at Google they do this in part through open labs called "Wheel of Misfortune" that helps spread troubleshooting/triage best practices.*

- *Reducing toil should be a key focus; you can't do that if you aren't tracking the time spent on repetitive tasks ripe for automation.*

How SRE Relates to DevOps

Do we see Site Reliability Engineering (SRE) as the future of DevOps? Definitely not. DevOps is really a broad set of principles and practices; SRE is a very specific implementation of those principles and practices. The two are not mutually exclusive. You can look at all these DevOps principles and achieve it by applying SRE.

Applying SRE Principles

In the book *Accelerate*, the authors separated out four key metrics that make for a successful team: lead time, MTTR, batch size, and change success rate. All of these metrics boil down to continuous delivery – how quickly can we make changes, and how fast can we recover when things go awry?

But we look too much at this desired outcome – we're releasing very often, with a low rate of failure – and sometimes lose sight of how we get there. It's that implementation space where SRE fills a gap. Applying SRE principles is like having a brake on the car; we can say, "Hey, there's a corner coming up; slow down and let's handle this safely." We'll go slow and steady for a bit, then speed up once we're on better ground.

We commonly hear people say, "Oh, SRE works for you, because you're Google – a massive, web-native company." But there are SRE approaches you can do at any size of company, even without a dedicated SRE team. There are some patterns and principles we wanted to stress, which is why we wrote both SRE books – particularly around how to manage and embrace risk, and how to establish a balanced SLO and an error budget policy. These things are fundamental to a well-running SRE team, and it's something your customers need.

Two Modes of Development

SREs don't take direct responsibility for releases, and our job isn't just to be a brake on development. In fact, we operate in two modes. The first mode is if a system is consistently within its error SLO and not consuming enough of its error budget – that's actually hampering our innovation. So, SRE should be advocating for increasing the speed of the pipeline – indeed, taking more risks. Congratulations, we're in that sweet spot that DevOps is aiming for, low friction releases. We are a well-performing team.

But the second mode is often the default mode: that mode is the opposite of stepping on the gas – the ability to slow down. If a system is constantly running out of error budget, then we need to slow down new feature releases and instead invest development effort into making the system more stable and reliable. The rate of failure is simply too high; it's not sustainable. We have to do whatever it takes to make the system more reliable, and not defer this work as debt. That's the fourth attribute we want with SRE (and promised by DevOps) – a low rate of failures in our production releases.

Error Budgets

One of the most frequent questions we got after publishing our first book had to do with forming an error budget policy. It's actually a concept that's pretty easy to apply at other organizations.

You can't get away from the fact that when it comes to instability, releases are one of the primary causes. If we stop or gate releases, the chance of a release causing a problem goes way down. If things are going fine, it's the SRE's job to call out that we're being TOO reliable – let's take more risks. And then, when we've run out of error budget, we want to have a policy agreed upon in advance so we can slow down the train.

We've seen this error policy take a number of different shapes. At one company we engaged with that's very Agile-focused, when they know a system isn't meeting customer expectations, developers can only pull items off the backlog if they're marked as a postmortem action item. Another company uses pair programming a lot. So, during that error budget overage period – the second mode – they mandate that one pair must be devoted purely to reliability improvements.

Now, that's not how we do it at Google – but it's totally effective. We see companies like Atlassian, IBM, and VMware all using error budgets and talking about it in public forums. One thing is for sure though: this policy needs to be explicit, in writing, agreed upon in advance – and supported by management. It's so, SO important to have this discussion before you have the incident.

Business stakeholders and execs sometimes fight for zero downtime – 100% availability. So, let's say you're a mobile gaming platform. Any downtime for you means money lost and perhaps customers out the door. So, how are you going to get to 100% reliability? Your customers aren't getting 99.9% reliability out of their phones. How are you going to fix that? Once you point out that people won't even notice a small amount of downtime in all likelihood, you end up with a financial argument, which has an obvious answer. I can spend millions of dollars for nearly no noticeable result, or accept a more reasonable availability SLO and save that money and stress in trying to attain perfection.

A competent SRE embraces risk. Our goal is not to slow down or stop releases. It's really about safety, not stability just for its own sake. Going back to that car analogy: if your goal is 100%, then the only thing we can do is jam on the brakes, immediately. That's a terrible approach to driving if you think about it – it's not getting you where you need to be. As difficult as it is to think about, even pacemaker companies cannot be 100% defect free; they have a documented, acknowledged failure rate. It might be one in 100M pacemakers that fail, but it still happens, and that 99.9999% success rate is still the number they strive for. What matters in these critical cases is not to achieve perfection, but to understand what failures will occur and have a plan for responding when they do.

Blameless Postmortems

It's counterproductive to blame other people, as doing so ends up hiding the truth. And it's not just blaming people – it's too easy sometimes to blame systems. This habit is emotional – it gives us a warm fuzzy feeling to come up with one pat answer. But at that point, we stop listing all the other factors that could have contributed to the problem.

We don't perform postmortems for each and every incident at Google – only when we think it has a root cause that's identifiable, and that it could be applicable to other outages – something we can actually learn from. We're very careful not to make never-ending lists of everything that can go wrong, and to pick out the really important things that need to be addressed. And your action items need to be balanced. Some should be comprehensive, some should be structural, some should be short-term fixes, and they can't all be red hot in priority. Let's say you have a lower priority action item that would need to be done by another team, for example. You might legitimately want to defer on that, instead of wasting political capital trying to drop work on other teams outside your direct control.

It's vitally important to keep postmortems on the radar of your senior leadership. We have a daily standup meeting in one area here at Google, where management looks over anything that's happened in the past few days. We go through each postmortem, people present on the issue and the follow-up items they've identified, and management weighs in and provides feedback. This makes sure that the really important fixes are tracked through to completion.

SRE Antipatterns

The magical title change is something that crops up quite often. For example, you know how sometimes developers are given a book or sent to a training class, and then a month later they're labeled as "Agile"? That same thing happens in the SRE world. Sometimes, we see companies taking sysadmins, changing one or two superficial things, and labeling them "DevOps Engineers" or some other shiny new title. But nothing around them has really changed – incentives haven't changed, and executives have not bought in to making changes that are truly going to be lasting and effective.

Another antipattern is charging ahead without getting that signoff from management. Executive level engagement on the SRE model, especially the part that has teeth – SLOs and Error Budgets – is a critical success/failure indicator. This is how we gauge whether we're in the first working model (we're reliable enough; let's go faster) or in our second working model (customers are suffering; give us the resources we need). A numerical error budget – a target that is agreed upon and very specific consequences that happen when that budget gets violated – needs to be consistently enforced, from the top.

A lot of times we find that it doesn't take a lot of convincing to get executives on board, but you do have to have that conversation. Leaders often have a need to see their company's product as reliable. We talk to them and help them quantify that reliability with metrics rather than just gut feel. We also drive home the fact that once a system becomes unreliable, it can be months or even years until we can bring it back to a reliable state. These are complex systems, and keeping them running smoothly requires constant attention.

Another antipattern that thankfully we don't see too often is where SRE becomes yet another silo – a gatekeeper. It's really important to cross-pollinate knowledge so production knowledge is shared. If just one group controls any and all production or release ownership and jealously guards that privilege, we've failed. So, at Google, we do something called "Mission Control," where developers can join an SRE team for one to two quarters. It's a great way of disseminating knowledge and getting coders to see what it's like on the other side of the fence.

DIRT and Gamedays

We find that it's absolutely vital to practice for failure. Netflix and others obviously have had a lot of success with Simian Army and Chaos Monkey, where SREs are whacking production systems at random to test availability. We use this approach somewhat at Google with our annual DIRT exercises: disaster recovery testing that's company-wide. But locally, we use something less intimidating for newbies and entirely theoretical and very low-key: something we call a Wheel of Misfortune exercise.

Wheel of Misfortune works almost like a Dungeons and Dragons table top game. It's held once a week, and lots of SREs show up at the arena as onlookers because it's fun. There's a gamemaster present, who throws the scenario – something that actually happened, not too long ago – on a whiteboard. An SRE takes on the role of a "player," someone who's handling incident response. As they walk through how they'd handle troubleshooting the incident and debugging, the gamemaster responds with what happens. A lot of times, the gaps come down to documentation – where's the playbook for this system? – and the appropriate training. What information would have helped that support team get to a root cause faster? It's great for the audience, because it's very engaging and collaborative – a great group socialization exercise. We always end up with lots of creative action items that help us down the road.

Production Application Support

We do feel that it's vital that development teams do some kind of production support. We might say that 5% of the production work must be done by developers, but that's really just a generic goal. The real aim here is to break down that palace wall, that silo between developers and operations. Many people assume that at Google every team has SREs, but that's not the case. In fact, our default model is 100% developer-supported services end to end – SREs are really used more for high-profile, public-facing, or mission-critical systems. The more dev ownership of production you can get, the more you'll be able to sustainably support production.

Reducing Toil

Reducing toil is always top of mind for us. Any team tasked with operational work will have some degree of toil – manual, repetitive work. While toil can never be completely eliminated, it can and should be watched carefully. Left unchecked, toil naturally grows over time to consume 100% of a team's resources. So, it's vital to the health of the team to focus relentlessly on tracking and reducing toil. That's not a luxury; it's actually necessary for us to survive.

At Google, we keep a constant eye on that toil/project work dichotomy, and we make sure that toil is capped. We've found that a well-run SRE team should be spending no more than 50% of its time on toil. A poorly run SRE team might end up with 95% toil. That leaves just 5% of time for project work. At that point you're bankrupt – you don't have enough time to drive down your toil or eliminate the things that are causing reliability issues; you're just trying to survive, completely overwhelmed. So, part of that policy you agree upon with your stakeholders must be enforcing that cap on toil, leaving at least half of your capacity for improving the quality of your services. Failing to do that is definitely an antipattern, because it leads to becoming overwhelmed by technical debt.

Brian Blackman, Microsoft

Brian works as a Senior Consultant for Microsoft Premier. As an Azure development and DevOps consultant, he works with Independent Software Vendors (ISV), Enterprises, and Partners where his specialty is DevOps. Brian's focus is assisting customers in establishing a vision for DevOps, assessing where they currently stand, and then working with them to develop a roadmap to attain their vision.

Lessons for Your Roadmap

- *Leaders are comfortable with the challenges that come with open, honest communication*

- *Connect your asks to dollars and the magic word "waste" in talking with execs*

- *Identify a good pilot opportunity and a strong champion for air cover*

- *Use value stream mapping to identify lead time and cycle time as a first step*

- *Spend the time to put together a solid plan everyone can commit to*

- *DevOps and TDD go together like PB&J*

- *The cloud is not a prereq for DevOps – neither is microservices nor container*

- *If it doesn't save money or make money, it's an engineering led exercise – deprioritize in favor of business value-driven features*

What I Learned from the Military

My story – well, I came from the OEM division, that's really hands on – including working with Windows Mobile, Windows for Automotive as a program manager. It was great stuff: very close to the metal, working right with automotive systems from a hardware / software interface point of view. At Microsoft Consulting Services (MCS), I got into SQL Server at a deep level and really buffed up my development side. I started really getting into ALM in 2003; I'd been following Brian Harry for years, even before he joined us at Microsoft and met with him in Raleigh when it was just three people sitting down and talking about what was going to become TFS. I knew ALM was really going to take off with Team System, which was what it was called at this point. I was the first guy who even knew what ALM was when I joined my current team – now, we have a whole stable of people; we can't hire them fast enough it seems.

Before that though I served in the US Army for about 12 years, starting in 1974. I'd just turned 17, and 5 days after my birthday I went into the service. Being a good soldier really comes down to the same qualities it takes to be a good IT person. Just for example, you must have absolute honesty and open communication because lives depend on it. So, I didn't mind a subordinate telling me I was a butthole – hey, maybe he's telling me something I need to hear!

The second thing had to do with that now cliched saying, "Be All You Can Be." There really was nothing to prevent me from being anything I wanted to be, anything the team needed me to be. The military taught me that growth mindset. You really can do anything you want to do – they will pave the way for you to do that.

They instill cross training as a discipline. I went from being an infantryman to a medic, and then to communications. That's learning, and those are the challenges that really get me up in the morning and excited. And it's great for the team. I never could say to someone on my squad, you're light weapons not heavy weapons, so I can't talk to you about radios and communications. Well, what if you lose someone on the team? Somebody needs to take over that slot.

In one training exercise, I was leading the team when we were trying to take a hill – the senior leaders then promptly had me "killed." Now what? That really forces the team to improvise and rely on others. The self-confidence that gives you to find all these abilities you didn't know you had – well, you don't often get that in the private sector.

Common Failure Points with DevOps

The failure points in DevOps that I see, they're exactly the same ones I see with Agile adoption. One of the most common is the lack of planning. One company I'm working with currently is just getting started. But I can already tell they're going to be successful; their executives are committed, they've built a holistic plan much like we did at Microsoft, and they're really committed to growing new skillsets and education. They're going to win because the top leadership is sending a consistent message; other places, the executives are giving it lip service and it's really a grass roots effort; those have a very high failure rate.

A few months back I visited another company that's almost 10 years along in their DevOps effort. My contact is all in, and so is his manager – but that's as far as it goes. The pushback and friction he faces is enormous. I go onsite, share our success stories and those of other companies, and then look at what they're doing and provide feedback. And we've had to be very frank – unless you get executive sponsorship you are going to be spinning your wheels, fighting a lot of resistance to change, which in turn will create waste. Ten years along, and they are still stuck in this very fixed mindset.

That's two companies with very different trajectories, all because of executive buy-in.

Getting Executive Buy-In

To overcome this, I engage with the executives on their level and speak their language – not that of an IT person or a developer. I must use the terms that are key to them. Delivering business value. Delivering more value that causes the customers to buy more, to have them upgrade. To reduce the impact of defects. Showing them how the cost of fixing things early vs after shipping.

We've had decades of studies showing the cost differences in catching defects early in software development and how it equates directly to money. In a way this, is a lot like when we work with executives on the adoption of test-driven development. It's the same problem really: *why are we doing something that looks like it will cost me more money up front?*

You need to present this to them as, you are going to make more money and save more money in the end. You're going to have greater customer loyalty, increased sales, reduce the cost of your bottom lines, drive up your stock price – that's what they want and need to hear.

The number one point that I want to bring out is waste. Executives get this instinctively once you connect your deployment practices with waste. Here's the waste, and if you eliminate this, look as the payoff – that gets you the buy in you needed.

Getting to Lead Time

When we're engaging with a customer, we always start with a value stream analysis. It's really vital to get to the lead time – once a customer gives me a request, how long does it take me to get to it – and cycle time, how long does it take to get that feature into production. Those are always the two metrics we're trying to improve and we keep it top of mind.

But from there it, becomes very client specific. For a team that's been doing things in Agile for a while, our approach is going to be very different than for a team that is still stuck in waterfall. So, we do a two-part assessment; one of their ALM processes and Agile/DevOps maturity, and a second one a more client-specific risk analysis. From that assessment, we start to build out a plan – what we will focus on, what the milestones will look like, and who owns things.

That last point is really key. I want a customer name attached to almost anything; that's a way bigger struggle than getting a company to adopt moving to the cloud. But it's absolutely vital – without clear ownership, the plan isn't going to move forward.

A Fresh Start

Our basic approach with these DevOps roadmaps is to handle things like we do with Agile – we start small, hopefully with a new team and a greenfield project – we get our iterations going, and refactor as we go along. The basic idea is to find a good candidate for a fresh start, you get some traction and momentum built up – and out of this team you assemble some champions, people indoctrinated and totally bought into DevOps as a process.

To change the culture of a large org and get on a DevOps journey, you need champions – then you take those people and infiltrate other teams with them, and spread that success, that new way of doing things, elsewhere.

Plan the Work, Work the Plan

My military background taught me to put a lot of work into building a plan – that's our starting point – and then as things progress, we change the plan and adapt. That's key with these roadmaps – to have the right people, committed, and to have key milestones. When we do our assessments one of the first things that pops up is the people part of things – does everyone have what they need as far of training? The answer is usually no, and it's a lot of work to get everyone on the same page. That could be a milestone by itself – "By the end of April, everyone will have had an opportunity to go through training."

The key point here in planning is not to get bogged down. We're trying to turn the lights on. The more we turn the lights on, the less resistance we are going to face. By this, I mean – transparency, dashboarding, and a key understanding and agreement on where we are, where we want to go, and how we're going to get there. Everyone needs to understand what is the plan and the change that is going to happen, and what is expected from them.

Inevitably, when people hear "plan," they think, "oh you mean project planning." And that's totally not the case! The plan can be verbal, not even written down – but you must have a plan to get there. And it can't be – "let's do DevOps – everybody get there on their own." You have a plan when you're going to work on your car right? Or work with your children. Is it written? No, but you do have a plan. This is not project management. But it is a plan – based on gaps you found in your assessments. Your deliverables could be, teams formed, or everyone trained by X date.

Testing and Automation

Test automation is another common obstacle for most organizations. My first 10 years at Microsoft I would preach until I was blue in the face that you should automate everything, which is possible with a 3-year release cycle. When Agile came around, all that got thrown out the window, and testers got left in the dust. And now with DevOps – you flatten things out, where everyone has the same title – software design engineer. Everyone on the team is a developer regardless of what you do. And testing is now part of the job description of every person on the team.

Nowadays, I no longer say, "You MUST automate EVERYTHING!" – it's just not possible anymore in most cases. You have to figure out where you're going to get the most value from testing and focus on that. With TDD, you're working on a test layer while the development is happening because both those roles are embedded with the team – DevOps and TDD go together like peanut butter and jelly. The cycle is so short now that testing the UI layer and lots of brittle acceptance tests makes almost no sense.

That shift has been a huge challenge for most organizations I visit. We still see siloes where testing is kept separate and code is thrown over the wall – even if the developer and the tester are one cubicle apart. I think there's one team I worked with in Portland that had integrated testing teams with the developers – their code coverage metric was 100%, and they always kept it at that level.

But that's just one company out of the hundreds of companies that I've worked with! Every other customer I've worked with, they box off the testers and keep them separate. And it just doesn't work… Let the deep testers do what they do well – higher level integration level testing and testing in production. For example, with the Azure DevOps program team, with feature flags, we ship with it turned off, then turn on the next sprint, using rings – internal first, then select customers, etc.

Architectural Decision Points

I don't feel like "if you're doing DevOps right you must go to the cloud." I can implement the same thing in my org without the cloud and still be successful. I also don't feel like you need to adopt microservices to be successful. Bold statement here – I don't think DevOps has anything to do with architecture. DevOps can be successful regardless of how you are building your solution.

Just for example, the UI for Visual Studio isn't built as a microservice. But when we build new feature sets, a lot of them are built as microservices for scalability. Microservices are terrific as a model, and it's no different than what we were taught in college when it comes to programming – don't make this behemoth method – make a method that is much smaller, more easily traceable within the code, and more easily changeable. Microservices gives us that and really improves scalability.

The same thing is true with containers, like Docker and Kubernetes. These technologies are great if you can do it as an architectural change – I believe in those solutions, they're fantastic, but there's no way I'm going to take something and rearchitect it just because it's a better solution. Often, we have to drill down and ask – is this a business solution or is it an engineering exercise? Which means is it making us money, or saving us money? If not, whether it's "better" or not, you should drop it.

Feedback and Learning

We talked about flow – another key piece is getting feedback. Most companies simply don't think to implement things to see that they're getting consistent, frequent feedback from customers. In your customer facing apps, do they have a way of providing feedback – a smiley face, or a direct way to call on a new feature? I don't see orgs doing enough around the feedback loop; if they do have a feedback loop its manual, with long delays and full of waste and misinterpretation.

Another short-circuit to the learning process some companies fall into is with analytics. I'm still seeing a lot of people rolling their own analytics. That's ridiculous – they really need to be using a vendor! I don't care who you use, dammit, just use pick one. Trust with one vendor is a key aspect of Deming's teachings. You really can't put enough stress on how important it is to get feedback, more often, more accurately to the people that need it. In Lean Manufacturing, this isn't as big of a deal – you can't change a car platform every month – but in software you can and should be adjusting and changing almost by the day.

The Roots of DevOps

DevOps is a really powerful movement, and people often don't realize how long its roots are. Twenty years ago, we had something called "MSF Mindsets" that had some very simple principles:

- Foster a team of peers
- Focus on business value
- Keep a solution perspective
- Take pride in workmanship
- Learn continuously
- Internalize qualities of service
- Practice good citizenship
- Deliver on your commitments

You know, I still go back to that list of guidelines when I get stuck. In a lot of ways, what we see today in DevOps inherits quite a bit from these simple daily ways of working with others.

John-Daniel Trask, Raygun

John-Daniel Trask is cofounder and CEO of Raygun, a New Zealand-based company that specializes in error, crash, and performance monitoring. John-Daniel (or JD) started out with repairing PCs out of college, to working as a developer, to finally starting several very successful businesses, including what became Mindscape and its very successful monitoring product, Raygun.

Lessons for Your Roadmap

- Real focus on the customer experience is still very rare; using monitoring to reduce the most common errors forces empathy and creates a better performing business.

- DevOps isn't purely about tools, nor is it only about culture. You'll need great process and software to complement the behavior changes you're looking for.

- Use stories and personas to keep a coherent experience and eliminate dead ends, especially those driven purely by perceived technical advantages.

- Engineers need to understand the language of business and put their asks in terms of specifics that matter to the executive layer: cost savings, revenue opportunities, and waste eliminated.

- Think carefully before you roll your own monitoring layer: Does this add value to the business, or create value for the customer?

Is DevOps Culture First?

I definitely run into a lot of zealots who swing one side or another. Some people pound the table and say that DevOps is nothing about tools, that it's all culture and fluffy stuff. These are usually the same people who think a DevOps team is an absolute abomination. Others say it's all about automation and tooling.

Personally, I'm not black and white on it. I don't think you can go and buy DevOps in a box; I also don't think that "as long as we share the same psychology, we've solved DevOps."

Let's take the whole idea of a DevOps team being an antipattern for example. For us it's not that simple – it's very easy, on a 16-person startup, to say that a DevOps team is a horrible idea. Well, of COURSE you'd think that, for you cross team communication is as easy as turning around in your chair! But let's take a larger enterprise, 50,000 people or so, with hundreds of engineering teams. You can't just hand down "we're doing DevOps" as an edict and it's solved.

Far from being an antipattern, I've seen DevOps teams be a very successful as a template, something that helps spread the good word by example and train up individual engineering teams to adopt DevOps. Just to take one example, this worked very well with a top ten-sized software company – it was terrific as a culture incubator.

The Role of Empathy

It's quite shocking how little empathy there is by most software engineers for their actual end users. You would think the stereotypical heads-down programmer would be a dinosaur, last of a dying breed, but it's still a very entrenched mindset.

I sometimes joke that for most software engineers, you can measure their entire world as being the distance from the back of their head to the front of their monitor. There's a lack of awareness and even care about things like software breaking for your users, or a slow loading site. No, what we care about is – how beautiful is this code that I've written, look how cool this algorithm is that I wrote.

We sometimes forget that it all comes down to human beings. If you don't think about that first and foremost, you're really starting off on the wrong leg.

One of the things I like about Amazon is the mechanisms they have to put their people closer to the customer experience. We try to drive that at Raygun too. We often have to drag developers to events where we have a booth. Once they're there, the most amazing thing happens – we have a handful of customers come by and they start sharing about how amazing they think the product is.

You start to see them puff out their chests a little – life is good! And the customers start sharing a few things they'd like to see – and you see the engineers start nodding their heads and thinking a little. We find those engineers come back with a completely different way of solving problems, where they're thinking holistically about the product, about the long-term impact of the changes they're making.

Unfortunately, the default behavior is still to avoid that kind of engagement, it's still out of our comfort zone.

Using Personas to Weed Out Red Herrings

I don't know if we talk enough in our industry about weeding out bad feedback. We often get requests from our customers to do things like dropping a data grid with RegEx on a page. That's the kind of request that comes from the nerdiest of the nerds – and if we were to take that seriously, think of the opportunity cost and what it would do to our own UX!

We weed out requests like this by using personas. For our application, we think in terms of either a CEO, a tech lead, or an operator. Each has their own persona and backstory, and we've thought out their story end to end and how they want to work with our software.

For the CXO level, the VP's, the directors – these are people who understand their whole business hinges on the quality of their software. They need to keep this top of mind at the very top levels of decision-making. For this person, there are graphs and charts showing this strategic level fault and UX information, all ready to drop into reports to the executive board. Then, there's the mid-tier – these are your tech leads, the Director of Engineering – they need to know both high-level strategic 30K foot information, and a summary of key issues. The cutting edge though is that third tier, your developer or operator. This person needs to have information when something goes bump in the night. For them, you have stack traces, profiling raw data, user request waterfalls. Without that information, troubleshooting becomes totally a stab in the dark.

Lots of companies use personas, I know. They're really critical to filter out noise and focus on a clear story that will thrill your true user base.

Using Error Reports to Drive a Better Performing Business

Most of the DevOps literature and thinking I see focuses entirely on build pipelines, platform automation, the deployment story, and that's the end of it. Monitoring and checking your application's real-world performance and correcting faults usually just gets a token mention, very late in the game. But after you deploy, the story is just beginning!

I hate to say this – but I think we're still way behind the times when it comes to having true empathy with our end users. It's surprising how entrenched that mindset of monitoring being an afterthought or a bolt-on can be. Sometimes, we'll meet with customers, and they'll say that they just aren't using any kind of monitoring, that it's not useful for them. And we show them that they're having almost 200,000 errors a day – impacting 25,000 users each day with a bad experience.

It's always a much, much larger number than they were expecting – by a factor of 10 sometimes. Yet somehow, they've decided that this isn't something they should care about. A lot of these companies have great ideas that their customers love – but because the app crashes nonstop, or is flaky, it strangles them. You almost get the thinking that a lot of people would really rather not know how many problems there really are with what they're building.

Yet time and again, we see companies that really care about their customers excel. Let's say I take you back in time to 2008, and I give you $10,000 to invest in any company you want. Are you going to put that into Microsoft, Apple, Google, or Domino's Pizza? Well guess what – Dominos has kicked the butt of all those big tech companies with their market cap growth rate!

The reason why is in the DNA of Domino's – they devote all their attention into ensuring their customers have a great experience. Their online ordering experience is second to none. And that all comes from them being customer obsessive, paying attention to finding where that experience is subpar and fixing it. It's never a coincidence that customer centric companies consistently outperform and dominate.

What's forced us as an industry to change and drive a better user experience is Google, believe it or not. They started publishing a lot of research and data around application errors, performance, and prioritizing well-performing sites. This democratized things that data scientists were just starting to figure out themselves. And it seemed like overnight, a lot of people cared very much that their web site not be dog slow – because otherwise, it wouldn't be on the first page results of a web search, and their sales would tank. But folks often didn't care about performance or the end user experience – until Google forced us to.

What If We're Starting from Square One?

What would I say to the company that is starting from ground zero when it comes to DevOps? I'm picturing here a shop where they take ZIP files and remote desktop onto VM's and copy-paste their deployments. If that's the case – I like to talk about what are the small things you could put into place that would dramatically improve the quality of life on the team. These are big impact, low-cost type improvements. So where would I start?

First would come automating the deployments. Just in reliability alone, that's a huge win. Suddenly, I have real peace of mind. I can roll out releases and roll them back with a single button push, and it's totally repeatable as a process. If I'm an on-call engineer, being able to roll out a patch through a deployment process that runs automatically at 3 a.m. is a world of difference from manually pushing assets.

The second thing I would do is set up some basic metrics with a tool like StatsD. You don't need to allocate a person to spend several days – it's a Friday afternoon kind of thing to start with. When you start tracking something – anything! – and put it up on the wall that's when people start to get religion. We saw this ourselves with our product – once we put up some monitors with some of the things coming from StatsD, like the number of times users were logging in and login failures. And it was like watching an ultrasound monitor of your child. People started gathering around, big smiles on their faces – things were happening, and they felt this connection between what they were doing and their baby, out there in the big bad old world. Right away, some of that empathy gap started to close.

Third would come crash reporting. There's just no excuse not to put this into place – it takes like 10 minutes, and it cuts out all that waste and thrash in troubleshooting and fuels an improvement culture.

Talking Business

What I wish more engineering teams understood is how to communicate in the language of business. I'm not asking developers to get an MBA in their off hours – but please TRY to frame things in terms of dollars, economic impact, or cost to the customer. Instead we say, "this shiny new thing looks like it could be helpful." It's no wonder engineering talent often feel like the business won't allow them to get the tools they want – it's like you're speaking another language to the folks with the check book.

There's a reason why we often have to beg to get our priorities on the table from the business. We haven't earned the trust yet to get "a seat at the table," plain and simple. We tend to be very maxed out, overwhelmed, and we're pretty cavalier with our estimates around development. This reflects technology – which is fast moving, there's so much to learn, and it's not in a stable state. But when engineers hem and haw about their estimates or argue for prioritizing pet projects that are solely tech driven, it makes us look unreliable as a partner in the business. We haven't learned yet to use facts and tie our decisions into saving money or getting an advantage in the market.

Always keep this in mind – any business person can make the leap to dollars. But if you're making an argument and you are talking about code – that's a bridge too far. It's too much to expect them to make that jump from code to customer to dollars. If you tell me you need React 16, that won't sell. But if you say 10% of your customers will have a better experience because of this new feature – any business person can look at that and make the connection, that could be 5,000 customers that are now going to have a better experience. You don't have to be Bill Gates to figure out that's a good move!

Actionable Monitoring Data

Let's get down to brass tacks – how do I make this monitoring data actionable? We wouldn't think about putting planes in the air without a black box – some way of finding out after something goes wrong what happened, and why. That's what crash monitoring is, and it's incredibly actionable. You know the health of your deployment cycle, you can respond faster when changes are introduced that degrade that customer experience.

Message	Last seen	Count	Users
My errors `0` Active `43` Resolved `9` Ignored `0` Permanently ignored			
Script error.	29 minutes ago	51	34
Cannot read property 'length' of undefined	4 hours ago	37	36
ReferenceError: "Hammer" is not defined. (https:/...	2 days ago	2	2
$animatedElements is undefined	4 hours ago	20	16
UET is not defined	6 hours ago	5	3
$(...) is undefined	4 hours ago	18	14
e.element[0].getContext is not a function	3 days ago	10	1
Cannot read property 'LoadQueue' of undefined	15 hours ago	48	41
AJAX Error: error POST /ABTest/Success	17 hours ago	5	5
(9EC0670B-3955-4168-B87A-6449A462DF49)a[0] t...	19 hours ago	2	1

(Above courtesy Raygun Software)

Let's say you are seeing 100,000 errors a month. Once you group them by root cause, that overwhelming blizzard of problems gets cut down to size which is smaller than you'd think. You may have 1000 distinct errors, but only ten actual, honest-to-goodness bugs. Then, you break it down by user, and that's when things really settle out. You might find that one user is using a crappy browser extension that's blocking half your scripts – that isn't an issue really, and not one you can fix for them. But then there's that one error that's happened only 500 times – but it's hitting 250 of your customers. That's a different story! So, you're shifting your conversation already from how many errors you're seeing to the actual number of customers you're impacting – that's a more critical number, and one that everyone from your CEO down understands. And it's actionable. You can – and you should – take those top two or three bugs and drop it right into your dev queue for the next sprint.

This isn't rocket science, and it isn't hard. Reducing technical debt and improving speed is just a matter of listening to what your own application is telling you. By nibbling away on the stuff that impacts your customers the most, you end up with a hyper reliable system and a fantastic experience, the kind that can change the entire game. One company we worked with started to just take the top bug or two off their list every sprint and it was dramatic – in 8 weeks, they reduced the number of impacted customers by 96%!

Think about that – a 96% reduction in 2 months. Real user monitoring, APM, error and crash reporting – this stuff isn't rocket science. But think about how powerful a motivator those kinds of gains are for behavioral change in your company. Data like that is the golden ticket you need to get support from the very top levels of your company.

One of my early mentors was Rod Drury, who founded Xero right here in Wellington, New Zealand. He says all the time: "It's not the big that eat the small, it's the fast that eat the slow." That's what DevOps is about – making your engineering team as reliably fast as possible. To get fast, you have to have a viable monitoring system that you pay close attention to. Monitoring is as close as you can get in this field to scratching your own itch.

Buy vs. Build

What about building vs. buying a monitoring system? I'll admit that I'm biased on the subject, running a SAAS-based monitoring business. But I do find it head-scratching when I talk to people that are trying to build their own. I ask them, "how many people are you putting on this?" And they tell me – oh, four people, say a 6-month project. And then I say, "what are their names?" They look at me funny and ask why – I tell them, "I've had 40 people working on this for 5 years – apparently now I could fire them and hire your people!" Back in 2005, it made total sense to roll your own, since so much of the stuff we use nowadays didn't exist. But the times have changed. Even self-hosting as its issues. Let's say you decide to go down the ELK stack route. Well, that means running a fairly large elastic instance, which is not a set-and-forget type system. It's a pain in the ass to manage, and it's not a trivial effort.

To me, it also is answering the wrong question. There's one question that should be the foundation for any decision an engineering team makes: *does this create value for our customer?* Is our customer magically better off because we made the decision to build our own? I think – for most companies – probably building a robust monitoring system has little or nothing to do with answering that question. It ends up being a distraction, and they spend far more to get less viable information.

Should We Track Everything?

Etsy says "if it moves, track it." Should we track everything, just in case it's needed later? I'm pragmatic on this – if you're small, tracking everything makes sense. Where it goes wrong is where the sheer amount of data clogs our decision-making.

Then, folks start to think about sampling data. However, what I often see is someone sitting in a chair, looking off into the distance and says – "yeah, I think about 10% of the data would give us enough." Rarely do we see them breaking out Excel and talking about what would be *statistically significant* – people tend to make gut calls. Many of us have forgotten statistics, but there is a lot of really great mathematics that help you make better decisions – like calculating what a statistically significant sampling rate might be.

If you're tracking everything you possibly could with real user monitoring for example, it can be a real thicket – a nightmare, there's so many metric streams. You trip over your own shoelaces when something goes wrong – there's just so much detail, you can't find that needle in the haystack quickly. This is where you need *both* aggregate and raw data – to see high-level aggregates and spot trends, but then be able to drill in and find out why something happened at the subatomic level. We still see too many tools out there that offer that great strategic view and it's a dead end – you know something happened, but you can't find out exactly what's wrong.

Closing Thoughts

I never get tired of tying everything back to the customer, to the end user experience. It's so imperative to everything you're doing. There is literally no software written today for any reason other than providing value to humans. Even machine to machine IOT systems are still supporting a human being ultimately.

Human beings are the center of the universe. But you wouldn't know that by the way we're treated by most of the software written for us. Great engineers and great executives grasp that. They know that to humans, the interface is the system – everything else simply does not matter in the end. So, they never let anything get in the way of improving the end user experience.

John Weers, Micron

John Weers is Senior Manager of DevOps and Software Quality at Micron. He works to build highly capable teams that trust each other, build high quality software, deliver value with each sprint, and realize there's more to life than work.

Lessons for Your Roadmap

- *Nobody gets it right the first time and there is no checklist. It takes patience and experimentation*
- *Determine what success means from a business perspective – and eliminate everything else*
- *Quality first, then speed*
- *Use tools as an incentive in selling specific benefits*
- *Matrixed cross-functional teams help avoid siloization in shared service orgs*
- *If it comes easy, it doesn't stick!*

Kickstarting a DevOps Culture

Some initial background – I lead on a team of passionate DevOps engineers/managers who are tasked with making our DevOps transformation work. While our group is only officially about 5 months old, we've all been working this separately for quite a while.

About every 2 weeks, we have a group of about 15 DevOps experts that get together and talk – we call them the "design team." That's a critical touch point for us – we identify some problems in the organization, talk about what might be the best practice for them, and then use that as a base in making recommendations. So, that's how we set up a common direction and coordinate, but we each speak for and report to a different piece of the org. That's a very good thing – I'd be worried if we were a separate group of architects, because then we'd get tuned out as "those DevOps guys." It's a different thing altogether if a recommendation is coming from someone working for the same person you do!

We've made huge strides when it comes to being more of a learning-type organization – which means, are we risk-friendly, do we favor experimentation? When there's a problem, we're starting to focus less on root cause and "how do we prevent this disaster from happening again" – and more on, what did we learn from this? I see teams out there trying new things, experimenting with a new tool for automation – and senior management has responded favorably.

Our movement didn't kick off with a bang. About 5 years ago, we came to the realization that our quality in my area of IT was poor. We knew quality was important but didn't understand how to improve it. Some of the software we were deploying was overly complex and buggy. In another area, the issue wasn't quality but time – the manual test cycle was too long, we're talking weeks for any release.

You can tell we're making progress by listening to people's conversations – it's no longer about testing dates or coverage percentages or how many bugs we found this month, but "how soon can we get this into production?" – most of the fear is gone of a buggy release as we've moved up that quality curve. But it has been a gradual thing. I talked to everyone I could think of at conferences, about their experiences with DevOps. It took a lot of trial and error to find out what works with our organization. No one that I know of has hit on the magical formula right off the bat; it takes patience and a lot of experimentation.

Start with Testing

Our first effort was to target testing – automated testing, in our case using HP's UFT and Quality Center platform. But there never was an all-hands-on-deck, call to "Do DevOps!" – that did happen, but it came 2 years later. We had to lay down the groundwork by focusing first on quality, specifically testing.

We're 5 years along now, and we are making progress, but don't kid yourself that growth or a change in mindset happens overnight. Just the phrase "Shift Left" for example – we did shift our quality work earlier in the development process by moving to unit testing and away from UI/Regression testing. We found that it decreased our bugs in production by a very significant amount.

We went through a few phases – one where we had a small army of contractors doing test automation and regression testing against the UI layer. Quality didn't improve, because of the he-said/she-said type interactions between the developers and QA teams in their different silos. We tried to address interactions between different applications and systems with integration testing, and again found little value. The software was just too complex. Then, we reached a point where we realized the whole dynamic needed to be rethought.

So, we broke up the QA org in its entirety and assigned QA testers on each of our agile teams and said – you guys will sink or swim as a team. Our success with regression testing went up dramatically, once we could write tests along with the software as it was being developed. Once a team is accountable for their quality, they find a way of making it happen.

We got resistance and kickback from the developers, which was a little surprising. There was a lot of complaint when we first started requiring developers to write unit tests along with their code of it not being "value added" type activity. But we knew this was something that was necessary – without unit tests, by the time we knew there was a problem in integration or functional testing, it would often be too late to fix it in time before it went out the door.

So, we held the line, and now those teams that have a comprehensive unit testing suite are seeing very few errors being released to production. At this point, those teams won't give up unit testing because it's so valuable to them.

"Shift Left" doesn't mean throwing out all your integration and regression testing. You still need to do a little testing to make sure the user experience isn't broken. "Shift Left" means test earlier in the process, but in my mind it also means that "our team" owns our quality.

Culture and Energy Are the Limiting Points

If you want to "Do DevOps" as a solo individual, you'll fail. You need other experts around you to share the load and provide ideas and help. A group is stronger than any individual.

Can I say – the tool is not the problem, ever? It's always culture and energy. What I seem to find is, we can make progress in any area that I or another DevOps expert can personally inject some energy into. If I'm visible, if I talk to people, if I can build a compelling storyline – we make rapid progress. Without it, we don't. It's almost like starting a fire – you can't just crumple up some newspaper, dump some kindling on it, light a match and walk away. You've got to tend it, constantly add material, or blow on it to get something going.

We're spread very thin; energy and time are limited, and without injecting energy things just don't happen. That's a very common story – it's not that we're lazy, or bad, or stupid – we work very hard, but there's so much work to be done we can't spare the cycles to look at how we're going about things. Sometimes, you need an outside perspective to provide that new idea, or show a different way.

Lead by Listening

One of the base principles of DevOps is to find your area of pain and devote cycles into automating it. That removes a lot of waste, human defects, errors when you're running a deployment. But that doesn't resonate when I work with a team that's new to DevOps. I don't walk in there with a stone tablet of commandments, "here's what you should do to do DevOps." That's a huge turn-off.

Instead, I start by listening. I talk to each team and ask them how they go about their work, what they do, how they do it. Once we find out how things are working, we can also identify some problems – then we can come in and we can talk about how automation can address that problem in a way that's specific to that team, how DevOps can make their world better. They see a better future and they can go after it.

Tools As an Incentive

I just said the tool isn't the problem, but that doesn't mean it's not a critical part of the solution. I'm a techie at heart, and I like a shiny new tool just as much as the next person. You can use tools as incentives to get new changes rolling. It's a tough sell to walk into a meeting and pitch unit testing as a cure to quality issues if they take a long time to write. But if we talk about using Visual Studio Enterprise and how it makes unit tests simple and it's able to run them real time, now it becomes easier to do unit testing than to test the old way. If we can show how these tools can shrink testing to be an afterthought instead of a week, now we have your attention!

About a year ago, our CIO set a mandate for the entire organization to excel at both DevOps and Agile. But the architecture wasn't defined, no tools were specified. Which is terrific – DevOps and Agile is just a way of improving what we can do for the business. We now see different teams having different tech stacks and some variation in the tools based on what their pain point is and what their customers are needing. As a rule, we encourage alignment where it makes sense around either a technology stack or with a common leader. That provides enough alignment that teams can learn from each other and yet look for better ways of solving their issues.

The rule is that each main group in IT should favor a toolchain but should choose software architecture that fits their business needs. In one area, for example, the focus is on getting changes into production as fast as possible. This is the cutting edge of the blade, so automation and fast turnaround cycles are everything. For them, microservices are a terrific option and the way that their development happens – it fits the business outcomes they want.

Do You Need the Cloud?

They'll tell you that DevOps means the cloud; you can't do it without rapid provisioning which means scalable architecture and massive cloud-based datacenters. But we're almost 100% on-prem. For us, we need to keep our software, especially R&D, privately hosted. That hasn't slowed us down much. It would certainly be more convenient to have cloud-based data centers and rapid provisioning, but it's not required by any means.

Metrics We Care About

We focus on two things – lead time (or cycle time in the industry) and production impact. We want to know the impact in terms of lost opportunity – when the fab slows down or stops because of a change or problem. That resonates very well with management; it's something everyone can understand.

But I tell people to be careful about metrics. It's easy to fall in love with a metric and push it to the point of absurdity! I've done this several times. We've dabbled in tracking defects, bug counts, code coverage, volume of unit testing, number of regression tests – and all of them have a dark side or poor behavior that is encouraged. Just for example, let's say we are tracking and displaying volume of regression tests. Suddenly, rather than creating a single test that makes sense, you start to see tests getting chopped up into dozens of tests with one step in them so the team can hit a volume metric. With bug counts – developers can classify them as misunderstood requirement rather than admitting something was an actual bug. When we went after code coverage, one developer wrote a unit test that would bring the entire module of code under test and ran that as one gigantic block to hit their numbers.

We've decided to keep it simple – we're only going to track these two things – cycle time and production impact – and the teams can talk individually in their retrospectives about how good or bad their quality really is. The team level is also where we can make the most impact on quality.

I've learned a lot about metrics over the years from Bob Lewis' IS Survivor columns. Chief among those lessons is to be very, very careful about the conversation you have with every metric. You should determine what success looks like and then generate a metric that gives you a view of how your team is working. All subsequent conversations should be around "if we're being successful" and not "are we achieving the metric." The worst thing that can happen is that I got what I measured.

PMO Resistance

Sometimes, we see some resistance from the BSA/PM layer. That's usually because we're leading with our left foot – the right way is to talk about outcomes. What if we could get code out the door faster, with a happier team, with less time testing, with less bugs? When we lead with the desired outcome, that middle layer doesn't resist, because we're proposing changes that will make their lives easier.

I can't stress this enough – focus on the business outcomes you're looking for and eliminate everything else. Only pursue a change if the outcome fits one of those business needs.

When we started this quality initiative, initially our release cycle averaged – I wish I was exaggerating – about 300 days. We would invest a huge amount of testing at every site before we would deploy. Today, we have teams with cycle times under 10 days. But that speed couldn't happen unless our quality had gone up. We had to beef up our communication loop with the fab so if there was a problem, we can stop it before it gets replicated.

The Role of Communication

You can't overstate credibility. As we create less and less impact with changes we deploy, our relationship with our customers in the business gets better and better. Just for example, 3 years ago, we had just gone through a disastrous communication tool patch that had grounded an entire site for hours. We worked through the problems internally, and then I came to a plant IT director a year later and told them that we thought the quality issues were taken care of and enlisted their help.

Our next deployment required 5 minutes of downtime and had limited sporadic impact. And that's been the last real impact we've had during software deployment for this tool in almost 3 years – now our deployments are automated and invisible to our users. Slowly building up that credibility and a good reputation for caring about the people you're impacting downstream has been a big part of our effort.

Cross-Functional Teams

It's commonly accepted that for DevOps to work you must be cross-functional. We are like many other companies in that we use a Shared Services model – we have several agile teams that include development, QA roles, an infrastructure team, and Operations which handles trouble tickets from the sites – each with their own leader. This might be a pain point in many companies, but for us it's just how we work. We've learned to collaborate and share the pain so that we're not throwing work over the fence. It's not always perfect, but it's very workable.

For example, in my area every week we have a recap meeting which Ops leads, where they talk about what's been happening in production and work out solutions with the dev managers in the room. In this way, the teams work together and feel each other's pain. We're being successful, and we haven't had to break up the company into fully cross-functional groups.

Purists might object to this – we haven't combined Development and Operations, so can we really say that we are "doing DevOps"? If it would help us drive better business outcomes, that org reshuffling would have happened. But for us, since the focus is on business outcomes, not on who we report to, our collaboration cross team is good and getting better every day. We're all talking the same language, and we didn't have to reshuffle. We're all one team. The point is to focus on the business outcomes, and if you need to reorg, it will be apparent when teams talk about their pain points.

If It Comes Easy, It Doesn't Stick

Circling back to energy – sometimes, I sit in my office and wish that culture was easier to change. It'd be so great if there was a single metric we could align on, or a magical technique where I could flip a switch and everyone would get it and catch fire with enthusiasm. Unfortunately, that silver bullet doesn't exist.

Sometimes, I listen to Dave Ramsey on my way in to work – he talks about changing the family tree and getting out of debt. Something he said though resonated with me – "If it comes easy, it doesn't stick." If DevOps came easy for us, it wouldn't really have the impact on our organization that we need. There's a lot of effort, thought, suffering – pain, really – to get any kind of outcome that's worth having.

As long as you focus on the outcome, I believe DevOps is a fantastic thing for just about any organization. But, if you view it as a recipe that you need to follow, or a checklist – you're on the wrong track already, because you're not thinking about outcomes. If you build from an outcome that will help your business and think backwards to the best way of reaching that outcome – then DevOps is almost guaranteed to work.

Jon Cwiak, Humana Inc

Jon works as an Enterprise Cloud Architect at Humana, where he helps people realize ideas by converting ones and zeros into measurable customer outcomes by helping people do things smarter, cheaper, and faster with tools. He's active in the technology community, including speaking at technical events including NEWDUG, NEWDUG Code Camp, That Conference, TechOnTap, AITP, and many others. Humana is a health solutions company focused on helping people achieve lifelong well-being.

Lessons for Your Roadmap

- *Success means proving you are adding value*
- *Feature toggles add so much to safety – deployment and release are two separate stages*
- *Start with VC, then CI, and auto deployments. Then, move to config management and db deployments*
- *Unit testing is your safety net. Use carrots like easier onboarding to push adoption*
- *Microservices help move the engineering team closer to the customer*
- *Have a yearly DevOps Day for your company*
- *Two metrics to live by – lead time and cycle time. Track and drill down on these constantly*
- *Group accountability and self-policing trump top-down written policies*
- *Selfishness and laziness are actually survival traits!*

Success Means Proving Our Value

I'm an enterprise software architect on our enterprise DevOps enablement team at Humana Inc, a large health insurance company based out of Kentucky. We are in the midst of a translation from the traditional insurance business into what amounts to a software company specializing in wellness and population health.

Our main function is to promote the right practices among our engineering teams. So, I spend a big part of each week reinforcing to groups the need for hygiene – that old cliché about going slow to go fast. Things like branching strategy, version control, configuration management, dependency management – those things aren't sexy but we've got to get it right.

It's been said that software is about two things – building the right thing and building the thing right. My group's mission is all about that second part – we provide the framework, all the tools, platforms, architectural patterns and guidance on how to deliver cheaper, faster, smarter.

Some of our teams though have been doing work in a particular way for 15 years; it's extraordinarily hard to change these indoctrinated patterns. What we are finding is, we succeed if we show we are adding value. Even with these long-standing teams, once they see how a stable release pipeline can eliminate so much repetitive work from their lives, we begin to make some progress.

Crowdsourced DevOps

We are a little different in that there was no trumpet call of "doing DevOps" from on high – instead it was crowdsourced. Over the past 5 years, different teams in the org have independently found a need to deliver products and services to the org at a faster cadence.

The big picture that's changed for us as a company is the realization that doing this big-bang, waterfall, shipping everything in 9 months or more mega-events just doesn't cut it anymore.

We used to do those vast releases – a huge flow of bits like water, we called it a tsunami release. Well, just like with a real tsunami, there's this wave of devastation after the delivery of these large platforms all at once that can take months of cleanup. We've changed from tsunami thinking to ripples with much faster, more frequent releases.

Start with Version Control

When the team first started up in 2012, the first thing we noticed was that everything was manual. And I mean everything – change requests, integration activity, testing. There were lots of handoffs, lots of Conway's Law at work.

So, we started with the basics. For us, that was getting version control right – starting with basic hygiene practices, doing things in ways that decouple you from the way in which the software is being delivered. Just as an example, we used to label releases based on the year, quarter, and month where a release was targeted for. If suddenly a feature wasn't needed – just complete integration hell trying to pull it out. There's lots of merges and drama as we were backing things out.

To address this, we moved toward semantic versioning, where products are versioned regardless of when they're delivered. Since this involved dozens of products and a lot of reorganization, getting version control right took the better part of 6 months for us. But it absolutely was the ground level for us being able to go fast.

Release Management

Next up was fixing the way the devs worked. We had absolutely no confidence in the build process because it was xcopy manual deployments – so there was no visibility, no accountability, and no traceability. This worked great for the developers, but terrible for everyone else having to struggle with "it works on my machine!"

It became obvious that continuous integration was the next rung on the ladder for us, and we started with a real enterprise build server. Getting to a common build system was enormously painful for us; don't kid yourself that it's easy. It exposed, application by application, all the gaps in our version control, a lot of hidden work we had to race to keep ahead of. But once the smoke cleared, we'd eliminated an entire category of work. Now, version control was the source of fact, the build server artifacts were reliable and complete. Finally, we had a repeatable build system that we could trust.

It wasn't magic, and we still struggle at times with long-lived feature branches. It's a recurring pain point for us; we call it the integration credit card. Teams charge to this credit card in rushing out releases, and it inevitably leads to drama at release time, some really long weekends. In a lot of cases, the team knows this is bad practice and they definitely want to avoid it, but because of cross dependencies they're kind of forced into keeping these long-lived branches around.

The other issue is contention, which usually is an architecture issue. We're moving toward a one repo, one build pipeline and decomposing software down to its constituent parts to try to reduce this, but decoupling these artifacts is not an overnight kind of thing.

Configuration Management

The third rung of the ladder was configuration management. It took some bold steps to get our infrastructure under control. Each application had its own unique and beautiful configuration, and no two environments were alike – dev, QA, test, production, they were all different. Trying to figure out where these artifacts were and what the proper source of truth was required a lot of weekends playing "Where's Waldo"!

Introducing practices like configuration transforms gave us confidence we could deploy repeatedly and get the same behavior, and it really helped us enforce some consistency. The movement toward a standardized infrastructure – no snowflakes, everything the same, infrastructure as code – has been a key enabler for fighting the config drift monster.

Using feature toggles changes the way we view change management. We've always viewed delivery as the release of something. Now we can say, the deployment and the release are two different activities. Just because I deploy something doesn't mean it has to be turned on. We used to view releases as a change, which means we needed to manage them as a risk. Feature toggles flips the switch on this where we say, deployments can happen early and often and releases can happen at a different cadence that we can control, safely. What a game-changer that is!

The Resistant Data Layer

The data layer has been one of the later pieces to the puzzle for us. With our move to the cloud, we can't wait for the thumb of approval from a DBA working apart from the team. So, teams are putting their database under version control, building and generating deployable packages through DACPACs or ReadyRoll, and the data layer just becomes another part of the release pipeline.

I think over time that traditional role of the DBA will change, and we'll see each team having a data steward and possibly a database developer; it's still a specialized need, and we need to know when a data type change will cause performance issues for example, but the skillset itself will get federated out.

Working with COTS

COTS products and DevOps totally go together. Think about it from an ERP perspective – where you need to deliver customizations to an ERP system, or Salesforce.com or whatever BI platform you're using. The problem is, these systems weren't designed in most cases to be delivered in an agile fashion. These are all big bang releases, with lots of drama, where any kind of meaningful customization is near taboo because it'll break your next release.

To bridge this gap, we tell people not to change but add – add your capabilities and customizations as a service, and then invoke thru a middleware platform. So, you don't change something that exists, you add new capabilities and point to it.

Lots of vendors are trying to sell DevOps In A Box – buy this product, magic will happen. But they don't like to talk about all the unsexy things that need to be done to make DevOps successful – 4 years to clean up version control, for example. It's kind of a land grab right now with tooling – some of those tools are great in unicorn space but not so well with teams that were using long lived feature branches.

BiModal IT

Gartner's concept of bimodal IT I struggle with, quite frankly. It's true you can't have a one size fits all risk management strategy – you don't want a lightweight web site going through the long review period you might need with a legacy mainframe system of record for example. But the whole concept that you have this bifurcated path of one team moving at this fast pace, and another core system at this glacial pace – that's just a copout I think, an excuse to avoid the modern expectations of platform delivery.

Testing

The big blocker for most organizations seems to be testing. Developers want to move at speed, but the way we test – usually manually – and our lack of investment in automated unit tests creates these long test cycles which in turn spawns these long-lived release branches. The obvious antidote are feature toggles to decouple deployment from delivery.

I gave a talk a few years back called "King Tut Testing" where we used Mike Cohn's testing pyramid to talk about where we should be investing in our testing. We are still in the process of inverting that pyramid – moving away from integration testing and lessening functional testing, and fattening up that unit testing layer. A big part of the journey for us is designing architectures so that they are inherently testable, mockable. I'm more interested in test-driven design than I am in test-driven development personally, because it forces me to think in terms of – how am I going to test this? What are my dependencies, how can I fake or mock them so that the software is verifiable?

The carrot I use in talking about this shift and convincing them to invest in unit testing is, not only is this your safety net, it's a living, breathing definition of what the software does. So, for example, when you get a new person on the team, instead of weeks of manual onboarding, you use the working test harness to introduce them to how the software behaves and give them a comfort level in making modifications safely.

The books don't stress enough how difficult this is. There's just not the ROI to support creating a fully functional set of tests with a brownfield software package in most cases. So, you start with asking, where does this hurt most? – using telemetry or tools like SonarQube. And then you invest in slowing down, then stopping the bleeding.

End-to-End Support

Operations support in many organizations tends to be more about resource utilization and cost accounting – how do I best utilize this support person so he's 100% busy? And we have ticketing systems that create a constant source of work for Operations and activity. The problem with this siloed thinking is that the goal is no longer developing the best software possible and providing useful feedback; it's now closing a ticket as fast as possible. We're shifting that model with our move to microservices to teams that own the product and are responsible for maintaining and supporting it end to end.

Numbers That Matter

There's lots of metrics to choose from, but two metrics stand out – and they're not new or shocking. Lead time and cycle time. Those two are the standard we always fall back on, and the only way we can tell if we're really making progress. They won't tell us where we have constraints, but it does tell us which parts of the org are having problems. We're going after those with every fiber of our effort. There's other line of sight metrics, but those two are dominant in determining how things are going.

We do value stream analysis and map out our cycle time, our wait time, and handoffs. It's an incredibly useful tool in terms of being a bucket of cold water right to the face – it exposes the ridiculous amount of effort being wasted in doing things manually. That exercise has been critical in helping prove why we need to change the way we do things. Its specific, quantitative – people see the numbers and get immediately why waiting 2 weeks for someone to push a button is unacceptable. Until they see the numbers, it always seems to be emotional.

Growing Culture Organically

A DevOps team isn't an antipattern like people say. Centralizing the work is not scalable, that is definitely an antipattern. But I love the mission our team has, enabling other groups to go faster. It's kind of like being a consulting team – architectural guidance and consulting, practices. It's incredibly rewarding to help foster this growing culture within our company; we are seeing this kind of organic center of excellence spring up. Just as an example, every year we do an internal DevOps Day. That's been so great for us in spreading enthusiasm. I highly recommend it.

The subject of the definition of DevOps inevitably comes up. We like Donovan Brown's definition and that's our standard. One of the things I will add is, DevOps is an emergent characteristic. It's not something you buy, not something you do. It's something that emerges from a team when you are doing all the right things behind the scenes, and these practices all work together and support each other.

We're still not there yet when it comes to setting a consistent definition of done, but we're getting there. Giving people 300-page binders, or a checklist, or templated tasks so developers have to check boxes – we've tried them all, and they're just not sustainable.

The model that seems to work is where the team is self-policing, where a continuous review is happening of what other people on the team are doing. That kind of group accountability is so much better than any checklist.

You have to be careful though – it's successful if the culture supports these reviews as a learning opportunity, a public speaking opportunity, a chance to show and tell. In the wrong culture, peer reviews or code demos becomes a kind of group beat-down where we are criticizing and nitpicking other people's investment.

Laziness As a Survival Skill

What I like to tell people is, be like the best developers out there, and be incredibly selfish and lazy. If you're selfish, you invest in yourself – improving your skillset, in the things that will give you a long-term advantage. If you're lazy, you don't want to work harder than you have to. So, you automate things to save yourself time. Learning and automation are two very nice side effects of being lazy and selfish, and it's a great survival trait!

Michael Goetz, Chef

Lessons for Your Roadmap

- *Map the flow of ideas to cut through siloes and get people thinking about business value*

- *Break your work down into much smaller pieces – commit to a true min viable product*

- *It's the middle layer that will make or break your initiatives*

- *Fight against "steamlining" – it's a false efficiency*

- *Real growth comes internally – consultants can't be in the driver's seat*

- *CoE's are great – if they're community driven. Think DevOps Days and weekly open demos*

- *Break down moves to infrastructure as codes into small phases*

- *Resist the allure of purely tech driven initiatives*

DevOps Is an Extension of Agile

My team at Chef is responsible for existing customers – we make sure they're successful both with our software and the underlying transformation they're attempting.

At the end of the day, DevOps is cutting through process and siloization to deliver faster, and only work on things of direct value to the business. Instead of saying "hey, you all need to work together" and do trustfalls or retreats – we get everyone aligned on the same page with what the organization is supposed to be doing. It always stuns me on the level of unpreparedness that exists within most enterprise orgs for trying to do this – even in our second decade of handling agile development.

I always look at DevOps just being an extension of Agile – really its about growing the amoeba of your org wider and wider so everyone is looking at working on a very specific discrete thing that provides value. So, instead of a dev walking by saying, "Hey, I wrote this software and now it needs to be deployed" – now we see, how we build our infrastructure directly impacts the customer experience.

How We Onboard

We try to do a vertical approach. We get brought in by the executive layer that wants us to set up a workshop with their teams. We'll take everyone from individual contributor on up; we require the executive sponsor to attend. We spend a few days working through the basics of product development and obtaining customer value. This is so how they can map how what they do directly impacts customer value.

We spend a lot of time helping them break work into smaller pieces – again that's very agile – but I find many agile teams don't break down work discretely enough. We go through exercises to help them really break down what they're shipping into the smallest possible chunk – a muscle most have never had to exercise. We also use value stream mapping, but we don't call it that; when people hear terms, they haven't heard before they tend to come in with preconceived notions.

The Value of Transparency

One of the biggest failure points I see is that people often don't make their work visible enough. If you don't know what people are working on across the team, that creates a natural siloization which reduces ability to collaborate. Not being completely transparent across the org is one of the biggest pitfalls that I've seen.

Now, what causes that kind of resistance to transparency? Usually, it comes down to org structural alignments and incentives. Most companies out there are operating in a shared services model. That's designed to keep up with demands on a workforce, like a factory line. With this model, the incentives and the things that are a priority for them becomes less about providing value to customers and more about managing the work queue.

There's a little fear there too – many teams aren't sure how efficient they are, and they may not want to lift that rock to see what's scurrying around underneath. There's a little bit of the old "don't look at wizard behind the curtain" – if you're just producing results and no one knows what you are doing, it's very easy to control your destiny and grow your little kingdom with more headcount, more budget. Most director-level people I work with came up in the age of creating an ever-growing team – so that's my career path, my goal is to lead a big army and become a SVP of network operations.

Getting Buy-In from the Middle

The resistance we get comes from a surprising source. It's easy to get buy-in and motivation at the exec level, and usually at the team/individual level. Where things break down is the middle management layer – if you can't get their buy in you are sunk. If you can't get the senior managers to the senior director level buying in and partnering, you are never going to do a DevOps transformation; it'll never happen. The siloes will live on. The message gets so muddied in the middle.

One time I was on this project – they set up a good org structure, they start getting results, people are happy, and the whole thing goes off the rails because the middle management level insists on maintaining the status quo. Now that scaled agile framework is taking off, I sometimes get a little scared that it might run into the same challenges we see with DevOps – you get past the squad level, and things really break down unless you have exec level and middle layer support.

Another common failure point I see is not continuing to feed the innovation appetite of your individual contributors. I've seen a lot of repetitive task IT teams just flourish at first – they go through a big transform effort, they love it, they like their jobs a lot more. Then, it stops. They get some efficiencies, they're able to do some cool new tech – which all of us love – and then after about a year – the company says, we're going to operationalize, make this efficient, which in other words means the learning stops and things get stale. These individual contributors get bored – I want to do new fun stuff, not the old fun stuff – change stalls, and you start getting talent attrition.

Struggling to Scale

So, we covered a few common stumbling blocks – lack of buy-in from middle management layer, work not visible, not allowing continued growth from contributors. Another is the lack of knowledge around how to do internal consulting and onboarding.

I've watched organizations create a great DevOps platform. The team operating the system is doing really well. Good patterns and practices, maybe not documented but it is working – then when they bring in new business units things start to unravel. They just don't have the skillset in house to be consultative and coaching. "Here's the tools, go have fun" – they really struggle coaching them or putting them through bootcamp so this second team doesn't have to take the 6 months or a year of experimenting and failing the first team had to suffer through to get to that point.

Encouraging Learning

You really can't stress this enough – the companies I've seen that are successful take learning seriously and build a plan around it. They run bootcamps or dojos – where they take groups at a time and say, for the next 2 weeks we're going to teach you about CI/CD and version control, and we're going to work in this way – from today forward.

This must be internally taught – it can't come from the outside, from consultants. We try to do a training or engagement with a dedicated group of people – and get them to a place where they're dedicated to it, living it, in their house. Then leave them with the path to set up their own internal consulting agency or center of excellence.

Some people get a little allergic when I say CoE or communities of practice because they've been burned in the past. If you organize it where it's a top-down, very rigid, outward focused – this is your coding style, your pipelines will look like this, if you have any questions come to us and we'll give you the right answer – yeah, that is a problem. Those efforts tend to die out pretty quickly.

The ones that live longer are where there's a few people in the core – the visionaries – kind of helping move things along and give structure, but it is set up as a kind of organic movement, a potluck, where everyone is bringing something to the table to discuss.

Show and Tell

We try to encourage weekly demos. And they're informal. Anyone in the company can show whatever they're working on, anyone in the company can find out what's going on. It always follows the same pattern – at first people are super skeptical, "no one wants to see my Bash script that automates the setup of network devices." But with a little helpful shove they show their work and whoa, people are interested.

The community starts out slow, and then somebody sees something they find interesting, and they tell other people. Then, these weird offline conversations start happening. Hey, that's super neat, how you do that? It's about showing off your work regardless of the state its in. I've had people show off presentation decks, how they automated the creation and updating of legal docs.

It sparks creativity, allowing you to spot things you may not be aware of that may impact your work. We really encourage internal DevOps days and these kinds of small meetups. This builds that transparency and community you are looking for.

Infrastructure As Code

There's always a strong pull to this concept of a set of golden images. Of course, this is a solid concept but in actual practice, many companies struggle with it. Much like the Container wave – they're immutable, you build them, it does its thing, and then you kill it. But this assumes a level of maturity and rigor that most orgs can't handle. Even in the cloud, most simply aren't ready for the rapid creation and destruction of resources like this, and you get old defunct instances spiraling out of control, a maintenance and governance nightmare.

A common misunderstanding is that you need to rebuild your environments every time you do a build from that "golden image" template. Well, if it takes you 45 minutes to install software on a system, no amount of automation will make that go faster if you're installing from scratch every time. We say, build it with a tool – a dry run build – and use that to snap a chalk line: these are our build times on this date. Now, you have your first step: the image creation process.

But you won't do that every time; that's just a process you will run on a regular schedule – perhaps daily, or weekly, or monthly. To cover the gaps in between destroying and recreating these images, you go to step 2 – configuration management.

Configuration Management

Run software that detects variances and enforces it, bringing your systems in line. If you don't follow something like this process, almost immediately you'll have drifts. How our software works at Chef is – you form a policy set, configure your system to match that, detect changes, and correct them. Four phases essentially.

Chef's perfectly capable of detecting and correcting variances immediately. It's very common for companies to want a pause button though – they want to know, but they also want to decide when that correction happens.

That does seem like an antipattern, but it goes to point – there are steps in the journey to DevOps. You want your company to jump 100% into fully automated, no one logging onto VM's manually? That's great on a small team, but I have yet to see it work on a large-scale org. The turning radius is very wide for most larger companies – you have to give them a way to proceed in this journey at a pace that is viable for them, so people aren't burned out, bored, disillusioned.

Gradual Is the Word

This is a slap in the face to all those Agile purists out there: Antipatterns are fine, as long as that's not where you stop. Just for example, a DevOps team is an antipattern, no question. But isn't that better than not having DevOps at all? As long as you're improving, I'm not going to judge you. I don't live in your shoes or live your life.

Question every piece of work you're taking on, and fight against the technologists who instinctively want to complicate things. We all want the latest and greatest tech candy, more efficiency, more speed. But check that – is this the 80 or the 20 part of the 80/20 rule? You could be taking on a lot of activity for very little real value.

Sometimes, you want to enforce some things for a set period of time to change some behavior. "We're going to do these retrospectives for x number of months." Then you back off, stop enforcing it. That allows time for modification and adjustment. If you go too light – no enforcement or guidance – you get a lot of variation and people get confused.

There Are No Silver Bullets in Software

This is going to sound a little weird coming from a software company but the overemphasis on the "magic tool," the one true software to rule them all, just doesn't hold water anymore. My thinking is, you always have the right tool for the job at the time period where you are using it.

I've seen folks live with Chef and Puppet and Ansible. This whole idea that, we're a 100% Chef or Puppet shop – that's just not real anymore. People are used to finding the tool for the right job – that's why JavaScript and OS web frameworks are proliferating the way they are. Over time, if it becomes a big issue you might do some pruning and consolidations, but it's better to not waste energy on it until then. There are differentiators, yes, but there's a lot of commonality. It's kind of like "what's the best programming language" – it's totally a subjective question.

One caveat though is, don't have two tools doing the same thing at the same time – two configuration management tools for example, or two release pipeline or monitoring software. What you want is a tool that reinforces the cultural change you are trying to make, and vice versa.

Do We Need a DevOps Manifesto?

It is a little weird that we're so far along and there's no common definition or manifesto for DevOps, but I see why that is. There's a natural inclination to not make a manifesto because then it becomes a Bible, something zealots can use to win arguments, and the meaning is lost. There's a lot of pullback from people not wanting to go back down the path Agile went down – it's too programmatic and thematic, do it this way, etc.

I get the need for being prescriptive – but there's a difference between being descriptive and prescriptive. Just for example, you should have automated testing. That's a descriptive capability you'd want – testing is nonnegotiable, DevOps won't work without it. There's certain patterns and practices that are common, and I get the desire to have it defined, but I'm not sure I agree with it. Let's work quickly and efficiently to deliver value to our customers. That's it!

Chef's always been about those two core concepts – taking an idea and shipping it as fast as possible. I love that we can write a recipe in Chef once and have it run anywhere – onprem, a Docker container, AWS, Azure. It's the ultimate in portability.

One little note here is that this does require trust, and the assumption that people are fundamentally good. Guess what – surprise! – not everyone is that way. Not everyone has essentially good and pure motives. You can insulate from that risk somewhat but not always; that human quality has broken more than one DevOps effort I've been involved in.

Michael Stahnke, Puppet

Lessons for Your Roadmap

- *DevOps is really about optimizing how people work together*
- *Unit tests are a great litmus test, but don't neglect your more useful higher level testing*
- *Containerization is great for a consistent API-driven framework; it's not a panacea*
- *Consistency is more important than perfection*
- *Microservices are almost a requirement for larger, more complex apps*
- *Monitoring begins with thinking about the customer's definition of success*
- *Tie your asks around business value and dollars*
- *Think about approval gates and how to segregate minor tasks from larger, more risky changes*

The Heroes Are Gone

I'm the Director of Engineering at Puppet; basically, I'm in charge of both the enterprise side of things and the platform architecture itself. I've been with Puppet for about 7 years. Before that, I worked as a sysadmin for a large enterprise – it was a big change going from a company of 110,000 to Puppet, which was just 35 people at the time!

I was at the first US DevOps days in 2009 and spoke there. Even back then, I felt that a lot of people were missing the boat – there's so much potential for DevOps even for companies not doing large-scale web deployments. I still feel that way.

Back in 2011–2013, a lot of infrastructure teams had that one person, the lynchpin that holds it all together, the hero. Now, it seems like we're talking more to groups where that person doesn't exist – the entire team are more 9-to-5ers. When they go home, they're thinking about picking up their kids or planning dinner; they're not up at 11 p.m. writing scripts. For this audience, you just can't reach them the same way we used to. They want more of a prescriptive guidance, a recipe they can follow. Maybe, the right approach in that case is an executive mandate or a leadership team or consultant-driven practice with Deloitte or Accenture.

It does keep me up at night sometimes though. DevOps Days used to be more homegrown, the best of the best, and we were trying different things and sharing what we learned, without thinking there was a silver bullet that works every time, with every team. Nowadays it's sometimes an echo chamber, where we're all repeating the same things to each other but it's just not resonating with the enterprises we belong to. And there's a lot of people we're leaving behind.

Worst Practices Are More Interesting

Usually, when things go off the rails with DevOps it's because incentives are misaligned with what you're trying to do. To me, it comes down to internal motivation – *do you want to be demonstrably better today than yesterday?* Everything is culture side for me.

You can't pattern yourself after Etsy or Google. Guess what – they're terrible at certain things, the same as you are. They just don't talk about it onstage. The big unspoken secret of our movement is, no one, absolutely NO ONE is the best at DevOps. Everyone is still learning and trying to do their thing.

The presentations I perk up for are the ones that are honest, what I call the Worst Practice talks. I want to know where people screwed up, the mistakes that set them back, what got swept under the rug or the shit behind the curtain that isn't working well that you desperately need to fix. That's so much better than the ego-driven "ain't my company cool, I'm such a visionary, you should want to be like me" type presentations.

Tech and Collaboration

Today, DevOps is still talked about like it's a software delivery style. I don't see it that way – I see it as defining the way people work together. You can do DevOps with a mainframe and COBOL and JCL; I don't need CI/CD for that.

But defining how people should interact and how they optimize their work and collaborate, to me that's the real potential offered with DevOps. It's not tech. Tech is cool, glossy, beautiful, but what's way more important is showing leaks in the process. What handoffs are there? Why are they there, and have you tried getting rid of them? How do you handle security audits and change control boards, and what cost do they have with your workflow? To me that's a much more interesting problem than boasting about using Chef, Puppet, blah blah.

I'll say it again – tech isn't all that important for how DevOps works. It's an enabler and change agent – a powerful engine – but the key part really is optimizing how people work together and collaborate.

And we underestimate how difficult these conversions are. Just adopting source control for an infrastructure team can be a multiyear effort. And it's damn difficult to reach that experienced, battle-hardened engineer who's been with the company for ages. They like SSH'ing onto the box, typing commands, that works for them. Shifting that mental model to checking out and deploying infra code with every change seems much slower – changing that mindset is way, way harder than tooling.

Testing

Let's take unit tests. It's fantastic you've got 90% code coverage, that's great – but does it do what you want? Are you invoking the code at the right spot? By far, the hardest part of continuous delivery is testing and everyone, I mean EVERYONE just glosses over it. It's damn hard, unglamorous work, and there is no generic way of testing everything. But testing is where it starts and ends – let's say you're deploying ten times a day, are you that confident in your tests, or in your ability to rework?

I'm going to risk the pitchforks and torches here and just say, I honestly care a lot less about unit tests than most. They're great as specifications and to demonstrate something works as its designed – but we've had times where Puppet's had 16K unit tests running and the build still fails in prod, so it didn't catch what we needed. We use it as a litmus test, and it gives our devs fast feedback. But I stress with our engineers to spend time at the system and integration level – are we actually solving the problem for the customer?

Infrastructure As Code

I'm not a big believer in the mythical golden set of builds. First off, stability by itself is a really crappy goal. A better question is – what's your current state? Where do you want to be? What are the characteristics you're after? I'm betting you don't really want to have a golden image of Windows that stays static for months. You want a Windows image that's up to date and conforms to all your standards. You want up-to-date user accounts and security patches. In almost zero cases, a set of golden images is really not the destination you should be shooting for.

Something else that may shock some people. Docker and Kubernetes are being touted right now as magical – "it works on my machine" is no longer a problem! Well, guess what, that often ends up NOT being the case. It allows developers to be lazy and think they can just plop their laptop on production. So, they do all these things that are really horrible and think containerization will make their work portable and secure.

My prediction is, we're going to see some major security issues over the next few years. It won't be the fault of Docker or Kubernetes, but it'll be an exploit based on a vulnerability with the images themselves. The good thing about containerization is, it means what we develop comes with a pretty well documented set of APIs'. As a Kubernetes admin, I know there's certain common characteristics of the app and the handoffs and edge interfaces all look the same – whether its SAP, an Apache webserver, some homegrown utility – it has a common set of characteristics due to it running on Kubernetes. That by itself is super valuable.

I often say, "consistency is more important than perfection." As an admin, I'd rather have a bad thing done 100x the same terrible way, than the right thing done once and who the hell knows what the other 99 configs look like?

Microservices

Microservices are all the rage right now as well, and in many cases they work great. I'd say at a large scale it's almost a requirement. How else are you going to get 1000 engineers to work together on a single monolith? The only real answer is to have your interaction points become an API.

It also makes sense at smaller scales. With startups for example, you're iterating and moving so quickly – changing the payment process for example without changing the frontend is such a great win for enabling velocity. I will say though that it is much harder to have many things online and available vs. a few things online and available. And people underestimate that complexity with distributed computing, all the time.

My prediction for 2019 is, you'll see a big company get off the microservice bandwagon because the ROI just isn't working out for them. It does remind me a bit of the early 2000s, when availability clustering started becoming a thing. For the first 50 clusters we built, every time we turned them on, it killed our availability. With microservices I say – if you're good at it, it's awesome, it's amazing. If you're not good at it, it's a never-ending pain in the butt. You end up with a distributed failure model, not a more resilient infrastructure.

Monitoring

I love monitoring and I hate how often it gets put last or gets swept under the table. If you think about it, it's just testing but it's done in production. So just like with testing – don't think plain vanilla metrics – but think about what you need to do to make sure the application is running correctly from the user's perspective. Then, implement some way of watching that in your monitoring.

I know Etsy and John Allspaw were fond of saying, "if it moves, graph it!" That works great if you're EMC and sell storage, but for me that's a terrible idea most of the time. I mean, how much of that data can I really use in a meaningful way, aggregate and make decisions off of it? I am really careful with the questions I ask and the data that I gather and keep.

And think about the way you are presenting this information to the people that matter in your company. You want to steer toward a measurable outcome that matters to people. For example, don't try to sell MTTR by itself. If I say I need to have more worker roles added to this process, or more servers in the background – that's great for techies but not for the people writing the checks. But if I say it costs me this much every time this problem happens, then I get strong feedback. What would it cost to fix this? Then, we can talk about our options and have a discussion. But if something's important, I do try to convert it to dollars – that's the universal language of business.

That's something I wish more developers understood. We need to think about the long-term maintenance costs of the things we build more. Over time, the cost of development gets rounded to zero in comparison with the cost of operating and maintaining the system.

Operations teams have a better understanding of business value and maintenance costs than developers do. If we really understood the language of business – we could get the backing we need to produce better quality software and keep our tech debt in check.

Culture Wars and CAB Gates

It's a cliché but unfortunately true – political or organizational problems are the hardest problems to solve. Because bureaucracy and risk avoidance are so entrenched, people find ways of working around it, not through it. You don't write a change ticket because it'd get flagged for approval, you just do the work in the background. If an exec has a dashboard outside his office showing availability and you need to take down the service, you put up a static pic showing everything is OK for a week or so.

I absolutely hate CAB meetings and I think they're from the age of dinosaurs. In the best-case scenario, let's say for the same app you have two changes going out in parallel and there'd be a broken dependency – and that's caught in the CAB meeting. Awesome!

But think – how often does that come up? I'm guessing, not that often. Usually people talk to each other and it's addressed in a standup. Approvals and gates from a superior or your boss' boss- how is it that they have any idea of what they're approving? Usually, they're signing off because they trust their direct report's approval. Well, if you trust them, why do you need to approve each and every action?

I used to file most of my changes months ahead of times for standard actions for preapproval – things like adding user accounts, making firewall changes, updating DNS entries. Then, I started thinking more big-picture, and instead of thinking about approvals and checkoffs we'd think about our external dependencies – policy auditing, security, change control boards – and how to better rope them in so they aren't dragging on our velocity.

It's been said, with DevOps you first optimize yourself and the way you do your work. Then, you move on to optimizing your team, then your team's interactions with other teams. Start figuring out – what matters to these people, and how can I bring DevOps to the people that are approving these changes every day? How can I get these SOX auditors to be collaborative vs. combative? Let's talk about risk and what we're trying to automate, instead of man-to-man combat between a systems professional and an auditor.

Ask, what's the cost of being wrong on a particular approval? Let's say it's not a minor change but a large one, say replacing core switching in the data center – how can we segregate these things to speed up our flow on minor tasks while protecting ourselves with major changes? What if we moved the change control meeting to a Slack channel?

Hiring for Compatibility

You can't overstate enough how important it is to hire the right people. And I look for that learning-oriented mindset, first and foremost. Their responses need to show a willingness to learn and adapt, a can-do, positive attitude. Some people come in cynical, and that's not healthy for any company. Or maybe they've been stuck with some crappy process for months and months, and it just infects them and you can't get rid of it. It would be great to hire people you'd want to have drinks with, but that's not what I'm looking for – primarily it's compatibility, will you fit with the way the team operates?

There's a reason why most leading companies use interview panels, and it's not to create a gauntlet. One person simply can't make an informed, solid decision on fit, because we're talking about group dynamics here. For example, I typically am drilling in on culture, but some other panels are more deep-dive on problem-solving or whiteboarding. We'll actually have the candidate sit beside the support person doing the interviewing, and they'll pull a ticket off the support queue and work on it together – the candidate will suggest some fixes, and they'll go back and forth. It's a great way of figuring out how they think and solve problems.

I try to find out what they're passionate about. I ask, "tell me about the coolest thing you've ever built." Notice I didn't qualify that by asking if it was at work, school, or home. I like to understand if they're blindly enthusiastic or if they know the pros and the cons – like with distributed computing, are they aware of the shortcomings with latency, state management, caching, and some mitigation strategies they like? And I ask about the characteristics they liked in their favorite manager, and the things they hated in the manager they struggled with. How often do you expect to receive feedback? What's the type of feedback you like best? How does the culture at your previous company either empower or disempower you? What are your career goals, where do you see yourself in 5 years?

One of my favorite bizarro interview questions is asking my techy candidates, "what's the difference between Nagios and Jenkins fundamentally?" I get two reactions – the "you don't know what you're talking about," or "hmm, that's interesting, let's talk about that." Once we drill down to the answer – both schedule jobs off a GUI – we can start talking about what you would do with either and why. It's a great way of challenging their preconceptions and sparking an honest discussion.

I think interviewing and selecting the right people is the one thing I've improved at the most over the past 7 years. Back then, we had only 35 people – now we're at 550 and turned over about 250 people on top of that. That's a lot of change. And I think I've hired about 75 people, and of those I regret very few – only about three people that for one reason or another didn't make it.

And I've been lucky in keeping people, but it goes in fits and starts. For 6 years, I never had a direct report quit. Then, we had a bunch of people drop out like flies. Burnout, or our QA/test framework changing – for one reason or another, it stopped being fun a while ago. It's best to let them leave and do what you can to address why they left so it doesn't crop up again.

My mantra is, if you're in Operations and you don't care about what your business does, go find a different job. We're so much better at our jobs when we care about business outcome instead of "I get to work on Unix or AIX blah blah." If you know what it is your company actually does – produce tractors, cars, software, whatever – and you can connect what you do to that function, you're going to actually care about it and it'll be much more rewarding and productive.

Munil Shah, Microsoft

At the time of this interview, Munil was the Director of Engineering of Visual Studio Team Services. He's currently Senior Vice President of Engineering at UiPath, a leader in enterprise Robotic Process Automation, heading up UiPath's US engineering centers. In addition, he leads the company's Cloud portfolio and global engineering practices.

Munil has over 25 years of experience building large-scale software, distributed systems, and Cloud services. Previously, he held various engineering leadership roles at Microsoft. As Partner Director of Engineering in Microsoft's Cloud and AI division, he led engineering for Azure DevOps and TFS products. As General Manager in Bing Advertising, he oversaw the launch of Bing Ads platform and its growth to multibillion dollar business. Earlier in his career, he held various engineering leadership positions in Windows, starting as a developer on the Windows networking stack.

Munil graduated with a Master's degree in Computer Science from University of Arizona. He lives in Seattle with his wife and two children. When he is not building Cloud software, you can find him reaching for mountain peaks all over the world as he loves hiking and photography. He has also invested in over dozen startups as a member of SWAN venture funds.

Lessons for Your Roadmap

- *Odds are, either testing or the build management system is your pain point*

- *Put a stake in the ground and force good unit testing going forward*

- *Make it easy on your teams by providing training and investing in good frameworks*
- *Gamify your quality by running Bug Bashes*
- *Never unhook from the business to "focus on quality" – deliver new value constantly*
- *Complex branching structures will murder your delivery rate*
- *Use dashboarding and scorecards to guard against complacency*
- *Constantly weed out your flaky or inefficient tests*

Testing May Not Be Cool, But It Is Necessary

At the end of the day, as an engineering director I'm concerned about two things: productivity – how much can we get done? – and secondly, how quickly can we get an idea into production and get the feedback we need. Once we understand that life cycle, the loop from an idea coming into development, walking as code through release environments and then out to production, then we can look at it and ask the vital question: where is the bottleneck? Often, it ends up being testing.

And I'm convinced that the bottleneck in most engineering systems is either testing or the build management system. The problem is, people don't want to do testing, it's not glamorous. The perception is that there's low ROI, and it's usually a massive effort – wading through 15 years of legacy code and revamping it. I can honestly say though – for us, there was no alternative but to roll up our sleeves and do it – it's been the key factor in everything we've accomplished, the velocity we've been able to reach.

So, it doesn't matter if it's cool or not – you have to focus on that bottleneck and optimize it, if you want to move at speed. I'm happy to say, testing is cool now – where it was kind of the forgotten man 5 years ago. It's something we talk about and think about, all the time.

The Microsoft Shift Left Movement

With Visual Studio, we started the switch to Agile back in 2010 or so. About 3 years in, we found that our features were getting out fast enough – but the CI/CD pipeline was gumming things up. We were really struggling with passing quality standards. So, say about 2014, we began flattening things out. We'd always had separate dev, test, and project management groups on each team – and everyone realized, that's just not the way to build services; these separate disciplines were actually one.

Combining things and making sure everyone had the same title and mission was a big help, but that still left our quality and this absurdly long test cycle. So, at the same time that we flattened the org – the timing really was quite perfect, but it was kind of accidental – there was this powerful incentive to do something about our testing collateral.

There was a lot of skepticism when we first published this idea, that we'd be relying more on unit testing going forward. We got a lot of "we tried this before, it didn't work" and "unit testing won't work in this case" type responses. We tried to avoid a lot of religious debate about this and made it pragmatic. And we didn't try blowing away our 27,000 integration and functional tests overnight – that was a huge investment that we couldn't remove overnight.

But we did put a stake in the ground, insisting that any new code going out the door had to be accompanied with unit tests. And we invested in showing teams how to write unit tests effectively, that are extendable and actually work. We spend time showing how we run testing, deployment, architecture, and security – but we don't get prescriptive. We don't straitjacket our people into one specific way of writing a unit test.

We used to do a crazy amount of performance testing and integration testing in lab environments, simulating real-world usage with synthetic loads, and it was killing us. What's more we weren't finding a lot of actual bugs with it! We spent so much time trying to maintain those expensive integration environments and chasing bugs that weren't real. For us, we've found no substitute for actual, real-world production environments – testing in production is a big part of moving at speed.

We run bug bashes too – that's where teams take a few days and try to find as many bugs as they can. We give awards out – gold medal for finding the most bugs, or the most bugs in other teams' work. Gamifying things like this helps us avoid that kind of blinders-on way we view our product when we're just testing our own feature, or treating bugs as a hateful flaw that must be hidden from others. No, it's a byproduct of our work! It's kind of like cleaning up a messy room – you just have to roll up your sleeves and tidy up, that's a bug bash.

Pitfalls Avoided

I don't want anyone to read this and think, "Oh, unit testing will solve our problems." It's really two parts – the second part was improving the way we ran releases. Visual Studio made this leap from shrinkwrapped software that came in a jewel case, to Visual Studio Team Services – VSTS, a service. That was huge, because now we can roll out changes in an incremental fashion, and we could build in a massive amount of telemetry to keep us honest about our quality. We progressively reveal features through release rings and feature flags. Those are guardrails – if we found gaps, or quality misses, we typically found them very early on – our own engineering team are the first ones impacted, we're on Ring 0 – so we could fix the test collateral.

That's not saying functional tests aren't in use today. It's just that we've flipped that Mike Cohn testing pyramid – 4 years ago, we had about 37K functional tests. That number has shrunk to about 3000 functional tests today – we call them L2 or L3 tests, and they go after very specific end-to-end scenarios. They're slow running though and come with a high cost. We don't like testing Ux, but test against business logic wherever possible.

And we do – this will shock some people – manual exploratory testing for some key releases, which we don't try to automate. Sometimes there's no substitute for someone poking around. But, we are allergic to any test that's either slow or unreliable. We set a time threshold, and any new unit test that can't run within this time limit gets kicked out so it doesn't gum up our CI system.

And it must run reliably – if a test runs OK 500 times, but then fails once – intermittently – that's not a test we can use. It gets yanked, and a bug is automatically filed for a developer to investigate and fix.

Quality Deserves Your Best People

Many times we see the most junior person on the team in charge of testing. That's not how we did it – we decided early on, this was a priority for Microsoft, so it needed top-level attention. I put my most senior engineer, a deep-level systems architect, on this problem, with the mission to drive this migration. He and the rest of the team built a framework as a kind of living standard and started working team by team to dig into specific issues, trying to understand where unit testing wouldn't work and how to tweak the framework so it could be more flexible.

Using a senior person, someone with credibility and a deep-level understanding of the product, was a key decision point – formerly, the QA team just simply didn't have that level of knowledge and authority. We asked nicely, and then enforced, some behavior changes around unit testing – and then, once people realized "hey, it's easier to write and maintain unit test code than these functional tests" – there was almost a race in the organization to see which team could be first to dismantle and replace the old, creaky test layer with unit tests.

It boggles my mind when companies tell me, "Oh we have a team in India that does the testing, and we get a report back on bugs." To me that's a fundamental part of the engineering system that you are choosing to ignore, to outsource – you just can't do that. Think about all the real problems that get swept under the rug, the opportunity cost from all the feedback you're never seeing!

You Can't Take a Timeout

One of the failure points I've seen with some other companies trying a "Shift Left" movement is the desire to timebox something. They'll say, let's take a team offline, and for the next 6 months we're going to focus entirely on getting our quality problems under control.

There's a couple of problems with that – first off, that likely won't be all the time you need – our effort took us almost 3 years of continual work, a really significant effort, and we went down the rabbit hole without any idea of how long it would take – just that it needed to be done. Trying to fit an artificial cap or milestone on a quality effort like this nearly always backfires, and you end up leaving it unfinished – a big reason why some companies perceive unit testing as an expensive dead end.

A second reason is that it's unbelievably expensive to take a team of engineers down for months at a time like this, which creates pressure to hurry up and "finish" as a project something that is really a way of doing work. It's unrealistic to stand down a team like this.

At Microsoft, we never stopped shipping. We got a lot of hard questions months in on whether it was working, if it was worth the cost, questions about ROI – but we stuck to the overall strategy, a strategy that our upper management knew about and was bought into, 100%.

To help us in what seemed like a never-ending journey, we did set little mini-milestones. We categorized and separated out our tests into categories. First, we pulled out what we called the P0 tests first – those were the ones that we needed to run, all the time. We refactored or replaced these, and that's what we used to prove that the strategy would work.

Then, we moved on – we said, OK, by April 1, we want to see all our P1s converted. There were times when some teams did struggle to hit these goals – we'd meet with them, and sometimes make some exceptions – but our feature work and refactoring our test layer all went on in parallel.

Only the Fast and Reliable Survive

Another common mistake is these deep, really complex branching structures. We used to do that, and it was like death by a thousand cuts – the integration debt from all these low-lying branches that we'd have to pay against constantly.

Now, it's a different story – every engineer merges against master. That's indispensable – to merge to master, you have to be absolutely sure you won't break it – so that forces a large amount of automated unit tests to prevent problems on check-in. And for that to work, you need to make sure these tests can run fast, every time you do a pull request. So, only the fast and reliable tests survive; everything else you weed out.

All that good behavior comes from having the master, the mainline always being in a shippable state – that concept is crucial for us. We do use and ship from release branches – we have to have those for hotfixes and to simulate a particular version on demand. But the concept of a feature branch is verboten to us; every engineer knows they can trust and build from master and know it has the same level of quality as any release branch.

Think about it this way. Let's say you're an engineer, and you just wrote some code and check it in. But there's this long integration cycle and test cycle that then kicks off. Two weeks later, someone comes to you with a list of bugs. That's very interruption driven and disruptive to your workflow; by that time, you may not even remember why you made those changes, or even where they were. But if you get feedback almost immediately – say within 90 minutes that your check-in is integrated to mainline, and it looks good – that gives you confidence that you can change things, safely. And there's a lot less waste due to context switching.

Your Developers Are Users Too

I started out by talking about our concerns around productivity as management. We're laser focused on the productivity of our developers; everything we do is based on that. I'm constantly talking to the engineers, asking – what did you do today? How can I help make you more productive? Maybe that means a larger monitor, or a tweak to our engineering system. And if it turns out they're working on a bug list from two weeks ago – whoa, that's not a fun day. I wonder what we can do to improve that?

Fighting Complacency

It's always an ongoing struggle to fight against complacency, plateauing. We fight this in three ways.

First comes monitoring and visibility. We have dashboards to show our CI runs and we keep them visible. If there's a broken build it shows up big and red and gets a lot of attention. But a bigger worry for us is bloat; let's say you've added tests to where your pull requests now take 15 minutes, and then 30 minutes. If an engineer has to wait half an hour for a pull request, or to merge to master, I guarantee you they will find a way to get around that.

So, we very carefully monitor the time it takes to create a pull request; the time it takes to self-host; the time it takes to merge back to main. We constantly talk about ways to trim that time down in our engineering staff meetings – dropping or refactoring tests, or new tech that can speed things up. It does require a constant investment of time and money to keep things running fast – so an engineer can create a pull request in 5-10 minutes, for example – the time it takes to get a cup of coffee.

The second thing to worry about is flaky tests. We write flaky tests all the time – tests that intermittently fail, or run long. We used to struggle with that all the time, and it led to people not trusting the system and ignoring red lights. So, we have a system that automatically yanks flaky tests; we want every test we run to be fast and useful in detecting problems early on.

Third, sometimes the tests are written in a way that are ineffective – they don't prevent bugs from being pushed out. Because we're running frequent releases, like multiple times a day – bad quality shows up almost immediately, and it's visible both with livesite issues – customers calling – and on our scorecard.

Running our software as a service means we can't hide from bad code, which often just means inadequate testing that needs to be built up. And scorecards that are visible to everyone – like management, and other teams – keep us honest. It's a key part of us managing scale – it's not about how many features you can push out the door, but the things that actually matter to our end users.

Nathen Harvey, Chef

Nathen Harvey, VP of Community Development at Chef, helps the community whip up an awesome ecosystem built around the Chef platform. Nathen also spends much of his time helping people learn about the practices, processes, and technologies that support DevOps, continuous delivery, and high velocity organizations. Prior to joining Chef, Nathen spent a number of years managing operations and infrastructure for a diverse range of web applications. Nathen is a co-host of the Food Fight Show, a podcast about Chef and DevOps. Chef is the leader in Continuous Automation software, an innovator in cloud native operations, and one of the founders of the DevOps movement. Chef is powered by an awesome community and open source software engines: Chef for infrastructure, Habitat for cloud native operations, and InSpec for compliance.

Lessons for Your Roadmap

- *Trust your config management tool to corral runaway drift*
- *Before changing a tool, look at past outages and what would have fixed them*
- *DevOps Dojo – focus on one key feature, get it out the door in 6 weeks*
- *Be open and honest about failure and learn from mistakes*
- *Quality begins with effective, regular peer reviews*

How We Approach Projects

I'm the VP of Community Development with Chef – I'm charged with helping build and grow our community, both the commercial and the Open Source side of things. A lot of companies out there see the energy and excitement, the sense of camaraderie, around open source and are trying to replicate that with their own DevOps efforts.

When we come onsite, you can start with a simulation but it's so much more interesting to work with the real thing. Often, we begin by picking out one idea or feature that's really going to deliver a lot of value. Then, we identify all the people that have to touch that idea to get it out the door and we lock them in a room. That means, if someone has to open a port on a firewall, and it could take them days to get to that with their backlog – well, they'd better be there, physically in the room. The idea is to do a complete release of one specific feature in 6 weeks. We're talking post-its on a whiteboard, very minimal tech here so we don't get lost in the tooling. But this kind of an exercise helps get your active supporters, the practitioners, really bought into things.

It also helps with identifying specifically how each person adds value. I've been a sysadmin in the past, so my job is racking and stacking servers right? Well, that's not exciting – its kind of like being a dev lead and graded on how many lines of code you can churn out. That's just not a lot of reason to get out of bed in the morning. But once you see the value the customer is going to get out of your actions, directly – well, that eliminates a lot of blockers.

Let's say I'm a mainframe programmer, the same person that Bimodal IT concept Gartner talks about is meant to address. As a practitioner, do I understand who my customer is, and is that driving my work? If success is 99.9% uptime, then I'm not going to be into DevOps and I'm not going to care about moving faster. That message won't resonate with me.

Trust the System

One of the common problems I see is fearing the system. For example, with Chef, or Puppet, or any other config management tool out there – we can automatically remove any variances with your systems, easily. At one place I used to work, we had infrastructure as code, with an agent running and keeping things up to date. But we got scared of the risk, so we turned it off. And any time we'd make a change, we'd have to add new code, spin up an agent to test against to confirm it was good – and then apply it to production. But by that time there could have been all kinds of changes in production that weren't in that test. So, we made a change – we decided to run config mgmt. all the time in production, trust our monitoring, and trust our reaction time and our ability to recover.

To get to that point where you really trust the tool – and trust yourself – probably the best place to start is looking at your last outage and the postmortem process you followed. Can you now detect that issue faster, recover faster? Zero in on those questions, and if there's a gap in tooling – THEN you buy software that will fill that particular need.

Getting Executive Buy-In

One of the key DevOps principles is that we treat failure as an opportunity to learn. So, getting that executive buy-in – well, you can't overstate how vital that is. You need time and space to try something new; you promise to this exec sponsor that you'll carefully monitor what your pilot team will be doing, and what's more you'll have regular demo days open to the entire company. As that team gets up to speed and demonstrates that we can fail, be honest about that failure, AND learn from those mistakes so we can recover more quickly. That gets the rest of the organization curious and excited.

The DORA annual report is fascinating as well when it talks about the Westrum study in 2004 and how organizations think. So sometimes we talk about information sharing. Are responsibilities across teams shared? How do you deal with messengers carrying bad tidings – are they shot, or thanked?

I get the same heebie-jeebies about Bimodal IT that I do about Centers of Excellence. To me – you don't want to be an engineer on the turtle, slow side of things – you want to be on the rabbit side of things. So, if there's a "Center of Excellence" and you're not on it – that's pretty exclusionary. It's much better to have a Community of Practice instead.

Acting Like a Startup

We strongly recommend running DevOps Dojos – a program where you can run through all the tools and learn by doing for 6 weeks – the same startup program I mentioned earlier. Then, the people you've invited to this program go back to their original team and bring this new way of doing things.

Just as an example – Verizon runs an annual DevOps Challenge contest. They set out some cool, aggressive goals at the beginning of the year – maybe a focus on CI/CD, or security, a big theme – and they give out projects for teams to self-select. As the year goes on, they start winnowing down the finalists – from 64, to 32, to 12. And then they bring in outside panelists – I was one, a few months back – to judge their finalists and choose a winner. Obviously, that requires some scale; you can't do that with a team of 12! But it's becoming obvious, DevOps isn't just for garage companies or startups – it's more mainstream enterprise than ever.

Numbers We Like

There's a few metrics we like at Chef, all focusing around speed, efficiency, and risk. We ask some questions:

- Speed: How frequently are you deploying? How long does it take from the time code is committed to the repository, to when its in production?

- Efficiency – how often does a change cause an outage or an incident in production? How long does it take you to recover when there's an outage? (MTTR)

- Risk – How long does it take you to figure out there's a problem in prod? (MTTD) How frequently are you auditing your systems for compliance?

People get really confused about that last one – let me explain. Traditionally, companies audit once a quarter – this could be for internal policy compliance, security, whatever. And let's say that auditor walks out the door end of December – they won't be back until April. In those 3 months, the systems will change, and it's likely the systems have drifted outside of controls. Now, there's this mad rush to bring them back into compliance with policy. So, there's this up and down wave throughout the year, and you're only compliant when the auditor is physically in the room. So that last question is key – that drift causes a lot of waste and rework that can be avoided.

Does DevOps Mean NoOps?

There's a common misconception that – we're doing DevOps now, so we're going to become generalists. No, we need specialists – we just need to learn how to work together as a broader team. What do we need to do together to better serve the customer?

That's the power of that word DevOps – two words we mush together. How do we Dev better? That's about experiments, learning better ways of doing things. And what about improving Ops? In the past, developers didn't care about production outages – my job was to ship the feature, I shipped, end of story! But now developers have to care about how things are behaving in production. Your two best tools to get each side to see across the fence are effective demos and postmortems.

Back when I was a sysadmin, one of the things I used to do was go out for lunch with the developers. And sometimes they'd spend an entire hour arguing over what would make a good unit test vs. a bad one. At the time I was writing all this infrastructure code in Chef, and people started asking why I wasn't writing unit tests against it. And I just froze up! I finally said, you know what, I've got an hour to spare here – I can either write a crappy, inadequate unit test, or I can write a Nagios alert. So, I was able to get ahead of problems in production, but I couldn't prevent them.

It took me a while to realize that the worst unit test was the one you didn't write. That's something you have to practice, to work at to get better. It's like with software development – if I showed you code that you wrote 2 years ago, or 10 years ago, you wouldn't say – whoa, that was outstanding, clearly the pinnacle of my career. Code is a continual experiment, and it's always changing – and we're always improving, through practice, making it a part of your regular routine. Unit testing was like that for me – kind of like when you weren't using version control, and once you finally do – you look back and wonder why you weren't doing it earlier, how you lived without it.

Code Reviews

If you want to get to continuous delivery, you start with effective code reviews. Of course, you should have a release pipeline. But that's meaningless until you can assess what the code is doing, and if it's not too clever. Clever code is terrific until it breaks, and then you need that genius engineer that wrote it 6 months ago to fix it, because they're the only one that can understand it!

Once you're doing regular code reviews, you can come up with practices, opportunities for improvement or automation. Can we bring in static analysis tools? Should we use spaces or tabs with our conventions? Pick one, and then build it into the pipeline as part of a release gate. I do think you need to enforce it – it really helps if you have some clear rules in place, a guardrail.

Infrastructure and Automation

With any framework – and that includes Chef – you need to avoid blindly implementing something as a best practice. You can't just buy some software, or go to a book, or copy what another company does as a solution. The challenge is to think critically about the problem you are trying to solve – and then you can identify and apply a framework that will help you solve that problem.

A common misconception is to think that you can write IAC once and be done with it. Think of it as code, which it is – as your understanding grows, and the solutions and environments change, you'll have to change that codeset as well. It's just not something you can set and forget.

Do you need to really clamp down and enforce a set of "golden images"? Well that's a tradeoff. If you allow a hundred different versions of Tomcat, or the .NET Framework, you're increasing your operational complexity. If you choose to constrain these and enforce some consistency, you're going to help reduce complexity, but you're also reducing your developer's capacity to innovate.

So, there's a tradeoff there. A large financial institution that I've worked with went through a number of years where they allowed their teams to go off and solve their business problems completely independently. But then they started looking at the number of AWS accounts – not subscriptions, accounts – they had and realized there was an opportunity there to streamline. The key then is to make the official, blessed way the easy way, so the developers don't have incentive to find workarounds.

The biggest thing I continue to struggle with is, there is no silver bullet. You know and understand your org better than anyone else – so you're in the best and probably only position to solve those problems. You can bring in Chef, Gene Kim, or any number of expensive consultants – but in the end, no one is going to come and save you. The only way out is through hard work, and the only one able to really do that work is you. It's hard work, no question, but you're going to learn a lot, and it's going to be fun!

Nigel Kersten, Puppet

Nigel came to Puppet from Google HQ in Mountain View, where he was responsible for the design and implementation of one of the largest Puppet deployments in the world. At Puppet, Nigel was responsible for the development of the initial versions of Puppet Enterprise and has since served in a variety of roles, including head of

product, CTO, and CIO. He's currently the VP of Ecosystem Engineering at Puppet. He has been deeply involved in Puppet's DevOps initiatives and regularly speaks around the world about the adoption of DevOps in the enterprise and IT organizational transformation.

Lessons for Your Roadmap

- Remember optimism bias – things are likely not running as smoothly as you think!

- DevOps doesn't require brilliance, just steady hard work and discipline

- Continuous Delivery is the single most productive goal for your life cycle

- A pioneering, experimental phase is natural

- Guard your time – your goal isn't automation but thinking long term with your investments

- Start with your scripted environments in VC, then optimize one pain point at a time in your deployment cycle

The Deep End of the Pool

I grew up in Australia; I was lucky enough to be one of those kids that got a computer. It turns out that people would pay me to do stuff with them! So, I ended up doing just that – and found myself at a local college, managing large fleets of Macs and handling a lot of multimedia and audio needs there. Very early in my career, I found hundreds of people – students and staff – very dependent on me to be The Man, to fix their problems. And I loved being the hero – there's such a dopamine hit, a real rush! The late nights, the miracle saves – I couldn't get enough.

Then the strangest thing happened – I started realizing there was more to life than work. I started getting very serious about music, to the point where I was performing. And I was trying a startup with a friend on the side. So, for a year or two, work became – for the first time – just work. Suddenly I didn't want to spend my life on call, 24 hours a day – I had better things to do! I started killing off all my manual work around infrastructure and operations, replacing it with automation and scripts.

That led me to Google, where I worked for about 5 years. I thought I was a scripting and infrastructure ninja – but I got torn to shreds by the Site Reliability Engineers there. It was a powerful learning experience for me – I grew in ways I couldn't have anywhere else. For starters, it was the deep end of the pool. We had a team of four managing 80,000 machines. And these weren't servers in a webfarm – these were roaming laptops, suddenly appearing on strange networks, getting infected with malware, suffering from unreliable network connections. So, we had to automate – we had no choice about it. As an Ops person, this was a huge leap forward for me – it forced me to sink or swim, really learn under fire.

Then, I left for Puppet – I think I was employee #13 there – now we're at almost 500 and growing. I'm the Chief Technical Strategist, but that's still very much a working title – I run engineering and product teams and handle a lot of our community evangelism and architectural vision. Really though it all comes down to trying to set our customers up for success.

Impoverished Communication

I don't think our biggest challenge is ever technical – it's much more fundamental than that, and it comes down to communication. There's often a real disconnect between what executives think is true – what they are presenting at conferences and in papers – and what is actually happening on the ground. There's a very famous paper from the Harvard Business Review back in the 1970s that said that communication is like water. Communication downward is rarely a problem, and it works much better than most managers realize. However, open and honest communication up the chain is hard, like trying to pump water up a hill. It gets filtered or spun, as people report upward what their manager wants to believe or what will reflect well on them – and next thing you know you have an upper management layer that thinks they are well informed but really is in an echo chamber. Just for example, take the Challenger shuttle disaster – technical data that clearly showed problems ahead of the explosion were filtered out, glossed over, made more optimistic for senior management consumption.

We see some enterprises out there struggling, and it becomes this very negative mindset – "oh, the enterprise is slow, they make bad decisions, they're not cutting edge." And of course that's just not true, in most cases. These are usually good people, very smart people, stuck in processes or environments where it's difficult to do things the right way. Just for example, I was talking recently to some very bright engineers trying to implement change management, but they were completely stuck. This is a company that is about 100,000 people – for every action, they had to go outside their department to get work done. So, piecemeal work was killing them – death by a thousand cuts.

Where to Start

In most larger enterprises aiming for complete automation, end to end, is somewhat of a pipe dream – just because these companies have so many groups and siloes and dependencies. But that's not saying that DevOps is impossible, even in shared services type orgs. This isn't nuclear science, it's like learning to play the piano. It doesn't require brilliance, it's not art – it's just hard work. It just takes discipline and practice, daily practice.

I have the strong impression that many companies out there SAY they are doing DevOps, whatever that means – but really it hasn't even gotten off the ground. They're still on Square 1, analyzing and trying to come up with the right recipe or roadmap that will fit every single use case they might encounter, past, present, and future. So, what's the best way forward if you're stuck in that position?

Well, first off, how much control do you have over your infrastructure? Do you have the ability to provision your VM's, self-service? If so, you've got some more cards to play with. Assuming you do – you start with version control. Just pick one – ideally a system you already have. Even if it's something ancient like Subversion – if that's what you have, use it as your one single source of truth. Don't try to migrate to latest and greatest hipster VC system. You just need to be able to programmatically create and revert commits. Put all your shell scripts in there and start managing your infrastructure from there, as code.

Now, you've got your artifacts in version control, and you're using it as a single repository, right? Great – then talk to the people running deployments on your team. What's the most painful thing about releases? Make a list of these items, and pick one and try to automate it. And always prioritize building blocks that can be consumed elsewhere. For example, don't attempt to start by picking a snowflake production webserver and trying to automate EVERYTHING about it – you'll just end up with a monolith of infrastructure code you can't reuse elsewhere, your quality needle won't budge. No, instead you'd want to take something simple and in common and create a building block out of it.

For example, time synchronization – it's shocking, once you talk to Operations people, how something so simple and obvious as a timestamp difference between servers can cause major issues – forcing a rollback due to cascading issues or a troubleshooting crunch because the clocks on two servers drifted out of synch and it broke your database replication. That's literally fixed in Linux by installing a single package and config. But think about the reward you'll get in terms of quality and stability with this very unglamorous but fundamental little shift.

Take that list and work on what's causing pain for your on-call people, what's causing your deployments to break. The more you can automate this, the better. And make it as self-service as possible – instead of having the devs fire off an email to you, where you create a ticket, then provision test environments – all those manual chokepoints – wouldn't it be better to have the devs have the ability to call an API or click on a web site button and get a test environment spun up automatically that's set up just like production? That's a force multiplier in terms of improving your quality right at the get-go.

Now you've got version control, you can provision from code, you can roll out changes and roll them back. Maybe, you add in inventory and discoverability of what's actually running in your infrastructure. It's amazing how few organizations really have a handle on what's actually running, holistically. But as you go, you identify some goals and work out the practices you want to implement – then choose the software tool that seems the best fit.

Continuous Delivery Is the Finish Line

The end goal though is always the same. Your target, your goal is to get as close as you can to Continuous Integration / Continuous Delivery. Aiming for continuous delivery is the most productive single thing an enterprise can do, pure and simple. There's tools around this – obviously working for Puppet I have my personal bias as to what's best. But pick one, after some thought – and play with it. Start growing out your testing skills, so you can trust your release gates.

With COTS products, you can't always adopt all of these practices – but you can get pretty close, even with big-splash, multi-GB releases. For example, you can use deployment slots and script as much as you can. Yes, there's going to be some manual steps – but the more you can automate even this, the happier you'll be.

Over time, kind of naturally, you'll see a set of teams appear that are using CI/ CD, and automation, and the company can point to these as success stories. That's when an executive sponsor can step in and set this as a mandate, top down. But just about every DevOps success story, we've seen goes through this pioneering phase where they're trying things out squad by squad and experimenting – that's a good thing. You can't skip this, no more than a caterpillar can go right to being a butterfly.

DevOps Teams

At first, I really hated the whole DevOps Team concept – and in the long term, it doesn't make sense. It's actually a common failure point – a senior manager starts holding this "A" team up as an example. This creates a whole legion of haters and enemies, people working with traditional systems who haven't been given the opportunity to change like the cool kids – the guys always off at conferences, running stuff in the cloud, blah blah. But in the short term, it totally has its place. You need to attach yourself to symbols that make it clear you're trying to change. If you try to boil the ocean or spin it out with dozens of teams, it gets diluted and your risk rises; it could lose credibility. Word of mouth needs to be in your favor, kind of like band t-shirts for teenagers. So, you can start with a small group initially for your experiments – just don't let it stay that way too long.

But what if you DON'T have that self-provisioning authority? Well, there's ways around that as well. You see departments doing things like doing capacity planning and reserving large pools of machines ahead of time. That's obviously suboptimal, and it's disappearing now that more people are seeing what a powerful game-changer the cloud and self-provisioned environments are. The point is – very rarely are we completely shackled and constrained when it comes to infrastructure.

Automation and Paying Off Technical Debt

It's all too easy to get bogged down in minutiae when it comes to automation. I said earlier that DevOps isn't art, it's just hard work – and that's true. But focus that hard work on the things that really matter. Your responsibility is to make sure you guard your time and that of the people around you. If you're not careful, you'll end up replacing this infinite backlog of manual work you have to do with an infinite amount of tasks you need to automate. That's really demoralizing, and it really hasn't made your life that much better!

Let's take the example of a classic three-tier web app you have onprem. And you've sunk a lot of time into it so that now it fails every week vs. every 6 months – terrific! But for that next step – instead of trying to automate it completely end to end, which you could do – how could you change it so that its more service oriented, more loosely coupled, so your maintenance drops even more and changes are less risky? Maybe building part of it as a microservice, or putting up that classic Martin Fowler strangler fig, will give you this dramatic payoff you would never get with grinding out automation for the sake of automation and never asking if there's a better way.

Paying off technical debt is a grind, just like paying off your credit card and paying off the mortgage. Of course, you need to do that – but it shouldn't be all you do! Maybe, you'll take some money and sink it into an investment somewhere, and get that big boost to your bottom line. So, instead of mindlessly just paying off your technical debt, realize you have options – some great investment areas open to you – that you can invest part of your effort in.

Optimism Bias and Culture

This brings us right back to where we started, communication. There is a fundamental blind spot in a lot of books and presentations I see on DevOps, and it has to do with our optimism bias. DevOps started out as a grassroots, community-driven movement – led and championed by passionate people that really care about what they're doing, why they're doing it. Pioneers like this are a small subset of the community though – but too often we assume "everyone is just like us"! What about the category a lot of people fall in – the ones who just want to show up, do their job, and then go home?

If we come to them with this crusade for efficiency and productivity, it just won't resonate with the 9 to 5 crowd. They like the job they have – they do a lot of manual changes, true, but they know how to do it, it guarantees a steady flow of work and therefore income, and any kind of change will not be viewed as an improvement – no matter how you try to sell it. You could call this "bad," or just realize that not everyone is motivated by the same things or thinks the same way. In your approach, you may have to mix a little bit of pragmatism in with that DevOpsy-starry eyed idealism – think of different ways to reach them, work around them, or wait for a strong management drive to collapse this kind of resistance.

Rob England, The IT Skeptic

Rob England B.Sc., CITP is an independent IT management consultant, trainer, and commentator based in Wellington, New Zealand. He usually works with his partner, Dr Cherry Vu. Together as a team, they brand themselves as Teal Unicorn, transforming organizations to new ways of working and managing.

Rob is an internationally recognized thought leader in DevOps and IT Service Management (ITSM) and a published author of seven books and many articles. He is best known for his controversial blog and alter-ego, the IT Skeptic. Rob labels himself a "DevOps anticryptoequinologist" – he's interested in DevOps for horses, not unicorns.

Lessons for Your Roadmap

- *Use big public storytelling events and relentless optimism to keep momentum going in Year 2*

- *PubSec success story – start with a single coordinated release, then self service dev environments, then testing*

Slow Down to Match Your Org's Pace

I've always been working with IT: developers, databases, systems management. I have been working with ITIL for years. With my previous vendor employer, we had such a diverse portfolio that I ended up supporting every kind of technology on earth. As a result, I've been a generalist rather than a specialist for many years. Then I went out on my own as a consultant and writer 12 years ago. My blog gets about 40K unique visitors a month; I was lucky enough to get in on the DevOps wave very early on.

A lot of my customers are public sector. In organizations, if you're too much of an irritant, there's a kind of organizational immune system – all these white cells come out of the woodwork and shut you down, smother you, even eject you. So, one of my first learning lessons was to slow down the pace to what the org can handle.

Watch out for that second year too! it gets harder in that second, critical year. The first year is usually all roses – you get all the early adopters onboard, lots of progress get made. The second year is a different story. All the low-lying fruit has been picked in terms of technical challenges, and difficult challenges like infrastructure as code, testing, and working with huge systems of record and legacy apps start adding to the load. And you start encountering some real resistance within the company – like a train starting up, taking the slack out of the couplers one wagon at a time, the load gets heavier and heavier until by year 2 you're now pulling along the whole org instead of just a small team of enthusiasts. There's a lot more inertia there to overcome.

My magic cure for overcoming this is simple – relentless optimism! You need to keep the executives onboard and keep up that awareness of success that's so critical to keep momentum going. I'm a big fan of storytelling and getting people up on big public stages in the organization to tell their story.

Tool Selection in DevOps

Technology makes us more efficient and more effective. But it doesn't solve problems on its own. People get very passionate about technology when you work at a tech company – it becomes very personal, and they lose objectivity. I refuse to get entangled in arguments about the pros and cons of various tools. This is really a closed problem: there is always a solution, you just need to find it. People, practices, systems, culture is an open problem, where there may not even BE a solution – it's much more challenging!

For me, DevOps is a very human-centric thing. People talk about how hippie and undefined it can be, but that's part of what appeals – restoring your faith in human goodness, treating people as a valuable part of a team. That's what Gene Kim calls Humane IT – those ethics really appeal to me.

DevOps is made possible by technology, it can't be done without it – but the heart of it really is changing the way people feel and the way they're treated. That all comes from Agile, with retrospectives, accepting input from the team, how to work together best in small groups. That's the power of DevOps – it combines that human part from Agile with the systems thinking from Lean. Technology is only there to make that flow happen.

Speeding Up Cycle Time

One public sector customer of mine experienced the project from hell that had some ugly consequences on go live, impacted the business, hurt IT badly. Everyone had agreed that this must never happen again. But we're talking complex apps here and 20 years of legacy code; massive systems that were all intertangled. You can't just jump to microservices in this case. But they couldn't stay where they were. What to do?

The CIO announced that they were going to solve this by doing DevOps – in their case, that meant a single, integrated release, every 6 weeks. And the first release would happen in 6 weeks. All hell broke loose! In 6 weeks, I think about half of their software made it out the door. But, it all worked. 6 weeks after that, they had 60% of the code shipped; now, they've done a dozen releases. These larger systems release now every 4 weeks, and they'll get to weekly. They've improved quality by orders of magnitude. We're now at about 80% code coverage of the core integration systems.

The first 6 months involved no automation or even continuous integration. It was focusing on people, behavior, process, life cycles. To get to weekly cycles obviously, we'll need to automate, but huge progress was made just by focusing on process.

First, we began by creating a self-service integration environment, where developers have full control and can do anything they want to integrate their code. There was some resistance to this, but once they got to this stage – now they can write code without having to ask a sysprod to migrate code.

Testing was the second hurdle; instead of having a separate environment for security and another for performance, they consolidated them all into a single testing environment. This cut down on wait time and mismatch issues, significantly.

Where We Are So Far

As far as DevOps being successful – well, of course it is. There's a hype curve with every new idea that we saw with Agile, and ITIL before that. You go through overinflated expectations, to the trough of disillusionment – I think we are heading down that slope right now with DevOps, where people are saying "This doesn't work!" But things will level out to a rational state.

I'm very positive about the DevOps Enterprise Summit – every year it gets better. You watch organizations coming back every year and track their journey. It's a very positive story, very enriching. I'm a professional skeptic, but I've seen DevOps work and I know how powerful it is.

Ryan Comingdeer, Five Talent

Ryan Comingdeer is the CTO of Five Talent Software, a thriving software consultancy firm based in Oregon with a strong focus on cloud development and architecture. Ryan has 20 years of experience in cloud solutions, enterprise applications, IoT development, web site development, and mobile apps.

Lessons for Your Roadmap

- *Honest retrospectives build trust*
- *A true MVP is something you're ashamed of. Most development teams are still releasing weeks of work, not hours*
- *A faster release cycle speaks for itself.*
- *Documentation is still important to set expectations and a guardrail for your engineers*
- *Blame is the enemy of learning and communication*
- *Automate everything; it's the only way to deliver at scale*
- *Gamedays rock to catch gaps in your readiness – they should be standard part of your pre-release checklist*

Obstacles in Implementing Agile

Last week, I was talking to a developer at a large enterprise who was boasting about their adoption of Agile. I asked him – OK, that's terrific – but how often do these get out the door to production? It turns out that these little micro changes get dropped off at the QA department, and then are pushed out to staging once a month or so… where it sits, until it's deemed ready to release and the IT department is ready – once a quarter. So that little corner was Agile – but the entire process was stuck in the mud.

The first struggle we often face when we engage with companies is just getting these two very different communities to talk to one another. Often, it's been years and years of the operations department hating on the development team, and the devs not valuing or even knowing about business value and efficiency. This is hard work but understanding that philosophy and seeing the other side of things is that vital first step.

I know I've won in these discussions – and this may be 12 meetings in – when I can hear the development team agreeing to the operations teams goals, or an Operations guy speaking about development requirements. You have to respect each other and view work as a collaborative effort.

For the development teams, often they're onboard with change because they recognize the old way isn't working. Often times, the business throws out a deadline – "get this done by April 1st" – and when they try to drill into requirements, they get an empty chair. So, they do the best they can – but there's no measurable goals, no iterative way of proving success over an 18-month project. So, they love the idea of producing work often in sprints – but then we have to get them to understand the value of prototyping, setting interim deliverables and work sizing.

Then, we get to the business stakeholders and have to explain – this is no longer a case where we can hand off a 300-page binder of requirements and ask a team to "get it done." The team is going to want us involved, see if we're on the right track, get some specific feedback. Inevitably, we get static over this – because this seems like so much more work. I mean, we had it easy in the old days – we could hand off work and wait 12 months for the final result. Sure, the end result was a catastrophic failure, and everybody got fired, but at least I wasn't hassled with all these demos and retrospectives every 2 weeks! That instant feedback is really uncomfortable for many leaders – there's no insulation, no avoidance of failure. It does require a commitment to show up and invest in the work being done as it's being done.

Retrospectives for me are one of the best things about Agile. I wish they were done more often. We do two, one internally, then a separate one with the customer so we're prepared – and we're upfront, here's where we failed, here's the nonbillable time we invested to fix it. You would think that would be really damaging, but we find it's the opposite. The best thing a consulting company can do is show growth, reviewing successes and failures directly and honestly to show progress. Our relationships are based on trust – the best trust building exercise I've seen yet is when we admit our failure and what we're going to do to fix it. I guarantee you our relationship with the customer is tighter because of how we handled a crisis – vs. attempting to hide, minimize, or shift blame.

Implementing DevOps

It's very common that the larger organizations we work with aren't sure of where to start when it comes to continuous integration or CD. Where do I begin? How much do I automate? Often, it comes down to changing something like checking in a new feature say after 2 weeks of work. That's just not going to cut it – what can we deliver in 4 hours?

That being said, CI/CD is Step 1 to DevOps; it's fundamental. Infrastructure as Code is further down the list – it takes a lot of work, and it's sometimes hard to see the value of it. Then, you start to see the impact with employee rotation and especially when you have to rollback. And think about how much easier it makes it when you have to rollback changes – you can see what was changed and when; without it, you might be stuck and have to fix a problem in place. The single biggest selling point for Infrastructure as Code is security; you can demonstrate what you're doing to regulate environments, you can show up to an audit prepared with a list of changes, who made them and what they were, and a complete set of security controls.

A True MVP

Most of the companies we work with come to us because they've got a huge backlog of aging requests, these mile-long wish lists from sales and marketing teams. We explain the philosophy behind DevOps and the value of faster time to market, small iterations, and more stable environments and a reliable deployment process. Then, we take those huge lists of wishes and break them down into very small pieces of work and have the business prioritize them. There's always one that stands out – and that's our starting point.

The first sprint is typically just a proof of concept of the CI/CD tools and how they can work on that top #1 feature we've identified. The development team works on it for perhaps 2 days, then sysops takes over and uses our tooling to get this feature into the sandbox environment and then production. This isn't even a beta product, it's a true MVP – something for friends and family. But it's an opportunity to show the business and get that feedback that we're looking for – is the UI ok? How does the flow look? And once the people driving business goals sit down and start playing with the product on that first demo, 2 weeks later, they're hooked. And we explain – if you give us your suggestions, we can get them to staging and then onto production with a single click. It sells itself – we don't need long speeches.

The typical reaction we get is – "great, you've delivered 5% of what I really want. Come back when it's 100% done." And the product is a little underwhelming. But that's because we're not always sticking to the true definition of a minimum viable product (MVP). I always say, "If an MVP is not something you're ashamed of, it's not a MVP!" Companies like Google and Amazon are past masters at this – they throw something crude out there and see if it sticks. It's like they're not one company but 1000 little startups. You've got to understand when to stop and get that feedback.

I've seen customers go way down in the weeds and waste a ton of money on something that ends up just not being viable. One customer I worked with spent almost $250K and a year polishing and refactoring this mobile app endlessly, when we could have delivered something for about $80K – a year earlier! Think of how the market shifted in that time, all the insights we missed out on. Agile is all about small, iterative changes – but most companies are still failing at this. They'll make small changes and then gate them so they sit there for months.

When we start seeing really progress is when the product is released ahead of deadline. That really captures a lot of attention – whoa, we wanted this app written in 15 months, you delivered the first version in two weeks – 9 months in we can see we're going to be done 4 months early because of our cadence.

Starting Small

So, here's my advice – start small.

Let me give you one example – we have one customer that's a classic enterprise – they've been around for 60 years, and it's a very political, hierarchical climate, very waterfall oriented. They have 16 different workloads. Well, we're really starting to make progress now in their DevOps transformation – but we never would have made it if we'd tried this all-in massive crusade effort. Instead, we took half of one workload, as a collection of features and said – we're going to take this piece and try something new. We implemented Agile sprints and planning, setup automated infrastructure, and CI/CD. Yeah, it ruffled some feathers – but no one could argue with how fast we delivered these features, and how much more stable they were, and how happy the customers were because we involved them in the process.

The biggest problem we had was – believe it or not – getting around some bad habits on having meetings for the sake of having meetings. So, we had to set some standards – what makes for a successful meeting? What does a client acceptance meeting look like?

Even if you're "just a developer" or "just an ops guy," you can create a lot of changes by the way you engage with the customer, by documenting the pieces you fill in, by setting a high standard when it comes to quality and automation.

Documentation

I find it really key to write some things down before we even begin work. When a developer gets a 2-week project, we make sure expectations are set clearly in documentation. That helps us know what the standards of success are, gets QA on the same page – it guides everything that we do.

I also find it helps us corral the chaos caused by runaway libraries. We have a baseline documentation for each project that sets the expectation of the tools we will use. Here, I'll just say – it's harder to catch this when you're using a microservice architecture, where you have 200 repos to monitor for the Javascript libraries they're choosing. Last week, we found this bizarre PDF writer that popped up – why would we have two different PDF generators for the same app? So, we had to refactor so we're using a consistent PDF framework. That exposed a gap in our documentation, so we patch that and move on.

Documentation is also a lifesaver when it comes to onboarding a new engineer. We can show them the history of the project, and the frameworks we've chosen, and why. Here's how to use our error logging engine, this is where to find Git repos, etc. It's kept very up to date, and much of it is customer facing. We present the design pattern we'll be using; here's the test plans and how we're going to measure critical paths and handle automated testing. That's all set and done before Day 1 with the customer so expectations are in line with reality.

We do use a launch checklist, which might cover 80% of what comes up – but it seems like there's always some weird gotchas that crop up. We break up our best practices by type – for our Microsoft apps, IOT, monoliths, or mobile – each one with a little different checklist.

It's kind of an art – you want just the right amount, not too much, not too little. When we err, I think we tend to over-document. Like most engineers, I tend to overdo it as I'm detail oriented. But for us, documentation isn't an afterthought; they're guardrails. It sets the rules of engagement, defines how we're measuring success. It's saved our bacon, many times!

Microservices

You can't just say "microservices are only for Netflix and other big companies." It's not the size of the team, but the type of the project. You can have a tiny one-developer project and implement it very successfully with microservices.

It does add quite a bit of overhead, and there's a point of diminishing returns. We still use monolith type approaches when it comes to throwaway proofs of concept; you can just crank it out.

And it's a struggle to keep these services discrete and finite. Let's say you have a small application. How do you separate out the domain modules for your community area and say an event directory so they're truly standalone? In the end, you tend to create a quasi-ORM, where your objects have a high dependency on each other; the microservices look terrific at the app or the UI layer, but there's a shared data layer. Or you end up with duplicated data, where the interpretation of "customer" data varies so much from service to service.

Logging is also more of a challenge – you have to put more thought into capturing and aggregating errors with your framework.

But, in general, microservices are definitely a winner and our choice of architecture. Isolation of functionality is something we really value in our designs; we need to make sure that changes to invoicing won't have any effect on inventory management or anything else. It pays off in so many ways when it comes to scalability and reliability.

Testing

We have QA as a separate functional team; there's a ratio of 25 devs to every QA person. We make it clear that writing automated unit tests, performance tests, security tests – that's all in the hands of the developers. But manual smoke tests and enforcing that the test plans actually does what it's supposed to is all done by the QA dept. We're huge fans of behavior-driven development, where we identify a test plan, lay it out, the developer writes unit tests, and QA goes through and confirms that's what the client wanted.

With our environments, we do have a testing environment set up with dummy data; then, we have a sandbox environment, with a 1-week-old set of actual production data where we do performance and acceptance testing. That's the environment the customer has full access to. We don't do performance testing against production directly. We're big fans of using software to mimic production loads – anywhere from 10 users/sec to 10K users/sec, along with mocks and fakes with our test layer design.

Continuous Learning

To me, continuous learning is really the heart of things. It goes all the way back to the honest retrospectives artifact in scrum – avoiding the blame game, documenting the things that can be improved at the project or process level. It's never the fault of Dave, that guy who wrote the horrible code – why did we miss that as a best practice in our code review? Did we miss something in how we look at maintainability, security, performance? Are lead developers setting expectation properly, how can we improve in our training?

Blame is the enemy of learning and communication. The challenge for us is setting the expectation that failure is an expected outcome, a good thing that we can learn from. Let's count the number of failures we're going to have and see how good our retrospectives can get. We're going to fail, that's OK – how we learn from these failures?

Usually, our chances of winning come down to one thing – a humble leader. If the person at the top can swallow their pride, knows how to delegate, and recognizes that it will take the entire team to be engaged and solve the problem – then, a DevOps culture change is possible. But if the leader has a lot of pride, usually there's not much progress that can be made.

Monitoring

Monitoring is too important to leave to end of project; that's our finish line. So, we identify what the KPI's are to begin with. Right now, it revolves around three areas – performance (latency of requests), security (breach attempts), and application logs (errors returned, availability, and uptime). For us, we ended up using New Relic for performance indicators, DataDog for their app layer KPIs, and Amazon's Inspector. OWASP has a set of tools they recommend for scanning; we use these quite often for our static scans.

Sometimes, of course, we have customers that want to go cheap on monitoring. So, quite often, we'll just go to app level errors; but that's our bare minimum. We always log, sometimes we don't monitor. We had this crop up this morning with a customer – after a year or more, we went live, but all we had was that minimal logging. Guess what, that didn't help us much when the server went down! Going bare-bones on monitoring is something customers typically regret, because of surprises like that. Real user monitoring, like you can get with any cloud provider, is another thing that's incredibly valuable checking for things like latency across every region.

Production Support by Developers

Initial on-calls support is handled in-house by a separate Sysops team; we actually have it in our agreement with the customer that application developers aren't a part of that on-call rotation. If something has made it through our testing and staging environments, that knocks out a lot of potential errors. So, 90% of the time, a bug in production is not caused by a code change; it's something environmental – a server reboot, a firewall config change, a SSL cert expires. We don't want to hassle our developers with this. But, we do have them handle some bug triage – always during business hours though.

Let's just be honest here – these are two entirely separate disciplines, specialties. Sysops teams love ops as code and wading through server error logs – developers hate doing that work! So, we separate out these duties. Yes, we sometimes get problems when we move code from a dev environment to QA – if so, there's usually some information missing that the dev needs to add to his documentation in the handoff to sysops.

And we love feature flags and canary releases. Just last week, we rolled out an IOT project to 2000 residential homes. One feature we rolled out to only the Las Vegas homes to see how it worked. It works great – the biggest difficulty we find is documenting and managing who's getting new features and when, so you know if a bug is coming from a customer in Group A or B.

Automation

For us, automating everything is the #1 principle. It reduces security concerns, drops the human error factor, and increases our ability to experiment faster with infrastructure our codebase. Being able to spin up environments and roll out POCs is so much easier with automation. It all comes down to speed. The more automation you have in place, the faster you can get things done. It does take effort to set up initially; payoff is more than worth it. Getting your stuff out the door as fast as possible with small, iterative changes is the only really safe way; that's only possible with automation.

You would think everyone would be onboard with the idea of automation over manually logging on and poking around on VMs when there's trouble, but – believe it or not – that's not always the case. And sometimes our strongest resistance to this comes from the director/CTO level!

First, we review compliance with customer – half the game is education. We ask them if they're aware of what GDPR is – for 90% of our customers, that's just not on their radar, and it's not really clear at this point what compliance means specifically in how we store user information. So, we give them papers to review and drop tasks into our sprints to support compliance for the developers and the sysops team with the CI/CD pipeline.

Gamedays

Most of my clients aren't brave enough to run something like Simian Army or Chaos Monkey on live production systems! But we do gamedays, and we love them. Here's how that works:

I don't let the team know what the problem is going to be, but one week before launch – on our sandbox environments, we do something truly evil to test our readiness. And we check how things went – did alerts get fired correctly by our monitoring tools? Was the event logged properly? How did the escalation process work, and did the right people get the information they needed fast enough to respond? Did they have the access they needed to make the changes? Were we able to use our standard release process to get a fix out to production? Did we have the right amount of redundancy on the team? Was the runbook comprehensive enough, and were the responders able to use our knowledgebase to track down similar problems in the past to come up with a remedy?

The whole team loves this, believe it or not. We learn so much when things go bump in the night. Maybe, we find a problem with auto healing, or there's an opportunity to change the design so the environments are more loosely coupled. Maybe, we need to clear up our logging, or tune our escalation process, or spread some more knowledge about our release pipeline. There's always something, and it usually takes us at least a week to fold in these lessons learned into the product before we do a hard launch. Gamedays are huge for us – so much so, we make sure it's a part of our statement of work with the customer.

For one recent product, we did three Gamedays on sandbox and we felt pretty dialed in. So, 1 week before go-live, we injected a regional issue on production – which forced the team to duplicate the entire environment into a completely separate region using cold backups. Our SLA was 2 hours; the whole team was able to duplicate the entire production set from Oregon to Virginia datacenters in less than 45 minutes! It was such a great team win; you should have seen the celebration.

Sam Guckenheimer, Microsoft

Sam Guckenheimer is the Product Owner for Azure DevOps. In this capacity, he acts as the chief customer advocate, responsible for strategy of the next releases of these products, focusing on DevOps, Pipelines and Agile.

Lessons for Your Roadmap

- *Find your North Star. Commit to a long effort, and every 6 months set three to four goals to show stairstep progress toward that goal*

- *It's very challenging to find the right metrics to drive against*

- *Keep track of your people's job satisfaction and happiness*

- *Servant leadership – good leaders look for ways of making their team's jobs easier*

- *Have a clear, written definition of done – they're consistent guardrails for every team*

Avoid Massive Reorgs

One thing I want to start with – it really annoys me when I read grandiose claims that DevOps is broken in some way. We know that's just not the case – Gartner tells us at least half of enterprises have something going on with DevOps and they all want to do more. If you look at Agile, which began with the Agile Manifesto back in 2001 – and compare it with where it was as a movement a decade later in 2011 – well, that would look very much like where we are at today, about 10 years after DevOps first began as a concept back in 2009. The trends are really clear, and our success rate and the maturity of the tools and processes part is only going to go up.

It's just not true when some say you have to "blow up the organization" to make DevOps work. Change is necessary – you have to get rid of all the handoffs, the waste, and really follow the Lean model with disintermediating developers from production and from customers. But that doesn't mean you need to make drastic moves and that's not how we did it at Microsoft. It can be done in an evolutionary way.

Most companies don't have the luxury of saying, "let's blow it up" and just jettison decades of code with their legacy applications and start over. That's your lifeblood! I know that was true with us on the Azure DevOps team; we had to go about things in a very gradual way, so we didn't threaten the jugular of our company.

Find Your North Star

Six years ago we found our North Star – how we wanted to go about delivering value using the DevOps mindset – and we pointed to it, saying "we want to be a world class engineering organization." Everything we've done since then, every major decision we've made, has been built around measuring our progress toward that mission.

Jez Humble has joked a few times about some companies trying to "sprinkle magical microservices fairy dust" over things to magically get cloud services architecture. I have to say – there was no fairy dust for us. It required progressive change, some very conscious hard engineering changes, and walking the walk.

Just for example, overhauling our test portfolio and moving to Git took 3 years. We kept deprecating and replacing older, slow tests with the faster ones incrementally – sprint by sprint, test by test. Now, it takes us about 7 minutes to run 70K unit tests before a developer commits to master. But the value is incredible for us – before that, we had these long-running integration tests that had never run completely green, that always required manual intervention and was killing our release flow.

Everything – our refactoring from monolith to microservices, our safe deployment practices, building a life cycle culture, even our datacenter standup automation – required a lot of work and a multiyear commitment, persistence despite setbacks. We knew though where the "North Star" was, and we were committed. Our approach was – set the goal, measure the progress, and keep going until we get there.

Production Support

Shifting to a production support mindset was a big change and of course not everyone was onboard, especially at first. We knew that would be our most important and critical win – making sure the delivery teams were onboard and happy with what was going on. We measured this as one of our first KPIs. We would do regular surveys of engineering satisfaction and go into depth about their jobs, how tooling was supporting their jobs, the process was supporting their jobs – and what we saw was a steady rise in satisfaction.

Just for example on this, one of the things we measured was alerting frequency – are we getting to the right person the first time? That's something we are always watching – if you're waking people up at 2 in the morning, it had better be the right person. We needed to make sure that we are paying attention to the things that matter to people's lives and their satisfaction with their jobs.

When you're genuine, you get a genuine response. This all helps build that high-trust culture that Gene Kim and others have emphasized as key.

The concept of servant leadership has been a big part of our change; good managers care about their team and look for ways to make their jobs easier. That's the Andon cord philosophy – anyone on the floor can pull that cord, stop the line if needed – and the manager comes over, the root cause is identified and rolled into the process so future incidents don't happen. So, in our case – we don't close out livesite incidents for example until the fix is identified and in the backlog so it won't happen again.

Setting Goals and Metrics

Our North Star remains fixed, but we are always redefining how we want to get there. Every 6 months, we select, epic by epic, three or four goals that define success for us over the next 6 months, and the specific metrics that will define them. We publish these, and they're flowed all the way up the management chain. Those goals and metrics on an epic level don't change for those 6 months. Each person on the feature crews know which epics they're working on and can ask each sprint – what are the next few things we need to do to move the needle along these goals? They look ahead about three sprints in terms of what they're trying to do – no more than that. That level of planning is key for us to make progress in an iterative way and minimize disruption.

In the beginning, we thought it was really not a big deal to figure out the metrics and focus on the right thing and so forth. It turns out that finding the right metrics is as complicated as designing the right feature. It's really not obvious what in terms of measurement and what you're striving for. Very frequently, you don't have an out of the box way of doing the telemetry – so you need to instrument for the business APIs you want.

A really clear example on this – one of the metrics that we're interested in is, how many developers are working on projects that are doing continuous delivery to Azure? That's a very hard thing to count. You have to make several leaps of instrumentation and joins in order to answer that. Asking the question clearly and getting a way of gathering data on it is a real engineering problem – and one that typically is made to sound much simpler and less of an obstacle than it really is on the web or in books about lean customer analytics.

This goes way, way beyond your standard # of site visitors or simple generic use cases for a web site. Until you start getting down to brass tacks and define what the things are that we care about as a business and why – it's difficult to appreciate how challenging it is to come up with the right measurables.

Value Stream Mapping

I'm going to shock you a little here – we don't do normal value stream mapping here. My observation is that value stream mapping is really effective when you want to get people on the same page and get some momentum going toward a DevOps movement. Once you show people – wow, it takes us 60 days to get something to production, and most of that is wait time – 5 days for approval here, 7 days for testing here – that's great to get everyone to see the elephant in the room. It never fails to shock people once they see how huge that bucket of idle time is!

For us, we're past that initial shock phase. We focus heavily on all the things that value stream mapping attacks in terms of handoffs, idle time vs. process time, etc. – but it is definitely not something you need to do on an ongoing basis, in my opinion.

Two Key Antipatterns

I see two key failings that sometimes trips organizations up. First, people often think in terms of formulas – you need to do X with the people, Y with the process, and Z with the tools – and think of each of these as being independent pillars, that you can tackle one at a time in phases. It ends up being counterproductive, making things more complicated and lengthening things, because in reality all these things are interrelated and need to be thought of together.

My advice is to fight the tendency to take a single practice, however good, and try to implement it in isolation. Think in terms of all three columns as supporting a single building together; each improvement should touch on people, process, and tools in some way and make it a little better. Focus on the quick wins – try to stairstep your maturity, building something small that quickens that release cycle and delivers feedback faster.

The second antipattern is not getting the right balance of leadership and delegation. You need to have obvious skin in the game from leadership, and initiative from individual practitioners. Think back to that great book *Drive* by Dan Pink, which stressed the leadership value between Autonomy, Mastery, and Purpose. You are going to need to spark people and get them enthusiastic, active, and feeling like they control their destiny – autonomy.

It's really part art and science, because that autonomy has to be balanced with purpose, which is driven consistently and forcefully by management. And if you look at most of the current execs at Microsoft, you will see that they practice both high empathy and engage deep technically organizations.

Mission is key for us, but it goes beyond just a few words or a slogan. We put up guardrails, very clear rules of the road that specifies "here is what you need to do to check your code into master." We have a very clear definition of done that is common in every team – "code delivered with tests and telemetry and deployed in production worldwide."

This is the exact opposite of "it works on my machine" – and everyone knows it. If you're doing new work, there's a set of common services we provide, including sample code and documentation. So, no one has to reinvent the wheel when it comes to telemetry for example – you might improve on it, but you would never have to deliver this from scratch, it's reused from a common set of services organizations.

Seth Vargo, Google

Seth Vargo is a Developer Advocate at Google. Previously, he worked at HashiCorp, Chef Software, CustomInk, and a few Pittsburgh-based startups. He is the author of Learning Chef and is passionate about reducing inequality in technology. When he is not writing, working on open source, teaching, or speaking at conferences, Seth enjoys spending time with his friends and advising nonprofits.

Lessons for Your Roadmap

- *Start small and learn what works with your culture*
- *Improve your MTTD and MTTR with gamedays and chaos exercises*
- *Alerts must be very specific and actionable*
- *Every release involves a balance of risk and opportunity; SRE makes this explicit*
- *Find out how to gauge customer satisfaction; that should be your touchstone for KPI's*
- *Blameless postmortems are the only way to get helpful remediation action steps*

DevOps and the SRE Movement

I'm a Developer Advocate for Google. The role is a cycle between evangelization through blogs and conferences, direct customer engagements, and providing feedback to product teams on what's hitting the mark (or what's not). It's very rewarding – almost like being a traveling product manager, where your stakeholder is the community and you represent their voice.

There's a bit of fuss about the difference between DevOps and Site Reliability Engineering (SRE), which I frankly don't understand. We already know what DevOps is about – breaking down silos, sharing blame, reducing MTTD/ MTTR, leveraging tooling, and automation. The challenge though, especially for large enterprises, is that it's not prescriptive. DevOps says for us to reduce MTTD, but it doesn't tell us to use, for example, Prometheus for logging, PagerDuty for alerting, etc. In this way, DevOps is similar to an abstract class or interface in programming. Our SRE discipline at Google is a very prescriptive way to do DevOps. To put it in coding terms, "class SRE implements DevOps." SRE is a concrete implementation of that DevOps interface; it's a very strict set of guidelines and rules of how to implement DevOps at scale, and it's opinionated.

I don't necessarily agree when people say that SRE is the future of DevOps, even though I love the SRE discipline and it works so well for us. There are other DevOps implementations coming out of Facebook and VictorOps that can happily coexist with the SRE discipline. So SRE is not DevOps 2.0 – it's just one specific recipe for doing DevOps. There's lots of other ways that work, equally valuable.

And we have to admit the challenge large, established enterprises face, is huge. The word "entrenched" doesn't even cover it. We're talking about 150 years of corporate culture, everything based on incentives around competition. Do you want that raise? Do you want more vacation time, a better office? Then, you have to step on your peers to get ahead. That culture doesn't just go away overnight. You can't just step in and say, "everybody gets along now, we're all about learning and not using people as stepping stones anymore." There's a lot of history of unhealthy competition and fear that has to be unlearned first.

No company starts out with yearly deployments; all these struggling companies, when they first started, were likely incredibly agile – even before that movement existed! Services and software got rolled out the door frequently, but then there's that one customer or account that is such a large value that you'll do anything to keep them. Now, we have to start slowing down releases because we care more about availability than we do augmenting these services. It builds up tension between the people that build services and those that keep it running. This ultimately leads to slowing or halting releases and adding unnecessary processes in the release process.

Tips for Adopting DevOps

First off, don't boil an ocean. Often times, CTO/CIOs catch fire and announce that SRE is the way of the future, and that they're going to reorganize with cross functional teams across an entire enterprise – hundreds of teams. Don't do that! Think about your DevOps or SRE transition in the same way that you'd release software. You wouldn't just dump it all out there at once.

You'd take a small subset of users and get it bulletproof before you did a grand rollout. Do the same thing when adopting a new discipline like SRE – take a low performing team and hand them some books and videos – ask them to take this on as a challenge.

If that team is successful, you can gradually expand outward. You want that organic growth; otherwise, any failure in the system at scale is exacerbated. Let's say you hit a roadblock with legal and compliance – or "where dreams go to die," as I call it. What's the more likely scenario for success – if one team is trying this as an experiment, or if there's 20 teams all hammering at the door? Start small and learn from what works with your culture.

Preparedness and Disaster Testing

Part of the SRE discipline is preparing for disaster, so we often do internal drills to see if our fail safes actually work. As more organizations adopt microservices and containers, the probability for failure increases. With tools like Kubernetes, auto-healing is easier… but the probability for cascading failure actually increases. We often have linchpins in these complex large systems – a single point of failure – where a single subsystem dies and brings down the entire system as a result.

This is why testing in production and introducing chaos is so important. If you practice high availability concepts – redundancy, failover, all the theory in the world – but never test, you don't know if it's actually going to work! I often work with organizations that have very clear processes for backing up and restoring data. When I ask them if they ever run DR scenarios, I get a blank stare. "No, we've never done that"… so, how do you know if it works?! What happens if halfway through your recovery, you realize your backup has corrupted data? Suddenly, what you thought was an hour or so of work turns into days of downtime as you manually repair data. That false sense of security cane be incredibly damaging to an organization.

Escalation paths are also really important. In a large distributed system, the things that break first might not be the thing that's actually broken. Having a tiered response model – who do I go to if I get paged, and if I realize it's a problem with another system – what's the handoff process? You can't have an incident sitting there for 45 minutes while you're trying to locate the team on point.

We have an internal system to track our incidents what was done. This helps us go back and see what happened, who participated and in what role, and build a running log of checkpoints. I like to call it Crash Bandicoot – it shows at what times we deploy a fix, at what point errors were reduced to 10%, etc. That system is open to most engineers at Google.

Blameless Postmortem Culture

People won't take risks if there's a fear of drastic failure. If we want people to experiment to get better performance, we have to convince them that if they mess something up, they won't get fired. If every outage is treated as opportunity to blame someone, we'll never learn anything.

There are some very well-publicized incidents where an engineer caused a major outage by running a command against production. If you go into the postmortem looking to blame the engineer, that's the wrong approach. This was fundamentally a problem with the architecture, with safety, not a human problem. Why did this user have read/write access to every row and table in the production system? Why does the staging database live on the same subnet as the production database? These questions become action items or specific steps that can improve the overall reliability and health of the system. But if your developers are afraid that if they break something they'll get fired — they're not going to be on the top of their game, they're going to suck at their jobs, because you have a fear-based culture.

One interesting factoid about Google — SWEs and SREs use the exact same toolchain. Every device has the same base instance, with the same set of CLI tools and source controls — no matter what your role is. Tooling, automation, and visibility — it's all kept the same.

Metrics and Monitoring

We track KPIs for services on a few different levels. The first is our SLI — Service Level Indicator — which shows latency, uptime, number of healthy vs. unhealthy request, etc. Second is SLO — Service Level Objectives — which is an integration of those SLIs over time where we say ratio of 500 server responses must be <5% for rolling 5-minute period. If we violate that — that spills into availability, our SLA, the third level. We measure everything — we have monitoring, disk, CPU usage, etc. — but the things that we measure, vs. the things we monitor, vs. the things we alert on are very different. We may log everything, we may only monitor a subset of these logs — and of that subset, only a fraction can trigger an alert. We have access to data if we need it — but we don't alert an SRE if our CPU usage exceeds 95% for a few seconds.

Signal to noise ratio is a very important piece of the SRE puzzle as well — you should only be alerted for actionable things. Even if an instance goes down — let's say 1 going down out of 10 — we don't alert an operator. We're at a slightly reduced redundancy, but why should we make someone up in middle of night for something that can be fixed it in the morning or is self-healing?

People often think about SRE as just being that hard cap, the error budget, but it really goes beyond that. Just having a number around availability starts this conversation between the product engineering and SRE teams. Let's say it's 95% availability – that's a lot of room, perfect for an alpha product. We can move quickly, take hours to fix a bug – let's have that conversation early. But for another product, say one with four 9's of availability, we need to slow down our shipping and rethink our entire process, because now availability and quality of service become the dominant concern. That availability target directly defines how quickly we can move.

Be careful about how you measure success. It's easy to look at things like Net Promoter Scores or sales figures to justify success; ultimately, what we should be caring about is customer satisfaction. But always keep in mind – yes, collect a ton of data, so you can make better informed decisions. Just remember that you don't know what you don't know. Every change is introducing a risk; we have to have conversations about what that risk could entail.

Lastly, it frustrates me that people focus on number of deployments a day as a success metric. "If you're deploying 10 million times a day you're doing DevOps!" No. That doesn't matter to your customers at all. They want value. So, does your site work? Are you delivering the features they want? Don't get caught up in the wrong metrics. Things like test code coverage, build deploy numbers, even build failures – they don't mean anything compared to customer satisfaction. Find out how to measure that – everything else is just signals, useful information but not the real definition of success.

Tyler Hardison, Redhawk Network Security

Tyler Hardison is the CTO of Redhawk Network Security. He's had a long career and has worked at every position from support desk to CIO, from small teams to large enterprises. Redhawk Network Security delivers practical information security services, including the best information technology solutions, regulatory expertise, and cybersecurity professionals in the Pacific Northwest. Redhawk works with organizations of all sizes to help develop security infrastructure and programs to

secure their information, assets, and reputation. Redhawk's proven security program methodology and technology integration allows customers to build world-class security programs that include assessment and compliance, managed security services, and network engineering.

Lessons for Your Roadmap

- *Split teams up if they grow past eight people*
- *Use kindergarten rules in code reviews*
- *Real leadership shows up when things break*
- *Security comes first — there's no excuse for not having it be part of your daily work*
- *Shared services is not a deal breaker — virtual cross-functional teams can work if they're aligned*
- *TDD is amazing for greenfield projects*
- *Interview and select inquisitive, learning focused people*

Back when I started out as a network administrator, DevOps wasn't a word yet, but if you were a good sysadmin you were already learning how to script and program things to make things more repeatable and predictable. So, I picked up some C# and Perl scripting chops to balance my background in Unix; then, I started branching out into databases and RDBMS, especially Oracle.

When the bank I was working for then started its first foray into internal development — up until then they'd outsourced everything — I started their internal web services development team, from the ground up. And that was a fantastic experience — I still stay in touch with my old team over there, and their current lead is a good friend of mine. Somehow though I always find my way back into development. Right now, I'm CTO wearing a couple of hats, managing the service delivery team as well as product development and software development for the portal, where we define our strategy and implement certain aspects that give us an edge in our field.

One thing that I keep coming back to is the importance of the unit. It's so much better to maintain small teams focused on a particular function vs. divisions and fleets of developers or testers — it's always better to have a small group of ninjas vs. a massive army of infantry. With the small teams I like to work on — we're talking a max of 8 — communication works so much better. You can pivot, change, and redirect the way you work, and you can onboard new people in a flash. So, if my teams grow past that magic number of 8, I start looking for ways to divide them — maybe one team handles IOS development, and another the API. Almost right away you start seeing the benefits – suddenly the whole team is working on the same mandate, and you stop seeing brain drain. There's a reason why SWAT teams are the size they are.

Code Reviews

Team dynamics can be fragile, and you have to work to keep the dynamic positive. For example, we knew regular code reviews were important and wanted to make them positive and upbuilding, a learning experience vs. a beatdown by the silverback devs. At the time we had about four or five projects running at a time. Each week, we would either nominate a volunteer or have a specific developer scheduled if it involved some cool new feature or library. The way we set up our weekly code reviews was with the clear understanding along kindergarten rules – everyone has to be polite. You're picking apart someone's sandcastle, something they've spent time on and are proud of. So, don't go kicking it down; play nice. It's a balance – you want it to be useful and have some teeth to prevent bad code smells from replicating, but you also don't want to show disrespect or be overly critical. Sometimes, there's legitimate reasons why the person writing that code approached it from a completely different perspective, and his or her solution is perfectly valid. So, we would encourage questions that would gather detail about the context, questions like:

- "Have you considered …" (not, "Why did you…")
- "What was your thought process when you started this?"
- "Why did you choose that particular library over others?"

We'd make sure that this was recent work, not ancient history from months ago, and not original work, not code that any developer had inherited. And we wouldn't shy away from keeping it spicy every now and then if there was an issue with a release – say there was some delay, or a code that somehow slipped by QA and got out the door – we'd have the developer present what went wrong and why as a learning point. But we encouraged empathy; everyone in that room had released horribly visible and embarrassing bugs at some point in their career. The point was to learn for next time, not to crucify the poor guy.

The best part was that, once some senior leaders and myself set the tone, I could kick back and watch the team enforce civility and professionalism in these reviews. I remember we were reviewing one of our Perl apps, and the work had been done by a junior developer. It wasn't elegant, but it wasn't terrible – you could understand what was going on and the reasoning behind why it was written the way it was. Well, we happened to have in the room that day someone from a different team we'd brought in to get his advice. This programmer had been on the initial eCommerce launch for the bank 12 years back and had a ton of experience. Well, he just rips into him – my God, you're using inline CSS, that's terrible, and on and on. A whole laundry list of issues, which he had in writing and was passing around, and as he's going through this diatribe it gets really quiet in the room. Finally, one of the devs on my team – not a manager – piped up and said, "Hey, I want to share something with you. This is not how we run our team. We've invited you as a guest, and we are asking you to remember that none of us are professional web developer like you. We are absolutely relying on your expertise to become better, but please show some consideration."

Well, the hairs on back of my head stood up; I was so thrilled with what I was hearing, and who it was coming from. The team wasn't beating up on him as a gang, but it also wasn't clamming up and submitting to behavior that wasn't acceptable in our playground. And this senior developer turns and apologizes – and later came to me and said he was sorry again, that peer reviews on his team had always been fairly antagonistic and hypercritical – that's the way his manager liked it. I think he was even more impressed when that junior developer had him stop by later and showed him that all his suggestions had been implemented. I started seeing him at more of our code reviews, and we saw this great transformation where we started getting a great flow of ideas between our teams. A year and a half later, one of this other team's biggest projects failed very visibly, where the latest version of this new online banking platform just fell over on Day 1. We'd been working together as part of our peer reviews, and it was from the standpoint of empathy – so it was easy and natural for us to work jointly on a resolution. That all came from positive, useful, regular peer reviews.

Crunch Time – How Do We React to Failure?

A lot of managers don't realize what a fundamental difference it makes – how we react when there's an outage or a failure. Sometimes, you'd swear that the poor coder is a puppy and it's everyone's job to rub his nose in it when there's a screwup. It leads to people being afraid to do anything, it leads to strained or blocked communication and collaboration, and inevitably to a lot of turnover. That banking team I mentioned happens to work in a very challenging environment, where there's all kinds of security constraints and regulatory standards – but they have very low turnover. That trust is part of the team fabric, and it all starts with showing mutual respect during the tough times.

As a manager, you have to delegate a lot. But I loved listening in on those calls as an observer and hearing how the team was interacting; this was raw, unfiltered, and I knew how things were actually going with the project. This wasn't something I could just hand off to a project manager to handle. It's the old telephone game; as a manager you are always receiving information that's filtered or spun to some extent. More CEOs are catching on that living in an echo chamber where nothing but good news is being reflected back at us is not a good thing; if a team is filtering out details, whether maliciously or not, it creates a dangerous condition where management is buying into a fake, sunny version of reality. Those daily standups and peer reviews were too important to miss – now I knew the bad news firsthand and could tell my senior management layer exactly how things really were.

Security

On security, sometimes your biggest holes can be on something totally off your radar – code you don't even own. COTS products sometimes give me a headache. We had a vendor once tell us not to put a web app firewall in front of their product. That's a bizarre position to take – you're asking me to trust your code implicitly, that it'll do the right thing all the time. Well, the code you give us might be controlled, but the danger are the things you didn't know – the Oracle vulnerability that you weren't patched up for, or the exploit that you hadn't scanned for. For me, with that word "DevSecOps," it really boils down to – security is now everyone's responsibility. Even if you're a small business taking credit card orders, you have to offload risk to a vendor or find ways of securely processing PI. And if your vendor isn't willing to accept your conditions, you need to find a different vendor. Just tell them straight up, if you're not willing to do this, I'll go elsewhere – that should be a part of your contract negotiation from the get-go. Make it a condition – if we find a security hole, you have X days to fix it. Now, this is changing thanks to the Target and Equifax data breaches, but still this is not top of mind for a lot of enterprises and people out there.

Security should be a byword, and it's never been easier to integrate. There are good frameworks that can help us identify security risks that didn't exist 5 years ago, and there's just no excuse for not using one. OWASP with its top 10 proactive security controls is the best – it's even ranked in order, from most important to least. But when you talk to DevOps gurus about security, they just roll their eyes – security is something pushed on them, and it cramps their style. But really, it's no different from code development, and done right it actually adds a little excitement to the routine. Do it at the very beginning and start with a risk assessment of the data. What are you trying to protect? If you're trying to map stars or you're storing GIS data, that's no big deal. But if it's healthcare related or you've got credit card information you're handling, your security protocols had better be at the top of its game. And with most teams, you don't have to do it all. If you love data, focus on that – or if you're more of a UI specialist, that's what your security efforts should target.

For CI, we're using GitLab at the moment, and Docker containers for our internal development. GitLab works very well for us. I get a dev environment created for me, very neat merging to master, repeatable deploys to production. It's fairly quick for us with these tools to resolve bugs and get hotfixes into production, usually anywhere from 30 minutes to a few hours if its complex. Docker I just can't say enough about. Rolling back is so easy — when there's a problem, we pull the cord and revert back to an older version of the container. That takes all the pressure off of trying to run out a hotfix with a production down system.

Testing and Dedicated QA Teams

I don't agree that it's necessarily an antipattern to have a separate QA team. For example, we used to have BSAs acting as QA internal in every team. Well, a BSA's goals primarily are to get product out the door as soon as possible — that's not a great position to focus on quality. So, for the first time, we created a QA team that would service both the internal and eCommerce web development teams. This QA team had an entirely different direct report, so you'd think we'd be at odds right away — that's a silo right? Only, we made it very clear that QA would need to be involved in the development work from the first day. So as they're meeting with the business stakeholders and mapping out their requirements, you'd have the devs madly scribbling out the functional expectations — and the QA person was taking notes about what the final product should look like; and they'd be there at standups and at follow-up meetings, writing their tests and refining them in parallel with the code being stood up, and participating in peer reviews. We didn't have siloing, and our quality really took off.

On testing, I absolutely follow TDD if I can start the project from the ground up. Using it is terrific practice, and it's definitely less overhead than pair programming — you're going to be more disciplined about how you're structuring your functions, and it's actually a protection for the developer — now, we can deliver results to spec; we can prove the solution is working exactly as designed. But if you're going into a project late game, it's very difficult to ramp up to that level. I'm facing that now with one of my projects. Once we hit a point of stability and the feature sets are locked, we'll likely peel them off into microservices, each with a battery of unit tests. We'll put in the results we want, have it run red, then add the code to make it green. But you don't always need that kind of overhead, and sometimes you truly can't control the environment. You won't need TDD if you're writing a report off a SQL database for example. But if you're working on a true backbone system, definitely go down the TDD road.

Valuable Traits in Hiring

There's a saying in golf — you drive for show, putt for dough. I like to apply that to software design and the qualities we look for in people we hire. It's great to be that brilliant process engineer and automate the hell out of everything you touch – that's the long drive, and it'll get attention. But it's the short game, the putting, that sets apart the great golfers. So, are you good at the day to day stuff, are you disciplined, are you a good problem solver? That's the real firepower you want on the team.

I wish we as managers would pay more attention to who we hire. You want to make sure these are people you actually want to spend time with. So, I look for a few specific character traits when I interview, not just ability. For starters, empathy. Does this person understand the reasons for failure and how it should be approached? So, I often ask, "how do you resolve conflict with another team member if you don't agree? When have you had a disagreement with a team member, how did you fix it? Let's say you both are 100% convinced that you're in the right, and the problem isn't going away – how will you resolve this?" What I'm looking for here is if they'll hear the other person out and try to understand where they're coming from. Maybe, they'll look for a third party to arbitrate, or allow this other person to try their solution first. Whatever solution this person proposes, we're looking for exactly the same thing Google values – strong opinions, lightly held. Anyone on the team needs to be able to listen and be willing to compromise in the best interests of the team.

The ability to communicate, both remotely and in person, also comes in very high. We do a lot of work remote, and I need to be able to understand where a person is coming from. How will this person be able to communicate bad news or manage expectations with a difficult customer for example?

Next up comes competence. I don't drag up the "top 50 C# interview questions" on Google; that's a complete waste of time. What we're looking for is good problem solvers. So, we give them exactly the same level of details that a customer gives us about a problem or a new design and let them noodle through it and give us a solutions design on a whiteboard. Pretty quick, you know how their mind works – are they looking for novelty, or simplicity? I find that folks looking for novelty tend to produce overly complex solutions.

Your best interviews are with people that ask lots of qualifying questions. I'll never forget this one time where we presented one of our favorite use cases – a large Java project, written by someone else, fairly well designed and architected but all the type declarations are strings. What would you do with this project? Well, this one engineer thinks this over and answers, "I'm going to figure out why they used strings." We were just flabbergasted and asked him why. He said, "It's too easy to dismiss that design automatically as stupid. But maybe everything they're getting is a string, so they have to do a lot of data conversion. It's worth a little poking around to answer that before you launch on a full-scale rewrite." That was such a great answer. Sometimes, you want a rockstar or ninja programmer to add on, and sometimes you want someone like that – a silent guru who'll say 3 words and you're like, whoa!

Ask them about learning too. I loved asking people with strong NodeJs experience. Let's say you're faced with a PHP web site that's breaking down, how would you go about it? The people I liked were the ones who clearly relished the idea of studying up on PHP and learn along the way.

We would look at the candidate's ability to select their initial tools and apply patterns. Let's say the customer has asked for this reporting solution in NodeJs – but does it really need to be that involved? Can we work with the customer to scale down to a solution that's a better fit for the nee? I'd always be scanning for ego. If I asked someone how they would go about establishing an SSL connection with a NodeJs project, and I started hearing "Well, I would start to write a wrapper around SSL" – no, that's just the wrong answer. Someone else has written this, you should be pulling a package from somewhere instead of reinventing the wheel. There's just no excuse for spending days or weeks getting stuck on a problem that's been solved elsewhere – good designers and architects know when and where to go for high quality components.

But for senior architects, you really want to know about their big wins. So, I often ask, "what is the largest thing you've worked on where you <u>did</u> have to reinvent the wheel?" Every senior person should have something in their arsenal they can point to that they've created that never existed before. Good architects will be able to point you to their GitHub repository or blog where they've written something amazing. People like that are very rare in the marketplace; when you find them, land them and keep them.

The Future of DevOps

It's hard to put my finger on what future shape DevOps will take, 10 years from now. Without a formal definition and common understanding of DevOps, everyone seems to have a little different point of view. Maybe, what's missing so far is addressing what DevOps isn't. When we have execs coming to us and saying, "we really need DevOps in this org!" – I always take a step back and ask them why. What is it that's missing that you hope DevOps will solve? Right now, it's very much viewed as a panacea, which can lead to dashed expectations.

It's also pretty clear on Reddit and elsewhere that not having an official job description or definition of DevOps as a profession is hurting us, especially new practitioners. A lot of the jobs out there I see are looking for a real grab bag – this person needs to be able to code, administer servers and networks, be Cisco and Amazon certified, automate, and kickstart a culture movement. Well, that Swiss Army knife master expert just doesn't exist; it creates a real barrier to entry that shouldn't exist.

I do love writing code though. That first 95% of a project is just so much damn fun. It's just you and your IDE, spinning away on this feature. You last looked at the clock at 11 in the morning, now it's 9 p.m., and you just realized you missed lunch and didn't even notice. You're completely in the zone, flying, cranking out work, and solving problems. I think we can all agree that the middle phase of a project – where the code is between 95% and 100% developed, and you're having to debug a ton – can be a grind. But the ramp-up and the end phase, when your baby is finally out the door and making money – it's just glorious.

Index

A

CPSIA information can be obtained
at www.ICGtesting.com
Printed in the USA
LVHW081929011019
632858LV00005B/11/P

9 781484 243879